—THE SAVE & PROSPER RUGBY UNION WHO'S WHO 1994/95

Compiled and edited by
Alex Spink

CollinsWillow

An Imprint of HarperCollins*Publishers*

First published in 1994 by
CollinsWillow
an imprint of HarperCollins*Publishers*
London

A CIP catalogue record for this book
is available from the British Library

ISBN 0 00 218539 3

Photographs provided by Allsport

Printed in Great Britain by
Butler & Tanner Ltd, Frome and London

CONTENTS

PREFACE

THE fifth edition of the *Rugby Union Who's Who* carries within its pages a clear and concise message from the world's best players: 'We want effective leadership and we want it now.'

While Rugby Union spirals in global appeal – witness the Ivory Coast's remarkable qualification for the World Cup finals – the players in the sport's heartland grow increasingly restless. Confusion is the name of the game, inconsistency the cancer endangering its soul.

On the field referees vary alarmingly in their views on how the game should be played. Off the field there is an even greater dichotomy in what countries permit their players to get up to.

At the top end, Rugby Union is in a right mess. The players don't know if they are coming or going. But while blame is sprayed towards referees and the Unions, the real guilt lies with the game's overlords, the International Board.

In any walk of life, what the boss says, goes. Therein lies Rugby Union's problem. The IB rarely says anything, other than 'interpret as you see fit'. As Ian Beer, erstwhile president of the Rugby Football Union, put it: 'The IB have given no impression to the people involved that they have any teeth. My overriding concern is their lack of backbone.'

The Rugby Union Who's Who has long campaigned for firm leadership. It's spokesmen, the game's very best players, have repeatedly warned of the perils of laissez-faire, be it over financial interpretations away from the park, or rule interpretations on it.

No-one has taken a blind bit of notice.

As a direct result, certain players have been stitched up, literally and metaphorically, both on and off the field, while certain others have enjoyed themselves handsomely. The concept of a 'level playing field' has been not so much kicked into touch as hoofed out of the stadium.

And now, at a time when we should be rejoicing at the prospect of the third World Cup, our anticipation is overrun with apprehension. The sport is at a crossroads. The importance of its next move cannot be overstated.

The IB needs to be dismantled, piece by piece, and reassembled, replacing the current archaic, worn-out parts with the most modern available – recent internationals, who know the implications of committing to modern-day Test rugby. It is not so much a nice idea as an absolute must.

Right now, these implications vary dramatically according to your geographical position. In the four Home Unions players sacrifice everything – family life, job prospects etc – for minimal return. Many actually lose out from representing their country.

Take Scotland's tour captain Andy Reed who, on the eve of departure for Argentina in May 1994, told me: 'Since last December I have tried desperately to find a job but as yet no luck. In this age, who wants to employ a free loader? Rugby has always come first but I've reached the point where I have to start thinking about settling down, getting a home.'

But what of the privileges which accompany Test status? 'A load of free kit which doesn't even fit,' dismissed the tartan British Lion. 'The Unions make an absolute fortune out of the players. There must be a realistic appreciation of how much time and effort is put into playing top-level rugby.'

Down Under and in South Africa, not to mention France and Italy, such an appreciation certainly exists. The Unions are more liberal. Fringe benefits abound. And the aforementioned Beer is bitter. 'If I had my way I would have expelled one or two of the major rugby nations from the Board,' he said.

'The way the All Blacks are organising themselves for next year's World Cup, with contracts, is supposedly within the rules of the IB but I don't believe it is and have told the IB. I have also written asking them to look into the reports about Natal players receiving $800 each to beat England.'

Only a revamped IB, drawing on selfless individuals with the interests of the players, not themselves, at heart, can rebuild the shattered reputation of a largely discredited governing body.

Get the composition of the Board right and the rest should be simple. Decide on policies and pass them into law. Then everyone – be they Unions or individuals, Northern or Southern hemisphere – abides because they have to. Dissenters can toe the line or watch the World Cup on television. Everyone knows exactly where they stand.

Which is more than could be said of England in South Africa last summer. They might as well have toured Mars, so alien were the interpretations they encountered. The talk off the field was of money-making opportunities, allegations abounding of win bonuses and lucrative contracts to play in the new Republic. The actual rugby was equally foreign.

The standard of local refereeing was abysmal, on at least one occasion verging on the criminal and if the RFU did make an error of judgement in conceding the moral high ground (taken during the visit to Blighty of the '93 All Blacks) over the Tim Rodber affair (they did), that could not mask the alarming incompetence in officiating which paved the way for the troubles.

'Having had to get to grips with the New Zealand way for the British Lions, like rucking the man off the ball, we were faced with South African refs who did not allow you to ruck,' commented England's Ben Clarke, who was equally bemused by line-out policing.

He added: 'The International Board must come up with a ten-point plan to simplify and standardise the key laws in the game – and make sure they are applied. What we want is consistency. Instead we have chaos. The IB should take a leaf from cricket's book and set up an elite pool of six or so international referees, selected because they are the best in the world.'

Quite so. A global game must have universal, one-for-all, rules. No buts. It should not be dangerous to pit together representatives from opposite hemispheres. At the moment it is.

Yet, paradoxically, Peter Brook, chairman of the 1991 World Cup referee appointments panel, boasted that achieving consistency was 'probably the easiest thing in the whole tournament.'

He explained: 'We did not want to the referees to talk about the Northern Hemisphere–Southern Hemisphere divisions. We wanted them to work out a common approach to satisfy our main requirements.

'By the quarter-finals of the tournament, whether popular or unpopular, players, coaches and managers knew that for the first time in their lives, they had consistency in the application and the interpretation of the law. As a consequence, from the quarter-finals on we had fewer penalties and better games.'

All of which was a far cry from South Africa '94, though not, one trusts, South Africa '95 when the whole world will be in attendance, either in person or via satellite. It is imperative for the future well-being of Rugby Union that the sport puts up a united front. As things stand, that will be a neat trick.

For all the above reasons, 1993/94 was not a vintage year for the sport. The change to the turnover law altered the face of Rugby Union, and not for the better. It reduced the disparity between good and poor sides but had the effect of lessening the spectacle. Wales against France in Cardiff was an epic with few peers.

Indeed, Wales's resurgence was one of the highlights, as was the performance of supposedly 'little' Italy in Australia last summer, where they so nearly hijacked the first Test from the world champions. Still, Test shocks abounded: Ireland's win at Twickenham, Australia's defeat in Bordeaux, New Zealand's loss at Twickenham, Canada's victory in Cardiff, England's extraordinary win in Pretoria, France's defeat in Toronto and Argentina's series sweep of Scotland.

To find out what the players thought of the campaign, check out their detailed profiles between pages 119–419. Remember, only those who won Test caps during the season – June 1993 to June 1994 – are featured. The borderline cases (squad members and A-teamers) are logged in the Appendix (pages 420–437).

Exclusive interviews with each of the eight national team captains – Michael Lynagh, Will Carling, Olivier Roumat, Michael Bradley, Sean Fitzpatrick, Gavin Hastings, François Pienaar and Ieuan Evans – appear on pages 10–118.

The most up-to-date global results service available is situated at the rear of the book (pages 451–478), charting the campaign in chronological order up to and including last summer's tours. And, this being World Cup season, everything you need to know about the greatest show on earth is to be found on pages 438–450.

Sources of reference for this tome were: *Rothmans Rugby Union Yearbooks* (1985-94, Queen Anne Press/Headline, editor Stephen Jones), the *Guinness Rugby Union Fact Book* (Guinness, Chris Rhys), *Radio New Zealand Sport Rugby Annual* (23rd edition, Moa, Bob Howitt), *History of New Zealand Rugby*, Volume 4, 1980-91 (Moa, R.H.Chester & N.A.C.McMillan), *McEwan's Rugby Record 1993-94* (IMA/Bill McMurtrie) and *Welsh Brewers Ltd Rugby Annual for Wales 1993-94* (Arwyn Owen).

I would like to extend my considerable gratitude to the players – and especially national captains – for their continued co-operation and goodwill in the production of this book. Without you guys this would be a doodle pad. On the other side of the touchline, my thanks go to the essential Greg Campbell, Wynne Gray, Chris Thau, Jonathan Goslett, Tony Roche, Karen Giles, the Big Eight unions, Westgate Sports, Michael Humphrey + Partners, Slattery PR, *Rugby World*, *Rugby News*, Bill Cotton and Programme Publications, Tom Whiting, Rachel Smyth, Allsport, *Today* newspaper and my colleagues in the British media. But most of all, to Karen, Tom and Jenny for your enduring tolerance.

Alex Spink
June 1994

FOREWORD

PAUL BATEMAN
Chief Executive, Save & Prosper Group

Welcome to this fifth edition of *The Save & Prosper Rugby Union Who's Who*. I trust that you will find it informative, amusing and above all good value at under £10.

As Save & Prosper enters its tenth year of rugby sponsorship, we celebrate with four internationals at Twickenham – Romania, Canada, France and Scotland – and of course the end of season Save & Prosper Middlesex Sevens.

With World Cup preparation very much in mind, we have an interesting Five Nations competition in prospect. This tournament's fascination lies in its unpredictability. Few forecast England's defeat last season at the hands of Ireland at Twickenham, or indeed the spectacular resurgence of Wales.

Let's hope that our Five Nations rugby continues to entertain and surprise.

Finally, I would like to wish Geoff Cooke well on his retirement as England team manager. His influence on English rugby has been immense. I believe that only with the benefit of hindsight will the size of his achievement be fully appreciated.

THE CAPTAINS REVIEW
THE 1993/4 SEASON

ENGLAND

Will Carling

GEOFF COOKE deserved a Five Nations title to take with him into retirement. Unfortunately, after a season of remarkable contrasts, England did not.

It was ten years since we had last beaten New Zealand, and 12 years since our last home defeat by Ireland. Both runs were broken in a campaign in which we rode a rollercoaster of fortune. We went five matches without a try – 438 try-less minutes taking us uncomfortably close to a most unwanted national record – and we committed daylight robbery when stealing out of Murrayfield with the spoils.

Yet all things considered I was proud of what we achieved. At the start of the season I would gladly have accepted the position in which we ended up. Of course I would love to have won all five games rather than four, but I don't know whether we would have learned as much as we have done. Believe me, we gained an awful lot from losing, which for a young squad will stand us in good stead in future.

We started strongly, we finished strongly, and although we had a few downs in the middle, that's no bad thing for the development of the side.

From a personal perspective, I was excited coming into the 1993/94 season. The Lions experience was not what I'd expected but I really enjoyed it, because it taught me a lot about myself.

> *'Being dropped [by the Lions] took me to the lowest I've been in international rugby…From the media point of view I'd had an easy run, and this was the first time things had gone wrong for me. I'd like to feel I handled it all right, but it wasn't easy'*

More than anything it refreshed me. Being dropped took me to the lowest I've been in international rugby. But I actually started to enjoy playing again in the last few games. Of course I was disappointed that I'd played so badly out there, but in a way it did me a lot of good.

From the media point of view I'd had an easy run, and this was the first time things had gone wrong for me. I'd like to feel I handled it all right, but it wasn't easy. Being dropped is never easy.

Not being Lions captain gave me the chance to get to know players from other countries. I'd missed out on the '89 Lions owing to injury, and not having that chance remains one of my biggest regrets. It's hard to get to know people who've only known me as England captain, sitting on the top table.

I came into the new season really wanting to show myself – and a few other people, I suppose – that I could still play a bit. And after England's relatively poor 1992/93 campaign, I was more confident that we were equipped to the adapt to the new rules. I was excited about the potential in the side. It was a question of whether we could gel together, and whether we had the mental edge – the mental hardness that distinguishes really great sides.

New Zealand possess that quality, and they represented our first challenge of the season. I had no doubt we could beat the All Blacks in a one-off game (although had it been a three-game series, that might have been different) provided we could get ourselves right mentally – which is why our 15–9 victory didn't come as a shock to me.

The Lions knew how to beat them; in fact, I think most people know how to beat them. But putting the theory into practice is less easy. They put you under tremendous pressure, and it's a question of putting them under that same pressure and making as few unforced errors as possible; retaining the ball in contact, and making your tackles. They play a fairly basic game, the Blacks, but they play it incredibly well.

> 'The Lions knew how to beat New Zealand; in fact, I think most people know how to beat them. But putting the theory into practice is less easy... The All Blacks play a fairly basic game, but they play it incredibly well'

Our win raised expectations beyond a level we could cope with. There again, these days the pressure is always on England. But that did not excuse the fact that we let ourselves down against Scotland and Ireland. We simply weren't as focused in our build-up to those games as we had been when preparing for New Zealand.

The Murrayfield game (won 15–14) was horribly reminiscent of the ill-fated 1990 Grand Slam decider. But until you've been through that experience, you can talk to people until you're blue in the face without it meaning anything to them. We played them tapes of 1990, we did everything we could; but we couldn't change the fact that they hadn't been there, that they hadn't been involved.

It's like me watching a 1970s rugby game and people saying that is what such and such an opponent is capable of. I look at it and think 'That's not relevant to me'. Until you play in the Five Nations and realize the intensity of it, it is really very hard to transmit that intensity to the younger players. We certainly didn't manage it.

Collectively, we were not right for that game. And to make matters worse, we didn't learn the lesson for the Irish game either. If we're being totally honest with ourselves, we thought 'Oh well, we got away with it against Scotland; we're good enough to get away with it again'. Players didn't learn the lessons, and as a squad we weren't focused enough. It was as though we felt 'Right, we've got a good team; let's go out and play'.

Against New Zealand we were incredibly focused in what we were doing in every area of the field. We knew what our roles were. We didn't against Scotland and Ireland.

Injuries, of course, did us no favours. Dean Richards, Ben Clarke, Tim Rodber and Nigel Redman each missed at least one game. And I would like to believe that, had we had the pack that played against New

Zealand throughout the Five Nations Championship, team performances might have been different.

Richards, Rodber and Redman were all missing at Murrayfield, where Jon Callard's late late kick got us out of jail. It was a magnificent strike from over 40 metres under the greatest pressure. I was certainly glad I didn't have to take it, but because he was kicking well at that stage, I just handed him the ball with the words 'It's easy'.

I was fairly philosophical as he lined up the kick. In my mind I was preparing for a defeat. But as soon as he hit it, I knew it was going over. Once it did, there was a huge surge of adrenalin mixed with relief.

Against Ireland (lost 12–13) we'd forgotten that you have to refocus before each game on what you're trying to do. What are the players' roles? What is the gameplan? What are the variations you can bring to it? We didn't have enough idea of how we were going to score the points, and it caught up with us. We thought we could almost play it off the cuff because we had a lot of good players, but international rugby doesn't work like that.

> *'If we're being totally honest with ourselves, we thought "Oh well, we got away with it against Scotland; we're good enough to get away with it again against Ireland"…We thought we could almost play it off the cuff because we had a lot of good players. But international rugby doesn't work like that'*

Our failure to turn pressure situations into tries was frustrating, because we were creating the chances but just not taking them. But more frustrating was the fact that we were then being labelled as a 'boring team'. You need just a little bit of luck every now and again, and it just wasn't going our way. But that wasn't for any lack of effort.

Under the new rules you have to be a very good side to go out and play an expansive game and win. The laws make it very easy to play a constricted game and get away with it. It's very easy now to close a game down, and that's a real shame.

But there's no doubt we are adapting accordingly. We went to Paris and closed the game down to win it. Mind you, we've done that on our last four visits and come home with a result each time. We have run the ball, but only when the game's been won.

You play a constricted game in Paris because what the French love to do is run. It amuses us that we get criticism for it when, without being arrogant, no one else has won a championship match out there for almost 20 years.

'I was shattered [when Geoff Cooke quit]. Not for the reasons people think – that I'm meant to be Geoff's boy, and this that and the other. But because I had a tremendous respect and a deep loyalty to the man...I never felt I got that close to him...It was almost like a business relationship'

Prior to the Paris game (won 18–14) we were hit by the bombshell that Geoff Cooke would be retiring from the post of England manager at the end of the Five Nations campaign, rather than after the 1995 World Cup as we had expected.

I was shattered. Not for the reasons people think – that I'm meant to be Geoff's boy, and this that and the other. But because I had a tremendous respect and a deep loyalty to the man.

In fact, the senior players were fairly surprised how reserved both Geoff and I were with each other. I never felt I got that close to him, and he probably felt the same. I think we both realized he might have to drop me from the England side at some point, as he did on the Lions tour. Thus we were reluctant to cross over that line. It was almost like a business relationship.

Geoff was a tremendous leading light as far as English rugby was concerned. He had the courage and the foresight to change it all, and an awful lot of our success is down to him. But he also had good players, and I think it would be most unwise for someone to come in and radically change something which had proved to be successful.

His sudden announcement did not fill me with dread at being an endangered species – although, I suppose, at the back of my mind there was this question mark over what on earth was going to happen after Geoff. No, I was shattered more because I believed Geoff was going to take us through to the World Cup.

The other feature of the Paris build-up was Pierre Berbizier's extraordinary attack on Brian Moore, branding him an *agent provocateur*. Personally, I didn't hear about it at the time – which was a great shame, because it robbed me and a lot of the other lads of a good evening's entertainment.

On a more serious note, Brian was right when he said Berbizier's ranting reflected a weakness in the French psyche. They seem to get very wound up about playing England – especially in Paris. In actual fact, I honestly prefer to play them in the Parc des Princes rather than at Twickenham, because they're more relaxed at our place. They don't have this incredible burden of expectation, and therefore they're more dangerous. In Paris, they seem to get so wound up emotionally that they lose their ability to play.

The press acclaimed Rob Andrew's match-winning performance: a poor display, they argued, would have cost him his Test place. People also said that if England didn't win it would be the end of my captaincy.

Did it bother us? Well no, not really, because as far as we were concerned, worrying about matters outside our control wasn't going to change anything. You can't afford to carry such emotional baggage into an international. You wouldn't be able to walk out of the tunnel if you did, for fear of failure. You have got to remain positive. I believed we would win, I felt in my mind I was playing well during the year: so I was positive.

Having beaten France, we knew we were back on course for the championship but for the small matter of having to beat Wales by 16 clear points in the title decider. Our philosophy, though, was just to win the game, to play well and to develop from the French game. The 16-point factor was irrelevant to my mind, and I would have been slightly annoyed had any of the other players not felt the same. I figured that if we played well enough the points would come anyway.

With our first-choice pack at last reunited, they put in a performance to rival that against New Zealand. Dean at number 8, with Tim and Ben either side, gives us a great balance and they play so well off him.

In the backs, I was especially pleased to see Tony Underwood come back so strongly after a difficult year, and to witness Ian Hunter relish playing in his favourite position of fullback. But the most pleasure came from the end of our try drought against Wales (won 15–8). It might surprise some observers to learn that we actually do want to score tries.

The inexperience of the side still manifested itself in our failure to take all our chances. We need to develop a mental ruthlessness before the World Cup, and I have high hopes that our summer tour to South Africa will have proved the breeding ground for a new mean streak. Time will tell.

ENGLAND (P6 W4 D0 L2 F84 A85):

(H)	v	New Zealand	(Twickenham, 27.11.93)	won	15–9
(A)	v	Scotland	(Edinburgh, 5.2.94)	won	15–14
(H)	v	Ireland	(Twickenham, 19.2.94)	lost	12–13
(A)	v	France	(Paris, 5.3.94)	won	18–14
(H)	v	Wales	(Twickenham, 19.3.94)	won	15–8
(A)	v	South Africa	(Pretoria, 4.6.94)	won	32–15
(A)	v	South Africa	(Cape Town, 11.6.94)	lost	9–27

England in South Africa (tour record: P8 W3 D0 L5 F152 A165):

(A)	v	Orange Free State	(Bloemfontein, 18.5.94)	lost	11–22
(A)	v	Natal	(Durban, 21.5.94)	lost	6–21
(A)	v	Western Transvaal	(Pretoria, 25.5.94)	won	26–24
(A)	v	Transvaal	(Pretoria, 28.5.94)	lost	21–24
(A)	v	South Africa B	(Kimberley, 31.5.94)	lost	16–19
(A)	v	Eastern Province	(Port Elizabeth, 7.6.94)	won	31–13

All Blacks in England (tour record: P8 W7 D0 L1 F175 A103):

(A)	v	London	(Twickenham, 23.10.93)	won	39–12
(A)	v	Midlands	(Leicester, 26.10.93)	won	12–6
(A)	v	South-West	(Redruth, 30.10.93)	won	19–15
(A)	v	Northern	(Liverpool, 2.11.93)	won	27–21
(A)	v	England A	(Gateshead, 7.11.93)	won	26–12
(A)	v	Emerging England	(Gloucester, 23.11.93)	won	30–19
(A)	v	Combined Services	(Devonport, 1.12.93)	won	13–3

ENGLAND A (P6 W3 D0 L3 F95 A98):

(A)	v	Canada	(Vancouver, 25.5.93)	lost	12–15
(A)	v	Canada	(Ottawa, 5.6.93)	won	19–14
(H)	v	New Zealand	(Gateshead, 7.11.93)	lost	12–26
(A)	v	Italy A	(Piacenza, 4.2.94)	won	15–9
(H)	v	Ireland A	(Richmond, 18.2.94)	won	29–14
(A)	v	France A	(Paris, 5.3.94)	lost	8–20

England A in Canada (tour record: P5 W4 D0 L1 F123 A57):

(A)	v	British Columbia	(Victoria, 22.5.93)	won	26–10
(A)	v	British Columbia XV	(Vancouver, 26.5.93)	won	26–11
(A)	v	Ontario	(Toronto, 2.6.93)	won	40–7

ENGLAND EMERGING PLAYERS (P3 W2 D0 L1 F128 A56):

(H)	v	New Zealand	(Gloucester, 23.11.93)	lost	19–30
(H)	v	Spain	(Richmond, 6.2.94)	won	86–17
(H)	v	Canada A	(Richmond, 20.3.94)	won	23–9

ENGLAND U-21 (P4 W3 D0 L1 F130 A48):

(H)	v	Ireland	(Gateshead, 7.11.93)	won	22–15
(A)	v	Holland	(Leiden, 17.4.94)	won	56–14
(A)	v	Italy	(Rovigo, 7.5.94)	won	43–6
(A)	v	France	(Rouen, 11.5.94)	lost	9–13

ENGLAND STUDENTS (P3 W1 D0 L2 F62 A74):

(H)	v	Ireland	(Bournemouth, 18.2.94)	won	23–9

| (A) | v | France | (Dunkirk, 4.3.94) | lost | 17–36 |
| (H) | v | Wales | (Oxford, 18.3.94) | lost | 22–29 |

ENGLISH COLLEGES (P1 W0 D0 L1 F13 A31):

| (H) | v | Irish | (Southampton, 17.2.94) | lost | 13–31 |

ENGLAND COLTS (P4 W2 D1 L1 F45 A44):

(A)	v	Italy	(Brescia, 12.3.94)	won	13–12
(A)	v	Wales	(Cardiff, 27.3.94)	lost	10–15
(A)	v	Scotland	(Waterloo, 9.4.94)	won	11–6
(H)	v	France	(Moseley, 23.4.94)	drew	11–11

ENGLAND 18 GROUP (P4 W4 D0 L0 F81 A36):

(H)	v	Wales	(Bournemouth, 22.3.94)	won	22–3
(A)	v	Scotland	(Kelso, 30.3.94)	won	22–12
(A)	v	France	(Cahors, 2.4.94)	won	14–13
(H)	v	Ireland	(Durham, 13.4.94)	won	23–8

ENGLAND 16 GROUP (P2 W1 D1 L0 F26 A11):

| (H) | v | Portugal | (Castlecroft, 31.3.94) | won | 15–0 |
| (H) | v | Wales | (London Welsh, 8.4.94) | drew | 11–11 |

ENGLAND 16 GROUP A (P2 W2 D0 L0 F36 A16):

| (H) | v | Portugal A | (Castlecroft, 31.3.94) | won | 27–8 |
| (H) | v | Wales A | (London Welsh, 8.4.94) | won | 9–8 |

ENGLAND WOMEN (P5 W5 D0 L0 F172 A39):

(–)	v	Russia★	(Edinburgh, 11.4.94)	won	66–0
(–)	v	Scotland★	(Edinburgh, 15.4.94)	won	26–0
(–)	v	Canada★	(q/f: Edinburgh, 17.4.94)	won	24–10
(–)	v	France★	(s/f: Gala, 20.4.94)	won	18–6
(–)	v	USA★	(f: Edinburgh, 24.4.94)	won	38–23

★ England win second Women's World Cup

DOMESTIC RUGBY

CIS DIVISIONAL CHAMPIONSHIP

	P	W	D	L	F	A	Pts
South-West	3	3	0	0	85	36	6
London	3	2	0	1	62	60	4
North	3	1	0	2	68	60	2
Midlands	3	0	0	3	26	85	0

* South West beat London 25–17 in decider at Twickenham

COURAGE CLUB CHAMPIONSHIP

Division One:	P	W	D	L	F	A	Pts
Bath	18	17	0	1	431	181	34
Leicester	18	14	0	4	425	210	28
Wasps	18	10	1	7	362	340	21
Bristol	18	10	0	8	331	276	20
Northampton	18	9	0	9	305	342	18
Harlequins	18	8	0	10	333	287	16
Orrell	18	8	0	10	327	302	16

Gloucester	18	6	2	10	247	356	14
London Irish	18	4	0	14	217	391	8
Newcastle Gosforth	18	2	1	15	190	483	5

champions: Bath; *relegated:* L Irish, N Gosforth

Division Two:	**P**	**W**	**D**	**L**	**F**	**A**	**Pts**
Sale	18	13	2	3	438	160	28
West Hartlepool	18	13	2	3	389	271	28
Saracens	18	11	1	6	299	238	23
Wakefield	18	8	3	7	347	240	19
Moseley	18	9	1	8	266	220	19
Nottingham	18	8	1	9	254	326	17
Waterloo	18	6	2	10	231	346	14
London Scottish	18	6	0	12	232	325	12
Rugby	18	5	1	12	186	302	11
Otley	18	4	1	13	235	449	9

promoted: Sale (champions), West Hartlepool; *relegated:* Rugby, Otley

Div 3 – *promoted:* Coventry (c), Fylde; *rel:* Havant, Redruth
Div 4 – *promoted:* Clifton (c), Harrogate; *rel:* Sheffield, Sudbury

CUP FINALS:

Pilkington Cup
Bath 21, Leicester 9, (Twickenham, 7.5.94)

CIS County Championship
Yorkshire 26, Durham 3 (Twickenham, 16.4.94)

Pilkington Shield
Malvern 8, Old Hamptonians 6 (Twickenham, 7.5.94)

Women's RFU National Cup
Richmond 18, Saracens 10

England new boy Steve Ojomoh moves menacingly forward during Ireland's 13–12 win.

1980:

I	W24–9	Twickenham	19 Jan	t: Scott, Slemen, SJ Smith
				c: Hare 3
				p: Hare 2
F	W17–13	Paris	2 Feb	t: Carleton, Preston
				p: Hare
				dg: Horton 2
W	W 9–8	Twickenham	16 Feb	p: Hare 3
S	W30–18	Edinburgh	15 Mar	t: Carleton 3, Slemen, Smith
				c: Hare 2
				p: Hare 2

1981:

W	L19–21	Cardiff	17 Jan	t: Hare
				p: Hare 5
S	W23–17	Twickenham	21 Feb	t: Davies, Slemen, Woodward
				c: Hare
				p: Hare 3
I	W10–9	Dublin	77 Mar	t: Dodge, Rose
				c: Rose
F	L12–16	Twickenham	21 Mar	p: Rose 4
Arg(1)	D19–19	Buenos Aires	30 May	t: Woodward 2, Davies
				c: Hare 2
				p: Hare
Arg(2)	W12–6	Buenos Aires	6 Jun	t: Davies
				c: Hare
				p: Hare 2

1982:

A	W15–11	Twickenham	2 Jan	t: Jeavons
				c: Dodge
				p: Rose 3
S	D 9–9	Edinburgh	16 Jan	p: Dodge 2, Rose
I	L15–16	Twickenham	6 Feb	t: Slemen
				c: Rose
				p: Rose 3
F	W27–15	Paris	20 Feb	t: Woodward, Carleton
				c: Hare 2
				p: Hare 5
W	W17–7	Twickenham	6 Mar	t: Carleton, Slemen
				p: Hare 3
US[+]	W59–0	Hartford	19 Jun	t: SJ Smith 2, Swift 2, Scott 2, Carleton, Rendall, Wheeler
				c: Hare 7
				p: Hare 2
				dg: Cusworth
Fj[+]	W60–19	Twickenham	16 Oct	t: Trick 3, Swift 2, Gadd 2, Scott, SJ Smith, Cusworth, Dodge, Colclough
				c: Hare 6

1983:

F	L15–19	Twickenham	15 Jan	**p:** Hare 4
				dg: Cusworth
W	D13–13	Cardiff	5 Feb	**t:** Carleton
				p: Hare 2
				dg: Cusworth
S	L12–22	Twickenham	5 Mar	**p:** Hare 3
				dg: Horton
I	L15–25	Dublin	19 Mar	**p:** Hare 5
NZ	W15–9	Twickenham	19 Nov	**t:** Colclough
				c: Hare
				p: Hare 3
C⁺	W27–0	Twickenham	15 Oct	**t:** Youngs, Winterbottom, penalty try
				c: Hare 3
				p: Hare 3

1984:

S	L 6–18	Edinburgh	4 Feb	**p:** Hare 2
I	W12–9	Twickenham	18 Feb	**p:** Hare 3
				dg: Cusworth
F	L18–32	Paris	3 Mar	**t:** R Underwood, Hare
				c: Hare 2
				p: Hare 2
W	L15–24	Twickenham	17 Mar	**p:** Hare 5
SA(1)	L15–33	Port Elizabeth	2 Jun	**p:** Hare 4
				dg: Horton
SA(2)	L9–35	Johannesburg	9 Jun	**p:** Hare 3
A	L3–19	Twickenham	3 Nov	**p:** Barnes

1985:

F	D 9–9	Twickenham	2 Feb	**p:** Andrew 2
				dg: Andrew
W	L15–24	Cardiff	20 Apr	**t:** Smith
				c: Andrew
				p: Andrew 2
				dg: Andrew
S	W10–7	Twickenham	16 Mar	**t:** Smith
				p: Andrew 2
I	L10–13	Dublin	30 Mar	**t:** R Underwood
				p: Andrew 2
NZ(1)	L13–18	Christchurch	1 Jun	**t:** Harrison, Teague
				c: Barnes
				p: Barnes
NZ(2)	L15–42	Wellington	8 Jun	**t:** Hall, Harrison
				c: Barnes 2
				dg: Barnes

1986:

W	W21–18	Twickenham	17 Jan	**p:** Andrew 6
				dg: Andrew
S	L6–33	Edinburgh	15 Feb	**p:** Andrew 2
I	W25–20	Twickenham	1 Mar	**t:** Richards 2, penalty try, Davies
				c: Andrew 3

F	L10–29	Paris	15 Mar	p: Andrew t: Dooley p: Barnes 2
J+	W39–12	Twickenham	11 Oct	t: R Underwood, Hall, Bailey, Richards, Rees, Salmon c: Rose 6 p: Rose

1987:

I	L0–17	Dublin	7 Feb	
F	L15–19	Twickenham	21 Feb	p: Rose 4 dg: Andrew
W	L12–19	Cardiff	7 Mar	p: Rose 4
S	W21–12	Twickenham	4 Apr	t: penalty try, Rose c: Rose 2 p: Rose 3
A★	L6–19	Sydney	23 May	t: Harrison c: Webb
J★	W60–7	Sydney	30 May	t: R Underwood 2, Rees, Salmon, Richards, Simms, Harrison 3, Redman c: Webb 7 p: Webb 2
US★	W34–6	Sydney	3 Jun	t: Winterbottom 2, Harrison, Dooley c: Webb 3 p: Webb 4
W★	L3–16	Brisbane	8 Jun	p: Webb

1988:

F	L9–10	Paris	16 Jan	p: Webb 2 dg: Cusworth
W	L3–11	Twickenham	6 Feb	p: Webb
S	W 9–6	Edinburgh	5 Mar	p: Webb 2 dg: Andrew
I(a)	W35–3	Twickenham	19 Mar	t: Oti 3, R Underwood 2, Rees c: Webb, Andrew 3 p: Webb
I(b)	W21–10	Dublin	23 Apr	t: R Underwood, Harding c: Webb 2 p: Webb 3
A(a1)	L16–22	Brisbane	29 May	t: R Underwood, Bailey c: Webb p: Webb 2
A(a2)	L8–28	Sydney	12 Jun	t: Richards, R Underwood
Fj	W25–12	Suva	17 Jun	t: R Underwood 2, Barley c: Barnes 2 p: Barnes 3
A(b)	W28–19	Twickenham	5 Nov	t: R Underwood 2, Morris, Halliday c: Webb 3 p: Webb 2

1989:

S	D12–12	Twickenham	4 Feb	p: Andrew 2, Webb 2
I	W16–3	Dublin	18 Feb	t: Moore, Richards

				c: Andrew
				p: Andrew 2
F	W11–0	Twickenham	4 Mar	t: Carling, Robinson
				p: Andrew
W	L9–12	Cardiff	18 Mar	p: Andrew 2
				dg: Andrew
R	W58–3	Bucharest	13 May	t: Oti 4, Guscott 3, Probyn, Richards
				c: Hodgkinson 8
				p: Hodgkinson
				dg: Andrew
Fj	W58–23	Twickenham	4 Nov	t: R Underwood 5, Skinner, Bailey, Linnett, Ackford, Guscott
				c: Hodgkinson 5, Andrew
				p: Hodgkinson 2

1990:

I	W23–0	Twickenham	20 Jan	t: R Underwood, Probyn, Egerton, Guscott
				c: Hodgkinson 2
				p: Hodgkinson
F	W26–7	Paris	3 Feb	t: R Underwood, Guscott, Carling
				c: Hodgkinson
				p: Hodgkinson 4
W	W34–6	Twickenham	17 Feb	t: Carling, R Underwood 2, Hill
				c: Hodgkinson 3
				p: Hodgkinson 4
S	L7–13	Edinburgh	17 Mar	t: Guscott
				p: Hodgkinson
It[+]	W33–15	Rovigo	1 May	t: Oti, Buckton, Back, Andrew
				c: Hodgkinson 4
				p: Hodgkinson 2
				dg: Andrew
Arg(a1)	W25–12	Buenos Aires	28 Jul	t: Ryan, Oti
				c: Hodgkinson
				p: Hodgkinson 5
Arg(a2)	L13–15	Buenos Aires	4 Aug	t: Hodgkinson, Heslop
				c: Hodgkinson
				p: Hodgkinson
Ba+	W18–16	Twickenham	29 Sep	t: Richards, Hodgkinson
				c: Hodgkinson 2
				p: Hodgkinson 2
Arg(b)	W51–0	Twickenham	3 Nov	t: R Underwood 3, Guscott 2, Hill, Hall
				c: Hodgkinson 7
				p: Hodgkinson 3

1991:

W	W25–6	Cardiff	19 Jan	t: Teague
				p: Hodgkinson 7
S(a)	W21–12	Twickenham	16 Feb	t: Heslop
				c: Hodgkinson
				p: Hodgkinson 5
I	W16–7	Dublin	2 Mar	t: R Underwood, Teague

				c: Hodgkinson
				p: Hodgkinson 2
F	W21–19	Twickenham	16 Mar	t: R Underwood
				c: Hodgkinson
				p: Hodgkinson 4
				dg: Andrew
Fj	W28–12	Suva	20 Jul	t: Probyn, R Underwood, Andrew
				c: Webb 2
				p: Webb 2
				dg: Andrew 2
A(a)	L15–40	Sydney	27 Jul	t: Guscott
				c: Webb
				p: Webb 3
USSR[+]	W53–0	Twickenham	7 Sep	t: Oti 2, Guscott 2, R Underwood 2, Skinner 2, Andrew
				c: Andrew 4, Hodgkinson 3
				p: Hodgkinson
NZ*	L12–18	Twickenham	3 Oct	p: Webb 3
				dg: Andrew
It*	W36–6	Twickenham	8 Oct	t: R Underwood, Guscott 2, Webb
				c: Webb 4
				p: Webb 4
US*	W37–9	Twickenham	11 Oct	t: R Underwood 2, Carling, Skinner, Heslop
				c: Hodgkinson 4
				p: Hodgkinson 3
F*	W19–10	Paris	19 Oct	t: R Underwood, Carling
				c: Webb
				p: Webb 3
S(b)*	W 9–6	Edinburgh	26 Oct	p: Webb 2
				dg: Andrew
A(b)*	L6–12	Twickenham	2 Nov	p: Webb 2
1992:				
S	W25–7	Edinburgh	18 Jan	t: R Underwood, Morris
				c: Webb
				p: Webb 4
				dg: Guscott
I	W38–9	Twickenham	1 Feb	t: Webb 2, Morris, Guscott, R Underwood, Halliday
				c: Webb 4
				p: Webb 2
F	W31–13	Paris	15 Feb	t: Webb, R Underwood, Morris, penalty try
				c: Webb 3
				p: Webb 3
W	W24– 0	Twickenham	7 Mar	t: Carling, Skinner, Dooley
				c: Webb 3
				p: Webb 2
C[†]	W26–13	Wembley	17 Oct	t: Hunter 2, Guscott, Winterbottom
				p: Webb 2

SA	W33–16	Twickenham	14 Nov	**t:** T Underwood, Guscott, Morris, Carling **c:** Webb 2 **p:** Webb 3

1993:

F	W16–15	Twickenham	16 Jan	**t:** Hunter **c:** Webb **p:** Webb 3
W	L 9–10	Cardiff	6 Feb	**p:** Webb 2 **dg:** Guscott
S	W26–12	Twickenham	6 Mar	**t:** Guscott, R Underwood, T Underwood **c:** Webb **p:** Webb 3
I	L 3–17	Dublin	20 Mar	**p:** Webb
NZ	W15–9	Twickenham	27 Nov	**p:** Callard 4 **dg:** Andrew

1994

S	W15–14	Edinburgh	5 Feb	**p:** Callard 5
I	L12–13	Twickenham	19 Feb	**p:** Callard 4
F	W18–14	Paris	5 Mar	**p:** Andrew 5 **dg:** Andrew
W	W15–8	Twickenham	19 Mar	**t:** R Underwood, Rodber **c:** Andrew **p:** Andrew
SA(1)	W33–15	Pretoria	4 Jun	**t:** Clarke, Andrew **c:** Andrew 2 **p:** Andrew 5 **dg:** Andrew
SA(2)	L9–27	Cape Town	11 Jun	**p:** Andrew 3

* World Cup matches
+ Non-cap tests
† Five-point try introduced from this game onwards

IRELAND

Michael Bradley

IRELAND could have won the Triple Crown and yet we might just as easily have collected the Wooden Spoon. Such was the fickle nature of the 1994 Five Nations Championship. As it was we achieved neither, but did have the considerable consolation of at last beating England at Twickenham.

The impartial will rightly remember the title race for the return of Wales to the winners' enclosure. And well deserved it was too. But for us Irish, 1994 will be remembered as the year our run of Twickenham failures stretching back to 1982 came to an end.

It was a remarkable result set in the context of the rest of the championship season. We beat no-one else, while England beat everyone. They are an excellent side, and one which, I really believe, has a first-rate chance of winning the World Cup in South Africa.

What particularly impresses me about them is the way they cope with being under such tremendous pressure to win all the time. Wales captain Ieuan Evans wrote in last year's edition that to become a force in world rugby you have to be able to handle the favourite's tag – to win when it is expected of you.

England, with the exception of their meeting with us, achieved just that. They won four games out of five – beating New Zealand and France away – and still came in for heavy criticism. I don't mind saying that had we had their season we would have been thrilled.

Ieuan's point was that if you go out at home with what is perceived as a 50–50 chance of winning, home advantage really should tell. And he's quite right. That was why we set ourselves a minimum target of four points in the championship.

We looked at our two games scheduled for Lansdowne Road - against Wales and Scotland – and felt we should win both. That achieved, anything gained away from Dublin would be seen as a bonus.

Yet in the event we won neither. So, applying Evans' line of thinking, our team has some way to go when it comes to being a global force. Certainly there is still a lot of learning for us to do, but we are not blind to the fact, and we do have the ability to learn.

> *'I do believe we have a duty to entertain in international rugby; but the priority must be the result. I don't think many supporters (outside England anyway) would quibble if their side won all four championship games without scoring a try'*

Statistics can, of course, be used to prove just about anything. Take, for example, our recent Test record. Of our last seven internationals we have won four, drawn one and lost only two – a pretty fair return. But if you choose to make your judgement on the state of Irish rugby over an 18-game period, you can add another 11 losses – not so clever.

But the principle of ensuring you win your home games is sound. And we were very conscious of the need to do exactly that when Romania opened our international season in Dublin before Christmas (won 25–3).

Bearing in mind what had happened to Scotland (lost 15–51 to New Zealand) and Wales (lost 24–26 to Canada) about the same time, you can be sure a victory was our only firm objective. Don't get me wrong: I do believe we have a duty to entertain in international rugby; but the priority must be the result. I don't think many supporters (outside England anyway) would quibble if their side won all four championship games without scoring a try.

Defences are very well organized, and fitter and faster than in the past. Coaching is becoming more professional and tactics more advanced.

The problem against Romania – we managed only one try, through Simon Geoghegan – was that they killed our ball repeatedly and in so doing created goal-kicking chances which Eric Elwood exploited (six successes plus a conversion). We were disappointed with the second half because we seemed to be merely going through the motions. It did not help, of course, that on Romania's last visit, back in 1986, Ireland had won 60–0.

Our previous results in Paris meant rather less pressure on us when our Five Nations campaign kicked off in a city where Ireland had only won once since 1952. Mindful of that depressing fact, we took with us to the Parc des Princes a very limited gameplan, but one constructed with a view to actually winning the game.

I've played in Paris in games which have been over at half-time, when it was just a case of keeping the opposition out for as long as you possibly could because they were going to win anyway. But this time we competed against France for most of the contest. Our gameplan was effective for 70-odd minutes.

Considering the effort we put in, their two late scores (which stretched their lead from 15–23 to a flattering 15–35) were soul-destroying. It reflected a bad performance which ours hadn't been.

> 'I've played in Paris in games which have been over at half-time, when it was just a case of keeping the opposition out for as long as you possibly could because they were going to win anyway. But this time we competed against France for most of the contest'

The game against Wales (lost 15–17) was very much a tale of two goalkickers, Elwood and Neil Jenkins, but we were comfortably in the lead at one stage and wasted gilt-edged chances to pull decisively clear. I remember us getting caught in possession near their line at a time when one more score might have broken them. They then came down the field and scored.

Make no mistake, we created enough chances in the Welsh game to have won. But we were let down by one particular weakness – the fact that when we get in the opposition 22 we aren't able to put away our chances as regularly as we would like. So the game was lost simply because on two occasions we didn't take our chances when five yards from their line. The management were understandably furious. Coach Gerry Murphy said it was ridiculous that international players could not score when five yards out.

Wales deserved to win the game – definitely – because they stuck at their task very well. But nonetheless it was an opportunity that we missed, even if it did unwittingly serve a useful purpose in focusing our minds that bit more at Twickenham.

People were actually talking about dropping Eric Elwood after the Wales game – a game in which he kicked five superb penalty goals (an Irish record for the fixture) but was remembered only for hitting the post with a late attempt and thereby letting Wales off the hook.

It was a ridiculous notion then, and even more so two weeks later when he produced a cracking performance, not just a kicking one, against England at Twickenham (won 13–12). He deserved tremendous credit for that. He would have had a major valley and a major peak inside two weeks. But if nothing else, last season created an experienced international player at number 10 for Ireland. You have to go down before you can appreciate the ups.

> *'Some have accused us of relying too much on Eric [Elwood], but you play to your strengths, and Eric's ability to kick the ball is part of our armoury... A lot of teams can be said to rely on kicking – the "Irish game" perhaps more than most because it relies on getting into positions from which we can sustain controlled pressure situations, and from which penalties so often result'*

Some have accused us of relying too much on Eric, but you play to your strengths, and Eric's ability to kick the ball is part of our armoury when we go onto a pitch. A lot of teams can be said to rely on kicking – the 'Irish game' perhaps more than most because it is reliant on getting into positions from which we can sustain controlled pressure situations, and from which penalties so often result.

The whole day at Twickenham was amazing. Having been involved in 1988, when we lost 3–35, having led 3–0 at half-time, it was particularly satisfying for me. What with Wales beating France in Cardiff, it was a good day to be an underdog – and important, too, as we had worked so hard without any reward against either France or Wales. On paper we looked as though we'd played badly because of the result, which was hugely unfair. After that, to beat England was a huge confidence booster, rescuing a season which had been heading towards disaster.

It was a very different game from our 1993 win in Dublin. We were more confident we could perform this time. They had the support, but we had had the rocket under us from our coach after not taking our chances against Wales. Consequently we went out with the instilled attitude that if you take your chances it'll be difficult for the opposition to win.

Simon Geoghegan had a phenomenal game, which will do him the world of good. The most telling moment in the match was his tackle on Rob Andrew, but his try, which effectively won us the match, will be remembered longer.

The one match I was worried about at the start of the season was the visit of Scotland (drew 6–6). Pre-season, many viewed it as a potential Wooden Spoon decider, and this worried me, as Scotland were the team that had given us our worst beating the previous season. They had completely dominated us in all aspects of the game, and I'd say it was one of the easiest games they'd ever had at Murrayfield.

So taken in that context, the draw was actually a step forward for us. Scotland are very dangerous when they're down, and they proved it at Lansdowne Road. They should have won the game. I'm quite sure Gavin would be disappointed with that result – the more so because they played very well for 60 minutes, and because they no doubt felt they should have been playing like that all season.

We showed tremendous character in salvaging a point while playing into the wind in the second half. But it still reflected a lack of professionalism that we did not win the game given our previous result – further food for thought as the World Cup draws ever closer.

Mick Galwey has eyes only for the loose ball in Paris, supported by Neil Francis (left) and Terry Kingston.

IRELAND (P7 W2 D1 L4 F105 A136):

(H)	v	Romania	(Dublin, 14.11.93)	won	25–3
(A)	v	France	(Paris, 15.1.94)	lost	15–35
(H)	v	Wales	(Dublin, 5.2.94)	lost	15–17
(A)	v	England	(Twickenham, 19.2.94)	won	13–12
(H)	v	Scotland	(Dublin, 5.3.94)	drew	6–6
(A)	v	Australia	(Brisbane, 5.6.94)	lost	13–31
(A)	v	Australia	(Sydney, 11.6.94)	lost	18–32

Ireland in Australia (tour record: P8 W2 D0 L6 F177 A252):

(A)	v	Western Australia	(Perth, 18.5.94)	won	64–8
(A)	v	New South Wales	(Waratah, 22.5.94)	lost	18–55
(A)	v	ACT	(Canberra, 25.5.94)	lost	9–22
(A)	v	Queensland	(Brisbane, 29.5.94)	lost	26–29
(A)	v	Australia B	(Mount Isa, 1.6.94)	lost	9–57
(A)	v	NSW Country	(Lismore, 8.6.94)	won	20–18

IRELAND A (P3 W0 D0 L3 F33 A73):

(A)	v	Scotland	(Ayr, 28.12.93)	lost	9–24
(H)	v	Wales	(Donnybrook, 4.2.94)	lost	10–20
(A)	v	England	(Richmond, 18.2.94)	lost	14–29

Irish Development Squad in Africa (tour record: P7 W6 D0 L1 F219 A103):

(A)	v	Mashonaland	(Harare, 21.7.93)	won	22–10
(A)	v	Zimbabwe A	(Harare, 24.7.93)	won	20–6
(A)	v	Namibia B	(Windhoek, 28.7.93)	won	38–21
(A)	v	Namibia A	(Windhoek, 31.7.93)	lost	19–33
(A)	v	SA Rural Dev.XV	(Nelspruit, 4.8.93)	won	23–18
(A)	v	SA Central Prov.XV	(Pietersburg, 7.8.93)	won	53–15
(A)	v	SA Development XV	(Brakpan, 11.8.93)	won	44–0

IRELAND U-21 (P3 W1 D0 L2 F44 A55):

(H)	v	England	(Gateshead, 7.11.93)	lost	15–22
(H)	v	Wales	(Blackrock, 4.2.94)	lost	5–27
(H)	v	Scotland	(Old Belvedere, 4.3.94)	won	24–6

IRELAND STUDENTS (P1 W0 D0 L1 F9 A23):

(H)	v	England	(Bournemouth, 18.2.94)	lost	9–23

IRISH COLLEGES (P1 W1 D0 L0 F31 A13):

(A)	v	English	(Southampton, 17.2.94)	won	31–13

IRELAND YOUTH (P2 W2 D0 L0 F22 A11):

(A)	v	Wales	(Bridgend, 3.4.94)	won	12–6
(H)	v	Scotland	(Belfast, 9.4.94)	won	10–5

IRELAND SCHOOLS (P3 W2 D0 L1 F52 A41):

(H)	v	Wales	(Dublin, 30.3.94)	won	14–13
(H)	v	Scotland	(Limerick, 4.4.94)	won	30–5
(A)	v	England	(Durham, 13.4.94)	lost	8–23

IRELAND WOMEN (P4 W2 D0 L2 F29 A115):

(–)	v	Scottish Students★	(Burnbrae, 13.4.94)	won	18–5

(−)	v	France*	(Burnbrae, 15.4.94)	lost	0–31
(−)	v	United States*	(q/f: Edinburgh, 17.4.94)	lost	0–76
(−)	v	Japan*	(3/4: Edinburgh, 24.4.94)	won	11–3

* second World Cup

DOMESTIC RUGBY

INTER-PROVINCIAL CHAMPIONSHIP

	P	W	D	L	F	A	Pts
Leinster	4	3	0	1	72	40	4
Munster	4	3	0	1	91	71	6
Ulster	4	2	0	2	84	59	4
Exiles	4	1	0	3	71	80	2
Connacht	4	0	0	4	42	110	0

IRISH PROVINCES v SCOTTISH DISTRICTS

Glasgow 22, Munster 17 (Glagow); Scottish North & Midlands 19, Connacht 20 (Dunfermline); Leinster 8, Edinburgh 13 (Dublin); Ulster 44, South of Scotland 26 (Belfast); Edinburgh 39, Ulster 13 (Hawkhill); South of Scotland 16, Leinster 26 (Melrose); Connacht 25, Glasgow 47 (Galway); Munster 6, Scottish North & Midlands 13 (Cork).

Irish fullback Conor O'Shea opens his legs and shows his class against Romania at Lansdowne Road.

SENIOR CUP FINALS
Ulster Cup: Dungannon 14, Instonians 10 (Ravenhill, 23.4.94)
Munster Cup: Sunday's Well 20, Young Munster 9 (Musgrave Park, 30.4.94)
Leinster Cup: Terenure College 12, Greystones 8 (7.5.94)
Connacht Cup: Connemara 10, Galway Corinthians 14 (8.5.94)

INSURANCE CORPORATION ALL-IRELAND CHAMPIONSHIP

Division One:	P	W	D	L	F	A	Pts
Garryowen	10	8	0	2	172	108	16
Cork Constitution	10	7	0	3	201	123	14
Blackrock College	10	7	0	3	137	99	14
Dungannon	10	5	0	5	181	130	10
Lansdowne	10	5	0	5	162	167	10
St Mary's College	10	5	0	5	157	163	10
Young Munster	10	5	0	5	102	149	10
Shannon	10	4	0	6	107	104	8
Old Wesley	10	4	0	6	114	138	8
Greystones	10	4	0	6	97	156	8
Wanderers	10	1	0	9	141	234	2

champions: Garryowen; *relegated:* Wanderers, Greystones.

Division Two:	P	W	D	L	F	A	Pts
Instonians	10	8	0	2	205	100	16
Sunday's Well	10	8	0	2	184	118	16
Ballymena	10	7	0	3	214	125	14
Old Belvedere	10	7	0	3	141	125	14
Bangor	10	5	0	5	122	189	10
Terenure College	10	4	1	5	149	112	9
Malone	10	4	1	5	125	141	9
Old Crescent	10	4	0	6	173	150	8
Dolphin	10	4	0	6	139	144	8
Galwegians	10	3	0	7	113	124	6
Ballina	10	0	0	10	72	309	0

promoted: Instonians (c), Sunday's Well; *relegated:* Ballina, Galwegians

Div 3: *promoted:* UCD (c), Bective Rangers; *relegated:* Sligo, Collegians, Portadown
Div 4: *promoted:* Monkstown and Waterpark; *relegated:* none

1980:

E	L9–24	Twickenham	19 Jan	**p:** Campbell 3
S	W22–15	Dublin	2 Feb	**t:** Keane, Kennedy
				c: Campbell
				p: Campbell 3
				dg: Campbell
F	L18–19	Paris	1 Mar	**t:** McLennan
				c: Campbell
				p: Cambell 3
				dg: Campbell
W	W21–7	Dublin	15 Mar	**t:** Irwin, O'Driscoll, C Fitzgerald
				c: Campbell 3
				p: Campbell
R+	D13–13	Dublin	18 Oct	**t:** F Quinn
				p: Campbell 3

1981:

F	L13–19	Dublin	7 Feb	**t:** MacNeill
				p: Campbell 3
W	L8–9	Cardiff	21 Feb	**t:** Slattery, MacNeill
E	L6–10	Dublin	7 Mar	**dg:** Campbell, MacNeill
S	L9–10	Edinburgh	21 Mar	**t:** Irwin
				c: Campbell
				p: Campbell
SA(1)	L15–23	Cape Town	30 May	**t:** McGrath, McLennan
				c: Campbell 2
				p: Campbell
SA(2)	L10–12	Durban	6 Jun	**t:** O'Brien
				p: Quinn 2
A	L12–16	Dublin	21 Nov	**p:** Ward 4

1982:

W	W20–12	Dublin	23 Jan	**t:** Ringland, Finn 2
				c: Campbell
				p: Campbell 2
E	W16–15	Twickenham	6 Feb	**t:** MacNeill, McLoughlin
				c: Campbell
				p: Campbell 2
S	W21–12	Dublin	20 Feb	**p:** Campbell 6
				dg: Campbell
F	L9–22	Paris	20 Mar	**p:** Campbell 3

1983:

S	W15–13	Edinburgh	15 Jan	**t:** Kiernan
				c: Campbell
				p: Campbell 3
F	W22–16	Dublin	19 Feb	**t:** Finn 2
				c: Campbell
				p: Campbell 4
W	L9–23	Cardiff	5 Mar	**p:** Campbell 2, MacNeill

E	W25–15	Dublin	19 Mar	t: Slattery, Campbell
				c: Campbell
				p: Campbell 5

1984:

F	L12–25	Paris	21 Jan	p: Campbell 4
W	L9–18	Dublin	4 Feb	p: Campbell 3
E	L9–12	Twickenham	18 Feb	p: Ward 3
S	L9–32	Dublin	3 Mar	t: Kiernan
				c: J Murphy
				p: J Murphy
A	L9–16	Dublin	10 Nov	p: Kiernan 3

1985:

S	W18–15	Edinburgh	2 Feb	t: Ringland 2
				c: Kiernan 2
				p: Kiernan
				dg: Kiernan
F	D15–15	Dublin	2 Mar	p: Kiernan 5
W	W21–9	Cardiff	16 Mar	t: Crossan, Ringland
				c: Kiernan 2
				p: Kiernan 3
E	W13–10	Dublin	30 Mar	t: Mullin
				p: Kiernan 2
				dg: Kiernan
J(1)[+]	W48–13	Osaka	26 May	t: Ringland 3, Matthews 2, Kiernan,
				MacNeill, C Fitzgerald
				c: Kiernan 5
				p: Kiernan 2
J(2)[+]	W33–15	Tokyo	2 Jun	t: Kiernan 2, Mullin, Anderson
				c: Kiernan 4
				p: Kiernan 3
Fj[+]	W16–15	Dublin	19 Oct	t: Bradley
				p: Kiernan 4

1986:

F	L9–29	Paris	1 Feb	p: Kiernan 3
W	L12–19	Dublin	15 Feb	t: Ringland
				c: Kiernan
				p: Kiernan 2
E	L20–25	Twickenham	1 Mar	t: Ringland, Mullin, McCall
				c: Kiernan
				p: Kiernan 2
S	L9–10	Dublin	15 Mar	t: Ringland
				c: Kiernan
				p: Kiernan
R	W60–0	Dublin	1 Nov	t: Crossan 3, Mullin 2, Dean 2,
				Anderson, Bradley, MacNeill
				c: Kiernan 7
				p: Kiernan 2

1987:

| E | W17–0 | Dublin | 7 Feb | t: Kiernan, Matthews, Crossan |

				c: Kiernan
				p: Kiernan
S	L12–26	Edinburgh	21 Feb	t: Lenihan
				c: Kiernan
				p: Kiernan
				dg: Kiernan
F	L13–19	Dublin	21 Mar	t: Ringland, Bradley
				c: Kiernan
				p: Kiernan
W(a)	W15–11	Cardiff	4 Apr	t: Dean, Mullin
				c: Kiernan 2
				p: Kiernan
W(b)*	L6–13	Wellington	25 May	p: Kiernan 2
C*	W46–19	Dunedin	30 May	t: Bradley, Crossan 2, Spillane, Ringland, MacNeill
				c: Kiernan 5
				p: Kiernan 2
				dg: Kiernan, Ward
T*	W32–9	Brisbane	3 Jun	t: MacNeill 2, Mullin 3
				c: Ward 3
				p: Ward 2
A*	L15–33	Sydney	7 Jun	t: MacNeill, Kiernan
				c: Kiernan 2
				p: Kiernan

1988:

S	W22–18	Dublin	16 Jan	t: Mullin, MacNeill, Bradley
				c: Kiernan 2
				p: Kiernan
				dg: Kiernan
F	L6–25	Paris	20 Feb	p: Kiernan 2
W	L9–12	Dublin	5 Mar	t: Kingston
				c: Kiernan
				p: Kiernan
E(a)	L3–35	Twickenham	19 Mar	dg: Kiernan
E(b)	L10–21	Dublin	23 Apr	t: S Smith, MacNeill
				c: Kiernan
WS	W49–22	Dublin	29 Oct	t: Crossan 2, Kiernan, Matthews, Mullin, Francis, McBride, Sexton
				c: Kiernan 4
				p: Kiernan 2
				dg: Sexton
It	W31–15	Dublin	31 Dec	t: Crossan 2, Matthews 2, Aherne
				c: Cunningham
				p: Danaher 2
				dg: Dean

1989:

F	L21–26	Dublin	21 Jan	t: Mullin
				c: Kiernan
				p: Kiernan 5
W	W19–13	Cardiff	4 Feb	t: Mannion, Dean

				c: Kiernan
				p: Kiernan 3
E	L3–16	Dublin	18 Feb	p: Kiernan
S	L21–37	Edinburgh	4 Mar	t: Mullin 2, Dunlea
				c: Kiernan 3
				p: Kiernan
C⁺	W24–21	Victoria	2 Sep	t: Dunlea, Sexton
				c: Kiernan 2
				p: Kiernan 4
US⁺	W32–7	New York	9 Sep	t: Dunlea, Mannion, Crossan, Bradley
				c: Kiernan 2
				p: Kiernan 3
				dg: B Smith
NZ	L6–23	Dublin	18 Nov	p: B Smith 2

1990:

E	L0–23	Twickenham	20 Jan	
S	L10–13	Dublin	3 Feb	t: J Fitzgerald
				p: Kiernan 2
F	L12–31	Paris	3 Mar	p: Kiernan 4
W	W14–8	Dublin	24 Mar	t: S Smith, McBride, Kingston
				c: Kiernan
Arg	W20–18	Dublin	27 Oct	t: Hooks, Kiernan
				p: Kiernan 4

1991:

F	L13–21	Dublin	2 Feb	t: S Smith
				p: Kiernan 3
W	D21–21	Cardiff	18 Feb	t: Clarke, Mullin, Geoghegan, Staples
				c: B Smith
				p: B Smith
E	L7–16	Dublin	2 Mar	t: Geoghegan
				p: B Smith
S	L25–28	Edinburgh	16 Mar	t: Crossan, Robinson, Geoghegan, Mullin
				c: B Smith 3
				dg: B Smith
Na(1)	L6–15	Windhoek	20 Jul	t: penalty try
				c: Mullin
Na(2)	L15–26	Windhoek	27 Jul	t: Staples, Cunningham
				c: Staples 2
				dg: Curtis
Z★	W55–11	Dublin	6 Oct	t: Robinson 4, Geoghegan, Popplewell 2, Curtis
				c: Keyes 4
				p: Keyes 5
J★	W32–16	Dublin	9 Oct	t: O'Hara, Mannion 2, Staples
				c: Keyes 2
				p: Keyes 4
S(b)★	L15–24	Edinburgh	12 Oct	p: Keyes 4
				dg: Keyes
A★	L18–19	Dublin	20 Oct	t: Hamilton

				c: Keyes
				p: Keyes 3
				dg: Keyes

1992:

W	L15–16	Dublin	18 Jan	**t:** Wallace
				c: Keyes
				p: Keyes 3
E	L9–38	Twickenham	1 Feb	**t:** Keyes
				c: Keyes
				p: Keyes
S	L10–18	Dublin	15 Feb	**t:** Wallace
				p: Keyes 2
F	L12–44	Paris	21 Mar	**p:** McAleese 4
NZ(1)	L21–24	Dunedin	30 May	**t:** Cunningham 2, Staples
				c: Russell 3
				p: Russell
NZ(2)	L6–59	Wellington	6 Jun	**t:** Furlong
				c: Russell
A[†]	L17–42	Dublin	31 Oct	**t:** Wallace
				p: Russell 4

1993:

S	L 3–15	Edinburgh	16 Jan	**p:** Malone
F	L 6–21	Dublin	20 Feb	**p:** Malone 2
W	W19–14	Cardiff	6 Mar	**t:** Robinson
				c: Elwood
				p: Elwood 3
				dg: C Clarke
E	W17–3	Dublin	20 Mar	**t:** Galwey
				p: Elwood 2
				dg: Elwood 2
R	W25–3	Dublin	14 Nov	**t:** Geoghegan
				c: Elwood
				p: Elwood 6

1994

F	L15–35	Paris	15 Jan	**p:** Elwood 5
W	L15–17	Dublin	5 Feb	**p:** Elwood 5
E	W13–12	Twickenham	19 Feb	**t:** Geoghegan
				c: Elwood
				p: Elwood 2
S	D 6–6	Edinburgh	5 Mar	**p:** Elwood 2
A(1)	L13–31	Brisbane	5 Jun	**t:** Johns
				c: Elwood
				p: Elwood, O'Shea
A(2)	L18–32	Sydney	11 Jun	**t:** Francis, Clohessy
				c: O'Shea
				p: O'Shea
				dg: O'Shea

★ World Cup matches

[+] Non-cap tests

[†] Five-point try introduced from this game onwards

SCOTLAND

Gavin Hastings

DON'T brand us as failures, even if we did not win an international in five attempts. To call us that suggests we did not achieve anything, and that is not the case. We stared into the abyss, walked through a tunnel of gloom, and emerged stronger for the experience.

Scotland has to accept that we are not capable of beating sides that we probably could have done four or five years ago when we had truly world class players in our ranks. We don't have such a team again yet. There are no world-class replacements for David Sole, Finlay Calder, John Jeffrey, Derek White or Sean Lineen. We have to face the fact that we are in a period of transition and need to build up gradually again.

The stark reality is that, right now, no one international match is any easier for Scotland than the rest. Every time we play, we have to go out with sufficient dedication and tactical nouse to enable us to win. Nothing can be left to chance, no matter who the opposition.

I'm not saying I want our supporters to lower their expectations, to resign themselves to second best – the public perception of Scotland winning at home has been very strong over the last few years and I don't want to change that. I'm aiming to ensure we again build up a proud record at Murrayfield, starting this Autumn against the Springboks.

What I am saying is that if we beat Ireland as opposed to, say, England, the achievement should be no less lauded, because our preparation will have been equally thorough for both games.

That said, I would be lying if I tried to pretend that certain defeats did not hurt more than others. And in the case of the 1993/94 campaign it was the New Zealand and England losses that I found especially painful.

> *'The All Black game was marred by ill-judged team selection on our part – while England's visit to Murrayfield saw us robbed by what I will forever consider to have been a refereeing blunder'*

For different reasons, too. The All Black game (lost 15–51) was marred for me by ill-judged team selection on our part – while England's visit to Murrayfield (lost 14–15) saw us robbed by what I will forever consider to have been a refereeing blunder. To tell the truth, I secretly feared we might be in for a depressing afternoon against New Zealand, having learned so much about them in the summer of 1993 while captaining the British Lions. But our cause was certainly not helped by that team selection.

I can only think the selectors got carried away by the performance of Scotland A in only losing 9–20, three days after our district champions, The South, had been pasted 84–5 by the tourists' midweek XV. Five or six of the A team were promoted into the senior ranks the following week. I hasten to add that I had no input into the selection, and that I was as bemused as anyone when the teamsheet appeared. How they could justify moving my brother Scott from centre to wing, for example, totally defeated me.

I know just how hard it is to raise your game two weeks in a row against the All Blacks. The Lions were not capable of it, so these A-team players were certainly not going to be capable of doing it. Experience had also taught me that the All Blacks always leave something in reserve for the Test matches. They know they are judged by their performances in internationals, and that, not surprisingly, is where their record is so strong.

New Zealand took every scoring opportunity against us, and I can tell you, conceding 50 points at home hurt like hell. But it wasn't so much the scoreline as the manner by which it was compiled. I don't like being humiliated on a rugby pitch, and I felt that we were on 20 November.

Despite making seven changes, our fortunes barely improved on our next outing, against Wales (lost 6–29). The weather on the opening day of the 1994 Five Nations Championship was absolutely miserable in Cardiff, and in those conditions their bigger pack was always likely to influence the outcome. What I will say, on a positive note, is that after the Welsh game we were, however belatedly, at least in a position of being able to recognize our optimum strength. And thereafter the forwards improved in every match. It was the backs who let down the cause.

> *'I know just how hard it is to raise your game two weeks in a row against the All Blacks. The Lions were not capable of it, so our A-team players promoted for the Test were certainly not going to be capable of it'*

The visit of England, conquerors of the same All Black side which had dispatched us, provoked a sudden and dramatic improvement. In many respects it was like the Grand Slam game of 1990 in that we were the underdogs and given absolutely no chance. But fortified by the return of scrum-half Gary Armstrong, and by the additions of Anglo-Scots forwards Alan Sharp, Andy Reed and Peter Walton, we repaired much of our damaged pride.

When Gregor Townsend, starting his first game at outside-half, landed a spectacular dropped goal in injury time, what had been an outrageous dream appeared poised to become reality. For it then to be taken away from us by a highly contentious refereeing decision, capitalized upon by the boot of England full-back Jon Callard, must rank as the most disappointing moment I've ever experienced on a rugby field. It was a refereeing decision no Scot agreed with – and certainly I will never agree with it. Kiwi official Lindsay McLachlan adjudged a Scottish hand to have fingered ruck ball, but I maintain that what he saw was an English cuff.

I know it's easy to say that if we had won that game the season would have been different, but it may well have been. The harsh and cruel manner of that defeat totally knocked the stuffing out of us. And never mind that it was against England. We would have felt equally aggrieved had we gone down to Ireland in the same manner.

Indeed, it was Dublin to which we turned next, but our bid for a sixth straight win over the Irish was undermined by a strong wind, which turned the contest into a lottery. Having said that, we put ourselves in a position to win by trailing only 0–3 after a first half played into the elements. To fail to exploit that position, even if the 6–6 draw did snap our losing streak, was a considerable disappointment – not least because it condemned us to a Wooden Spoon decider against France, of all teams, in Edinburgh.

> *'For victory over England to be taken away from us by a highly contentious refereeing decision must rank as the most disappointing moment I've ever experienced on a rugby field'*

Many observers had felt we would pick up the Wooden Spoon the previous season. But having avoided the ignominy then, we had no place to hide this time round – not after a 12–20 loss to the French gave them their first Murrayfield triumph in 16 years.

In defence of our campaign, we were terribly harshly dealt with by injuries. We lost first-choice wing forward Iain Morrison with a broken leg, closely followed by Rob Wainwright, who had had a magnificent game against England. All of a sudden we were onto our third openside. A country the size of Scotland, with our very limited number of players, simply cannot afford such losses.

A hard-luck season, then, but Scotland does not need pity. And anyone who takes us lightly does so at their peril. All I ask in the coming season is for Scotland to learn from their mistakes, to make sensible team selections, and to have a term free of injuries. For us to have a chance in any given game, we must have our top players on the park.

Scotland scrum-half Gary Armstrong makes available second-phase ball against England, with Ian Smith supplying the cover.

41

SCOTLAND'S INTERNATIONAL SEASON 1993/94

SCOTLAND (P7 W0 D1 L6 F85 A156):

(H) v New Zealand	(Edinburgh, 20.11.93)	lost	15–51
(A) v Wales	(Cardiff, 15.1.94)	lost	6–29
(H) v England	(Edinburgh, 5.2.94)	lost	14–15
(A) v Ireland	(Dublin, 5.3.94)	drew	6–6
(H) v France	(Edinburgh, 19.3.94)	lost	12–20
(A) v Argentina	(Buenos Aires, 4.6.94)	lost	15–16
(A) v Argentina	(Buenos Aires, 11.6.94)	lost	17–19

Scotland in Argentina (tour record: P6 W1 D1 L4 F123 A125):

(A) v Buenos Aires	(Buenos Aires, 25.5.94)	drew	24–24
(A) v Cuyo	(Mendoza, 28.5.94)	lost	11–25
(A) v Córdoba	(Córdoba, 31.5.94)	won	40–14
(A) v Rosario	(Rosario, 7.6.94)	lost	16–27

All Blacks in Scotland (tour record: P4 W4 D0 L0 F186 A41):

(A) v South of Scotland	(Gala, 10.11.93)	lost	5–84
(A) v Scottish Dev XV	(Edinburgh, 16.11.93)	lost	12–31

SCOTLAND A (P4 W2 D0 L2 F60 A56):

(H) v New Zealand	(Glasgow, 13.11.93)	lost	9–20
(A) v Italy	(Rovigo, 18.12.93)	lost	15–18
(H) v Ireland	(Ayr, 28.12.93)	won	24–9
(A) v France	(Rennes, 20.2.94)	won	12–9

SCOTLAND U–21 (P3 W0 D0 L3 F36 A93):

(A) v Wales	(Glamorgan Wdrs, 14.1.94)	lost	0–36
(A) v Ireland	(Dublin, 4.3.94)	lost	6–24
(A) v Italy	(San Dona di Piave, 2.4.94)	lost	30–33

SCOTLAND U-19 (P2 W0 D0 L2 F21 A36):

(A) v England	(Waterloo, 9.4.94)	lost	6–11
(H) v Wales	(Stirling, 16.4.94)	lost	15–25

SCOTLAND U-18 (P3 W0 D0 L3 F25 A87):

(A) v Wales	(Llanwern, 4.1.94)	lost	8–35
(H) v England	(Kelso, 30.3.94)	lost	12–22
(H) v Ireland	(Limerick, 4.4.94)	lost	5–30

SCOTLAND WOMEN (P4 W2 D0 L2 F68 A39):

(–) v Russia★	(Edinburgh, 13.4.94)	won	57–0
(–) v England★	(Edinburgh, 15.4.94)	lost	0–26
(–) v Wales★	(q/f: Edinburgh, 17.4.94)	lost	0–8
(–) v Canada★	(s/f: Edinburgh, 24.4.94)	won	11–5

★ second World Cup

DOMESTIC RUGBY

McEWAN'S INTER-DISTRICT CHAMPIONSHIP
Final: South 28, Glasgow 14 (Melrose). 3rd/4th play-off: Edinburgh 28, North & Midlands 25 (Melrose). **Semi-finals:** Glasgow 21, Edinburgh 6 (Hughenden); South 37, North & Midlands 13 (Jedburgh)

SCOTTISH DISTRICTS vs IRISH PROVINCES

Glasgow 22, Munster 17 (Glagow); Scottish North & Midlands 19, Connacht 20 (Dunfermline); Leinster 8, Edinburgh 13 (Dublin); Ulster 44, South of Scotland 26 (Belfast); Edinburgh 39, Ulster 13 (Hawkhill); South of Scotland 16, Leinster 26 (Melrose); Connacht 25, Glasgow 47 (Galway); Munster 6, Scottish North & Midlands 13 (Cork)

McEWAN'S CLUB CHAMPIONSHIP

Division One	P	W	D	L	F	A	Pts
Melrose	13	12	0	1	410	192	24
Gala	12	9	0	3	274	214	18
Edinburgh Academicals	13	8	1	4	265	183	17
Heriot's FP	12	7	0	5	230	224	14
Watsonians	13	7	0	6	276	337	14
Stirling County	12	6	1	5	227	163	13
Hawick	12	6	1	5	218	178	13
Jed-Forest	13	6	0	7	231	199	12
Currie	12	6	0	6	230	285	12
Stewart's-Melville FP	13	5	1	7	157	190	11
Boroughmuir	12	5	0	7	214	228	10
West of Scotland	13	4	1	8	235	279	9
Kelso	13	4	0	9	175	296	8
Selkirk	13	0	1	12	138	312	1

champions: Melrose; *relegated:* Kelso, Selkirk

Division Two	P	W	D	L	F	A	Pts
Glasgow High/Kelvinside	13	13	0	0	440	115	26
Dundee High School FP	12	11	0	1	395	80	22
Kirkcaldy	13	10	0	3	277	150	20
Edinburgh Wanderers	13	8	0	5	214	251	16
Musselburgh	13	7	0	6	204	185	14
Peebles	13	6	0	7	206	219	12
Glasgow Academicals	13	5	1	7	237	276	11
Wigtownshire	13	5	0	8	172	241	10
Haddington	12	5	0	7	146	220	10
Grangemouth	13	4	1	8	201	293	9
Biggar	13	3	2	8	203	240	8
Preston Lodge FP	13	4	0	9	158	291	8
Clarkston	13	4	0	9	158	357	8
Ayr	13	3	0	10	168	261	6

promoted: GHK (champions), Dundee HSFP; *relegated:* Clarkston, Ayr

Div 3 – *promoted:* Gordonians (c), Corstorphine; *relegated:* Howe of Fife, Perthshire

Div 4 – *promoted:* Trinity Acads (c), Edinurgh Univ; *relegated:* Cartha Queen's Park, Leith Acads

Div 5 – *promoted:* Duns (c), Glenrothes; *relegated:* Aberdeenshire, Lenzie

Div 6 – *promoted:* Allan Glen's (c), Cumbernauld; *relegated:* Moray, Lasswade

Div 7 – *promoted:* Annan (c), Aberdeen Univ; *relegated:* Dalkeith, Montrose & District

CUP FINALS

Alloa Brewery Cup:
Boroughmuir 42, Dundee HSFP 18 (Meggatland, 7.5.94)

Castlemaine XXXX Trophy:
Forrester 22, Garnock 6 (7.5.94)

1980:

I	L15–22	Dublin	2 Feb	**t:** Johnston 2 **c:** Irvine 2 **p:** Irvine
F	W22–14	Edinburgh	16 Feb	**t:** Rutherford, Irvine 2 **c:** Irvine, Renwick **p:** Irvine 2
W	L6–17	Cardiff	1 Mar	**t:** Renwick **c:** Irvine
E	L18–30	Edinburgh	15 Mar	**t:** Tomes, Rutherford **c:** Irvine 2 **p:** Irvine 2

1981:

F	L9–16	Paris	17 Jan	**t:** Rutherford **c:** Renwick **p:** Irvine
W	W15–6	Edinburgh	7 Feb	**t:** Tomes, penalty try **c:** Renwick 2 **p:** Renwick
E	L17–23	Twickenham	21 Feb	**t:** Monro 2, J Calder **c:** Irvine **p:** Irvine
I	W10–9	Edinburgh	21 Mar	**t:** Hay **p:** Irvine **dg:** Rutherford
NZ(1)	L4–11	Dunedin	13 June	**t:** Deans
NZ(2)	L15–40	Auckland	20 Jun	**t:** Hay **c:** Irvine **p:** Irvine 2 **dg:** Renwick
R	W12–6	Edinburgh	26 Sep	**p:** Irvine 4
A	W24–15	Edinburgh	19 Dec	**t:** Renwick **c:** Irvine **p:** Irvine 5 **dg:** Rutherford

1982:

E	D 9–9	Edinburgh	16 Jan	**p:** Irvine 2 **dg:** Rutherford
I	L12–21	Dublin	20 Feb	**t:** Rutherford **c:** Irvine **p:** Renwick 2
F	W16–7	Edinburgh	6 Mar	**t:** Rutherford **p:** Irvine 3 **dg:** Renwick
W	W34–18	Cardiff	20 Mar	**t:** J Calder, Renwick, Pollock, White, Johnston **c:** Irvine 4 **dg:** Renwick, Rutherford

A(1)	W12–7	Brisbane	3 Jul	**t:** Robertson
				c: Irvine
				p: Irvine
				dg: Rutherford
A(2)	L9–33	Sydney	10 Jul	**p:** Irvine 3
Fj⁺	W32–12	Edinburgh	25 Sep	**t:** Dods 2, Johnston, F Calder, Beattie
				c: Dods 3
				p: Dods
				dg: Rutherford

1983:

I	L13–15	Edinburgh	15 Jan	**t:** Laidlaw
				p: Dods 2
				dg: Renwick
F	L15–19	Paris	5 Feb	**t:** Robertson
				c: Dods
				p: Dods
				dg: Gossman 2
W	L15–19	Edinburgh	19 Feb	**t:** Renwick
				c: Dods
				p: Dods 3
E	W22–12	Twickenham	5 Mar	**t:** Laidlaw, Smith
				c: Dods
				p: Dods 3
				dg: Robertson
NZ	D25–25	Edinburgh	12 Nov	**t:** Pollock
				p: Dods 5
				dg: Rutherford 2

1984:

W	W15–9	Cardiff	21 Jan	**t:** Paxton, Aitken
				c: Dods 2
				p: Dods
E	W18–6	Edinburgh	4 Feb	**t:** Johnston, Kennedy
				c: Dods 2
				p: Dods 2
I	W32–9	Dublin	3 Mar	**t:** Laidlaw 2, penalty try, Robertson, Dods
				c: Dods 3
				p: Dods 2
F	W21–12	Edinburgh	17 Feb	**t:** J Calder
				c: Dods
				p: Dods 5
R	L22–28	Bucharest	12 May	**t:** Leslie, Dods
				c: Dods
				p: Dods 3
				dg: Robertson
A	L12–27	Edinburgh	8 Dec	**p:** Dods 4

1985:

I	L15–18	Edinburgh	2 Feb	**p:** Dods 4
				dg: Robertson
F	L3–11	Paris	16 Feb	**p:** Dods

W	L21–25	Edinburgh	2 Mar	**t:** Paxton 2 **c:** Dods 2 **p:** Dods **dg:** Rutherford 2
E	L7–10	Twickenham	16 Mar	**t:** Robertson **p:** Dods

1986:

F	W18–17	Edinburgh	17 Jan	**p:** G Hastings 6
W	L15–22	Cardiff	1 Feb	**t:** Duncan, Jeffrey, G Hastings **p:** G Hastings
E	W33–6	Edinburgh	15 Feb	**t:** Duncan, Rutherford, S Hastings **c:** G Hastings 3 **p:** G Hastings 5
I	W10–9	Dublin	12 Mar	**t:** Laidlaw **p:** G Hastings 2
R	W33–18	Bucharest	30 Mar	**t:** Jeffrey, S Hastings, Deans **c:** G Hastings 3 **p:** G Hastings 5

1987:

I	W16–12	Edinburgh	21 Feb	**t:** Laidlaw, Tukalo **c:** G Hastings **dg:** Rutherford 2
F(a)	L22–28	Paris	7 Mar	**t:** Beattie, S Hastings **c:** G Hastings **p:** G Hastings 4
W	W21–14	Edinburgh	21 Mar	**t:** Beattie, Jeffrey **c:** G Hastings 2 **p:** G Hastings 2 **dg:** Rutherford
E	L12–21	Twickenham	4 Apr	**t:** Robertson **c:** G Hastings **p:** G Hastings 2
Sp⁺	W25–7	Edinburgh	19 Apr	**t:** Duncan, Tukalo, Deans, Paxton **c:** G Hastings 3 **p:** G Hastings
F(b)*	D20–20	Christchurch	23 May	**t:** White, Duncan **p:** G Hastings 4
Z*	W60–21	Wellington	30 May	**t:** Tait 2, Duncan 2, Tukalo 2, Paxton 2, Oliver, G Hastings, Jeffrey **c:** G Hastings 8
R*	W55–28	Dunedin	2 Jun	**t:** G Hastings 2, Tukalo, Duncan, Tait 2, Jeffrey 3 **c:** G Hastings 8 **p:** G Hastings
NZ*	L3–30	Christchurch	6 Jun	**p:** G Hastings

1988:

I	L18–22	Dublin	16 Jan	**t:** Laidlaw, S Hastings **c:** G Hastings 2 **p:** G Hastings 2
F	W23–12	Edinburgh	6 Feb	**t:** G Hastings, Tukalo

46

				p: G Hastings 4
				dg: Cramb
W	L20–25	Cardiff	20 Feb	**t:** F Calder, Duncan
				p: G Hastings 4
E	L 6–9	Edinburgh	5 Mar	**p:** G Hastings 2
A	L13–32	Edinburgh	19 Nov	**t:** G Hastings, Robertson
				c: G Hastings
				p: G Hastings

1989:

W	W23–7	Edinburgh	21 Jan	**t:** Armstrong, White, Chalmers
				c: Dods
				p: Dods 2
				dg: Chalmers
E	D12–12	Twickenham	4 Feb	**t:** Jeffrey
				c: Dods
				p: Dods 2
I	W37–21	Edinburgh	4 Mar	**t:** Tukalo 3, Jeffrey, Cronin
				c: Dods 4
				p: Dods 3
F	L3–19	Paris	19 Mar	**p:** Dods
Fj	W38–17	Edinburgh	28 Oct	**t:** Stanger 2, K Milne, Gray, G Hastings, Tukalo
				c: G Hastings 4
				p: G Hastings 2
R	W32–0	Edinburgh	9 Dec	**t:** Stanger 3, White, Sole
				c: G Hastings 3
				p: G Hastings 2

1990:

I	W13–10	Dublin	3 Feb	**t:** White 2
				c: Chalmers
				p: Chalmers
F	W21–0	Edinburgh	17 Feb	**t:** F Calder, Tukalo
				c: Chalmers 2
				p: Chalmers 2, G Hastings
W	W13–9	Cardiff	3 Mar	**t:** Cronin
				p: Chalmers 3
E	W13–7	Edinburgh	17 Mar	**t:** Stanger
				p: Chalmers 3
NZ(1)	L16–31	Dunedin	16 Jun	**t:** Lineen, Gray, Sole
				c: G Hastings 2
NZ(2)	L18–21	Auckland	23 Jun	**t:** Stanger, Moore
				c: G Hastings 2
				p: G Hastings 2
Arg	W49–3	Edinburgh	10 Nov	**t:** Stanger 2, K Milne 2, Moore, Armstrong, Gray, G Hastings, Chalmers
				c: G Hastings 5
				p: G Hastings

1991:

F	L9–15	Paris	19 Jan	**p:** Chalmers 2

				dg: Chalmers
W	W32–12	Edinburgh	2 Feb	**t:** Chalmers, White 2, Armstrong
				c: Chalmers, G Hastings
				p: Chalmers, G Hastings 2
				dg: Chalmers
E(a)	L12–21	Twickenham	16 Feb	**p:** Chalmers 4
I(a)	W28–25	Edinburgh	16 Mar	**t:** G Hastings, Stanger, S Hastings
				c: Chalmers 2
				p: Chalmers 3, G Hastings
R	L12–18	Bucharest	31 Aug	**t:** Tukalo
				c: Dods
				p: Dods 2
J★	W47–9	Edinburgh	5 Oct	**t:** S Hastings, Stanger, Chalmers, penalty try, White, Tukalo, G Hastings
				c: G Hastings 5
				p: Chalmers, G Hastings 2
Z★	W51–12	Edinburgh	9 Oct	**t:** Tukalo 3, Turnbull, Stanger, S Hastings, Weir, White
				c: Dods 5
				p: Dods 2
				dg: Wyllie
I(b)★	W24–15	Edinburgh	12 Oct	**t:** Shiel, Armstrong
				c: G Hastings 2
				p: G Hastings 3
				dg: Chalmers
WS★	W28–6	Edinburgh	19 Oct	**t:** Jeffrey 2, Stanger
				c: G Hastings 2
				p: G Hastings 4
E(b)★	L6–9	Edinburgh	26 Oct	**p:** G Hastings 2
NZ★	L6–13	Cardiff	30 Oct	**p:** G Hastings 2
1992:				
E	L7–25	Edinburgh	18 Jan	**t:** White
				p: G Hastings
I	W18–10	Dublin	15 Feb	**t:** Stanger, Nicol
				c: G Hastings 2
				p: G Hastings 2
F	W10–6	Edinburgh	7 Mar	**t:** Edwards
				p: G Hastings 2
W	L12–15	Cardiff	21 Mar	**p:** G Hastings, Chalmers 2
				dg: Chalmers
A(1)	L12–27	Sydney	13 Jun	**t:** Wainwright
				c: G Hastings
				p: G Hastings 2
A(2)	L13–37	Brisbane	21 Jun	**t:** Lineen, Sole
				c: Chalmers
				p: Chalmers
1993:				
I[†]	W15–3	Edinburgh	16 Jan	**t:** Stark, Stanger
				c: G Hastings
				p: G Hastings

F	L 3–11	Paris	6 Feb	**p:** G Hastings
W	W20–0	Edinburgh	20 Feb	**t:** Turnbull
				p: G Hastings 5
E	L12–26	Twickenham	6 Mar	**p:** G Hastings 3
				dg: Chalmers
NZ	L15–51	Edinburgh	20 Nov	**p:** G Hastings 4, Chalmers
1994				
W	L 6–29	Cardiff	15 Jan	**p:** G Hastings 2
E	L14–15	Edinburgh	5 Feb	**t:** Wainwright
				p: G Hastings 2
				dg: Townsend
I	D 6–6	Dublin	5 Mar	**p:** G Hastings 2
F	L12–20	Edinburgh	19 Mar	**p:** G Hastings 4
Arg(1)	L15–16	Buenos Aires	4 Jun	**p:** M Dods 5
Arg(2)	L17–19	Buenos Aires	11 Jun	**t:** Logan
				p: Shiel 2, M Dods
				dg: Townsend

★ World Cup matches
⁺ Non-cap tests
† Five-point try introduced from this game onwards

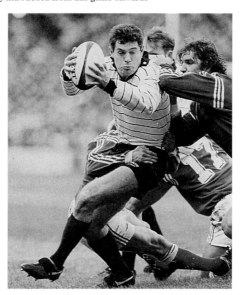

Scotland captain Gavin Hastings celebrates his 50th cap with some French chums at Murrayfield. France won 20–12.

WALES

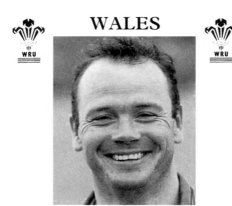

Ieuan Evans

BRINGING the Five Nations Championship title back to Wales in 1994 was a victory for our refusal to put up with mediocrity any longer.

The horrors of our tours to New Zealand (1988) and Australia (1991) and the last World Cup, plus six years without a championship crown, had left the morale of the proudest of rugby nations battered and bruised. Some even suggested the Welsh game was in terminal decline.

That was far from the truth, as thankfully we have since proved, but our return to being truly competitive was only achieved after two years spent painstakingly rebuilding our confidence.

First we developed a defence we could trust, as England discovered at Cardiff Arms Park in 1993. And that spawned the confidence a year later to go forward with the ball. Welsh players have always had the ability to handle the ball well – likewise to beat men. It was a question of eliminating the fear of failure from our minds and putting that inherent ability into practice.

The management worked on this, stressing that the goal for the 1993/94 season would be to achieve a positive try count. The thinking was that by scoring tries you score a massive psychological blow against the opposition. Unlike a penalty goal, which you are usually given by your opponents, tries have to be won. And to win them, especially against modern defences, provides a major adrenalin surge.

So the fact that we went into the season confident in our defence's ability, not only to hold out but to regain possession and set the attack away again, was significant indeed. That 'safety net' made everybody's job easier because it removed the panic when we had the ball.

> *'Welsh players have always had the ability to handle the ball well – likewise to beat men. It was a question of eliminating the fear of failure from our minds and putting that inherent ability into practice'*

It is vital when you are in possession, especially in key areas of the field, that you keep your composure – that you remain patient, bide your time, and don't try things when they're not on. But that all stems from confidence – hence everything we worked on was designed to increase our inner self-belief. It has taken two years – self-belief cannot be achieved overnight – but the psychological battle is being won.

I think we could be very proud that, at a time when no other championship nation save France was scoring tries, we were racking them up. And long may it continue.

The tone was set in our curtain-raiser against Japan (won 55–5). Although they are not one of the leading rugby-playing nations in the world, the fixture provided us with an ideal opportunity to start off in a manner that would stand us in good stead in the tougher contests ahead. Nine tries was a pleasing haul.

Next up was Canada (lost 24–26) and our one major blip. No excuses – we didn't perform. We got conned into playing a style of game that suited them – a physical, battering ram-type game – rather than one that suited us, with our physique and style. We were drawn into this bruising encounter and they came away with the victory. It was a sharp lesson learned. We played badly and allowed ourselves to be led down the wrong path. They gave us channels to run into and trapped us in them.

There were a number of changes which we had to make as a result of our failure to exert control that night. We did not need to be told that as the home side we should have been dictating the pace.

I said in my Captain's Review last year that we must be able to wear the favourite's tag comfortably if we are to move up in the world order. Against Canada we patently failed, although by the end of the season, when we were expected to trounce Portugal and Spain in the World

Cup qualifying ties and did, we proved we were heading in the right direction.

> *'To the players it was unthinkable that Alan Davies and Bob Norster could be sacked, as they had worked so hard to make this team into something. They had achieved minor miracles in restoring us into some sort of shape, and they deserved better'*

Perhaps the most alarming consequence of that wet Cardiff night was that Canada's victory put the futures of coach Alan Davies and manager Bob Norster firmly on the line. To the players it was unthinkable that they could be sacked, as they had worked so hard, basically from scratch, together with assistant Gareth Jenkins, to make this team into something by formulating a pattern which suited us.

When they came on board after the disastrous tour of Australia in 1991, Welsh rugby really was in the depths of despair. They had achieved minor miracles in restoring us into some sort of shape, and we all agreed they really deserved better.

But we also knew that it had been our display against Canada which had so damaged their cause. We carried that burden of guilt over Christmas and into the New Year period, when the speculation intensified that managerial changes were on the cards. The nearer it came to the Five Nations Championship, the more committed we became to saving their bacon by performing above expectation.

This was a strong part of our motivation against Scotland (won 29–6). We felt for Alan and Bob because they had stuck by us. They had been loyal and consistent as far as selection was concerned, sticking with players who had not performed to the height of their ability. Eventually, as the history books show, those players repaid that faith – and I can tell you, they did so as much for the management as for themselves.

Against Scotland we were praised for our ball-handling in atrocious conditions. But as I have already mentioned, that is something Welsh players have always been good at. So it was a question of us playing to our strengths, although I concede it has taken a long time for us to do that satisfactorily. To have done so in the driving rain that submerged the Arms Park, scoring three tries in the process, was great to see.

Our next port of call was Dublin (won 17–15), where you are always assured of a battle. It's fair to say that if you are under any other impression, you more often than not come to grief. We produced the necessary battling performance, of which we were very proud, and Neil Jenkins, who claimed all our points, kicked wonderfully well.

People have said that Eric Elwood's kick which struck an upright late on, when we were two points ahead, saved us from defeat. Not so. I firmly believe that had that kick gone over we would still have won. We were camped in the Irish 22 throughout the remaining minutes, and had we had to score again we would have done. As it was we were more content with retaining possession at their end of the field. I would go so far as to say that it was one of the best ten-minute spells Wales have played since I came into the team back in 1987.

> *'I know from experience that when the French get on a roll, they rarely allow teams to score at the other end. The feeling of joy, mixed with relief, when Nigel Walker hared away to score the winning try, will remain with me for years'*

But the highlight of our season was still to come, a fortnight later, when France came to Cardiff confidently anticipating their 13th successive win against us. None of our side had ever won against the French and none of them had ever lost to us – not even Philippe Sella with his world-record haul of caps. He has now.

Bearing in mind all our injuries (Nigel Davies, Wayne Proctor and I were all missing from the side which had won in Dublin), Wales produced an immense performance (won 24–15), which showed me how mentally mature we had become. We refused to let the changes affect either our game or the newly found belief in our collective ability.

What most impressed me was the way we came back after France had built up a momentum in the second half. I know from experience that when the French get on a roll, they rarely allow teams to score at the other end. The feeling of joy, mixed with relief, when Nigel Walker hared away to score the winning try, will remain with me for years.

It was a pleasure to see two teams who wanted to play the way the game should be played, and I think everyone enjoyed it. I would have to pick out Scott Quinnell's performance as being particularly impressive, made that little bit extra special by his early wonder try.

Victory meant that we would go to Twickenham with a chance of our first Grand Slam in 16 years – the Triple Crown and the Championship itself. To add further spice, England could also take the title if they could win by 16 clear points.

We had a month to ponder the prospect, which with hindsight was a double-edged sword. It might have given us extra time to prepare, but it also left us more time to mull over the enormity of what was at stake, and to become embroiled in the media speculation which, naturally enough, was rife.

> *'The fact that we finished top only on points-difference should not detract from the achievement. By winning three of our four games convincingly we had taken out an insurance covering our Twickenham visit and I was disappointed that certain people questioned our right to be champions'*

England, had been unfairly castigated in the press for their try-less campaign, and we were under no illusions as to how good they were potentially. That said, after losing 8–15 we were more disappointed with our own performance because we failed to win enough ball. We did score a beautifully simple try, and in the end there was only one score between us. Who knows what could have happened had one or two more bounces gone our way? England deserved to win the game but we deserved to win the championship.

The fact that we finished top only on points-difference should not detract from the achievement. By winning three of our four games convincingly we had taken out an insurance covering our Twickenham visit, and I was disappointed that certain people questioned our right to be champions.

There could certainly be no questioning our right to be in the World Cup, even if we did have to qualify. We left no room for any doubt by winning through at the expense of Portugal (102–11) and Spain (54–0).

At the start of 1993/94 I thought we were capable of having a good season, and we proved it to ourselves. But there's no use in having just one good season. We must continue to build and develop. It is important for the future of the game in Wales that we reach the top of world rugby, and that in so doing we hopefully put a smile back on the faces of more than just Welshmen.

WALES (P15 W12 D0 L3 F511 A209):

(A)	v	Zimbabwe	(Bulawayo, 22.5.93)	won	35–14
(A)	v	Zimbabwe	(Harare, 29.5.93)	won	42–13
(A)	v	Namibia	(Windhoek, 5.6.93)	won	38–23
(H)	v	Japan	(Cardiff, 16.10.93)	won	55–5
(H)	v	Canada	(Cardiff, 10.11.93)	lost	24–26
(H)	v	Scotland	(Cardiff, 15.1.94)	won	29–6
(A)	v	Ireland	(Dublin, 5.2.94)	won	17–15
(H)	v	France	(Cardiff, 19.2.94)	won	24–15
(A)	v	England	(Twickenham, 19.3.94)	lost	8–15
(A)	v	Portugal	(Lisbon, 18.5.94)	won	102–11
(A)	v	Spain	(Madrid, 21.5.94)	won	54–0
(A)	v	Canada	(Toronto, 11.6.94)	won	33–15
(A)	v	Fiji	(Suva, 18.6.94)	won	23–8
(A)	v	Tonga	(Nuku'alofa, 22.6.94)	won	18–9
(A)	v	Western Samoa	(Apia, 25.6.94)	lost	9–34

WALES A (P5 W5 D0 L0 F168 A42):

(H)	v	Japan	(Llanelli, 29.9.93)	won	61–5
(H)	v	North of England	(Pontypool, 13.10.93)	won	24–8
(A)	v	Ireland A	(Donnybrook, 4.2.94)	won	20–10
(H)	v	Canada A	(Cardiff, 12.3.94)	won	42–11
(H)	v	France A	(Cardiff, 18.3.94)	won	21–8

Wales development squad in France (tour record: P3 W2 D0 L1 F83 A59):

(A)	v	French Students	(Bayonne, 20.5.93)	won	30–29
(A)	v	Côte des Basques	(Dax, 23.5.93)	won	41–8
(A)	v	Aquitaine XV	(Mimizan, 25.5.93)	lost	12–22

WALES U-21 (P2 W2 D0 L0 F63 A5):

(H)	v	Scotland U-21	(Glamorgan Wdrs, 14.1.94)	won	36–0
(A)	v	Ireland U-21	(Carlow, 4.2.94)	won	27–5

WALES STUDENTS (P2 W2 D0 L0 F46 A28):

(H)	v	France	(Cardiff, 18.2.94)	won	18–6
(A)	v	England	(Oxford, 18.3.94)	won	28–22

WALES U-19 (P1 W1 D0 L0 F25 A15):

(A)	v	Scotland	(Stirling, 16.4.94)	won	25–15

WALES YOUTH (P4 W2 D0 L2 F53 A64):

(H)	v	Italy Youth	(Newport, 27.2.94)	won	24–14
(A)	v	France Juniors	(Le Puy, 12.3.94)	lost	8–28
(H)	v	England Colts	(Cardiff, 27.3.94)	won	15–10
(H)	v	Ireland Youth	(Bridgend, 3.4.94)	lost	6–12

WALES SCHOOLS U-18 (P4 W2 D0 L2 F75 A55):

(H)	v	Scotland	(Llanwern, 4.1.94)	won	35–8
(H)	v	France	(Swansea, 18.2.94)	won	24–11
(A)	v	England	(Bournemouth, 22.3.94)	lost	3–22
(A)	v	Ireland	(Dublin, 30.3.94)	lost	13–14

WALES SCHOOLS U-16 (P1 W0 D1 L1 F11 A11):

(A)	v	England	(Twickenham, 9.4.94)	drew	11–11

WALES SCHOOLS U-16 'A' (P1 W0 D0 L1 F8 A9):

(A)	v	England A	(London Welsh, 8.4.94)	lost	8–9

WALES WOMEN (P5 W3 D0 L2 F53 A96):

(–)	v	Canada★	(Gala, 11.4.94)	won	11–5
(–)	v	Kazakhstan★	(Gala, 13.4.94)	won	29–8
(–)	v	Scotland★	(q/f: Edinburgh, 17.4.94)	won	8–0
(–)	v	USA★	(s/f: Gala, 20.4.94)	lost	5–56
(–)	v	France★	(3/4: Edinburgh, 24.4.94)	lost	0–27

★ second World Cup

DOMESTIC RUGBY

HEINEKEN CLUB CHAMPIONSHIP

Division One:	P	W	D	L	F	A	Pts
Swansea	22	20	0	2	549	264	40
Neath	22	17	2	3	581	286	36
Pontypridd	22	17	1	4	571	299	35
Cardiff	22	15	2	5	668	240	32
Llanelli	22	13	1	8	461	366	27
Bridgend	22	10	1	11	466	434	21
Newport	22	8	1	13	362	472	17
Newbridge	22	7	1	14	367	440	15
Pontypool	22	7	0	15	312	626	14
Dunvant	22	6	1	15	288	464	13
Aberavon	22	6	1	15	242	464	13
Cross Keys	22	0	0	22	239	751	0

champions: Swansea; *relegated:* Dunvant, Cross Keys

Division Two:	P	W	D	L	F	A	Pts
Treorchy	22	20	1	1	425	200	41
Abertillery	22	15	1	6	473	242	31
Maesteg	21	12	1	8	354	253	25
South Wales Police	21	12	0	9	361	311	24
Narberth	22	10	0	12	273	294	20
Tenby United	22	10	0	12	308	366	20
Llanharan	22	9	2	11	259	349	20
Ebbw Vale	22	8	2	12	279	312	18
Penarth	22	9	0	13	291	372	18
Llandovery	22	8	1	13	269	370	17
Mountain Ash	22	8	0	14	275	333	16
Glamorgan Wanderers	22	6	0	16	262	418	12

promoted: Treorchy (champions), Abertillery; *relegated:* Mountain Ash, Glamorgan Wanderers

Div 3 – *promoted:* Abercynon (c), Bonymaen; *relegated:* Tumble, St Peter's
Div 4 – *promoted:* Builth Wells (c), Caerphilly; *relegated:* Garndiffaith, Wrexham

SWALEC CUP FINAL
Cardiff 15, Llanelli 8 (Cardiff, 7.5.94)

PRYSG-WHITBREAD CUP FINAL
Wattstown 15, Hartridge HSOB 6 (Cardiff, 23.4.94)

1980:

F	W18–9	Cardiff	19 Jan	**t:** E Rees, Holmes, D S Richards, G Price
				c: G Davies
E	L8–9	Twickenham	16 Feb	**t:** E Rees, Squire
S	W17–6	Cardiff	1 Mar	**t:** Holmes, Keen, D S Richards
				c: Blyth
				p: Fenwick
I	L7–21	Dublin	15 Mar	**t:** Blyth
				p: Fenwick
NZ	L3–23	Cardiff	1 Nov	**p:** Fenwick

1981:

E	W21–19	Cardiff	17 Jan	**t:** G Davies
				c: Fenwick
				p: Fenwick 4
				dg: G Davies
S	L6–15	Edinburgh	7 Feb	**dg:** Fenwick 2
I	W 9–8	Cardiff	21 Feb	**p:** G Evans 2
				dg: Pearce
F	L15–19	Paris	7 Mar	**t:** D S Richards
				c: G Evans
				p: G Evans 3
A	W18–13	Cardiff	5 Dec	**t:** R Moriarty
				c: G Evans
				p: G Evans 3
				dg: G Davies

1982:

I	L12–20	Dublin	23 Jan	**t:** Holmes
				c: G Evans
				p: G Evans
				dg: Pearce
F	W22–12	Cardiff	6 Feb	**t:** Holmes
				p: G Evans 6
E	L7–17	Twickenham	6 Mar	**t:** JR Lewis
				dg: G Davies
S	L18–34	Cardiff	20 Mar	**t:** Butler
				c: G Evans
				p: G Evans 4

1983:

E	D13–13	Cardiff	5 Feb	**t:** Squire
				p: Wyatt 2
				dg: Dacey
S	W19–15	Edinburgh	19 Feb	**t:** S Jones, E Rees
				c: Wyatt
				p: Wyatt 3
I	W23–9	Cardiff	5 Mar	**t:** Wyatt, Holmes, E Rees
				c: Wyatt
				p: Wyatt 3

F	L9–16	Paris	19 Mar	t: Squire
				c: Wyatt
				p: G Evans
J⁺	W29–24	Cardiff	22 Oct	t: Hadley, Brown, Dacey, Bowen, Giles
				c: Wyatt 3
				p: Wyatt
R	L6–24	Bucharest	12 Nov	p: G Evans 2

1984:

S	L9–15	Cardiff	21 Jan	t: Titley
				c: H Davies
				p: H Davies
I	W18–9	Dublin	4 Feb	t: Ackerman
				c: H Davies
				p: H Davies 2, Bowen 2
F	L16–21	Cardiff	18 Feb	t: H Davies, Butler
				c: H Davies
				p: H Davies 2
E	W24–15	Twickenham	17 Mar	t: Hadley
				c: H Davies
				p: H Davies 4
				dg: Dacey 2
A	L9–28	Cardiff	24 Nov	t: Bishop
				c: Wyatt
				p: Wyatt

1985:

S	W25–21	Edinburgh	2 Mar	t: Pickering 2
				c: Wyatt
				p: Wyatt 4
				dg: G Davies
I	L9–21	Cardiff	16 Mar	t: P Lewis
				c: G Davies
				p: G Davies
F	L3–14	Paris	30 Mar	p: Thorburn
E	W24–15	Cardiff	20 Apr	t: J Davies, Roberts
				c: Thorburn 2
				p: Thorburn 3
				dg: J Davies
Fj	W40–3	Cardiff	9 Nov	t: P Davies 2, Titley, Holmes, Hadley, James, Pickering
				c: Thorburn 3
				p: Thorburn 2

1986:

E	L18–21	Twickenham	17 Jan	t: Bowen
				c: Thorburn
				p: Thorburn 3
				dg: J Davies
S	W22–15	Cardiff	1 Feb	t: Hadley
				p: Thorburn 5
				dg: J Davies
I	W19–12	Dublin	15 Feb	t: P Lewis, P Davies

				c: Thorburn
				p: Thorburn 3
F	L15–23	Cardiff	1 Mar	p: Thorburn 5
Fj	W22–15	Suva	31 May	t: J Davies, Bowen
				c: Bowen
				p: Dacey 3
				dg: J Davies
T	W15–7	Nuku'alofa	12 Jun	t: P Moriarty
				c: Dacey
				p: Bowen 2, Dacey
WS	W32–14	Apia	14 Jun	t: Titley 2, Bowen, R Moriarty
				c: Dacey 2
				p: Dacey 3
				dg: J Davies

1987:

F	L9–16	Paris	7 Feb	p: Thorburn 3
E	W19–12	Cardiff	7 Mar	t: S Evans
				p: Wyatt 5
S	L15–21	Edinburgh	21 Mar	t: M Jones
				c: Wyatt
				p: Wyatt 2
				dg: J Davies
I	L11–15	Cardiff	4 Apr	t: I Evans, Norster
				p: Wyatt
I(b)*	W13–6	Wellington	25 May	t: Ring
				p: Thorburn
				dg: J Davies 2
T*	W29–16	Palmerston North	29 May	t: Webbe 3, Hadley
				c: Thorburn 2
				p: Thorburn 2
				dg: J Davies
C*	W40–9	Brisbane	3 Jun	t: I Evans 4, Bowen, Hadley, Devereux, A Phillips
				c: Thorburn 4
E(b)*	W16–3	Brisbane	8 Jun	t: Roberts, Jones, Devereux
				c: Thorburn 2
NZ*	L6–49	Brisbane	14 Jun	t: Devereux
				c: Thorburn
A*	W22–21	Rotorua	18 Jun	t: Roberts, P Moriarty, Hadley
				c: Thorburn 2
				p: Thorburn 2
US	W46–0	Cardiff	7 Nov	t: Bowen 2, Clement 2, Webbe, Young, P Moriarty, Norster
				c: Thorburn 4
				p: Thorburn 2

1988:

E	W11–3	Twickenham	6 Feb	t: Hadley 2
				dg: J Davies
S	W25–20	Cardiff	20 Feb	t: J Davies, I Evans, Watkins
				c: Thorburn 2

I	W12–9	Dublin	5 Mar	p: Thorburn dg: J Davies 2 t: P Moriarty c: Thorburn
F	L9–10	Cardiff	19 Mar	p: Thorburn dg: J Davies t: I Evans c: Thorburn
NZ(1)	L3–52	Christchurch	28 May	p: Thorburn p: Ring
NZ(2)	L9–54	Auckland	11 Jun	t: J Davies c: Ring p: Ring
WS	W24–6	Cardiff	12 Nov	t: N Davies 2, J Davies, C Davies c: Thorburn 4
R	L9–15	Cardiff	10 Dec	t: Devereux c: Thorburn p: Thorburn

1989:

S	W23–7	Edinburgh	21 Jan	t: Hall p: Bowen
I	L13–19	Cardiff	4 Feb	t: M Jones p: Thorburn 3
F	L12–31	Paris	18 Feb	p: Thorburn 4
E	W12–9	Cardiff	18 Mar	t: Hall c: Thorburn p: Thorburn 2
NZ	L9–34	Cardiff	4 Nov	p: Thorburn 3

1990:

F	L19–29	Cardiff	20 Jan	t: Titley p: Thorburn 4 dg: D Evans
E	L6–34	Twickenham	17 Feb	t: P Davies c: Thorburn
S	L9–13	Cardiff	3 Mar	t: Emyr c: Thorburn p: Thorburn
I	L8–14	Dublin	24 Mar	t: Ford, G O Llewellyn
Na(1)	W18–9	Windhoek	2 Jun	t: Thorburn, Bridges c: Thorburn 2 p: Thorburn 2
Na(2)	W34–30	Windhoek	9 Jun	t: Emyr 2, O Williams, penalty try c: Thorburn 3 p: Thorburn 3 dg: Clement
Ba	L24–31	Cardiff	6 Oct	t: Thorburn c: Thorburn p: Thorburn 5 dg: D Evans

1991:

E	L6–25	Cardiff	19 Jan	**p:** Thorburn, N Jenkins
S	L12–32	Edinburgh	2 Feb	**t:** Ford
				c: Thorburn
				p: Thorburn 2
I	D21–21	Cardiff	16 Feb	**t:** Arnold, N Jenkins
				c: Thorburn 2
				p: Thorburn 2
				dg: N Jenkins
F(a)	L3–36	Paris	2 Mar	**p:** Thorburn
A(a)	L6–63	Brisbane	21 Jul	**p:** Thorburn
				dg: A Davies
F(b)	L9–22	Cardiff	4 Sep	**t:** Collins
				c: Ring
				p: Ring
WS★	L13–16	Cardiff	6 Oct	**t:** Emyr, I Evans
				c: Ring
				p: Ring
Arg★	W16–7	Cardiff	9 Oct	**t:** Arnold
				p: Ring 3, Rayer
A(b)★	L3–38	Cardiff	12 Oct	**p:** Ring

1992:

I	W16–15	Dublin	18 Jan	**t:** S Davies
				p: N Jenkins 3
				dg: C Stephens
F	L9–12	Cardiff	1 Feb	**p:** N Jenkins 3
E	L0–24	Twickenham	7 Mar	
S	W15–12	Cardiff	21 Mar	**t:** Webster
				c: N Jenkins
				p: N Jenkins 3
It[++]	W43–12	Cardiff	7 Oct	**t:** Clement, I Evans, Gibbs, C Stephens, Webster, S Davies, Rayer
				c: C Stephens 4
				p: C Stephens 2
A	L6–23	Cardiff	21 Nov	**p:** C Stephens 2

1993:

E	W10–9	Cardiff	6 Feb	**t:** I Evans
				c: N Jenkins
				p: N Jenkins
S	L 0–20	Edinburgh	20 Feb	
I	L14–19	Cardiff	6 Mar	**t:** I Evans
				p: N Jenkins 3
F	L10–26	Paris	20 Mar	**t:** Walker
				c: N Jenkins
				p: N Jenkins
Z(1)	W35–14	Bulawayo	22 May	**t:** Moon, Hill, Proctor, P Davies
				c: N Jenkins 3
				p: N Jenkins 2
				dg: A Davies
Z(2)	W42–13	Harare	29 May	**t:** G O Llewelyn 2, Bidgood, J Davies, N Jenkins, S Davies

				c: N Jenkins 3
				p: N Jenkins 2
Na	W38–23	Windhoek	5 Jun	t: Lewis 2, Hill, Proctor, Moon
				c: N Jenkins 2
				p: N Jenkins 3
J	W55–5	Cardiff	16 Oct	t: I Evans 2, Gibbs 2, Moon, Clement, Lewis, Rayer, N Jenkins
				c: N Jenkins 5
C	L24–26	Cardiff	10 Nov	p: N Jenkins 8

1994

S	W29–6	Cardiff	15 Jan	t: Rayer 2, I Evans
				c: N Jenkins
				p: N Jenkins 4
I	W17–15	Dublin	5 Feb	t: N Jenkins
				p: N Jenkins 4
F	W24–15	Cardiff	19 Feb	t: Quinnell, Walker
				c: N Jenkins
				p: N Jenkins 4
E	L 8–15	Twickenham	19 Mar	t: Walker
				p: N Jenkins
P=	W102–11	Lisbon	18 May	t: Walker 4, I Evans 3, Hall 3, R Jones 2, Taylor, Quinnell, Llewelyn, penalty try
				c: N Jenkins 11
S=	W54–0	Madrid	21 May	t: Quinnell, I Evans 3, Walker, G Jenkins, penalty try
				c: N Jenkins 5
				p: N Jenkins 3
C	W33–15	Toronto	11 Jun	t: I Evans, Hall 2
				c: N Jenkins 3
				p: N Jenkins 4
Fj	W23–8	Suva	18 Jun	t: Rayer, Collins
				c: A Davies 2
				p: A Davies 3
T	W18–9	Nuku'alofa	22 Jun	p: N Jenkins 6
WS	L9–34	Apia	25 Jun	p: N Jenkins 3

* World Cup
= World Cup qualifier
† Five-point try introduced from this game onwards

FRANCE

Olivier Roumat

Speaking with Chris Thau

FROM my viewpoint France's season started well and ended in disarray. We won a Test series in South Africa, shared the spoils with the world-champion Wallabies, and beat Romania twice. Yet much of our good work was undone in the Five Nations Championship.

We were told we had failed our public and supporters by not providing a spectacle, and this I totally refute. But it affected the team. Instead of people supporting us, and trying to understand what we were trying to achieve, they criticized us for 'lack of flair'. We felt pushed, trying to run before we could walk. We stopped doing the basics properly and tried to do the fancy stuff – and that proved very damaging.

It was all a far cry from the previous summer in South Africa, where our policy of 'returning to basics' had reaped rich reward. We returned home feeling that we had matured into a meaningful side – one that understood the game better, was less prone to making mistakes, and was more aware of its means and capabilities.

Our autumn displays against Australia added weight to this belief. In a word, we grew up and we proved we could look after ourselves. After all that, to come within one defeat of the championship Wooden Spoon, and for me to be dropped for that crucial Scotland game, was a great disappointment.

The year, rather than season (because these days international

63

rugby is a year-round business), effectively began in South Africa, although we had beaten Romania 37–20 in Bucharest with three tries from the 'Pau Rocket' Philippe Bernat-Salles.

The previous year we had shared a home series against the Springboks, so we knew it would be tough going. And as most of the players were exhausted after a very demanding 1992/93 season, our coaches wisely kept changing the side around during the early games.

I captained the side in Port Elizabeth in the first match against Eastern Province. I was both flattered and delighted. Given my chequered career in the French team, I had not expected such an honour. We did not play particularly well, but it is always like that in the first game on tour. Some had forecast aggro because Adri Geldenhuys, the Eastern lock forward, had bashed Abdel Benazzi in the Lyon Test the previous autumn. But there was none. In fact, perhaps the most significant aspect of the game was that we won.

Jean-François ('Jeff') Tordo made his long-awaited return next time against Western Province in Cape Town, and took over the captaincy. But it was a fateful return. A dreadful performance on our part was totally overshadowed by the incident involving Gary Pagel, one of the Province props, who appeared to test his studs on Tordo's face. A lot has been said about the incident, but I cannot accept that anyone would deliberately put a fellow player out of the game. I honestly believe that it was an accident – a very ugly and dangerous accident. I cannot believe it was deliberate.

> *'A lot has been said about the incident when Gary Pagel appeared to test his studs on Jeff Tordo's face, but I cannot accept that anyone would deliberately put a fellow player out of the game. I honestly believe that it was an accident – a very ugly and dangerous accident'*

Pagel was suspended but then, foolishly, transformed a rugby matter – unfortunate and sad – into a legal issue, which became the theme of the tour. Instead of concentrating on games, we kept reading in newspapers about Pagel's appeals and the legal tragi-comedy that followed.

Once Jeff Tordo had left the field (he required 50 stitches to his mouth, nose and cheek in a two-hour plastic-surgery operation), I took over the captaincy and retained it until the end of the tour.

Initially, the tour to South Africa was designed as a build-up for the World Cup. At the beginning of the tour, that was our main theme: developing a strong side capable of challenging England, Australia or New Zealand in 1995. But as the tour wore on, it took on a different meaning.

We lost the third game of the tour to South Africa B – the first defeat in my short career as captain. We did not play too badly, but the truth was that the South Africans wanted to win more than we did.

We drew the following game, against the Orange Free State in Bloemfontein, but in bizarre circumstances. A spectator ran onto the field and physically prevented David Berty, our left wing, from scoring a try!

> 'Nothing could prepare us for the atmosphere at Ellis Park in Johannesburg. When I ran out onto the field, the sound of the crowd hit me like a physical blow. The pressure was immense. The South Africans obviously felt that the first Test draw had been an accident, and they decided to throw everything at us'

Although statistically the tour was not too impressive, from a human viewpoint it proved a tremendous success in the sense that it allowed us to develop a great camaraderie within the squad, and allowed several young players to prove themselves at the highest level.

Though we lost to Northern Transvaal, the result actually did us a major favour. The South Africans read too much into the defeat, and thought we would be easy meat in the first Test in Durban the following weekend. How wrong they were.

The international at Kings Park (drew 20–20) was one of the most intense games in which I have ever played. The atmosphere was electric. By then we had lost two seasoned campaigners in Laurent Seigne (damaged knee) and Abdel Benazzi (in hospital with infected wound). Yet, still, our forwards had a tremendous game. Philippe Benetton tackled his heart out; Laurent Cabannes was immense at the tail of the lineout; Stephane Graou, in only his second international, did not give an inch; and Olivier Merle, who had replaced Abdel, was a tower of strength.

I played my normal game; in other words I did not do anything out of the ordinary. I jumped, I won my ball, I pushed in the scrum, I tackled and I ran. However, I did also give the guys a useful tip. South

Africa had spent the last five minutes camped on our line, and before one of a succession of scrums I sensed that they would go for the pushover try. I told my forwards that we had to be ready, and they really came up trumps. The Springbok pack tried every trick in the book but could not dislodge us. In fact, at one point we actually pushed them back and won the put-in.

So to the decisive Test (won 18–17) played in the boiling cauldron of Ellis Park, Johannesburg, the biggest rugby ground in the world. Our build-up was tremendous, for which credit must go to Pierre Berbizier, Christophe Mombet and Guy Laporte, who instilled in the side a tremendous sense of pride and achievement.

But nothing could prepare us for the atmosphere at Ellis Park. When I ran out onto the field, the sound of the crowd hit me like a physical blow. The pressure was immense. The South Africans obviously felt that the first Test draw had been an accident and they decided to throw everything at us. They did exactly that and the first 20 minutes were hell.

> 'The second Test against South Africa saw one of the most magnificent defensive efforts ever by a French team. We succeeded in getting back to basics. From now on we could work towards adding what the British call "the French flair"'

They scored an excellent try on the left after about five minutes, followed by a penalty, and it looked as though we were in trouble. But we talked amongst ourselves, agreeing that this was something we had all expected, and that if we could do the basics right and defend properly, we could prevail.

Sure enough, we bounced back into the contest by taking the game to them. Their lineout was operating better than it had been in the first Test, but – crucially – we enjoyed a 20-minute spell on top. We carried on with the same simple but effective plan, and took the lead early in the second half. Neither side scored tries in that period but I have to say I have never run so much in my life.

They came to within a point of us with about ten minutes to go, and tried everything on us. But we stood firm and absorbed everything. It was one of the most magnificent defensive efforts ever by a French team. We had succeeded in getting back to basics. From now on we could work towards adding what the British call 'the French flair'.

We took a break after the tour in order to recharge our batteries for the Autumn campaign. We did play Romania in Brive but, unlike in the Spring contest in Bucharest, they were not as well prepared. We beat them rather easily (won 51–0) and got ourselves in top gear for the big encounter with the world-champion Wallabies in Bordeaux.

Games against Australia have taken on a special meaning for France since our wonderful semi-final win in the 1987 World Cup, and despite the fact that Philippe Sella, the king of centres, was the only survivor from six years ago, we wanted to prove that this French team could scale such heights.

But at that stage Australia had a superior side. This did not mean they couldn't be beaten in a one-off game, or that they weren't vulnerable in the World Cup. What it did mean was that in a Test series, while they could be surprised in one game (as they were, losing 13–16 in Bordeaux), they would most likely bounce back (as they did, winning 24–3 in Paris).

> *'Our concentration has improved, our comprehension has developed, our discipline is better, we don't give away silly penalties as we used to, and we play an intelligent game similar to the great generation of the 1980s…The collective force is superior to the sum of individual talents. This is the ultimate accolade of a team'*

It was pleasing that we maintained our record of never having lost a Test series to Australia on home soil. But again, the real achievement was in human terms.

Our concentration has improved, our comprehension has developed, our discipline is better, we don't give away silly penalties as we used to, and we play an intelligent game similar to the great generation of the 1980s. What has happened to this French side, which is full of talented individuals, is that the collective force is superior to the sum of individual talents. This is the ultimate accolade of a team.

But we were not the finished, fully mature article, and the proof was provided by the 1994 Five Nations Championship. We beat the Irish (35–15) rather easily in Paris, but the old theme in the French media about the 'dull France' has re-emerged.

We lost to a very keen and motivated Wales (15–24) because we made mistakes – too many mistakes. We had a dreadful first half but we bounced back in the second. We played better rugby than the Welsh and controlled the game most of the time. But we made basic mistakes which allowed them to punish us. Suddenly, everything that had been achieved the previous summer seemed lost. The media started baying for blood.

The following game against England (lost 14–18) was another aberration, which signalled the end of my spell as captain of France. We lost, although again we could have won. This became the new French theme.

> 'We played better rugby than the Welsh and controlled the game most of the time. But we made basic mistakes which allowed them to punish us. Suddenly, everything that had been achieved the previous summer seemed lost. The media started baying for blood'

We did not make as many mistakes as we had in Cardiff, but we failed to score when a try could have made the difference. We allowed them to control the game, but one should give credit to Rob Andrew, who was magnificent. I felt that our forwards were on a par with the English, although perhaps my contribution in the lineout was not as impressive as it could have been.

I have to say that the words of the French Rugby Federation president, Monsieur Lapasset, who criticized the players for not trying hard enough, really hurt. We lost, but not through a lack of effort.

I paid the ultimate price by being dropped for the game in Scotland (won 20–12) and it was embarrassing to be kicked out like that in full flight. I am confident that they made a mistake, and they will have to live with it. I have nothing to blame myself for, but I am now back at square one, having yet again to prove myself.

That was my goal last summer on the tour of New Zealand, the launching pad for our World Cup campaign. France has both the talent and the know-how to win the World Cup, even if we do have to rebalance our act after our last Five Nations campaign.

FRANCE'S INTERNATIONAL SEASON 1993/94

FRANCE (P11 W6 D1 L4 F245 A171):

(A)	v	Romania	(Bucharest, 20.5.93)	won	37–20
(A)	v	South Africa	(Durban, 26.6.93)	drew	20–20
(A)	v	South Africa	(Johannesburg, 3.7.93)	won	18–17
(H)	v	Romania	(Brive, 9.10.93)	won	51–0
(H)	v	Australia	(Bordeaux, 30.10.93)	won	16–3
(H)	v	Australia	(Paris, 6.11.93)	lost	3–24
(H)	v	Ireland	(Paris, 15.1.94)	won	35–15
(A)	v	Wales	(Cardiff, 19.2.94)	lost	15–24
(H)	v	England	(Paris, 5.3.94)	lost	14–18
(A)	v	Scotland	(Edinburgh, 19.3.94)	won	20–12
(A)	v	Canada	(Ottawa, 5.6.94)	lost	16–18

France in South Africa (tour record: P8 W4 D2 L2 F169 A159):

(A)	v	Eastern Province	(Port Elizabeth, 9.6.93)	won	18–8
(A)	v	Western Province	(Cape Town, 12.6.93)	won	12–6
(A)	v	South Africa B	(East London, 15.6.93)	lost	22–35
(A)	v	Orange Free State	(Bloemfontein, 19.6.93)	drew	22–22
(A)	v	Northern Transvaal	(Pretoria, 22.6.93)	lost	19–38
(A)	v	SA Development XV	(Welkom, 29.6.93)	won	38–13

FRANCE A (P3 W1 D0 L2 F37 A41):

(H)	v	Scotland A	(Rennes, 20.2.94)	lost	9–12
(H)	v	England A	(Paris, 5.3.94)	won	20–8
(A)	v	Wales A	(Cardiff, 18.3.94)	lost	8–21

FRANCE U-21 (P1 W1 D0 L0 F13 A9):

(H)	v	England	(Rouen, 11.5.94)	won	13–9

FRANCE STUDENTS (P2 W1 D0 L1 F42 A35):

(A)	v	Wales	(Cardiff, 18.2.94)	lost	6–18
(H)	v	England	(Dunkirk, 4.3.94)	won	36–17

FRANCE JUNIORS (P2 W1 D1 L0 F39 A19):

(H)	v	Wales Youth	(Le Puy, 12.3.94)	won	28–8
(A)	v	England Colts	(Moseley, 23.4.94)	drew	11–11

FRANCE 18-GROUP (P2 W0 D0 L2 F24 A38):

(A)	v	Wales	(Swansea, 18.2.94)	lost	11–24
(H)	v	England	(Cahors, 2.4.94)	lost	13–14

FRANCE WOMEN (P5 W4 D0 L1 F239 A18):

(–)	v	Scottish Students★	(Burnbrae, 11.4.94)	won	76–0
(–)	v	Ireland★	(Burnbrae, 15.4.94)	won	31–0
(–)	v	Japan★	(q/f: Edinburgh, 17.4.94)	won	99–0
(–)	v	England★	(s/f: Gala, 20.4.94)	lost	6–18
(–)	v	Wales★	(3/4: Edinburgh, 24.4.94)	won	27–0

★ second World Cup

Club Championship final (Parc des Princes, Paris, 28.5.94)
Toulouse (6) 22 (try: Cazalbou; conversion: Deylaud, penalty goals: Deylaud 3;
dropped goals: Deylaud 2)
Montferrand (9) 16 (try: Juillet; penalty goals: Pradier 3; conversion: Pradier)
(attendance: 48,000)

*Michael Lynagh tries desperately to clear his lines as opposite number Alain Penaud hovers
above during Australia's 24–3 defeat of France in Paris.*

1980:

W	L 9–18	Cardiff	19 Jan	**t:** Marchal
				c: Caussade
				dg: Caussade
E	L13–17	Paris	2 Feb	**t:** Averous, Rives
				c: Caussade
				p: Caussade
S	L14–22	Edinburgh	16 Feb	**t:** Gallion, Gabernet
				p: Gabernet
				dg: Caussade
I	W19–18	Paris	1 Mar	**t:** Gourdon 2
				c: Aguirre
				p: Aguirre 2
				dg: Pedeutour
SA	L15–37	Pretoria	8 Nov	**t:** Dintrans
				c: Vivies
				p: Vivies 3
R	L 0–15	Bucharest	23 Nov	

1981:

S	W16–9	Paris	17 Jan	**t:** Blanco, Bertranne
				c: Caussade
				p: Vivies, Gabernet
I	W19–13	Dublin	7 Feb	**t:** Pardo
				p: Laporte 2, Gabernet
				dg: Laporte 2
W	W19–15	Paris	7 Mar	**t:** Gabernet
				p: Laporte 3, Gabernet 2
E	W16–12	Twickenham	21 Mar	**t:** Lacans, Pardo
				c: Laporte
				dg: Laporte 2
A(1)	L15–17	Brisbane	5 Jul	**t:** Mesny
				c: Gabernet
				p: Blanco, Gabernet
				dg: Vivies
A(2)	L14–24	Sydney	11 Jul	**t:** Lacas, Elissalde
				dg: Elissalde, Sallefranque
R	W17–9	Narbonne	1 Nov	**t:** Elissalde 2, Blanco
				p: Gabernet 2
NZ(1)	L9–13	Toulouse	14 Nov	**p:** Laporte 2
				dg: Gabernet
NZ(2)	L6–18	Paris	21 Nov	**p:** Laporte, Blanco

1982:

W	L12–22	Cardiff	6 Feb	**t:** Blanco
				c: Sallefranque
				p: Sallefranque, Martinez
E	L15–27	Paris	20 Feb	**t:** Pardo
				c: Sallefranque
				p: Sallefranque 2

				dg: Lescarboura
S	L7–16	Edinburgh	6 Mar	t: Rives
				p: Sallefranque
I	W22–9	Paris	20 Mar	t: Blanco, Mesny
				c: Gabernet
				p: Blanco 2, Gabernet 2
R	L9–13	Bucharest	31 Oct	t: Fabre
				c: Camberabero
				dg: Camberabero
Arg(1)	W25–12	Toulouse	14 Nov	t: Sella 2, Esteve, Blanco
				p: Blanco, Camberabero
				dg: Camberabero
Arg(2)	W13– 6	Paris	20 Nov	t: Begu, Blanco
				c: Camberabero
				p: Camberabero

1983:

E	W19–15	Twickenham	15 Jan	t: Esteve, Sella, Paparemborde
				c: Blanco 2
				p: Camberabero
S	W19–15	Paris	5 Feb	t: Esteve 2
				c: Blanco
				p: Blanco 3
I	L16–22	Dublin	19 Feb	t: Blanco, Esteve
				c: Blanco
				p: Blanco 2
W	W16–9	Paris	19 Mar	t: Esteve
				p: Blanco 3
				dg: Camberabero
A(1)	D15–15	Clermont-Ferrand	13 Nov	p: Lescarboura 3
				dg: Lescarboura, Lafond
A(2)	W15– 6	Paris	20 Nov	t: Esteve
				c: Lescarboura
				p: Gabernet, Lescarboura 2

1984:

I	W25–12	Paris	21 Jan	t: Gallion, Sella
				c: Lescarboura
				p: Lescarboura 4
				dg: Lescarboura
W	W21–16	Cardiff	18 Feb	t: Sella
				c: Lescarboura
				p: Lescarboura 4
				dg: Lescarboura
E	W32–18	Paris	3 Mar	t: Codorniou, Sella, Esteve, Bergu, Gallion
				c: Lescarboura 3
				p: Lescarboura
				dg: Lescarboura
S	L12–21	Edinburgh	17 Mar	t: Gallion
				c: Lescarboura
				p: Lescarboura

NZ(1)	L9–10	Christchurch	16 Jun	**dg:** Lescarboura **t:** Blanco **c:** Lescarboura **p:** Lescarboura
NZ(2)	L18–31	Auckland	23 Jun	**t:** Lescarboura 2, Bonneval **p:** Lescarboura 2
R	W18–3	Bucharest	11 Nov	**t:** Sella, Lescarboura **c:** Lescarboura 2 **p:** Lescarboura 2

1985:

E	D9–9	Twickenham	2 Feb	**dg:** Lescarboura 3
S	W11–3	Paris	16 Feb	**t:** Blanco 2 **p:** Lescarboura
I	D15–15	Dublin	2 Mar	**t:** Esteve, Codorniou **c:** Lescarboura 2 **p:** Lescarboura
W	W14–3	Paris	30 Mar	**t:** Esteve, Gallion **p:** Lescarboura 2
Arg(1)	L16–24	Buenos Aires	22 Jun	**t:** Blanco, Bonneval **c:** Lescarboura **p:** Lescarboura 2
Arg(2)	W23–15	Buenos Aires	29 Jun	**t:** Codorniou, Erbani, Berbizier, Blanco **c:** Lescarboura 2 **p:** Lescarboura
J(1)[*]	W50–0	Dax	19 Oct	**t:** Lafond 4, Fabre, Cassagne, Codorniou, Rodriguez, Detrez, Dubroca **c:** Camberabero 5
J(2)[*]	W52–0	Nantes	26 Oct	**t:** Camberabero 2, Lafond 2, Charvet 2, Dintrans 2, Fabre, Rodriguez **c:** Camberabero 6

1986:

S	L17–18	Edinburgh	17 Jan	**t:** Berbizier, Sella **p:** Laporte 2 **dg:** Laporte
I	W29–9	Paris	1 Feb	**t:** Berbizier, Marocco, Sella **c:** Laporte **p:** Laporte 3, Blanco **dg:** Lafond
W	W23–15	Cardiff	1 Mar	**t:** Sella, Lafond 2, Blanco **c:** Laporte 2 **dg:** Laporte
E	W29–10	Paris	15 Mar	**t:** Sella, Blanco, penalty try, Laporte **c:** Laporte 2 **p:** Laporte 3
R(a)	W25–13	Lille	12 Apr	**t:** Charvet, Bonneval, Sella, Erbani, Lagisquet **c:** Laporte **p:** Laporte
Arg(1)	L13–15	Buenos Aires	31 May	**t:** Bonneval **p:** Laporte 3

Arg(2)	W22–9	Buenos Aires	7 Jun	t: Lescarboura, Sella, Debroca
				c: Lescarboura 2
				p: Lescarboura 2
A	L14–27	Sydney	21 Jun	t: Blanco 2, Sella
				c: Lescarboura
NZ(a)	L9–18	Christchurch	28 Jun	dg: Lescarboura 3
R(b)	W20–3	Bucharest	25 Oct	t: Andrieu, Blanco, Berot
				c: Berot
				p: Berot 2
NZ(b1)	L7–19	Toulouse	8 Nov	t: Sella
				p: Berot
NZ(b2)	W16–3	Nantes	15 Nov	t: Charvet, Lorieux
				c: Berot
				p: Berot 2

1987:

W	W16–9	Paris	7 Feb	t: Mesnel, Bonneval
				c: Berot
				p: Berot 2
E	W19–15	Twickenham	21 Feb	t: Bonneval, Sella
				c: Berot
				p: Berot 2
				dg: Mesnel
S(a)	W28–22	Paris	7 Mar	t: Bonneval 3, Berot
				p: Berot 3
				dg: Mesnel
I	W19–13	Dublin	21 Mar	t: Champ 2
				c: Berot
				p: Berot 3
S(b)★	D20–20	Christchurch	23 May	t: Sella, Berbizier, Blanco
				c: Blanco
				p: Blanco 2
R(a)★	W55–12	Wellington	28 May	t: Charvet 2, Lagisquet 2, Sella, Andrieu, Camberabero, Erbani, Laporte
				c: Laporte 8
				p: Laporte
Z★	W70–12	Auckland	2 Jun	t: Modin 3, Camberabero 3, Charvet 2, Dubroca, Rodriguez 2, Esteve, Laporte
				c: Camberabero 9
Fj★	W31–16	Auckland	7 Jun	t: Lorieux, Rodriguez 2, Lagisquet
				c: Laporte 3
				p: Laporte 2
				dg: Laporte
A★	W30–24	Sydney	13 Jun	t: Lorieux, Sella, Lagisquet, Blanco
				c: Camberabero 4
				p: Camberabero 2
NZ★	L9–29	Auckland	20 Jun	t: Berbizier
				c: Camberabero
				p: Camberabero
S(c)[+]	L12–15	Galashiels	26 Sep	t: Mesnel
				c: Bianchi
				p: Bianchi 2

R(b)	W49–3	Agen	11 Nov	t: Berot, Lagisquet 2, Andrieu 2, Ondarts, penalty try
				c: Berot 6
				p: Berot 3

1988:

E	W10–9	Paris	16 Jan	t: Rodriguez
				p: Berot 2
S	L12–23	Edinburgh	6 Feb	t: Lagisquet
				c: Berot
				p: Berot
				dg: Lescarboura
I	W25–6	Paris	20 Feb	t: Blanco, Lagisquet, Sella, Camberabero, Carminati
				c: Camberabero
				dg: Berot
W	W10–9	Cardiff	19 Mar	t: Lescarboura
				p: Lafond 2
Arg(a1)	W18–15	Buenos Aires	18 Jun	t: Dintrans
				c: Berot
				p: Berot 4
Arg(a2)	L6–18	Buenos Aires	25 Jun	p: Berot 2
Arg(b1)	W29–9	Nantes	5 Nov	t: Blanco 2, Cecillon, Lagisquet, Rodriguez
				c: Berot 3
				p: Berot
Arg(b2)	W28–18	Lille	11 Nov	t: Sanz, Cecillon, Andrieu, Sella
				c: Berot 3
				p: Berot 2
R	W16–12	Bucharest	26 Nov	t: Blanco, Lagisquet
				c: Berot
				p: Berot 2

1989:

I	W26–21	Dublin	21 Jan	t: Lagisquet 2, Blanco, Lafond
				c: Lafond 2
				p: Lafond 2
W	W31–12	Paris	18 Feb	t: Blanco 2, Berbizier, Dintrans
				c: Lafond 3
				p: Lafond 2
				dg: Mesnel
E	L0–11	Twickenham	4 Mar	
S	W19–3	Paris	19 Mar	t: Berbizier, Blanco, Lagisquet
				c: Berot 2
				p: Berot
USSR*	W18–16	Valence	20 May	t: Roumat
				c: Lafond
				p: Lafond 3, Camberabero
NZ(1)	L17–25	Christchurch	17 Jun	t: Blanco 2, Cecillon
				c: Berot
				p: Berot
NZ(2)	L20–34	Auckland	1 Jul	t: Rouge-Thomas, Cecillon

				p: Blanco 4
BL	L27–29	Paris	4 Oct	t: Blanco, Benetton, Camberabero
				c: Camberabero 3
				p: Camberabero 3
A(1)	L15–32	Strasbourg	4 Nov	p: Camberabero 4
				dg: Camberabero
A(2)	W25–19	Lille	11 Nov	t: Lagisquet, Andrieu
				c: Lacroix
				p: Lacroix 5

1990:

W	W29–19	Cardiff	20 Jan	t: Lafond, Sella, Camberabero, Lagisquet, Rodriguez
				c: Camberabero 3
				p: Camberabero
E	L7–26	Paris	3 Feb	t: Lagisquet
				p: Charvet
S	L0–21	Edinburgh	17 Feb	
I	W31–12	Paris	3 Mar	t: Mesnel 2, Lagisquet
				c: Camberabero 2
				p: Camberabero 5
R	L6–12	Auch	24 May	p: Lescarboura 2
A(1)	L9–21	Sydney	9 Jun	p: Camberabero 3
A(2)	L31–48	Brisbane	24 Jun	t: Blanco 2, Armary, Lacombe
				c: Camberabero 3
				p: Camberabero 3
A(3)	W28–19	Sydney	30 Jun	t: Camberabero, Mesnel
				c: Camberabero
				p: Camberabero 2, Blanco
				dg: Camberabero 3
NZ(1)	L3–24	Nantes	3 Nov	p: Camberabero
NZ(2)	L12–30	Paris	10 Nov	p: Camberabero 3
				dg: Camberabero

1991:

S	W15–9	Paris	19 Jan	p: Camberabero 2
				dg: Blanco, Camberabero 2
I	W21–13	Dublin	2 Feb	t: Lagisquet, Cabannes
				c: Camberabero 2
				p: Camberabero 3
W(a)	W36–3	Paris	2 Mar	t: Blanco, Saint-André, Mesnel, Roumat, Sella, Lafond
				c: Blanco, Camberabero 2
				p: Camberabero 2
E	L19–21	Twickenham	16 Mar	t: Saint-André, Camberabero, Mesnel
				c: Camberabero 2
				p: Camberabero
R(a)	W33–21	Bucharest	22 Jun	t: Blanco, Camberabero, Cecillon, Simon
				c: Camberabero
				p: Camberabero 5
US(1)	W41–9	Denver	13 Jul	t: Blanco 2, Lafond, Saint-André, Champ, Courtiols, Cecillon, Mesnel

				c: Camberabero 3
				p: Camberabero
US(2)	W10–3	Colorado Springs	20 Jul	t: Mesnel, Blanco
				c: Camberabero
W(b)	W22–9	Cardiff	4 Sep	t: Blanco, Camberabero, Saint-André
				c: Camberabero 2
				p: Camberabero 2
R(b)★	W30–3	Beziers	4 Oct	t: penalty try, Saint-André, Roumat, Lafond
				c: Camberabero
				p: Camberabero 4
Fj★	W33–9	Grenoble	8 Oct	t: Lafond 3, Sella 2, Camberabero
				c: Camberabero 3
				p: Camberabero
C★	W19–13	Agen	13 Oct	t: Lafond, Saint-André
				c: Camberabero
				p: Camberabero, Lacroix 2
E★	L10–19	Paris	19 Oct	t: Lafond
				p: Lacroix 2

1992:

W	W12–9	Cardiff	1 Feb	t: Saint-André
				c: Lafond
				p: Viars
				dg: Penaud
E	L13–31	Paris	15 Feb	t: Viars, Penaud
				c: Viars
				p: Viars
S	L 6–10	Edinburgh	7 Mar	p: Lafond 2
I	W44–12	Paris	21 Mar	t: Penaud 2, Viars 2, Cecillon, Cabannes, Sadourny
				c: Viars 5
				p: Viars 2
R	W25–6	Le Havre	28 May	t: Saint-André, Cadieu, Galthie, penalty try
				c: Viars, Lacroix 2
				p: Viars
Arg(a1)†	W27–12	Buenos Aires	4 Jul	t: Deylaud, Viars
				c: Deylaud
				p: Viars 4
				dg: Penaud
Arg(a2)	W33–9	Buenos Aires	11 Jul	t: Saint-André, Viars, Hueber
				c: Viars 3
				p: Viars 3
				dg: Hueber
SA(1)	L15–20	Lyon	17 Oct	t: Penaud 2
				c: Viars
				p: Viars
SA(2)	W29–16	Paris	24 Oct	t: Penaud, Roumat
				c: Lacroix 2
				p: Lacroix 5
Arg(b)	L20–24	Nantes	14 Nov	t: Gonzales, Galthie, Sella

				c: Viars
				p: Viars

1993:

E	L15–16	Twickenham	16 Jan	t: Saint-André 2
				c: Camberabero
				p: Camberabero
S	W11–3	Paris	6 Feb	t: Lacroix
				p: Camberabero 2
I	W21–6	Dublin	20 Feb	t: Saint-André, Sella
				c: Camberabero
				p: Camberabero 2
				dg: Camberabero
W	W26–10	Paris	20 Mar	t: Benetton 2, Lafond
				c: Lafond
				p: Lacroix 3
R(a)	W37–20	Bucharest	20 May	t: Bernat-Salles 3, Cecillon
				c: Viars 4
				p: Viars 3
SA(1)	D20–20	Durban	26 Jun	t: Saint-André
				p: Lacroix 5
SA(2)	W18–17	Johannesburg	3 Jul	p: Lacroix 4
				dg: Lacroix, Penaud
R(b)	W51–0	Brive	9 Oct	t: Bernat-Salles 3, Sella, Loppy, Merle
				c: Lacroix 6
				p: Lacroix 3
A(1)	W16–3	Bordeaux	30 Oct	t: Hueber
				c: Lacroix
				p: Lacroix
				dg: Penaud, Sadourny
A(2)	L 3–24	Paris	6 Nov	p: Lacroix

1994

I	W35–15	Paris	15 Jan	t: Benetton, Saint-André, Lacroix, Merle
				c: Lacroix 3
				p: Lacroix 3
W	L15–24	Cardiff	19 Feb	t: Roumat, Sella
				c: Lacroix
				p: Lacroix
E	L14–18	Paris	5 Mar	t: Benazzi
				p: Lacroix 3
S	W20–12	Edinburgh	19 Mar	t: Sadourny, Saint-André
				c: Lacroix, Montlaur
				p: Lacroix 2
C	L16–18	Ottawa	5 Jun	t: N'Tamack
				c: Lacroix
				p: Lacroix 3

* World Cup matches
⁺ Non-cap tests
† Five-point try introduced from this game onwards

AUSTRALIA

Michael Lynagh

Speaking with Greg Campbell

ALTHOUGH the Wallabies lost three of the eight Tests played during 1993, one more than we had suffered throughout the two previous seasons, it still wasn't a bad campaign considering many of the extraordinary hurdles we faced in a long and extremely tiring season.

Of course there were disappointments, particularly the Test losses and the number of injuries we encountered. But overall the team displayed tremendous courage and determination.

There was no better example of this than when we trailed a very strong South African team one-nil in our best-of-three home series. We came through to win. And these never-say-die qualities were reproduced later in the season when we beat France to square the two-Test series by a record margin in Paris, where no previous Wallaby team had won.

Lesser teams would not have been able to cope with this pressure, and it was a tribute to all involved that we had the tenacity to come back and prove that we are still a major force in world rugby.

For me, looking at all eight Tests, the best feature of our rugby was the consistently high standard of our forward play. I have no hesitation in stating that every one of our forwards is a weapon – which is quite something, especially as we also have backs who on their day are without peer.

Apart from having such a strong all-round arsenal, we have also developed a wide range of ways to win matches. We do not simply rely on either back or forward, but we have the capacity to alter our tactics to suit the occasion and the need. By comparison, teams like the All Blacks play the same way every time, and there is really no great surprise element to their game. The same cannot be said of the Wallabies.

> *'We have developed a wide range of ways to win matches... We have the capacity to alter our tactics to suit the occasion and the need... Teams like the All Blacks play the same way every time, and there is really no great surprise element to their game'*

There was, however, one disappointing feature of our play during the year, and that was that it often took us until late in a series to start performing to our best. We must learn to adopt the attitude that every game is important, and not wait until a do-or-die situation before we finally play to our potential and capacity.

If we had adopted the correct attitude, it would have made everything so much easier. All Black teams have had the belief that winning was their God-given right. We must become more ruthless in our approach to winning and not wait until we're trailing in a series before we start performing.

Like all sides we had our setbacks along the way. Losing John Eales and Willie Ofahengaue, two of our best forwards in recent years, was disruptive, and on top of that I was sidelined against the All Blacks and for the Test series against the Springboks after being rushed to hospital for emergency surgery. There were also other players who either missed games or carried injuries along the way. But as Bob Dwyer says, adversity opens the door to opportunity, and there were several players who took the chance they were given.

Garrick Morgan was one such player.

At the beginning of the season, Garrick faced stiff competition to win Test selection ahead of either John Eales or Rod McCall. But once given that chance, he needed no second invitation. So much so, in fact, that many judges named him the best player in the world in 1993.

Garrick's tremendous form now presents the problem that we need to perm two from three outstanding locks in Eales, McCall and Morgan – though I hasten to add that this is only a problem for the selectors, and one which I don't think will cause too much heartache.

Queensland flanker Ilie Tabua was another who took his chance fabulously. His Test debut performance at Ballymore, in our second Test defeat of South Africa, was one that every player would dream to experience.

The emergence of players such as Garrick and Ilie underlines the improved depth in the Wallaby squad, which is indeed heartening. Playing depth has been a problem in past years, and we were most fortunate that our only real injury worry during the 1991 World Cup campaign was Nick Farr-Jones. And Nick did manage to play most games.

> *'We must learn to adopt the attitude that every game is important, and not wait until a do-or-die situation before we finally play to our potential and capacity...All Black teams have had the belief that winning was their God-given right. We must become more ruthless in our approach to winning'*

I'm pleased to report that our pool of talent is deepening. In fact, talent is oozing all over Australia, and the Australian Rugby Football Union is doing a fine job in bringing it to the surface. This season, for example, both New South Wales and Queensland have improved B-game fixture lists, and the Emerging Wallabies will again tour (when they travel to Africa at the end of the year).

Australia approached the 1993 season with the full knowledge that every opposing team would be hellbent on beating us because we are the World Cup holders. The other nations are now aspiring to the levels we set in 1991 and we are well aware that they are catching up. As of 1994, the competition is a lot closer among the leading national teams. That is why we need to step up a gear from 1991 in order to stay ahead of the competition. If we do not improve from the standard which brought us World Cup triumph, we will be beaten.

Tonga were our first international opponents of 1993, at Ballymore. I was pleased to be able to play again with the team, having missed the end of the 1992 tour to Ireland and Wales on account of a shoulder injury sustained at Lansdowne Road. I then developed a hernia problem, which required a minor operation before the Tongan match. Anyway, we beat them 52–14, which was a good result. Like many of the Pacific Island sides, Tonga are not easy to play against, as they have no set pattern of play.

After that, to lose the Bledisloe Cup 10–25 to New Zealand only a fortnight later was very disappointing – the more so for me, as I was taken to hospital while we were in camp and missed the game. Retaining the Cup was always going to be a tall order, as we arrived in Dunedin just two days before a one-off match, having played only one Test in our build-up. By contrast, the All Blacks had just completed a Test series win over the British Lions.

Another game we found difficult was the first Test against South Africa in Sydney, as it was the first time we had played an international under lights. But despite our 12–19 loss we learned a lot from the experience, and it transpired that the series was one of the best ever seen in Australia.

'We need to step up a gear from 1991 in order to stay ahead of the competition. If we do not improve from the standard which brought us World Cup triumph, we will be beaten'

The second Test (won 28–20) in Brisbane saw us faced with a desperate situation. We needed to win to keep the series alive. After an early setback, when Joel Stransky scored a 50-metre interception try,

The Wallaby front row packs down during France's shock 16–11 win in Bordeaux.

the guys turned the match around, with Jason Little scoring two super tries. Victory accomplished, we returned to Sydney for the deciding Test (won 19–12) and played a well-controlled game.

Much was made of Nick Farr-Jones' return to the the side against the All Blacks and the Springboks. It was tough on Brett Johnstone, Peter Slattery's deputy, but Nick had always said that he would be available for reselection if needed. He was only sticking to his word. As it turned out, Nick was a major factor in our winning the series, as his experience and direction was first class.

The Springboks were a completely different team from the one we had played in Cape Town 12 months earlier. You only needed to look at the team sheet to see that. They are now a strong and very competitive outfit, and they're not far from the money. I believe they will continue to improve, and given their fanatical support base, they are going to be very difficult to beat.

Next up was the tour to France, but en route we stopped off in North America, where we experienced the most extreme climatic change I have ever encountered. The first match against the American Eagles (won 26–22) at Riverside outside Los Angeles was played in a heatwave. I don't think I've ever played in hotter conditions. Yet only days later we played Canada B in freezing Calgary, where the wind went right through you. We may have played on colder days in the past, but the 40-degree change in temperature that confronted us was hard to deal with.

However, we kept winning, our efforts culminating in a 43–16 Test defeat of Canada. I was really struck by how much they had improved in such a short space of time. I can remember when they toured Australia in 1985 and we thrashed them by more than 50 points. They've got some good players and they're well organized, as Wales will need no reminding.

The tour of France was my third, having previously been there in 1983 and 1989. Now this was a trip I thoroughly enjoyed, not least because the French are more prepared nowadays than they have been in the past with the meals and accomodation. I remember that in 1983 our lock David Hillhouse was presented with a medal after the second Test by the team for being the only Wallaby player to have survived two tours of France.

While the touring conditions are far better, the rugby hasn't become any easier, with matches against a variety of national selections. But this was the most successful ever Wallaby tour of France, as we lost only one match outside the Tests.

'Our first-Test loss to France will always go down in our minds as a classic case of the better team losing the game. We had five or six real scoring opportunities but only accepted one or two. On the other hand, France had only two real chances and took them both'

The most frustrating result was the 16–13 first Test loss in Bordeaux. It will always go down in our minds as a classic case of the better team losing the game. We had five or six real scoring opportunities but only accepted one or two. On the other hand, France had only two real chances and took them both.

However, by the time of the second Test in Paris (won 24–3), we figured that belatedly we had the French sorted out. We changed a few things tactically and made a few other alterations, and were rewarded with a very satisfying win.

It was a great way for our fullback Marty Roebuck to bow out. He scored a try and kicked a conversion and four penalty goals in a fantastic performance. He couldn't have wished for a higher note on which to finish his career.

But some of us go on, and the countdown to the World Cup continues with a very busy run-up to South Africa, in the form of six Test matches against four different countries. Our challenge is to improve sufficiently to remain ahead of the rest.

AUSTRALIA (P8 W5 D0 L3 F201 A125):

(H)	v	Tonga	(Brisbane, 3.7.93)	won	52–14
(A)	v	New Zealand	(Dunedin, 17.7.93)	lost	10–25
(H)	v	South Africa	(Sydney, 31.7.93)	lost	12–19
(H)	v	South Africa	(Brisbane, 14.8.93)	won	28–20
(H)	v	South Africa	(Sydney, 21.8.93)	won	19–12
(A)	v	USA*	(California, 2.10.93)	won	26–22
(A)	v	Canada	(Calgary, 9.10.93)	won	43–16
(A)	v	France	(Bordeaux, 30.10.93)	lost	13–16
(A)	v	France	(Paris, 6.11.93)	won	24–3

* Non-cap

Wallabies in North America (tour record: P3 W3 D0 L0 F109 A41):

(A)	v	Canada A	(Calgary, 6.10.93)	won	40–3

Wallabies in France (tour record: P8 W6 D0 L2 F204 A141):

(A)	v	Aquitaine XV	(Dax, 16.10.93)	won	30–15
(A)	v	South West	(Agen, 20.10.93)	won	20–19
(A)	v	Languedoc XV	(Narbonne, 23.10.93)	won	35–18
(A)	v	French Select	(Grenoble, 26.10.93)	won	24–23
(A)	v	Cote d'Azur	(Toulon, 2.11.93)	lost	15–21
(A)	v	French Barbarians	(Clermont-Ferrand, 11.11.93)	won	43–26

Australia U-21 (P1 W1 D0 L0 F31 A8):

(A)	v	New Zealand Colts	(Auckland, 31.7.93)	won	31–8

Australia U-19 (P1 W1 D0 L0 F22 A20):

(H)	v	New Zealand U-19	(Brisbane, 8.7.93)	won	22–20

Australia Universities (P1 W0 D0 L1 F3 A68):

(A)	v	New Zealand Universities	(Wellington, 7.7.93)	lost	3–68

Australia Schools (P2 W2 D0 L0 F83 A12):

(A)	v	New Zealand Schools	(Rotorua, 1.10.93)	lost	7–32

Australia U-16 (P1 W0 D0 L1 F12 A18):

(A)	v	New Zealand U-16	(Palmerston North, 25.9.93)	lost	12–18

1993 SUPER 10 TOURNAMENT
'New South Wales and Queensland fail to shine' – see page 113.

DOMESTIC RUGBY

Sydney Grand Final
Gordon 23 (try: Murdoch; penalty goals: Wallace 6)
Warringah 19 (tries: McKeown, Carroll; penalty goals: Walton 3)

Brisbane Grand Final
Southern Districts 27 (tries: Horan, Perrin, Skeggs, penalty try; conversion: Mandrusiak 2; penalty goal: Mandrusiak)
Sunnybank 8 (try: McKinnon; penalty goal: Saunders)

1980:

Fj	W22–9	Suva	24 May	**t:** Martin, Moon **c:** P E McLean **p:** P E McLean 3 **dg:** P E McLean
NZ(1)	W13–9	Sydney	21 Jun	**t:** Hawker, Martin **c:** Gould **dg:** M Ella
NZ(2)	L9–12	Brisbane	28 Jun	**t:** Moon **c:** Gould **p:** Gould
NZ(3)	W26–10	Sydney	12 Jul	**t:** Grigg 2, O'Connor, Carson **c:** Gould 2 **p:** Gould **dg:** M Ella

1981:

F(1)	W17–15	Brisbane	5 Jul	**t:** Poidevin, O'Connor, Moon **c:** P McLean **p:** Richards
F(2)	W24–14	Sydney	11 Jul	**t:** Hall, O'Connor **c:** P McLean 2 **p:** P McLean 4
I	W16–12	Dublin	21 Nov	**t:** O'Connor **p:** P McLean 3 **dg:** Gould
W	L13–18	Cardiff	5 Dec	**t:** Slack, M Cox **c:** P McLean **p:** P McLean
S	L15–24	Edinburgh	19 Dec	**t:** Poidevin, Moon, Slack **p:** P McLean

1982:

E	L11–15	Twickenham	2 Jan	**t:** Moon 2 **p:** P McLean
S(1)	L7–12	Brisbane	3 Jul	**t:** Hawker **p:** Hawker
S(2)	W33–9	Sydney	10 Jul	**t:** Gould 2, O'Connor **c:** P McLean 3 **p:** P McLean 5
NZ(1)	L16–23	Christchurch	14 Aug	**t:** Hawker, Campese **c:** Gould **p:** Gould 2
NZ(2)	W19–16	Wellington	28 Aug	**t:** G Ella, Campese **c:** Gould **p:** Gould 3
NZ(3)	L18–33	Auckland	11 Sep	**t:** Gould **c:** Gould **p:** Gould 3 **dg:** Hawker

1983:

US	W49–3	Sydney	9 Jul	t: Campese 4, Slack 2, Ross, Roche, Hanley c: Gould 4, Campese dg: M Ella
Arg(1)	L3–18	Brisbane	31 Jul	dg: Campese
Arg(2)	W29–13	Sydney	8 Aug	t: Moon 2, Roche, Campese, penalty try c: Campese 3 p: Campese
Fj	W16–3	Suva	xx Aug	t: Campese p: Lynagh 4
NZ	L8–18	Sydney	20 Aug	t: Slack, Poidevin
It	W29–7	Padova	22 Oct	t: Hawker 2, Moon, Williams, M Ella c: M Ella 3 p: M Ella
F(1)	D15–15	Clermont-Ferrand	13 Nov	t: Roche c: Campese p: Campese dg: M Ella, Hawker
F(2)	L6–15	Paris	20 Nov	p: Campese dg: M Ella

1984:

NZ(1)	W16–9	Sydney	21 Jul	t: Reynolds, Moon c: M Ella p: M Ella dg: Gould
NZ(2)	L15–19	Brisbane	4 Aug	t: M Ella c: M Ella p: M Ella 2, Campese
NZ(3)	L24–25	Sydney	18 Aug	t: Campese c: M Ella p: M Ella 5, Campese
E	W19–3	Twickenham	3 Nov	t: M Ella, Poidevin, Lynagh c: Lynagh 2 p: Lynagh
I	W16–9	Dublin	10 Nov	t: M Ella p: Lynagh dg: M Ella 2, Lynagh
W	W28–9	Cardiff	24 Nov	t: Lawton, Tuynman, M Ella, Lynagh c: Gould 3 p: Gould 2
S	W37–12	Edinburgh	8 Dec	t: Campese 2, Farr–Jones, M Ella c: Lynagh 3 p: Lynagh 5

1985:

C(1)	W59–3	Sydney	15 Jun	t: Burke 2, Lane 2, Grigg 2, Calcraft, Farr-Jones, Kassulke c: Lynagh 7 p: Lynagh 3
C(2)	W43–15	Brisbane	23 Jun	t: Burke 3, Grigg, Cutler, Tuynman,

				Farr-Jones
				c: Lynagh 3
				p: Lynagh 2
				dg: Lynagh
NZ	L9–10	Auckland	29 Jun	t: Black
				c: Lynagh
				p: Lynagh
Fj(1)	W52–28	Brisbane	10 Aug	t: Farr-Jones 2, Reynolds, Cutler, Lawton, Papworth, Grigg
				c: Knox 3
				p: Knox 3
				dg: Knox 2, Campese
Fj(2)	W31–9	Sydney	17 Aug	t: Campese 2, Grigg, McIntyre, Cutler
				c: Knox
				p: Knox 3

1986:

It	W39–18	Brisbane	1 Jun	t: Campese 2, Tuynman, McIntyre, Moon, Burke
				c: Lynagh 6
				p: Lynagh
F	W27–14	Sydney	21 Jun	t: Campese
				c: Lynagh
				p: Lynagh 6
				dg: Lynagh
Arg(1)	W39–19	Brisbane	6 Jul	t: Papworth 2, Grigg, Campese
				c: Lynagh 4
				p: Lynagh 5
Arg(2)	W26–0	Sydney	12 Jul	t: Campese 2, Tuynman
				c: Lynagh
				p: Lynagh 4
NZ(1)	W13–12	Wellington	9 Aug	t: Campese, Burke
				c: Lynagh
				p: Lynagh
NZ(2)	L12–13	Dunedin	23 Aug	p: Lynagh 3
				dg: Lynagh
NZ(3)	W22–9	Auckland	6 Sep	t: Leeds, Campese
				c: Lynagh
				p: Lynagh 4

1987:

SK	W65–18	Brisbane	17 May	t: Burke 3, Grigg 2, Slack 2, Cook, Gould, B Smith, Miller, James, Farr-Jones
				c: Smith 5
				p: Smith
E*	W19–6	Sydney	23 May	t: Campese, Poidevin
				c: Lynagh
				p: Lynagh 3
US*	W47–12	Brisbane	31 May	t: penalty try, Smith, Slack, Leeds 2, Papworth, Campese, Codey
				c: Lynagh 6
				p: Lynagh

J*	W42–23	Sydney	3 Jun	**t:** Slack 2, Tuynman, Burke 2, Grigg, Hartill, Campese
				c: Lynagh 5
I*	W33–15	Sydney	7 Jun	**t:** McIntyre, Smith, Burke 2
				c: Lynagh 4
				p: Lynagh 3
F*	L24–30	Sydney	13 Jun	**t:** Campese, Codey
				c: Lynagh 2
				p: Lynagh 3
				dg: Lynagh
W*	L21–22	Rotorua	18 Jun	**t:** Burke, Grigg
				c: Lynagh 2
				p: Lynagh 2
				dg: Lynagh
NZ	L16–30	Sydney	25 Jul	**t:** Papworth
				p: Leeds 3
				dg: Hawker
Arg(1)	D19–19	Buenos Aires	31 Oct	**t:** Williams, Cutler, Lynagh
				c: Lynagh 2
				p: Lynagh
Arg(2)	L19–27	Buenos Aires	7 Nov	**t:** Williams 2
				c: Lynagh
				p: Lynagh 3

1988:

E(a1)	W22–16	Brisbane	29 May	**t:** Williams
				p: Lynagh 6
E(a2)	W28–8	Sydney	12 Jun	**t:** Campese, G Ella, Lynagh, Carter
				c: Lynagh 3
				p: Lynagh 2
NZ(1)	L7–32	Sydney	3 Jul	**t:** Williams
				p: Lynagh
NZ(2)	D19–19	Brisbane	16 Jul	**t:** Grant, Williams
				c: Leeds
				p: Leeds 3
NZ(3)	L9–30	Sydney	30 Jul	**t:** Walker
				c: Lynagh
				p: Leeds
E(b)	L19–28	Twickenham	5 Nov	**t:** Leeds, Campese, Grant
				c: Lynagh 2
				p: Lynagh
S	W32–13	Edinburgh	19 Nov	**t:** Lawton 2, Campese 2, Gourley,
				c: Lynagh 3
				p: Lynagh 2
It	W55–6	Milan	3 Dec	**t:** Campese 3, Niuqila 3, Leeds, Gourley, Lynagh
				c: Lynagh 8
				p: Lynagh

1989:

BL(1)	W30–12	Sydney	1 Jul	**t:** Walker, Gourley, Maguire, Martin
				c: Lynagh 4
				p: Lynagh

BL(2)	L12–19	Brisbane	8 Jul	**dg:** Lynagh **t:** Martin **c:** Lynagh **p:** Lynagh 2
BL(3)	L18–19	Sydney	15 Jul	**t:** Williams **c:** Lynagh **p:** Lynagh 4
NZ	L12–24	Auckland	5 Aug	**t:** Campese **c:** Lynagh **p:** Lynagh 2
F(1)	W32–15	Strasbourg	4 Nov	**t:** Horan 2, Williams, Campese **c:** Lynagh 2 **p:** Lynagh 4
F(2)	L19–25	Lille	11 Nov	**t:** Kearns, Farr–Jones **c:** Lynagh **p:** Lynagh 3

1990:

F(1)	W21–9	Sydney	9 Jun	**t:** Martin **c:** Lynagh **p:** Lynagh 5
F(2)	W48–31	Brisbane	24 Jun	**t:** Carozza, Cornish, Gavin, Little, penalty try, Campese **c:** Lynagh 6 **p:** Lynagh 4
F(3)	L19–28	Sydney	30 Jun	**t:** Campese, Daly **c:** Lynagh **p:** Lynagh 2 **dg:** Lynagh
US	W67–9	Brisbane	8 Jul	**t:** Lynagh 2, Williams 2, Daly, McKenzie, Kearns, Gavin, Little, Farr-Jones, Slattery, Campese **c:** Lynagh 8 **dg:** Campese
NZ(1)	L6–21	Christchurch	21 Jul	**p:** Lynagh 2
NZ(2)	L17–27	Auckland	4 Aug	**t:** Horan, Ofahengaue **p:** Lynagh 2 **dg:** Lynagh
NZ(3)	W21–9	Wellington	18 Aug	**t:** Kearns **c:** Lynagh **p:** Lynagh 5

1991:

W(a)	W63–6	Brisbane	21 Jul	**t:** Lynagh 2, Kearns 2, Gavin 2, Ofahengaue, Horan, Roebuck, Campese, Egerton, Little **c:** Lynagh 6 **p:** Lynagh
E(a)	W40–15	Sydney	27 Jul	**t:** Campese 2, Ofahengaue 2, Roebuck **c:** Lynagh 4 **p:** Lynagh 4
NZ(a1)	W21–12	Sydney	10 Aug	**t:** Gavin, Egerton **c:** Lynagh 2

				p: Lynagh 3
NZ(a2)	L3–6	Auckland	24 Aug	p: Lynagh
Arg*	W32–19	Llanelli	4 Oct	t: Campese 2, Horan 2, Kearns
				c: Lynagh 3
				p: Lynagh 2
WS*	W 9–3	Pontypool	9 Oct	p: Lynagh 3
W(b)*	W38–3	Cardiff	12 Oct	t: Roebuck 2, Slattery, Campese, Horan, Lynagh
				c: Lynagh 4
				p: Lynagh 2
I*	W19–18	Dublin	20 Oct	t: Campese 2, Lynagh
				c: Lynagh 2
				p: Lynagh
NZ(b)*	W16–6	Dublin	27 Oct	t: Campese, Horan
				c: Lynagh
				p: Lynagh 2
E*	W12–6	Twickenham	2 Nov	t: Daly
				c: Lynagh
				p: Lynagh 2

1992:

S(1)	W27–12	Sydney	13 June	t: Campese 2, Carozza, Lynagh
				c: Lynagh
				p: Lynagh 3
S(2)	W37–13	Brisbane	21 Jun	t: Carozza 2, Horan 2, Eales
				c: Lynagh
				p: Lynagh 5
NZ(1)†	W16–15	Sydney	14 Jul	t: Campese, Horan
				p: Lynagh 2
NZ(2)	W19–17	Brisbane	19 Jul	t: Carozza 2
				p: Lynagh 3
NZ(3)	L23–26	Sydney	25 Jul	t: Farr-Jones, Herbert
				c: Lynagh 2
				p: Lynagh 3
SA	W26–3	Cape Town	23 Aug	t: Carozza 2, Campese
				c: Lynagh
				p: Lynagh 3
I	W42–17	Dublin	31 Oct	t: Campese, McKenzie, Little, Kelaher, Horan
				c: Roebuck 4
				p: Roebuck 3
W	W23–6	Cardiff	21 Nov	t: Wilson, McCall, Campese
				c: Roebuck
				p: Roebuck 2

1993

T	W52–14	Brisbane	3 Jul	t: Campese 2, Carozza, Little, Gavin, Morgan, Johnstone
				c: Roebuck 3, Lynagh
				p: Roebuck 3
NZ	L10–25	Dunedin	17 Jul	t: Horan
				c: Kelaher

				p: Kelaher
SA(1)	L12–19	Sydney	31 Jul	p: Roebuck 4
SA(2)	W28–20	Brisbane	14 Aug	t: Little 2, Horan
				c: Roebuck 2
				p: Roebuck 3
SA(3)	W19–12	Sydney	21 Aug	t: Horan
				c: Roebuck
				p: Roebuck 4
US[+]	W26–22	California	2 Oct	t: Wilson, Howard, Tabua, Lea
				c: Lynagh 3
C	W43–16	Calgary	9 Oct	t: Campese 3, Horan, Daly, D Smith
				c: Lynagh 2
				p: Lynagh 3
F(1)	L13–16	Bordeaux	30 Oct	t: Gavin
				c: Lynagh
				p: Lynagh 2
F(2)	W24–3	Paris	6 Nov	t: Roebuck, Gavin
				c: Roebuck
				p: Roebuck 4
I(1)	W33–13	Brisbane	5 Jun	t: Tabua, Lynagh, Burke, Campese, Smith
				c: Lynagh
				p: Lynagh 2
I(2)	W32–18	Sydney	11 Jun	t: D Herbert, Wilson, Tabua
				c: Lynagh
				p: Lynagh 5

* World Cup
[+] Non-cap tests
[†] Five-point try introduced from this game onwards

Michael Lynagh sets his sights on goal in Bordeaux, where France won 16–13.

NEW ZEALAND

Sean Fitzpatrick
Speaking with Wynne Gray
(*New Zealand Herald*)

THE All Blacks had endured a period of grace in 1992 from the New Zealand rugby public. It was our first season together as a new-look squad under a new coach – a time for regrouping after the unsatisfactory ending to our second World Cup campaign the year before.

If we enjoyed the 1992 honeymoon, things changed abruptly last year. We had been given the benefit of getting ourselves organized, but in 1993 the public and private demands were great. We were expected to win and win well, especially as the Lions were not considered to be too much of a threat. They had proved otherwise with their series results but that did not wear with the critics. That made it difficult for the team, as we were still struggling in a couple of areas while being bombarded from all directions for results.

However, the Lions did us some favours by demonstrating to some of the less-experienced members of our squad that playing Tests for the All Blacks was not just a matter of pulling on the black jersey. We got a shock in the first Test in Christchurch (won 20–18) before Grant Fox sneaked us home, but it was after the second Test loss in Wellington (7–20) that we really felt the full brunt of the New Zealand public's wrath.

At no time did we underestimate the Lions, but I can now see that they gave us a much tougher series that many had envisaged. They exposed us in certain areas, and gave us problems which, ironically, helped our progress. We were forced to work harder, and look more at our gameplans and tactics, rather than just coast through as we might have done if we had not been troubled during the series.

It showed in the final Test, at Eden Park, Auckland, when with our backs to the walls we came out firing and determined not to make the same sorts of errors which had plagued us throughout the series. We won (30–13), and in so doing showed we were capable of playing controlled rugby despite being an inexperienced unit.

We learned as we went through the season, but there are times when experience is an unparalleled commodity in tight Test matches. It is an ingredient to be tapped when the unexpected arises, or when the pressure really comes on, as it does at that level of rugby. Our final Test of the year against England at Twickenham (lost 9–15) may be a case in point, when some of the younger players were found wanting.

Some people would argue that rugby is becoming more and more a young man's game as the pressure of business and family increases. Such outside influences can divert minds and cause some players to drop by the wayside, and this obviously gives the keen younger men a chance. But there is still nothing that can replace the experience of playing a large number of games in the cauldron of international rugby.

You have to constantly want to be an All Black, and make a strong commitment at the start of each season. I decide first whether I still have the hunger for Test rugby, and only then whether I can afford the time away from work. The 1994 international calendar for the All Blacks is not so bad – there is only one overseas jaunt, to Australia for the Bledisloe Cup – but the training programme does not let up.

> 'You have to constantly want to be an All Black, and make a strong commitment at the start of each season. I decide first whether I still have the hunger for Test rugby, and only then whether I can afford the time away from work'

My regime starts at 6.15 am most days, with a two-hour workout and then training several days a week. But while it is a big sacrifice in terms of time, I still have the same desire to be an All Black that I had when I first broke through in 1986. That drives me, and the other guys have to have that commitment too. There is no such thing as a free ride with the All Blacks.

After the Lions, we were visited by Western Samoa (won 35–13). They came with a fizz and a rattle for the first Test between the two countries. It was a hugely physical game but we kept our composure. We were in a no-win situation really, as everyone expected us to win. But we did realize some of our potential. Our concentration was good, Grant Fox (with 25 points) was again masterful, and we successfully negotiated another step in our young side's education.

Next up were the Aussies (won 25–10), playing for the Bledisloe Cup in Dunedin. Some of the Wallabies reckoned we had set an ambush for them by scheduling the game way down south. The Dunedin mayor even got in on the act by sending the visitors some whisky and hot water bottles. I wonder what the mayor of Sydney will send us this year!

> 'Some of the Wallabies reckoned we had set an ambush for them by scheduling the Bledisloe Cup game way down south. The Dunedin mayor even got in on the act by sending the visitors some whisky and hot water bottles'

I think we read the Dunedin Test well. We used ideas we had tried in training, and fully deserved to regain the trophy. Maybe the Wallabies were underprepared, but as one of them said some time ago, you don't give a sucker an even break.

By that stage of the year – mid-July – we had played five Tests but still had a huge amount of rugby left: the climax of our national championship programme, followed by an eight-week trip to England, Scotland and Wales.

Our season had begun in March with the new Super-10 tournament, and we did not stop until the Barbarians match in early December. It was far too long, and there was no way the players could stay in peak form throughout. There had to be flat periods. At least, this year there is light at the end of the tunnel: the programme will all be over by October and then we can plan for the World Cup.

I think deep down the team struggled to get motivated for the tour to the United Kingdom. Once we were there, we played steadily, winning the Test against Scotland (51–15) in style. But we played a shocker against England. Why?

I think they just overpowered us and hit us with a few moves we were not prepared for. We did not have players with sufficient experience to combat some of England's moves. We did not have the players to deal with their playing the ball on the ground or killing it. England simply denied us the ball or any possession that was of any use. Their thirst for victory was greater than the All Blacks.

> *'I think deep down the team struggled to get motivated for the tour to the United Kingdom. England overpowered us... Their thirst for victory was greater than the All Blacks'*

That Test for England presented them with a similar situation to that faced by the All Blacks before the final Test against the Lions. England had been written off all week, while we were coming off a good win – and deep down, as much as you try to convince yourself you are in a good frame of mind, you have to admit that England had the greater urgency.

Although we already knew we were tired, that defeat was the greatest disappointment of the year. It wrecked our tour when victory would have given us an impeccable record.

There were also other problems. We got slated for Phil de Glanville's facial injury in the game against South West England at Redruth, and we were labelled 'the dirtiest team to tour the UK'. I don't think any of that nonsense affected the All Blacks, although the description hurt and was hard to accept. We actually felt sorry for UK sides and their media, who seemed to have missed a great chance to promote the sport. Everything seemed negative.

Mind you, there is a very different attitude to rugby in the UK. Players seem to revel in a tight game with a three-point margin where there are 50 penalties and no tries. They and some officials seem to think that is a wonderful sort of contest. But I stick by the comments I made after the Lions series. I don't enjoy that sort of boring rugby. It makes you wonder why some players even bother with the game. It still amazes me, and I stick by my observations that the Lions series was uninspiring rugby.

This season offers us some breathing space before the next World Cup – although the All Blacks face another daunting programme, with that tournament in South Africa in May followed by a proposed trip to France at the end of the year. Not that I think anybody is looking past the World Cup.

The All Blacks are in reasonable shape, a good number of players have been exposed to Test rugby, and if you compare our situation before the first World Cup, then we are on schedule. In 1986, rugby in New Zealand was in disarray, yet the following year we won the inaugural World Cup.

We are not set, but we are more settled, confident and committed to the cause. There are still some players to be juggled, but with the likes of Richard Loe and Mike Brewer back, and with exciting teenage talent like Jonah Lomu, we should raise a solid team. But it all comes down to coping with pressure, and candidates will have to be living and breathing rugby for the next 18 months.

> *'There is a very different attitude to rugby in the UK. Players seem to revel in a tight game with a three-point margin where there are 50 penalties and no tries. They and some officials seem to think that is a wonderful sort of contest...I don't enjoy that sort of boring rugby...It makes you wonder why some players even bother with the game'*

The All Blacks bred an exceptional team for the opening World Cup triumph in 1987, and that group came out of the previous year's uncertainty. So the formula is there, and there is no reason why we cannot follow a similar track this time round.

From a personal standpoint, I have found captaining the All Blacks to be a most demanding task, though that is not an indication that I would like any other scenario. But in terms of on-field leadership, the All Blacks are looking for more lieutenants – people like Brewer, who are prepared to offer suggestions and are prepared to give them a shot.

The beauty of the 1987 All Blacks was that few of the players needed to be led. Now we have two or three leaders and the rest are followers. This is a key area which needs to be addressed if we are to regain the World Cup.

NEW ZEALAND (P7 W5 D0 L2 F177 A104):

(H)	v	British Lions	(Christchurch, 12.6.93)	won	20–18
(H)	v	British Lions	(Wellington, 26.6.93)	lost	7–20
(H)	v	British Lions	(Auckland, 3.7.93)	won	30–13
(H)	v	Australia	(Dunedin, 17.7.93)	won	25–10
(H)	v	Western Samoa	(Auckland, 31.7.93)	won	35–13
(A)	v	Scotland	(Edinburgh, 20.11.93)	won	51–15
(A)	v	England	(Twickenham, 27.11.93)	lost	9–15

British Lions in New Zealand (tour record: P13 W7 D0 L6 F314 A285):

(–)	v	North Auckland	(Whangarei, 22.5.93)	won	30–17
(–)	v	North Harbour	(Auckland, 26.5.93)	won	29–13
(–)	v	New Zealand Maoris	(Wellington, 29.5.93)	won	24–20
(–)	v	Canterbury	(Christchurch, 2.6.93)	won	28–10
(–)	v	Otago	(Dunedin, 5.6.93)	lost	24–37
(–)	v	Southland	(Invercargill, 8.6.93)	won	34–16
(–)	v	Taranaki	(New Plymouth, 16.6.93)	won	49–25
(–)	v	Auckland	(Auckland, 19.6.93)	lost	17–29
(–)	v	Hawke's Bay	(Napier, 22.6.93)	lost	17–29
(–)	v	Waikato	(Hamilton, 29.6.93)	lost	10–38

All Blacks in England and Scotland (tour record: P13 W12 D0 L1 F386 A156):

(A)	v	London & SE Division	(Twickenham, 23.10.93)	won	39–12
(A)	v	Midlands Division	(Leicester, 26.10.93)	won	12–6
(A)	v	South-West Division	(Redruth, 30.10.93)	won	19–15
(A)	v	Northern Division	(Liverpool, 2.11.93)	won	27–21
(A)	v	England A	(Gateshead, 7.11.93)	won	26–12
(A)	v	South of Scotland	(Galashiels, 10.11.93)	won	84–5
(A)	v	Scotland A	(Glasgow, 13.11.93)	won	20–9
(A)	v	Scottish Development XV	(Edinburgh, 16.11.93)	won	31–12
(A)	v	Emerging England XV	(Gloucester, 23.11.93)	won	30–19
(A)	v	Combined Services	(Devonport, 1.12.93)	won	13–3
(A)	v	Barbarians	(Cardiff, 4.12.93)	won	25–12

Western Samoa in New Zealand (tour record: P9 W7 D0 L2 F455 A131):

(–)	v	Buller-West Coast	(Westport, 4.7.93)	won	72–0
(–)	v	Marlborough	(Blenheim, 7.7.93)	won	128–0
(–)	v	Wanganui	(Wanganui, 14.7.93)	won	30–0
(–)	v	New Zealand XV	(Rotorua, 18.7.93)	lost	13–37
(–)	v	Counties	(Pukekohe, 21.7.93)	won	41–22
(–)	v	King Country	(Te Kuiti, 24.7.93)	won	57–21
(–)	v	Poverty Bay	(Gisborne, 27.7.93)	won	53–6

New Zealand Divisional XV (P7 W6 D0 L1 F245 A118):

(A)	v	Tongan Development XV	(Nuku'alofa, 16.10.93)	won	66–0
(A)	v	Tongan President's XV	(Nuku'alofa, 19.10.93)	lost	18–21
(A)	v	Western Fiji XV	(Nadi, 23.10.93)	won	31–29
(A)	v	Eastern Fiji XV	(Suva, 26.10.93)	won	39–3
(A)	v	Cook Islands Pres. XV	(Rarotonga, 28.10.93)	won	30–24
(A)	v	Cook Islands	(Rarotonga, 30.10.93)	won	26–15
(A)	v	Western Samoa Country	(Apia, 3.11.93)	won	35–26

New Zealand Colts (P1 W0 D0 L1 F8 A31):
(H) v Australia U-21	(Auckland, 31.7.93)	lost	8–31

New Zealand U-19 (P1 W0 D0 L1 F20 A22):
(A) v Australia U-19	(Brisbane, 8.7.93)	lost	20–22

New Zealand Youth (P8 W7 D0 L1 F252 A147):
(A) v Southern California	(Long Beach)	won	44–34
(A) v Leinster U-21	(Dublin)	won	47–28
(A) v Munster U-21	(Limerick)	lost	16–19
(A) v Ireland	(Dublin, 26.10.93)	won	22–6
(A) v Ulster U-21	(Belfast)	won	24–21
(A) v Connacht Development XV	(Galway)	won	31–13
(A) v Eastern Districts U-21	(Cardiff)	won	26–13
(A) v Wales	(Pontypridd, 9.11.93)	won	42–13

New Zealand Universities (P2 W1 D0 L1 F78 A51):
(H) v Australian Universities	(Wellington, 7.7.93)	won	68–3
(H) v Western Samoa	(Wellington, 11.7.93)	lost	10–48

New Zealand Schools (P2 W2 D0 L0 F83 A12):
(H) v England Schools	(Dunedin, 21.7.93)	won	51–5
(H) v Australia Schools	(Rotorua, 1.10.93)	won	32–7

New Zealand U-16 (P1 W1 D0 L0 F18 A12):
(H) v Australia U-16	(Palmerston North, 25.9.93)	won	18–12

1993 SUPER 10 TOURNAMENT
'Auckland beaten in final' – see page 113.

England captain Will Carling tags 'Inga the Winger' (alias Va'iga Tuigamala) during the 15–9 Twickenham win.

NATIONAL MUTUAL CHAMPIONSHIP

Division One:	P	W	D	L	F	A	Pts
Waikato	8	6	0	2	219	106	26
Auckland	8	6	0	2	356	131	25
North Harbour	8	6	0	2	257	161	24
Otago	8	5	1	2	221	141	23
Wellington	8	4	1	3	174	166	20
Canterbury	8	4	0	4	188	235	16
King Country	8	3	0	6	90	317	9
Taranaki	8	3	0	6	175	338	8
Hawke's Bay	8	0	0	8	157	242	3

Final: Auckland 27, Otago 18 (Auckland, 10.10.93). **Semi–finals:** Otago 36, Waikato 22 (Dunedin, 2.10.93); Auckland 43, North Harbour 20 (Auckland, 3.10.93).

Division Two:	P	W	D	L	F	A	Pts
North Auckland	8	7	0	1	322	162	29
South Canterbury	8	6	0	2	238	138	25
Counties	8	6	0	2	401	135	24
Bay of Plenty	8	6	0	2	318	189	24
Manawatu	8	4	1	3	224	242	18
Southland	8	3	0	5	199	230	14
Nelson Bays	8	2	0	6	182	275	9
Wairarapa Bush	8	0	2	6	105	300	4
Poverty Bay	8	0	1	7	80	398	3

Final: Counties 38, Bay of Plenty 10 (Rotorua, 9.10.93). **Semi-finals:** Bay of Plenty 41, North Auckland 26 (Rotorua, 2.10.93); Counties 33, South Canterbury 18 (Pukekohe, 3.10.93).

Division Three
Promoted: Horowhenua. Final: Wanganui 9, Horowhenua 15 (Wanganui, 9.10.93).
Semi-finals: Horowhenua 30, Mid-Canterbury 22 (Levin, 2.10.93); Wanganui 30, Thames Valley 14 (Wanganui, 2.10.93).

National Sevens (final): Canterbury 34, Otago 19 (Palmerston North, 7.3.93).

Ranfurly Shield: Holders – Waikato (Auckland's run ended after 62 wins).
Horowhenua 17, Auckland 80 (Levin, 3.4.93); Buller 3, Auckland 48 (Westport, 6.4.93); Auckland 69, Hawke's Bay 31 (Auckland, 5.6.93); North Otago 5, Auckland 139 (Oamaru, 1.9.93); Auckland 51, Wellington 14 (Auckland 11.9.93); Auckland 6, Waikato 17 (Auckland, 18.9.93); Waikato 28, Otago 11 (Hamilton, 26.9.93).

1980:

A(1)	L9–13	Sydney	21 Jun	p: Codlin 3
A(2)	W12–9	Brisbane	28 Jun	t: Reid
				c: Codlin
				p: Codlin 2
A(3)	L10–26	Sydney	12 Jul	t: Fraser
				p: Codlin 2
Fj(a)[+]	W30–6	Suva	23 Jul	t: Fraser 3, Allen, B Robertson
				c: Codlin 2
				p: Codlin 2
Fj(b)[+]	W33–0	Auckland	30 Sep	t: Osborne 2, K Taylor 2, Wylie, Woodman
				c: Valli 3
				p: Valli
C[+]	W43–10	Vancouver	11 Oct	t: M Shaw 3, Mourie, Haden, Osborne, S Wilson, Fraser
				c: Rollerson 4
				p: Rollerson
US[+]	W53–6	San Diego	Oct	t: Woodman 3, Osborne 2, Wilson, Allen, Old
				c: Codlin 6
				p: Codlin 3
W	W23–3	Cardiff	1 Nov	t: Mourie, Fraser, Allen, Reid
				c: Rollerson 2
				p: Rollerson

1981:

S(1)	W11–4	Dunedin	13 Jun	t: Wilson, Loveridge
				p: Hewson
S(2)	W40–15	Auckland	20 Jun	t: Wilson 3, Hewson 2, Robertson, Mourie
				c: Hewson 6
SA(1)	W14–9	Christchurch	15 Aug	t: Rollerson, Wilson, Shaw
				c: Rollerson
SA(2)	L12–24	Wellington	29 Aug	p: Hewson 4
SA(3)	W25–22	Auckland	12 Sep	t: Wilson, Knight
				c: Rollerson
				p: Hewson 3, Rollerson
				dg: Rollerson
R	W14–6	Bucharest	24 Oct	t: Salmon, Dalton
				p: Hewson
				dg: Rollerson
F(1)	W13–9	Toulouse	14 Nov	t: Wilson
				p: Hewson 2
				dg: Hewson
F(2)	W18–6	Paris	21 Nov	t: penalty try, Wilson
				c: Hewson 2
				p: Hewson 2

1982:

A(1)	W23–16	Christchurch	14 Aug	**t:** Mexted, Mourie, Pokere, Fraser **c:** Hewson 2 **p:** Hewson
A(2)	L16–19	Wellington	28 Aug	**t:** Shaw, Fraser **c:** Hewson **p:** Hewson 2
A(3)	W33–18	Auckland	11 Sep	**t:** Hewson, Shaw **c:** Hewson 2 **p:** Hewson 5 **dg:** Hewson, Smith

1983:

BL(1)	W16–12	Christchurch	4 Jun	**t:** Shaw **p:** Hewson 3 **dg:** Hewson
BL(2)	W9–0	Wellington	18 Jun	**t:** Loveridge **c:** Hewson **p:** Hewson
BL(3)	W15–8	Dunedin	2 Jul	**t:** Wilson **c:** Hewson **p:** Hewson 3
BL(4)	W38–6	Auckland	16 Jul	**t:** Wilson 3, Hewson, Hobbs, Haden **c:** Hewson 4 **p:** Hewson 2
A	W18–8	Sydney	20 Aug	**t:** Taylor **c:** Hewson **p:** Hewson 4
S	D25–25	Edinburgh	12 Nov	**t:** Fraser 2, Hobbs **c:** Deans 2 **p:** Deans 3
E	L9–15	Twickenham	19 Nov	**t:** Davie **c:** Deans **p:** Deans

1984:

F(1)	W10–9	Christchurch	16 Jun	**t:** Taylor **p:** Hewson 2
F(2)	W31–18	Auckland	23 Jun	**t:** B Smith, Dalton, Taylor **c:** Hewson 2 **p:** Hewson 5
A(1)	L9–16	Sydney	21 Jul	**p:** Hewson 2 **dg:** Hewson
A(2)	W19–15	Brisbane	4 Aug	**t:** Pokere **p:** Deans 5
A(3)	W25–24	Sydney	18 Aug	**t:** Clamp, Stone **c:** Deans **p:** Deans 5

1985:

E(1)	W18–13	Christchurch	1 Jun	**p:** Crowley 6
E(2)	W42–15	Wellington	8 Jun	**t:** Green 2, Kirwan, Mexted, Hobbs, Shaw

				c: Crowley 3
				p: Crowley 3
				dg: Smith
A	W10–9	Auckland	29 Jun	t: Green
				p: Crowley 2
Arg(1)	W33–20	Buenos Aires	26 Oct	t: Kirwan 2, Hobbs, Crowley
				c: Crowley
				p: Crowley 4
				dg: Fox
Arg(2)	D21–21	Buenos Aires	2 Nov	t: Kirwan 2, Mexted, Green
				c: Crowley.
				p: Crowley

1986:

F(a)	W18–9	Christchurch	28 Jun	t: Brewer
				c: G Cooper
				p: G Cooper
				dg: Botica 2, G Cooper
A(1)	L12–13	Wellington	9 Aug	t: Brooke-Cowden
				c: G Cooper
				p: G Cooper 2
A(2)	W13–12	Dunedin	23 Aug	t: Kirk
				p: G Cooper 2
				dg: G Cooper
A(3)	L9–22	Auckland	6 Sep	p: Crowley 3
F(b1)	W19–7	Toulouse	8 Nov	t: Shelford
				p: Crowley 3
				dg: Stone, Crowley
F(b2)	L3–16	Nantes	15 Nov	p: Crowley

1987:

It★	W70–6	Auckland	22 May	t: Kirk 2, Kirwan 2, Green 2, M Jones, Taylor, McDowell, Stanley, A Whetton, penalty try
				c: Fox 8
				p: Fox 2
Fj★	W74–13	Christchurch	27 May	t: Green 4, Gallagher 4, Kirk, Kirwan, A Whetton, penalty try
				c: Fox 10
				p: Fox 2
Arg★	W46–15	Wellington	1 Jun	t: Kirk, Z Brooke, Stanley, Earl, Crowley, A Whetton
				c: Fox 2
				p: Fox 6
S★	W30–3	Christchurch	6 Jun	t: Gallagher, A Whetton
				c: Fox 2.
				p: Fox 6
W★	W49–6	Brisbane	14 Jun	t: Kirwan 2, Shelford 2, Drake, Brooke–Cowden, Stanley, A Whetton
				c: Fox 7
				p: Fox
F★	W29–9	Auckland	20 Jun	t: Kirk, Kirwan, M Jones

				c: Fox
				p: Fox 4
				dg: Fox
A	W30–16	Sydney	25 Jul	**t:** Fitzpatrick 2, Kirwan, Green
				c: Fox
				p: Fox 3
				dg: Fox

1988:

W(1)	W52–3	Christchurch	28 May	**t:** Kirwan 4, Wright 2, Gallagher, Deans, Shelford, G Whetton
				c: Fox 6
W(2)	W54–9	Auckland	11 Jun	**t:** Kirwan 2, Wright 2, Taylor, Deans, M Jones, McDowell
				c: Fox 8
				p: Fox 2
A(1)	W32–7	Sydney	3 Jul	**t:** Kirwan 2, McDowell, A Whetton, Schuster
				c: Fox 3
				p: Fox 2
A(2)	D19–19	Brisbane	16 Jul	**t:** M Jones, Wright, Kirwan
				c: Fox 2
				p: Fox
A(3)	W30–9	Sydney	30 Jul	**t:** Deans, Gallagher, Kirwan
				c: Fox 3
				p: Fox 4

1989:

F(1)	W25–17	Christchurch	18 Jun	**t:** Wright 2, A Whetton
				c: Fox 2
				p: Fox 3
F(2)	W34–20	Auckland	1 Jul	**t:** Stanley, Deans, Fitzpatrick, A Whetton
				c: Fox 3
				p: Fox 4
Arg(1)	W60–9	Dunedin	15 Jul	**t:** Gallagher 3, Kirwan 2, Wright 2, penalty try, M Jones 2
				c: Fox 7
				p: Fox 2
Arg(2)	W49–12	Wellington	29 Jul	**t:** Wright 2, Deans 2, Gallagher, Kirwan, A Whetton
				c: Fox 6
				p: Fox 3
A	W24–12	Auckland	5 Aug	**t:** Gallagher, Loe
				c: Fox 2
				p: Fox 4
W	W34–9	Cardiff	4 Nov	**t:** Innes 2, Bachop, Wright
				c: Fox 3
				p: Fox 4
I	W23–6	Dublin	18 Nov	**t:** Gallagher, Wright, Shelford
				c: Fox
				p: Fox 3

1990:

S(1)	W31–16	Dunedin	16 Jun	**t:** Kirwan 2, Crowley, I Jones, Fox
				c: Fox 4
				p: Fox
S(2)	W21–18	Auckland	23 Jun	**t:** Loe
				c: Fox
				p: Fox 5
A(1)	W21–6	Christchurch	21 Jul	**t:** Fitzpatrick, Crowley, Innes, Kirwan
				c: Fox
				p: Fox
A(2)	W27–17	Auckland	4 Aug	**t:** Fitzpatrick, Z Brooke, G Bachop
				c: Fox 3
				p: Fox 2
				dg: Fox
A(3)	L9–21	Wellington	18 Aug	**p:** Fox 2
				dg: Fox
F(1)	W24–3	Nantes	3 Nov	**t:** Innes, A Whetton
				c: Fox 2
				p: Fox 3
				dg: Fox
F(2)	W30–12	Paris	10 Nov	**t:** Crowley, M Jones
				c: Fox 2
				p: Fox 6

1991:

Arg(1)	W28–14	Buenos Aires	6 Jul	**t:** Wright, Earl
				c: Fox
				p: Fox 5
				dg: Crowley
Arg(2)	W36–6	Buenos Aires	13 Jul	**t:** Z Brooke, M Jones, Kirwan, Wright
				c: Fox 4
				p: Fox 4
A(a1)	L12–21	Sydney	10 Aug	**t:** I Jones
				c: Fox
				p: Fox 2
A(a2)	W 6–3	Auckland	24 Aug	**p:** Fox 2
E⋆	W18–12	Twickenham	3 Oct	**t:** M Jones
				c: Fox
				p: Fox 4
US⋆	W46–6	Gloucester	8 Oct	**t:** Wright 3, Timu, Earl, Purvis, Tuigamala, Innes
				c: Preston 4
				p: Preston 2
It⋆	W31–21	Leicester	13 Oct	**t:** Z Brooke, Tuigamala, Hewitt, Innes
				c: Fox 3
				p: Fox 3
C⋆	W29–13	Lille	20 Oct	**t:** Timu 2, McCahill, Kirwan, Z Brooke
				c: Fox 3
				p: Fox
A(b)⋆	L6–16	Dublin	27 Oct	**p:** Fox 2
S⋆	W13–6	Cardiff	30 Oct	**t:** Little
				p: Preston 3

1992:

Wd(1)	L14–28	Christchurch	18 Apr	**t:** Turner, Tuigamala
				p: Fox 2
Wd(2)	W54–26	Wellington	22 Apr	**t:** G Cooper 2, Loe 2, Pene, Clarke 2, Tuigamala, Larsen, Strachan
				c: G Cooper 6, Fox
Wd(3)	W26–15	Auckland	25 Apr	**t:** Pene, Kirwan, Loe, Clarke
				c: G Cooper 2
				p: G Cooper 2
I(1)	W24–21	Dunedin	30 May	**t:** Henderson, Bunce 2, Clarke
				c: G Cooper 4
I(2)	W59–6	Wellington	6 Jun	**t:** Bunce 2, Pene 2, I Jones, Clarke, Timu, M Cooper 2, Kirwan, Strachan
				c: M Cooper 6
				p: M Cooper
A(1)[†]	L15–16	Sydney	14 Jul	**t:** Tuigamala, Bunce
				c: Fox
				p: Fox
A(2)	L17–19	Brisbane	19 Jul	**t:** Timu, Kirwan
				c: Fox 2
				p: Fox
A(3)	W26–23	Sydney	25 Jul	**t:** Bunce, Joseph
				c: Fox 2
				p: Fox 3
				dg: Fox
SA	W27–24	Johannesburg	15 Aug	**t:** Z Brooke, Kirwan, Timu
				c: Fox 3
				p: Fox 2

1993

BL(1)	W20–18	Christchurch	12 Jun	**t:** Bunce
				p: Fox 5
BL(2)	L 7–20	Wellington	26 Jun	**t:** Clarke
				c: Fox
BL(3)	W30–13	Auckland	3 Jul	**t:** Bunce, Fitzpatrick, Preston
				c: Fox 3
				p: Fox 3
A	W25–10	Dunedin	17 Jul	**t:** Fitzpatrick, Bunce
				p: Fox 5
WS	W35–13	Auckland	31 Jul	**t:** Stensness, Z Brooke
				c: Fox 2
				p: Fox 7
S	W51–15	Edinburgh	20 Nov	**t:** Wilson 3, Ellis 2, Bunce, Z Brooke
				c: Cooper 4, Wilson
				p: Cooper 2
E	L 9–15	Twickenham	27 Nov	**p:** Wilson 3

★ World Cup matches
[+] Non-cap tests
[†] Five-point try introduced from this game onwards

SOUTH AFRICA

François Pienaar
Speaking with Chris Thau

I SPENT much of my first year as captain trying to change the way rugby people think in South Africa. My goal was to introduce a degree of perspective. The history and tradition of our game is one whereby winning is the only acceptable option. I wanted the emphasis to be changed so that quality play could be appreciated regardless of the result.

If the Springboks lose, the public decide that someone must be guilty and a scapegoat must be found – and the captain is there to take the flak. I accept that, but it doesn't mean I have to like it. I feel that our media has been largely responsible for this unhealthy situation, and I asked them to help our public change their way of thinking. I know the people's expectations will never change. But their perception can.

This is why, just before the first Test against France in Durban, I made an appeal to the South African journalists to support my attempt to overcome the divisive effects of the entrenched provincialism created by the years of isolation, and to help us convince the public that success will only arrive when the quality has been achieved.

You can play well and still lose. That is as much a part of the game as is winning. The essence of the message I was trying to put across to the public was 'Look for quality rather than a win. The winning will come, because it's part and parcel of a quality game.'

There was plenty of quality to admire in our play during '93. We won a Test in Australia and swept Argentina 2–0 in South America. However, there was also disappointment as we lost the home series to France, and also let the Wallabies recover to win the Australian series.

> *'You can play well and still lose. That is as much a part of the game as is winning. The essence of the message I was trying to put across to the public was, look for quality rather than a win. The winning will come, because it is part and parcel of a quality game'*

The year for me had started outside the international fold, although I was captain of a Transvaal side which won the Super-10 crown and the Currie Cup. I was delighted to be selected for the Springboks, but to be appointed captain on my debut was something special. It is every South African's dream to captain the Springboks. I was in tears when I heard the news, as were my mother and father.

But I quickly realized that my problems had only begun. Rugby football is more than a religion in South Africa, it is the soul of the nation. We are possessed by rugby and we are very proud of our rugby heritage. Being Transvaal skipper had not prepared me for Springbok captaincy, which involves having to cope with the extreme demands of the South African public. There is an obsessive expectation of success among our supporters, irrespective of circumstances and parameters.

When I ran out at Kings Park, leading the Springboks for the first time in that Test against France (drew 20–20), I was gripped by fear – the fear of failure. I kept asking myself, 'Did I do my homework properly? Will the team play according to plan? Is the plan correct? Have the guys accepted me as captain?' and many more questions besides.

With hindsight, I regret I was so tense and scared. I could not enjoy the occasion as much as I wanted. The tension was expressed in my decision to go for a pushover try at the end of the game, when we were given a scrum near to the French line. The score was 20–20, and my apprehensions were reflected in my decision to go for the safest option – scrummaging. We'd had a good scrummaging session the day before, and I felt that we could shove them backwards.

We failed, and now, again with hindsight, I feel we should have initiated a back-row move instead. I use the word hindsight a lot, but this is just to emphasize our lack of experience. We have learnt a lot since.

The second Test (lost 17–18) was even more painful than the first. We lost when we should have won. We were the better side, but for reasons that defeat me we simply turned the engine off after roaring into a ten-point lead.

'When I ran out at Kings Park, leading the Springboks for the first time in that Test against France (drew 20–20), I was gripped by fear – the fear of failure'

Three players had been dropped after the first Test – Rudi Visagie, Kobus Wiese and Ian Macdonald – but Hannes Strydom, Nico Wegner and Deon Lotter came in, and all three had great games.

Lotter cleaned out Laurent Cabannes at the tail of the lineout – an area in which we had previously been exposed – while Strydom and Wegner shared the lineout ball with French giants Olivier Roumat and Olivier Merle, who had dominated us in the first Test. We scored a brilliant try through wing James Small, but we lost the penalty count. In the first Test we had been refereed by New Zealander Lindsay McLachlan. But in the second we were penalized by Englishman Ed Morrison for a rucking style which had seemed perfectly acceptable to Mr McLachlan.

This was my second international game, both as a player and as a captain, and to be honest I didn't feel that it was that much different from a top provincial game in the Currie Cup. It was faster, but not much harder physically. However, it was mentally very tough for me, as just before the game I learned of the death of my friend Stef Nel in a car crash. He died together with another budding talent, Cameron Oliver. I felt numb. I could hardly pull myself together. The grief was unbelievable.

Soon after the French series we left for Australia. In the first Test (won 19–12) the Wallabies did not know what to expect from us. We kept changing the positions in the lineout, and we punched the blindside as we had worked on in practice. It worked a treat and we scored three tries to their none.

The Wallabies did not know what had hit them, but by the second Test (won 28–20) they had worked out our pattern and they strangled our lineout. We deservedly lost to a better side. We were not outplayed, but one has to say that the scoreline flattered us. It did not reflect the degree of superiority enjoyed by the Wallabies.

Towards the end of the game James Small was sent off for what was formally described as 'back-chatting'. In other words, he was rude to the referee – the same Mr Morrison who had handled our second-Test defeat against France. Small became the first Springbok to be sent off in an international, and we could imagine the reaction back home. It was a harsh decision by any standard. Small might have been slightly obnoxious, but he was not involved in any act of violence or disobedience.

> *'James Small became the first Springbok to be sent off in an international, and we could imagine the reaction back home. It was a harsh decision by any standard. Small might have been slightly obnoxious, but he was not involved in any act of violence or disobedience'*

In the third Test (lost 12–19) our lack of experience proved to be the deciding factor. The guys knew that the night after the game we were going to fly out. And instead of concentrating on the task at hand, we spent the morning packing and making arrangements for the bags to be taken to the airport.

All the same, we played very well, and again outscored them on the try count. We had made a point of talking beforehand to referee Morrison about the aspects of the game he felt we had to tidy up, as well as about some of the points we wanted to make. We pointed out that at two-man lineouts on our throw-in, Wallaby scrum-half Nick Farr-Jones stood at hooker while Tim Gavin was at scrum-half. And as soon as we threw the ball in, Gavin moved in and contested the ball. Morrison assured us that he was going to deal with it instantly. As I recall, he did punish them once, after which he forgot, I think. We did play well when we had the ball, but again we suffered from a lack of primary possession, lineout in particular. That cost us the game.

We returned home to a barrage of criticism, the like of which I had never seen before. But I kept saying that we'd played as well as we could, and that we needed more time to sort out our problems.

Soon after that Transvaal played and beat Natal in the Currie Cup final. It was one of the most intense and physically demanding games I have ever played in (I never experience such intensity in our games abroad). Very often the game crossed that fine dividing line between physical and brutal. In the second half I was tackled blindly. I hit a knee as I went down and suffered concussion.

> 'Transvaal beat Natal in the Currie Cup final. It was one of the most intense and physically demanding games I have ever played in. Very often the game crossed that fine dividing line between physical and brutal'

Just a week later we left for Argentina. According to International Board rules I had to sit it out for three weeks. So I found myself as non-playing captain, and I didn't really know how to handle it. Vice-captain Tiaan Strauss took over, but despite his best efforts our build-up to the first Test was comparatively poor.

I did not feel the squad was focused enough, so I called a meeting in Tucuman. We sat down and discussed our goals and how to achieve them. We all agreed that we were playing each match as it came, that we were lethargic, and that for many of us the tour was very much an anti-climax after the Currie Cup final.

For you to understand my philosophy better, I ought to explain that I approach rugby in the same way as I approach business, setting goals at the beginning of the season. I also set out the means by which I intend achieving them. Everything is clear-cut. I believe in the value of group therapy as a means of developing a strong collective – hence the chat in Tucuman. My philosophy in the Transvaal team is that we talk to each other rather than about each other. It is vital for the skipper is to keep all channels of communications open.

We had a bruising encounter against Tucuman – the so-called Battle of Tucuman, which I'm sure most touring teams must have experienced. But we kept our cool, concentrated, and won both the battle and the game.

In the first Test (won 29–26) we started very well. I made my comeback from injury and we looked like running away with the game. But as we eased into the comfort zone we started to think about other things. Complacency crept in, and instead of running the ball as before, we kept kicking against the wind and into their hands. That brought Argentina back into the game and gave the scoreline a flattering look.

In the second Test (won 52–23) we decided to run the ball, and it was a great game of rugby football. The team played like a dream. It would be unfair to name names. All the guys played their hearts out, and in a way the team spirit started to resemble the atmosphere we have in the Transvaal team. There is respect and loyalty in the Transvaal side, with open channels of communication. That is the kind of rugby we were aiming to play as Springboks. We knew all along we could do it, but it was very satisfying to prove it to everyone else.

> *'There is respect and loyalty in the Transvaal side, with open channels of communication. That is the kind of rugby we were aiming to play as Springboks. We knew all along we could do it, but it was very satisfying to prove it to everyone else'*

The side made a quantum leap in quality during 1993. But we must now stop experimenting with selection and get on with preparing the side for the World Cup. We must forget about our provincial outfits, and start thinking like South Africans first and Transvaalers (or Natalians or whatever) second.

I would dearly love to lead the team in the World Cup. Having it in South Africa is both a bonus and an incentive. We will be able to win it provided we are positive about it and stop bickering among ourselves.

South African scrum-half Joost van der Westhuizen gets the ball away during the historic First Test against England in Pretoria.

SOUTH AFRICA (P7 W3 D1 L3 F169 A146):

(H)	v	France	(Durban, 26.6.93)	drew	20–20
(H)	v	France	(Johannesburg, 3.7.93)	lost	17–18
(A)	v	Australia	(Sydney, 31.7.93)	won	19–12
(A)	v	Australia	(Brisbane, 14.8.93)	lost	20–28
(A)	v	Australia	(Sydney, 21.8.93)	lost	12–19
(A)	v	Argentina	(Buenos Aires, 6.11.93)	won	29–26
(A)	v	Argentina	(Buenos Aires, 13.11.93)	won	52–23

Springboks in Australia (tour record: P12 W9 D0 L3 F527 A147):

(A)	v	Western Australia	(Perth, 14.7.93)	won	71–8
(A)	v	South Australia	(Adelaide, 17.7.93)	won	90–3
(A)	v	Victoria	(Melbourne, 21.7.93)	won	78–3
(A)	v	New South Wales	(Sydney, 24.7.93)	lost	28–29
(A)	v	NSW Country	(Orange, 31.7.93)	won	41–7
(A)	v	ACT	(Canberra, 4.8.93)	won	57–10
(A)	v	Queensland	(Brisbane, 8.8.93)	won	17–3
(A)	v	Queensland Country	(Mackay, 11.8.93)	won	63–5
(A)	v	Sydney	(Penrith, 18.8.93)	won	31–20

Springboks in Argentina (tour record: P6 W5 D0 L1 F243 A142):

(A)	v	Cordoba	(Cordoba, 27.10.93)	won	55–37
(A)	v	Buenos Aires	(Buenos Aires, 30.10.93)	lost	27–28
(A)	v	Tucuman	(Tucuman, 2.11.93)	won	40–12
(A)	v	Rosario	(Rosario, 9.11.93)	won	40–26

SOUTH AFRICA B (P1 W0 D0 L1 F22 A31):

(A)	v	Uruguay	(Montevideo, 6.11.93)	lost	22–31

PROVINCIAL INTERNATIONAL RUGBY

1993 SUPER 10 TOURNAMENT

Final: Transvaal (10) 20, Auckland (7) 7
Ellis Park, Johannesburg, 22 May 1993

Pool A: Western Samoa 27, Queensland 19 (Apia, 3.4.93); Otago 22, Auckland 63 (Dunedin, 10.4.93); Queensland 21, Auckland 22 (Brisbane, 17.4.93); Natal 56, Western Samoa 13 (Durban, 17.4.93); Auckland 18, Western Samoa 10 (Auckland, 24.4.93); Otago 13, Natal 35 (Dunedin, 25.4.93); Auckland 22, Natal 6 (Auckland, 30.4.93); Queensland 20, Otago 8 (Brisbane, 1.5.93); Natal 32, Queensland 15 (Durban, 8.5.93); Western Samoa 30, Otago 20 (Apia, 8.5.93).

	P	W	D	L	F	A	Pts
Auckland	4	4	0	0	125	59	16
Natal	4	3	0	1	129	63	12
Western Samoa	4	2	0	2	80	113	8
Queensland	4	1	0	3	75	89	5
Otago	4	0	0	4	63	148	0

Pool B: Waikato 29, North Harbour 24 (Hamilton, 3.4.93); Transvaal 42, Northern Transvaal 22 (Pretoria, 3.4.93); New South Wales 17, Waikato 13 (Sydney, 17.4.93);

Transvaal 39, North Harbour 13 (Johannesburg, 17.4.93); Northern Transvaal 45, New South Wales 20 (Pretoria, 23.4.93); Transvaal 30, Waikato 15 (Johannesburg, 24.4.93); Waikato 18, Northern Transvaal 28 (Hamilton, 1.5.93); North Harbour 16, New South Wales 17 (Takapuna, 1.5.93); North Harbour 29, Northern Transvaal 14 (Takapuna, 7.5.93); New South Wales 3, Transvaal 10 (Sydney, 8.5.93).

	P	W	D	L	F	A	Pts
Transvaal	4	4	0	0	121	53	16
New South Wales	4	2	0	2	57	84	9
Northern Transvaal	4	2	0	2	109	109	8
North Harbour	4	1	0	3	82	99	6
Waikato	4	1	0	3	75	99	5

DOMESTIC RUGBY

CURRIE CUP
Final: Natal (9) 15, Transvaal (3) 21 (Kings Park, Durban, 16 October 1993)

Natal: A Joubert; J Small, P Müller, D Muir, C van der Westhuizen; J Stransky, K Putt; L Muller, J Allan, G Kebble, M Andrews, S Atherton, W Bartmann (capt), A Blakeman, G Teichman.
Scorer – Penalty goals: Stransky 5.

Transvaal: G Johnson; C Dirks, J Mulder, B Fourie, P Hendriks; H le Roux, J Roux; H Rodgers, U Schmidt, B Swart, H Strydom, K Wiese, F Pienaar (capt) (D Lotter 46), I MacDonald, R Straeuli.
Scorers – Try: Johnson, Schmidt. Conversion: Johnson. *Penalty goals:* Johnson 3.

Referee: F Burger (Western Province).

Urban Section:	P	W	D	L	F	A	Pts
Natal	10	9	0	1	340	187	18
Transvaal	10	8	0	2	320	227	16
Eastern Province	10	5	0	5	227	243	10
Northern Transvaal	10	4	0	6	225	263	8
Western Province	10	2	0	8	220	249	4
Orange Free State	10	2	0	8	199	310	4

Central A Section:	P	W	D	L	F	A	Pts
Western Transvaal	6	5	0	1	174	123	10
Border	6	3	0	3	162	134	6
Northern Free State	6	3	0	3	143	161	6
Eastern Transvaal	6	1	0	5	86	146	2

Central B Section:	P	W	D	L	F	A	Pts
South East Transvaal	8	6	0	2	191	137	12
Griqualand West	8	6	0	2	197	149	12
Boland	8	4	0	4	164	145	8
Vaal Triangle	8	3	0	5	182	192	6
Far North	8	1	0	7	136	249	2

Rural A Section:	P	W	D	L	F	A	Pts
East Orange Free State	6	6	0	0	239	107	12
Stellaland	6	4	0	2	221	146	8
North East Cape	6	4	0	2	183	121	8

South West Districts	6	3	0	3	158	180	6
Lowveld	6	2	0	4	161	176	4
Northern Natal	6	2	0	4	138	163	4
North West Cape	6	0	0	6	91	298	0

Currie Cup roll of honour (since 1980):

1980 Northern Transvaal
1981 Northern Transvaal
1982 Western Province
1983 Western Province
1984 Western Province
1985 Western Province
1986 Western Province
1987 Northern Transvaal
1988 Northern Transvaal
1989 Western Province
1990 Natal
1991 Northern Transvaal
1992 Natal
1993 Transvaal

LION CUP

Quarter-finals (5.6.93): Border 3, Northern Transvaal 70; Western Province 10, Natal 24; North East Cape 3, Orange Free State 95; Eastern Province 12, Transvaal 33. *Semi-finals* (28.8.93): Orange Free State 33, Natal 55; Northern Transvaal 25, Transvaal 48. *Final* (18.9.93): Transvaal 20, Natal 11.

South Africa A against England, with Johan Roux under pressure from opposite number Steve Bates.

1980:

SAm(a1)	W24–9	Johannesburg	26 Apr	**t:** T du Plessis, Mordt, Germishuys **c:** Botha 3 **p:** Botha **dg:** Botha
SAm(a2)	W18–9	Durban	3 May	**t:** M du Plessis **c:** Botha **p:** Botha **dg:** Botha 3
BL(1)	W26–22	Cape Town	31 May	**t:** Louw, W du Plessis, Van Heerden, Germishuys, Serfontein **c:** Botha 3
BL(2)	W26–19	Bloemfontein	14 Jun	**t:** Louw, Stofberg, Germishuys, Pienaar **c:** Botha 2 **p:** Botha 2
BL(3)	W12–10	Port Elizabeth	28 Jun	**t:** Germishuys **c:** Botha **p:** Botha **dg:** Botha
BL(4)	L13–17	Pretoria	12 Jul	**t:** W du Plessis **p:** Pienaar 2, Botha
SAm(b1)	W22–13	Montevideo	18 Oct	**t:** Stofberg, Gerber, Berger **c:** Botha 2 **p:** Botha **dg:** Botha
SAm(b2)	W30–16	Santiago	26 Oct	**t:** Mordt 2, Germishuys 2, Gerber, M du Plessis **c:** Botha 3
F	W37–15	Pretoria	8 Nov	**t:** Pienaar, Germishuys, Serfontein, Stofberg, Kahts **c:** Botha 4 **p:** Botha 3

1981:

I(1)	W23–15	Cape Town	30 May	**t:** Gerber 2, Louw **c:** Botha **p:** Botha 3
I(2)	W12–10	Durban	6 Jun	**p:** Botha **dg:** Botha 3
NZ(1)	L9–14	Christchurch	15 Aug	**t:** Bekker **c:** Botha **dg:** Botha
NZ(2)	W24–12	Wellington	29 Aug	**t:** Germishuys **c:** Botha **p:** Botha 5 **dg:** Botha
NZ(3)	L22–25	Auckland	12 Sep	**t:** Mordt 3 **c:** Botha 2 **p:** Botha 2

US	W38–7	Glenville		t: Mordt 3, Geldenhuys, Germishuys 2, Beck, Berger c: Botha 3

1982:

SAm(1)	W50–18	Pretoria	27 Mar	t: Gerber 3, Mordt 2, Oosthuizen, C du Plessis, W du Plessis c: Botha 6 p: Heunis dg: Botha
SAm(2)	L12–21	Bloemfontein	3 Apr	t: Gerber c: Botha p: Botha 2

1984:

E(1)	W33–15	Port Elizabeth	2 Jun	t: Gerber, C du Plessis, Louw c: Heunis 3 p: Heunis 5
E(2)	W35–9	Johannesburg	9 Jun	t: Gerber 3, Stofberg, Sonnekus, Tobias c: Heunis 3, Tobias p: Heunis
SAm(1)	W32–15	Pretoria	20 Oct	t: Louw, Gerber, Serfontein, Heunis, Mallet c: Tobias 2, Gerber p: Tobias 2
SAm(2)	W22–13	Cape Town	27 Oct	t: C du Plessis, Ferreira, Mordt, Gerber p: Tobias 2

1986:

Cv(1)	W21–15	Cape Town	10 May	t: C du Plessis c: Botha p: Botha 3 dg: Botha 2
Cv(2)	L18–19	Durban	17 May	t: Reinach c: Botha p: Botha 4
Cv(3)	W33–18	Pretoria	24 May	t: Schmidt, Botha, Gerber, Reinach c: Botha 4 p: Botha 3
Cv(4)	W24–10	Johannesburg	31 May	t: Wright c: Botha p: Botha 5 dg: M du Plessis

1989:

Wd(1)	W20–19	Cape Town	26 Aug	t: Knoetze, Botha, Smal c: Botha p: Botha 2
Wd(2)	W22–16	Johannesburg	1 Sep	t: Heunis, M du Plessis c: Botha p: Botha 3 dg: Botha

1992:

NZ[†]	L24–27	Johannesburg	15 Aug	**t:** Gerber 2, P Müller
				c: Botha 3
				p: Botha
A	L3–26	Cape Town	22 Aug	**p:** Botha
F(1)	W20–15	Lyon	17 Oct	**t:** Gerber, Small
				c: Botha 2
				p: Botha
				dg: Botha
F(2)	L16–29	Paris	24 Oct	**t:** Gerber
				c: Botha
				p: Botha 2
				dg: Botha
E	L16–33	Twickenham	14 Nov	**t:** Smit
				c: Botha
				p: Botha 2
				dg: Botha

1993

F(1)	D20–20	Durban	26 Jun	**t:** Schmidt
				p: van Rensburg 5
F(2)	L17–18	Johannesburg	3 Jul	**t:** Small
				p: van Rensburg 4
A(1)	W19–12	Sydney	31 Jul	**t:** Small 2, Muller
				c: van Rensburg 2
A(2)	L20–28	Brisbane	14 Aug	**t:** Olivier, Stransky
				c: Stransky 2
				p: Stransky 2
A(3)	L12–19	Sydney	21 Aug	**t:** Small, Pienaar
				c: Stransky
Arg(1)	W29–26	Buenes Aires	6 Nov	**t:** Small 2, van der Westhuizen, Joubert
				c: Stransky 3
				p: Stransky
Arg(2)	W52–23	Buenes Aires	13 Nov	**t:** Strauss 2, Small 2, Williams van der Westhuizen, Johnson
				c: Johnson 4
				p: Johnson 3

1994

E(1)	L15–32	Pretoria	4 Jun	**p:** Joubert 5
E(2)	W27–9	Cape Town	19 Jun	**t:** H le Roux, Joubert
				c: Joubert
				p: H le Roux 3, Joubert 2

* World Cup matches
· Non-cap tests
† Five-point try introduced from this game onwards

THE PLAYERS A-Z

KEY TO INDIVIDUAL STATISTICS

Take the case of Mark Davies (right) as an example*. Mark was first capped at senior level for Wales in 1982, won 2 caps last season, and has 34 caps in all, with 61 points to his credit. In 1994, Mark toured the South Seas with Wales. However, he played in the 1986 IRB Centenary match in Cardiff (Lions 7, The Rest 15) which has been included as a Lions cap. In 1992 he played one Test in the series against New Zealand.

Each player has his caps listed in order, plus a breakdown of his points tally, again in chronological order. For example, Mark marked his debut against France in 1982 with two tries and a penalty goal. If a nation is

Wales (1982)		
Last Season	2 caps	3 pts
1994	Tour to South Seas	
Career	34 caps	61 pts
Lions 1983		
1986		
1992	1 Test	0 pts

Caps (34): **1982** F, E, S, W **1983** NZ(1,2), E, F, W, S **1984** W, F, E, S, Fj **1987** S, E, W, wc–T, W, A **1989** W, S, E, F, Arg(1,2), Fj **1991** F, S, J, W **1993** E, F

Points (61 – 9t, 5c, 4p, 1dg) **1982** F(2t, 1p) S(1t), W(1t) **1983** NZ(1:1dg), E(2t) **1989** Fj(2p) **1991** F(1t), W(2t) **1993** F(1p)

played more than once in the same year, the statistic is recorded in one of two ways. For a 3-match series against, say, Australia, the statistic reads: A(1,2,3). If our player has previously turned out against the Aussies in the same year, that statistic reads: A(a), followed by A(b1,b2,b3). This makes identification possible when it comes to points scored, e.g. A(b3:1t) means that our player has scored a try against Australia in the third Test of the second series.

---

* The qualification for entry in *The Save & Prosper Rugby Union Who's Who* is involvement in any Test match of any player from the Big Eight nations during the 1993/94 season (June 1993–June 1994). Players' statistics *do* include summer tours (excluding France to NZ, South Africa to NZ, and Australia's home series against Italy). Details of A-team players are logged in the Appendix section (pp 420–437).

Allan, J.   South Africa

Full Name: John Allan
Province: Natal
Club: Glenwood Old Boys (SA)
Position: Hooker
Height: 6ft (1.83m)
Weight: 15st (91kg)
Occupation: Computer consultant with ABS Computers (Durban)
Born: Glasgow, 25.11.63
Family: Claire (wife)
Family links with rugby: Brothers both play – William in Italy and Richard for Empangeni in Durban, SA
Former clubs: Northern Transvaal Defence (SA), Edinburgh Academicals
International debut (for Scotland): New Zealand 31, Scotland 16, 1990
International debut (for SA): Australia 12, South Africa 19, 1993
Five Nations debut: Scotland 32, Wales 12, 1991
Best moment in rugby: Representing Scotland in 1991 World Cup
Worst moment in rugby: Snapping knee ligaments playing in club game (1988)

Scotland (1990)		
Career	9 caps	0 pts
South Africa (1993)		
Last Season	5 caps	0 pts
Career	5 caps	0 pts

Caps	(Scotland–9): **1990** NZ(1) **1991** W, I(a), Ro wc–J, I(b), WS, E, NZ
Caps	(S Africa–5): **1993** A(1R) Arg(1,2R) **1994** E(1,2)
Points	Nil

Most respected opponent: Uli Schmidt (Transvaal & South Africa)
Serious injuries: Snapped knee ligaments
Best memory last season: Helping Natal beat England 21–6 at Kings Park
Other sporting achievements: Softball for Scotland Schools
Suggestions to improve rugby: On-field – take steps to prevent negative rugby by penalizing players for killing opposition ball by award of automatic penalty in front of posts
Notable landmarks in rugby career: Springbok hooker in both Tests against England last summer, less than two years on from opposing them for Scotland in the World Cup semi-final. Glasgow-born John made his South African debut against Australia in Sydney (31.7.93) as a last-minute replacement for Uli Schmidt, a player for whom he has the utmost respect. South Africa won that game (19–12) – one of seven starts made by John in Oz. But he did not reappear

in the Test side until the autumn tour to Argentina (starting the first Test and coming on as a 52nd-minute replacement in the second), where the Springboks completed a 2–0 series sweep. John had returned to the Republic in the summer of 1992 to live with his wife Claire, having collected the last of his nine Scotland caps in the World Cup third/fourth place play-off against New Zealand at Cardiff (30.10.91). He had figured in five of Scotland's six Cup ties before being usurped by perennial rival Kenny Milne for the '92 Five Nations Championship. He warmed the replacements bench throughout the latter, as he had done in 1990/91 season, when he also became replacement for Scotland B against Ireland and France, before making his full debut in first Test at Dunedin on summer tour of New Zealand (lost 16–31, 16.6.90). Five Nations debut came the following season against Wales (2.2.91). Captained South African Barbarians against Wales (1993)

Touchlines: Reading

Allen, M. R. New Zealand

Full Name: Mark Richard Allen
Province: Taranaki
Position: Loosehead prop
Height: 6ft ½ in (1.84m)
Weight: 17st 11lb (113kg)
Occupation: Auto-electrician
Born: 27.7.67
International debut: New Zealand 35, Western Samoa 13, 1993
Best moment in rugby: Winning the second division with Taranaki in 1992
Worst moment in rugby: Being relegated to second division in first place
Biggest influence on career: People who know what they're talking about
Best memory last season: Winning first cap against Western Samoa
Notable landmarks in rugby career: One of the characters of New Zealand rugby, Mark is known as 'Bull' throughout the Land of the

New Zealand (1993)

Last Season	1 cap	0 pts
Career	1 cap	0 pts

Caps (1): **1993** WS(TR)

Points Nil

Long White Cloud, and revered in his home province of Taranaki. He enjoys running with the ball almost as much as he loves greens; he is a committed vegetarian. He skippered his province to the 1992 second-division title, beating Counties 12–0 in the final at New Plymouth (3.10.92), having finished the regular season with seven wins from eight starts (Bull scoring ten tries). He toured Canada with the NZ Development squad in 1990, and went on to appear in non-cap internationals against Romania and the Soviet Union as well as the two 'tests' against England B in 1992. He was called into the All Black squad for the 1993 series against the British Lions, having captained Taranaki against the tourists in New Plymouth in June of that year. But had to wait until Western Samoa's visit for his Test debut. One of the first to benefit from the new temporary replacement law, he came on for two short bursts (for Craig Dowd and Graham Purvis) during the 35–13 win in Auckland on 31 July, and the cap was his. He missed the remainder of season with a broken jaw (inflicted by Waikato's Graham Purvis), but was included in the All Black party which won 12 of 13 games in England and Scotland (October–December 1993). Mark was an unused replacement in both Tests, unable to dislodge first-choice loosehead Craig Dowd, but did play in wins over Midlands, North, South of Scotland, Scotland A (replacement), Scottish Development XV and Emerging England XV. He has a secret desire to be a winger

Touchlines: Food (that I don't have to cook), hours and hours of hard rugby training in the cold and wet, golf

Andrew, C. R.   England

Full Name: Christopher Robert Andrew
Club: Wasps
Position: Outside-half
Height: 5ft 9in (1.76m)
Weight: 12st 8lb (80kg)
Occupation: Associate director with Debenham, Tewson and Chinnock (chartered surveyors)
Born: Richmond, Yorkshire, 18.2.63
Family: Sara (wife) and Emily (daughter)
Family links with rugby: Brothers (Richard and David) play for Headingley
Former clubs: Middlesbrough, Cambridge University (Blues: 1982, 83, 84), Nottingham, Gordon (Sydney, Aus), Toulouse (Fr)
International debut: England 22, Romania 15, 1985

Five Nations debut: England 9, France 9, 1985

Best moment in rugby: Beating France 21–19 at Twickenham to win 1991 Five Nations Grand Slam

Worst moment in rugby: Losing 1990 Grand Slam decider 13–7 to Scotland (losing the World Cup final was disappointing but in a different way); losing England place (1992/93)

Most embarrassing moment: Missing 9 out of 10 kicks at goal for Nottingham at Beeston against London Welsh in fourth round of 1985 John Player Cup (lost 11–12)

Most respected opponent: Michael Lynagh (Australia)

Other sporting achievements: Played first-class cricket for Yorkshire 2nd XI and Cambridge University, 1984 and 1985 (as captain). Scored 101 n.o. for University against Notts at Trent Bridge (1984)

Best memory last season: England's defeat of All Blacks

Should rugby's amateur rules be revised? Yes

To what degree should players benefit? Players should be allowed to take advantage of commercial activities. It's not about making fortunes out of the game – the sums are largely peanuts – it's the principal of being able to benefit from our massive commitment to rugby. The game is a multi-million-pound industry and should be administered accordingly

Advice for International Board: Reduce the number of offences for which kicks at goal are permitted. Be careful not to go too far with rule changes designed to speed up the game and make it more entertaining. XV-a-side needs to maintain a distinct identity from Sevens. End the season with Five Nations (in March–April). Remove the ten-yard law for offside for players in front of ball (revert to old law)

Notable landmarks in rugby career: World's most-capped outside-half (58 of his 59 caps in the No 10 jersey), who resumed the goal-kicking duties for England during the 1994 Five Nations Championship after a five-year break. He celebrated with 18 points (5p,1dg) against France in his first game back (5.3.94) as England won their fourth straight Paris match. But it was his performance in the first Test against South Africa (4.6.94) that really stood out. His 27 points were an English record, his 19th dropped goal (17 for England,

England (1985)		
Last season	7 caps	62 pts
1994	tour to South Africa	
Career	59 caps	210 pts
Lions 1989	2 Tests	8 pts
1993	3 Tests	3 pts

Caps (59): **1985** Ro, F, S, I, W **1986** W, S, I, F **1987** I, F, W wc–J(R), US **1988** S, I(1,2), A(a1,a2), Fj,A(b) **1989** S, I, F, W, Ro, Fj. Lions–A(2,3) **1990** I, F, W, S, Arg(b) **1991** W, S, I, F, Fj, A(a) wc–NZ, It, US, F, S, A(b) **1992** S, I, F, W, C, SA **1993** F, W. Lions–NZ(1,2,3). NZ **1994** S, I, F, W, SA(1,2)

Points (210 – 2t,12c,42p,17dg): **1985** Ro(4p,2dg), F(2p,1dg), S(2p), I(2p), W(1c,2p,1dg) **1986** W(6p,1dg), S(2p), I(3c,1p) **1987** F(1dg) **1988** S(1dg), I(1:3c) **1989** S(2p), I(1c,2p), F(1p), W(2p,1dg), Ro(1dg), Fj(1c). Lions–A(2:1c,1p,1dg) **1991** F(1dg), Fj(1t,2dg) wc–NZ(1dg), S(1dg) **1993** Lions–NZ(2:1dg). NZ(1dg) **1994** F(5p,1dg), W(1c,1p), SA(1:1t,2c,5p,1dg), SA(2:3p)

two for Lions) was a world record, and he became the first Englishman to achieve a 'full house' of try, conversion (2), penalty goal (5) and dropped goal in a Test. He replaced injured Paul Dean (13.6.89) on the triumphant Lions tour of Australia in 1989, and played in last two Tests (1c,1p,1dg in Brisbane second Test). Either side of trip Down Under, captained England to win 58–3 in Romania (13.5.89) and British Lions XV to 29–27 success over France (4.10.89) in French Revolution Bicentennial match. Captained Wasps to 1989/90 Courage Championship and London to 1990 Divisional Championship (having represented North in 1985 and 1986). Moved family, work and rugby to Toulouse after 1991 World Cup but returned with job early in 1992/93 season. Subject to 120-day re-qualification rule, which prevented his playing League rugby and doubtless affected his form. Deposed by Stuart Barnes midway through 1993 Five Nations Championship but gained his revenge when he became first-choice No 10 for Lions in New Zealand that summer, playing in all three Tests

Touchlines: Gardening and DIY

Andrews, K. S. South Africa

Full Name: Keith Steven Andrews
Club: Villagers
Province: Western Province
Position: Tighthead prop
Height: 5ft 11in (1.80m)
Weight: 16st 7lb (105kg)
Occupation: Accountant
Born: Molteno, 3.5.62
International debut: England 33, South Africa 16, 1992
Notable landmarks in rugby career: Having made his debut against England at Twickenham (14.11.92), Keith's Test career went from strength to strength in 1993, with the only blip coming when he was one of two Springboks sent off during the 40–12 tour triumph over Argentine province Tucuman (2.11.93). Played in four of South Africa's six games in South America (also against Córdoba and Rosario), having appeared eight times on the summer tour of Australia – outings in each of the three Tests plus starts

South Africa (1992)

Last Season	6 caps	0 pts
Career	7 caps	0 pts

Caps (7): **1992** E **1993** F(1,2), A(1R,2,3), Arg(2)

Points Nil

against South Australia, Victoria, NSW Country, Queensland and Queensland Country. Although only a replacement first time against Argentina, he took over from Transvaal's Balie Swart for the second international in Buenos Aires (13.11.93) – his sixth cap of the year (having played in both home Tests against France in June and July). Educated at Selbourne College in the South African district of East London, Keith played 95 times for Western Province before being selected by Boks to tour France and England in 1992, during which the Cape Town-based player appeared in eight of the 13 games

Armary, L. France

Full Name: Louis Armary
Club: Lourdes
Position: Prop, hooker
Height: 6ft (1.83m)
Weight: 15st 7lb (94kg)
Occupation: Business executive
Born: Lourdes, 24.7.63
International debut: France 55, Romania 12, 1987
Five Nations debut: Scotland 23, France 12, 1988
Notable landmarks in rugby career: Scored the one and only international try for France in 48–31 second-Test reversal at hands of Australia at Ballymore Oval, Brisbane (24.6.90). Represented France in two different positions during 1991/92 season: at hooker against Wales in non-cap Test in Cardiff (4.9.91), and at loosehead prop at Murrayfield and in Paris against Ireland after first-choice Gregoire Lascube had been suspended for his dismissal against England. In 1992/93, however, he remained at loosehead throughout the ten-match campaign (including France's 1993 Five Nations title triumph) before missing the spring trip to Bucharest. Reinstated, Louis

France (1987)

Last Season	7 caps	0 pts
Career	40 caps	4 pts

Caps (40): **1987** wc–Ro(a), Ro(b) **1988** S, I, W, Arg(b1,b2), Ro **1989** W, S, A(1,2) **1990** W, E, S, I, A(1,2,3), NZ(1) **1991** W(b) **1992** S, I, R, Arg(a1,a2), SA(1,2), Arg(b) **1993** E, S, I, W, SA(1,2), R(b), A(1,2) **1994** I, W

Points (4 – 1t): **1990** A(2:1t)

wore No 1 jersey throughout South Africa and Australia Test series, neither of which France lost. But after reaching the 40-cap milestone against Wales last season, he was sidelined by injury for remainder of 1994 championship. Eleven of his 40 appearances have come at hooker, so his 29 propping caps leave him well short of the 55 gained by French record holder Robert Paparemborde. Louis was a member of France's 1991 World Cup squad, but one who did not get off the bench. A former captain of France B (in 27–18 win over Scotland B in Albi) and of France A in FIRA Championship

Armstrong, G. Scotland

Full Name: Gary Armstrong
Club: Jed-Forest
Position: Scrum-half
Height: 5ft 8in (1.73m)
Weight: 13st 10lb (87kg)
Occupation: Lorry driver with Mainetti (UK)
Born: Edinburgh, 30.9.66
Family: Shona (wife), Darren James (son) and Nicole (daughter)
Family links with rugby: Father (Lawrence) played for Jed-Forest. Brother (Kevin) plays for Jed-Forest, and formerly Scotland U-21s
Former club: Jed Thistle
International debut: Scotland 13, Australia 32, 1988
Five Nations debut: Scotland 23, Wales 7, 1989
Best moment in rugby: Beating England to win 1990 Grand Slam
Worst moment in rugby: Knee injury suffered against Currie (11.1.92), which put me out of the Five Nations Championship
Most repected opponent: Pierre Berbizier (ex-Agen & France)
Biggest influence on career: Family – mum, dad and wife
Serious injuries: Torn knee, ankle

Scotland (1988)

Last Season	2 caps	0 pts
Career	30 caps	16 pts
Lions 1989		

Caps (30): **1988** A **1989** W, E, I, F, Fj, Ro **1990** I, F, W, E, NZ(1,2), Arg **1991** F, W, E, I, Ro wc–J, I, WS, E, NZ **1993** I, F, W, E **1994** E, I

Points (16 – 4t): **1989** W(1t) **1990** Arg(1t) **1991** W(1t) wc–I(1t)

ligaments, damaged elbow, three-quarter tear of medial ligament in left knee (v Currie, Riverside Park, 11.1.92), damaged right thumb ligaments and tendon (v Ireland, 1994)
Best memory last season: Beating Auckland for District Select XV. Only team to have beaten them on my first game back at scrum-half

Should rugby's amateur rules be revised? Yes

To what degree should players benefit? Compensation for time lost, and off-field benefits should be permitted, but no direct payment for playing

Should referees be rewarded? Yes, at top level, to act as an incentive for up-and-coming officials

Advice for International Board: Give players more time to learn new rules before changing them. Far too many new rules have been introduced, though I'm happy that try was increased to five points. Conversion should still be increased to three points to encourage an even more open game. Scrap the 90-degree wheel law. There needs to be a more unified interpretation of laws by referees

Notable landmarks in rugby career: When a player of Gary's calibre quits Test rugby ahead of time, it's a fair bet someone will try and talk him out of it. So it was last season, when arguably the world's best scrum-half stood down, citing family and business commitments. Scotland were promptly walloped by New Zealand (51–15) and Wales (29–6), and with alarm bells sounding all around he was persuaded to return. Suddenly Scotland came within an ace of beating England. But a hand injury sustained in 6–6 draw against Ireland (in which he was acclaimed man of the match) forced him out for the rest of the season, including the 1994 tour to Argentina. Had previously made a splendid recovery from a torn knee ligament, which had kept him out of 1992 Five Nations campaign and summer tour to Australia, and was widely considered the outstanding player in the 1993 Championship. Automatic choice for 1993 Lions, but the cruel hand of fate touched him again and he was forced to withdraw with a groin injury sustained in the Five Nations opener against Ireland. Represented Scotland at U-18, Youth, U-21 and twice at B level in 1988, v Italy (scoring try hat-trick in 37–0 win) and France. Selected to tour Australia with 1989 Lions, scoring five tries in five games, but unable to budge Welshman and good friend Robert Jones from Test team. An integral part of Scotland's 1990 Five Nations Grand Slam-winning side, and leading light in '91 Murrayfield World Cup run to the semi-finals

Touchlines: Golf

Arnold, P.   Wales

Full Name: Paul Arnold
Club: Swansea
Position: Lock
Height: 6ft 5in (1.95m)
Weight: 15st 9lb (99kg)
Occupation: Rugby development officer for Swansea RFC
Born: Morriston, 28.4.68
Family: Single
International debut: Namibia 9, Wales 18, 1990
Best moment in rugby: Going to Namibia after injured Gareth Llewellyn withdrew
Worst moment in rugby: Missing out on selection for 1992 Five Nations squad
Most respected opponent: David Waters (Newport & Wales)
Biggest influence on career: Richard Moriarty (Swansea & Wales)
Best memory last season: Returning to Test side against Spain
Suggestions to improve rugby: On-field – permit non-powered scrum if team loses prop; abandon new mauling rule (it is ridiculous);

Wales (1990)		
Last Season	2 caps	0 pts
1994	Tour to Canada/South Seas	
Career	13 caps	8 pts

Caps (13): 1990 Na(1,2), Ba 1991 E, S, I, F, A(a) wc–Arg, A(b) 1993 F(R) 1994 wc(q)–Sp. Fj

Points (8 – 2t): 1991 I(1t). wc–Arg(1t)

permit support for jumpers in lineout. Off-field – consider introducing win bonuses (I believe the game will go semi-professional by next World Cup); keep encouraging the kids

Notable landmarks in rugby career: Returned to Test arena in Wales's 54–0 defeat of Spain (Madrid, 21.5.94) in World Cup qualifier, having previously toured to Zimbabwe and Namibia in 1993, and despite only having played 16 minutes of Test rugby during the 1992/93 season (as a 64th-minute replacement for Mark Perego in the final game of the campaign, against France). Gained experience playing in New Zealand (summer 1989). Quickly climbed up representative ladder after making Wales Under-21 debut in 24–10 defeat of Scotland at Ayr (28.4.90). Within five weeks had won a full cap, playing in the 18–9 first-Test win over Namibia in Windhoek (2.6.90). Added a B cap in Leiden when helped beat Netherlands 34–12 (2.12.90). Made Five Nations debut the following season against Grand Slam '91 England and scored first-Test try later in the Championship in the 21st minute of the 21–21

draw with Ireland in Cardiff (16.2.91). Toured Australia in summer 1991 and played twice in World Cup, scoring the solitary Welsh try in a 16–7 win over Argentina (9.10.91). Overlooked for 1992 Championship. Helped Swansea beat touring Wallabies 21–6 (4.11.92)
Touchlines: Sunday soccer, indoor five-a-side, indoor cricket, squash, swimming

Back, N. A.   England

Full Name: Neil Antony Back
Club: Leicester
Position: Openside flanker
Height: 5ft 10in (1.78m)
Weight: 14st (84kg)
Occupation: Senior pensions supervisor with AXA Equity and Law, Coventry
Born: Coventry, 16.1.69
Family: Single
Former club: Nottingham
International debut: Scotland 14, England 15, 1994
Five Nations debut: As above
Best moment in rugby: Winning 1992/93 Pilkington Cup final
Worst moment in rugby: Losing 1993/94 Cup final to Bath
Most respected opponent: Andy Robinson (Bath & England)
Serious injuries: Broken arm (aged 16); 21 stitches to ear (1992); broken right thumb (1994)
Other sporting achievements: Cricket for Coventry and Warwickshire Schools

England (1994)

Last Season	2 caps	0 pts
Career	2 caps	0 pts

Caps   (2): **1994** S, I

Points Nil

Best memory last season: Full debut against Scotland
Should rugby's amateur rules be revised? No, scrapped
To what degree should players benefit? Players shouldn't be out of pocket in any way; off-field activities should be allowed; international players should receive some form of benefit; regulations are too tight. Other international sportsmen are raking it in; we receive no financial reward
Should referees be rewarded? Yes. There are very few good referees, and there needs to be some incentive to bring new ones into the game
Advice for International Board: Not happy with way rules are implemented.

Although it's one rule for all, they allow nations to interpret these as they see fit. That is not good enough. One for all should mean just that, regardless of the hemisphere in which you play

Notable landmarks in rugby career: Neil had waited a long time for 5 February 1994, the day when a player who'd been told he was too small to grace the international stage did exactly that. He had won 12 caps in England's second XV, dating back to his B debut against the Emerging Wallabies in 1990, a year after hed claimed a hat-trick of tries as England's first ever Under-21 side walloped their Romanian counterparts in sunny Bucharest. He had played, too, for England Under-18s (1985-87) and England Colts (1987/88), starred for the centenary Barbarians against England (September 1990), and even scored a try for an England XV in their 33–15 defeat of Italy in 1990. But what he hungered for more than anything was a full cap. Nothing else would suffice. Hence the satisfaction that February afternoon in Edinburgh when he finally achieved his goal. So disappointed had he been to have missed the All Blacks visit to Twickenham the previous November that he had taken the advice of three fitness advisors and devised a programme that would have him in tip-top shape for 5 February. What a shame after such a long wait that England should turn in such a poor performance, despite Jon Callard's injury-time winner. If anything they were worse on Neil's second outing, when Ireland won at Twickenham for the first time since 1982. The upshot was that England's management reverted to the 'big is beautiful' script; Neil was discarded, and not even retained for the summer tour to South Africa. But don't bet against his return

Touchlines: Training five days a week for rugby. Weight training, golf, equestrian sports (girlfriend has three horses)

Scotland starlet Gregor Townsend evades Eric Elwood in Dublin.

Bayfield, M. C.   England

Full Name: Martin Christopher Bayfield
Club: Northampton
Position: Lock
Height: 6ft 10in (2.08m)
Weight: 18st 2lb (115kg)
Occupation: Police constable with the Bedfordshire Constabulary
Born: Bedford, 21.12.66
Family: Helena (wife), Rosanna (daughter) and Polly (daughter)
Former clubs: Metropolitan Police, Bedford
International debut: Fiji 12, England 28, 1991
Five Nations debut: Scotland 7, England 25, 1992
Best moment in rugby: Lions' second-Test defeat of New Zealand (1993)
Worst moment in rugby: Being dropped by England (1994)
Most respected opponent: Paul Ackford (Harlequins, England & *Sunday Telegraph*)
Best memory last season: Finding out that the neck injury I suffered in New Zealand, and which I had feared would end my career, had cleared

England (1991)		
Last Season	4 caps	0 pts
1994	Tour to South Africa	
Career	16 caps	0 pts
Lions 1993	3 Tests	0 pts

Caps (16): **1991** Fj, A **1992** S, I, F, W, C, SA **1993** F, W, S, I. Lions–NZ (1,2,3) **1994** S, I, SA(1,2)

Points Nil

Should rugby's amateur rules be revised? Yes
To what degree should players benefit? Players should be entitled to be paid for anything they do short of actually playing. There is no reason why we should not be reimbursed for loss of earnings, and even given a free holiday with the family each year
Should referees be rewarded? Yes – paying the officials would lead to improved quality
Advice for International Board: Ensure that laws apply across the board. Permit lifting in lineout. It is a bit of an art, and everyone does it anyway
Notable landmarks in rugby career: The tallest forward to play for England graduated to British Lion status on the '93 tour to New Zealand, after just two seasons as his country's first-choice lock, and played in all three Tests of a series in which the hosts had the edge. Martin, whose representative career had been

launched on the back of three games for the England 18 Group, represented Midlands Division and British Police for three seasons, toured with British Police to Italy (1989) and broke into England's B set-up during 1990/91 season, playing against Emerging Australians (12–12, Wasps 4.11.90) and Italy (12–9, Waterloo 27.3.91). Progressed to England squad for the 1991 tour to Fiji and Australia, playing in both Tests after Wade Dooley had sustained a hand injury. Missed out on the World Cup squad, but following Paul Ackford's retirement booked a permanent berth alongside Dooley in England's 1992 Grand Slam XV. Reverted to England B for summer of '92 tour to New Zealand, where he played in both 'Test' losses to the All Black XV (lost 18–24, Hamilton, 28.6.92; lost 18–26, Pukekohe, 5.7.92). Returned to the senior side once back in Blighty, and played the full season, doubling his cap tally to a dozen, before being one of 16 Englishmen measured for Lions' blazers. Less dominant on his return, however. Injury to neck and spine, sustained in a fall in New Zealand, kept him out of the famous defeat of the All Blacks. After returning for two Tests, he was displaced by Nigel Redman, arguably England's premier forward of the 1993/94 season. Returned to top form, however, on last summer's tour of South Africa

Touchlines: Weight training

Benazzi, A. France

Full Name: Abdelatif Benazzi
Club: Agen
Position: No 8, flanker
Height: 6ft 6in (1.98m)
Weight: 17st 5lb (111kg)
Occupation: Sales representative
Born: Oujda, Morocco, 20.8.68
Former club: Cahors
International debut: Australia 21, France 9, 1990
Five Nations debut: England 21, France 19, 1991
Notable landmarks in rugby career: Sent off after 14 minutes of full debut in first Test against Australia in Sydney. But modest 14-day ban meant he was able to play in next two Tests of the series at flanker. Switched to second row for visit of All Blacks to Nantes (1990), and it was six internationals before he finally adopted his favoured No 8 berth. Came to France by way of Czechoslovakia where, while on tour with Morocco, he met up with a touring fourth-division French club. On learning

he wanted to play in France, they advised him to join Cahors. This he did before switching, a year later, to Agen, for whom he appeared in the 1990 French Cup final. Represented Morocco in the African zone of the 1991 World Cup qualifying rounds (against Belgium in Casablanca), and then France in the final stages. Became the first Moroccan to play at Twickenham when making Five Nations debut for France in the 1991 Grand Slam decider. Suspended indefinitely during 1991/92 season by the French Federation after being sent off for fighting with Eric Champ in an Agen-Toulon Cup match (2.5.91). The ban ruled him out of France's summer tour of Argentina, but he was back in the engine room shortly afterwards, coming on as replacement for Jean-Marie Cadieu in the Test loss to South Africa in Lyon (17.10.91). Started the next six internationals, playing in historic home loss to Argentina but also in 1993 Championship triumph. However, lost Test place on '93 summer tour to South Africa after an infected wound required a stay in hospital. Returned to side for Autumn series against Australia, and was ever-present thereafter, scoring first Test try in 18–14 home loss to England (Paris, 5.3.94), before heading off on tour to Canada and New Zealand last summer

France (1990)		
Last Season	7 caps	5 pts
1994	Tour to Canada/NZ	
Career	25 caps	5 pts

Caps (25): **1990** A(1,2,3), NZ(1,2) **1991** E, US(1R,2) wc–Ro, Fj, C **1992** SA(1R,2), Arg(b) **1993** E, S, I, W, A(1,2) **1994** I, W, E, S, C

Points (5 – 1t): **1994** E(1t)

Benetton, P.   France

Full Name: Philippe Benetton
Club: Agen
Position: Flanker, No 8
Height: 6ft 3in (1.90m)
Weight: 15st (95kg)
Occupation: Sports instructor with Agen council
Born: Cahors, 17.5.68
Former club: Cahors
International debut: France 27, British Lions 29, 1989
Five Nations debut: England 16, France 15, 1993
Notable landmarks in rugby career: France's Player of the Season, Philippe, played in nine of the ten internationals in 1993/94, missing only the May '93 visit to

Bucharest. During that run he occupied all three back-row positions and celebrated his fourth Test try in the 35–15 defeat of Ireland (Paris, 15.1.94). Had marked his senior debut with a try against the 1989 British Lions, masquerading as a Home Unions XV, in the Paris floodlit international staged to mark the bicentenary of the French Revolution. In common with Abdel Benazzi, Michel Courtiols and Denis

France (1989)

Last Season	10 caps	5 pts
1994	Tour to Canada/NZ	
Career	21 caps	19 pts

Caps (21): **1989** BL **1991** US(2) **1992** Arg(a1,a2R), SA(1R,2), Arg(b) **1993** E, S, I, W, SA(1,2), R(b), A(1,2) **1994** I, W, E, S, C

Points (19 – 4t): **1989** BL(1t) **1993** W(2t) **1994** I(1t)

Charvet, he began his playing career with Cahors before switching to Agen in 1988. At international level Philippe graduated through Under-21 and B set-ups. He missed out on the 1990 and 1991 Five Nations Championships, unable in the latter to displace Xavier Blond from the blindside berth. However, he re-emerged on France's 1991 tour to North America, winning his second cap in the 10–3 second-Test win over the US Eagles. The match, staged in Colorado Springs, was abandoned at half-time due to lightning. Although included in the 26-man '91 World Cup squad, he remained redundant through France's four matches, and continued in the same vein at first after former club mate Pierre Berbizier succeeded Jacques Fouroux as national coach. However, not only did he return to Test favour in 1992/93, he played in the last nine internationals. Having missed the contest with Romania at Le Havre in May '92, he toured Argentina and played in both Tests, in the second as a 59th-minute replacement for Jean-Marie Cadieu. He was benched for the next game – the defeat by South Africa at Lyon – but again came on in the second period, this time for Jean-François Tordo. From that time on he became first-choice blindside and finished the season on a high: France won the 1993 Championship and Philippe scored two tries in the title-clinching 26–10 defeat of Wales (Paris, 20.3.93). Toured with France to South Africa (1993) and Canada/New Zealand (1994)

Benezech, L. France

Full Name: Laurent Benezech
Club: Racing Club de France
Position: Loosehead prop
Height: 6ft 1in (1.85m)
Weight: 16st 4lb (99kg)
Occupation: Publicist
Born: Pamiers, 19.12.66
Former club: Toulouse
International debut: France 18, England 14, 1994
Five Nations debut: As above
Notable landmarks in rugby career: Laurent started life as a second-row forward, but was unable to find a place in the Toulouse engine room during his teenage days. So he took the decision to 'bulk up' and was rewarded with a place on the loosehead side of the front row. Four years after joining Toulouse from Ariege in 1985, he again switched allegiances, this time to the capital and the flamboyant Racing Club de France. The move was immediately rewarded as Racing captured the French championship

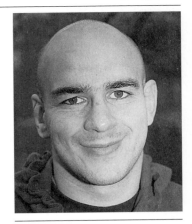

France (1994)

Last Season	3 caps	0 pts
1994	Tour to Canada/NZ	
Career	3 caps	0 pts

Caps (2): **1994** E, S, C

Points Nil

in 1990 and Laurent was selected for France A's tour to Namibia. It was not until 1993 that the senior selectors came calling, including him in the tour party for the historic trip to born-again South Africa. However, a foot injury meant that the former French Student and French Armed Forces player had to call off, so missing a famous series win. No such rejections last season, though, when he was called into a French side, reeling after defeat in Cardiff, to pack down against arch-rivals England in Paris. He impressed, not least opposite number Victor Ubogu, and held his place for the Championship finale against Scotland in Edinburgh, before heading to Canada and New Zealand with the summer tour

Bernat-Salles, P.   France

Full Name: Philippe Bernat-Salles
Club: Pau
Position: Wing
Height: 5ft 11 ½ in (1.81m)
Weight: 11st 8lb (74kg)
Occupation: Commercial agent
Born: 17.7.70
International debut: France 20,
Argentina 24, 1992
Five Nations debut: None
**Notable landmarks in rugby
career:** The 'Pau Rocket', Philippe
burst explosively onto the Test
scene, scoring six tries in his first five
internationals. But don't remind
Romania, as each of his two
appearances against them yielded a
try hat-trick: in Bucharest (won
37–20, 20.5.93) and in Brive (won
51–0, 9.10.93). Established himself
as a permanent fixture in the French
side until a trapped nerve in his neck
curtailed his 1993/94 season, forcing
him out of the last three
Championship games. Philippe first
earned full international recognition

France (1992)

Last Season	6 caps	15 pts
Career	8 caps	30 pts

Caps (8): **1992** Arg(b) **1993** R(a),
SA(1,2), R(b), A(1,2) **1994** I

Points (30 – 6t): **1993** R(a:3t), R(b:3t)

against Argentina, not in South America as he would have initially hoped –
having toured there with France in the summer of '92 (scoring tries against
Córdoba, Buenos Aires and Cuyo) – but at Nantes, where the Pumas came,
saw and historically conquered on 14 November 1992. France lost 20–24 –
their first ever home loss to the Pumas – and Philippe was one of many who
paid the price for team failure. He was dropped down a notch on the
representative ladder, and turned out on the right wing for France B at Leicester
(15.1.93), where England A triumphed 29–17 (11 months on from his B debut
against Scotland in the 27–18 win in Albi). Reunited with Scotland in April
1993 as a member of the French team which contested the World Cup Sevens
at Murrayfield

Berty, D.   France

Full Name: David Berty
Club: Toulouse
Position: Wing
Height: 5ft 11in (1.80m)
Weight: 13st 5lb (85kg)
Occupation: PR representative
Born: 11.6.70
International debut: France 12,
New Zealand 30, 1990
Five Nations debut: None
**Notable landmarks in rugby
career:** Continued to flirt with
international selection last season,
adding only his third cap in four
years in the 51–0 rout of Romania in
Brive (9.10.93). His debut had come
on the left wing against New
Zealand on 10 November 1990. The
All Blacks triumphed easily in the
Parc des Princes, and David
subsequently lost his place in the
squad for the 1991 Five Nations
Championship. However, he
continued an association with the
national A and B teams which had
yielded B caps against Wales and
Scotland in the 1989/90 season. It was not until 20 May 1992 that he returned
to the senior XV, coming on as a 37th-minute replacement for Sebastien Viars
in the 25–6 defeat of Romania at Le Havre. Thereafter, he was overlooked for
the two-Test series against South Africa, despite helping France B to a 24–17
win over the Springboks in Bordeaux on 4 October, the visit to Nantes of
Argentina and the 1993 Five Nations Championship – though he did represent
France at Murrayfield in the 1993 World Cup Sevens

France (1990)

Last Season	1 cap	0 pts
Career	3 caps	0 pts

Caps (3): **1990** NZ(2) **1992** R(R) **1993** R(b)

Points Nil

137

Bidgood, R. A. Wales

Full Name: Roger Anthony Bidgood
Club: Newport
Position: Centre
Height: 6ft (1.83m)
Weight: 14st 4lb (91kg)
Occupation: Fireman at Whitchurch Fire Station
Born: Caerphilly, 15.9.65
Family: Deborah (wife)
Former clubs: Glamorgan Wanderers Youth, Pontypridd, Pontypool (two spells), Cardiff
International debut: Wales 15, Scotland 12, 1992
Five Nations debut: As above
Best moment in rugby: Finally making Wales debut, five years after first selected
Worst moment in rugby: Missing potential debut (Wales 11, Ireland 15, Cardiff 1987) after match was postponed
Most embarrassing moment in rugby: Tackling a goal post and being taken to hospital with concussion
Most respected opponent: Tony Bond (ex-Askeans & England)
Biggest influence on career: Tom Hudson (Newport coach)
Serious injuries: Shoulder operation – tendon shortened (1988)
Suggestions to improve rugby: On-field – happy with five points for a try, as it promises to make the game more exciting for players and spectators alike. Off-field – as long as I keep my place in the Welsh team I am happy
Notable landmarks in rugby career: Thought his chances of a Wales cap had gone when freezing weather postponed Wales's 1987 Championship match against Ireland. Had been selected in place of the injured John Devereux, but by the time the match was rearranged Devereux was fit. Won two Wales Youth caps (v F, E) in 1984 whilst with Glamorgan Wanderers. During time at Pontypool, represented Wales B twice against France B: at Pontypridd in October 1986 (won 13–10) and at Begles in October 1987 (lost 0–26). Helped Newport win 1990/91 Heineken League division one title in his first season with the club, and belatedly received his first full cap against Scotland (21.3.92). Roger, who has also represented Monmouthshire Counties, Crawshays and the Barbarians, took his cap tally to four with appearances against Zimbabwe (two)

Wales (1992)

Last Season	1 cap	0 pts
Career	5 caps	5 pts

Caps (5): 1992 S 1993 Z(1,2), Na, J

Points (5 – 1t): 1993 Z(2:1t)

and Namibia on the 1993 summer tour, scoring a try in 42–13 second-Test defeat of Zimbabwe in Harare (29.5.93). Added fifth cap last season as 73rd-minute replacement for captain Ieuan Evans in 55–5 defeat of Japan (Cardiff, 16.10.93), having also turned out against Japan for Wales A in 61–5 win (Llanelli, 29.9.93). Toured Africa with Barbarians last summer
Touchlines: Snooker

Boobyer, N. Wales

Full Name: Neil Boobyer
Club: Llanelli
Position: Centre
Height: 5ft 10in (1.78m)
Weight: 12st (76kg)
Occupation: Student at Bridgend Technical College
Born: Bridgend, 11.6.72
Family: Single
Family links with rugby: Father (Brian) played for Tondu and Bridgend Sports
International debut: Zimbabwe 13, Wales 42, 1993
Five Nations' debut: None
Best moment in rugby: Making full Wales debut in Harare on 29 May 1993
Worst moment in rugby: Missing out on selection for Wales Youth against Italy
Most respected opponent: Mike Hall (Cardiff & Wales)
Best memory last season: Picking up two full caps in Zimbabwe and Namibia

Wales (1993)		
Last Season	4 caps	0 pts
Career	4 caps	0 pts

Caps (4): 1993 Z(2), Na **1994** Fj, T

Points Nil

Advice for International Board: Reduce worth of penalty goal to two points
Notable landmarks in rugby career: Made full Wales debut on 1993 tour to Africa, appearing in 42–13 second-Test win over Zimbabwe (Harare, 29.5.93), partnering Newport's Roger Bidgood in midfield. Picked up second cap against Namibia (won 38–23, Windhoek, 5.6.93) in addition to turning out against Zimbabwe B (one try), Namibia B (two tries) and the South African Barbarians. Before that, had played a full and active role for Wales Under-19s, turning out against Scotland and then touring to Canada and playing against the host nation. There was also a Welsh Youth cap (won against Japan) for the

family sideboard before, in 1991/92, Neil was selected to represent Wales Under-21s against Scotland Under-21s (17.4.92) – a match in which the Welsh extended their monopoly in the fixture to six wins from six starts. Helped Llanelli to League and Cup double in 1992/93. Represented Wales A against North of England (won 21–13, Pontypool, 14.10.92), as 14th-minute replacement for clubmate Ian Jones in 11–24 loss to Australia (Cardiff, 7.11.92), in 42–11 defeat of Canada A (scoring two tries) at Cardiff (12.3.94), and in the 21–8 defeat of France (Cardiff, 18.3.94) which completed a 1993/94 'A' Grand Slam. Toured with Wales last summer to Canada, Fiji, Tonga and Western Samoa, appearing in middle two Tests.

Touchlines: Golf, swimming, football

Bowen, S. $\qquad$ Australia

Full Name: Scott Bowen
State: New South Wales
Club: Southern Districts
Position: Outside-half
Height: 5ft 9in (1.76m)
Weight: 12st 10lb (76kg)
Occupation: Trainee in Sports Fashions Group
Age: 26
Family: Single

Australia (1993)		
Last Season	3 caps	0 pts
Career	3 caps	0 pts

Caps (3): **1993** SA(1,2,3)

Points Nil

International debut: Australia 12, South Africa 19, 1993
Best moment in rugby: Being chosen for first Test against South Africa in 1993
Worst moment in rugby: Being plagued by hamstring injuries in 1992 – only playing 10 games
Most respected opponent: Hennie Le Roux (Transvaal & South Africa)
Best memory of 1993: Winning third Test against South Africa
Serious injuries: Hamstring (1992) **Notable landmarks in rugby career:** Australia's No 10 jersey was

something of a hot potato in 1993, with no less than three players donning it. One of these was Scott, whose chance came in the eagerly awaited home series against South Africa. Wallaby captain Michael Lynagh had started campaign at outside-half against Tonga before his late withdrawal from the Bledisloe Cup game against New Zealand in Dunedin gave Queensland's Pat Howard his chance. The result – a 10–25 loss – did him no favours, but the following week Scott's contribution (partnering Nick Farr-Jones at half-back) to New South Wales' 29–28 defeat of the Springboks (Sydney, 24.7.93) did wonders for his cause. Despite Australia's shock defeat in the first Test (31.7.93) the selectors stood by him, and their faith was repaid as the Wallabies bounced back to win the series. Scott then embarked on Australia's autumn tour of North America and France, but with Lynagh restored to rude health, found his opportunities limited. In all he made three appearances, starting with the 40–3 win over Canada A in freezing Calgary (6.10.93). He marked his debut in France with a try as Aquitaine's colours were lowered in Dax (won 30–15, 16.10.93), but had less to shout about at Grenoble, where he failed to finish his third outing (26.10.93) when replaced by Jason Little during Australia's 24–23 win

Tours: 1993 – North America and France.
Touchlines: Tennis, golf, beach, spending time with girlfriend

---

Bracken, K. P. P. England

Full Name: Kyran Paul Patrick Bracken
Club: Bristol
Position: Scrum-half
Height: 5ft 10 ½ in (1.78m)
Weight: 13st (78kg)
Occupation: Law graduate at University of West of England
Born: Dublin, 22.11.71
Family: Single
Former club: Waterloo (minis)
International debut: England 15, New Zealand 9, 1993
Five Nations debut: Scotland 14, England 15, 1994
Best moment in rugby: Final whistle of New Zealand game (1993)
Worst moment in rugby: Getting dropped after Ireland game
Most embarrassing moment: Having shorts ripped off against Ireland
Other sporting achievements: Tennis for Jersey Youths
Most respected opponent: Robert Jones (Western Province & Wales)
Serious injuries: Broken nose (when 18), ankle ligaments (v New Zealand, 1993)
Best memory last season: Beating All Blacks on debut
Should rugby's amateur rules be revised? Yes
To what degree should players benefit? Should be compensated for time given to rugby; off-field activities should be allowed, but not direct payment for playing
Should referees be rewarded? Should be compensated for time given to rugby, although I don't know if that will improve standards

England (1993)

Last Season	3 caps	0 pts
Career	3 caps	0 pts

Caps (3): **1993** NZ **1994** S, I

Points Nil

Notable landmarks in rugby career: Thrust into the limelight after the late withdrawal of Dewi Morris prior to England's international with New Zealand at Twickenham (27.11.93), having originally been selected as a first-time bench reserve. Responded with fairy-tale performance, all the more impressive for the fact that he could hardly walk after having his right ankle stamped on by Jamie Joseph in the early stages. Kyran, who had played for the South West and England A against the All Blacks earlier in the tour, ignored the obvious pain and went on to celebrate England's 15–9 win before hobbling away on crutches. 'To be honest, I thought I was going to have to go off early in the game', he recalled. 'Towards the end, I was just living on adrenalin'. His second and third caps coincided with far-from-satisfactory performances by England against Scotland and Ireland, the upshot of which was the return of Morris for the remainder of the championship. But Kyran, who had graduated through Lancashire, North Schools and England 16 Group as an outside-half, and had captained England 18 Group in 1989/90, remained in the squad and was included in the summer-tour squad to South Africa, although exams later forced his withdrawal. Played for Bristol in 1992/93 UAU final at Twickenham before touring Canada with England A and Australia with England Under-21s
Touchlines: Cinema, football

Bradley, M. T. Ireland

Full Name: Michael Timothy Bradley
Club: Cork Constitution
Position: Scrum-half
Height: 5ft 10in (1.78m)
Weight: 13st 2lb (83kg)
Occupation: Sales and marketing executive with Top Security Ltd (Cork)
Born: Cork, 17.11.62
Family: Gillian (wife)
Family links with rugby: Father (Austin) played for Cork Constitution, and also played amateur international soccer for Ireland
International debut: Ireland 9, Australia 16, 1984
Five Nations debut: Scotland 15, Ireland 18, 1985

Best moment in rugby: Captaining Cork Constitution to 1990/91 All-Ireland League victory and beating England in Dublin (1993)
Worst moment in rugby: Ireland losing 3–35 to England at Twickenham in

1988, having led 3–0 at half-time

Most respected opponent: Nick Farr-Jones (NSW & Australia)

Serious injuries: Torn ankle ligaments (1990)

Best memory last season: Beating England 13–12 at Twickenham

Should rugby's amateur rules be revised? Yes

To what degree should players benefit? Remuneration for time lost to rugby. At international level some form of bonus payment should be considered because of increased commit-ments at top end. Irish rugby could not sustain a professional game, but we are losing out in our workplaces. I've seen junior partners who have been passed over for a senior partnership because of their rugby commitments. In my own work situation I have twice asked my employers whether they want me to get involved again. On each occasion they have said 'yes', but had their answer been 'no', then that would have been it. Employers should definitely be reimbursed, and put on a pedestal for all they do for us

Should referees be rewarded? In the same way as players

Advice for International Board: More for the Unions really – listen to players' problems, and act on this rather than just paying homage to the notion

Notable landmarks in rugby career: Succeeded Phil Danaher as Ireland captain during 1992 tour to New Zealand, and has retained the honour throughout the past two Five Nations Championships and last summer's tour to Australia. Deserves much credit for his role in upturning Irish fortunes. His finest hour came in the 17–3 win over England at Lansdowne Road, an occasion he marked by becoming Ireland's most-capped scrum-half (29). Has since taken the tally to 36, with a full book of appearances last season, including the famous 13–12 win over England at Twickenham (19.2.94). Played four games for Irish Schools and captained them on 1980 tour of Australia. Captained Irish U-19s and U-21s. Completed journey up representative ladder with appearances for U-25s and B (1983 against Scotland). Chosen as replacement for Ireland in 1984 before having played provincial rugby for Munster. Played in Ireland's 1985 Triple Crown-winning side. Returned to Ireland's B team in 1990/91 and captained side to victories over Argentina (27–12, Limerick 20.10.90) and England (24–10, Old Belvedere 1.3.91). Scored try in defeat of touring Pumas. Led Cork Constitution to 1990/91 All-Ireland League title. Played in both Tests on '92 New Zealand tour, taking over the captaincy for the second match, in Wellington. Ireland lost 6–59, and Michael lost his place for next outing, against Australia in Dublin. However, he returned as skipper for the 1993 International Championship, leading the side to morale-boosting wins over Wales and England

Touchlines: Golf, landscaping in Robert Kennedy's garden (summer house)

Ireland (1984)

Last Season	7 caps	0 pts
1994	Tour to Australia	
Career	36 caps	16 pts

Caps (36): **1984** A **1985** S, F, W, E **1986** F, W, E, S, Ro **1987** E, S, F, W(a) wc–W(b), C, T, A **1988** S, F, W, E(a) **1990** W **1992** NZ(1,2) **1993** S, F, W, E, R **1994** F, W, E, S, A(1,2)

Points (16 – 4t): **1986** Ro(1t) **1987** F(1t) wc–C(1t) **1988** S(1t)

Brial, M. C.   Australia

Full Name: Michael Cameron Brial
State: New South Wales
Club: Eastern Suburbs
Position: Flanker, No 8
Height: 6ft 3in (1.90m)
Weight: 16st 7lb (105kg)
Occupation: Futures broker for
Fay, Richwhite Australia
Age: 22
Family: Single
International debut: France 16,
Australia 13, 1993
Best moment in rugby: Making
first international start in second-
Test win over France in Paris
Worst moment in rugby: Losing
two consecutive Grand Finals to
Randwick
Best memory in 1993: Wallaby
performance in Paris
Serious injuries: Lucky to date –
minor knee problem in October 1992
Suggestions to improve rugby:
Just a word to the administrators –
remember that the stadiums are full
of spectators who are watching 30 players playing rugby

Australia (1993)

Last Season	2 caps	0 pts
Career	2 caps	0 pts

Caps (2): **1993** F(1R,2)

Points Nil

Notable landmarks in rugby career: Six years after being an Australian Schools team mate of Tim Horan and Jason Little, he joined the midfield dynamos in Australia's Test XV on the 1993 autumn tour of France. Michael, who also spent two years representing Australia's Under-21 side (1990-91), was given his debut as a half-time replacement for injured Queenslander Ilie Tabua in Bordeaux (30 October), where a sub-par Wallaby performance was well on course to gifting victory (16–13) to the French. With Tabua not recovering in time, Michael kept his place for the return, seven days later, where a vastly improved Australia triumphed 24–3 in Paris's Parc des Princes stadium. Apart from his two caps, Michael remained active on a tour which had started in North America, where he appeared in the Wallaby side which downed Canada A 40–3 in freezing Calgary (6.10.93). When the tour moved on to France, he featured in the 20–19 defeat of South West France in Agen (20.10.93), the 24–23 win against a French Selection in Grenoble (26.10.93) and the 15–21 loss to Côte d'Azur in Toulon (2.11.93). Born and bred in the NSW Country, he represented their Origin side before taking his rugby skills to Sydney
Touchlines: Love the sunshine, beach and surf in no particular order

Brooke, R. M.　　　　　New Zealand

Full Name: Robin Brooke
Province: Auckland
Position: Lock
Height: 6ft 5 ½ in(1.96m)
Weight: 17st 13lb (109kg)
Born: 10.1.67
Family links with rugby: Zinzan (brother) plays for Auckland and New Zealand (23 caps, 35 pts); Martin (brother) a former New Zealand triallist
International debut: New Zealand 59, Ireland 6, 1992
Best moment in rugby: Getting named to play my first Test while visiting Zinzan in hospital
Worst moment in rugby: Losing to Australia 15–16 in first Test of 1992 Bledisloe Cup
Most embarrassing moment: Walking into a clear glass door in front of 500 people at Ellis Park while the speeches were on
Notable landmarks in rugby career: Injury disrupted the latter part of Robin's 1993 season;

New Zealand (1992)

Last Season	5 caps	0 pts
Career	10 caps	0 pts

Caps (10): **1992** I(2), A(1,2,3), SA **1993** BL(1,2,3), A, WS

Points Nil

although a member of New Zealand's tour to England and Scotland, he was unable to take any active part. His frustration was compounded by fact he had become first-choice All Black lock, alongside former North Auckland secondary schools team mate Ian Jones, during the course of the year, playing all three Tests against the British Lions; he had helped wrestle the Bledisloe Cup back from world champions Australia (25–10) in Dunedin on 17 July, and picked up his tenth cap in the 35–13 defeat of Western Samoa that same month. He had settled remarkably easily into the Test side in 1992, having been given his chance against Ireland in Wellington on 6 June. It might have come earlier for Robin had he not missed the national trials in favour of club commitments in Italy. As one of three All Black debutants that June day – along with Auckland prop Olo Brown and Waikato fullback Matthew Cooper – he helped rout the Irish 59–6. His performance earned him a berth on the tour to Australia, where he played alongside Jones in all three matches of the Bledisloe Cup series. But it was in Johannesburg on 15 August that Robin enjoyed his finest hour: with brother Zinzan, he was the star performer as New Zealand beat South Africa for the first time on African soil, 27–24. In addition to the Tests he turned out in the wins over Western Australia (80–0), New South Wales (41–9) and Queensland (26–19), while in South Africa he enjoyed that winning feeling against Junior South Africa (25–10) in Pretoria. A member of the New Zealand Maoris since 1988

Touchlines: Golf, family, travel, basketball

Brooke, Z. V. New Zealand

Full Name: Zinzan Valentine Brooke
Club: Marist
Province: Auckland
Position: No 8, flanker
Height: 6ft 3in (1.90m)
Weight: 15st 9lb (99kg)
Occupation: Courier
Born: Waiuku, 14.2.65
Family links with rugby: Martin (brother) is a former New Zealand triallist; Robin plays for Auckland, Maoris and New Zealand (10 caps)
International debut: New Zealand 46, Argentina 15, 1987
Serious injuries: Broken ankle (1991)
Notable landmarks in rugby career: Auckland captain, who confirmed himself as one of the world's great back-row players on New Zealand's tour to England and Scotland in 1993. Yet only after starting off in the 'dirt trackers' XV – a result of having lost his Test place after the series win over the '93 British Lions. Only a replacement – albeit one who was utilized – for the third Test win in Auckland, he sat out the Bledisloe Cup victory over Australia before coming on as a replacement against Western Samoa,

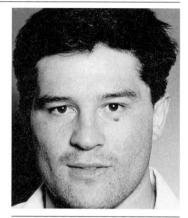

New Zealand (1987)

Last Season	6 caps	10 pts
Career	23 caps	35 pts

Caps (23): **1987** wc–Arg **1989** Arg(2R) **1990** A(1,2,3), F(1R) **1991** Arg(2), A(a1,a2). wc–E, It, C, A(b), S **1992** A(2,3), SA **1993** BL(1,2,3R), WS(R), S, E

Points (35 – 8t): **1987** wc–Arg(1t) **1990** A(2:1t) **1991** Arg(2:1t). wc–It(1t), C(1t) **1992** SA(1t) **1993** WS(R:1t), S(1t)

and scoring a try. On tour in the UK he captained the midweek XV, but after coming on in the first two Saturday games and then scoring four tries in the 84–5 defeat of South of Scotland, he won a Test place at openside flanker against both Scotland (scoring his eighth inter-national try) and England. A

product of the 1985 New Zealand Colts team, he has represented Auckland since 1986, and the All Blacks since scoring one of their six tries in the 46–15 win over Argentina on his debut in June 1987, at the inaugural World Cup. Came to the fore when he succeeded captain Wayne Shelford at No 8 after the Scotland series in 1990. But although he played in all three Tests against Australia that year, he was injured and replaced in the first Test against France in Nantes. Returned strongly in 1991, after recovering from a broken ankle, and was the All Blacks first-choice No 8 through the World Cup – a personal campaign which featured tries against Italy and Canada. An impressive Sevens player, he captained New Zealand to victory in the 1989 and 1990 Hong Kong Sevens. Made ten appearances on the All Blacks tour of Australia and South Africa in 1992, playing in three of the four Tests
Touchlines: Competing at anything

Brouzet, O. France

Full Name: Olivier Brouzet
Club: Grenoble
Position: Lock
Height: 6ft 8in (2.03m)
Weight: 18st 7lb (113kg)
Occupation: Student
Born: Béziers, 22.11.72
Former club: Seyssins
International debut: Scotland 12, France 20, 1994
Five Nations debut: As above
Notable landmarks in rugby career: Olivier was summoned last season by French selectors desperate to avert a catastrophic Wooden Spoon. Murrayfield, the final port of call in France's Five Nations campaign, was the setting for the 'Spoon decider' against winless Scotland, and with Olivier offering his considerable bulk (6ft 8in and 18st 7lb) defeat was comfortably averted. He comes from a rich sporting lineage, his father Yves being the former French athletics champion who has held the national

France (1994)

Last Season	1 cap	0 pts
1994	Tour to Canada/NZ	
Career	1 cap	0 pts

Caps (1): **1994** S

Points Nil

shot-putt record for 24 years. Olivier plays alongside the former lumberjack in the Grenoble team that reached the 1992/93 French championship final, losing

147

to Castres. He helped France win the 1992 Students World Cup, and as recently as February 1993 was in the French Under-21 side which whipped their Scottish counterparts 67–9 in Dijon. Was promoted to replacement for the 1994 Championship opener against Ireland in Paris (15.1.94), having been a member of the France A gold medal-winning side at the 1993 Mediterranean Games. Toured with France last summer to Canada and New Zealand

Brown, O. M.   New Zealand

Full Name: Olo Max Brown
Province: Auckland
Position: Tighthead prop
Height: 6ft ½ in (1.85m)
Weight: 15st 11lb (100kg)
Born: Western Samoa, 24.10.67
International debut:
New Zealand 59, Ireland 6, 1992
Best moment in rugby: Beating South Africa in 1992
Worst moment in rugby: Losing the Ranfurly Shield (17–6 to Waikato) after eight years
Biggest influence on career: Ponsonby RFC
Most respected player: Colin Meads
Notable landmarks in rugby career: Retained his position as the All Blacks' first-choice tighthead throughout 1993, despite missing part of the season (including 35–13 defeat of his country of origin, Western Samoa) with a neck injury. First represented the All Blacks in 1990 when, having been flown out

New Zealand (1992)

Last Season	6 caps	0 pts
Career	11 caps	0 pts

Caps (11): **1992** I(2), A(1,2,3), SA
1993 BL(1,2,3), A, S, E

Points Nil

to join the tour of France as a replacement, he was thrust into the fray against France A in the Stade Marcel Deflandre, La Rochelle. The date was 6 November, and the tourists won 22–15. Three months earlier he had helped Auckland beat the touring Australians 16–10 at Eden Park. Although he was overlooked for the Argentina tour and the World Cup in 1991, a fine display for the Saracens team which beat a New Zealand XV 20–15 in one of the national trial matches speeded his return to the big time. Having also helped Auckland destroy Ireland 62–7 at Eden Park (23 May), weighing in with one of his team's 11 tries, he made his Test debut soon after (6 June) when selected in place of Richard Loe for the second International against the Irish in Wellington, which resulted in a 59–6 win for the host nation. Auckland team mate Robin Brooke and Waikato's Matthew Cooper also made their debuts that day. After that Olo was retained for the tour of Australia and South Africa, figuring as first-choice tighthead in the nine weekend engagements, including all four Test matches. Failed to score any points, but his contribution in terms of strength enabled the All Blacks to achieve an edge over their Wallaby rivals in the scrum

Bunce, F. E. New Zealand

Full Name: Frank Eneri Bunce
Province: North Harbour
Position: Centre
Height: 6ft 1in (1.85m)
Weight: 14st 10lb (93kg)
Born: Auckland, 4.2.62
Family links with rugby: Steve (brother) plays for Western Australia
Former nation: Western Samoa
Former province: Auckland
Former club: Manukau
International debut (NZ): New Zealand 24, Ireland 21, 1992
Worst moment in rugby: The death of my father before he could see me become an All Black
Most respected opponents: John Kirwan (Auckland & NZ) and Philippe Sella (Agen & France)
Notable landmarks in rugby career: Among the game's great midfield defenders, Frank also boasts a prolific strike rate, with ten tries in 16 Tests since switching allegiance from Western Samoa after the 1991 World Cup. Ever-present throughout 1993, he claimed tries against the Lions (2), Australia and Scotland. It is hard to believe that it

Western Samoa (1991)		
Career	4 caps	4 pts
New Zealand (1992)		
Last Season	7 caps	20 pts
Career	16 caps	46 pts

Caps (16): **1992** Wd(1,2,3), I(1,2), A(1,2,3), SA **1993** BL(1,2,3), A, WS

Points (46 – 10t): **1992** I(1:2t), I(2:2t), A(1:1t), A(3:1t) **1993** BL(1:1t), BL(3:1t), A(1t), S(1t)

took six years, after his debut for Auckland in a Ranfurly Shield game against Horowhenua at Eden Park, for his All Black Test debut, against a World XV. But it was his two-try show against Ireland in the following series which

149

confirmed him as a class act. Mind you, the 30-year-old was no novice that day at Carisbrook. Frustrated at his lack of opportunities in the New Zealand national set-up he had declared his allegiance for Western Samoa in the '91 World Cup and featured strongly in each of their four games – against Wales, Australia, Argentina and Scotland – and claiming a try in the 35–12 win over the Pumas. Any notion that his heroics in the 24–21 defeat of Ireland at Dunedin were a flash in the pan was dispelled in the second Test when he weighed in within another try-brace. Frank has since gone from strength to strength, playing in ten of the All Blacks' fixtures on their tour of Australia and South Africa (scoring five tries), and bagging tries in the All Blacks' first and third Test wins over the 1993 British Lions. His penetrative qualities and brick-wall defending make him a perennial target for the Rugby League scouts, and he was indeed courted in 1991. Fortunately for the All Blacks, he resisted the overtures, and is bound to be one of the cornerstones around which they build their '95 World Cup challenge

Burke, M.   Australia

Full Name: Matthew Burke
State: New South Wales
Club: Eastwood
Position: Fullback (and outside centre)
Height: 6ft (1.83m)
Weight: 15st 1lb (91kg)
Occupation: Eastwood rugby development officer
Born: 26.3.73
Family: Single
International debut: Australia 19, South Africa 12, 1993
Best moment in rugby: Running on for my first Test against South Africa
Most respected opponent: All of them
Best memory last season: Going through a French tour winning nine out of eleven games
Suggestions to improve rugby (on-field): With the nature of the mark, a fair catch could be played in the air, similar to that in Australian Rules.

Australia (1993)

Last Season	4 caps	0 pts
Career	4 caps	0 pts

Caps (4): 1993 SA(3R), F(1) **1994** I(1,2)

Points (5 – 1t): **1994** I(1:1t)

Notable landmarks in rugby career: A utility back who greatly impressed during Australia's 1993 tour of North America and France, prompting Wallaby coach Bob Dwyer to describe him as 'a real investment for the future'. He added, 'Against Languedoc he gave one of the greatest displays of fullback play by a young man it's ever been my pleasure to witness'. Matt also appeared at centre for New South Wales in their thrilling 29–28 defeat of the touring Springboks (24.7.93) – a performance that led to his first cap as a replacement in the decisive third-Test victory over South Africa in Sydney (21.8.93) – and for the Wallabies in their 40–3 win against Canada A in Calgary (16.10.93). Other appearances on tour came at fullback in the non-cap Test against the US Eagles at Riverside, California (won 26–22, 2.10.93), against South-West France at Agen (won 20–19, 20.10.93), and against Languedoc in Narbonne (won 35–18, 23.10.93). In the latter game he retired injured and was replaced by Marty Roebuck, the man whom he controversially displaced in the Australian side for the first Test against France in Bordeaux (30.10.93). The Wallabies lost and Roebuck, with his superb goalkicking ability, was recalled to save the series

Touchlines: Golf, skiing, watching television

Burnell, A. P. Scotland

Full Name: Andrew Paul Burnell
Club: London Scottish
Position: Prop
Height: 6ft 1in (1.85m)
Weight: 16st 8lb (105kg)
Occupation: Sales director with
Anglo-Scottish Finance (Reading)
Born: Edinburgh, 29.9.65
Family: Single
Former clubs: Marlow, Harlequins,
Leicester
International debut: England 12,
Scotland 12, 1989
Five Nations' debut: As above
Best moment in rugby: Beating
England to win 1990 Grand Slam
Worst moments in rugby:

Scotland losing 3–19 to France in
1989; London Scottish getting relegated from English Second Division (1988/89); missing 1992 tour to Australia due to torn knee medial ligament sustained in 12–15 defeat by Wales in '92 Five Nations Championship finale
Most respected opponent: David Sole (Edinburgh Acads & Scotland) – good scrummager, great ball player, superb captain

Serious injuries: Ruptured disc in back (1989, required surgery); acute tear in knee medial ligament (1992)

Best memory last season: Staying in Division Two with London Scottish after beating Saracens in final game

Should rugby's amateur rules be revised? Yes

To what degree should players benefit? Should be compensated for time lost, and permitted to benefit from off-field activities, but do not sanction payment for playing

Should referees be rewarded? Yes – it would improve standards

Advice for International Board: Clamp down on scrummage collapsing, awarding penalty if shoulder dips below hip

Notable landmarks in rugby career: Still 14 caps short of Sandy Carmichael's 50-cap national best for a prop, but at a time of such transition in Scotland's ranks, is already regarded as a senior figure in the tartan pack. A British Lion in 1993, Paul played against North Harbour, Canterbury, Otago, Auckland and Waikato, but missed out on Test honours against All Blacks. Missed out on nothing in 1993/94 season, however, except league relegation after sterling end-of-season rally by London Scottish, whom he skippers this season. Scored on first-team debut for Leicester and Scotland B debut in 26–3 win over Italy in L'Aquila (1989). Twice helped London Scottish win promotion, as 1989/90 Third Division and 1991/92 Second Division champions, and featured in their triumphant 1990/91 Middlesex Sevens side. Toured with Scotland to Zimbabwe (1988), New Zealand (1990), having been ever-present tighthead in Grand Slam campaign, and Argentina (1994), but missed tours to Japan (1989) and Australia (1992) through injury. Prior to knee ligament tear against Wales (21.3.92) had played in 24 of Scotland's most recent 26 cap internationals, including all six World Cup games

Touchlines: Cinema-going

Scotland (1989)		
Last Season	7 caps	0 pts
1994	Tour to Argentina	
Career	36 caps	0 pts
Lions 1993		

Caps (36): **1989** E, I, F, Fj, Ro **1990** I, F, W, E, Arg **1991** F, W, E, I, Ro wc–J, Z, I, WS, E, NZ **1992** E, I, F, W **1993** I, F, W, E, NZ **1994** W, E, I, F, Arg(1,2)

Points Nil

Cabannes, L.   France

Full Name: Laurent Cabannes
Club: Racing Club de France
Position: Flanker
Height: 6ft 2in (1.88m)
Weight: 14st 2lb (89.5kg)
Occupation: Public relations officer
Born: Reims, 6.2.64
Former club: Pau
International debut: France 12,
New Zealand 30, 1990
Five Nations' debut: France 15,
Scotland 9, 1991
**Notable landmarks in rugby
career:** A seriously torn thigh
muscle messed up 1993/94 for
Laurent, one of the most mobile and
effective loose forwards in the game.
Having helped France to their
historic series win in South Africa
(1993), he sustained the injury in
September and was sidelined for the
next five months. But he was
recalled at the earliest possible
opportunity, and played the final
two championship matches, against
England and Scotland. Laurent
made his senior debut for Pau at the
age of just 17. In 1992/93, in
addition to further enhancing his
reputation with a hefty contribution

France (1990)

Last Season	5 caps	0 pts
1994	Tour to Canada/NZ	
Career	29 caps	8 pts

Caps (29): **1990** NZ(2R) **1991** S, I, W, E, US(2), W wc–Ro, Fj, C, E **1992** W, E, S, I, R, Arg(a2), SA(1,2) **1993** E, S, I, W, R(a), SA(1,2) **1994** E, S, C

Points (8 – 2t): **1991** I(1t) **1992** I(1t)

to France's Five Nations title triumph, he also turned out for France at Murrayfield in the World Cup Sevens tournament. Laurent, whose two international tries have come in spectacular style against Ireland, has travelled far in rugby pursuit, playing the club game in South Africa and in the south west region of France for Pau. But it was with Racing that his representative career burgeoned, scoring a try as the Paris side won the 1990 French Club Championship – their first success in 31 years. He was also on the side which finished runners-up in 1987, the year after he had begun playing France B rugby (against Wales B at Pontypridd). But it was only in November 1990 that he broke into the senior ranks as a replacement for Abdel Benazzi in the second Test against New Zealand in Paris

Callard, J. E. B.   England

Full Name: Jonathan Edward Brooks Callard
Club: Bath
Position: Fullback
Height: 5ft 10in (1.78m)
Weight: 12st 7lb (79kg)
Occupation: Schoolmaster at Downside
Born: Leicester, 1.1.66
Family: Gail (wife)
Family links with rugby: Brother (Nigel) plays for Newport
International debut: England 15, New Zealand 9, 1993
Five Nations debut: Scotland 14, England 15, 1994
Best moment in rugby: Beating All Blacks on debut
Worst moment in rugby: Being dropped after Ireland defeat (1994)
Most respected opponent: Gavin Hastings (Watsonians & Scotland)
Serious injuries: Fractured patella (1992)
Other sporting achievements: Junior cricket for Monmouthshire
Best memories last season:
Kicking the last-ditch penalty goal which won the 1994 Calcutta Cup; winning English league and cup double with Bath

England (1993)

Last Season	3 caps	39 pts
1994	Tour to South Africa	
Career	3 caps	39 pts

Caps (3): **1993** NZ **1994** S, I

Points (39 – 13p): **1993** NZ(4p) **1994** S(5p), I(4p)

Should rugby's amateur rules be revised? Yes
To what degree should players benefit? Broken-time payments and full expenses (travel, washing, missed work opportunities due to training etc), but no payment for playing
Should referees be rewarded? Definitely, if it means disparity in their standards will be eliminated
Advice for International Board: Demand that all rugby-playing nations abide by the same rules
Notable landmarks in rugby career: A man for the big occasion, Jon marked his Twickenham debut in 1990 with a try in Bath's Pilkington Cup final triumph, and marked his England debut at Twickenham (27.11.93) with the five penalty goals which beat New Zealand 15–9. Save for a wayward pass which gifted the Blacks a try against England A, Jon enjoyed their tour, as he landed eight penalty goals against them wearing the colours of South West Division and the national

A team. But he saved his finest hour for his Five Nations debut at Murrayfield (5.2.94), when he pulled the Calcutta Cup out of the fire. Scotland looked for all the world to have upset the considerable odds stacked against them when Gregor Townsend's injury-time dropped goal nudged them 14–12 ahead. But, remarkably, there was still time for referee Lindsay McLachlan to award England one more penalty, 40 metres out. 'For a few awful seconds I wanted to run and hide', remembers Jon of the moment when Will Carling turned to him and said 'Here, it's easy: get on with it'. 'But you can't hide, you have to conquer yourself', added the former Newport player, who had made his debut as an 18-year-old against Bath. He dutifully obliged, before embarking on a well-deserved celebratory jig. How fitting for a man who not so long ago had been 'lost' in the third team at Chipping Sodbury. However, Jon's season turned thereafter, as he was one of the victims of the purge which followed Ireland's sensational Twickenham win. He joined England's tour of South Africa as emergency replacement for David Pears, and despite having kicked 17 points in his three games, will remember the trip for the 25 stitches which put his face back together after being stamped on by an Eastern Province boot

Touchlines: Bandit golfer

Campese, D. I.   Australia

Full Name: David Ian Campese
State: New South Wales
Clubs: Randwick (Aus: since 1986),
Mediolanum Milan (It: since 1988)
Position: Wing, fullback
Height: 5ft 10in (1.77m)
Weight: 13st 5lb (85kg)
Occupation: Partner in Campo's
Sports Store
Born: 21.10.62
Family: Tony (father), Joan
(mother), Mario (brother), Lisa
(sister), Corinne (sister)
Former clubs: Queanbeyan
(1980–86), Petrarca (Padua, It:
1984–87)
International debut: New Zealand

23, Australia 16, 1982
Best moments in rugby: Debut in first Test v New Zealand in 1982, when scored try; 1989 Hong Kong Sevens Player of Tournament; 1991 World Cup.
Worst moment in rugby: Being dropped for first Test v France in 1990
Most embarrassing moment: Dropping ball at Cardiff v 1988 Barbarians with try line in sight

155

Most respected opponent: Hugo Porta (Argentina)
Serious injuries: Dislocated shoulder (1985), ankle (1987), knee (1992)
Other sporting achievements: 1981 ACT Schools Golf Championship
Suggestions to improve rugby: On-field – allow playing the ball on the ground; stop locks marking wingers under current maul law. Off-field – install professional rugby administrators
Notable landmarks in rugby career: The world's leading Test try-scorer with 58, Campo is also Australia's most-capped player, with 82 appearances to his name. Shares with Greg Cornelsen the Aussie record for the most tries scored in a single Test, with his four against the US Eagles in 1983. One of a growing number of full-time rugby players, who follow the winter season around the globe by playing their 'trade' in both hemispheres. Campo started with Queanbeyan before joining Randwick in 1987. His State allegiance also switched from Australian Capital Territory to New South Wales. Made his international debut against New Zealand back in 1982, and has been a thorn in his opponents' flesh ever since – not least in the 1991 World Cup,

Australia (1982)		
Last Season	10 caps	30 pts
Career	82 caps	285 pts

Caps (82): 1982 NZ(1,2,3) **1983** US, Arg(1,2), NZ, It, F(1,2) **1984** Fj, NZ(1,2,3), E, I, W, S **1985** Fj(1,2) **1986** It, F, Arg(1,2), NZ(1,2,3) **1987** wc–E, US, J, I, F, W. NZ **1988** E(1,2), NZ(1,2,3), E, S, It **1989** BL(1,2,3), NZ, F(1,2) **1990** F(2,3), US, NZ(1,2,3) **1991** W, E, NZ(1,2). wc–Arg, WS, W, I, NZ, E **1992** S(1,2), NZ(1,2,3), SA, I, W **1993** T, NZ, SA(1,2,3), C, F(1,2) **1994** I(1,2)

Points (285 – 58t,8c,7p,2dg): 1982 NZ(1:1t), NZ(2:1t) **1983** US(4t,1c), Arg(1:1p), Arg(2:1t,3c,1p), It(3c,1p), F(1:1c,1p), F(2:1p) **1984** Fj(1t), NZ(2:1p), NZ(3:1t,1p), S(2t) **1985** Fj(1:1dg), Fj(2:2t) **1986** It(2t), F(1t), Arg(1:1t), Arg(2:2t), NZ(1:1t), NZ(3:1t) **1987** wc–E(1t), US(1t), J(1t), F(1t) **1988** E(a2:1t), E(b:1t), S(2t), I(3t) **1989** NZ(1t), F(1:1t) **1990** F(2:1t), F(3:1t), US(1t,1dg) **1991** W(a:1t), E(a:2t). wc–Arg(2t), W(b:1t), I(2t), NZ(b:1t) **1992** S(1:2t), NZ(1:1t), SA(1t), I(1t), W(1t) **1993** T(2t), C(3t) **1994** I(1:1t)

when six tries in six appearances helped Australia win the Webb Ellis Cup. They also led to his being declared both the Player of the Tournament and the Australian Society of Rugby Writers' Player of the Year, with a similar accolade from the British Rugby Writers in the form of the Pat Marshall Memorial Award. Dropped only once – for the first Test against France in 1990 – he was ever-present throughout Australia's eight-Test campaign in 1992, adding to his try tally against Scotland, New Zealand (first Test), South Africa (No 50), Ireland and Wales. His other Wallaby outings came against Western Transvaal, Northern Transvaal (two tries), Eastern Province, Leinster (two tries), Ulster, Connacht and (at Twickenham) the Barbarians. An unbroken run in 1993 included the third try hat-trick of his career, against Canada (won 43–16, Calgary, 9.10.93), having claimed two against Tonga (won 52–14, Brisbane, 3.7.93)
Touchlines: Golf

Carling, W. D. C.   England

Full Name: William David Charles Carling
Club: Harlequins
Position: Centre
Height: 5ft 11lb (1.81m)
Weight: 14st 2lb (89.5kg)
Occupation: Runs own management training/personal development company: 'Insight'
Born: Bradford-on-Avon, Wiltshire, 12.12.65
Family: Julia (wife)
Family links with rugby: Father (Bill) played for Cardiff
Former club: Durham University
International debut: France 10, England 9, 1988
Five Nations debut: As above
Best moments in rugby: England beating Australia 28–19 in my first game as captain; leading England to back-to-back Grand Slams; 1993 Lions selection
Worst moment in rugby: Losing 1990 Grand Slam decider to Scotland; being dropped by 1993 Lions
Most embarrassing moment: Not touching down try for Harlequins against Rosslyn Park at Twickenham after crossing line in 1990 Middlesex Sevens
Most respected opponent: Denis Charvet (Toulouse & France)
Serious injuries: Leg fracture (1989)

England (1988)

Last Season	7 caps	0 pts
1994	Tour to South Africa	
Career	49 caps	29 pts
Lions 1993	1 Test	0 pts

Caps (49): **1988** F, W, S, I(1,2), A(a2), Fj, A(b) **1989** S, I, F, W, Fj **1990** I, F, W, S, Arg(a1,a2), Arg(b) **1991** W, S, I, F, Fj, A(a) wc–NZ, It, US, F, S, A(b) **1992** S, I, F, W, C, SA **1993** F, W, S, I. Lions–NZ(1). NZ **1994** S, I, F, W, SA(1,2)

Points (29 – 7t): **1989** F(1t) **1990** F(1t), W(1t) **1991** wc–US(1t), F(1t) **1992** W(1t), SA(1t)

Best memory last season: Beating All Blacks
Should rugby's amateur rules be revised? They should be made comprehensible!
To what degree should players benefit? Players should be allowed to benefit from rugby-related activities because everything we do is naturally related to rugby. But we do not want to be paid to play
Should referees be rewarded? No
Advice for International Board: I have no idea of their influence on world

rugby at the moment. I still don't understand the off-the-field legislation. There should be player involvement in law changes and in the administration of the game. It seems so logical to me, yet they ignore it. The general level of coaching in English club rugby must be raised – were still too stuck in our ways. We must learn from other countries. Better communication is needed, and everyone, regardless of hemisphere, should play by the same rules

Notable landmarks in rugby career: England's most-capped centre (49) and holder of the world record for most international wins as captain (31 in 42 games), Will rebounded from the disappointment of being dropped by 1993 Lions (after first-Test loss to All Blacks) to lead England to victory over same opponents (27.11.93). Retained captaincy through indifferent Five Nations campaign before leading side to sensational 32–15 first-Test defeat of South Africa in Pretoria (4.6.94). Began playing career as a six-year old with Terra Nova School Under-11s. At 15 he was the first fifth-former to play in Sedbergh's first XV (three years in team; experienced only two defeats), before captaining England 18 Group (1984) and moving on to Durham University (on an Army scholarship, reading psychology), where he switched to fullback. Northern Division selectors Geoff Cooke and Dave Robinson advised playing centre, where he has remained ever since. Bought himself out of Army (2nd Lt heading towards Royal Regiment of Wales) when told he would not be able to play representative rugby. Helped England B beat France B (22–9, Bath, 20.2.87). Became England's youngest captain for 57 years (since P D Howard of Old Millhillians, 1931) when handed the reins aged 22 years and 11 months for England's 28–19 win over Australia (5.11.88). Captain in two Grand Slams and in 1991 run to World Cup final. Confessed on Radio 4's Desert Island Discs (May 1992) that if cast away he would want with him Tolkein's book *The Hobbit*, Louis Armstrong's record *What a Wonderful World*, and a flotation tank

Touchlines: Painting (sketching and inks), social golf

Carozza, P. V.   Australia

Full Name: Paul Vincent Carozza
State: Queensland
Club: Western Districts
Position: Wing
Height: 5ft 6in (1.66m)
Weight: 12st 8lb (80kg)
Occupation: School sports promotional officer with Queensland Department of Education
Born: 14.4.66
Family: Peter (father), Beryl (mother), John (brother), Maria (sister)
Former clubs: None
International debut: France 9, Australia 21, 1990
Best moment in rugby: 1992 Bledisloe Cup second Test – scoring both tries in 19–17 win over All Blacks
Worst moment in rugby: Missing 1991 World Cup selection
Most embarrassing moment: My cricket skills at an after-session cricket game
Most respected opponent: John Kirwan (Auckland & New Zealand)
Serious injuries: Groin (1991), hamstring (1993)

Australia (1990)

Last Season	2 caps	5 pts
Career	15 caps	41 pts

Caps (15): **1990** F(1,2,3), NZ(2,3) **1992** S(1,2), NZ(1,2,3), SA, I, W **1993** T, NZ

Points (41 – 9t): **1990** F(2:1t) **1992** S(1:1t), S(2:2t), NZ(2:2t), SA(2t) **1993** T(1t)

Other sporting achievements: GPS athletics competitor
Suggestions to improve rugby: Off-field – compensate players for financial loss due to touring etc
Notable landmarks in rugby career: Paul was always going to have to struggle to emulate his superb campaign in 1992, but he would have expected better than the hand fate dealt him. After playing against Tonga (scoring his ninth Test try) and New Zealand, he badly tore a hamstring in the first Test against the touring Springboks, and having recovered was then omitted from the autumn tour squad to North America and France. It was a far cry from '92, when he burst back onto the Test scene (after a one-off cap in 1990 against France, when David Campese was dropped for the only time in his Test career) by scoring three tries against the touring Scots in the Wallabies' 2–0 series win. From there he was voted the Chivas Regal Man-of-the-Series as Australia regained the Bledisloe Cup with a 2–1 series defeat of the All Blacks. He bagged

two tries in the 19–17 second-Test win at Brisbane – a series-clinching performance – and repeated the feat against South Africa, in Cape Town on 22 August, when the Springboks were handed their heaviest ever Test defeat (26–3). Whilst in the Republic he also played in the wins over Northern Transvaal and Eastern Province. Paul, who achieved the rare feat of representing his country before his State (Queensland), maintained his ever-present Test status in Ireland and Wales, on a tour in which he also turned out against Leinster, Ulster, Swansea and the Barbarians. First toured with the Wallabies (to South America) back in 1987, and appeared in England and Scotland on the 1988 trip

Touchlines: Surfing

Catt, M. J.   England

Full Name: Michael John Catt
Club: Bath
Position: Centre, outside-half
Height: 5ft 10in (1.78m)
Weight: 13st 2lb (79kg)
Occupation: Marketing executive with Johnson's News
Born: Port Elizabeth, 17.9.71
Family: Single
International debut: England 15, Wales 8, 1994
Five Nations debut: As above
Best moment in rugby: Winning first England cap
Worst moment in rugby: None
Most respected opponent: Graham Dawe (Bath & England)
Biggest influence on career: Brothers Richard, Douglas and Peter
Other sporting achievements: Triathlon for Eastern Province (Under-21 champion)
Best memory last season: Whole day of Pilkington Cup final
Should rugby's amateur rules be revised? Yes

England (1994)

Last Season	1 cap	0 pts
1994	Tour to South Africa	
Career	1 cap	0 pts

Caps (1): **1994** W(R)

Points Nil

To what degree should players benefit? Should have compensation for time lost to rugby; all off-field activities should be given green light
Should referees be rewarded? Yes
Advice for International Board: Return maul law to the way it was (as has

160

been done with ruck law); implement rules and make sure they are adhered to all around the globe

Notable landmarks in rugby career: Stunning debut season in top flight, having moved to the Recreation Ground from Eastern Province, South Africa, and immediately establishing himself as deputy to Stuart Barnes. Born in Port Elizabeth, he holds a British passport thanks to his English mother. A stand-off by design, Mike has flourished at centre in the star-studded Bath side. However, it was at No 10 that he appeared for South West England against New Zealand (30.10.93), although he reverted to centre for England A's challenge to the tourists at Gateshead the following weekend. Completed his hat-trick of appearances against the All Blacks with stand-off outing for England Emerging Players (Gloucester, 23.11.93). Returned to South Africa with England last summer, having toured Australia with England's Under-21 side in 1993, scoring a try in their 'Test' win. It took him only nine domestic appearances to get himself nominated for England's preliminary squad to play New Zealand, and although he didn't figure in the final 21, he was drafted into the squad for the 1994 Five Nations Championship, warming the bench in each game before coming on in the 76th minute of the title decider against Wales as a replacement for Rob Andrew. Had time to miss a penalty kick at goal. Central figure in Bath's 1993/94 league and cup double-winning side

Touchlines: Drinking

Cecillon, M. France

Full Name: Marc Cecillon
Club: Bourgoin-Jallieu
Position: No 8, flanker, lock
Height: 6ft 3in (1.90m)
Weight: 15st 2lb (96kg)
Occupation: Schoolmaster
Born: Bourgoin-Jallieu, 30.7.59
International debut: France 25, Ireland 6, 1988
Five Nations' debut: As above
Notable landmarks in rugby career: An indefatigable player who refuses to go quietly. Last summer he set off on another tour, this time to Canada and New Zealand, after a season in which he turned 35 and picked up a further eight caps to take his tally to 40. Appointed captain for the 1992 summer and autumn Tests

against Argentina (on tour in July) and South Africa (at Lyon and Paris in

October), but was succeeded in that position by Jean-François Tordo thereafter. Still, Marc retained his place in the side at No 8 and played a full part in France's Championship triumph. Starting out, he had had to wait more than eight years between first representing France B – in December 1979 against Wales (won 33–12) in Bourg-en-Bresse – and making his full debut against Ireland in Paris in 1988. In between, he busied himself with regular tours of duty for France A in the FIRA Championship, before embarking on a cap-less world tour with France in

France (1988)
Last Season	7 caps	0 pts
1994	Tour to Canada/NZ	
Career	40 caps	33 pts

Caps (40): **1988** I, W, Arg(a2), Arg(b1,b2), Ro **1989** Ro, I, E, NZ(1,2), A(1) **1990** S, I, E(R) **1991** Ro, US(1), W wc–E **1992** W, E, S, I, R, Arg(a1,a2), SA(1,2) **1993** E, S, I, W, R(a), SA(1,2), R(b), A(1,2) **1994** I, W

Points (33 – 8t): **1988** Arg(b1:1t), Arg(b2:1t) **1989** NZ(1:1t), NZ(2:1t) **1991** Ro(1t),US(1:1t) **1992** I(1t) **1993** R(a:1t)

1986. A Jack of virtually all scummage trades and master of a good many, Marc's 22 caps include 17 at No 8, 11 at flanker and three at lock. Before 1991 he appeared only sporadically, collecting four Championship caps in three seasons. All that changed in 1991/92, when he was recognized as a vital member of the French squad, as well as being the oldest. Indeed, so highly was he regarded that a place was made for him in the 26-man World Cup party, despite the then coach Jean Trillo knowing his torn thigh muscle would rule him out of the three Pool games

Chalmers, C. M.　　　　　Scotland

Full Name: Craig Minto Chalmers
Club: Melrose
Position: Outside-half
Height: 5ft 11in (1.80m)
Weight: 13st 6lb (85kg)
Occupation: Marketing advisor with Scottish Power
Born: Galashiels, 15.10.68
Family: Lucy (wife), Sam (son)
Family links with rugby: Father (Brian) coaches at Melrose
International debut: Scotland 23, Wales 7, 1989
Five Nations debut: As above
Best moments in rugby: Winning 1990 Grand Slam by beating England; winning 1989/90, 1991/92,

1992/93 and 1993/94 Scottish Championships with Melrose

Worst moment in rugby: Being dropped by 1989 Lions, after playing in first Test against Australia (lost 12–30); breaking arm at Twickenham (6.3.93) to be ruled out of '93 Lions selection; being dropped by Scotland (1994)

Most respected opponent: Michael Lynagh (Queensland & Australia)

Biggest influence on career: Father, Ian McGeechan, Jim Telfer

Serious injuries: Torn knee cartilage, strained groin, dead leg, double break of right forearm (1993), partially torn cruciate knee ligament (1994)

Scotland (1989)		
Last Season	2 caps	3 pts
Career	35 caps	120 pts
Lions 1989	1 Test	6 pts

Caps (35): **1989** W, E, I, F, Fj **1990** I, F, W, E, NZ(1,2), Arg **1991** F, W, E, I, Ro wc–J, Z, I, WS, E, NZ **1992** E, I, F, W, A(1,2) **1993** I, F, W, E, NZ **1994** W

Points (120 – 4t,7c,24p,6dg): **1989** W(1t,1dg) **1990** I(1c,1p), F(2c,2p), W(3p), E(3p), Arg(1t) **1991** F(2p,1dg), W(1t,1c,1p,1dg), E(4p), I(2c,3p) wc–J(1t,1p), I(1dg) **1992** W(1dg,2p), A(2:1c,1p) **1993** E(1dg), NZ(1p)

Best memory last season: Winning Scottish league title for third straight year with Melrose. Otherwise it was a hellish year for me with injuries

Should rugby's amateur rules be revised? Yes. Things are changing in rugby, and people in authority can see that. I recommended last year that trust funds be introduced for international players – something per match, to be collected at the end of your career. SRU have made huge strides and should be applauded. They have taken the bull by the horns and shown other nations the way forward

To what degree should players benefit? I don't why we should not be paid for playing

Should referees be rewarded? Yes. Pay them a fee similar to that received by their counterparts in soccer. Good referees add to the enjoyment of the game

Advice for International Board: One rule for all, regardless of hemisphere. Play game without flankers (give me more room to run)

Notable landmarks in rugby career: By his own admission, Craig had a disappointing 1993/94 campaign, suffering the ignominy of being dropped for first time since his Scotland debut in 1989, and being dogged by injury, which ruled him out of summer tour to Argentina. He paid price for playing when less than 100% fit against Wales, and was not required thereafter. A far cry from 6 March 1993, when he was considered odds-on to become British Lions' first-choice stand-off in New Zealand that summer. A double break of his right forearm, playing against England at Twickenham – the last Test hurdle for Scotland before selection was made – put paid to that. The injury also meant he was a spectator as Melrose were crowned Scottish club champions for the third time in four seasons. They won it again last term. The youngest player ever to represent Scotland B – as a 19-year-old in the 18–12 defeat of France B at Chalon-sur-Saône (20.3.88) – having already turned out for Scottish Schools, Under-18, Under-19 and Under-21. Scored a try and dropped goal

on full debut against Wales (21.1.89), having marked first XV debut for Melrose with three dropped goals against Harrogate. Earned selection to 1989 Lions tour of Australia, and kicked six points in first Test before being replaced by Rob Andrew for remainder of series. Still, he played in seven matches of the 12-match programme. In Scotland's Grand Slam No 10 in 1990, kicked three penalty goals in never-to-be-forgotten decider against England. Toured with Scotland to New Zealand (1990), North America (1991) and Australia (1992)
Touchlines: Golf (12-handicap), ten-pin bowling

Clarke, B. B. England

Full Name: Benjamin Bevan Clarke
Club: Bath
Position: No 8
Height: 6ft 5in (1.95m)
Weight: 16st 13lb (107kg)
Occupation: Works for National Power, Swindon
Born: Bishop's Stortford, 15.4.68
Family: Single
Family links with rugby: Father (Bevan) played for Bishop's Stortford and is now club chairman
Former clubs: Bishop's Stortford, Saracens
International debut: England 33, South Africa 16, 1992
Five Nations debut: England 16, France 15, 1993
Best moment in rugby: Lions' second Test defeat of All Blacks; England's win over All Blacks (both 1993)
Worst moment in rugby: Damaging shoulder and missing England XV's game against an Italy XV in Rovigo (1.5.90)
Most respected opponent: Dean Ryan (Wasps & England)
Biggest influence on career: Tony Russ (my coach at Saracens)

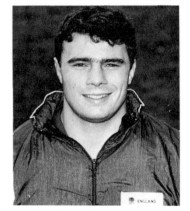

England (1992)

Last Season	6 caps	5 pts
1994	Tour to South Africa	
Career	11 caps	5 pts
Lions 1993	3 Tests	0 pts

Caps (11): **1992** SA **1993** F,W,S,I. Lions–NZ(1,2,3). NZ **1994** S,F,W, SA(1,2)

Points (5 – 1t): **1994** SA(1:1t)

Serious injuries: Sprung shoulder joint, torn ligaments
Other sporting achievements: Swimming for Hertfordshire
Best memory last season: Beating France in Paris; Bath's league and cup double

Should rugby's amateur rules be revised? Yes

To what degree should players benefit? Compensate players or employers for time lost to rugby

Advice for International Board: Better policing of line-outs by referees. Sceptical of new mauling rule: no one I know at Colts level, where they have experience of it, is in favour. Talk to players before introducing such regulations

Notable landmarks in rugby career: Further cemented his reputation as one of world's great players with a 1993/94 campaign which saw him acclaimed as the outstanding British Lion in New Zealand, and as the most dynamic and dependable of performers in an England side which beat New Zealand, Scotland, France, Wales and South Africa (scoring maiden try in first Test). England did lose to Ireland but Ben wasn't playing. Little wonder he was named among the five players of the year by the Rugby Almanack of New Zealand. Within five caps of his England debut (14.11.92) he had been snapped up by the Lions for their safari in New Zealand – a country he had previously visited in 1992 with England B, though he did not pick up a 'Test' scalp (lost 18–24, Hamilton, 28.6.92; lost 18–26, Pukekohe, 5.7.92). In his formative years Ben represented Hertfordshire Colts, Under-21 and full teams while with Bishops Stortford. On joining Saracens at the start of 1990/91, he was selected for London Division, Public School Wanderers, Penguins, England Students and England B. Toured Australia (1991) with London, and was a member of the 1992 England B Grand Slam-winning side which accounted for Spain, Ireland B, France B and Italy B (scored tries v Sp, I). Helped Bath achieve league and cup double last season

Touchlines: Golf, squash, hockey

Wales replacement Mike Rayer skids over the Scottish try-line, with Kenny Logan in tow, to score one of his two tries in the 29–6 win.

Clarke, E.   New Zealand

Full Name: Eroni Clarke
Province: Auckland
Position: Centre, wing
Height: 6ft 1in (1.86m)
Weight: 14st 2lb (90kg)
Born: 31.3.69
International debut: New Zealand 54, World XV 26, 1992
Notable landmarks in rugby career: Eroni was a product of New Zealand's post-1991 World Cup revolution. Drafted into the squad for the 1992 centenary series, after a superb All Black trial, he was untrapped in the second Test at Wellington on 22 April and responded with two tries as the All Blacks triumphed 54–26 to make amends for their 14–28 loss in the opening match. His was the outstanding performance, and he was deservedly retained for the series decider in Auckland three days later, when he again made the try sheet, with one of New Zealand's four in a 26–15 win. The man who had scored 40 points in 11 games for Auckland in 1991, as well as a try in

New Zealand (1992)

Last Season	4 caps	5 pts
Career	8 caps	25 pts

Caps (8): **1992** Wd(2,3), I(1,2) **1993** BL(1,2), S(R), E

Points (25 – 6t): **1992** Wd(2:2t), Wd(3:1t), I(1:1t), I(2:1t) **1993** BL(2:1t)

a New Zealand XV's 60–30 win over Romania (Auckland, 9.6.91), was now on a roll, and luckless Ireland were next in his path. Sure enough, a try in each Test against the Emerald Isle took his tally to five in four Tests. His own luck changed on the tour of Australia and South Africa. Although he made eight appearances – scoring tries against Western Australia, Australian Capital Territory (2) and the Victorian XV – he lost his Test place to North Harbour's Walter Little. He flirted with favour in 1993, winning a wing berth in the first Test starting line-up against the Lions before switching to centre for the second game of the series. Although he scored New Zealand's only try, he was dropped after the 7–20 loss in Wellington and replaced by Auckland team-mate Lee Stensness. He reappeared on the autumn tour to England and Scotland, coming on as a 78th-minute replacement for the injured Matthew Cooper at Murrayfield, and holding his place (in Cooper's enforced absence) at Twickenham. He also played in six of the 11 other games, scoring a try against Emerging England at Gloucester.

Clement, A. Wales

Full Name: Anthony Clement
Club: Swansea
Position: Outside-half, fullback
Height: 5ft 9in (1.75m)
Weight: 13st 8lb (86kg)
Occupation: Contract hire consultant, C. M. Day Ltd, Swansea
Born: Swansea, 8.2.67
Family: Debra (wife)
Family links with rugby: Father (Malcolm) played for Bonymaen; brother (Michael) plays for Bonymaen
Former club: Morriston Youth
International debut: Wales 46, US Eagles 0, 1987
Five Nations debut: England 3, Wales 11, 1988
Best moments in rugby: Scoring two tries for Wales on debut. Helping Wales beat Australia 16–10 in quarter-finals of 1990 Hong Kong Sevens. Beating Scotland (21.3.92) to end three-year winless run at Arms Park. Call-up to '93 Lions; Swansea beating Australia (14.11.92)
Worst moments in rugby: Being dropped by Wales for the second time (before 1988/89 Five Nations Championship) when playing well. Having my name blackened for 48 hours during 1992/93 season when accused of drug involvement. Being dropped by Wales for the third time

Wales (1987)

Last Season	9 caps	5 pts
1994	Tour to Canada/South Seas	
Career	30 caps	16 pts
Lions 1989		
1993		

Caps (30): **1987** US(R) **1988** E, NZ, WS(R), Ro **1989** NZ **1990** S(R), I(R), Na(1,2) **1991** S(R), A(a:R), F(b) wc–WS, A(b) **1992** I, F, E, S **1993** I(R), F, J, C **1994** S, I, F. wc(q)–Sp. C(R), T, WS

Points (16 – 3t,1dg): **1987** US(R:2t) **1990** Na(2:1dg) **1993** J(1t)

Most respected opponent: Mike Rayer (Cardiff & Wales)
Serious injuries: Hamstring strain, shin fracture (Swansea v Australia, 14.11.92, and didn't come off)
Best memory last season: Swansea's Heineken title triumph; captaining Swansea for the first time in the absence of the injured Stuart Davies
Should rugby's amateur rules be revised? They have to be revised
To what degree should players benefit? We should be compensated for time lost to work – it's the way it's going. Too much pressure on employers. Yes, we should be able to earn money from off-the-field activities, and be paid an

international match fee

Should referees be rewarded? Compensation or a match fee would improve the standard of refereeing. It is also a huge demand on their time

Advice for International Board: They are improving – slowly. Tradition has been a stumbling block to progress, but after the 1995 World Cup matters will be improve quickly. There can be no hiding the fact that during the Five Nations Championship the game is semi-professional for those involved. Financial assistance is required for the commitment both of players and companies. I disagree with decision to leave maul ruling, as it encourages negative play. Sides struggling to win can too easily adopt a negative attitude. Referees should officiate more in the spirit of the game than to the letter of the law: as long as the ball is not in maul for too long, don't blow

Notable landmarks in rugby career: A 1993 British Lion who claimed third Test try in 55–5 win over Japan (Cardiff, 16.10.93) and played next three games at fullback before being ousted by long-time rival Mike Rayer. However, injury to Nigel Davies allowed Tony to continue, albeit as a centre, against France. But Davies returned for 1994 Five Nations decider against England, and Tony was dropped down to the bench. Sustained stress fracture of left shin in 1993 after early part of a season in which he had scored one of Wales XV's seven tries against Italy (Cardiff, 7.10.92) and helped Swansea wallop the touring Wallabies 21–6 (14.11.92). Rayer deputized, and made a favourable impression until losing place to Clement (who had also replaced him against Ireland) for Paris match. Touring New Zealand with Lions, Tony turned out against North Auckland, Canterbury, Otago, Southland, Taranaki, Hawke's Bay and Waikato. Had also been a member of 1989 series-winning Lions squad in Australia. Toured South Africa with World XV in same year. But it was not until 1991/92 season that he finally secured much-cherished fullback slot, after returning from Wales' horrible tour of Australia. Turned out against Western Samoa and Australia during 1991 World Cup and proved a major success in 1992 Five Nations Championship. Equally impressive for Swansea, who won 1991/92 Heineken Championship. Joined All Whites in 1985, having played six games for Welsh Youth the previous year. Captained Wales Under-20s, and also represented Wales Under-21s and B (three times)

Touchlines: Soccer, cricket

Clohessy, P. M. N.   Ireland

Full Name: Peter Martin Noel Clohessy
Club: Young Munster
Position: Tighthead prop
Height: 5ft 11in (1.80m)
Weight: 16st (102kg)
Occupation: Company director with TMM Ltd
Born: Limerick, 22.3.66
Family: Anna (wife), Luke (son)
Family links with rugby: Grandfather (Peter O'Hallaran) won Munster Senior Cup medal with Garryowen
Former club: Garryowen
International debut: Ireland 6, France 21, 1993
Five Nations debut: As above
Best moment in rugby: Beating 1992 Wallabies with Munster
Worst moment in rugby: Being suspended for 12 weeks after trial by video playing for Young Munster against St Mary's College in All-Ireland League
Most embarrassing moment: Above dismissal

Ireland (1993)

Last Season	6 caps	5 pts
1994	Tour to Australia	
Career	9 caps	5 pts

Caps (7): **1993** F, W, E **1994** F, W, E, S, A(1,2)

Points (5 – 1t): **1994** A(2:1t)

Most respected opponent: Louis Armary (Lourdes & France)
Serious injuries: Slipped disc, broken leg and arm
Best memory last season: Beating England at Twickenham
Should rugby's amateur rules be revised? No, scrapped
To what degree should players benefit? Should be compensated for time lost to rugby, and permitted to benefit from off-field activities
Should referees be rewarded? No. They should all be shot!
Advice for International Board: Keep up the good work
Notable landmarks in rugby career: Graduated through Irish Under-23 (1989 v Italy, Ravenhill) and B ranks to full side in 1992/93 season, after helping Munster beat touring Australians 22–19 at Thomond Park, and Young Munster win All-Ireland Championship. Debut against France came three years after Ireland B debut in 22–22 draw with Scotland B at Murrayfield (9.12.89). Big breakthrough followed provincial appearances against Ulster, Leinster and Connacht, and came in wake of Ireland's desperately poor defeat by Scotland at Murrayfield. Paul McCarthy was the player to pass over

tighthead duties. Peter retained No 3 jersey for the remainder of the Championship, and should have been picked for 1993 British Lions tour to New Zealand. A ten-week suspension (for stamping) ruled him out of last season's Test opener against Romania (14.11.93), but he regained jersey from Garrett Halpin by time of 1994 Five Nations Championship. Spent last summer touring Australia with Ireland, and claimed first international try in 32–18 second-Test loss to Wallabies in Sydney (11.6.94)

Touchlines: Watersports, especially waterskiing

Coker, T. Australia

Full Name: Troy Coker
State: Queensland
Clubs: Southern Districts (Aus),
Harlequins (Eng)
Position: Lock, back row
Height: 6ft 6in (1.98m)
Weight: 17st 13lb (114kg)
Occupation: Industrial Relations
Advocate with Carter Newell
Solicitors
Born: 30.5.63
Family: Single
Former clubs: GPS (Brisbane:
1981–84), Western Districts
(1985–91), Oxford University
(1988–89)
International debut: Australia 19,
England 6, 1987
Best moments in rugby: Winning
1991 World Cup and 1992 Bledisloe
Cup series
Worst moment in rugby:
Snapping cruciate ligament in right
knee (Argentina, 1987) after full
recovery from left-knee operation
the previous year
Most embarrassing moment:
Blocking attempted dropped goal
with my groin region during club match in Brisbane
Most respected opponent: Ian Jones (North Auckland & New Zealand)
Serious injuries: Left knee reconstruction (1986), right knee reconstruction (1987-88)
Other sporting achievements: Oxford rowing 1990-91

Australia (1987)

Last Season	2 caps	0 pts
Career	15 caps	0 pts

Caps (15): **1987** wc–E, US, F, W **1991** NZ(a2). wc–Arg,WS, NZ(b), E(b) **1992** NZ(1,2,3), W(R) **1993** T, NZ

Points Nil

Suggestions to improve rugby: On-field – get referees to realize that they have had a good game if people/players did not notice they were there. They are there to administer the rules, not shove them down our throats!

Notable landmarks in rugby career: A familiar face to English audiences, having represented Oxford University (along with now retired Wallaby Brian Smith) in the 1988 and 1989 Varsity matches, and Harlequins since 1990 (helping them to a 1991 Pilkington Cup final victory over Northampton). Embroiled in controversy during 1993/94 domestic season in England, when he claimed to be the victim of a premeditated act of foul play during the league clash between Quins and Bath. It was claimed he suffered eye gouging, and that there were severe scratch marks around his eyes. First played for Australia in the 1987 World Cup, winning caps at No 8 against England, the United States, France and Wales. Thereafter, despite touring in 1987 and 1990, did not add a fifth cap to his tally until 1991, when he replaced Tim Gavin at No 8 against New Zealand in Auckland. Something of a utility forward in the Wallabies' triumphant World Cup campaign: employed at lock in the Pool victories over Argentina and Western Samoa, before reverting to No 8 for the semi-final defeat of New Zealand and the final win over England. His travels around the scrum continued when he opened 1992 at blindside in the 16–15 first-Test defeat of the All Blacks in Sydney. From there he switched flanks to fill the openside berth for the remainder of the Bledisloe Cup-winning series. Displaced thereafter by a combination of Willie O and David Wilson, he nonetheless played against Wales in Cardiff (albeit as a 56th-minute replacement for Wilson). Appearances against Tonga and New Zealand in 1993 failed to bring him his first international points

Touchlines: Rugby 12 months a year

France's front row against Scotland: Laurent Seigne, Jean-Marie Gonzales and Laurent Benezech.

Cooksley, M. S.   New Zealand

Full Name: Mark Cooksley
Province: Counties
Position: Lock
Height: 6ft 7 ½ in (2.02m)
Weight: 18st 2lb (115kg)
Born: 11.4.71
International debut: New Zealand 14, World XV 28, 1992
Notable landmarks in rugby career: The biggest man in New Zealand's squad for the 1992 tour of Australia and South Africa, Mark made his Test debut in the first match of the centenary series in Christchurch (18 April). The good news ended there, as the All Blacks were beaten 28–14, and Mark, although teaming up with North Auckland's Ian Jones to get the better of Frenchmen Olivier Roumat and Marc Cecillon, sustained an injury. Fit for the aforementioned tour, he made seven appearances – against Western Australia (scored try), ACT, Victoria, Queensland B, Sydney, Natal and Central Unions –

New Zealand (1992)

Last Season	3 caps	0 pts
Career	4 caps	0 pts

Caps   (4): **1992** Wd(1) **1993** BL(2,3R), A

Points Nil

improving as the trip progressed. Graduated through the age-group ranks at second-division Counties, developing into a strong lock and number-four jumper, though also well versed in the front-jumping duties. Represented New Zealand at Under-19 level and NZ Colts 1990-91. One of his great memories is 11 August 1991 in Christchurch, when he played on the Colts side which demolished their Australian counterparts 61–9. First All Black trial came in 1991, and he helped Saracens trial team beat New Zealand XV 20–15 at Napier in 1992. Partook in New Zealand Maoris' two tours in 1992 (one internal, the other to the Pacific Islands), but had to wait until 1993 before adding to his cap tally when selected ahead of Ian Jones for the second Test against the British Lions. Lasted only half of Wellington defeat before Jones replaced him. Roles reversed in deciding Test when Mark came on for Jones 20-minuted in New Zealand's 30–13 Auckland win. Kept place for Bledisloe Cup defeat of Australia (Dunedin, 17.7.93), but did not tour England and Scotland in autumn.

Cooper, M. J.   New Zealand

Full Name: Matthew James Cooper
Province: Waikato
Club: Marist (Hamilton)
Position: Fullback, centre, wing
Height: 6ft 2in (1.88m)
Weight: 14st 13lb (95kg)
Born: 10.10.66
Family links with rugby: Greg
(brother) plays for Otago and New
Zealand
Former provinces: Otago, Hawke's
Bay
International debut: New Zealand
59, Ireland 6, 1992
Best memory in rugby: Ending
Auckland's dominance of the
Ranfurly Shield in 1993
Suggestions to improve rugby:
Make goal posts wider or bend
outwards at the top
**Notable landmarks in rugby
career:** Record-breaking start to
Test career in second Test against
Ireland at Wellington in 1992.
Having displaced brother Greg at
fullback, he responded with 23
points in 59–6 win. His tally – two

New Zealand (1992)

Last Season	4 caps	14 pts
Career	6 caps	37 pts

Caps (6): **1992** I(2), SA(R) **1993** BL(1R,3TR), WS(TR), S

Points (37 – 2t,10c,3p): **1992** I(2:2t,6c,1p) **1993** S(4c,2p)

tries, six conversions and a penalty goal – represented a world record for a Test
debutant. Matthew, who finished second to his fraternal rival in the 1992 New
Zealand domestic charts, with 260 points (6t,59c,38p,1dg) to Greg's 291, at
least had the satisfaction of taking national championship honours with
Waikato, 40–5 against his brother's Otago side in front of 30,000 fans at
Hamilton. In that game he kicked three penalty goals and converted all four
tries. Matthew's national squad involvement began as far back as 1987, when
he represented the All Blacks as a centre in Tokyo against Japan B, where the
tourists triumphed 94–0, and in Kyoto in the 96–3 win over the Asian
Barbarians. He scored a total of three tries. Returned to set-up in 1992 after
Trial in which he contributed 23 points to a winning cause. Took to 11 his total
All Black appearances, with nine outings during the 1992 tour of Australia and
South Africa, including his second cap as a temporary replacement against the
Springboks. Ended tour as second-top scorer (with 71 points), a feat he
repeated in 1993 when bagging 76 points (11c,18p) in England and Scotland
(dirt tracker Shane Howarth topped the charts with 81). Matt had already taken

his cap haul to five with three more replacement outings (two temporary) against the Lions (whom he'd helped Waikato thrash) and Western Samoa, before a tour in which his brilliant kicking form showed him to be the new Grant Fox. Landed 14 points (4c,2p) against Scotland (won 51–15, 20.11.93), but a groin injury (sustained in 78th minute at Murrayfield) kept him out of England game. It was perhaps no coincidence that New Zealand lost (15–9)

Copsey, A. H.   Wales

Full Name: Anthony Hugh Copsey
Club: Llanelli
Position: Lock
Height: 6ft 7in (2.01m)
Weight: 17st (105kg)
Occupation: Sales representative with Konica Peter Llewellyn (Swansea)
Born: Romford, Essex, 25.1.65
Family: Amanda (wife)
Family links with rugby: Brother (Peter) plays for Old Edwardians
Former clubs: Old Edwardians, Cardiff Institute
International debut: Ireland 15, Wales 16, 1992
Five Nations debut: As above
Best moment in rugby: Winning first cap in Dublin
Worst moment in rugby: Every time I am on a losing side
Most embarrassing moment: Press finding out about the tattoo on my behind
Most respected opponent: Wade Dooley (Preston Grasshoppers & England)
Biggest influence on career: Andy Sankey and Steve Drake (school teachers)

Wales (1992)

Last Season	8 caps	0 pts
1994	Tour to Canada/South Seas	
Career	16 caps	0 pts

Caps (16): **1992** I, F, E, S, A **1993** E, S, I, J, C **1994** E(R). wc(q)–P, Sp(R). Fj, T, WS (R)

Points Nil

Serious injuries: Over 50 career stitches, dislocated collarbone, fractured ribs
Best memory last season: Being in Wales squad that won Five Nations title
Should rugby's amateur rules be revised? No, scrapped
To what degree should players benefit? Players should be paid to play. There's too much hypocrisy at present. Let's be honest and bring it all out into the open

Should referees be rewarded? I believe match fees would encourage new-comers to the officiating business, and consequently standards would rise. They need better training and to have their performances analysed to help iron out mistakes and differences in interpretation. Give more power to touch judges

Advice for International Board: Don't really know what they do, which is an indictment of them in itself. What I do know is that there is a big difference between rugby in the two hemispheres

Notable landmarks in rugby career: Member of Wales' 1994 Five Nations title-winning squad, though appeared only once, as replacement for Emyr Lewis in final game against England (Twickenham, 19.3.94). Had played in both autumn Tests, against Japan and Canada, before being usurped by Phil Davies. Also turned out for Wales A in 61–5 defeat of Japan (Llanelli, 29.9.93). Joined Llanelli (1989/90) via county rugby for Essex Colts and Eastern Counties Under-21s. Moved to work in Wales in 1986, and then enrolled at South Glamorgan Institute (Human Movement), allowing him to represent Welsh Colleges and England Students, with whom he toured Namibia. Former member of London Division squad. Selected for England Development squad before opting for Wales. Represented centenary Barbarians against Scotland at Murrayfield (drew 16–16, 7.9.91), Cork Constitution and Old Wesley. Ever-present in Wales' 1992 Five Nations campaign, and was heading for a similar record in 1993 Championship before losing his place for the final game in Paris. A member of Llanelli's 1992/93 League and Cup-winning side

Touchlines: Basketball, water-polo

Cronin, D. F.   Scotland

Full Name: Damian Francis Cronin
Club: London Scottish
Position: Lock
Height: 6ft 6in (1.98m)
Weight: 17st 10lb (112.5kg)
Occupation: Sales manager with Walcot Reclamation Ltd (Bath)
Born: Wegberg, West Germany, 17.4.63
Family: Annie (wife), Callum (6 months)
Family links with rugby: Father is a past president of Ilford Wanderers
Former clubs: Ilford Wanderers, Bath
International debut: Ireland 22, Scotland 18, 1988
Five Nations debut: As above

Best moment in rugby: Winning 1990 Grand Slam with Scotland; being selected for the Lions

Worst moment in rugby: Being dropped by Scotland during 1991 World Cup

Most embarrassing moment: Getting ball knocked out of my hands as I was going over to score a try against Wellington (1990)

Most respected opponent: Wade Dooley (Preston Grasshoppers & ex-England)

Scotland (1988)

Last Season	1 cap	0 pts
Career	29 caps	8 pts

Lions 1993

Caps (29): **1988** I, F, W, E, A **1989** W, E ,I, F, Fj, Ro **1990** I, F, W, E, NZ(1,2) **1991** F, W, E, I, Ro wc–Z **1992** A(2) **1993** I, F, W, E, NZ

Points (8 – 2t): **1989** I(1t) **1990** W(1t)

Serious injuries: Ligament damage in both knees; staple put in right knee

Best memory last season: Getting picked to tour with British Lions; winning last two league matches against Saracens and West Hartlepool for London Scottish to stay up

Other sporting achievements: Drove in celebrity race round Brands Hatch; won Victor Ludorum three years in a row at school

Should rugby's amateur rules be revised? Yes

To what degree should players benefit? Should be compensated; should be able to benefit from off-the-field activities; should receive a wage for playing an international

Should referees be rewarded? Yes, and it should improve standards

Advice for International Board: If I was living in the Southern Hemisphere, I would think they were doing a marvellous job. Look seriously at the commercialization of rugby in support of players. Some sort of trust fund for international players. Do not change the lineout: it is a lottery, which is half the fun. Those who survive are technicians who learn to survive. Better off working on keeping the game flowing more. Make people stay on their feet more and make referees more aware of players, especially flankers, coming over the top

Notable landmarks in rugby career: Not much to remember of Damian's 1993/94 Test season, having picked up his one cap in record 51–15 loss to New Zealand (Murrayfield, 20.11.93). Thereafter he was not required – a far cry from previous season, when his strong form had prompted a British Lions tour place in New Zealand, and appearances against North Auckland, NZ Maoris, Southland, Taranaki, Hawke's Bay and Waikato. Had done well to return to rugby after fracturing base of spine aged 22. Built reputation in Scotland with performances for Anglo-Scots, having become eligible thanks to Lothian-based grandparents. Helped 1987 Anglos beat French at Cupar, and was included in Scottish XV which achieved a similar feat. Toured with Scotland to Zimbabwe in 1988, captaining them against Mashonaland District. Toured Japan (1989) and New Zealand (1990). Ever-present alongside Chris Gray in Scotland second row during 1991 Five Nations Championship after missing early-season win (49–3) over Argentina through injury, but was largely kept out of 1991 World Cup campaign and 1992 Championship by Doddie Weir and Neil Edwards. Lust for game returned on moving from Bath to London Scottish.

Helped them win promotion back to division one in 1991/92, before touring Australia with Scotland in 1992 and recapturing Test place
Touchlines: DIY (restoring the house), golf, squash, antiques

Crowley, D. J.   Australia

Full Name: Daniel (Dan) James Crowley
State: Queensland
Club: Southern Districts
Position: Tighthead prop
Height: 5ft 8in (1.73m)
Weight: 16st 3lb (103kg)
Occupation: Police officer, Queensland Police Service
Born: 28.8.65
Family: Lisa (wife), Jessica (daughter)
Former clubs: None, Souths since 1972
International debut: Australia 30, British Lions 12, 1989
Best moment in rugby: First cap
Worst moment in rugby: Losing third Test (series decider) to 1989 British Lions
Most respected opponent: All of them
Suggestions to improve rugby: On-field – no kicking out on the full from anywhere; make the backs do some work

Australia (1989)

Last Season	1 cap	0 pts
Career	7 caps	0 pts

Caps (7): 1989 BL(1,2,3) 1991 wc–WS 1992 I, W 1993 C(R)

Points Nil

Notable landmarks in rugby career: Dan was the man who presented Her Majesty the Queen with a miniature football prior to Australia's World Cup final win over England in 1991, having made just the one tournament appearance against Western Samoa. Indeed, his links with the United Kingdom stretch back to 1989, when he made his debut against the British Lions and retained his place through the three-Test series. That same year he toured Canada and France, but was stood down for the 1990 trip across the Tasman Sea. With Tony Daly and Ewen McKenzie pretty much shoring up the Test propping duties, Crowley's outings have been restricted to just four appearances since the '89 Lions left Oz in triumph. He was a reserve in all Tests in 1991. However, he ended 1992 on a high when, with Daly missing the tour to Ireland and Wales, he wore the loosehead's jersey in both internationals. Dan had himself been unavailable for the historic visit to South Africa in August, but once in Britain was one of the busiest players on duty: appearing also against Leinster, Munster, Ulster and Connacht on the Irish leg, and Wales B and Llanelli once the tourists switched their attentions to the Principality. Perhaps his proudest moment came with a try in the 30–20 defeat of the Barbarians at a packed Twickenham. The highlight of his 1993 campaign was coming on as a 59th-minute replacement for Daly against Canada in Calgary (won 43–16, 9.10.93)

Touchlines: Work

Cunningham, V. J. G.   Ireland

Full Name: Vincent John Gerald Cunningham
Club: St Mary's College
Position: Centre, outside-half
Height: 6ft (1.83m)
Weight: 14st 1lb (85kg)
Occupation: Bank official with Allied Irish
Born: Dublin, 14.3.67
Family: Single
Family links with rugby: Father played for (and coached and selected) St Mary's
International debut: Ireland 10, England 21, 1988
Five Nations debut: Scotland 15, Ireland 3, 1993
Best moment in rugby: Winning first cap in Millennium match; beating England (Dublin, 1993); British Lions call-up (1993)
Worst moment in rugby: Breaking hand in training to miss Ireland's tour to North America (1989); knee injury (January '94) which put me out for rest of season
Most respected opponent: Philippe Sella (Agen & France)
Serious injuries: Broken hand (1989); right knee reconstruction (1994)
Other sporting achievements: Cricket for Irish Schoolboys

Ireland (1988)

Last Season	2 caps	0 pts
Career	16 caps	14 pts

Lions 1993

Caps (16): **1988** E(b), It **1990** Arg(R) **1991** Na(1,2) wc–ZJ(R) **1992** NZ(1,2), A **1993** S, F, W, E, R **1994** F

Points (14 – 3t,1c): **1988** It(1c) **1991** Na(2:1t) **1992** NZ(1:2t)

178

Best memory last season: Watching Ireland's win at Twickenham

Should rugby's amateur rules be revised? Yes

To what degree should players benefit? Compensation for time lost, and permission to benefit from off-field activities, but no direct payment for playing

Should referees be rewarded? Yes. Same position as players regarding commitment, but not convinced it will improve standards

Advice for International Board: As a body their integrity is undoubted, but it's such a large organization that it's very difficult to keep up to date with law changes. There's always going to be a time lag. We need to enjoy the same leniency as Southern Hemisphere nations. It is a necessity if a country like Ireland is to compete at the same level. At present we cannot. Players work 9-to-5, then go training. Other countries allow players to get together more often. We can't compete with that. It's amateur versus professional. Talent may be similar at the outset, but the time and dedication they're able to devote leaves us trailing

Notable landmarks in rugby career: Replacement for 1993 British Lions who first found fame as outside-half in first Irish Schools team to beat Wales. Played in Irish touring side which beat France four seasons ago. Has amassed 16 caps since debut against England in 1988 Dublin Millennium match. Toured Namibia with Ireland (1991), playing in both Tests (scoring try in second), and added a further couple of caps in World Cup. Scored Ireland U-25s' try in 12–10 defeat of US Eagles (Limerick, 10.3.90), and landed conversion in 36–17 defeat of Spain (Limerick, 8.9.90). Kicked penalty goal in Ireland B's 16–0 defeat of Scotland (Ravenhill, 22.12.90). Toured to New Zealand (1992) with Ireland and was very nearly responsible for one of the great shocks in the game's history. He scored two tries, and 'no-hopers' Ireland led 12–0 in the first Test (Dunedin, 30.5.92) before New Zealand edged home 24–21. Retained his place in Irish midfield throughout 1992/93 campaign, sharing in wins over Wales and England. Also played major role in Irish VII which came within a whisker of final in inaugural World Sevens tournament at Murrayfield (April 1993). Injury wrecked last season for Vinnie, ruling him out of three-quarters of championship, plus summer tour to Australia, after he had played against Romania and France

Touchlines: Enjoy horse racing at Leopardstown and Phoenix Park, cricket, golf

Daly, A. J.   Australia

Full Name: Anthony (Tony) John Daly
State: New South Wales
Club: Randwick
Position: Loosehead prop
Height: 5ft 10in (1.78m)
Weight: 16st 3lb (103kg)
Occupation: Sales consultant with Carmin Office Furniture
Born: 7.3.66
Family: Shannon (wife)
Former clubs: Wests (1985-86), Gordon (1987-90), Easts (1991-92)
International debut: New Zealand 24, Australia 12, 1989
Best moment in rugby: 1991 World Cup victory
Worst moment in rugby: Not playing in 1991 Grand Final with Easts
Most respected opponent: Olo Brown (Auckland & New Zealand)
Serious injuries: Broken ankle (1988); disc protrusion (1992)
Suggestions to improve rugby: Off-field – more investments for players; more media for the game
Notable landmarks in rugby career: Moved to within four games of becoming Australia's most-capped prop, with ten appearances in last season alongside NSW team mates Phil Kearns and Ewen McKenzie in what remained an unchanged front row. He even chipped in with a try (his fourth) in the 43–16 defeat of Canada (Calgary, 9.10.93), though it won't go down as his most notable score. That, without doubt, came in the 1991 World Cup final, when he scored the only try of Australia's 12–6 win. A breakaway wing-forward in his school days at St Joseph's College, he was transformed into a prop when playing under former Wallaby front-rower John Griffiths at Western Suburbs in Sydney. So well did he master the art that he was plucked from the relative obscurity of club rugby in 1989, and asked to prop against Richard Loe in the All Black Test at Eden Park. He has rarely, if ever, taken a backwards step since, amassing 33 caps despite not being available to tour Ireland and Wales in the autumn of 1992.

Australia (1989)		
Last Season	10 caps	5 pts
Career	35 caps	17 pts

Caps (35): **1989** NZ, F(1,2) **1990** F(1,2,3), US, NZ(1,2,3) **1991** W(a), E(a), NZ(a1,a2) wc–Arg, W(b), I, NZ(b), E(b) **1992** S(1,2), NZ(1,2,3), SA **1993** T, NZ, SA(1,2,3), C, F(1,2) **1994** I(1,2)

Points (17 – 4t): **1990** F(3:1t), US(1t) **1991** wc–E(b:1t) **1993** C(1t)

Among his other fond memories are the 1992 Bledisloe Cup series win against New Zealand (though not their one-off loss at Dunedin in '93) and the defeats of South Africa in 1992 (by a record 26–3 margin) and 1993 (a 2–1 series decision)

Touchlines: Tennis, movies, socializing

Danaher, P. P. A.   Ireland

Full Name: Philip Paul Anthony Danaher
Club: Garryowen
Position: Centre
Height: 5ft 11in (1.81m)
Weight: 14st (84kg)
Occupation: Director of Premier Peat Products Ltd (Nenagh)
Born: Limerick, 5.10.65
Family: Married
Former clubs: Abbeyfeale, Lansdowne
International debut: Ireland 22, Scotland 18, 1988
Five Nations debut: As above
Best moments in rugby: Winning 1991/92 All-Ireland League with Garryowen; beating England (1993)
Worst moment in rugby: Losing to Wales (1994)
Most embarrassing moment: Touching ball down behind line and conceding 5-yard scrum against Wales (ref was wrong!)
Most respected opponent: Jeremy Guscott (Bath & England)
Biggest influence on career: Don Spring (Dublin University & Ireland No 8, 1978-81)

Ireland (1988)

Last Season	7 caps	0 pts
Career	23 caps	6 pts

Caps (23): **1988** S, F, W, WS, It **1989** F, NZ(R) **1990** F **1992** S, F, NZ(1), A **1993** S, F, W, E, R **1994** F, W, E, S, A(1,2)

Points (6 – 2p): **1988** It(2p)

Serious injuries: Broken both ankles, serious hamstring injuries
Other sporting achievements: Badminton at national level while at school; Gaelic football for Limerick (helped them reach 1991 Munster Cup final against Kerry)
Best memory last season: Beating England at Twickenham, and specifically when Simon Geoghegan scored his try
Should rugby's amateur rules be revised? Yes

To what degree should players benefit? There should be no payment for playing, but I would expect full reimbursement for loss of earnings, as well as full permission to benefit from available off-field activites

Should referees be rewarded? Yes, some form of reimbursement for them would also be appropriate. But they must be more universal in their interpretations. Improve coaching of schools and age-group levels

Advice for International Board: None. We've got a good deal in Ireland. We've interpreted the new rules to suit our style of play

Notable landmarks in rugby career: Still searching for first Test try after 23 starts, yet remains a rock in Irish midfield. Last season he was an ever-present in the No 12 jersey, while three players shored up the other centre duties (Vinnie Cunningham, Mark McCall and Maurice Field). Succeeded Phil Matthews as Ireland captain for final game of 1992 Five Nations Championship, against France in Paris (21.3.92). Ireland lost 44–12 to complete whitewashed Wooden Spoon. Then led side to New Zealand for summer tour, having previously toured to France and North America. Skippered Irish to sensational 12–0 lead over All Blacks in first Test at Dunedin. After he had gone off injured in the 35th minute, New Zealand recovered, just, to scrape home 24–21. Missed second Test, but recovered fitness in time to lead side in 17–42 loss to Australia (31.10.92). Subsequently relinquished captaincy to Michael Bradley. Collected first international honours in 1982 when represented Ireland Schools (v E, W). Left Garryowen for Lansdowne, in 1984 but returned four years later. The 1987/88 season brought his Munster debut and first full cap (at fullback) against Scotland (16.1.88). Missed out on 1991 World Cup, but toured to Australia with Ireland last summer

Touchlines: Social golf, walking my pet English sheepdog Boris

New Zealand's golden boy Jeff Wilson keeps the ball alive during a Murrayfield debut which brought him three tries.

Davies, A.   Wales

Full Name: Adrian Davies
Club: Cardiff
Position: Outside-half
Height: 5ft 10in (1.78m)
Weight: 12st 7lb (79kg)
Occupation: Surveyor with
Chesterton International
Born: Bridgend, 9.2.69
Family: Single
Family links with rugby: Brother
(Graham) plays for Llanharan;
brother (Lloyd) played for
Cambridge University
Former clubs: Pencoed Youth,
Neath
International debut: Wales 24,
Barbarians 31, 1990
Five Nations debut: None
Best moment in rugby: Winning
1993/94 Swalec Cup final with
Cardiff
Worst moment in rugby: 1990
Varsity match
Most respected opponent: Aled
Williams (Swansea & Wales A)
Biggest influence on career: Ron
Waldron (coach at Wales U-19s &
Neath) and Cardiff coach Alec Evans

Wales (1990)

Last Season	3 caps	13 pts
1994	Tour to Canada/South Seas	
Career	7 caps	19 pts

Caps (7): **1991** Ba(R), A **1993** Z(1,2), J, C **1994** Fj

Points (19 – 2c,3p,2dg): **1991** A(1dg) **1993** Z(1:1dg) 1994 Fj(2c,3p)

Serious injuries: Neck problem for one and a half years
Other sporting achievements: Football Blue at Cambridge (offered trials
with Leeds United and Sheffield Wednesday aged 16), having played for Wales
U-15s
Best memory last season: Day after our Cup final defeat of Llanelli; no one
had given us a chance and the self-satisfaction was immense
Should rugby's amateur rules be revised? Yes
To what degree should players benefit? Anything short of being paid to play.
We'd be under no less pressure if the game was totally professional – public
expectation of internatonal players is the maximum. I would say England's
rugby players these days are under the same pressure as their national football
team. For us to compete with Southern Hemisphere nations, we must sort out
the situation. Players must certainly not lose out by playing top-level rugby. It
is a joke when nations tour short-handed because certain players cannot afford
time off work

Should referees be rewarded? Yes. If theirs was a profession, standards would assuredly increase. At present, they're in a worse boat than even the players

Advice for International Board: Listen to the experienced international players. There is much benefit to be gained from hearing what the likes of Ieuan Evans and Will Carling think. It is irresponsible to ignore what the players have to say

Notable landmarks in rugby career: Still looking for first appearance in Five Nations Championship, despite having won six caps. Played in both autumn Tests last season, against Japan and Canada, but defeat in latter led to wholesale changes before start of '94 Five Nations, including switch of Neil Jenkins from centre to outside-half. Adrian captained Wales at U-18, U-19 and U-21 levels. Kicked four penalty goals for Wales B in 15–28 loss to France B at La Teste (12.11.89). Made full debut for Wales when coming on as 47th-minute replacement for Mark Ring during 24–31 loss to Barbarians (6.10.91), and dropped a goal against Australia in Wales's 6–63 record reversal in Brisbane (21.7.91). Included in Welsh World Cup squad, but talent was not utilised. Switched from Neath to Cardiff seeing a perfect opportunity, with their great back division, to be in a position to take hold of a game and run the show. Captained Cambridge to 17–11 win over Oxford in 110th Varsity Match (10.12.92), kicking nine points. Played also in 1990 and 1991 Varsity matches. Kicked one conversion and two penalty goals on one Wales A appearance in 1992/93, but still lost 28–29 to Ireland A at Newport (5.3.93). Toured with Wales to Africa in 1993 and dropped a goal in 35–14 first-Test win over Zimbabwe (Bulawayo, 22.5.93), but outside-half berth again went to Jenkins after second Test in Harare. Scored one of Wales's eight tries in 56–17 defeat of South African Barbarians (Windhoek 9.6.93). Helped Cardiff win 1993/94 Swalec Cup with final defeat of holders Llanelli at end of season in which played twice on Wales A's grand slam surge. Scored 14 points (2t,2c) in 61–5 rout of Japan, and 12 points (1t,2c,1p) in 42–11 defeat of Canada

Touchlines: Cricket, piano, trumpet

Davies, J. D.   Wales

Full Name: John David Davies
Club: Neath
Position: Tighthead prop
Height: 6ft (1.83m)
Weight: 16st 7lb (100kg)
Occupation: Farmer
Born: Carmarthen, 1.2.69
Family: Veronica (wife)
Family links with rugby: Cousin
plays for Crymych
Former club: Crymych
International debut: Wales 21,
Ireland 21, 1991
Five Nations debut: As above
Best moment in rugby: Beating
France and winning Five Nations
title (both 1994)
Worst moment in rugby: Losing
1992/93 Swalec Cup final to Llanelli
Most embarrassing moment:
Being given an aerial view of Paris
during a scrum against France
Most respected opponent: Jason
Leonard (Harlequins & England)
Other sporting achievements:
Winning Wales's Strongest Man
in 1993
Best memory last season:
Winning Five Nations title

Wales (1991)		
Last Season	10 caps	0 pts
1994	Tour to Canada/South Seas	
Career	14 caps	5 pts

Caps (14): 1991 I, F 1993 F(R), Z(2),
J, C 1994 S, I, F, E. wc(q)–P, Sp.
C, WS

Points (5 – 1t): 1993 Z(2:1t)

Should rugby's amateur rules be revised? Yes
To what degree should players benefit? Expenses for time lost and
permission to benefit from all off-field activities – everyone else is doing it.
Should not be paid to play for country, but should receive some reward for your
performance from commercial activities for promoting the game
Should referees be rewarded? Should be compensated for time given to
rugby. Then hopefully more would be encouraged to take up the game
Advice for International Board: I don't know who they are, but they should
be more professional and promote game better. Make rules and adhere to them
strictly – at present there are ways of getting round amateur rules, which is
ridiculous. It's about time they woke up to fact that certain players are being
given money
Notable landmarks in rugby career: Established himself as first-choice
Welsh tighthead last season, and in so doing shared in Wales's 1994 Five

185

Nations Championship triumph and their World Cup qualifying success. Had toured with Wales to Zimbabwe and Namibia last summer, scoring his first international try in the 42–13 second-Test win over Zimbabwe (Harare, 29.5.93), and also turning out against Zimbabwe B and South Africa Barbarians. Last summer packed bags again and toured to Canada and South Pacific after helping Wales qualify for World Cup with wins in Portugal and Spain. First player from Crymych to represent Wales Youth, turning out against Ireland, France and England in 1987, and the same three opponents the following season. Joined Neath in 1987 and was included in Wales B squad in his first senior season. An Under-21 cap against Scotland in 1989 was followed by 'B' recognition in 34–12 win against Holland (1990/91), and against North of England in 1992/93. Graduated to senior side in 1991, playing against Ireland (drew 21–21) and France (lost 3–36) in Five Nations Championship.
Touchlines: Gardening, renovating houses

Davies, N. G. Wales

Full Name: Nigel Gareth Davies
Club: Llanelli
Positions: Centre, wing
Height: 6ft 1in (1.86m)
Weight: 13st 10lb (87kg)
Occupation: Management consultant with Dennis Morgans Associates, Swansea
Born: Llanelli, 29.3.65
Family: Married
Family links with rugby: Father played for Trimsaran
Former club: Trimsaran
International debut: New Zealand 54, Wales 9, 1988
Five Nations debut: Scotland 23, Wales 7, 1989
Best moment in rugby: Scoring second of two tries for Wales in 24–6 win over Western Samoa (1988)
Worst moment in rugby: Being dropped after Samoan game (1986)
Most respected opponent: Simon Halliday (ex-Harlequins & England) – so hard to mark
Other sporting achievements: County tennis (member of Llanelli LTC)

Wales (1988)

Last Season	9 caps	0 pts
1994	Tour to Canada/South Seas	
Career	14 caps	8 pts

Caps (14): **1988** NZ(2), WS **1989** S, I **1993** F **1994** S, I, E. wc(q)–P, Sp, C, Fj, T(R), WS

Points (8 – 2t): **1988** WS(2t)

Best memory last season: Returning to international fray against France
Should rugby's amateur rules be revised? Yes
To what degree should players benefit? Broken-time payments
Advice for International Board: More consideration should be given to players' families
Notable landmarks in rugby career: A key component in Wales's 1994 Five Nations Championship triumph, Nigel won rave reviews for his performances in free-scoring three-quarters. Brought into side after Wales's calamitous autumn defeat by, he played against Scotland, Ireland and England, and was less than impressed to be forced out of French game by injury. One Wales A appearance produced a try in 24–8 win against North of England (Pontypool, 13.10.93). His form was remarkable, as he had only been rescued from four years in Test wilderness on 20 March 1993, when deployed against France. Thereafter, was forced to pull out of summer tour to Zimbabwe and Namibia before departure. Graduated from Trimsaran Youth to Wales Youth, and passed through national Student and B levels before breaking into Test side in 1988 on disastrous tour to New Zealand. His debut came in second Test – a 54–9 thrashing in Auckland which clinched one of the most convincing 2–0 series results ever. On his return he ran in two tries as Wales defeated Western Samoa 28–6 at Cardiff. Following season made his Five Nations debut against Scotland at Murrayfield in a game Wales lost 23–7. Lost place after 19–13 home loss to Ireland that same season. Nigel, who toured Italy with Wales B in 1986/87, is very highly regarded on the club scene inside the Principality, and of late has been one of the central figures in Llanelli's triumphant exploits – not least their League and Cup double and victory over Australia in 1992/93
Touchlines: Reading, music, motocross

Scott Quinnell holds off Alain Penaud en route to his epic try against France.

Davies, P. T.   Wales

Full Name: Philip Thomas Davies
Club: Llanelli
Position: No 8, lock, flanker
Height: 6ft 3in (1.90m)
Weight: 17st 3lb (109kg)
Occupation: Marketing manager with M.R.J. Group Ltd (Cross Hands)
Born: Seven Sisters, 19.10.63
Family: Caroline (wife), Rebecca (daughter) and Danikka (daughter)
Family links with rugby: Wife Caroline is Jonathan Davies' sister
Former club: Sevens Sisters, South Wales Police
International debut: Wales 24, England 15, 1985
Five Nations debut: As above
Best moments in rugby: Captaining Llanelli to three Schweppes Challenge Cup triumphs (1988, 1991 and 1992) against Neath, Pontypool and Swansea respectively
Worst moment in rugby: Wales's 1990 whitewash
Most embarrassing moment: Having ball knocked from grasp by Kenfig Hill centre while touching down in 1992/93 Swalec Cup
Most respected opponent: Laurent Rodriguez (Dax & France)
Biggest influence on career: Gareth Jenkins (Llanelli coach)

Wales (1985)

Last Season	7 caps	0 pts
1994	Tour to Canada/South Seas	
Career	42 caps	21 pts

Caps (42): **1985** E, Fj **1986** E, S, I, F, Fj, T, WS **1987** F, E(a), I wc–T, C, NZ **1988** WS, Ro **1989** S, I, F, E, NZ **1990** F, E, S **1991** I, F(a), A(a), F(b) wc–WS, Arg, A(b) **1993** F, Z(1), Na **1994** S, I, F, E, C, Fj(R), WS

Points (21 – 5t): **1985** Fj(2t) **1986** I(1t) **1990** E(1t) **1993** Z(1:1t)

Serious injuries: Broken cheekbone, misplaced disc in neck, dislocated elbow
Other sporting achievements: Swam for West Wales Schools
Best memory last season: Final whistle of Scotland game. Tremendous feeling of satisfaction as we played ever so well
Should rugby's amateur rules be revised? Yes
To what degree should players benefit? Anything short of being paid to play. The time and effort required for rugby is becoming increasingly difficult to reconcile with other demands. We have mortgages to pay and lives to lead away from sport. Rugby wants a professional commitment, but so do our wage-

paying employers, who must take precedence. Rugby's demands have increased tenfold from when I started, and are now unreasonable, with training 5–6 days per week. It is becoming survival of fittest. I'm not saying we should turn back the clock to the days of more beer than training. Our enjoyment these days comes from winning and being successful. There was always a level of commitment, even 12 years ago when I started, but it's now more performance-related. Playing careers are bound to become shorter as a result

Should referees be rewarded? Same applies as for players

Advice for International Board: Talk to players before making laws; allow handling in rucks when it improves continuity of game

Notable landmarks in rugby career: Restored following November '93 home loss to Canada, Phil's return coincided with Wales's resurgence (actually, it was no coincidence). His first three games all ended in wins as Wales clinched 1994 Five Nations Championship. Wales's most-capped forward (overtaking Graham Price, 41) with 42nd appearance, against Western Samoa (Apia 25.6.94). First played for Wales at 16 Group. Former policeman. Broke into full Welsh squad in 1984. Marked second cap with two tries in 40–3 win over Fiji at the National Stadium (9.11.85). Jaw broken by punch in controversial Five Nations clash with England (Twickenham, 7.3.87). Dropped after playing in 1987 World Cup and became Wales B captain. Returned against Western Samoa in 1988 but missed that year's Championship. Retired from international arena when left out of team to play the centenary Barbarians (6.10.90), but returned during 1991 Five Nations, and held place through 1992 Australia tour and World Cup before being replaced by Swansea's Stuart Davies for 1992 Championship campaign. Llanelli's most-capped international has also represented Crawshays and the Barbarians. Stepped down as Scarlets' captain at end of 1991/92 season after five years in job (four Cup finals, three wins). Enjoyed fine 1992/93, helping Llanelli beat touring Wallabies 13–9 at Stradey (14.11.92), clinching the League and Cup double, and returning to Test side in time to tour Zimbabwe and Namibia over summer

Touchlines: Golf

Davies, S.   Wales

Full Name: Stuart Davies
Club: Swansea
Position: No 8
Height: 6ft 3in (1.90m)
Weight: 17st 4lb (110kg)
Occupation: Environmental Health Officer with Swansea City Council
Born: Swansea, 2.9.65
Family: Lorna (wife)
Family links with rugby: Father (Elwyn) played at centre for Swansea
Former club: South Glamorgan Institute
International debut: Ireland 15, Wales 16, 1992
Five Nations debut: As above
Best moments in rugby: Whole debut weekend in Ireland; leading Swansea to victory over touring Australia in 1992
Worst moments in rugby: Losing two successive WRU Schweppes Challenge Cup semi-finals (1990-91) and the next final
Most embarrassing moment:

Wales (1992)

Last Season	1 cap	0 pts
Career	12 caps	9 pts

Caps (12): **1992** I, F, E, S, A **1993** E, S, I, Z(1R,2), Na, J

Points (9 – 2t): **1992** I(1t) **1993** Z(2:1t)

Falling over when running out onto pitch for Swansea against All Blacks (21.10.89, lost 22–37)
Most respected opponent: Wayne Shelford (Northampton & New Zealand)
Biggest influence on career: My father
Serious injuries: Cartilage operation on each knee; torn medial ligaments in left knee; another two cartilage operations in 1993 (November and June)
Best memory last season: Lifting Heineken League for Swansea
Should rugby's amateur rules be revised? Yes, but I don't think rugby can sustain professionalism
To what degree should players benefit? I would play whatever, with or without, but it would be nice to receive compensation. We should be able to benefit from off-field activities. I would like to see the game follow the example set by athletics. However, I wouldn't want to be paid for playing for my country
Should referees be rewarded? Yes, anything that might encourage greater depth and improved standards would be a benefit. More discussion between players and referees is needed. Increased feedback from both sides can only improve on-field understanding

Advice for International Board: I'm not happy with them. Some of the law changes have reduced the quality of our game and they're very inconsistent. They're also slow on standardizing and don't equate. As my old teacher would say, 'Could do better'.

Notable landmarks in rugby career: Captained Swansea to Welsh league championship last season, having led them to a famous 21–6 win over Australia at St Helens (4.11.92). But Test fortunes were hit by injury and he made just one appearance, in 55–5 victory over Japan (Cardiff, 16.10.93). Had been dropped for final 1993 Championship game in Paris, but on summer tour to Zimbabwe and Namibia he played in all three internationals (scoring try in second Test against Zimbabwe) and also skippered side against Zimbabwe B and Namibia B. Knee trouble prompted his late withdrawal from last summer's tour to Canada and the South Pacific. Represented Wales at Under-15, Under-16 and Under-18 levels, and was an Under-21 squad member (1987). Attended South Glamorgan Institute, where turned out for Welsh Colleges, Students and Academicals. Selected for Wales B squad in 1989 but the match against France coincided with his wedding. Called into Wales squad post-1991 World Cup and played full 1992 Championship season at No 8, marking debut with winning try against Ireland in Dublin

Touchlines: Golf (22-handicap), seeing my wife, cinema, eating out

De Glanville, P. R.   England

Full Name: Philip Ranulph de Glanville
Clubs: Bath
Position: Centre
Height: 6ft (1.83m)
Weight: 13st 7lb (81kg)
Occupation: Marketing executive with Cow & Gate, Trowbridge
Born: Loughborough, 1.10.68
Family: Single
Family links with rugby: Father played for Loughborough and Rosslyn Park; now MD of Rhino scrum machines
Former clubs: Durham University, Oxford University
International debut: England 33, South Africa 16, 1992
Five Nations debut: Wales 10, England 9, 1993
Best moment in rugby: Beating New Zealand (1993)

Worst moment in rugby: Being stamped on my face during South West game against 1993 All Blacks

Most embarrassing moment: Losing match for Durham University on Canadian tour when dropped a goalbound penalty effort beneath posts, and University of Victoria scored try from resultant scrum

England (1992)

Last Season	7 caps	0 pts
Career	9 caps	0 pts

Caps (9): **1992** SA(R) **1993** W(R), NZ **1994** S, I, F, W, SA(1,2)

Points Nil

Most respected opponent: Philippe Sella (Agen & France)

Biggest influence on career: Parents

Best memory last season: Winning English league and cup double with Bath

Serious injuries: Broken arm, dislocated collarbone, eye gash (required 15 stitches)

Should rugby's amateur rules be revised? Yes

To what degree should players benefit? No player should lose out financially from playing rugby in this day and age

Should referees be rewarded? Yes, a match fee

Advice for International Board: Appoint independent arbitrator to deal with matters of discipline. My eye injury last season, caused by a boot, highlighted the fact that there is no procedure. We need a neutral body to examine such incidents. As for IRB themselves, we need a governing body which lays down the law. At present, Unions are split in way they handle their affairs

Notable landmarks in rugby career: Having earned his first two caps as a replacement, Phil came into his own in 1993/94. With the season-long injury to Jeremy Guscott, the former Oxford Blue was given an extended run alongside Will Carling, growing in confidence as the season progressed. However, he was lucky – not in being selected, but in being fit enough to be considered. Representing South West England against the touring All Blacks (30.10.93), he suffered a quite horrifying, sight-threatening eye injury at the bottom of a ruck. Fifteen stitches were required to keep his left eyelid intact, and there was a deep wound above and below the eye. It wasn't an accident, Phil insists. Amazingly, less than a month later, he faced up against the tourists again in the colours of England and enjoyed a sweet victory. Member of original England Under-21 side, scoring two tries against Romania Under-21s (won 54–13, Bucharest 13.5.89). Made England B debut as a 20-year old in 44–0 defeat of Italy (19.3.89). Helped underdogs Oxford University win 1990 Varsity match (11.12.90) and favourites Bath to win 1991/92 Pilkington Cup. Toured New Zealand with England B in summer of '92, playing in both 'Test' losses to the All Black XV, scoring a try in the second. Took England B appearances into double figures with cap against South Africa (7.11.92). Toured Canada with England A (1993)

Touchlines: Golf, cricket

Delaigue, Y.   France

Full Name: Yanne Delaigue
Club: Toulon
Position: Centre
Height: 5ft 11in (1.80m)
Weight: 12st 8lb (80kg)
Occupation: Student
Born: Toulon, 5.4.73
International debut: Scotland 12,
France 20, 1994
Five Nations debut: As above

France (1994)		
Last Season	1 cap	0 pts
1994	Tour to Canada/NZ	
Career	1 cap	0 pts

Caps (1): **1994** S

Points Nil

Notable landmarks in rugby career: Son of Gilles Delaigue, also a centre, who won two caps during the 1973 season against Japan and Romania, Yanne is one of the jewels in French rugby's crown. A playmaker *par extraordinaire*, he has turned Toulon's back division into one of the most exciting around since moving from outside-half to centre. Indeed, he was the guiding light behind Toulon's championship triumph in 1992, beating Biarritz in the final. At just 21, the youngest member of France's 1994 Five Nations squad, Yanne has made swift advances. As a teenager he scored a try against England 18 Group at Franklin Gardens, having gone from school team straight into the Toulon side alongside Aubin Hueber. Played a hefty role in the 67–9 rout of Scotland Under-21s by France Under-21s in Dijon (5.2.93,) and last season helped France A defeat their England second-string counterparts 20–8 in Paris (5.3.94). A fortnight later, with France staring a Five Nations Wooden Spoon square in the face, he was called upon to steer them clear of that unthinkable prospect. Given his debut in the splendidly refurbished Murrayfield, Yanne's upright elusive running was a feature of France's 20–12 win. Indeed, it was his break that made the opening try for Jean-Luc Sadourny. Knowing a good thing when they saw one, the relieved selectors re-enlisted their young star for the summer tour to Canada and New Zealand

Deylaud, C.   France

Full Name: Christophe Deylaud
Club: Toulouse
Position: Centre
Height: 5ft 9 ½ in (1.76m)
Weight: 11st 11lb (75kg)
Occupation: Civil servant
Born: 2.10.64
International debut: France 25,
Romania 6, 1992
Five Nations debut: None
Notable landmarks in rugby career: Won his Test recall with brilliant display in French Championship final, where he guided Toulouse to victory. He was promptly included in France's squad to tour Canada and New Zealand. However, in one-off Test against Canucks, with Christophe at No 10, France crashed 18–16 (Ottawa, 5.6.94). Previously this highly promising midfielder had failed to sustain his challenge for a Test place in 1992, having been initially blooded in the 25–6 defeat of Romania at Le Havre (28.5.92). He was retained for the summer tour to

France (1992)

Last Season	1 cap	0 pts
1994	Tour to Canada/NZ	
Career	5 caps	7 pts

Caps (5): 1992 R, Arg(a1,a2), SA(1) 1994 C

Points (7 – 1t,1c): 1992 Arg(a1:1t,1c)

Argentina, contributing a try and conversion to the 27–12 first-Test win in Buenos Aires (4.7.92), although he was later replaced by Christian Courveille, and retained his berth alongside Courveille for the 33–9 second-Test win the following week. Returned home with the praise of Robert Paparemborde ringing in his ears. Christophe is going to become a magnificent player in our back division, forecast the then team manager. He is an excellent link man, and his fast hands make him a very good distributor of the ball. Yet the visit of South Africa to Lyon (17.10.92) marked the beginning of the end of his season as France were downed 15–20 and Thierry Lacroix was drafted in to partner Franck Mesnel. Deylaud retained his place in the squad until Christmas, warming the bench against South Africa in Paris (24.10.92) and Argentina in Nantes (14.11.92), but was then excluded from the squad for France's victorious 1993 Five Nations Championship campaign. However, he did represent France in the inaugural World Cup Sevens tournament at Murrayfield (April 1993)

194

Dods, M.   Scotland

Full Name: Michael Dods
Club: Gala
Position: Fullback
Height: 5ft 11in (1.81m)
Weight: 12st 2lb (77kg)
Occupation: Medical Stores Manager
Born: Galashiels, 30.12.68
Family: Single
Family links with rugby: Brother (Peter) played 23 times for Scotland (1983-91, 210 points: 2t,26c,50p) and British Lions (1989)
International debut: Ireland 6, Scotland 6, 1994
Five Nations debut: As above
Best moment in rugby: Getting my first cap (v Ireland). I came on as a replacement for Gavin Hastings. I was only on the field for eight seconds and didn't even touch the ball
Worst moment in rugby: Having to come off in the above game
Most respected opponent: Mark Tetley

Scotland (1994)

Last Season	3 caps	18 pts
1994	Tour to Argentina	
Career	3 caps	18 pts

Caps (3): **1994** I(TR), Arg(1,2)

Points (16 – 6p): **1994** Arg(1:5p), Arg(2:1p)

Serious injuries: Broken collarbone (1988), nose (1990), broken thumb and hand (1993)
Best memory last season: Involvement on the international scene and winning the Melrose Sevens in April
Should rugby's amateur rules be revised? Yes
To what degree should players benefit? Should be compensated for time lost, able to earn money from off-the-field activities, and receive a wage for international duty
Should referees be rewarded? Yes, it might well improve standards
Advice for International Board: Leave the rules alone. All this chopping and changing isn't doing the game any good
Notable landmarks in rugby career: In arguably the briefest Test debut of all time, Mike came on as a temporary replacement for captain Gavin Hastings during the 6–6 draw with Ireland at Lansdowne Road (5.3.94) but it is questionable whether ball was in play at all before he returned to stands. Club form fully merited the chance, however brief. And he had waited patiently for nearly three years since touring with Scotland to North America in 1991, in

three games contributing 44 points, including 28 against Alberta. A chip off the old block, if British Lion and Scotland fullback brother Peter will excuse the 'old' reference, Mike is also a more than capable goalkicker under the glare of the international spotlight. He landed five penalty goals on his first start, against Argentina (lost 15–16, Buenos Aires, 4.6.94), and popped over a touchline penalty goal (his third of the game) to hand a 12–9 victory to Scotland A over France A (Rennes, 20.2.94). He also turned out for A team against touring All Blacks, kicking a penalty in 9–20 defeat (Glasgow, 13.11.93), and Italy, bagging all 15 points (five penalty goals) in 15–18 loss (Rovigo, 18.12.93). First played for Gala in 1987 when only 17 years old. First represented Scotland at Under-15 and Under-18 Schools grades, going on to win Under-21 honours in 1990. Toured to Argentina with Scotland (1994)

Touchlines: Golf (handicap 12), shooting, fishing

Dowd, C. New Zealand

Full Name: Craig Dowd
Province: Auckland
Club: Suburbs
Position: Loosehead prop
Height: 6ft 3 ½ in (1.91m)
Weight: 18st 11lb (115kg)
Occupation: Carpenter
Born: 26.10.69
International debut: New Zealand 20, British Lions 18, 1993
Best moment in rugby: Winning the Gallagher Shield
Best memory last season: Beating Australia to win Bledisloe Cup
Notable landmarks in rugby career: An avid pasta and potato eater, Craig announced his Test intentions by first relieving All Black Steve McDowell of his place in the Auckland scrum. That achieved, he set to work on the national slot and achieved his goal in time for the visit of the 1993 British Lions. A powerfully built, mobile player, Craig came up New Zealand's representative ladder, playing for

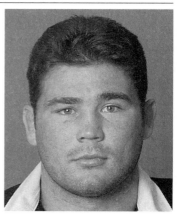

New Zealand (1993)

Last Season	7 caps	0 pts
Career	7 caps	0 pts

Caps (7): **1993** BL(1,2,3), A, WS, S, E

Points Nil

both New Zealand Colts (he was a team mate of England and Lions lock Martin Johnson) and the New Zealand XV; he was also a bench reserve against England

B in 1992. Since becoming an All Black there has been no removing him. An ever-present in the 2–1 series defeat of the Lions (his debut came in Christchurch on 12 June), Craig held his place for the eagerly awaited Bledisloe Cup showdown against World champions Australia, at Dunedin on 17 July. His front row colleagues were once again Auckland team mates Sean Fitzpatrick and Olo Brown, and the trio held firm as New Zealand raced to a satisfying 25–10 victory. Brown missed the next outing, a 35–13 defeat of Western Samoa in Auckland (31 July), but otherwise the front row remained unaltered throughout the year, as it lined up against Scotland and England on the autumn tour. England's 15–9 win, at Twickenham on 27 November, ended Craig's run of never having left the Test arena a loser. Among his targets in 1994/95 will be his first points at international level, although he could claim he is already off the mark. His one try of the British tour, at Cardiff on 4 December, came in the 25–12 win over the Barbarians in a fixture the Blacks' management had insisted on referring to as a third Test

Touchlines: Weight training, bodybuilding

Du Preez, R. J. South Africa

Full Name: Robert James Du Preez
Club: Harlequins (Durban)
Province: Natal
Position: Scrum-half
Height: 6ft (1.82m)
Weight: 14st 2lb (90kg)
Occupation: Insurance broker
Born: Potchefstroom, 19.7.63
International debut: South Africa 24, New Zealand 27, 1992
Former Provinces: Western Transvaal, Northern Transvaal
International debut: South Africa 24, New Zealand 27, 1992
Notable landmarks in rugby career: Lost Test place to Northern Transvaal's Joost van der Westhuizen when he missed 1993 tour to Argentina, having been an ever-present in No 9 Springbok jersey during home series against France and trip to Australia (where, in addition to three Tests, he also played against South Australia, Victoria and Queensland). Much

South Africa (1992)

Last Season	5 caps	0 pts
Career	7 caps	0 pts

Caps (7): **1992** NZ, A **1993** F(1,2), A(1,2,3)

Points Nil

197

travelled since leaving Potchefstroom Technical High School in his home town, having followed his Provincial debut (with Western Province in 1982) with a 78-match stint at Northern Transvaal, before moving on to Natal, where in 1992 he helped them to their second Currie Cup triumph in three years, by virtue of a 14–13 win over Transvaal at Ellis Park, Johannesburg (12.9.92). His opposite number that day was Garth Wright, with whom he toured France and England in the autumn, and who displaced him from the Test side for the three internationals. Prior to the tour, Robert was a member of the Springbok side which marked South Africa's return to legitimate international competition. Having figured in Natal's 25–43 loss to the touring All Blacks in Durban (1.8.92), he partnered Naas Botha at half-back in the 24–27 Test loss to New Zealand in Johannesburg (15.8.92). The following week he was in the side annihilated 26–3 by world champions Australia in Cape Town. Despite his failure to make the Test team in Europe, he was twice honoured with the captaincy – in the 36–15 win over Languedoc-Roussillon (Béziers, 20.10.92), and in the 15–18 loss to French Universities (Tours, 28.10.92)

Eales, J. A. Australia

Full Name: John Anthony Eales
State: Queensland
Club: Brothers
Position: Lock
Height: 6ft 7in (2.00m)
Weight: 16st 7lb (107kg)
Occupation: Promotions manager with G&E Hotels
Born: 27.6.70
Family: Jack (father), Rosa (mother), Bernadette (sister), Damian (brother), Antoinette (sister), Rosaleen (sister)
Former clubs: None (Brothers since 1988)
International debut: Australia 63, Wales 6, 1991
Best moments in rugby: First cap; 1991 World Cup; 1992 Bledisloe Cup

Worst moments in rugby: Injury v Llanelli in 1992 defeat; losing Eden Park Test to New Zealand
Most respected opponent: Ian Jones (North Auckland & New Zealand)
Serious injuries: Right a/c joint v World XV (April 1992); left shoulder v Llanelli (1992)
Should rugby's amateur rules be revised? Yes

To what degree should players benefit? If rugby is to continue to be as professional as it is, playing and training-wise (where currently we are on call for virtually 11 months of the year), it needs to give players some financial security. Many players have to make big sacrifices to go on tours **Notable landmarks in rugby career:** One of the world's foremost

Australia (1991)		
Last Season	2 caps	0 pts
Career	19 caps	4 pts

Caps (19): **1991** W(a), E(a), NZ(a1,a2) wc–Arg, WS, W(b), I, NZ(b), E(b) **1992** S(1,2), NZ(1,2,3), SA, I **1994** I(1,2)

Points (4 – 1t): 1992 S(2:1t)

lineout men, John announced himself in 1990 when winning the coveted Rothmans Medal Best-and-Fairest Award in Brisbane club rugby. His skills were appreciated by a wider audience when he toured Europe with the Emerging Wallabies, playing in the 12–12 draw with England B at Wasps. From there on he was included in the Aussies' World Cup training squad, and having made his debut in the record rout of Wales at Ballymore, he played all six matches in the Cup-winning side. His astonishing rise continued in 1992 when he was selected to play for the World XV in the Centenary Series against New Zealand. Unfortunately, he damaged a shoulder in the second Test – an injury which forced him to miss the entire 1993 campaign and kept him out until the visit to Ireland in June 1994. Started 1992 superbly when voted the Chivas Regal Man-of-the-Series against Scotland, having scored his first Test try in the 27–12 opening international win. Thereafter, toured South Africa – playing against Northern Transvaal and the Republic itself – and took his cap tally to 17 when he appeared in the 42–17 win over Ireland on 31 October. His other tour outings came against Leinster, Ulster (scored try), Swansea, Neath and Llanelli
Touchlines: Golf, cricket, reading

Edwards, N. G. B.   Scotland

Full Name: Neil George Barry
Edwards
Club: Northampton
Position: Lock
Height: 6ft 4in (1.93m)
Weight: 17st 5lb (105kg)
Occupation: Chartered surveyor
with Furnitureland of Catford
Born: Carshalton, Surrey, 20.8.64
Family: Single
Family links with rugby: Father
(Barry) played for Army and
Richmond
Former clubs: Rosslyn Park,
Harlequins
International debut: Scotland 7,
England 25, 1992
Five Nations debut: As above
Best moments in rugby:
Scotland's pushover try against
England on my debut; reaching
semi-finals with Barbarians at 1989
Hong Kong Sevens
Worst moments in rugby:
Captaining Harlequins to a 20–42
loss at the hands of Cambridge

Scotland (1992)		
Last Season	1 cap	0 pts
Career	6 caps	4 pts
Caps (6): **1992** E, I, F, W, A(1) **1994** W		
Points (4 – 1t): **1992** F(1t)		

University the day before the 1991 World Cup final; losing Scotland place
Most embarrassing moment: Singing 'Flower of Scotland' prior to Scottish
debut, I was smiling at someone in the crowd, totally lost my concentration and
started singing the wrong line
Most respected opponent: John Morrison (Bristol & England B)
Biggest influences on career: Father and Dick Best (Harlequins coach)
Serious injuries: Compressed neck vertebrae (November 1990)
Other sporting achievements: Soccer trial for Crystal Palace FC, as a
goalkeeper, when aged 18
Should rugby's amateur rules be revised? Yes
Advice for International Board: Ban wearing of long Australian Rugby
League studs, which are long, thin and much sharper, like stiletto heels, and
easily able to do severe damage to someone's back at the bottom of a ruck.
People forget that there are no rucks in RL, and we have to go to work on
Monday. Greater involvement of wives and girlfriends by Unions. Easier to get
blessing for periods away from them if they are made to feel special
Notable landmarks in rugby career: Made two entries into Test arena during

1993/94 season, and to contrasting ends. His first was to win sixth full cap, in 29–6 thrashing by Wales (Cardiff, 15.1.94), after which he was released from senior duties. The second came in colours of Scotland A, whom he powered to a 12–9 away victory over France (Rennes, 20.2.94). Had been outstanding in his debut international season in 1992, making five appearances and scoring winning try against France at Murrayfield on third start, on an afternoon in which he cleaned out not only the French lineout but also a bookmaker (£1,500) who had offered 40/1 odds against his scoring the first try. However, lost place to Damian Cronin after first-Test defeat by Australia (Sydney, 13.6.92). Spent five years with Rosslyn Park on leaving school aged 17. Made debut against Newport aged 19 when Paul Ackford left to join Harlequins. Represented England Students and British Polytechnics while studying at Oxford Poly before attending England's 1989 training camp in Portugal. The previous year he had helped Harlequins win John Player Special Cup at Twickenham in arguably best ever final against Bristol. Quins' coach Dick Best selected him for the London XV which beat the touring Wallabies, but with Messrs Ackford and Dooley firmly ensconced in the England set-up, Neil turned to his Scottish qualification (Dundonian grandparents). He impressed playing for the Anglo-Scots, Scotland B and the Junior Reds in the 1992 national trial, and was consequently one of four newcomers to be blooded in Calcutta Cup clash

Touchlines: Skiing, cricket

Ellis, M. C. G. New Zealand

Full Name: Marc Christopher Gwynne Ellis
Province: Otago
Club: University
Position: Outside-half, centre
Height: 5ft 11in (1.80m)
Weight: 13st 10lb (87kg)
Born: 8.10.71
International debut: Scotland 15, New Zealand 51, 1993
Best moment in rugby: Scoring two tries on Test debut
Worst moment in rugby: Losing to the side of my good friend/mentor Keith Quinn, St Pat's Silverstream (1989)
Most embarrassing moment: My television debut with Jase Gunn when I fell off the toy slide

Notable landmarks in rugby career: You know Marc is hungry to play for his country when his answer to 'Where would you like to play given the choice?' is 'Anywhere in the starting XV for the All Blacks would be good'. He wasn't joking, either. Having begun his provincial career

New Zealand (1993)		
Last Season	2 caps	10 pts
Career	2 caps	10 pts

Caps (2): **1993** S, E

Points (10 – 2t): **1993** S(2t)

on the wing, he toured Australia and South Africa in 1992 as a centre (making six appearances in all), and then moved to fly-half in 1993 when the All Blacks visited England and Scotland. It was in the No 10 slot that Marc made his Test bow. Having arrived in Britain as second choice behind fellow Otago tourist Stephen Bachop, by the time New Zealand ran out at Murrayfield on 20 November he was calling the shots. An impressive debut featured a brace of tries as Scotland were overwhelmed 51–15. Marc, who retained his place the following week for the 9–15 loss to England at Twickenham, made six other starts on the autumn tour, scoring against North of England (two tries), England A (dropped goal), South of Scotland (one try as a replacement) and Scotland A (one try), to finish the tour as joint leading try-scorer, on six, with Otago team-mate Jeff Wilson. Other tour outings came against the Midlands, and in Cardiff against the Barbarians – a fixture treated as a third Test match by the Kiwi management. The Blacks won 25–12. His association with the All Blacks had begun in April 1992, when he was selected for the national 'centenary' squad for the series against Ian McGeechan's World XV. The highlight of three years of provincial rugby with Otago would have to be the 37–24 defeat of the '93 Lions at Dunedin on 5 June

England's Lawrence Dallaglio charges through against Eastern Province during the tour match in Port Elizabeth.

Elwood, E. P.   Ireland

Full Name: Eric Paul Elwood
Club: Lansdowne
Position: Outside-half
Height: 6ft (1.83m)
Weight: 13st 5lb (84kg)
Occupation: Sales representative with Irish Distillers
Born: Galway, 26.2.69
Family: Single
Former club: Galwegians
International debut: Wales 14, Ireland 19, 1993
Five Nations debut: As above
Best moment in rugby: Winning first cap
Worst moments in rugby: Lansdowne's relegation from Division One of the 1991/92 All-Ireland League; losing semi-final of 1993 World Cup Sevens to Australia
Most respected opponent: Michael Lynagh (Queensland & Australia)
Biggest influences on career: Michael Casserely, Warren Gatland, Eddie O'Sullivan and Graham Taylor
Serious injuries: Chipped vertebrae in neck (1987)

Ireland (1993)

Last Season	7 caps	69 pts
1994	Tour to Australia	
Career	9 caps	92 pts

Caps (9): **1993** W, E, R **1994** F, W, E, S, A(1,2)

Points (92 – 4c,26p,2dg): **1993** W(1c,3p), E(2p,2dg), R(1c,6p) **1994** F(5p), W(5p), E(1c,2p), S(2p), A(1:1c,1p)

Other sporting achievements: Gaelic football and soccer for Galway
Best memory last season: Beating England at Twickenham
Should rugby's amateur rules be revised? Yes
To what degree should players benefit? Should be compensated for time lost, and be able to benefit from off-field activities – but no payment for playing. Too much strain on players to give required commitment and still satisfy employers. So many firms these days see rugby employees as liabilities rather than assets
Should referees be rewarded? Maybe they need some form of incentive – standards need improving
Advice for International Board: I don't know what job they do. I don't think the game is being played the way people want it to be. Not enough room on pitch, and not enough tries in Northern Hemisphere. It is very frustrating seeing

Southern Hemisphere nations enjoy benefits of more lax regulations. I like playing rugby and representing my country, but it would be nice to enjoy a similar slice of the cake. Like to see maul law refereed according to the spirit of the game and not to the letter of the law. But killing of the ball should always be penalized

Notable landmarks in rugby career: Prodigious goalkicker, who has carried Ireland's strike threat virtually single-handed for past two years. His nine starts have produced 92 points and inspired four victories, including two against England. He also kicked four penalty goals against All Blacks for Barbarians in 25–12 loss (Cardiff, 4.12.93). Having missed out on a Schools trial, Eric first wore an Ireland jersey on 30 September 1989 when on national U-21 side beaten 10–9 by Italian counterparts in Treviso. Bench reserve for following match v New Zealand U-21s (drew 13–13, 19.11.89). Connacht debut came in the same year, v Ulster. Progressed up international ladder in 1992/93 after series of impressive displays for Connacht: v Australia and throughout Inter-Provincial Championship. Missed national trial but was drafted onto Ireland bench for the visit to Dublin of France, and subsequently succeeded Niall Malone as outside-half. Headlined in games v Wales and England, not least because Ireland won both. He contributed 23 of the 36 points scored by the men in green, and was widely acclaimed. His omission from the Lions squad, named 48 hours after England's defeat in Dublin, was contentious, but he put disappointment behind him and enjoyed a fine season last time round. Twenty points against Romania (won 25–3, Dublin 14.11.93) were followed by five penalty goals against both France (lost 15–35) and Wales (lost 15–17). A further 14 points against England and Scotland ensured that he finished the five-Test 'regular' season with 64 of Ireland's 74 points

Touchlines: Gym, walking

Gavin Hastings (Scotland) and John Timu (New Zealand) dance the quick-step at Murrayfield.

Evans, I. C. — Wales

Full Name: Ieuan Cenydd Evans
Club: Llanelli
Position: Wing
Height: 5ft 10 ½ in (1.79kg)
Weight: 13st 5lb (85kg)
Occupation: Leasing executive with Autopia Contract Hire (Cwmbran)
Born: Pontardulais, 21.3.64
Family: Single
Family links with rugby: Father (John) played for Aberavon
Former club: Carmarthen Quins
International debut: France 16, Wales 9, 1987
Five Nations debut: As above
Best moments in rugby: Scoring the tries that (i) clinched Test series for 1989 Lions in Australia and (ii) beat England in Cardiff (1992)
Worst moment in rugby: New South Wales 71, Wales 8, 1991
Most respected opponent: David Campese (Randwick & Australia) – you can never let him out of your sight
Serious injuries: Recurring dislocated shoulder, broken leg
Best memory last season: Captaining Wales to Five Nations title
Should rugby's amateur rules be revised? Yes
To what degree should players benefit? Reimburse employers for employees' time spent away from work playing rugby. Employers are indirectly the sponsors of the game
Notable landmarks in rugby career: The *Rugby World & Post* 1992/93 Player of the Year, Ieuan might well have renewed the honour last season after skippering Wales to 1994 Five Nations title. Wales's 103rd captain when appointed under the management of Robert Norster and Alan Davies prior to 1991 World Cup, he became Principality's longest-serving leader when he took charge of last May's World

Wales (1987)		
Last Season	11 caps	50 pts
1994	Tour to Canada/South Seas	
Career	47 caps	92 pts
Lions 1989	3 Tests	4 pts
1993	3 Tests	0 pts

Caps (47): **1987** F, E(a), S, I(a) wc–I(b), C, E(b), NZ, A **1988** E, S, I, F, NZ(1,2) **1989** I, F, E. Lions–A(1,2,3) **1991** E, S, I, F(a), A(a), F(b) wc–WS, Arg, A(b) **1992** I, F, E, S, A **1993** E, S, I, F, J, C **1994** S, I, F, E. wc(q)–P, S, C, Fj, T, WS

Points (92 – 20t): **1987** I(a:1t) wc–C(4t) **1988** S(1t), F(1t) **1989** Lions–A(3:1t) **1991** wc–WS(1t) **1993** E(1t), I(1t), J(2t) **1994** S(1t). wc(q)–P(3t), S(3t), C(1t)

Cup qualifier in Portugal (celebrated with try hat-trick). Mission No 19 in charge (a 102–11 win) nudged him past Arthur 'Monkey' Gould, and 20th game (54–0 v Spain) produced a similar result: another three tries. Equalled Welsh try record, held jointly by Gareth Edwards and Gerald Davies, with 20th in 33–15 defeat of Canada (11.6.94). Early part of playing career severely hampered by injury – five dislocations and two operations. But played all three Tests in 1989 Lions series win (2–1) in Australia, scoring series-clinching try in final Test in Sydney (won 19–18, 15.7.89), and all three Tests in New Zealand with 1993 Lions. Missed whole of 1989/90 season through injury. Played in five matches in 1987 World Cup, scoring Welsh record-equalling four tries in 40–9 defeat of Canada, and contributed one (against Western Samoa) to Wales's 1991 Cup challenge. Scored six tries for Wales B in 1985 defeat of Spain (80–9) at Bridgend. National hero when running in winning try against England (6.2.93). Also crossed against Ireland in next Test at Arms Park (6.3.93) to account for two-thirds of Wales's entire try tally in 1992/93 season. At home, scored winning try as Llanelli beat Australia 13–9 (14.11.92) and shared in Scarlets' 1992/93 League and Cup double.
Touchlines: Tennis, cricket, squash, golf

Evans, R. L. Wales

Full Name: Richard (Ricky) Lloyd Evans
Club: Llanelli
Position: Loosehead prop
Height: 6ft 2in (1.88m)
Weight: 17st 3lb (109kg)
Occupation: Fireman in the Dyfed-Powys Brigade
Born: Cardigan, 23.6.61
Family: Married with son and daughter
Former clubs: Cardigan, Army
International debut: Wales 10, England 9, 1993
Five Nations debut: As above
Best moment in rugby: Beating England on debut in Cardiff
Worst moment in rugby: Not being included in Welsh squad for 1993 tour to Zimbabwe and Namibia

Most embarrassing moment: Coming on as replacement flanker for Llanelli, used hands to push ball back between legs at scrum
Most respected opponent: David Young (ex-Cardiff & Wales)

Serious injuries: Broken leg

Other sporting achievements: Longboat rowing for Aberporth LBC

Suggestions to improve rugby: Referees must hold tighter disciplinary reins

Notable landmarks in rugby career: Restored to national side (having been omitted from 1993 tour

Wales (1993)		
Last Season	9 caps	0 pts
1994	Tour to Canada/South Seas	
Career	13 caps	0 pts

Caps (13): **1993** E, S, I, F **1994** S, I, F, E. wc(q)–P, Sp. C, Fj, WS

Points Nil

to Zimbabwe and Namibia and two autumn internationals against Japan and Canada) and promptly played part in Wales's 1994 Five Nations title-winning run. Selectors learned their lesson and kept him in situ for World Cup qualifiers and summer tour to Canada and South Pacific. Spent nine years in Army (16–25) before playing for two years in Pembrokeshire League with Cardigan. Other causes represented are Army, Crawshays and both Wales and British Fire Brigades. Broke leg against Cambridge University in only his sixth game for Llanelli. Toured Canada with Wales B in 1989, making three appearances. Wore their colours again in 21–13 victory over North of England (Pontypool, 14.10.92), in 11–24 loss to Australia (Cardiff, 7.11.92), in 61–5 defeat of Japan (Llanelli, 29.9.93) and in 24–8 win against North of England (Pontypool, 13.10.93). Helped Llanelli beat '92 Wallabies in 13–9 win at Stradey en route to League and Cup double. Ricky, who finished fourth in the televised Strongest Man competition in 1992, made his Wales debut in 1993 Five Nations Championship as a result of Mike Griffiths's freak cycling accident in Lanzarote, in which he broke a collarbone to put himself out for campaign

Wales scrum-half Rupert Moon enjoys clean possession against France.

Farr-Jones, N. C.   Australia

Full Name: Nicholas (Nick)
Campbell Farr-Jones
State: New South Wales
Club: Sydney University
Position: Scrum-half
Height: 5ft 10in (1.78m)
Weight: 13st 3lb (84kg)
Occupation: Solicitor with Garland
Hawthorn Brahe
Born: 18.4.62
Family: Angela (wife), Jessica
(daughter)
Former clubs: None. Sydney
University since 1980
International debut: England 3,
Australia 19, 1984
Best moments in rugby: Winning
1991 World Cup; beating South
Africa by record score (26–3) in
August 1992; meeting ANC leader
Nelson Mandela during same tour
Worst moment in rugby: Losing
to 1989 British Lions
Most embarrassing moment:
Being photographed in the nude
talking to British Prime Minister
John Major
Most respected opponent: Gary
Armstrong (Jed-Forest & Scotland)
Serious injuries: None
Other sporting achievements:
Winning a chook in 1977 for the
best back-nine at the Australia Golf
Club
Suggestions to improve rugby:
On-field – administrators to consult
players, coaches and referees before
making law changes. Off-field – administrators to leave running of game to
professional marketing groups, providing the essence of rugby union is not lost

Australia (1984)

Last Season	4 caps	0 pts
Career	63 caps	37 pts

Caps (63): **1984** E, I, W, S **1985**
C(1,2), NZ, Fj(1,2) **1986** It, F,
Arg(1,2), NZ(1,2,3) **1987** SK.
wc–E, I, F, W(R). NZ, Arg(2)
1988 E(a1,a2), NZ(1,2,3), E(b),
S, It **1989** BL(1,2,3), NZ, F(1,2)
1990 F(1,2,3), US, NZ(1,2,3)
1991 W(a), E(b), NZ(a1,a2).
wc–Arg, WS, I, NZ(b), E(b)
1992 S(1,2), NZ(1,2,3), SA **1993**
NZ, SA(1,2,3)

Points (37 – 9t): **1984** S(1t) **1985**
C(1:1t), C(2:1t), Fj(1:2t) **1987**
SK(1t) **1989** F(2:1t) **1990** US(1t)
1992 NZ(3:1t)

Notable landmarks in rugby career: Retired as Australia's captain after
leading the side to a famous 26–3 win over South Africa in Cape Town. The
defeat was the heaviest ever suffered by the Springboks and victory completed
Nick's collection of scalps. However, he was persuaded to 'unretire' in 1993

(after successor Peter Slattery broke ribs playing against Tonga), saying: 'This team means too much to me for me not to make myself available if they want to play'. Played (though was not captain) in Bledisloe Cup loss to New Zealand, but bowed out (again) on high note after helping Australia edge an exciting home series against South Africa. The Wallabies' most-capped scrum-half, with 63 appearances to his name (though one came as a replacement wing), he also shares with Michael Lynagh the world-record halfback partnership of 47 games together. The seeds of a proud career were sown in 1981 when he moved into senior-grade rugby after only a year of Colts. He played for Australia Universities on tour in Britain before returning in 1984 as the Grand Slam scrum-half. An ever-popular Barbarians invitee, he was first appointed as Australian captain against England in 1988, and remained in charge until leaving the Newlands pitch on 22 August 1992

Touchlines: Golf, tennis

Field, M. J.   Ireland

Full Name: Maurice John Field
Club: Malone
Position: Centre, wing, fullback
Height: 6ft (1.83m)
Weight: 13st 2lb (84kg)
Occupation: Firefighter
Born: Greenisland, 24.2.64
Family: Gillian (wife), Rebekah (daughter)
Former club: NIFC
International debut: England 12, Ireland 13, 1994
Five Nations debut: As above
Best moment in rugby: Beating England at Twickenham on debut
Worst moment in rugby: Not being selected for Ireland's tour to New Zealand (1992)
Most respected opponent: Scott Hastings (Watsonians & Scotland)
Biggest influence on career: Mike Gibson, father and Bob Kurangi (team mate during NIFC days)
Best memory last season: Phonecall advising me of my full selection
Should rugby's amateur rules be revised? Yes

Ireland (1994)

Last Season	3 caps	0 pts
1994	Tour to Australia	
Career	3 caps	0 pts

Caps (3): **1994** E, S, A(1R)

Points Nil

209

To what degree should players benefit? Make sure we don't lose out financially through playing, that's all

Should referees be rewarded? Only as much as players; it's a recreation for us all

Advice for International Board: Allow us to compete on a level playing field with Southern Hemisphere nations; revise maul law

Notable landmarks in rugby career: Took full advantage of Test opportunity last season, helping Ireland to a two-match unbeaten run after they had started 1994 championship campaign with pair of losses. His promotion to centre berth followed injury to Vinnie Cunningham and selectors' decision to replace Bangor's Mark McCall after defeat by Wales in Dublin. So Maurice was given debut at Twickenham (19.2.94), where Ireland had not won since 1982. England were beaten 13–12 and Maurice was suitably chuffed. He retained his place for drab 6–6 home draw with Scotland (5.3.94), and was then invited to tour Australia last summer. A member of the Northern Ireland Fire Brigade, he started out with NIFC, playing for Ulster at Under-20 level in 1983. Following year, played for Ulster Under-23s, but then had to wait six years before senior provincial debut against Irish Exiles. Played in Ulster's defeat by Australia in 1992 and won first international honours in the Ireland A side beaten 20–10 by Wales counterparts at Donnybrook (4.2.94)

Touchlines: Golf (17 handicap)

Fitzpatrick, S. B. T.   New Zealand

Full Name: Sean Brian Thomas Fitzpatrick
Club: University
Province: Auckland
Position: Hooker
Height: 6ft (1.83m)
Weight: 14st 10lb (93kg)
Occupation: Marketing promotions officer
Born: Auckland, 4.6.63
Family: Bronwyn (wife)
Family links with rugby: Brian (father) won three caps as All Black five-eighth (1953 W; 1954 I, F)
International debut: New Zealand 18, France 9, 1986
Best memory in rugby: Beating Australia 30–16 in Sydney (25.7.87) – a great team performance

Earliest memory in rugby: Ball boy for my brother's team when I was three.

My father was also coach of that team – and no, my brother was not captain! **Notable landmarks in rugby career:** All Black Test hooker since 1986 and – incredibly – an ever-present since start of 1987 World Cup – a run which has taken him into third place on the list of most-capped All Blacks, two behind John Kirwan and Gary Whetton (equal on 58 appearances), the latter of whom, coincidentally, he succeeded as captain prior to the 1992 centenary series. Captaincy has rested well on his shoulders, adding a new dimension to his already immense performances. Sean, who is widely

New Zealand (1986)

Last Season	7 caps	10 pts
Career	56 caps	30 pts

Caps (56): **1986** F(a), A(1), F(b1,b2) **1987** wc–It, Fj, Arg, S, W, F. A **1988** W(1,2), A(1,2,3) **1989** F(1,2), Arg(1,2), A, W, I **1990** S(1,2), A(1,2,3), F(1,2) **1991** Arg(1,2), A(a1,a2). wc–E, US, It, C, A(b), S **1992** Wd(1,2,3), I(1,2), A(1,2,3), SA **1993** BL(1,2,3), A, WS, S, E

Points (30 – 7t): **1987** A(2t) **1989** F(2:1t) **1990** A(1:1t), A(2:1t) **1993** BL(3:1t), A(1t)

considered to be the world's premier lineout thrower, is the first Auckland hooker to pass the 100-appearance mark for the province – a total amassed since his debut in 1984. It was not until 1986 that he secured a regular provincial berth – a year which coincided with his Test debut, against France in Christchurch, while the Cavaliers were away in South Africa. He was displaced by the returning Hika Reid for the second and third Tests against the Wallabies later in the year, but reversed the roles for the tour of France, and has since resisted each and every pretender to his throne. Equalled NZ record for a hooker when he scored two tries in the 30–16 win over Australia in 1987. He was selected for New Zealand Schools in 1981, progressing to NZ Colts, whom he represented in 1983 (along with John Kirwan, Grant Fox and Murray Mexted) and captained the following year. His 1984 charges included Bernie McCahill, Frano Botica (now Wigan RL) and Paul Henderson. Captained the All Blacks on nine occasions during the 1992 tour to Australia (scoring two tries against NSW) and South Africa, in the process becoming the first New Zealander to skipper a winning side in the Republic. Despite the disappointment of Auckland finally relinquishing the Ranfurly Shield and England beating the Blacks at Twickenham, 1993 was generally another fine year for Sean. Auckland became national champions once more, New Zealand regained the Bledisloe Cup at Australia's expense, and won 12 of 13 tour games in England and Scotland

Touchlines: Golf, fishing, skin diving

Forster, S. T.　　　　New Zealand

Full Name: Stuart (Stu) Thomas
Forster
Province: Otago
Club: Southern
Position: Scrum-half
Height: 5ft 6 ½ in (1.70m)
Weight: 11st 11lb (75kg)
Born: 12.2.69
Former province: Hawke's Bay
International debut: Scotland 15,
New Zealand 51, 1993
Worst moment in rugby: Getting
thrashed by Waikato in final of 1992
New Zealand Championship
Most respected player: John Timu
– played with him at school and he
won games by himself, scoring tries
from everywhere
**Notable landmarks in rugby
career:** Renowned as a top-notch
sevens player (he played in '92
World Cup at Murrayfield) well
before the British Lions' roar was
muted in Dunedin (5.6.93) thanks
in no small measure to a superb
performance from 'Batman' (aka

New Zealand (1993)

Last Season	2 caps	0 pts
Career	2 caps	0 pts

Caps (2): **1993** S, E

Points Nil

Michael Keaton) lookalike Stu, a one-time Hawke's Bay player. An Otago side,
also including All Blacks Marc Ellis, John Timu and Arran Pene, won 37–24,
and those English and Scottish players in the Lions XV took note. The reason
was that five months later they were once again opposing the diminutive but
devastating runner as he arrived in Britain for the All Blacks' autumn tour as
one of the two selected scrum-halves. A bench reserve (behind Waikato's
Simon Crabb) for the New Zealand XV which swept their 1992 series with
England B, Stu's form in the defeats of London (won 39–12, Twickenham
23.10.93), North of England (won 27–21, Liverpool 2.11.93), England A (won
26–12, Gateshead 7.11.93) and Scotland A (won 20–9, Glasgow 13.11.93)
ensured that he displaced Wellington's Jon Preston (first choice in '93 against
the Lions, Australia and Western Samoa) from the No 9 berth for the two Tests
against Scotland (Edinburgh 20.11.93) and England (lost 9–15, Twickenham
27.11.93). He formed an all-Otago halfback partnership with Marc Ellis,
although most of his 62 provincial starts have been alongside another All Black
tourist, Stephen Bachop. A 1989 New Zealand Colt, Stu's team mates included
Craig Innes (now Leeds RL), Va'iga Tuigamala (now Wigan RL), John Timu,

Blair Larsen, Craig Dowd and English Lion Martin Johnson
Touchlines: Boogie boarding, water skiing, mountain biking, skiing, golf, tennis

---

Fox, G. J.   New Zealand

Full Name: Grant James Fox
Club: University
Province: Auckland
Position: Outside-half
Height: 5ft 9in (1.75m)
Weight: 11st 12lb (75kg)
Occupation: Sports marketing executive
Born: New Plymouth, Taranaki, 16.6.62
Family: Adele (wife), Kendall (daughter), Ryan (son)
International debut: Argentina 20, New Zealand 33, 1985
Serious injuries: Pelvis (1991)
Notable landmarks in rugby career: New Zealand's leading Test points scorer with 645 points – a total surpassed only by Australia's Michael Lynagh (813) – Grant is a former captain of New Zealand Schools, who represented NZ Colts in 1983 (along with Sean Fitzpatrick, John Kirwan and Murray Mexted). He first represented Auckland in 1982 when just 20 and has been a central figure in the Province's Ranfurly Shield monopoly since 1985 – the year in which he marked his Test debut with a dropped goal against Argentina, opposite another scoring legend, Hugo Porta (564 points). First represented the All Blacks on the 1984 tour of Fiji, when he turned out against a President's XV and an Eastern XV, scoring 27 points (3c,6p,1dg). With 126 points, Grant was the leading scorer in the 1987 World Cup, which New Zealand won. He kicked 17 points in the 29–9 final defeat of France on his home Eden Park pitch. Indeed, so impressive was his performance that, after the second World Cup, his 1987 records – total points (126), conversions (30) and penalty goals (21), as well as single-match totals for cons (ten) and pens (six) – remain supreme. His two-tournament total of 170 (126 + 44) betters second-best Lynagh by 22. If 1987 was his best-scoring year, with an average of 20 points through his seven appearances, it was closely followed by 1989 (average 17 points) and 1988 (average 15 points). Needed 35 fewer games than Don Clarke to pass the Kiwi legend's 1964 All Black record of 781 points, amassed in 89 games. His tally of well over 3,000 first-class points constitutes

another national best. Bitter at public criticism, he contemplated retirement at the end of a 1991 season undermined by a serious hip injury. Replaced by Walter Little after the first Test loss to World XV (1992), he displayed great character in returning after the Ireland series and excelling against Australia and South Africa. Brought his record-studded career to a close by steering New Zealand to a 2–1 series win over the '93 Lions and to a Bledisloe Cup victory against holders Australia. Went out with a bang, setting a then world record with seven penalty goals (and two conversions) in the 35–13 defeat of Western Samoa (Auckland 31.7.93)

New Zealand (1985)

Last Season	5 caps	69 pts
Career	46 caps	645 pts

Caps (46): **1985** Arg(1) **1987** wc–It, Fj, Arg, S, W, F. A **1988** W(1,2), A(1,2,3) **1989** F(1,2), Arg(1,2), A, W, I **1990** S(1,2), A(1,2,3), F(1,2) **1991** Arg(1,2), A(a1,a2). wc–E, It, C, A(b) **1992** Wd(1,2R), A(1,2,3), SA **1993** BL(1,2,3), A, WS

Points (645 – 1t,118c,128p,7dg): **1985** Arg(1:1dg) **1987** wc–It(8c,2p), Fj(10c,2p), Arg(2c,6p), S(2c,6p), W(7c,1p), F(1c,4p,1dg). A(1c,3p,1dg) **1988** W(1:6c), W(2:8c,2p), A(1:3c,2p), A(2:2c,1p), A(3:3c,4p) **1989** F(1:2c,3p), F(2:3c,4p), Arg(1:7c,2p), Arg(2:6c,3p), A(2c,4p), W(3c,4p), I(1c,3p) **1990** S(1:1t,4c,1p), S(2:1c,5p), A(1:1c,1p), A(2:3c,2p,1dg), A(3:2p,1dg), F(1:2c,3p,1dg), F(2:2c,6p) **1991** Arg(1:1c,5p), Arg(2:4c,4p), A(1:1c,2p), A(2:2p). wc–E(1c,4p), It(3c,3p), C(3c,1p), A(2p) **1992** Wd(1:2p), Wd(2:1c), A(1:1c,1p), A(2:2c,1p), A(3:2c,3p,1dg), SA(3c,2p) **1993** BL(1:5p), BL(2:1c), BL(3:3c,2p), A(5p), WS(2c,7p)

Jon Callard dispatches England's last-minute penalty winner against Scotland at Murrayfield.

Francis, N. P. J.   Ireland

Full Name: Neil Patrick John Francis
Club: Old Belvedere
Position: Lock
Height: 6ft 6in (1.98m)
Weight: 17st 12lb (113kg)
Occupation: Business executive with Gatehouse Finance
Born: Dublin, 17.3.64
Family: Single
Former clubs: London Irish, Manly (Aus)
International debut: Ireland 32, Tonga 9, 1987
Five Nations debut: Scotland 37, Ireland 21, 1989
Best moment in rugby: Winning 1981 Schools Cup final with Blackrock
Worst moment in rugby: Being dropped by Ireland on 1989 North American tour
Most respected opponent: Laurent Rodriguez (Dax & France)
Serious injuries: Broken vertebrae (out for two years)
Other sporting achievements: Javelin for Ireland (national junior and senior champion)

Ireland (1987)

Last Season	7 caps	5 pts
1994	Tour to Australia	
Career	27 caps	9 pts

Caps (27): **1987** wc–T, A **1988** WS, It **1989** S **1990** E, F, W **1991** E, S, Na(1,2) wc–Z, J, S, A **1992** W, E, S **1993** F, R **1994** F, W, E, S, A(1,2)

Points (9 – 2t): **1988** WS(1t) **1994** A(2:1t)

Notable landmarks in rugby career: Returned to front line in 1993/94 after injury had decimated the previous season from his viewpoint, and enjoyed a magnificent tour of Australia last summer. A previously enigmatic player, who had been in and out of favour since his debut in 1987 World Cup, he was consistently outstanding down under, and grabbed his second international try in the 32–18 second-Test loss to Sydney (11.6.94). Represented Irish Schools five times (1981-82), but back injury meant no representative rugby for four years from the age of 19, by which time he had already won Leinster Senior Cup medal with Blackrock. Did not represent Leinster until 1986. Scored try for Ireland Under-25s against Canada in 1986. Rejoined Blackrock from London Irish in 1989 and moved on to Old Belvedere last season. After debut in '87, not called upon again until October 1988, when scored only international try to date against touring Western Samoans. Sole Irish representative in Home Unions team which played Rest of

Europe at Twickenham in 1990 Romania Appeal match. Ever-present in 1991/92 season, including each 1991 World Cup tie, until final Five Nations match in Paris when Brian Rigney returned, thus breaking Neil's 11-game streak. Missed Ireland's tour to New Zealand in 1992, but visited Namibia (1991) and Australia (1994)

Fuls, H. T. South Africa

Full Name: Heinrich Theodorus Fuls
Club: RAU
Province: Transvaal
Position: Centre
Height: 6ft 3in (1.90m)
Weight: 14st 2lb (90kg)
Born: Bloemfontein, 8.3.71
International debut: South Africa 24, New Zealand 27, 1992
Notable landmarks in rugby career: Formed an unbreakable midfield partnership with Natal's Pieter Müller in 1993, during which the pair played in all of seven Springbok Tests. After home series defeat by France, Heinrich toured to Australia, making appearances outside Test arena against Western Australia, New South Wales and Queensland. On to Argentina, where he played in five of the six games, missing 27–28 loss to Buenos Aires and scoring try in 40–26 defeat of Rosario. A product of Grey College, Bloemfontein, he was one of the 17

South Africa (1992)

Last Season	7 caps	0 pts
Career	8 caps	0 pts

Caps (8): **1992** NZ(R) **1993** F(1,2), A(1,2,3), Arg(1,2)

Points Nil

players accorded the honour of carrying the South African banner back into international rugby. A bench reserve for the historic visit of New Zealand to Ellis Park, Johannesburg (15.8.92), Heinrich was brought into the fray as a last-minute replacement for Transvaal team mate James Small. The previous week he had played on the left wing as Junior South Africa went down 10–25 to the All Blacks in Pretoria. He missed out on the action against Australia (22.8.92), but returned to Ellis Park for the Currie Cup final (12.9.92) and scored Transvaal's only try in a 14–13 defeat by Natal. His next stop was France, where he appeared in five of Springboks' seven provincial engagements before crossing English Channel and turning out against England B (won 20–16,

Bristol, 7.11.92) as a 70th-minute replacement for Pieter Müller, and against Northern Division (won 19–3, Leeds, 10.11.92)

Gallart, P.   France

Full Name: Philippe Gallart
Club: Béziers
Position: Prop
Height: 6ft ½ in (1.85m)
Weight: 17st 5lb (105kg)
Occupation: IBM computer representative
Born: 18.12.62
Former club: Pezenas
International debut: France 6, Romania 12, 1990
Five Nations debut: Scotland 10, France 6, 1992
Notable landmarks in rugby career: Returned to international fray in 1994 Championship when Laurent Seigne, who had replaced him under identical circumstances in 1993, suffered injury. Philippe had been recalled in place of Philippe Gimbert against Scotland (7.3.92) for first time since being sent off by Clive Norling for punching Tim Gavin in the 48th minute of the 28–19 third-Test win against Australia in Sydney (30.6.90). For that misdemeanour a four-month

France (1990)

Last season	3 caps	0 pts
Career	15 caps	0 pts

Caps (15): **1990** Ro, A(1,2R,3) **1992** S, I, R, Arg(a1,a2), SA(1,2), Arg(b) **1994** I, W, E

Points Nil

suspension was meted out, ensuring that he played no part in the 1991 Five Nations campaign when only England stood between France and a fifth Grand Slam. Despite touring to North America in summer of '91, he was no less redundant, and failed to make the 26-man World Cup squad. However, the Paris debacle, which wrote Gimbert and Lascube out of the international script, allowed Gallart to restore a representative career which had begun, in Stade Patrice Brocas, Auch, with defeat against Romania (24.5.90). Injury forced him from the field prematurely, to be replaced by Pascal Ondarts, although he returned Down Under to play in two and a half Tests against the Wallabies. Having been voted 1992 Prop of the Year by French rugby writers, he promptly lost his place to Merignac's Seigne for 1993 Five Nations Championship, but only because of a serious calf injury

217

Galthie, F.   France

Full Name: Fabien Galthie
Club: Colomiers
Position: Scrum-half
Height: 5ft 10 ½ in (1.80m)
Weight: 12st 4lb (78kg)
Occupation: Executive
Born: Cahors, 20.3.69
International debut: Romania 21, France 33, 1991
Five Nations debut: Wales 9, France 12, 1992
Former club: Tournefeuille
Notable landmarks in rugby career: Became the first player from the Colomiers club (Parisian suburb) to be capped when, to the surprise of many, he succeeded Pierre Berbizier at No 9. It was widely anticipated that Henri Sanz, a former France B captain and long-standing understudy to le patron, would step up, but erstwhile coach Daniel Dubroca thought differently and successor Berbizier himself agreed. Consequently, Fabien was given his debut in Bucharest (22.6.91) and remained intact for

France (1991)

Last Season	3 caps	0 pts
Career	14 caps	9 pts

Caps (14): **1991** Ro, US(1) wc–Ro, Fj, C, E **1992** W, E, S, R, Arg(b) **1993** I, W, E

Points (9 – 2t): **1992** R(1t), Arg(b:1t)

eight of the next ten internationals, before Toulon's Aubin Hueber took over for Ireland's Championship visit to Paris (21.3.92) following mounting criticism of the incumbent. In his defence, Fabien was unable to settle into a halfback understanding because of the constantly changing identity of his stand-off, with Didier Camberabero, Thierry Lacroix and Alain Penaud all given a shot. He even captained France for part of the Five Nations game against England (15.2.92) when Philippe Sella was injured. Saw little Test action in 1992/93 (Hueber preferred), though was a try-scorer in both games he did play – against Romania (won 25–6, Le Havre, 28.5.92) and Argentina (lost 20–24, Nantes, 14.11.92). He was one of eight casualties after the Pumas' historic first win on French soil. Was bench reserve for both Tests against South Africa in summer of 1993, and was recalled for '94 Championship before again losing place, for final game against Scotland, to Perpignan's Alain Macabiau

Galwey, M. J.   Ireland

Full Name: Michael Joseph Galwey
Club: Shannon
Position: Lock, flanker
Height: 6ft 4in (1.95m)
Weight: 17st 5lb (110kg)
Occupation: Sales representative
with Hibernian Business Equipment
Born: County Kerry, 8.10.66
Family: Joan (wife)
Former club: Castle Island
International debut: Ireland 13,
France 21, 1991
Five Nations debut: As above
Best moments in rugby: Winning
first cap against French in Dublin
(2.2.91); scoring try in win against
England (20.3.93)
Worst moment in rugby: Losing
1988/89 Munster Cup final to
Constitution
Most respected opponent: Zinzan
Brooke (NZ)
Serious injuries: Damaged Achilles
tendon, knee ligaments (1992)
Other sporting achievements:
Winner of All-Ireland Gaelic
Football medal with Kerry in 1986
Best memories last season:
Ireland's two Championship wins

Ireland (1991)

Last Season	5 caps	0 pts
1994	Tour to Australia	
Career	19 caps	5 pts

Lions 1993

Caps (19): **1991** F, W, Na(2R) wc–J
1992 E, S, F, NZ(1,2), A **1993** F,
W, E, R **1994** F, W, E, S, A(1)

Points (5 – 1t): **1993** E(1t)

and Lions selection – win over England especially (We love beating England)
Should rugby's amateur rules be revised? Yes
To what degree should players benefit? We should be compensated, be
allowed to benefit from the game off the field, and receive a wage for
international duty. Why not?
Should referees be rewarded? Definitely. Referees are under a lot of
pressure, but if there was more in it for them, perhaps you would get a better
standard
Advice for International Board: There should be international rules that
apply across the board. The advantages that the Southern Hemisphere have
should be enjoyed by all
Notable landmarks in rugby career: British Lion status in 1993 (though he
was unable to win a Test place) was fitting reward for a memorable 1992/93
season, highlighted by his match-winning try against England in Dublin. Nick

Popplewell was the only other Irishman in the original Lions selection. A campaign which had begun with two Tests in New Zealand (1992) ended back in the Land of the Long White Cloud, albeit as a flanker. Selected to play with Munster U-20 whilst a member of Castle Island, he took possession of a Munster Senior Cup medal in three successive seasons, and was awarded a Shannon RFC cap for the achievement. Played for Ireland U-25s in wins over US Eagles (12–10, Limerick, 10.3.90) and Spain (36–17, Limerick, 8.9.90). First called into Irish squad for 1988 tour of France, but did not break into the senior team until the 1991 Five Nations Championship, playing against France and Ireland, having warmed the bench in season opener against Argentina. Made B debut in 1989 against Scotland at Murrayfield (drew 22–22, 9.12.89), and added caps against Argentina (scoring try), Scotland and England in 1990/91. Toured with Ireland to Namibia (1991), New Zealand (1992) and Australia (1994), the latter after a Test season in which he was ever-present. But lost place to Gabriel Fulcher for second Test in Sydney
Touchlines: Fishing the Kerry Lakes, golf

Gavin, B. T. Australia

Full Name: Bryant Timothy (Tim) Gavin
State: New South Wales
Clubs: Eastern Suburbs (Aus), Mediolanum Milan (It)
Position: No 8, lock
Height: 6ft 5in (1.96m)
Weight: 16st 12lb (107kg)
Occupation: Rugby development officer
Born: 20.11.63
Family: Single
Former clubs: None. Easts (Sydney) since 1983
International debut: Australia 19, New Zealand 19, 1988
Best moment in rugby: Beating England 40–15 at Sydney in 1991
Worst moment in rugby: Sustaining knee injury in club game before 1991 World Cup, which forced me to miss tournament
Most embarrassing moment: Being sidestepped by a grey-haired Italian at least ten years older than me
Most respected opponent: Wayne Shelford (New Zealand)
Serious injuries: Knee reconstruction (1991), thigh injury (1992)

Suggestions to improve rugby: On-field – change the tackle law, as these days players are picked because of their ability to kill the ball. Off-field – there must be financial reward for the time players put in at international level. Gone are the days of twice-a-week training and playing on the Saturday with a few beers afterwards **Notable landmarks in rugby career:** Debut was against All Blacks in 1988, but it was a further two years before the second-row turned No 8 (with more than a little help from

Australia (1988)

Last Season	10 caps	15 pts
Career	32 caps	35 pts

Caps (32): **1988** NZ(2,3), S, It(R) **1989** NZ(R), F(1,2) **1990** F(1,2,3), US, NZ(1,2,3) **1991** W(a), E(a), NZ(a1) **1992** S(1,2), SA, I, W **1993** T, NZ, SA(1,2,3), C, F(1,2) **1994** I(1,2)

Points (35 – 8t): **1990** F(2:1t), US(1t) **1991** W(a:2t), NZ(a1:1t) **1993** T(1t), F(1:1t), F(2:1t)

national coach Bob Dwyer) shook off the challenge of Steve Tuynman to secure a regular berth. Once in the side he wasted little time attracting a host of admirers, not least the Australian Society of Rugby Writers who voted him their Player of the Year in 1990. Tim was a racing certainty for the Aussies' 1991 World Cup squad before sustaining a knee injury in club colours and having to watch the crowning glory via satellite back home in Oz. Injury continued to frustrate him in 1992, when a bruised thigh kept him out of the 2–1 Bledisloe Cup series win. He recovered in time to tour South Africa, and made a wonderful start in the Republic, scoring two tries as the Wallabies downed Western Transvaal 46–13 in Potchefstroom (11.8.92). He did not reappear until the Test match in Cape Town (22.8.92), where the Wallabies handed the Springboks a frightful beating (26–3). From there he toured Ireland and Wales, playing in both internationals in addition to the wins over Leinster, Ulster (two tries), Wales B and the Barbarians, and the losses to Swansea and Llanelli. Stepped up his try-scoring rate in an injury-free 1993, touching down against Tonga and in both Tests of the shared autumn series against France
Touchlines: Fishing, skiing

Geoghegan, S. P.   Ireland

Full Name: Simon Patrick
Geoghegan
Club: London Irish
Position: Wing
Height: 6ft 1in (1.86m)
Weight: 13st (83kg)
Occupation: Trainee solicitor with
Rosling King
Born: Barnet, Herts, 1.9.68
Family: Single
Former club: Wasps (Colts)
International debut: Ireland 13,
France 21, 1991
Five Nations debut: As above
Best moment in rugby: Scoring try
on second full international
appearance for Ireland in 21–21
draw with Wales (16.2.91)
Worst moment in rugby: Seeing
Australia's Michael Lynagh score
last-gasp try to deny us victory in
1991 World Cup quarter-final
Most respected opponent: David
Campese (NSW & Australia)
Best memory last season: Scoring
try against England at Twickenham
**Should rugby's amateur rules be
revised?** Yes
**To what degree should players
benefit?** Both players and their

Ireland (1991)

Last Season	7 caps	10 pts
1994	Tour to Australia	
Career	23 caps	26 pts

Caps (23): **1991** F, W, E, S, Na(1)
wc–Z, S, A **1992** E, S, F, A **1993**
S, F, W, E, R **1994** F, W, E, S,
A(1,2)

Points (26 – 6t): **1991** W(1t), E(1t),
S(1t) wc–Z(1t) **1993** R(1t) **1994**
E(1t)

employers should be compensated fully for time lost to rugby. Favour allowing
off-field activities and also a wage for international games
Should referees be rewarded? Yes they should get a wage, but I don't think
this will help improve standards. Most are quite professional anyway. Most
problems stem from the revision of laws
Advice for International Board: I don't really know what they do. I have no
contact with them. Communications between Unions and players need to be
improved. Each Union has a different interpretation, which is unfair. There
should be uniformity
Notable landmarks in rugby career: Simon's return to form in 1993/94 was
a Godsend for Ireland. Without him the Irish wouldn't have scored a try all
season. With him, they managed two – against Romania and England – and you
don't need to be an Einstein to know which was the best received. Would have

added a third in second Test against Australia (11.6.94), but referee Joel Dume inexplicably chalked it off. Missed Ireland's tour to New Zealand in 1992, but returned to side for visit of world champions Australia to Dublin. Failed to emulate his previous scoring exploits in that game, or in his subsequent outings in the 1993 Five Nations Championship. Represented Ireland at Under-25, Students, B and full level. Quickly rose to prominence, with try-scoring debuts for Ireland U-25 (36–17 v Spain, Limerick, 8.9.90) and Ireland B (27–12 v Argentina, Limerick, 20.10.90). Quality inter-provincial performances for Connacht sped his progress into the senior national XV, for whom he opposed the Bayonne Express, Patrice Lagisquet, on his debut against France at Lansdowne Road (2.2.91). Scored tries in next three internationals, against Wales, Ireland and Scotland. Toured Namibia (1991) and Australia (1994), and played in 1991 World Cup, scoring in 55–11 World Cup defeat of Zimbabwe

Touchlines: Soccer (West Ham fan), cinema, theatre

Gonzales, J.-M.   France

Full Name: Jean-Michel Gonzales
Club: Bayonne
Position: Hooker, prop
Height: 5ft 7 ½ in (1.72m)
Weight: 13st 10lb (88kg)
Occupation: Salesman
Born: Bayonne, 10.7.67
International debut: Argentina 12, France 27, 1992
Five Nations debut: None
Former club: Cambo
Notable landmarks in rugby career: Until Jean-François Tordo's switch from flanker prior to the 1993 Five Nations Championship, France seemed unsure as to who they wanted to perform their hooking duties. Jean-Pierre Genet, the Racing Club de France rake, lost the

jersey on tour in Argentina, having done the honours against Romania at Le Havre in May, and coach Pierre Berbizier instead invited Jean-Michel to put in a bid. The Bayonne man played in both Tests in Buenos Aires against a poor Pumas side, and kept the job through the two-Test series with South Africa, despite the 15–20 loss France suffered at Lyon (17.10.92). But his time was nearly up. Had France not allowed Argentina, now themselves on tour, a historic first victory on French soil at Nantes on 14 November, he might have survived. As it was the Pumas won 24–20, and the hooker, despite scoring one of the home side's three tries, was one of eight casualties as the selectors wielded the broom. He did not reappear again subsequently, although he was granted a place on the bench at Parc des Princes (20.3.93) to watch France beat Wales 26–10 and clinch the inaugural Five Nations Cup. Reappeared at loosehead prop against Romania in Bucharest (20.5.93), where another serious injury to Tordo paved the way for Jean-Michel to reassert himself. He played the next nine Tests, and then toured to Canada and New Zealand last summer

France (1992)

Last Season	10 caps	0 pts
1994	Tour to Canada/NZ	
Career	16 caps	5 pts

Caps (16): 1992 Arg(a1,a2), SA(1,2), Arg(b) 1993 R(a), SA(1,2), R(b), A(1,2) 1994 I, W, E, S, C

Points (5 – 1t): Arg(b:1t)

Gordon, S. B.   New Zealand

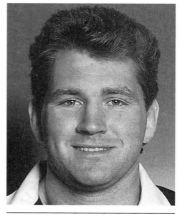

Full Name: Steven Bryan Gordon
Province: Waikato
Club: Taupiri
Position: Lock
Height: 6ft 6in (1.98m)
Weight: 17st 7lb (111kg)
Born: Te Awamutu, 16.6.67
International debut: Scotland 15, New Zealand 51, 1993
Best moment in rugby: Man-of-the-match award on debut for Waikato against Wellington as a 19-year-old
Worst moment in rugby: Missing 1992 All Black trial through injury
Most respected player: Colin Meads – legendary figure
Notable landmarks in rugby career: Ended a seemingly endless wait for his first New Zealand cap when partnering North Auckland's Ian Jones in the engine room against Scotland at Murrayfield (20.11.93). It was a satisfying moment after four All Black tours without a Test

New Zealand (1993)

Last Season	2 caps	0 pts
Career	2 caps	0 pts

Caps (2): 1993 S, E

Points Nil

appearance, mostly as deputy to Gary Whetton, New Zealand's most-capped player of all time. Some misfortune that: Whetton 58 caps, Gordon nil. Played five matches on the 1989 tour of Canada, Wales and Ireland under the captaincy of Wayne Shelford, appearing against British Columbia, Swansea, Newport, Munster and Ulster. One of the few players who attended the 1991 World Cup (in Britain and France) without getting a game, front-jumping Steve enjoyed greater success at provincial level. He helped Waikato, whom he first represented in 1987, to win the 1992 New Zealand Championship, beating Otago 40–5 in the final (Hamilton, 4.10.92), and then contributed mightily to the ending of Auckland's eight-year grip on the Ranfurly Shield the following year, in addition to sending the British Lions packing with tails firmly between legs, trounced 38–10 (Hamilton, 29.6.93). Not surprisingly, he was invited to tour England and Scotland in the autumn, and he established himself as a first choice from day one. Appearances in the victories against London (39–12, Twickenham, 23.10.93), South West England (19–15, Redruth, 30.10.93), England A (26–12, Gateshead, 7.11.93), South of Scotland (84–5, Gala, 10.11.93) and Scotland A (20–9, Glasgow, 13.11.93) served as a prelude to engagements in the two Tests, as well as the unofficial third Test against the Barbarians (won 25–12, Cardiff, 4.12.93)

Touchlines: Diving, fishing, water-skiing, skiing, basketball, eating out

---

Graou, S. France

Full Name: Stephane Graou
Club: Auch
Position: Prop, hooker
Height: 5ft 10in (1.78m)
Weight: 16st 6lb (100kg)
Occupation: Commercial officer
Born: Auch, 1.5.66
International debut: France 20, Argentina 24, 1992
Five Nations debut: None
Notable landmarks in rugby career: As storming starts to Test careers go, Stephane's must rate somewhere down the list, which is a pity, because he worked hard to put himself into the frame. A member of the French squad which won the 1988 Students World Cup, he

waited two years before touring Namibia with a French development squad. Finally he got his shot at the big time when selected to tour Argentina in 1992 with the senior squad, but rather than exploit the opportunity he had himself sent off against Cuyo, having come on as a replacement in the 30–32 loss in Mendoza (30.6.92). In all, he appeared in four of the eight tour games, but remained uncapped until the Pumas visited Nantes on 14 November. At half-time in a Test which was to make history for all the wrong reasons as far as France was concerned, he entered the fray as replacement for Philippe Gallart. But Argentina won 24–20 to register their first ever victory on French soil, and Stephane returned

France (1992)

Last Season	4 caps	0 pts
Career	5 caps	0 pts

Caps (5): **1992** Arg(b:R) **1993** SA(1,2), R(b), A(2R)

Points Nil

from whence he came. Merignac's Laurent Seigne was presented with the No 3 jersey for the 1993 Five Nations Championship, while the Auch skipper had to make do with replacement duties throughout the triumphant campaign, to add to those he carried out in South Africa's two-Test visit in October. It was against the 1993 Springboks that he returned, playing in both Tests on the summer tour. However, he lost his place to old foe Seigne after helping trounce Romania 51–0 in Brive (9.10.93). His final appearance of the term came as a 75th-minute replacement for Seigne in the second Test against Australia in Paris (6.11.93)

Griffiths, M.   Wales

Full Name: Michael Griffiths
Club: Cardiff
Position: Loosehead prop
Height: 5ft 11in (1.81m)
Weight: 16st 10lb (106kg)
Occupation: Self-employed builder with G D Griffiths, Rhondda (will go anywhere!)
Born: Tonypandy, 18.3.62
Family: Anne (wife), Joel Michael (son) and Luc Rhys (son)
Family links with rugby: Brother plays for Ystrad Rhondda
Former clubs: Ystrad Rhondda, Bridgend
International debut: Wales 24, Western Samoa 6, 1988
Five Nations debut: Scotland 23, Wales 7, 1989

Best moment in rugby: Winning first Welsh cap against touring Samoans (12.11.88)
Worst moments in rugby: Wales losing 6–34 to England at Twickenham (18.2.90); breaking collarbone in freak cycling accident and missing 1992/93

international season

Most embarrassing moment: Twice having to change shorts against France (1991/92) in front of the Princess of Wales

Most respected opponents: Jeff Probyn (Wasps & England) for his technique, and Iain Milne (Heriot's FP & Scotland) for his size and strength

Biggest influence on career: Ian Stephens and Merideth James (Bridgend)

Serious injuries: Broken ribs, fractured arm, twisted shoulder muscles, damaged ankle and knee ligaments

Other sporting achievements: Accomplished soccer player (centre-back)

Should rugby's amateur rules be revised? Yes

Advice for International Board: Abandon maul law – good mauling is an art. Look after players better. After all, they are the people who draw the crowds

Notable landmarks in rugby career: Mike's penchant for mountain biking wrecked his international hopes in 1992/93 when he suffered a broken collarbone as a result of a collision with Anthony Clement and Colin Stephens in a freak accident on Lanzarote's mountain roads in January during Wales's preparations for the 1993 Five Nations campaign. So, having propped on the loosehead side in the 6–23 loss to Australia in Cardiff (21.11.92), not forgetting against Italy on 7 October in a non-cap affair, his Test season was over until his return on last summer's tour of Zimbabwe and Namibia, where he appeared in all three Tests. Retained berth on return home, figuring against Japan and Canada, but was one of old guard swept from office following Canadian victory. Started career in back row but moved to front of scrum shortly before joining Bridgend. Moved to Cardiff for new challenges, and found them: playing for Crawshays, Wales B (in 12–18 loss to France B, Brecon, 29.10.88), Wales and 1989 Lions. Despite failing to oust David Sole in Test side, he played in six of the Lions' 12 games, including the final game (as a replacement) against the ANZAC XV. Played at tighthead against Barbarians (6.10.90). Only Welsh representative in Home Unions team which played Rest of Europe at Twickenham on behalf of Romania Appeal (won 43–18, 22.4.90). Missed the 1991 tour to Australia, but was quickly recalled for the duration of the World Cup and 1992 Five Nations Championship. Bench reserve for Barbarians against 1993 All Blacks (Cardiff, 4.12.93)

Touchlines: Mountain biking (!)

Wales (1988)		
Last Season	2 caps	0 pts
Career	25 caps	0 pts

Lions 1989

Caps (25): **1988** WS, Ro **1989** S, I, F, E, NZ **1990** F, E, Na(1,2), Ba **1991** I, F(a), F(b) wc–WS, Arg, A(b) **1992** I, F, E, S, A **1993** Z(1,2), Na, J, C

Points Nil

Guscott, J. C.   England

Full Name: Jeremy Clayton Guscott
Club: Bath
Position: Centre
Height: 6ft 1in (1.86m)
Weight: 13st 5lb (85kg)
Occupation: Marketing co-ordinator with British Gas
Born: Bath, 7.7.65
Family: Jayne (wife) and Imogen (daughter)
International debut: Romania 3, England 58, 1989
Five Nations debut: England 23, Ireland 0, 1990
Best moment in rugby: Try scored for 1989 Lions v Australia in second Test
Worst moment in rugby: Being dropped by Bath for semi-finals of 1989/90 Pilkington Cup
Most embarrassing moment: Any time I miss a tackle
Most respected opponent: All of them
Biggest influence on career: S J Halliday (ex-Harlequins & England)
Should rugby's amateur rules be revised? Yes
To what degree should players benefit? Allow players to earn money through off-field activities. The situation is improving, but there remains no overall consensus: each Union applies the rules as they see fit. The International Board should insist the same applies worldwide, but they seem to back away from confrontation

Advice for International Board: Reduce amount of offences in lineout, there must be 100-odd, when there should be no more than five or six, and it is such an annoying part of the game. Scrap 90-degree scrum wheel law

Notable landmarks in rugby career: Long-term groin injury ruled Jerry out of entire 1993/94 season and left him with no choice but to watch Bath team mate Phil de Glanville fill his boots throughout the campaign. Frustration

England (1989)		
Last Season	0 caps	0 pts
Career	28 caps	73 pts
Lions 1989	2 Tests	4 pts
1993	3 Tests	0 pts

Caps (28): **1989** Ro, Fj. Lions–A(2,3) **1990** I, F, W, S, Arg(b) **1991** W, S, I, F, Fj, A(a) wc–NZ, It, F, S, A(b) **1992** S, I, F, W, C, SA **1993** F, W, S, I. Lions–NZ(1,2,3)

Points (73 – 16t,2dg): **1989** Ro(3t), Fj(1t). Lions–A(2:1t) **1990** I(1t), F(1t), S(1t), Arg(b:2t) **1991** A(a:1t) wc–It(2t) **1992** S(1dg), I(1t), C(1t), SA(1t) **1993** W(1dg), S(1t)

doubtless heightened by fact that Bath won league and cup double in his absence. Selected to tour South Africa with England last summer, but had to withdraw as still unfit. An automatic selection for the 1993 Lions (playing in all three Tests) after super 1992/93 season, in which he bagged tries against Canada, South Africa and Scotland, and dropped a goal in defeat by Wales in Cardiff. For many, though, his most memorable contribution of the campaign was his part in the wonderful move which led to Rory Underwood's try against the Scots (6.3.93). Stuart Barnes' break and divine pass allowed Jerry to stretch his legs like the thoroughbred he is, unravel the tartan defence and then release Underwood. Started out with Bath's mini-section as a wing, aged seven. Meteoric rise in 1989 brought two caps for England B, three tries on full England debut in Bucharest, and one invitation from the British Lions (before capped by England). Scored crucial try in Brisbane (second Test, won 19–12, 8.7.89) to bring Lions back into the series, which they went on to win 2–1. Ever-present throughout England's back-to-back Grand Slams (1991-92), and wore No 12 jersey in 1991 World Cup final, having previously toured Australia (1991). Toured New Zealand with World XV (April 1992), playing in first two Tests, including famous 28–14 first-Test defeat of All Blacks. Collected fourth Pilkington Cup winners medal in 1992 to add to those collected in '87, '89 and '90

Touchlines: Golf

Hall, J. P. England

Full Name: Jonathan Peter Hall
Club: Bath
Position: Flanker, No 8
Height: 6ft 3in (1.90m)
Weight: 16st 4lb (99kg)
Occupation: Insurance executive with Colonial and Mutual
Born: Bath, 13.3.62
Family: Single
Family links with rugby: Father (Peter) and grandfather (Harry Vowles) played for Bath
International debut: Scotland 18, England 6, 1984
Five Nations debut: As above
Best moment in rugby: Winning first England cap and winning 1984 John Player Cup final (10–9 v Bristol)

Worst moment in rugby: Knee cartilage injury sustained during England training week in Lanzarote (1991) that required operation and put paid to international hopes for season

Most embarrassing moment: Playing in England Under-23 trial at Bisham Abbey on pitch which also had soccer markings. I ran to try-line and triumphantly touched ball down, only to discover I was still five metres short

Most respected opponent: Jeff Squire (ex-Pontypool & Wales)

Serious injuries: Knee cartilage (1990/91)

England (1984)

Last Season	1 cap	0 pts
Career	21 caps	8 pts

Caps (21): **1984** S(R), I, F, SA(1,2), A **1985** R, F, S, I, W, NZ(1,2) **1986** W, S **1987** I, F, W, S **1990** Arg(b) **1994** S

Points (8 – 2t): **1985** NZ(2:1t) **1990** Arg(b:1t)

Advice for International Board: Guidelines regarding amateurism must be clearly marked out. No grey areas, but black and white. Standards of refereeing worldwide must fall into line. Present situation (interpretations differing so markedly between northern and southern hemispheres) is both frustrating and dangerous

Notable landmarks in rugby career: First represented England as a 21-year old in 1984, having by-passed England B recognition. But after collecting 19 caps in the next three years, the remaining two caps took a painfully long time to arrive. Not until the autumn of 1990 was this most dependable of players accorded the honour of turning out again, and he celebrated with a try as Argentina were routed 51–0 at Twickenham (3.11.90). But just when he thought he was back in the fold, Lady Luck turned turned her back on him. Participating in a New Year training week in Lanzarote, John sustained knee ligament damage and was instantly ruled out of the international equation. However, he refused to quit, and fought his way back to the top last season after leading England A's tour to Canada in the summer of 1993, playing in both non-cap Tests. As captain of Bath he inspired the league and cup double, and he was appointed England A skipper for the match against New Zealand (Gateshead 7.11.93), which ended in a 26–12 defeat. He climbed the last rung of the representative ladder when returning to the full side for the start of the Five Nations Championship. But again there was disappointment, as he was made a scapegoat for England's poor showing at Murrayfield, where only Jon Callard's injury-time penalty goal rescued the Calcutta Cup

Touchlines: Hot-air ballooning, cycling

Hall, M. R.   Wales

Full Name: Michael Robert Hall
Club: Cardiff
Positions: Centre, wing
Height: 6ft 1in (1.86m)
Weight: 15st 3lb (96kg)
Occupation: Chartered surveyor with Cooke and Arkwright (Cardiff)
Born: Bridgend, 13.10.65
Family: Single
Former clubs: Bridgend, Maesteg, Cambridge University
International debut: New Zealand 52, Wales 3, 1988
Five Nations debut: Scotland 23, Wales 7, 1989
Best moments in rugby: Selection for 1989 British Lions; 1990 Hong Kong Sevens with Barbarians
Worst moments in rugby: Every time I go to Twickenham!
Most embarrassing moment: England 34, Wales 6 (record defeat at Twickenham, 17.2.90)
Most respected opponent: Philippe Sella (France)
Biggest influence on career: Brian Nicholas (coach at Bridgend)
Serious injuries: Hamstring tears
Other sporting achievements: Schoolboy honours at county level in soccer, basketball and cricket
Should rugby's amateur rules be revised? Yes, to clear up ambiguities in laws on amateurism

Wales (1988)		
Last Season	8 caps	25 pts
1994	Tour to Canada/South Seas	
Career	33 caps	33 pts
Lions 1989	1 Test	0 pts

Caps (33): **1988** NZ(R1,2), WS, Ro **1989** S, I, F, E, NZ. Lions–A(1) **1990** F, E, S **1991** A(a), F(b) wc–WS, Arg, A(b) **1992** I, F, S, A **1993** E, S, I **1994** S, I, F, E. wc(q)–P, Sp. C, T

Points (33 – 9t): **1989** S(1t), E(1t) **1994** wc(q)–P(3t). C(2t)

To what degree should players benefit? Players must be better looked after, with more sympathy from the Unions with regard to employers etc
Advice for International Board: Too many of the new rules are half-measures. The mauling rule encourages players to kill the ball. The lineout shambles still needs addressing
Notable landmarks in rugby career: Captained Cardiff to 1993/94 Swalec Cup triumph, having shared in Waless 1994 Five Nations Championship win weeks earlier. And finished excellent campaign by rediscovering try-scoring touch, with try hat-trick in World Cup qualifier against Portugal (won 102–11,

Lisbon, 17.5.94) and brace in 33–15 defeat of Canada (Toronto, 11.6.94). A 1989 Lion who failed to retain his place on 1993 tour, though not helped by being dropped by Wales for their final Five Nations game in Paris. Before that had started season on wing against Italy XV at Cardiff Arms Park (won 43–12, 7.10.92), before reverting to centre in Wales B side beaten 24–11 by Australia (7.11.92). He was in the same position when touring Wallabies met first-choice Welsh side, and retained his place through England, Scotland and Ireland games. Past captain of British Universities, Welsh Students and Wales U-21s. Two Blues at Cambridge (1987, 1988). Wales B against France in 1987 (lost 0–26). Represented 1989 Lions against Australia in first Test (lost 12–30). Toured to New Zealand (1988) and Australia (1991) with Wales, and to South Africa (1989) with World XV. Scored winning try against England (Cardiff, 18.3.89, won 12–9) to deny them 1989 Five Nations Championship. Tore hamstring on first appearance in 1990/91 season, and having recovered, promptly did it again. Returned to international duty Down Under in 91, and was ever-present thereafter until Paris match on 20 March 1993

Touchlines: Golf

Halpin, G. F. Ireland

Full Name: Garrett Francis Halpin
Club: London Irish
Position: Tighthead prop
Height: 6ft (1.83m)
Weight: 17st 6lb (111kg)
Occupation: Teacher at St George's College, Weybridge
Born: Dublin, 14.2.66
Family: Caroline (wife)
Former clubs: Rockwell College, Wanderers
International debut: England 23, Ireland 0, 1990
Five Nations debut: As above
Best moment in rugby: Winning first full cap, at Twickenham
Worst moment in rugby: London Irish's relegation from English League Division One (1993/94)
Most embarrasing moment: Scoring try on 22-metre line in 1991 at Ballymena
Most respected opponents: Louis Armary (Lourdes & France) and Jason Leonard (Harlequins & England)
Other sporting achievements: Irish International hammer thrower

(American Indoor Collegiate champion); represented Ireland in 1987 in World Athletics Championships (Rome); hockey coach

Best memory last season: Beating England at Twickenham, even though I was only on bench

Should rugby's amateur rules be revised? Yes

Ireland (1990)

Last Season	2 caps	0 pts
1994	Tour to Australia	
Career	7 caps	0 pts

Caps (7): **1990** E **1991** wc–J **1992** E, S, F **1993** R **1994** F

Points Nil

To what degree should players benefit? Should be compensated for time given up to rugby, allowed to benefit from off-field activities and receive an international match fee

Should referees be rewarded? Should receive a wage, as I think this would raise standards

Advice for International Board: More definitive rulings. Rugby is either amateur or professional, and I hate the half-hearted stance taken by various countries. Nations must become more unified in their interpretations

Suggestions to improve rugby: On-field – scrap 90-degree scrummage wheel law, as it slows game down and inspires dubious tactics

Notable landmarks in rugby career: Beneficiary of Peter Clohessy's early-season suspension, which allowed him to wear Ireland's No 3 jersey either side of Christmas 1993, against Romania and France. However, with Clohessy's return Garrett reverted to bench. Joined Wanderers on return from a sports scholarship with University of Manhattan in New York. Played four times for Ireland Schools (1983-84). Toured North America with Ireland (1989), scoring try in defeat of Mid West in Chicago. Won 1989/90 Leinster League and Cup double with Wanderers. Lost his place after debut against England at Twickenham (20.1.90), and had to be content with turning out in Ireland Under-25s' 36–17 win over Spain (Limerick, 8.9.90) and Ireland B's 27–12 win over Argentina (Limerick, 20.10.90). Ever-present on Irish replacements' bench during 1991 Five Nations Championship, and failed to make Test team on summer tour to Namibia. Played against Japan in 1991 World Cup and toured to Australia last summer, failing to make Test team but playing against New South Wales, ACT, Queensland, Australia B and NSW Country

Touchlines: Motor-biking, music

Hastings, A. G.   Scotland

Full Name: Andrew Gavin Hastings
Club: Watsonians
Position: Fullback
Height: 6ft 2in (1.88m)
Weight: 14st 7lb (92kg)
Occupation: Sports marketing
executive with the Carnegie
Partnership
Born: Edinburgh, 3.1.62
Family: Diane (wife)
Family links with rugby: Clifford
(father) played No 8 for Edinburgh
XV and Watsonians; Scott (brother)
plays for Watsonians, Scotland and
British Lions; Graeme (brother)
plays centre for Melbourne RFC
and Victoria State (Australia); Ewan
(brother) plays on wing for
Watsonians

Former clubs: Cambridge University, London Scottish
International debut: Scotland 18, France 17, 1986
Five Nations debut: As above
Best moments in rugby: Winning 1990 Grand Slam; 1989 British Lions' 2–1
series win in Australia; captaining Scotland (1992-94); captaining 1993 British
Lions to second-Test win over All Blacks
Worst moments in rugby: Missing kick in front of posts against England in
1991 World Cup semi-final at Murrayfield (26.10.91); losing to England's last
kick in 1994 Calcutta Cup clash (5.2.94)
Most embarrassing moment: Missing plane home from Ireland after B
international
Most respected opponents: The All Blacks, because of their record – I've only
beaten them twice in 12 attempts (NZ 14, World XV 28, 1992; NZ 7, British Lions
20, 1993)
Biggest influence on career: Parents (Clifford and Isobel)
Other sporting achievements: Appearing on TV in Trail Blazers (1988) and
in three Pro-Celebrity Golf competitions (1990, 1992, 1993)
Best memory last season: Captaining Lions in New Zealand
Should rugby's amateur rules be revised? Yes
To what degree should players benefit? All that matters is that everyone
competes on a level playing field. It is utter nonsense to talk about rugby-related
activities and non-rugby-related activities. You cannot differentiate between
the two. It is high time the IB acknowledge the widespread abuses, and cut out
all the hypocrisy that currently exists. Players should certainly not be

disadvantaged financially through playing rugby

Should referees be rewarded? They should be entitled to the same benefits as players

Advice for International Board: Deliberate knock-on should be punished with a penalty, not a free kick; there should be no difference in rule relating to ruck and maul

Notable landmarks in rugby career: Appointed captain of both Scotland and British Lions in 1992/93, so the following season was always likely to be an anti-climax. It was. Scotland picked up 1994 Five Nations wooden spoon. Had played all three Tests for the Lions against New Zealand, and come within a dodgy refereeing decision (at end of first game) of skippering series-winning team. Kicked six penalty goals in first Test, four in second Test win and five points in third Test loss. Despite Scotland's poor campaign last season, Gavin still extended national points-scoring record to a European-best 466, and reached 50-cap milestone against France (19.3.94). In 1986 set Scottish record for most points in a Five Nations season with 52. Won two Blues at Cambridge University (1984-85)

Scotland (1986)		
Last Season	5 caps	42 pts
Career	50 caps	466 pts
Lions 1986		
1989	3 Tests	28 pts
1993	3 Tests	35 pts

Caps (50): **1986** F, W, E, I, Ro **1987** I, F, W, E wc–F, Z, R, NZ **1988** I, F, W, E, A **1989** Fj, Ro. Lions–A(1,2,3) **1990** I, F, W, E, NZ(1,2), Arg **1991** F, W, E(a), I(a) wc–J, I(b), WS, E(b), NZ **1992** E, I, F, W, A(1) **1993** I, F, W, E. Lions–NZ (1,2,3). NZ **1994** W, E, I, F

Points (466 – 10t,60c,102p): **1986** F(6p), W(1t,1p), E(3c,5p), I(2p), Ro(3c,5p) **1987** I(1c), F(1c,4p), W(2c,2p), E(1c,2p) wc–F(4p), Z(1t,8c), Ro(2t,8c,1p), NZ(1p) **1988** I(2c,2p), F(1t,4p), W(4p), E(2p), A(1t,1c,1p) **1989** Fj(1t,4c,2p), Ro(3c,2p). Lions–A(1:2p), A(2:1t,1p), A(3:5p) **1990** F(1p), NZ(1:2c), NZ(2:2c,2p), Arg(1t,5c,1p) **1991** W(1c,2p), I(a:1t,1p) wc–J(1t,5c,2p), I(b:2c,3p), WS(2c,4p), E(b:2p), NZ(2p) **1992** E(1p), I(2c,2p), F(2p), W(1p), A(1:1c,2p) **1993** I(1c,1p), F(1p), W(5p), E(3p). Lions–NZ(1:6p), NZ(2:4p), NZ(3:1c,1p). NZ(4p) **1994** W(2p), E(2p), I(2p), F(4p)

and five caps for Scotland B, before establishing Scottish record with six penalty goals on full debut (17.1.86). Toured with Scotland to North America (1985), 1987 World Cup (where scored 62 points in four games), New Zealand (1990) and Australia (1992). Scored go-ahead try in second Test for 1989 Lions and 15 points in victorious decider. Kicked penalty for 1986 British Lions in 7–15 defeat by The Rest at Cardiff in match to celebrate centenary of IRFB. Played in '1989 Home Unions' 29–27 win over France (scored 22 points) and for 1989 Barbarians against All Blacks. Led London Scottish to 1989/90 Courage League division-three title, and Watsonians to promotion (1990/91) to McEwan's League division one. Captained Barbarians at 1991 Hong Kong Sevens. Represented 1992 World XV in three-Test series against All Blacks (NZRFU centenary celebrations), kicking penalty in 28–14 first-Test win and scoring try in second

Touchlines: Golf

Hastings, S. Scotland

Full Name: Scott Hastings
Club: Watsonians
Positions: Centre, wing, fullback
Height: 6ft 1in (1.86m)
Weight: 14st 4lb (93kg)
Occupation: Advertising and Public Relations account manager with Barker's, Scotland
Born: Edinburgh, 4.12.64
Family: Jenny (wife), Corey
Family links with rugby: Clifford (father) played No 8 for Edinburgh XV and Watsonians; Gavin (brother) plays for Watsonians, and captains Scotland and British Lions; Graeme (brother) plays centre for Melbourne RFC and Victoria State (Australia); Ewan (brother) plays on wing for Watsonians
Former club: Newcastle Northern
International debut: Scotland 19, France 18, 1986
Five Nations debut: As above
Best moments in rugby: 1989 Lions' Test series win; 1990 Grand Slam win with Scotland; playing in Hong Kong Sevens; receiving a pass from brother Gavin for Scotland against England; winning the Stockholm 10-a-sides with New Zealand Warblers in August last year
Worst moment in rugby: Sustaining hamstring injury on first appearance in 1987 World Cup (55–28 win v Romania)

Scotland (1986)

Last Season	4 caps	0 pts
Career	50 caps	28 pts
Lions 1989 1993	2 Tests	0 pts

Caps (50): **1986** F, W, E, I, Ro **1987** I, F, W wc–Ro **1988** I, F, W, A **1989** W, E, I, F, Fj, Ro. Lions–A(2,3) **1990** I, F, W, E, NZ(1,2), Arg **1991** F, W, E(a), I(a) wc–J, Z, I(b), WS, E(b), NZ **1992** E, I, F, W, A(1,2) **1993** I, F, W, E, NZ **1994** E, I, F

Points (28 – 7t): **1986** E(1t), Ro(1t) **1987** F(1t) **1988** I(1t) **1991** I(1t) wc–J(1t), Z(1t)

Most embarrassing moments: My 1987 World Cup injury, and finding out Gavin was my brother
Most respected opponents: Brendan Mullin (Blackrock & Ireland) – played opposite him ever since we captained our respective countries in a Schools international; Tim Horan and Jason Little
Biggest influence on career: Family's involvement in rugby
Serious injuries: Torn hamstring, cartilage operation (1985), broken cheekbone (1987 v Wales), fractured jaw and cheekbone (Lions v Otago, 1993;

4 hour operation to rebuild face)

Best memories last season: Selection for British Lions; winning the Stockholm 10s with NZ Warblers and the Old Belvedere International seven-a-side with Watsonians; skippering the Barbarians against the All Blacks on 4th December 1993, my birthday (unfortunately the SRU spoilt the occasion by requesting that I return to Edinburgh for a squad session the following day)

Should rugby's amateur rules be revised? Yes, to allow players to earn as little or as much money as is available in terms of advertising products or promoting the game of rugby

To what degree should players benefit? They should be compensated for time lost, able to benefit from off-the-field activities, and receive a £1000 international match fee (it's a nice round figure that has been bandied around); either that or a percentage of gate fees, sponsorship revenue and TV rights

Should referees be rewarded? Yes, they dedicate as much time to rugby as we do. It is the only way to improve standards. We should also reward coaches

Advice for International Board: They're not a strong enough body; they don't appear to impose their will, and as such I can only conclude that they have no apparent jurisdiction. Take all conversions in front of the posts. Put posts on dead-ball line so penalties cannot be kicked from the halfway line, and teams will be more inclined to run the ball. Increase try-worth to six points

Notable landmarks in rugby career: Shares with Sean Lineen the world record for an international centre partnership of 28 games (Lineen retired after 1992 Australia tour). No such fond memories of 1993/94 campaign, in which Scotland collected '94 Five Nations wooden spoon and Scott admitted to being humiliated playing out of position as a winger in 51–15 defeat by New Zealand (20.11.93). Captaining Barbarians against same All Black tourists (Cardiff, 4.12.93) was a far more accurate reflection of his international stock. Took his tally of caps to 50 (against France, 19.3.94) on same day as brother Gavin. Pair had become first Scottish brothers to play together in a Lions Test back in 1989. Selected to tour with 1993 Lions to New Zealand, under Gavin's captaincy, but returned early and in agony after sustaining a fractured cheekbone. Former Watsonians captain (1989/90), who helped Edinburgh to three Inter-District Championship 'grand slams' between 1986 and 1988. Also ex-skipper of Scottish Schools. Played three times for Scotland U-21s and once for Scotland B (at fullback in 9–0 win over Italy B, Glasgow, 7.12.85). Also played at outside-half, for Anglo-Scots, during time at Newcastle Polytechnic. Key cog in Scotland's 1990 Grand Slam machine, making famous try-saving tackle on England's Rory Underwood in Murrayfield decider. Within one cap of joining Jim Renwick (51) as Scotland's most-capped centre

Touchlines: Underwater hockey refereeing; golf (18 handicap – still a bandit on a good day, which isn't often), watching films, viticulture

Herbert, A. G. — Australia

Full Name: Anthony Gerard Herbert
State: Queensland
Club: GPS
Position: Centre, fullback
Height: 6ft (1.83m)
Weight: 13st 8lb (86kg)
Occupation: Sales and promotions representative with Castlemaine Perkins XXXX
Born: 13.8.66
Family: Suellen (wife), Rachael (daughter), Justine (daughter), James (son)
Family links with rugby: Brother (Daniel) scored try on Wallaby debut against Ireland (11.6.94)
International debut: Australia 65, South Korea 18, 1987
Best moment in rugby: Scoring try after coming on as replacement in third Test v New Zealand (1992)
Worst moment in rugby: Losing the above game 23–26
Most embarrassing moment: Acting as replacement breakaway in third Test of Bledisloe series and knowing when they were calling Zinzan Brooke in the lineouts but not capable enough to stop him
Most respected opponent: Don't get to play against many, but anyone chosen to play for his country deserves the utmost respect
Serious injuries: Damaged three transversus (abdominal) muscles (1992)
Other sporting achievements: Teamed up with Jason Little in Fiji to triumph against the odds and handicaps of Tim Horan and John Brass
To what degree should players benefit? Better compensation for elite players to enable them to produce greater results more consistently
Advice for International Board: Reduce value of penalty to two points
Notable landmarks in rugby career: In and out of the Wallabies' Test side during the past six years, his cap tally finally hit double figures in 1993 when, before being omitted from the squad to tour North America and France, he made two appearances as replacement. He came on for hamstring victim Paul Carozza during the Bledisloe Cup loss to New Zealand in Dunedin (17.7.93), and then tasted the spoils of victory after replacing two-try hero Jason Little in

Australia (1987)

Last Season	2 caps	0 pts
Career	10 caps	5 pts

Caps (10): 1987 SK(R). wc–F(R) **1990** F(1R), US, NZ(2,3) **1991** wc–WS **1992** NZ(3R) **1993** NZ(R), SA(2R)

Points (5 – 1t): **1992** NZ(3:1t)

238

the 28–20 second-Test victory against South Africa in Brisbane (14.8.93). This appearance completed a hat-trick of replacement outings, as he had collected his eighth cap in the third Test against New Zealand in Sydney the previous year. A dead rubber it might have been, with Australia having already sewn up the series, but Herbert seized his opportunity with both hands and claimed his first international try. Despite that the All Blacks won 26–23. Thereafter he failed to add to his Test match experience, the majority of which had been obtained in 1990, when he made appearances against France, the United States and New Zealand (twice). Despite his shortage of Test action in 1992, he turned out in the wins over Western Transvaal, Northern Transvaal and Eastern Province (scored try) in South Africa, and in the defeats by Munster and Swansea once the tour moved on to Britain

Touchlines: Golf and work

Hill, S. D. Wales

Full Name: Simon David Hill
Club: Cardiff
Position: Centre
Height: 5ft 11in (1.81m)
Weight: 13st 2lb (83kg)
Occupation: Dental student at Cardiff Medical College
Born: Barry, South Glamorgan, 27.5.68
Family: Single
Former club: Headingley
International debut: Zimbabwe 14, Wales 35, 1993
Five Nations debut: None
Best moment in rugby: Scoring try on Wales debut
Worst moment in rugby: Breaking nose and having to leave field after 15 minutes of 1990/91 game against Wasps
Best memory last season: Winning Test place on tour of Africa and retaining throughout
Notable landmarks in rugby career: Simon was a late call-up into the Wales squad for the 1993 summer

Wales (1993)		
Last Season	2 caps	0 pts
Career	5 caps	10 pts

Caps (5): **1993** Z(1,2), Na **1994** I(R), W

Points (10 – 2t): **1993** Z(1:1t), Na(1t)

---

tour to Zimbabwe and Namibia, but took his opportunity with both hands. He played in all six matches, including the three internationals against Zimbabwe

239

(two) and Namibia. To add to his joy, he bagged a try on his Test debut, in Bulawayo on 22 May, and added another in the 38–23 win over Namibia, in Windhoek on 5 June. Wales won all six matches, with Simon also turning out against Zimbabwe B (try in 64–13 win, Harare, 25 May), Namibia B (won 47–10, Windhoek, 2 June) and the South African Barbarians (39th-minute replacement for Wayne Proctor in 56–17 triumph). Played in two legs of Wales's 1994 Five Nations triumph, coming on as a 44th-minute replacement for Proctor in Dublin, and playing throughout famous 24–15 defeat of France in Cardiff (19.2.94). Previously represented Glamorgan and Headingley (while studying in Leeds). Included in Wales's preliminary 1991 World Cup squad. Bench reserve for Wales B during 34–12 win over Netherlands in Leiden (2.12.90). Finished 1993/94 season on a high after helping Cardiff beat Llanelli in Swalec Cup final

Touchlines: Lifeguards in summer

Hills, W. G. South Africa

Full Name: Willem (Willie) Gerhardus Hills
Club: Police
Province: Northern Transvaal
Position: Hooker
Height: 5ft 11in (1.80m)
Weight: 17st 5lb (110kg)
Occupation: Policeman
Born: Pretoria, 26.1.62
International debut: France 15, South Africa 20, 1992
Other sporting achievements: Provincial colours in softball and weightlifting
Notable landmarks in rugby career: Season ended early for Willie in 1993 after he tore knee ligaments in only second minute of 19–12 first-Test victory over Australia in Sydney (31.7.93). Prior to that had worn No 1 jersey in both Tests against France. Made swift progress after his provincial debut in 1990 for Northern Transvaal, no doubt aided by the Blue Bulls' Currie Cup-Lion Cup double in 1991. Educated at the Gardens

South Africa (1992)

Last Season	3 caps	0 pts
Career	6 caps	0 pts

Caps (6): **1992** F(1,2), E **1993** F(1,2), A(1)

Points Nil

School in Pretoria, he had played 30 matches for Northern Transvaal but none for South Africa before embarking on the Springboks' tour of France and England. He came close to a full debut against Australia (22.8.92), but having represented his province against the Wallabies the previous week (lost 17–24 in Pretoria), lost out to Blue Bulls team mate Uli Schmidt in selection at Cape Town. Schmidt, who also hooked against New Zealand, did not tour, and Hills needed no second invitation to take over. Appearances at prop against Aquitaine (won 29–22, Pau, 7.10.92), Midi-Pyrenées (won 18–15, Toulouse, 15.10.92) and French Universities (lost 13–18, Tours, 28.10.92) preceded his Test debut in the No 2 jersey at Lyon, where the Springboks beat France 20–15. He again had the hooking responsibilities the following week in Paris, when France rebounded with a 29–16 win, and a busy season was completed in England, with outings against the Midlands Division (won 32–9, Leicester, 4.11.92), England B (won 20–16, Bristol, 7.11.92) and at Twickenham England themselves (14.11.92, lost 16–33). Prior to injury against '93 Wallabies, Willie had turned out against South Australia (won 90–3, Adelaide, 17.7.93) and New South Wales (lost 29–28, Sydney, 24.7.93)

Hogg, C. D.   Scotland

Full Name: Carl David Hogg
Club: Melrose
Position: No 8, lock, flanker
Height: 6ft 4in (1.93m)
Weight: 16st (97kg)
Occupation: Civil engineer with Crouch Hogg and Waterman
Born: Galashiels, 5.7.69
Family: Single
Family links with rugby: Jim Telfer (uncle) played for Scotland (25 caps, 1964-70) and Lions (8 Tests, 1966-68)
International debut: Australia 27, Scotland 12, 1992
Five Nations debut: None
Best moment in rugby: Making Scotland debut on '92 Australian tour

Worst moment in rugby: Being well beaten by Randwick in 1990 Melrose Sevens, and Scotland being humiliated by All Blacks (1993)
Most respected opponent: John Jeffrey (Kelso & Scotland)
Serious injuries: Back operation to remove disc (1988), dislocated shoulder (1991)

Best memory last season: Scotland A 9, New Zealand 20, 1993; Melrose thrashing Currie to clinch fourth Scottish title in five years
Should rugby's amateur rules be revised? Yes
To what degree should players benefit? Some compensation, but not total. I don't want to see payments for playing, but we should be able to benefit from off-field activities
Should referees be rewarded? Compensated, but no direct payments. We can't have professional referees in an amateur game
Advice for International Board: Moving in right direction. We don't want to go overboard. It's an amateur game and that's the way it should stay. Danger of all-out professionalism, which would be asking for problems
Notable landmarks in rugby career: Became 19th Melrose player to be capped by Scotland when appeared at blindside in Scotland's two Test defeats against Australia on 1992 tour (12–27 and 13–37). Played in shadow Scotland side (A team) which beat Italy 22–17 at the Greenyards (19.12.92), and in Scotland A side which won well (22–13) in Dublin against Ireland counterparts (28.12.92). But he damaged ankle ligaments in latter match, and was forced to miss first Trial, then Championship opener against Ireland. Selectors subsequently opted not to disturb Weir-Turnbull-Morrison back-row combination, and although fit again Carl, remained on bench until last season, when jumped off to replace Damian Cronin 62 minutes into Scotland's humiliating 51–15 loss to New Zealand (Murrayfield, 20.11.93). Returned to bench for 1994 Five Nations Championship. Represented Scotland Schools (1986/87) and U-19s before breaking into Scotland Under-21 side (1989/90), and captained side in 10–24 loss to Wales at Ayr. Aged just 19 when appeared in 1989 Scottish Trial. Graduated to Scotland B during 1991/92 season, warming bench in Belfast before making debut in 10–31 home loss to France in unaccustomed surroundings of second row. Member of Scotland squad at 1992 Students World Cup in Italy. Toured with Scotland to Fiji, Tonga and Western Samoa (1993) – playing against Fiji Juniors, Tongan President's XV and Western Samoan President's XV – and to Argentina (1994), when broke back into Test side, appearing in both international defeats to Pumas
Touchlines: Golf, squash, soccer

Scotland (1992)

Last Season	3 caps	0 pts
Career	5 caps	0 pts

Caps (5): **1992** A(1,2) **1993** NZ(R) **1994** Arg(1,2)

Points Nil

Honiball, H.   South Africa

Full Name: Henry Honiball
Province: Natal
Position: Outside-half
Height: 6ft 3in (1.90m)
Weight: 14st 1lb (85kg)
Occupation: Farmer
Born: 1.12.65
International debut: Australia 19, South Africa 12, 1993

South Africa (1993)		
Last Season	2 caps	0 pts
Career	2 caps	0 pts

Caps (2): **1993** A(3R), Arg(2)

Points Nil

Notable landmarks in rugby career: Kicked Natal to victory over England last summer, with three penalty goals in their 21–6 defeat of the tourists at King's Park, Durban (21.5.94). By then he was a fully fledged Springbok, having been given his debut as a 48th-minute replacement for Natal team mate Peter Müller in the third-Test loss to Australia in Sydney (21.8.93), and having then made his first start in South Africa's No 10 jersey in the second-Test victory against Argentina in Buenos Aires (13.11.93) – a match the tourists won 52–23. He had warmed the bench in 29–26 first-Test defeat of Pumas a week earlier. Henry was one of the busiest Springboks in Australia, playing in no fewer than nine of the 12 fixtures: against Western Australia (won 71–8, Perth, 14 July), South Australia (won 90–3, Adelaide, 17 July), Victoria (won 78–3, Melbourne, 21 July), New South Wales (lost 29–28, Sydney, 24 July), NSW Country (won 41–7, Orange, 27 July), ACT (won 57–10, Canberra, 4 August), Queensland Country (won 65–5, Mackay, 11 August) and Sydney (won 31–20, Penrith, 18 August), and in the third Test. Missed out on 1993 Currie Cup final, which Natal lost 15–21 to Transvaal, but spent his autumn with the Springboks in South America, top-scoring on the tour. In his three starts he amassed 35 points from ten conversions and five penalty goals. The breakdown was thus: six conversions and a penalty goal against Córdoba (won 55–37, 27.10.93), and four conversions and four penalty goals against Tucumán (won 40–12, 2.11.93)

Horan, T. J.   Australia

Full Name: Timothy (Tim) James
Horan
State: Queensland
Club: Southern Districts
Position: Centre, five-eighth
Height: 6ft (1.83m)
Weight: 13st 8lb (86kg)
Occupation: Sales representative
with Castlemaine Perkins XXXX
Born: 15.5.70
Family: Katrina (wife), Lucy
(daughter)
Former clubs: None. Souths since
1988
International debut: New Zealand
24, Australia 12, 1989
Best moment in rugby: Winning
1991 World Cup
Worst moment in rugby: Losing
to New Zealand at Eden Park in
second Test of 1991 Bledisloe Cup
series
Most embarrassing moment:
Answering just one question on 'Sale
of the Century'
Most respected opponent: Jerry
Guscott (Bath & England)
Serious injuries: Knee (1990)
Suggestions to improve rugby:
Improve standards of refereeing
**Notable landmarks in rugby
career:** Suffered potentially career-
ending knee injury playing for
Queensland in 1994 Super-10 final

Australia (1989)

Last Season	8 caps	20 pts
Career	33 caps	70 pts

Caps (33): **1989** NZ, F(1,2) **1990** F(1),
NZ(1,2,3) **1991** W(a), E(a),
NZ(a1,a2). wc–Arg, WS, W(b),
I, NZ(b), E(b) **1992** S(1,2),
NZ(1,2,3), SA, I, W **1993** T, NZ,
SA(1,2,3), C, F(1,2)

Points (70 – 16t): F(1:2t) **1990** NZ(2:1t)
1991 W(a:1t). wc–Arg(2t),
W(b:1t), NZ(b:1t) **1992** S(2:2t),
NZ(1:1t), I(1t) **1993** NZ(1t),
SA(2:1t), SA(3:1t), C(1t)

against Natal, and is in major doubt for World Cup. Cruel luck for Tim, as he had established himself as world's premier centre, following up his quite outstanding 1992 campaign with a full book of appearances in 1993. And he continued to terrorize opposition defences, with four more tries – against New Zealand, South Africa (2) and Canada – taking his Test tally to 16. Once again, his midfield partnership with Southern Districts and Queensland team-mate Jason Little did the world champions no harm, although it could not prevent the Bledisloe Cup being lost to New Zealand, or South Africa winning the first Test in Sydney, or France snatching a share of their two-match autumn series.

Tim has proved a highly capable performer since being given his debut as a teenager against the All Blacks in 1989 – two years after helping Australia Under-17s beat their New Zealand counterparts 16–3. A World Cup winner in 1991 and an ever-present since. His glorious '92 included tries in the 16–15 first-Test win over New Zealand, and another in the 42–17 defeat of Ireland. Prior to those, he had represented the World XV against New Zealand in the first and third Tests of the '92 Centenary Series

Touchlines: Golf and family

Howard, P. W.   Australia

Full Name: Patrick William Howard
Club: Queensland University
State: Queensland
Position: Outside-half, five-eighth, inside-centre
Height: 5ft 10in (1.78m)
Weight: 14st 6lb (87kg)
Occupation: Pharmacy Student
Born: 14.11.73
Family: Single
International debut: New Zealand 25, Australia 10, 1993
Best moment in rugby: Debut Test against All Blacks (1993)
Worst moment in rugby: Getting dropped after above match
Most respected opponent: Grant Fox (ex-Auckland & New Zealand)
Best memories last season: Debuts for Queensland and Australia; Interstate Series win
Suggestions to improve rugby: On-field – change the new rules back to the old rules so that there are fewer back-rowers clogging the backline

Australia (1993)		
Last Season	1 cap	0 pts
Career	1 cap	0 pts

Caps (1): **1993** NZ

Points Nil

Notable landmarks in rugby career: Thus far a one-cap wonder, having made his debut as a late call-up in the 1993 Bledisloe Cup game against New Zealand in Dunedin (17.7.93). Captain Michael Lynagh withdrew at the 11th hour owing to illness, and young Pat was drafted in. New Zealand won 25–10, and the No 10 jersey was taken over by New South Wales's Scott Bowen. Nonetheless, Pat kept himself busy. He represented Queensland in their 17–3 defeat by the touring Springboks at Ballymore (8.8.93), and was then invited on Australia's autumn tour of North America and France. His first outing came as a centre in the non-cap Test against the US Eagles and he bagged a try in Australia's 26–22 win, played in severe heat at Riverside, California (2.10.93). From there he made four appearances in France: at centre against Aquitaine (won 30–15, Dax, 16.10.93), as a replacement for Constable in the 20–19 defeat of South West France (Agen, 20.10.93), at centre against a French Selection (won 24–23, Grenoble, 26.10.93), and back at fly-half in the 15–21 loss to Côte d'Azur (Toulon, 2.11.93)

Touchlines: Travelling and surfing

Hueber, A. France

Full Name: Aubin Hueber
Club: Lourdes
Position: Scrum-half
Height: 5ft 8in (1.70m)
Weight: 12st (76kg)
Occupation: Communications officer with Var Regional Council
Born: Tarbes, 5.4.67
International debut: Australia 19, France 28, 1990
Five Nations debut: France 44, Ireland 12, 1992
Notable landmarks in rugby career: Damaged knee ligaments restricted Aubin to Test appearances in only the first part of 1993/94 season: he played six times before the turn of the year (Romania twice, South Africa twice and Australia twice) and not at all after it. The highlight of his season was the try he scored in France's shock 16–13 defeat of the world-champion Wallabies (Bordeaux, 30.10.93). Had been France's first-choice scrum-half since making his Five Nations debut in 44–12 rout of Ireland in Paris (21.3.92). Although rested for subsequent engagement

France (1990)

Last Season	5 caps	5 pts
Career	19 caps	13 pts

Caps (19): **1990** A(3), NZ(1) **1991** US(2) **1992** I **1992** Arg(a1,a2), SA(1,2), Arg(b) **1993** E, S, I, W, R(a), SA(1,2), R(b), A(1,2)

Points (13 – 2t,1dg): **1992** Arg(a2:1t,1dg) **1993** A(2:1t)

against Romania at Le Havre, he played the next nine games – three against Argentina (two on tour in July 1992), two against South Africa and all four in France's triumphant 1993 Five Nations campaign. Scored try and dropped goal in 33–9 second-Test win over Pumas in Buenos Aires (11.7.92). Had succeeded Henri Sanz as France B scrum-half at Brecon (29.10.88) when Wales B were defeated 18–12. Again partnered Thierry Lacroix at half-back when the second string were undone 14–12 by Scotland B at Melrose (18.2.89), and was captain when Wales B were beaten 28–15 in La Teste (12.11.89). A year earlier he had appeared at Auch in a non-cap match against Ireland, and moved a step nearer cap recognition when selected to represent the Rest of the Europe against the Four Home Unions (lost 43–18) at Twickenham in a match organized to raise money for the Romania appeal (22.4.90). He again understudied Sanz when France toured Australia in 1990 and was given his long-awaited chance in the third Test, Jacques Fouroux's last match as coach, which the visitors won 28–19 (30.6.90) despite the dismissal of Philippe Gallart. He went on to play in the first Test against New Zealand (3.11.90) but was replaced by Sanz after France lost 3–24. A third cap followed, however, in the lightning-shortened second-Test win over the United States on France's pre-World Cup tour before Fabien Galthie pipped him to 1991 World Cup selection

Hull, P. A. England

Full Name: Paul Anthony Hull
Club: Bristol
Position: Fullback, outside-half, wing, centre
Height: 5ft 10in (1.78m)
Weight: 11st 11lb (70kg)
Occupation: RAF physical training instructor
Born: London, 17.5.68
Former club: Milton Keynes
International debut: South Africa 15, England 32, 1994
Five Nations debut: None
Best moment in rugby: Meeting president Nelson Mandela at Ellis Park prior to my debut and then beating South Africa
Worst moment in rugby: Missing 1988 John Player Cup final epic between Harlequins and Bristol through injury
Most embarrassing moment: Being kicked in the privates the first time my girlfriend watched me play

England (1994)

Last Season	2 caps	0 pts
1994	Tour to South Africa	
Career	2 caps	0 pts

Caps (2): **1994** SA(1,2)

Points Nil

Serious injuries: Torn ankle ligaments
Advice for International Board: Make game more professional
Notable landmarks in rugby career: Selected ahead of Jonathan Callard for last summer's England tour to South Africa after incumbent Ian Hunter withdrew from original selection; such swift progress did he make that coach Jack Rowell deployed him in the first Test – a record-breaking occasion in Pretoria (4.6.94). He proved utterly dependable on his debut – impressing with his strategic positioning and his confidence under the high ball – and it was no surprise that he was retained for the second Test, where his defence was possibly even better. It was easy to forget that Paul had been waiting patiently in the wings for four years for his chance, having been taken to Argentina with England's senior party back in 1990 and given outings against Buenos Aires, Cuyo and Córdoba. His England A debut had come the same year, in the 20–12 home loss to Fiji. Paul was also member of England's original Under-21 side which panned their Romanian counterparts 54–13 in Bucharest (13.5.89). His team mates that day included England internationals Phil de Glanville, David Pears, Neil Back and Tim Rodber, not forgetting Wales scrum-half Rupert Moon. Paul's stock rose last season with no less than four impressive showings against the 1993 All Blacks. On tour in South Africa he also turned out against Orange Free State, Western Transvaal, Transvaal and Eastern Province, scoring two tries in the latter contest, since dubbed 'the Battle of Port Elizabeth'
Touchlines: Soul music, nightlife

Hunter, I.   England

Full Name: Ian Hunter
Club: Northampton
Position: Fullback, wing, centre
Height: 6ft 2in (1.88m)
Weight: 14st 2lb (85kg)
Occupation: Commercial artist with KWS advertising/marketing agency
Born: Harrow, London 15.2.69
Family: Single
Family links with rugby: Father played in New Zealand
Former clubs: Windermere, Carlisle, Nottingham
Best moment in rugby: Selection for 1993 British Lions
Worst moment in rugby: Coming back from New Zealand after dislocating shoulder in first game

(v North Auckland) of '93 Lions tour (I had got myself so fit for that tour) **Most embarrassing moment:** Falling over for no reason in front of capacity crowd at Northampton just before kick-off **Most respected opponent:** Rory Underwood (Leicester, RAF & England)

England (1992)		
Last Season	2 caps	0 pts
Career	5 caps	15 pts
Lions 1993		

Caps (5): 1992 C 1993 F, W 1994 F, W

Points (15 – 3t): 1992 C(2t) 1993 F(1t)

Serious injuries: Dislocated shoulder (1992)

Best memory last season: Getting picked by England at fullback against Wales (19.3.94)

Should rugby's amateur rules be revised? Yes

To what degree should players benefit? I'm happy for the game to go professional. What's wrong with paying us for doing what we're good at, namely playing rugby?

Should referees be rewarded? Yes, a match fee

Advice for International Board: Stop tampering with rulebook, and if you do make rules, make sure everybody abides by them; leave no room for interpretation

Notable landmarks in rugby career: Desire to represent England at fullback was finally satisfied in last international of 1994 championship campaign, when injury to David Pears in the run-up to the game allowed him to switch from the wing. Responded with exciting display which justified his own billing as Wales were put to the sword. A career plagued by injury: Ian's tour of duty with the 1993 Lions in New Zealand lasted just 38 minutes before he dislocated his shoulder against North Auckland and returned home. Did not reappear in the England side until March, displacing Tony Underwood in the right wing berth against France in that Paris cauldron. Educated in Windermere, Ian had made his Test debut at Wembley on 17 October 1992, when England beat Canada 26–13. To compound his joy, he scored two tries (his opener, England's first ever five-point score). His other two caps also came on the right wing, against France and Wales in the 1993 Five Nations. Had been selected for South Africa game (14.11.92) but forced to withdraw with freak injury suffered in impromptu soccer match during club training. Interviewed by Des Lynam on Sportsnight as next star of English rugby, after scoring crucial try (off crossbar) in 16–15 defeat of French at Twickenham (16.1.93), he was then promptly dropped. Still, he had made sufficient impression to earn Lions selection. First appeared in New Zealand in summer of '92, when England A lost both 'Tests', despite Ian scoring two tries and a conversion in first Test. Took to 42 points his contribution to the England A cause with try on 12th appearance, against South Africa (7.11.92). Toured Australia with England (1991)

Touchlines: Athletics, cycling

Jardine, I. C.   Scotland

Full Name: Ian Carrick Jardine
Club: Stirling County
Position: Centre
Height: 6ft 1in (1.85m)
Weight: 14st 7lb (87kg)
Occupation: Secondary maths
teacher at Larbert HS
Born: Dunfermline, 20.10.64
Family: Ann (wife), Megan
(daughter)
Family links with rugby: Four
brothers (Stephen, Neil, Colin and
Aitken) play at Stirling
International debut: Scotland 15,
New Zealand 51, 1993
Five Nations debut: Wales 29,
Scotland 6, 1994
Best moment in rugby: Winning
first cap
Worst moment in rugby:
Scotland's record defeat coinciding
with my debut
Most embarrassing moment:
Accidentally drinking my wife's
contact lenses, which she had left in
a glass of water by our bed in the
hotel room, after a Scotland B game
when I was worse for wear

Scotland (1993)

Last Season	5 caps	0 pts
1994	Tour to Argentina	
Career	5 caps	0 pts

Caps (5): **1993** NZ **1994** W, E(R),
        Arg(1,2)

Points Nil

Most respected opponent: John Wright (Young Munster)
Serious injuries: Damaging collarbone last season, which meant I missed first
division-one game for Stirling in five years
Best memory last season: Running out onto Murrayfield for first time
Should rugby's amateur rules be revised? Yes
To what degree should players benefit? Anything short of being paid to play
Should referees be rewarded? Yes. They put in work like us and also deserve
some reward. It would also encourage an improvement in their performance,
which is imperative
Advice for International Board: Implement one-for-all rules. Revise maul
law, because it encourages forwards to hang off scrums, so cluttering midfield
Notable landmarks in rugby career: After seemingly years waiting for a
vacancy in Scottish midfield, Ian's chance finally arrived last season when Scott
Hastings was mysteriously moved to wing berth. How unfortunate, after such
a wait, that his debut should coincide with a 51–15 Murrayfield mauling at the

hands of New Zealand. Retained place for 1994 Five Nations opener against Wales, but even though that result was little better, he was relegated back onto bench to accomodate Doug Wyllie's return. Still, he picked up a third cap as a 71st-minute replacement for Scott Hastings against England (5.2.94). Replacement for Scotland U-21s (1986) and Scotland B in Italy (1988/89). Made B debut in 22–22 draw with Ireland B (9.12.89), and having been only bench reserve in 0–16 loss to Ireland B (22.12.90), he made the A team's No 12 jersey his own in 1992/93, turning out against Ireland B at Murrayfield (lost 19–29, 28.12.91) and in Albi against France B (3.2.92), where he scored try in 18–27 defeat. Helped Glasgow win 1989/90 Inter-District Championship. Toured with Scotland to Canada and the United States (1991), appearing against Alberta (won 76–7) and Ontario (won 43–3), and later to Argentina (1994).

Touchlines: Hill walking, cycling

Jenkins, G. R. Wales

Full Name: Garin Richard Jenkins
Club: Swansea
Position: Hooker
Height: 5ft 10in (1.78m)
Weight: 15st 2lb (96kg)
Occupation: Schools liason officer for Swansea RFC
Born: Ynysybwl, 18.8.67
Family: Helen (wife)
Family links with rugby: Father's uncle played for Wales. Mother's cousin propped for Wales and Lions
Former clubs: Ynysybwl, Pontypridd, King Country (NZ), Pontypool
Best moments in rugby: Winning first Welsh cap; scoring try for Swansea in win over 1992 Wallabies; winning 1994 Five Nations title
Worst moment in rugby: Losing place in Welsh team before 1993 Five Nations Championship
Most respected opponent: All of them
Other sporting achievements: Marbles champion at Treobart Junior School

Wales (1991)

Last Season	10 caps	5 pts
1994	Tour to Canada/South Seas	
Career	19 caps	5 pts

Caps (19): **1991** F(b) wc–WS(R), Arg, A(b) **1992** I, F, E, S, A **1993** C **1994** S, I, F, E. wc(q)–P, Sp. C, T, WS

Points (5 – 1t): **1994** wc(q)–Sp(1t)

Best memory last season: Beating Scotland and France in Cardiff
Notable landmarks in rugby career: For many he was the heart and soul of Waless pack during their 1994 Five Nations title run. Having been edged out by Andrew Lamerton for the curtain-raiser against Japan (Garin turned out against Japanese in A team which won 61–5 at Llanelli), he was reinstated. Even though his first game back coincided with Canada's shock win in Cardiff, he remained throughout season, celebrating his maiden Test try in the 54–0 World Cup qualifying win against Spain (Madrid, 21.5.94). Had lost place in Welsh side during 1992/93, after performing hooking duties in 43–12 win over Italy XV at Cardiff (7.10.92) and in 6–23 loss to Australia (21.11.92), also in National Stadium. Between two outings he helped Swansea to a famous win over Wallabies at St Helens, scoring one of All Whites' two tries in 21–6 victory (4.11.92). But come the 1993 Five Nations Championship, Pontypool's Nigel Meek earned the vote, with Llanelli's Lamerton as his bench deputy. Garin, a former coal miner, represented Boys Clubs of Wales U-18s and Glamorgan U-23s. He started his career with Ynysybwl, the birthplace of national coach Alan Davies, and in 1990 toured Kenya with Pontypool, having represented Pooler against 1989 All Blacks. Broke into Wales team at the start of the 1991/92 season, when Davies was appointed coach following the catastrophic 1991 Australia tour, and played in all eight games from the French 'floodlit' game through the 1991 World Cup to the 1992 Five Nations Championship (pack leader). Helped Swansea win the 1991/92 and 1993/94 Heineken League title
Touchlines: Soccer, cricket, weightlifting

Jenkins, N. R. Wales

Full Name: Neil Roger Jenkins
Club: Pontypridd
Position: Outside-half
Height: 5ft 10in (1.78m)
Weight: 13st 5lb (80kg)
Occupation: PR consultant with Just Rentals Ltd (Pontypridd)
Born: Church Village, Pontypridd, 8.7.71
Family: Single
International debut: Wales 6, England 25, 1991
Five Nations debut: As above
Best moment in rugby: Winning 1994 Five Nations title
Worst moment in rugby: Being sent off in 39th minute of 6–27 1991/92 Schweppes Cup semi-final

against Llanelli at Arms Park

Most respected opponents: Philippe Sella (Agen & France)

Biggest influences on career: Parents and two uncles

Best memory last season: Scoring try against ireland in Dublin

Should rugby's amateur rules be revised? Yes

To what degree should players benefit? Anything short of being paid to play; Unions should pay players wages when rugby takes them away from work, rather than expecting goodwill from employers

Should referees be rewarded? Yes, a match fee would serve as an incentive to improve standards of officiating; they deserve a lot of support

Wales (1991)

Last Season	11 caps	173 pts
1994	Tour to Canada/South Seas	
Career	26 caps	273 pts

Caps (26): **1991** E, S, I, F **1992** I, F, E, S **1993** E, S, I, F, Z(1,2), Na, J, C **1994** S, I, F, E. wc(q)–P, Sp. C, T, WS

Points (273 – 4t,37c,59p,1dg): **1991** E(1p), I(1t,1dg) **1992** I(3p), F(3p), S(1c,3p) **1993** E(1c,1p), I(3p), F(1c,1p), Z(1:3c,2p), Z(2:1t,3c,2p), Na(2c,3p), J(1t,5c), C(8p) **1994** S(1c,4p), I(1t,4p), F(1c,4p), E(1p). wc(q)–P(11c), Sp(5c,3p). C(3c,4p), T(6p), WS(3p)

Advice for International Board: Quite simply, all rules must apply to all nations – no buts

Notable landmarks in rugby career: Central to Wales's heroic 1994 Five Nations title win was the performance of Neil. Buoyed by his world record haul of eight penalty goals in 24–26 defeat by Canada (Cardiff, 10.11.93), Neil went to work with his boot after Christmas. He bagged 14 points against Scotland, all 17 against Ireland, 14 against France and three against England for a 48-point haul. What is perhaps more significant is that he missed hardly any. Added another 86 in end-of-season contests against Portugal, Spain, Canada and the South Seas. Had warmed up for season with 42 points in three Tests on Waless summer tour of Zimbabwe and Namibia. An ever-present for Wales in the last four Five Nations campaigns, and yet, remarkably, until the last season he had appeared in no other Tests (including 1991 World Cup). Represented Wales A team in 21–13 win over North of England at Pontypool (14.10.92), in which he contributed 11 points (1c,3p), and again last season at centre in 61–5 defeat of Japan at Llanelli, claiming 19 points (2t,3c,1p). Played for East Wales U-21s v West Wales, East Glamorgan and Wales Youth (1989/90). Broke into Wales U-21s in 1990/91, playing against New Zealand U-21 XV (14 pts: 4c,2p) and Scotland U-21 (15pts: 1t,1c,3p). In 1991/92 he added a second cap and ten points (2c,2p) in 22–15 win over Ireland U-21

Touchlines: Golf

Johns, P. S. Ireland

Full Name: Patrick Stephen Johns
Club: Dungannon
Position: Lock, No 8
Height: 6ft 6in (1.98m)
Weight: 16st 7lb (100kg)
Occupation: Dentist
Born: Portadown, 19.2.68
Family: Kirsty (wife)
Former clubs: Newcastle Univ, Gosforth, Dublin Univ
International debut: Ireland 20, Argentina 18, 1990
Five Nations debut: Scotland 15, Ireland 3, 1993
Best moments in rugby: First match for Ireland (Schools v Australia, 1988); wins over Wales and England (1993)
Worst moment in rugby: Waiting two years for second cap
Most embarrassing moment: Getting my shorts ripped off aged 13
Most respected opponent: Tim Horan (Queensland & Australia)
Serious injuries: Neck injury, broken wrist, knee cartilage (1992), two operations (1993/94) on left knee

Ireland (1990)

Last Season	7 caps	0 pts
1994	Tour to Australia	
Career	15 caps	0 pts

Caps (15): **1990** Arg **1992** NZ(1,2), A **1993** S, F, W, E, R **1994** F, W, E, S, A(1,2)

Points Nil

Best memory last season: Beating England at Twickenham – what else?!
Should rugby's amateur rules be revised? Yes
To what degree should players benefit? Should be compensated for loss of time, commitment and injury. Off-field benefits should be worked out on a team basis. If you're a part of the Irish team, money earned should go into a players' fund and be split. Only two or three players are marketable, but it's a team sport and they wouldn't be any good without the rest
Should referees be rewarded? No objection to them being paid, but no real feeling on the subject
Advice for International Board: Everyone should be on a par, though it's not likely to happen, because every union has a different opinion. It should be black and white with no grey areas. Everything should be out in open, not underhand
Notable landmarks in rugby career: Switched from lock to No 8 midway through 1993/94 season as Ireland moved to change their fortunes for the better, and after a 35–15 loss to France in Paris in which Paddy sustained an

eye injury that required an operation and forced him to take a week off work. He impressed us in his new position, as England were beaten at Twickenham and Scotland held at Lansdowne Road. Along with Nick Popplewell has been an ever-present on Irish side for past two seasons (from 1992 New Zealand tour through to 1994 Australia tour). Represented Ulster against 1989 All Blacks (lost 3–21, Ravenhill, 21.11.89) and Ireland Schools in 1986 against Japan (twice), Australia, England and Wales. Toured Canada with Dungannon (1989). Played for Ireland at Under-21 and Under-25 level (twice) in 1988/89 season. Also turned out for Irish Students and Universities while at Dublin University. Represented Ireland B in 22–22 draw with Scotland B at Murrayfield (9.12.89), and twice against England B: in 24–10 win at Old Belvedere (scoring try, 1.3.91) and at Richmond (No 8 in 15–47 loss, 31.1.92). First capped by Ireland against touring Argentina Pumas (27.20.90)
Touchlines: Painting, making wine

Johnson, G.   South Africa

Full Name: Gavin Johnson
Province: Transvaal
Position: Fullback
Height: 6ft 1in (1.85m)
Weight: 13st 5lb (80kg)
Age: 28
International debut: Argentina 23, South Africa 52, 1993

South Africa (1993)		
Last Season	1 cap	22 pts
Career	1 cap	22 pts

Caps (1): **1993** Arg(2)

Points (22 – 1t,4c,3p): Arg(2:1t,4c,3p)

Notable landmarks in rugby career: Made a record-equalling international debut, scoring 22 points in the Springboks' second-Test victory over Argentina in Buenos Aires (13.11.93). Gavin plundered a try, four conversions and three penalty goals to equal Gerald Bosch's South African single-Test points-scoring record. Moreover, Transvaal's reserve fullback was within one point of equalling the world record for points scored on a Test debut, established by All Black Matthew Cooper in New Zealand's 59–6 win over Ireland (Wellington, 6.6.92). One of three Springbok Test fullbacks on Transvaal's playing staff (Theo van Rensburg and Chris Dirks being the other two), Gavin only journeyed to South America as a late call-up replacing the injured Dirks, who broke his hand in the 'battle of Tucumán'. He had one warm-up game against Rosario (9.11.93) in which he weighed in with the second of five tries (the Springboks won 40–26 in front of a 4,000 crowd). From there it was on to Buenos Aires and his tour de force which silenced 30,000 home hopefuls

Johnson, M. O.   England

Full Name: Martin Osborne Johnson
Club: Leicester
Position: Lock
Height: 6ft 7in (2.01m)
Weight: 17st 12lb (109kg)
Occupation: Bank officer with Midland Bank (Market Harborough)
Born: Solihull, 9.3.70
Family: Single
Former clubs: Wigston, College Old Boys (NZ)
International debut: England 16, France 15, 1993
Five Nations debut: As above
Best moment in rugby: Making full debut against France at Twickenham (16.1.93)
Worst moment in rugby: Returning early from England tour to South Africa
Most respected opponent: Paul Ackford (ex-Harlequins & England)
Serious injuries: Dislocated left shoulder (April 1991) playing for Midlands U-21s v London U-21s; required operation and four months off

England (1993)		
Last Season	5 caps	0 pts
1994	Tour to South Africa	
Career	6 caps	0 pts
Lions 1993	2 Tests	0 pts

Caps (6): **1993** F. Lions–NZ(2,3). NZ **1994** S, I, F, W

Points Nil

Should rugby's amateur rules be revised? Yes
To what degree should players benefit? Use commonsense to resolve the amateurism question; do what is fair
Advice for International Board: Beware not to alter too much of the game. If we try to make too many changes in an attempt to pander to television etc, we run the risk of changing the face of the game, and that would be disastrous
Notable landmarks in rugby career: Spent 18 months playing out in New Zealand for College Old Boys (1990-91) and for King Country in Division Two of Inter-Provincial Championship, during which time he also represented NZ Colts against Australian counterparts on a two-week tour. Team mates included All Blacks Va'aiga Tuigamala, John Timu and Blair Larsen. Planned to remain only 12 months, but niggling shoulder complaint prolonged his stay. Had previously represented England Schools (1987-88) and 1989 England Colts (along with Damien Hopley and Steve Ojomoh) before heading Down

Under. On his return he played for England U-21, partnering Gloucester's David Sims in 94–0 rout of Belgium (1.9.91), before turning out (again alongside Sims) in England B's away wins against France B (15.2.92) and Italy B (7.3.92). But it was in the 1992/93 season that he really hit the big time. Expecting to play for England A against France A at Leicester (15.1.93), he was diverted to Twickenham, where Wade Dooley had withdrawn from the senior side with a thigh injury. With less than 24 hours notice, Martin was thrust into the Five Nations opener against France, and acquitted himself well, especially in second half. Returned to A team thereafter, playing in wins over Italy A, Spain and Ireland A, before touring to Canada and playing in both internationals. So impressive was he that, when Dooley returned home early from the clashing British Lions tour to New Zealand, Martin was quickly summoned and played in the final two Tests. Ever-present in England side in 1993/94, but came home early from summer tour to South Africa after being concussed in 24–21 loss to Transvaal

Johnstone, B. A. Australia

Full Name: Brett Andrew Johnstone
Clubs: Souths (Brisbane)
State: Queensland
Position: Scrum-half
Height: 5ft 10in (1.78m)
Weight: 13st 9lb (82kg)
Occupation: Brisbane-based retail merchandizer for Pepsi Cola (Australia)
Age: 22
Family: Michelle (wife)

Australia (1993)		
Last Season	1 cap	5 pts
Career	1 cap	5 pts

Caps (1): 1993 T(R)

Points (5 – 1t): 1993 T(R:1t)

International debut: Australia 52, Tonga 14, 1993
Best moment in rugby: Test debut against Tonga (1993)
Worst moment in rugby: Missing 1993 Wallaby tour
Most respected opponent: Graeme Bachop (Canterbury & New Zealand)
Best memory last season: Scoring try against Tonga on Test debut
Serious injuries: Five clavicle frac-tures (two in '88, one in '89, two in '90)
Suggestions to improve rugby: On-field – open the game up to be more free flowing. Off-field – financial assistance on a larger scale for players
Notable landmarks in rugby career: 1993 dawned full of promise for Brett, Queensland's reserve scrum-half, when he was included in the squad to face Tonga at Ballymore, Brisbane, on 3 July. Twenty minutes into the game, Peter Slattery, his State captain and the man keeping him out of the side, suffered broken ribs and Brett was called off the bench. He responded with one of seven tries in the 52–14 victory. However, that was the extent of his joy, as Nick Farr-Jones was controversially tempted out of retirement for the Bledisloe Cup

contest against New Zealand and the three-Test series against South Africa. Slattery then recovered in time to represent Queensland against the Springboks (lost 3–17, 8.8.93). To rub salt into his wounded ego, Brett was then overlooked for the autumn tour to North America and France, with the selectors plumping for Queensland Country's Mark Catchpole

Touchlines: Restoring old houses, tennis, travel

Jones, I. D. New Zealand

Full Name: Ian Donald Jones
Province: North Auckland
Club: Kamo
Position: Lock
Height: 6ft 6in (1.98m)
Weight: 16st 8lb (105kg)
Occupation: Builder
Born: Whangarei, 17.4.67
International debut: New Zealand 31, Scotland 16, 1990
Best memory in rugby: Winning first Test v France (1990) on the back of two straight losses
Worst memory in rugby: Being forced to leave field during third Test against 1993 Lions, knowing I would be out of Bledisloe Cup game v Australia
Notable landmarks in rugby career: An outstanding player since his early days, when he represented Whangarei Schools (1979) and North Island Under-18s. The teenage Jones broke into both the Kamo first XV and North Auckland Colts in 1986, and two years later made his bow for North Auckland, whom he now captains. Having marked his inaugural season of provincial rugby (1988) with four tries in eight matches, the Kamo Kid played in the 1989 All Black Trials, and

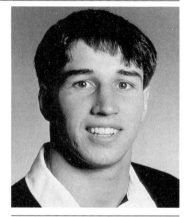

New Zealand (1990)

Last Season	6 caps	0 pts
Career	32 caps	12 pts

Caps (32): **1990** S(1,2), A(1,2,3), F(1,2) **1991** Arg(1,2), A(a1,a2). wc–E, US, It, C, A(b), S **1992** Wd(1,2,3), I(1,2), A(1,2,3), SA **1993** BL(1,2R,3), WS, S, E

Points (12 – 3t): **1990** S(1:1t) **1991** A(1:1t) **1992** I(2:1t)

was included in the squad for their tour to Wales and Ireland. Failed to make the Test side, but did make a lot of friends and consequently returned to Britain the following year as an invited guest of the centenary Barbarians, playing against England, Wales and Argentina. By then he had made his Test debut against Scotland at Dunedin, following the retirement of Murray Pierce, and celebrated with a try in the 31–16 win. Ian appeared in all seven All Black Tests in 1990, and toured Argentina the following year, starting both Tests. Scored a try in the 21–12 Bledisloe Cup first-Test defeat by Australia. An ever-present in the World Cup, he maintained his place throughout the nine-Test schedule in 1992, claiming his third international try in the second-Test romp over Ireland. Enjoyed an impressive tour of Australia and South Africa last season, edging highly rated Wallaby John Eales in the lineout. Made ten appearances on the tour, including one (a formidable display) as captain against Orange Free State at Bloemfontein. Extended his unbroken run in the New Zealand side to 29 caps, with appearances in each of the three Tests in the 2–1 series win over the 1993 Lions (though he was a half-time replacement in the middle match). Missed the Bledisloe Cup defeat of Australia, but returned for the final three missions of the year, including contests against Scotland and England. Six other starts on that British tour featured a try in the 25–12 tour-ending defeat of the Barbarians

Touchlines: Golf (person I'd most like to meet is Nick Faldo), water skiing, swimming

Wallabies' scrum-half Peter Slattery feeds his line during France's 16–11 win in Bordeaux.

Jones, R. L. Wales

Full Name: Richard Lyn Jones
Club: Treorchy
Position: Flanker
Height: 5ft 11in (1.80m)
Weight: 13st 12lb (83kg)
Occupation: Self-employed proprietor
Born: Cwmasfan, 5.6.64
Family: Helen (wife), Rhys (son) and Luke (son)
Family links with rugby: Father (Peter) played for Aberavon (1964-74); brother (Ashley) played for Welsh Youth and Aberavon
Former clubs: Neath (1983-90: 193 apps), Llanelli (1990-94: 103 apps)
International debut: Zimbabwe 14, Wales 35, 1993
Five Nations debut: None
Best moment in rugby: Llanelli's win over 1992 Wallabies
Worst moment in rugby: Watching Canada's Gareth Rees converting winning try in last minute against Wales

Wales (1993)		
Last Season	5 caps	0 pts
Career	5 caps	0 pts

Caps (5): 1993 Z(1,2), Na, J, C

Points Nil

Most embarrassing moment: Never been embarrassed
Other sporting achievements: Karate (brown belt), finished 1993 New York Marathon
Most respected opponent: Mark Ring (Pontypool & ex-Wales)
Serious injuries: Broken right leg (1984); cruciate left knee ligaments (detached from bone, 1993)
Best memory last season: Signing for Treorchy
Should rugby's amateur rules be revised? Yes
To what degree should players benefit? You should be compensated, and be able to benefit off-field, but receive no wage for playing, even if you're an international. In Ireland, Scotland and England, rugby is played by the middle class, who don't need the money anyway. In Wales it's played by working class
Should referees be rewarded? Yes, though in Wales standards are pretty good anyway
Advice for International Board: Happy with what they do
Notable landmarks in rugby career: Despite years of impressive domestic form, Lyn had to wait until a fortnight before his 29th birthday to win his first

cap. Opportunity finally knocked for Lyn on Wales's 1993 tour to Africa, when he played in all three Tests, beginning with his debut against Zimbabwe in Bulawayo (won 35–14, 22.5.93). A sports nut, Lyn was tempted into running the 1993 New York Marathon a matter of days after playing in Wales's shock 24–26 home defeat by Canada (Cardiff, 10.11.93), a result which did his future prospects no favours. Had made his home debut in 55–5 rout of Japan (Cardiff, 16.10.93), following an outing for Wales A in 61–5 defeat of hapless Japanese tourists (Llanelli, 29.9.93). Was ousted from No 7 jersey by Llanelli clubmate Mark Perego for 1994 Five Nations Championship, and after Christmas had to be content with A-team appearances against Ireland (won 20–10, Donnybrook, 4.2.94) and France (scored try in 21–8 win, Cardiff, 18.3.94). Gained Wales Youth caps before breaking into Wales B ranks on 1986 tour to Italy. Has also played club rugby in Australia, South Africa and Neath
Touchlines: Marathon running, cricket (a bit of a bowler)

Jones, M. N. New Zealand

Full Name: Michael Niko Jones
Province: Auckland
Position: Flanker, No 8
Height: 5ft 11in (1.80m)
Weight: 15st 2lb (96kg)
Born: Auckland, 8.4.65
Former country: Western Samoa
International debut: Western Samoa 14, Wales 32, 1986
International debut (NZ): New Zealand 70, Italy 6, 1987
Serious injuries: Damaged knee (1989)
Notable landmarks in rugby career: Missed the 1993 All Blacks tour to England and Scotland after breaking his jaw in three places in a training accident shortly before departure. So New Zealand were

denied the services of one of rugby's great wing-forwards. Auckland-born Michael had first come to people's attention playing in the colours of Western Samoa against Wales at Suva in 1986. By the following year New Zealand had snapped him up, and he was included in their World Cup-winning squad, scoring a try against Italy at Eden Park 30 minutes into his debut, and claiming the All Blacks' first, after 17 minutes of their 29–9 World Cup final win over France on the same Auckland field. Had been marked out as something special ever since his provincial debut in 1985, when he scored three tries against South

Canterbury. However, his climb to the very pinnacle of the world game was abruptly halted in 1989, when he sustained a serious knee injury playing against Argentina, having scored two tries in the 60–9 first-Test defeat of the Pumas at Carisbrook, Dunedin. The injury was described by his specialist as the equivalent of being hit by a truck doing 60 mph. As a consequence he missed the tour to Wales and Ireland, but returned 18 months later for the 1990 tour of France, during which he crossed for a try in the 30–12 second-Test victory in Paris. Made headlines on and off the paddock at the 1991 World Cup: having scored the only try

Western Samoa (1986)
Career 1 cap 0 pts
New Zealand (1987)
Last Season 5 caps 0 pts
Career 33 caps 36 pts

Caps (33): **1987** wc–It, Fj, S, F. A **1988** W(1,2), A(2,3) **1989** F(1,2), Arg(1,2) **1990** F(1,2) **1991** Arg(1,2), A(1,2). wc–E, US, S **1992** Wd(1,3), I(2), A(1,3), SA **1993** BL(1,2,3), A, WS

Points (36 – 9t): **1987** wc–It(1t), F(1t) **1988** W(2:1t), A(2:1t) **1989** Arg(1:2t) **1990** F(2:1t) **1991** Arg(2:1t). wc–E(1t)

of the tournament opener as England were beaten 18–12 in their own Twickenham backyard, he then declined to play in the quarter-final and semi-final ties against Canada and Australia respectively (the games fell on a Sunday – a day of rest in his book). This refusal to compromise his religious beliefs also caused him to miss the Brisbane Test against Australia in the 1992 Bledisloe Cup series. Prior to that training injury in 1993, Michael had helped the Blacks to beat the Lions (over three matches) and the Aussies to recapture the Bledisloe Cup

Jones, R. N.   Wales

Full Name: Robert Nicholas Jones
Clubs: Swansea (Wales), Western Province (SA)
Position: Scrum-half
Height: 5ft 8in (1.73m)
Weight: 11st 8lb (74kg)
Occupation: Business development executive with Swansea Building Society
Born: Trebanos, 10.11.65
Family: Megan (wife)
Family links with rugby: Father-in-law (Clive Rowlands) played for Wales and Lions; brother (Rhodri) plays for Neath
International debut: England 21, Wales 18, 1986

Five Nations debut: As above

Best moments in rugby: Captaining Wales; 1989 Lions winning decisive third Test against Australia

Worst moments in rugby: Captaining Wales in 1990 whitewash (very, very despondent); defeat by New Zealand in 1987 World Cup

Most embarrassing moment: Attempted dropped goal for Wales against Ireland – I hit the ground before the ball and sent it 3 yards; Paul Dean collected and initiated move which led to Irish try

Most respected opponents: Pierre Berbizier (ex-Agen & France) and Gary Armstrong (Jed-Forest & Scotland)

Biggest influence on career: Father (Cliff)

Other sporting achievements: Cricket for Wales at three age-groups

Best memories last season: Swansea's defeat of Wallabies and my late selection for Lions

Should rugby's amateur rules be revised? Yes, greater consideration should be given to players. Reconsider amateurism issue so that players can benefit away from play

To what degree should players benefit? Look after players' employers with tickets etc. WRU trying to be more forward-looking than other Unions, but they are governed by IRB. Moves still have to be made to improve the situation, because there are still very few player benefits considering the time put in. Commitments and time involved are ever-increasing. Yet athletes are able to benefit from their amateur sport

Advice for International Board: Reduce worth of penalty goal instead of increasing value of try. England winning 1991 Grand Slam with hardly any tries made a mockery of old scoring system. However, increasing try value has only served to make for a greater disparity between the major and the developing nations, discouraging the latter

Notable landmarks in rugby career: Joined Western Province, South Africa, last Spring, after a 1993/94 season spent predominantly on bench watching Waless Five Nations title triumph. However, he did enjoy nine minutes of action in Dublin as a replacement for Nigel Davies during Waless 17–15 victory (5.2.94), and then started first Test of season against Portugal in World Cup qualifier in Lisbon (won 102–11, 17.5.94). Celebrated with first try in seven years. Swansea's most-capped player (48) and former captain of the St Helens club as well as of Wales. Within five caps of joining rugby legend Gareth Edwards as Wales's most-capped scrum-half. Having been ommitted from final game of 1993 Championship in Paris, Robert's morale was boosted by

Wales (1986)

Last Season	2 caps	5 pts
Career	48 caps	9 pts
Lions 1989	3 Tests	0 pts
1993		

Caps (48): **1986** E, S, I, F, Fj, T, WS **1987** F, E(a), S, I(a), US wc–I(b), T, E(b), NZ, A **1988** E, S, I, F, NZ(1), WS, Ro **1989** I, F, E, NZ. Lions–A(1,2,3) **1990** F, E, S, I **1991** E, S, F(b) wc–WS, Arg, A(b) **1992** I, F, E, S, A **1993** E, S, I **1994** I(R). wc(q)–P

Points (9 – 2t): **1987** wc–E(1t) **1994** wc(q)–P(1t)

Lions selectors, who drafted him for New Zealand tour after his good friend Gary Armstrong withdrew with a groin injury. Turned out against North Auckland, Canterbury, Southland, Taranaki, Hawke's Bay and Waikato. First played for Swansea whilst still at Cwmtawe School, having already played for West Wales U-11s and Wales 12 Group. Represented Welsh Schools for two seasons before graduating, by way of Wales B in 1985, to senior XV for 1986 Five Nations Championship. Enjoyed outstanding World Cup (1987) and equally magnificent tour to Australia with 1989 Lions. Partnered Jonathan Davies in 22 internationals before latter switched codes. Missed Welsh tour of Namibia in 1991 through injury, but did go to Fiji, Tonga and Western Samoa (1986), New Zealand (1988) and Australia (1991)

Touchlines: Golf

Joseph, J. W. New Zealand

Full Name: Jamie Joseph
Province: Otago
Position: Flanker
Height: 6ft 5in (1.96m)
Weight: 16st 8lb (105kg)
Born: Blenheim, 21.11.69
Family links with rugby: Jim (father) played for New Zealand Maoris in 1960s
International debut: New Zealand 54, World XV 26, 1992
Notable landmarks in rugby career: Controversy has dogged Jamie from the start of his Test career. On his international debut against the World XV, in the second Test of the 1992 centenary series, he was spotted on the TV screen stamping, and for this he later received a four-week suspension from the Union's judiciary committee . A year on, dateline 27 November 1993 (his sixth Tour appearance), he was again guilty of stamping. Twickenham was the venue, England the opposition, and Kyran Bracken the victim, his ankle

New Zealand (1992)

Last Season	7 caps	0 pts
Career	13 caps	5 pts

Caps (13): **1992** Wd(2,3R), I(1), A(1R,3), SA **1993** BL(1,2,3), A, WS, S, E

Points (5 – 1t): **1992** A(3:1t)

crunched by Jamie's studs while the game was still in its infancy. The fact that the All Blacks management failed to make known any punishment prolonged the dissatisfaction over the incident. In between these two unsavoury incidents, Jamie made news (for the right reasons) on the All Blacks tour of Australia and South Africa. Lost out in selection stakes, first to Mike Brewer, his Provincial skipper, then to Andy Earl, in the first two tests against Australia, although he came on as a 65th-minute replacement for Brewer in Sydney. But he was awarded the start in the 'dead rubber' and scored a wonderful try. Against South Africa, too, he impressed. In all he made nine appearances on the trip, bagging a try in the 80–0 defeat of Western Australia. His other outings were against New South Wales, Victoria, Queensland, Natal and Junior South Africa. A latecomer to top-grade rugby, having completed only two seasons of First Division rugby at Otago, the 1991 national champions. He was acclaimed the Province's most improved player in 1992, and in the same year excelled in two national trials at Napier, finishing on the winning side for Fitzpatrick's XV and the Saracens team which beat a New Zealand XV 20–15. Completed an excellent campaign by following in his father's studprints and representing the New Zealand Maoris on their tour of the Pacific Islands

Joubert, A. S.   South Africa

Full Name: André Stoop
Province: Natal
Position: Fullback
Height: 6ft 3in (1.90m)
Weight: 14st 6lb (87kg)
Occupation: Bank official
Born: 15.4.64
International debut: Australia 19, South Africa 12, 1993
Former province: Orange Free State
Notable landmarks in rugby career: Played a central role in Natal's defeat of England last summer, kicking four penalty goals in the famous 21–6 win (21.5.94), having earlier scored 33 points in a '94 Super-10 match against Western Samoa. Claimed 28 points in two-Test series against England. Andre had first come to the notice of British audiences when he turned out for centenary Barbarians against Scotland at Murrayfield (7.9.91) and set up the most glorious try in

South Africa (1993)		
Last Season	4 caps	33 pts
Career	4 caps	33 pts

Caps (4): **1993** A(3), Arg(1) **1994** SA(1,2)

Points (33 – 2t,1c,7p): **1993** Arg(1:1t) **1994** SA(1:5p), SA(2:1t,1c,2p)

final minute. From underneath his own posts, he broke deep into the Scottish half to set up the match-saving score. Had to wait a further two years to gain Test recognition, when called up as a replacement for Transvaal's Theo van Rensburg on the Springboks tour of Australia. André scored two tries and two conversions in the 65–5 defeat of Queensland Country (Mackay, 11.8.93), and two conversions and four penalty goals in the 31–20 victory against Sydney (Penrith, 18.8.93). Much to his delight, he was then selected to play fullback in the decisive third Test (Sydney, 21.8.93). Unhappily, both for him and his compatriots, the Wallabies won 19–12. André then appeared in the Currie Cup final at King's Park, Durban (16.10.93), where Natal lost 15–21 to Transvaal in front of their own fans. He then headed off to Argentina with the South African tourists. He made three appearances in South America, against Buenos Aires (scoring try in 28–27 loss, 30.10.93), Rosario (won 40–26, 9.11.93), and (picking up his second cap) in the 29–26 first-Test victory (6.11.93), in which he bagged a try

Kearns, P. N. Australia

Full Name: Philip (Phil) Nicholas Kearns
State: New South Wales
Club: Randwick
Position: Hooker
Height: 6ft (1.83m)
Weight: 17st (108kg)
Occupation: Key account executive with Tooheys Ltd
Born: 27.6.67
Family: Keith, Nereda, Vicki (sister)
International debut: New Zealand 24, Australia 12, 1989
Best moments in rugby: Winning first cap; winning World Cup; 1992 Bledisloe series win
Worst moment in rugby: Losing second leg of 1991 Bledisloe Cup series 3–6, allowing New Zealand to retain trophy

Most embarrassing moment: Falling over as I moved in at a shot on goal
Serious injuries: Not enough room in this book
Suggestions to improve rugby: On-field – get rid of the maul law; change positional names back to the old ones. Off-field – pay players more
Notable landmarks in rugby career: Maintained his grip on the Wallabies' No 2 jersey through 1993, although relinquished the captaincy when Michael

Lynagh returned from injury. Phil had ended 1992 captaining the Aussies to a 23–6 win over Wales (Cardiff, 21.11.92), having been a Randwick reserve grade player only three years earlier. In 1989 he sprang from obscurity to hook against the All Blacks, and has remained in the line-up ever since. The Test captaincy, in the absence of injured Lynagh, capped a fine season in which he packed down alongside Randwick team mate Ewen McKenzie throughout, as he also did in '93. Like another Wallaby front-row player Dan Crowley, his only try came in the 30–20 win over the Barbarians at Twickenham (28.11.92) – a match in which he also carried out captaincy duties. Not since the last World Cup (against Argentina) has he registered a Test try. Needs four more caps to join P G Johnson (1959-71) on the 42-appearance threshold and thus become the joint most-capped hooker in Australian rugby history

Touchlines: Golf, surfing, reading

Australia (1989)		
Last Season	10 caps	0 pts
Career	38 caps	24 pts

Caps (38): **1989** NZ,F(1,2) **1990** F(1,2,3), US, NZ(1,2,3) **1991** W(a), E(a), NZ(a1,a2). wc–Arg, WS, W(b), I, NZ(b), E(b) **1992** S(1,2), NZ(1,2,3), SA, I, W **1993** T, NZ, SA(1,2,3), C, F(1,2) **1994** I(1,2)

Points (24 – 6t): **1989** F(2:1t) **1990** US(1t), NZ(3:1t) **1991** W(a:2t). wc–Arg(1t)

Kelaher, T. P.   Australia

Full Name: Timothy (Tim) Patrick Kelaher
State: New South Wales
Club: Randwick
Position: Fullback, centre
Height: 6ft (1.83m)
Weight: 12st 8lb (80kg)
Occupation: Trainee futures broker with All States Futures (Sydney)
Born: 24.7.70
Family: Michael (father), Lyn (mother), Andrew (brother), David (brother), Anthony (brother), Peter (brother), Elizabeth (sister)
Former clubs: None. Randwick since 1991
International debut: Australia 16, New Zealand 15, 1992
Best moment in rugby: Winning

first cap in opening Test of 1992 Bledisloe Cup series

Worst moment in rugby: Seriously injuring my kidney at start of 1991 season, which put me out for three months and ruled out my representative chances for that year

Serious injuries: Torn kidney (1991)

Australia (1992)

Last Season	1 cap	5 pts
Career	3 caps	10 pts

Caps (3): **1992** NZ(1), I(R) **1993** NZ

Points (10 – 1t,1c,1p): **1992** I(R:1t) **1993** NZ(1c,1p)

Notable landmarks in rugby career: Cruelly robbed of a chance to stake a long-term claim to the Australian fullback slot in 1993, when a ruptured stomach ulcer forced him out of the side one Test after he had been selected in preference to Marty Roebuck. His NSW colleague was dropped for the Bledisloe Cup match against New Zealand, and Tim responded with five points (1c,1p) in a 25–10 losing cause (Dunedin, 17 July). His subsequent injury paved the way for Roebuck's return and Tim was not seen again. Had been a member of the Emerging Wallabies party which toured England and Europe in 1990, although he was not in the side held 12–12 by England B at Wasps (4.11.90). Fellow tourists included Jason Little, Peter Slattery, Willie Ofahengaue, David Nucifora, Dan Crowley and John Eales. Had represented Australian Schools in 1989, and broke into first grade with Eastwood the following season. Switched club allegiances to Randwick in 1991, and played at hooker for Australia's Sevens team in 1992, before touring New Zealand with New South Wales. Renewed his acquaintance with the men in Black when given Test debut in the victorious 16–15 first leg of the 1992 Bledisloe Cup series (deputizing for the injured Roebuck) in Sydney on 4 July. With Roebuck restored to rude health,Tim fulfilled the role of backup on the tours to South Africa, Ireland and Wales. He kicked eight points (1c,2p) in the 24–17 defeat of Northern Transvaal and 14 points (1c,4p) in the 34–8 win over Eastern Province, and continued his scoring exploits when the tourists arrived in Britain. He contributed all 19 points (1t,1c,4p) in the 19–22 loss to Munster, 11 points in the 16–8 win at Neath, and shared the remaining 32 points amongst Connacht (3p), Swansea (2p) and Welsh Students (1t,4p). Ended the tour on a high note with a try after coming on as a half-time replacement for Michael Lynagh in the 42–17 win over Ireland

Touchlines: Training, beach

Kingston, T. J.   Ireland

Full Name: Terence John Kingston
Club: Dolphin
Position: Hooker
Height: 5ft 10in (1.78m)
Weight: 15st (91kg)
Occupation: Marketing manager for Kiernan Electrical, Ireland Ltd
Born: Cork, 19.9.63
Family: Single
Former club: Lansdowne
International debut: Ireland 6, Wales 13, 1987
Five Nations debut: Ireland 22, Scotland 18, 1988
Best moments in rugby: Captaining Ireland against Japan in 1991 World Cup; captaining Munster to victory over 1992 Wallabies
Worst moments in rugby: Being dropped from Irish team; Dolphin's failure to qualify for National League in 1989/90 play-off match
Most respected opponent: Sean Fitzpatrick (Auckland & New Zealand)
Best memories last season: Beating England at Twickenham

Ireland (1987)

Last Season	5 caps	0 pts
1994	Tour to Australia	
Career	18 caps	8 pts

Caps (18): **1987** wc–W, T, A **1988** S, F, W, E(a) **1990** F, W **1991** wc–J **1993** F, W, E, R **1994** F, W, E, S

Points (8 – 2t): **1988** W(1t) **1990** W(1t)

Should rugby's amateur rules be revised? Yes
To what degree should players benefit? Compensation, payment for off-field activities but no wage for playing
Should referees be rewarded? Yes. The more professional they are, the better their standard
Advice for International Board: None, they seem to be more in tune with modern-day life and rugby. An extra five metres should be added to all penalties as an increased deterrent and to encourage them team benefiting to take a fast, running ball while the opposition is retreating
Notable landmarks in rugby career: Finally established himself as Ireland's premier hooker, in succession to Steve Smith and John Murphy, who had for so long divided up the duties, playing in all five Tests in 1993/94, before losing out to Garryowen's Keith Wood on last summer's tour to Australia. Terry, whose first reign as No 2 was back in the 1988 Championship, was appointed vice-captain in 1992/93, and contributed to famous wins over Wales and

269

England. If those successes were not sufficient cause for celebration, he also skippered Munster to a 22–19 victory over the touring Australians (Cork, 21.10.92). Previously captained Ireland to a 32–16 World Cup win over Japan (Dublin, 9.10.91) in a 1991/92 season which he otherwise viewed from the bench, as Smith monopolized the No 2 jersey. In all, Terry has represented Irish Schools (1982), Ireland Under-21s (1984), Ireland Under-25s (1987, three caps), Ireland B (beat Argentina 27–12, Limerick, 20.10.90), and Ireland Full on 18 occasions since his debut in the 1987 World Cup (in place of injured Harry Harbison). Toured with Ireland to Namibia (1991), New Zealand (1992) and Australia (1994)

Touchlines: Golf (18 handicap), travel, fitness

Kirwan, J. J. New Zealand

Full Name: John Joseph Kirwan MBE
Clubs: Marist (NZ), Treviso (It)
Province: Auckland
Position: Wing
Height: 6ft 3in (1.90m)
Weight: 14st 7lb (92kg)
Occupation: Public relations officer
Born: Auckland, 16.12.64
Family: Fiorella (wife)
International debut: New Zealand 10, France 9, 1984
Serious injuries: Ruptured Achilles tendon (1984 and 1989)
Notable landmarks in rugby career: New Zealand's record try-scorer (34) and most-capped player (equal with Gary Whetton on 58 appearances), John suffered the ignominy of being dropped for the 1993 tour of England and Scotland in favour of 19-year old Otago reserve Jeff Wilson. His response to the news: 'I am totally devastated'. Previous to that, his exploits had been central to the success of the All Blacks ever since his debut in the side in 1984 against France at Lancaster Park. Only the previous season he had made his provincial debut in the Auckland centenary game against the President's XV, while still a Marist third XV player. Dropped out of the 1986 rebel Cavaliers tour to South Africa, and instead busied himself with three appearances against both Australia and France. His failure to score that year was corrected in 1987, when he collected a World Cup best of six tries (matched by compatriot Craig Green) as New Zealand surged to glory. Largely responsible for burying Wales on the

Principality's disastrous 1988 tour, scoring four tries in the 52–3 first-Test rout and adding another two as the second Test ended 54–9 in the hosts' favour. John maintained his record of at least one try per Test in 1988, with four in the three-match series against Australia. But his playing career was put on hold the following season: playing against Pontypool, he ruptured his Achilles tendon and was sidelined for six months. Quickly returned to his best with two tries on his comeback in 31–16 first-Test defeat of Scotland in 1990, and on the 1991 tour of Argentina he collected eight tries in five games. John, who has spent the last five 'summers' playing in Italy for Treviso and Sienna, toured Australia and South Africa in 1992. Last season, having shed a couple of stone, he helped the All Blacks beat the 1993 Lions by the odd Test in three and regain the Bledisloe Cup from Australia

New Zealand (1984)

Last Season	4 caps	0 pts
Career	58 caps	138 pts

Caps (58): **1984** F(1,2) **1985** E(1,2), A, Arg(1,2) **1986** F(a), A(1,2,3), F(b1,b2) **1987** wc–It, Fj, Arg, S, W, F. A **1988** W(1,2), A(1,2,3) **1989** F(1,2), Arg(1,2), A **1990** S(1,2), Arg(1,2,3), F(1,2) **1991** Arg(2), A(a1,a2). wc–E, It, C, A(b), S **1992** Wd(1,2,3), I(1,2), A(1,2,3), SA **1993** BL(2,3), A, WS

Points (138 – 34t): **1985** E(2:1t), Arg(1:2t), Arg(2:2t) **1987** wc–It(2t), Fj(1t), W(2t), F(1t). A(1t) **1988** W(1:4t), W(2:2t), A(1:2t), A(2:1t), A(3:1t) **1989** Arg(1:2t), Arg(2:1t) **1990** S(1:2t), A(1:1t) **1991** Arg(2:1t). wc–C(1t) **1992** Wd(3:1t), I(2:1t), A(2:1t), SA(1t)

Kruger, R.   South Africa

Full Name: Ruben Kruger
Province: Northern Transvaal
Position: Flanker
Height: 6ft 2in (1.88m)
Weight: 16st 2lb (98kg)
Occupation: Public relations officer
Born: 30.3.70
International debut: Argentina 26, South Africa 29, 1993
Notable landmarks in rugby career: An outstanding South African success story in 1993, Ruben scored 11 tries for the Springboks during the course of the year, yet his biggest value was in his versatility. Selected for the autumn tour to Argentina as a blindside

flanker, but answered the emergency call to fill the openside berth, and did so with great aplomb, wearing the No 7 jersey in both Test victories over the Pumas (Buenos Aires, 6 & 13.11.93). In all, Ruben appeared in five of the six tour engagements, claiming tries against Córdoba and Rosario. He had

South Africa (1993)		
Last Season	2 caps	0 pts
Career	2 caps	0 pts

Caps (2): 1993 Arg(1,2)

Points Nil

been even more prolific in Australia during the summer, running in nine tries in just six 'dirt-tracking' appearances: against South Australia (2), Victoria (2), NSW Country, ACT and Queensland Country (2). The only defence to withstand his pounding was that of Sydney in Penrith. Switched provincial loyalties on his return from Australia, moving from Orange Free State to Northern Transvaal

Lacroix, T. France

Full Name: Thierry Lacroix
Club: Dax
Position: Outside-half, centre
Height: 5ft 11in (1.80m)
Weight: 13st (78kg)
Occupation: Physiotherapist
Born: Nogaro, 2.3.67
International debut: France 15, Australia 32, 1989
Five Nations debut: France 36, Wales 3, 1991
Notable landmarks in rugby career: A big contributor to French cause in 1993/94, bagging 112 points in ten starts. His goal-kicking was largely responsible for France's historic Test series defeat of South Africa (1993), but also, it has to be said, for France's first loss to Wales

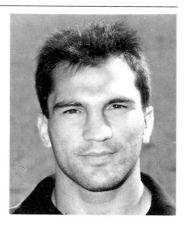

in 12 years. Toured Canada and New Zealand with France last summer (1994). Helped France win 1992 Students World Cup in Italy prior to turning out for France Espoirs in 24–17 win over touring Springboks in Bordeaux (4.10.92). In that game Thierry accounted for most of the points – kicking four penalty goals and converting one of Pierre Hontass two tries. His fortunes at senior level improved the longer the 1992/93 campaign lasted. A replacement in the first Test against South Africa, when France were beaten, he was brought in for the second Test to add some firepower, and responded with 19 points

(2c,5p) in 29–16 victory in Paris (24.10.92). Scored winning try against Scotland (6.2.93), and three penalty goals against Wales (20.3.93) as France won 1993 Five Nations Championship. Thierry had burst onto the international scene with 17 points – five penalty goals and a conversion – on his first start in France's 25–19 defeat of Australia in the second Test in Lille. His debut had come in the first Test as a replacement for Didier Camberabero. In spite of his prolific start, he had to wait until the 1991 Five Nations Championship for his third cap, when replacing Philippe Sella in the 36–3 win over Wales (2.3.91). He again replaced Sella against Wales in

France (1989)

Last Season	10 caps	112 pts
1994	Tour to Canada/NZ	
Career	22 caps	174 pts

Caps (22): 1989 A(1R,2) 1991 W(a:R), W(b:R). wc–R(b), C(R), E(b) 1993 SA(2) 1993 E, S, I, W, SA(1,2), R(b), A(1,2) 1994 I, W, E, S, C

Points (174 – 2t,16c,43p,1dg): 1989 A(2:1c,5p) 1991 wc–C(2p), E(2p) 1992 SA(2:2c,5p) 1993 S(1t), W(3p), SA(1:5p), SA(2:4p,1dg), R(b:6c,3p), A(1:1c,1p), A(2:1p) 1994 I(1t,3c,3p), W(1c,1p), E(3p), S(1c,2p), C(1c,3p)

the contest to celebrate the Arms Park's new floodlights (4.9.91), before further profiting from another's misfortune in the World Cup, as injury to Camberabero allowed him three further caps and the opportunity to kick four penalty goals, two each against Canada and quarter-final opponents England. Did not feature in Pierre Berbizier's 1992 Five Nations plans

Lamerton, A. E. **Wales**

Full Name: Andrew Edwin Lamerton
Club: Llanelli
Position: Hooker
Height: 6ft (1.83m)
Weight: 14st 10lb (93.5kg)
Occupation: Sales representative
Born: Pontypridd, 28.5.70
Family: Single
Family links with rugby: Father (Roger) played for Llantrisant and Mid-District
Former clubs: Beddau, Neath
International debut: France 26, Wales 10, 1993
Five Nations debut: As above
Best moment in rugby: Playing for

Wales

Worst moment in rugby: Finding out Llanelli prop Ricky Evans had not been picked to tour Zimbabwe and Namibia (1993)

Most embarrassing moment: Ripping shorts playing at Cardiff and being brought out pair two sizes too small. To everyone's amusement they got stuck halfway up my legs

Most respected opponent: Graham Dawe (Bath & England)

Biggest influence on career: David Fox (Llanelli hooker) – for pushing me

Suggestions to improve rugby: With maul rule, referees should not blow too early when the ball gets tied up. Give it a chance to come out. Referees also need to be more consistent in their officiating of the advantage law. It is very frustrating at present

Notable landmarks in rugby career: Wales's youngest hooker since 1947, having been capped in the final game of the 1993 Five Nations Championship against France in Paris, after excellent season which included helping Llanelli beat touring Australians 13–9 at Stradey (14.11.92). Continued run in national side on summer tour to Africa, figuring in all three Tests against Zimbabwe(2) and Namibia, as well as in 56–17 win over the South Africa Barbarians. However, on return home he managed just one more cap, in 55–5 defeat of Japan (Cardiff, 16.10.93), before being ousted by Swansea's Garin Jenkins. While at Bryncelynnog County School he played four times for Wales U-18s (1986/87), and having moved on to Beddau, picked up four Wales Youth caps(1987/88), scoring try against Canada. Represented Wales Under-21s twice v Scotland (1990-91), before which had featured in Llanelli side which gave 1989 All Blacks such a run for their money

Touchlines: Golf (26 handicap)

Wales (1993)		
Last Season	1 cap	0 pts
Career	5 caps	0 pts

Caps (5): **1993** F, Z(1,2), Na, J

Points Nil

Le Roux, H. P.   South Africa

Full Name: Hendrik (Hennie)
Pieter Le Roux
Province: Transvaal
Club: RAU
Position: Outside-half
Height: 5ft 10in (1.78m)
Weight: 12st 8lb (80kg)
Occupation: Student
Born: Grahamstown, 10.7.67
Former province: Eastern Province
International debut: South Africa
20, France 20, 1993
**Notable landmarks in rugby
career:** Hennie was hugely
impressive playing for both
Transvaal and South Africa against
England last summer. His lithe
running was behind much of the
best moves. Hennie, a former Junior
Springbok, went over in Ellis Park's
left corner for Transvaal's opening
try as England were beaten 24–21,
and he claimed 14 points in the 2nd
Test defeat of England. Actually
played in England the previous
season on a Springbok tour which

South Africa (1993)

Last Season	4 caps	14 pts
Career	4 caps	14 pts

Caps (4): **1993** F(1,2) **1994** E(1,2)

Points (14 – 1t,3p): **1994** E(2:1t,3p)

also took in France. He made six appearances and scored five points (one try).
His outings came against France B, (lost 17–24, Bordeaux, 4.10.92), Aquitaine
(won 29–22, Pau, 7.10.92), Provence-Côte D'Azur (won 41–12, Marseille,
13.10.92), Languedoc-Roussillon (won 26–15, Béziers, 20.10.92), French
Universities (lost 13–18, Tours, 28.10.92) and North of England (won 19–3,
Leeds, 10.11.92). However, he had to wait for his Test chance until France
visited the Republic in June and July of 1993. Selected to fill the No 10 jersey
in the absence of retired legend Naas Botha, Hennie played in both Tests (first:
drew 20–20, Durban, 26.6.93; second: lost 17–18, Johannesburg, 3.7.93). But
South Africa's failure even to share the series led to changes at outside-half, with
Natal's Joel Stransky taking over. Still, Hennie made six appearances on tour in
Australia (against South Australia, New South Wales, NSW Country, ACT,
Queensland Country and Sydney) and scored 14 points (2t,2c). His tries came
against South Australia and NSW. Played four out of the Springboks' six games
on their autumn tour of Argentina – against Córdoba, Buenos Aires, Tucumán
and Rosario – scoring tries against Córdoba and Rosario. Helped Transvaal win
1993 Currie Cup final, 21–15 over Natal (16.10.93)

Leonard, J.   England

Full Name: Jason Leonard
Club: Harlequins
Position: Loosehead prop
Height: 5ft 10in (1.78m)
Weight: 17st 2lb (109kg)
Occupation: Self-employed builder and joiner
Born: Barking, London, 14.8.68
Family: Single
Former clubs: Barking, Saracens
International debut: England 12, Fiji 20, 1989
Five Nations debut: Wales 6, England 25, 1991
Best moment in rugby: New Zealand 7, British Lions 20, 1993
Worst moment in rugby: Losing third decisive Test with Lions against All Blacks (13–30)
Most embarrassing moment: Being made songmaster on '93 Lions tour – I can't sing to save my life
Most respected opponent: Jeff Probyn (Wasps & England) – superb technique and physical abilities
Biggest influences on career: Mixture of Jeff Probyn, Paul Rendall, Gary Pearce, Brian Moore and John Olver
Serious injuries: Ruptured disc in neck (1991/92)

England (1990)

Last Season	7 caps	0 pts
1994	Tour to South Africa	
Career	32 caps	0 pts
Lions 1993	3 Tests	0 pts

Caps (32): **1990** Arg(a1,a2), Arg(b) **1991** W, S(a), I, F(a), Fj, A(a) wc–NZ, It, US, F(b), S(b), A(b) **1992** S, I, F, W, C, SA **1993** F, W, S, I. Lions–NZ(1,2,3). NZ **1994** S, I, F, W, SA(1,2)

Points Nil

Best memory last season: England's 18–14 win in Paris
Should rugby's amateur rules be revised? Yes
To what degree should players benefit? I don't want to be paid to play but, being self-employed, I don't want to lose money through playing rugby – somewhere in between
Should referees be rewarded? Yes, it would improve standards
Advice for International Board: If you have to tamper with rulebook at all, make rules that apply for everyone – none of this hemisphere divide; we should all be on a level playing field. Law-makers must consult players; that is rugby's biggest problem

Notable landmarks in rugby career: Only England forward to play in last 32 internationals – an unbroken run dating back to his debut against Argentina in July 1990. In that period he has played on two Grand Slam sides, in a World Cup campaign which culminated in an appearance in the final against Australia, and for the 1993 Lions throughout a three-Test series in New Zealand. Yet the period has also included an injury which seriously threatened his playing career. After the 1992 Championship a neck injury required delicate surgery, including a muscle graft, and forced him to take three months off work. He had experienced problems at Murrayfield against Scotland (18.1.92) and the disc finally ruptured against Wales (7.3.92). Surgeons replaced the ruptured disc with a piece of bone, then waited for it to bond with existing vertebra. He was off work for three months, but with no England tour was able to recover in good time before returning for Test against Canada at Wembley (17.10.92). Jason started his career at Barking, helping them win Essex Colts Cup before tasting success at Twickenham with Eastern Counties winning U-21 County Championship. Won 1989/90 Courage League division two title with Saracens, and sat on England U-21 bench in Romania (1989). Broke into England B ranks in 1989/90, winning caps against Fiji and France, and warming bench against USSR before being promoted to senior status on '90 tour of Argentina, when he made his debut in Buenos Aires

Lewis, E. W. Wales

Full Name: Emyr Wyn Lewis
Club: Llanelli
Position: Flanker, No 8
Height: 6ft 4in (1.93m)
Weight: 16st 8lb (101kg)
Occupation: Police officer with
Dyfed Powys Police Authority
Born: Carmarthen, 29.8.68
Family: Single
Former club: Carmarthen Athletic
International debut:
Wales 21, Ireland 21, 1991
Five Nations debut: As above
Best moments in rugby: Llanelli's
defeat of 1992 Wallabies; winning
first cap; Waless 1994 Five Nations
triumph

Worst moments in rugby: Missing
England game in 1992 due to food poisoning on eve of game (I had wanted to play in an England game since I was a little boy and had to wait until the following season); losing to England (1994) when Grand Slam and Triple

Crown was at stake

Most embarrassing moment: Running down sidelines in support of attack (while playing against Northampton, 1990/91) and falling over, twisting ankle in process

Most respected opponent: Dean Richards (Leicester & England)

Biggest influence on career: Peter Herbert (fitness coach) and Gareth Jenkins (Llanelli coach)

Serious injuries: 1993/94 was a nightmare season – suspected broken back v Pontypool (lost all feeling in feet and arms); strained knee ligaments v England; popped rib cartilage

Best memory last season: Beating France in Cardiff

Should rugby's amateur rules be revised? Yes

To what degree should players benefit? We should not lose money; in fact, players at top level should get a trust fund in recognition of time and effort they've invested into making grade

Should referees be rewarded? Pay referees fee commensurate with their level of performance rather than just handing out standard payment per match

Advice for International Board: Work harder on players' behalf. At the moment the amateurism question is a complete shambles

Notable landmarks in rugby career: An ever-present for Wales during 1993/94, a season in which Emyr discovered the art of Test try-scoring. After 17 internationals without crossing goal line, he bagged a try-brace in Wales's 38–23 win against Namibia (Windhoek, 5.6.93), and added a third as Wales crushed Japan 55–5 (Cardiff, 16.10.93). He played at No 8 that day, as he did against Canada (10.11.93), but was moved to blindside flanker for 1994 Five Nations Championship to accomodate Scott Quinnell at base of pack. Wales's 1991/92 Player of the Year also figured in Llanelli's 13–9 defeat of the touring Wallabies at Stradey (14.11.92), and in their 1992/93 League and Cup double. In the latter case, victory over Neath in the Swalec final was due to Emyr, an improbable hero, as he dropped a late goal to clinch victory. Missed playing for Welsh Schools because he was too old by two days. Could not play for Wales Youth either because still at school, but on leaving represented Wales at Under-20, Under-21 and B (for two minutes as replacement in 34–12 defeat of the Netherlands at Leiden, 2.12.90) before graduating to senior level. Emerged from disastrous 1991 (tour to Australia and World Cup) with reputation enhanced. Having played for less than a minute of Llanelli's 1989 Schweppes Cup final loss to Neath (after coming on as a replacement), he embarked on a hat-trick of Cup wins with the Scarlets in 1990/91 (scoring a try in defeat of Pontypool), 1991/92 and 1992/93

Touchlines: fishing (river spinning), shooting

Wales (1991)

Last Season	10 caps	5 pts
1994	Tour to Canada/South Seas	
Career	28 caps	15 pts

Caps (28): **1991** I, F(a), A(a), F(b) wc–WS, Arg, A(b) **1992** I, F, S, A **1993** E, S, I, F, Z(1,2), Na, J, C **1994** S, I, F, E. wc(q)–P, Sp. Fj, WS

Points (15 – 3t): **1993** Na(2t), J(1t)

Little, J. S.   Australia

Full Name: Jason Sidney Little
State: Queensland
Club: Southern Districts
Position: Centre, wing
Height: 6ft 1in (1.86m)
Weight: 14st 2lb (90kg)
Occupation: Marketing officer with Queensland Cotton Corp
Born: 26.8.70
Family: Roy (father), Pat (mother), Jonelle (sister), Ashley (brother), Steven (brother)
Former clubs: None. Souths since 1988
International debut: France 15, Australia 32, 1989
Best moment in rugby: Test debut v France
Worst moment in rugby: Breaking ankle v United States prior to 1990 New Zealand tour
Most embarrassing moment: Accused of enhancing a potential moustache whilst playing in Japan
Most respected opponent: Frank Bunce (North Harbour & New Zealand)
Serious injuries: Broken ankle (1990)
Other sporting achievements: Limited!

Australia (1989)

Last Season	8 caps	15 pts
Career	29 caps	32 pts

Caps (29): **1989** F(1,2) **1990** F(1,2,3), US **1991** W(a), E(a), NZ(a1,a2). wc–Arg, W(b), I, NZ(b), E(b) **1992** NZ(1,2,3), SA, I, W **1993** T, NZ, SA(1,2,3), C, F(1,2)

Points (32 – 7t): **1990** F(2:1t), US(1t) **1991** W(a:1t) **1992** I(1t) **1993** T(1t), SA(2:2t)

Suggestions to improve rugby: On-field – correct the maul rule

Notable landmarks in rugby career: Like club and state colleague Tim Horan, with whom he has formed arguably the world's best midfield partnership, his rise to prominence was helped in no small measure by a strong showing for Australia Under-17s in their 16–3 over New Zealand in 1987. Two years later he was in Britain with the Emerging Wallabies – playing in the 12–12 draw with England B at Wasps – and the same year he broke into the Test side at Strasbourg in the first match against France during a Wallabies' tour which also took in Canada. Unhappily for Jason, like Tim he also sustained a serious knee injury playing for Queensland in 1994 Super 10 final against Natal, and was sidelined for much of '94 season. Happier days included an appearance in the 1991 World Cup final at Twickenham, and he played an equally full role in the 1992 Bledisloe Cup triumph over holders New Zealand. Jason, who was reared in the Darling Downs region of Queensland, was an ever-present in the '92 Wallabies XV, scoring his fourth Test try in the 42–17 rout of Ireland in Dublin (31 October), and also fitting in tour appearances against Northern Transvaal, Leinster, Ulster (one try), Swansea, Neath (one try), Llanelli and the Barbarians. Retained centre berth throughout 1993, scoring tries against Tonga and South Africa (two in vital second Test at Ballymore)

Touchlines: Golf, movies, reading

Little, W. K.   New Zealand

Full Name: Walter Kenneth Little
Province: North Harbour
Club: Glenfield
Position: Centre, wing, outside-half
Height: 5ft 10 ½ in (1.79m)
Weight: 12st (76kg)
Occupation: Mechanic
Born: Takapuna, 14.10.69
Former province: Auckland
International debut: New Zealand 31, Scotland 16, 1990
Notable landmarks in rugby career: Mr Versatile in the New Zealand set-up, having appeared at outside-half, centre and wing in consecutive Tests last season. Walter was seen as the heir apparent to Grant Fox's No 10 jersey until the Auckland man decided his career was far from over. When Fox was dropped after New Zealand's first-Test beating at the hands of the World XV, Walter moved from centre into the vacant halfback berth, and guided the team to a centenary series win. He retained his job description for the 2–0 series defeat of Ireland before being selected again at centre for the tour

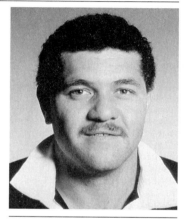

New Zealand (1990)

Last Season	2 caps	0 pts
Career	23 caps	9 pts

Caps (23): **1990** S(1,2), A(1,2,3), F(1,2) **1991** Arg(1,2), A(a1). wc–It, S **1992** Wd(1,2,3), I(1,2), A(1,2,3), SA **1993** BL(1), WS(R)

Points (9 – 2t): **1991** wc–S(1t) **1992** A(3:1t)

of Australia and South Africa as Fox returned to conduct affairs at first-five. During the trip he played in nine of the 16 matches, scoring tries against South Australia, Queensland, Junior South Africa, and best of all Australia in the third Test. His excellent 1992 was sandwiched in between two relatively disappointing years. In '91 he was replaced in the Test side by Bernie McCahill, following the 21–12 Bledisloe Cup loss to Australia, after a run of ten consecutive Tests. And in '93 a last-minute injury in the first-Test defeat of the British Lions put him out of contention for the rest of the series, and although he returned as a replacement for Lee Stensness during the victory over Western Samoa (31 July) in Auckland, he was not selected to tour England and Scotland in the autumn. Indeed, Britain has not been the happiest of hunting grounds for Walter, who made only two appearances in the 1991 World Cup, scoring the winning try as the All Blacks clinched third place in Cardiff at the expense of Scotland, whom Walter had come up against on his international debut at Dunedin in 1990. A year earlier, as the youngest member of the touring party to Wales and Ireland, 20-year old Walter did not make the Test side, though he was picked for bench duties at Cardiff and featured against the Barbarians at Twickenham – three months after having helping New Zealand Colts beat their Australian counterparts 38–15

Llewellyn, G. O.   Wales

Full Name: Gareth Owen Llewellyn
Club: Neath
Position: Lock
Height: 6ft 6in (1.98m)
Weight: 16st 8lb (105kg)
Occupation: Fitter/turner with British Steel (Port Talbot)
Born: Cardiff, 27.2.69
Family: Single
Family links with rugby: Brother (Glyn) plays for Neath and Wales; father (David), who was in Army with Will Carling's dad, is a qualified WRU coach
Former club: Llanharan
International debut: Wales 9, New Zealand 34, 1989
Five Nations debut: England 34, Wales 6, 1990
Best moment in rugby: Winning first Wales cap
Worst moment in rugby: Twice being dropped by Wales
Most embarrassing moment: Almost tripping over when running out at Cardiff for first cap
Most respected opponent: Bob Norster (ex-Cardiff & Wales)
Biggest influence on career: Llanharan RFC as a whole
Serious injuries: Dislocated collarbone, damaged pelvis

Best memory last season: Being asked to captain Wales on summer tour to Zimbabwe and Namibia
Should rugby's amateur rules be revised? Yes
Should referees be rewarded? Yes, if standards will improve as a consequence. Greater consistency needed in refereeing interpretations; ridiculous discrepancies exist at present
Advice for International Board: Take better care of players

Wales (1989)		
Last Season	11 caps	5 pts
1994	Tour to Canada/South Seas	
Career	30 caps	19 pts

Caps (30): **1989** NZ **1990** E, S, I **1991** E, S, A(a:R) **1992** I, F, E, S, A **1993** E, S, I, F, Z(1,2), Na, J, C **1994** S, I, F, E. wc(q)–P, Sp. C, T, WS

Points (19 – 4t): **1990** I(1t) **1993** Z(2:2t) **1994** wc(q)–P(1t)

Notable landmarks in rugby career: Outstanding 1992/93 campaign for Gareth culminated in his appointment to captain Wales on summer tour to Zimbabwe and Namibia, where he played in all three Tests (scoring two tries in 42–13 second-Test defeat of Zimbabwe in Harare). The Neath skipper's performance had been central in the famous 10–9 victory over England (Cardiff, 6.2.93), and his lineout exploits in particular took him to the threshold of Lions selection. To his credit, he did not let his standards slip one iota last season, playing in all nine internationals (pre-South Seas tour) and captaining the side with great distinction in Wales's glorious 24–15 defeat of France (Cardiff, 19.2.94). Added a fourth international try in Wales's 102–11 World Cup qualifying rout of Portugal (Lisbon, 17.5.94). Capped three times by Wales Youth. Toured New Zealand with Welsh U-19 team (1987), playing at No 8. Also played for Crawshays and Barbarians. Represented Wales against England and Scotland in 1990/91 before losing place to Paul Arnold. Has previously partnered brother Glyn in second row both for Neath and Wales. Toured Australia with Wales in 1991, coming on as a 20th-minute replacement for Phil Davies in 6–63 Test defeat to Wallabies. Omitted from Wales's World Cup squad in 1991, but recalled for 1992 Five Nations Championship as lock partner for Llanelli's Tony Copsey, and has remained ever since.
Touchlines: Golf, squash, weights

Logan, K. M.   Scotland

Full Name: Kenneth (Kenny)
McKerrow Logan
Club: Stirling County
Position: Fullback, wing
Height: 6ft 1in (1.85m)
Weight: 14st 2lb (85kg)
Occupation: Farmer at Powis
Mains Farm, Stirling
Born: 3.4.72, Stirling
Family: Single
International debut: Australia 37,
Scotland 13, 1992
Five Nations debut: England 26,
Scotland 12, 1993
Best moment in rugby: Winning
first cap in Australia
Worst moments in rugby: 1992
Scotland Trial when Scott Hastings
charged down my clearance kick and
scored a try; in the Scotland A game
against New Zealand, Tuigamala
went through me three times –
everyone thought I was playing
touch rugby
Most embarrassing moments:
Gregor Townsend dummying me in
the Gala-Stirling game (every time
he is shown on TV, that moment is replayed); playing touch rugby with
Tuigamala

Scotland (1993)

Last Season	7 caps	5 pts
1994	Tour to Argentina	
Career	9 caps	5 pts

Caps (9): **1992** A(2) **1993** E(R), NZ
1994 W, E, I, F, Arg(1,2)

Points (5 – 1t): **1994** Arg(2:1t)

Most respected opponent: Gary Armstrong (Jed-Forest & Scotland)
Biggest influence on career: Hamish Logan (cousin), who played ten years
for West of Scotland
Other sporting achievements: Turned down soccer trials (goalkeeper) with
Dundee United and Hearts to pursue rugby career
Best memory last season: Scotland against England at Murrayfield and my
tackle on Rory Underwood
Should rugby's amateur rules be revised? Yes
To what degree should players benefit? Compensation, the right to make
money when off the field, and an international wage. If I did not work for a
family concern, I could never take so much time off for rugby
Should referees be rewarded? If they start producing the goods on the pitch,
then maybe
Advice for International Board: I'm happy

Notable landmarks in rugby career: First Stirling County player to be capped when selected at fullback in place of the injured Gavin Hastings for 13–37 second-Test defeat by Australia during 1992 summer tour on which he played in seven of the eight games (four as wing, three as fullback). Thoroughly enjoyed the experience, his confidence high after making a try/match-saving tackle on Paul Carozza in the 15–15 draw with Queensland and earning widespread media acclaim. Cemented his place in Scotland side in 1993/94, playing in all five games, although only as a temporary replacement (again for Gavin) against New Zealand. Represented Scotland at U-18, U-19 (fullback v '91 Aussie Schools) and U-21 level, and captained Glasgow to 1991/92 U-21 Championship. Picked to tour Oz before playing in any national trial. 1993 Championship bench reserve before coming on at Twickenham as 60th-minute replacement for Scott Hastings. Won three Scotland A caps during 1992/93 campaign (scoring try in each game against Spain, Ireland and France), and again last season (against New Zealand, Italy, and (as fullback) Ireland). Toured with Scotland to Fiji, Tonga, Western Samoa (1993) – playing in all three non-cap internationals – and to Argentina (1994), scoring try in second test (Buenos Aires, 11.6.94)

Touchlines: Squash, weights, running 400-acre farm, golf (handicap 20)

Loppy, L.　　　　　　　　　　　　　France

Full Name: Leon Loppy
Club: Toulon
Position: Flanker, No 8
Height: 6ft 5in (1.95m)
Weight: 13st 10lb (83kg)
Occupation: Municipal employee
Born: Senegal, 19.4.66
International debut: France 51, Romania 0, 1993
Five Nations debut: None
Notable landmarks in rugby career: Highly rated wing-forward hailing from that rugby-playing stronghold of Senegal. Leon came to the attention of international observers for the first time during the 1992/93 season in the colours of France A. First he turns out against England A (Leicester, 15.1.93) in a

controversial match in which England overturns a 10–3 half-time deficit to win 29–17. Then he heads north-east to Aberdeen, where at Rubislaw Scotland A are put to the sword (20.3.93). Leon scores in neither match, saving his first international try for his full debut. Brive is the venue, the date 9 October 1993, and Romania the besieged opposition. France win 51–0 and Leon claims one of the six touchdowns. Poised for his Five Nations introduction, he then suffers an injury which puts him out of the opener against Ireland in Paris (15.1.94). By

the time he's fit, Agen's outstanding Philippe Benetton is back in the No 6 jersey, and Leon's only solace is a place on the bench at Cardiff, where Wales end 12 winless years against France with an epic 24–15 win. However, he is selected for the summer tour to Canada and New Zealand – a year after having toured to South Africa. He is nothing new to the Springboks, who encountered him twice on their 1992 visit to Europe. He helped France Espoirs score a famous 24–17 win at Bordeaux (4.10.92) and then had the tables turned on him, representing the Provence-Côte d'Azur XV beaten 41–12 in Marseille (13.10.92)

Lotter, D. South Africa

Full Name: Deon Lotter
Province: Transvaal
Position: Flanker
Height: 6ft 6in (1.97m)
Weight: 16st 13lb (103kg)
Occupation: Businessman
Born: 10.11.57
International debut: South Africa 17, France 18, 1993

Notable landmarks in rugby career: Experienced player whom Springbok coach Ian McIntosh drafted in after the pioneering round of matches against New Zealand, Australia, France and England in 1992. A member of the immensely powerful Transvaal union, which won the inaugural Super 10 Tournament in 1993 as well as the 1993 Currie Cup – though he appeared in neither last year's Currie Cup final (in which Transvaal beat Natal) nor the one prior to that (when they lost to Natal). It was during France's '93 tour to South Africa that Deon won his first cap, coming in for the second Test (Johannesburg, 3.7.93) as the Springboks tried to prove the first-Test draw was a freak result. It was: France won the return! Despite the set-back, he kept the No 7 jersey on the tour to Australia, playing in the first two Tests before losing the openside slot to Transvaal rival Ian MacDonald for the decider in Sydney. Other tour appearances came against South Australia (an occasion he marked with a try), New South Wales, ACT, Queensland and Sydney. Did not figure on the autumn tour to Argentina, as the selectors opted for a youth policy with the World Cup in mind

---

Lynagh, M. P. **Australia**

Full Name: Michael Patrick Lynagh
State: Queensland
Clubs: Queensland Univeristy (Aus), Benetton Treviso (It)
Position: Outside-half
Height: 5ft 10in (1.78m)
Weight: 12st 8lb (80kg)
Occupation: Commercial real-estate manager
Born: 25.10.63
Family: Single
Former clubs: None
International debut: Fiji 3, Australia 16, 1984
Best moments in rugby: 1984 Grand Slam tour; 1991 World Cup victory
Worst moment in rugby: 1987 World Cup
Most embarrassing moment: Running into the goal posts whilst trying to catch a kick in an under-age match
Most respected opponent: Grant Fox (Auckland & New Zealand)
Serious injuries: Broken collarbone (1983), dislocated shoulder (1992)
Other sporting achievements: Cricket for Queensland Schoolboys
Notable landmarks in rugby career: Australia's captain and the world's leading points scorer with 813 points. His total comprises 13 tries, 131 conversions, 157 penalty goals and nine dropped goals. With the gifted Mark Ella superglued to the Wallaby No 10 jersey, Michael was obliged to start international life as a centre, in Suva on 9 June 1984. He marked the occasion with three penalty goals and has been popping them over ever since. He missed the Bledisloe Cup series that year, but toured Great Britain and Ireland, where he appeared at centre in all four Tests of the Aussies' Grand Slam. His 21-point haul in the defeat of Scotland equalled the Wallaby single-match record held by Paul McLean. He upped it a couple of notches on his first-Test appearance at outside-half against Canada (15.6.85), when he registered 23 points (7c,3p), and by the end of 1990 he had twice enjoyed 24-point afternoons. Michael, who spends his Australian summers playing with Treviso in Italy, passed the 100-point barrier playing against the Italians (1.6.86). Has bagged 148 points in two World Cup tourna-ments, the second of which yielded a winners medal.

Helped Australia regain Bledisloe Cup from New Zealand in 1992, and succeeded Nick Farr-Jones as national skipper after the historic 26–3 rout of South Africa in Cape Town on 22 August. First Test in charge saw him last only 40 minutes against Ireland (won 42–17, Dublin, 31.10.92) before dislocating left shoulder and having to miss Cardiff Test. Resumed the captaincy in the 1993 season-opener against Tonga, but injury robbed him of his participation in the Bledisloe Cup match, which New Zealand won, and in South Africa's first visit to Oz since 1971. Returned to tour North America and France in the autumn, but was well below his best, and had to wait until last summer (against Ireland) to reach 800-point milestone

Touchlines: Surfing, golf, fishing, music, films

Australia (1984)

Last Season	6 caps	53 pts
Career	66 caps	813 pts

Caps (66): **1984** Fj, E, I, W, S **1985** C(1,2), NZ **1986** It, F, Arg(1,2), NZ(1,2,3) **1987** wc–E, US, J, I, F, W. Arg(1,2) **1988** E(a1,a2), NZ(1,3R), E(b), S, It **1989** BL(1,2,3), NZ, F(1,2) **1990** F(1,2,3), US, NZ(1,2,3) **1991** W(a), E(a), NZ(a1,a2). wc–Arg, WS, W(b), I, NZ(b), E(b) **1992** S(1,2), NZ(1,2,3), SA, I **1993** T, C, F(1,2) **1994** I(1,2)

Points (813 – 13t,131c,157p,9dg): **1984** Fj(3p), E(1t,2c,1p), I(1p,1dg), W(1t), S(3c,5p) **1985** C(1:7c,3p), C(2:3c,2p,1dg), NZ(1c,1p) **1986** It(6c,1p), F(1c,6p,1dg), Arg(1:4c,5p), Arg(2:1c,4p), NZ(1:1c,1p), NZ(2:3p,1dg), NZ(3:1c,4p) **1987** wc–E(1c,3p), US(6c,1p), J(5c), I(4c,3p), F(2c,3p,1dg), W(2c,2p,1dg). Arg(1:1t,2c,1p), Arg(2:1c,3p) **1988** E(a1:6p), E(a2:1t,3c,2p), NZ(1:1p), NZ(3:1c), E(b:2c,1p), S(3c,2p), It(1t,8c,1p) **1989** BL(1:4c,1p,1dg), BL(2:1c,2p), BL(3:1c,4p), NZ(1c,2p), F(1:2c,4p), F(2:1c,3p) **1990** F(1:1c,5p), F(2:6c,4p), F(3:1c,2p,1dg), US(2t,8c), NZ(1:2p), NZ(2:2p,1dg), NZ(3:1c,5p) **1991** W(a:2t,6c,1p), E(a:4c,4p), NZ(a1:2c,3p), NZ(a2:1p). wc–Arg(3c,2p), WS(3p), W(b:1t,4c,2p), I(1t,2c,1p), NZ(b:1c,2p), E(b:1c,2p) **1992** S(1:1t,1c,3p), S(2:1c,5p), NZ(1:2p), NZ(2:3p), NZ(3:2c,3p), SA(1c,3p) **1993** T(1c), C(2c,3p), F(1:1c,2p) **1994** I(1:1t,1c,2p), I(2:1c,5p)

England wing Ian Hunter evades the tackle of William Techoueyres in Paris.

Macabiau, A.   France

Full Name: Alain Macabiau
Club: Perpignan
Position: Scrum-half
Height: 5ft 9in (1.75m)
Weight: 12st 4lb (73kg)
Occupation: PE teacher
Born: Perpignan, 15.5.66
Former club: Nîmes
International debut: Scotland 12, France 20, 1994
Five Nations debut: As above
Notable landmarks in rugby career: Suffered tragic misfortune last season when suffering a family bereavement just hours before his selection to represent France for first time. Not surprisingly, Alain was a little distracted during his debut at Murrayfield (19.3.94), where France beat Scotland 20–12 to avoid the Wooden Spoon – the funeral had been held only days earlier. But he did enough to underline his potential, and was quickly reselected to tour Canada and New Zealand over the summer. Perpignan's

France (1994)

Last Season	2 caps	0 pts
1994	Tour to Canada/NZ	
Career	2 caps	0 pts

Caps (2): 1994 S, C

Points Nil

captain for the past three seasons, he earned his Test chance after the unfortunate Aubin Hueber had damaged knee ligaments. He had understudied the Toulon No 9 during France's 37–20 defeat of Romania in Bucharest (20.5.93), and was again called onto the bench, this time as deputy to Colomiers' Fabien Galthie, for the visit to Cardiff (19.2.94), where France lost to Wales for the first time in 13 contests. Shortly afterwards, he played a pivotal role in France A's 20–8 win over their England counterparts, landing two dropped goals (5.3.94). Alain has also represented French Students

McBride, W. D.   Ireland

Full Name: William Denis McBride
Club: Malone
Position: Flanker
Height: 5ft 11in (1.80m)
Weight: 13st 10lb (87kg)
Occupation: Mechanical engineer
with Ballylumford Power Ltd
Born: Belfast, 9.9.64
Family: Catrina (wife), Stephanie
Denise (daughter)
Family links with rugby: Brother
also plays
Former club: Queen's University
Belfast
International debut: Ireland 9,
Wales 12, 1988
Five Nations debut: As above
Best moments in rugby: Beating
England in 1993 and 1994
Worst moment in rugby: Second
half of Ireland's 3–35 defeat by
England in 1988, when we conceded
35 points without reply
Most embarrassing moment:
Ireland v England (1988)
Most respected opponents: David
Wilson (Queensland & Australia)
Other sporting achievements:
Completed the 1982 Belfast City
Marathon

Ireland (1988)

Last Season	5 caps	0 pts
1994	Tour to Australia	
Career	17 caps	8 pts

Caps (17): **1988** W, E, WS, It **1989** S **1990** F, W, Arg **1993** S, F, W, E, R **1994** W, E, S, A(1R)

Points (8 – 2t): **1988** WS(1t) **1990** W(1t)

Best memory last season: Final whistle at Twickenham
Should rugby's amateur rules be revised? Yes
To what degree should players benefit? Everything short of being paid to play
Should referees be rewarded? Why not? Some form of expenses. They're in same boat as players
Advice for International Board: It's very hard to enforce laws. Compare Ireland with France at club level: standards are not as good in Ireland and there's not as much as money. It's all down to the amount of money in the game. In countries like England and France there is the money, but for those of us who haven't got it, it doesn't matter what the rules are, there can be no rewards for players if no one is watching the game
Notable landmarks in rugby career: Injury ruled him out of Paris match

against France (15.1.94) last season, but he was hurried back into the side two weeks later against Wales. Having added four caps to his tally during 1993/94, he headed off on tour to Australia, hoping for better luck than his previous trip away with Ireland. That was in 1992, when he returned from New Zealand after just one game – the victim of a freak training accident when he broke a toe after catching a stud in Kelvin Leahy. Malone and Ulster captain, who returned to the Test arena after a three-year gap in the 1993 Five Nations Championship. First representative honours came for Ulster and Irish Schools sides in 1983. Graduated to Ulster Under-20s and Combined Provinces Under-21s in 1984/85 before making his senior Ulster bow against Connacht in 1987. Having impressed on the summer tour to France, which featured a 19–18 non-cap victory against the French, he was given his Test debut in the '88 Championship against Wales. Collected his first try third time out against Western Samoa, but lost his place after win over Italy. In and out of favour for the next four years before firmly taking possession of the No 7 jersey in 1992/93

Touchlines: Athletics (400 metres)

McCall, C. M. — Ireland

Full Name: Con Mark McCall
Club: Bangor
Position: Centre, outside-half
Height: 5ft 9in (1.75m)
Weight: 12st 7lb (79kg)
Occupation: Public servant
Born: Bangor, 29.11.67
Family: Single
Family links with rugby: Peter (brother) plays for QUB
International debut: New Zealand 24, Ireland 21, 1992
Five Nations debut: Ireland 15, Wales 17, 1994
Best moment in rugby: Winning first cap against New Zealand
Worst moment in rugby: Not being selected for last summer's Australia tour
Most respected opponent: Michael Lynagh (Australia)
Biggest influence on career: Bangor coach Ashley Armstrong – changed me from outside-half to centre when I was 23

Ireland (1992)

Last Season	1 cap	0 pts
Career	3 caps	0 pts

Caps (3): 1992 NZ(1R,2) **1994** W

Points Nil

Other sporting achievements: Irish Schools cricket with Vince Cunningham and Ciaran Clarke. Also played for Irish Universities and Irish Under-23s

Best memory last season: Test selection against Wales

Should rugby's amateur rules be revised? Yes

To what degree should players benefit? Those who devote so much time to rugby should be able to benefit from anything extra-curricular – no limit

Should referees be rewarded? Top-grade referees are under same scrutiny as Test players, so deserve similar recompense. But I don't think rewards would have any affect on standards

Advice for International Board: One rule for all, regardless of hemisphere. Maul law should be seriously looked at. Too many sides are kicking and killing the ball

Notable landmarks in rugby career: Arguably the unluckiest Test player in the Four Home Unions last season. Having toured Zimbabwe, Namibia and South Africa with Irish development squad in 1993, his excellent performances for Ulster returned him to the Test ranks for first time since playing in both Test defeats on 1992 tour of New Zealand. Did nothing wrong in 15–17 defeat by Wales (5.2.94) but was dropped: coach Gerry Murphy explained that he was too similar to Phil Danaher. However, that hardly explained his omission from the 1994 tour to Australia. Made Test debut (Dunedin, 30.5.92) as a 35th-minute replacement for injured skipper Danaher. Played five games in all on tour, kicking penalty goal in the Auckland landslide defeat. Returned home to represent Ulster against Australia at Ravenhill, but then contracted a viral infection which threatened his playing career. However, within two months he was back, and closed the season by adding Ireland A caps against Wales and England to those won in 1991/92 against Scotland and England. Followed up last season with A appearances against Scotland and England. Prior to that, played six times for Ireland Schools, captaining the side four times

Touchlines: Cricket (for Bangor CC)

McCall, R. J.   Australia

Full Name: Roderick (Rod) James McCall
State: Queensland
Club: Brothers (Brisbane)
Position: Lock
Height: 6ft 6in (1.98m)
Weight: 17st 5lb (110kg)
Occupation: Sales director with Walmac Printing Ltd
Born: 20.9.63
Family: Lorelle (wife), Meagan (daughter)
Former clubs: one. Brothers since 1980
International debut: France 15, Australia 32, 1989
Best moments in rugby: Winning 1987 Brisbane Grand Final and 1991 World Cup
Worst moment in rugby: Losing 3–6 to New Zealand at Eden Park in 1991, which cost us Bledisloe Cup
Most respected opponent: Paul Ackford (ex-Harlequins & England)
Serious injuries: Left knee dislocation (1988), left shoulder a/c (1991)
Other sporting achievements: Several centuries in golf
Suggestions to improve rugby:

Australia (1989)

Last Season	8 caps	0 pts
Career	34 caps	5 pts

Caps (34): **1989** F(1,2) **1990** F(1,2,3), US, NZ(1,2,3) **1991** W(a), E(a), NZ(a1,a2). wc–Arg, W(b), I, NZ(b), E(b) **1992** S(1,2), NZ(1,2,3), SA, I, W **1993** T, NZ, SA(1,2,3), C, F(1,2)

Points (5 – 1t): **1992** W(1t)

On-field – lose maul law. Off-field – get rid of archaic rugby administrators who change the rules without asking players and who uphold those which need changing (i.e. the ones who have no idea which direction the game is taking)
Notable landmarks in rugby career: Waited three years for his Test debut after first touring with Australia in 1986 to New Zealand. His call finally came in 1989, when he was given a chance in the first Test victory over France in Strasbourg. He needed no second invitation, and has since been a Test regular, alongside John Eales after 1991 – although the latter's absence through injury in 1993 meant Rod had to team up with fellow Queenslander Garrick Morgan. His honours have included a 1991 World Cup winners medal and a share in the 1992 Bledisloe Cup series win over the All Blacks. A full schedule in '92 saw him play all eight Tests – scoring his maiden international try in the 23–6 defeat of Wales in Cardiff – in addition to appearances against Northern Transvaal,

Leinster, Ulster, Wales B, Neath, Llanelli, Monmouthshire (as a replacement) and the Barbarians. His omnipresence last season took him to New Zealand, North America and France on Test business. But return of Eales in 1994 ended his run

Touchlines: Spending time with family

McCarthy, P. D. Ireland

Full Name: Paul David McCarthy
Club: Cork Constitution
Position: Tighthead prop
Height: 6ft (1.83m)
Weight: 17st 12lb (113kg)
Occupation: Service engineer for Hotpoint
Born: Cork, 27.8.63
Former club: Dolphin
International debut: New Zealand 24, Ireland 21, 1992
Five Nations debut: Scotland 15, Ireland 3, 1993
Best moments in rugby: Winning first cap in Dunedin; helping Ireland B beat England B 24–10 (1991), and Cork Con winning inaugural All-Ireland League (1990/91)
Worst moment in rugby: Losing Ireland place in 1993 to Peter Clohessy
Most respected opponent: Staff Jones (ex-Pontypool & Wales)
Best memory last season: Coming so close to beating All Blacks on my Ireland debut

Ireland (1992)

Last Season	1 cap	0 pts
Career	5 caps	0 pts

Caps (5): 1992 NZ(1,2), A 1993 S, R(R)

Points Nil

Suggestions to improve rugby: On-field – improve refereeing of scrum
Notable landmarks in rugby career: Not one of Paul's busiest seasons: Paul played only four minutes of Test rugby in 1993/94, coming on as a 76th-minute replacement for Nick Popplewell in 25–3 defeat of Romania (Dublin, 14.11.93). His misfortune continued from 1992/93, when he lost the Irish tighthead berth to Peter Clohessy during the '93 Five Nations Championship. The selectors change of mind followed Ireland's shocking defeat by Scotland (16.1.93). That was Paul's fourth consecutive Test appearance, having made his debut against the All Blacks (Dunedin, 30.5.92) during summer tour. On that day Ireland led 12–0 before eventually being reeled in and losing 24–21.

He played also in the 59–6 second-Test loss in Wellington the following week, and then against world champions Australia in a similarly heavy defeat (17–42) at Lansdowne Road on 31 October. Prior to his international call-up, he had won Schools Junior and Senior Cup medals, and had represented Munster in Irish Inter-Provincial Championships, and Ireland B against Scotland B, England B and Scotland B, scoring a try in the latter. An Irish World Cup triallist as far back as 1987, Paul shared in Cork Constitution's All-Ireland League triumph in 1991, having moved from Dolphin four years previously.
Touchlines: Shooting, fishing

Macdonald, A. E. D. Scotland

Full Name: Andrew Edward Douglas Macdonald
Clubs: Heriot's FP
Position: No 8, lock
Height: 6ft 8in (2.03m)
Weight: 17st 10lb (108kg)
Occupation: Chartered surveyor with Montagu Evans
Born: Nairn, 17.1.66
Family: Single
Former clubs: Loughborough University, London Scottish, Cambridge University
International debut: Scotland 15, New Zealand 51, 1993
Five Nations debut: None
Best moments in rugby: Winning 1989 Varsity match; first cap against New Zealand
Worst moment in rugby: Missing out on selection for Scotland tour to Australia (1992)
Most embarrassing moment: Being sent off and breaking hand simultaneously in UAU semi-final, then being headlined as a 'villain' in Times report

Scotland (1993)

Last Season	1 cap	0 pts
Career	1 cap	0 pts

Caps (1): **1993** NZ

Points Nil

Most respected opponent: Robert Norster (ex-Cardiff & Wales) – constantly defied logic to outjump taller opponents
Biggest influence on career: Ian Barnes's rucking scarf
Serious injuries: Broken hand, ankle ligaments, prolapsed disc (out for three months)

294

Other sporting achievements: Bowling Steve James (future cricket star with Glamorgan) in net practice

Best memory last season: Getting Test call-up

Should rugby's amateur rules be revised? Yes

To what degree should players benefit? Should be compensated, and be able to make money from the game, but not receive a wage for playing; it would be inappropriate unless it came from sponsorship or a bonus scheme

Should referees be rewarded? Yes, they should be paid, but I don't think it would necessarily improve standards. More would turn up for the money rather than through a genuine enthusiasm for the game

Advice for International Board: Leave the rules alone. Rugby has suffered more rule changes than any other sport apart from circuit cycling. Standards are dropping, it's just not entertaining. Get coaches more involved in selection. Relax amateur laws to help growth of game

Notable landmarks in rugby career: One of four Scotland forwards promoted to senior side for visit of New Zealand to Murrayfield (20.11.93) on evidence of A-team showing previous week, when All Blacks were held to 'only' a 20–9 scoreline in Glasgow, and promptly discarded in wake of 50–15 rout. It was especially disappointing for Andy, as he was the only one of the quartet making his Test debut. Had to content himself thereafter with second A-team outing against Italy in Rovigo (18.12.93), but Scotland lost that as well, 15–18. Capped by Scotland at U-21 and B level, and made four appearances on Scotland's six-match 1991 tour to North America, including both non-cap internationals against US Eagles (won 41–12 and scored try) and Canada (lost 19–24). Played against Scotland for centenary Barbarians at packed Murrayfield (7.9.91), and then went on Barbarians' Irish tour, opposing Old Wesley and Cork Constitution. Very close to full Scotland cap in 1992/93 season, but Neil Edwards earned nod instead after a better Trial. Represented Scotland B in four losing causes – once against Ireland B (0–16, Ravenhill, 22.12.90) and three times against France B (9–31, Oyonnax, 21.1.90; 10–31, Hughenden, 2.3.91; 18–27, Albi, 3.2.92) – and in one draw against Ireland B (22–22, Murrayfield, 9.12.89). Marked Scotland A debut (Murrayfield, 28.12.91) with try in 36–16 win over Spain

Touchlines: Keen ukelele player, golf (14 handicap)

Macdonald, I. South Africa

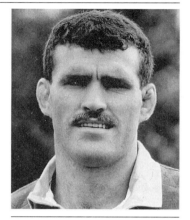

Full Name: Ian Macdonald
Club: Roodespoort
Province: Transvaal
Position: Flanker
Height: 6ft 5in (1.95m)
Weight: 17st 5lb (110kg)
Occupation: Teacher
Born: Pretoria, 22.2.68
International debut: South Africa 24, New Zealand 27, 1992
Notable landmarks in rugby career: 1993 was a patchy year for Ian. He helped Transvaal win the Currie Cup, beating Natal 21–15 in the final at King's Park, Durban (16.10.93), but he only appeared in two of South Africa's seven Test engagements, in the first Test against France and in the last against Australia; the Springboks won neither. Outings on the tour of Australia included those against Western Australia (scored two tries), Victoria, NSW Country, ACT, Queensland Country (try) and Sydney (try). Missed out on autumn

South Africa (1992)

Last Season	3 caps	0 pts
Career	5 caps	0 pts

Caps (5): **1992** NZ, A **1993** F(1), A(3) **1994** E(2)

Points Nil

tour to Argentina, but returned in 1994 for wonderful 27–9 second Test win over England (Cape Town, 11.6.94). Educated at Rhodesfield Technical High in Kemptonpark, Ian quickly proved himself a thoroughbred by breaking into the Transvaal side in 1989 and teaming up with Springbok back-row legend Jannie Breedt. Both men were selected by South Africa for their historic return to Test rugby against New Zealand at Ellis Park (15.8.92), a match which ended 24–27 in favour of the All Blacks, and again the following week in the heavy loss to Australia (23–26, Cape Town). Completing the back-row trio was Natal skipper Wahl Bartmann, but he turned on his colleagues the following month, leading Natal to a 14–13 win over Transvaal in a poor Currie Cup final (Johannesburg, 12.9.92). Ian's disappointment was compounded when he lost his breakaway Test place to Northern Transvaal's Adriaan Richter in France, and to Western Province giant Frederik Smit at Twickenham against England. However, he still made six appearances for the Springboks: against France B, Provence-Côte d'Azur (scored try), Languedoc-Roussillon, French Universities, the Midlands Division and the Northern Division

McIvor, D. J.   Scotland

Full Name: David John McIvor
Club: Edinburgh Academicals
Position: No 8, flanker
Height: 6ft 1in (1.85m)
Weight: 16st 9lb (101kg)
Occupation: Computer technician with Fife Police
Born: Kirkcaldy, 29.6.64
Family: Pauline (wife), Jamie (son) and David (son)
Former clubs: Dunfermline, Glenrothes
International debut: Scotland 7, England 25, 1992
Five Nations debut: As above
Best moment in rugby: Winning first cap in 1992 Calcutta Cup match
Worst moment in rugby: Being thrashed at home by New Zealand (1993)
Most embarrassing moment: Being called 'Grandad' by the opposition (because of my grey hair)
Most respected opponent: John Jeffrey (Kelso & ex-Scotland)
Biggest influence on career: Self-motivation
Best memory last season: Being capped against All Blacks
Should rugby's amateur rules be revised? No
To what degree should players benefit? Not at all
Should referees be rewarded? No
Advice for International Board: Reduce value of penalty goal to two points

Scotland (1992)

Last Season	1 cap	0 pts
1994	Tour to Argentina	
Career	5 caps	0 pts

Caps (5): **1992** E, I, F, W **1993** NZ

Points Nil

Notable landmarks in rugby career: Returned to Scotland side after more than a year's lay-off when selected at blindside flanker against New Zealand at Murrayfield (20.11.93). Unfortunately, his impressive performance of the previous week (playing for Scotland A in 9–20 loss to All Blacks) could not be emulated as New Zealand stepped up many gears to win 51–15. Disappeared almost without trace thereafter, surfacing three months later in Rennes wearing colours of Scotland A in superb 12–9 win over French counterparts (20.2.94). Had broken into Scotland side in 1992 Five Nations Championship. One of four new caps fielded against England (18.1.92). Played all four Championship games, and then spent summer touring with senior party in Australia, where lost No 6 jersey to Doddie Weir. Played first District game for North and

Midlands in 1986, having represented North/Midlands U-18s in 1982 and U-21s in 1985. Helped North/Midlands beat Anglo-Scots at Oxford (15.12.90) for first win in McEwan's Scottish Inter-District Championship since 1984. Made Scotland B debut against France in 10–31 defeat at Hughenden (2.3.91), and added second cap in 19–29 loss to Ireland B (Murrayfield, 28.12.91). Toured Argentina with Scotland (1994), playing against Cuyo, Córdoba (scored try) and Rosario

Touchlines: Golf (14-handicap), table-tennis

McKenzie, E. J. A. Australia

Full Name: Ewen James Andrew McKenzie
State: New South Wales
Clubs: Randwick (Aus: since 1985), Paris University (Fr: since 1993)
Position: Tighthead prop
Height: 6ft (1.82m)
Weight: 17st 5lb (110kg)
Occupation: Trainee waste management engineer with CGEA (France) and its affiliate COLLEX (Australia). Responsible for activities in industrial and domestic waste collection, transfer and recycling
Born: 21.6.65
Family: Sally (wife)
Former clubs: Harlequins (Melbourne, 1984)
International debut: France 9, Australia 21, 1990
Best moments in rugby: Beating NZ in 1991 World Cup semi-final; beating NZ in Wellington (1990); beating South Africa (1992); winning Bledisloe Cup (1992)
Worst moments in rugby: Losing Grand Final to Parramatta (1986); missing selection for 1986 Scotland Test; being dropped by NSW selectors in 1989; injury during British Lions tour

Australia (1990)

Last Season	10 caps	0 pts
Career	34 caps	9 pts

Caps (34): **1990** F(1,2,3), US, NZ(1,2,3) **1991** W(a), E(a), NZ(a1,a2). wc–Arg, W(b), I, NZ(b), E(b). **1992** S(1,2), NZ(1,2,3), SA, I, W **1993** T, NZ, SA(1,2,3), C, F(1,2) **1994** I(1,2)

Points (9 – 2t): **1990** US(1t) **1992** I(1t)

Most embarrassing moment: Tony Daly and I doing our fat percentage tests prior to the 1991 World Cup. (I should also mention that Phil Kearns managed, with Tony Daly alongside, to lose a tighthead in a sixth-grade trial match in 1993 – just in case they forget to mention it!)

Most respected opponent: The following opponents' attributes I have admired: entertaining – Tony Daly; story-telling – Peter Fatialofa; scrummaging – Frederico Mendez; athleticism – Steve McDowell; demeanor/ornament to the position – David Sole; dancing – Olo Brown; drinking games – Jeff Probyn; singing – Pascal Ondarts/Geoff Didier; most like to have a drink with – Jason Leonard (our paths have not crossed post-match despite two games against him)

Serious injuries: Posterior cruciate tear left knee (1987), medial ligament strain (1989), numerous other arthritic-type ailments that medicine has been unable to cure

Suggestions to improve rugby: On-field – exotic sevens tournament for tight-five only; more Barbarian-type fixtures; regular Northern Hemisphere v Southern Hemisphere fixtures; reduce dropped goal value to one point; universal trial by video; standardize elegibility for national teams; improve refereeing standards; get rid of the new maul turnover rule as it encourages negative play. Off-field – more efforts to improve the situation for wives and children; they suffer more from the effects of time given up to rugby

Notable landmarks in rugby career: The first born-and-bred Victorian since 1932 to represent Australia, Ewen moved to Sydney club Randwick in 1985 to further his rugby career, and five years later was rewarded with his first cap on the tour to France. Since those early days – a knee injury in 1989 had delayed his Test debut – he has built one of the most respected front-row partnerships in world rugby with fellow New South Walians Phil Kearns and Tony Daly. A measure of the esteem in which he is held was that the World XV included him in their side to play the All Blacks in the 1992 Centenary Series, a year after he had picked up a World Cup winners medal at Twickenham. A Test ever-present since then, scoring his second international try in the 42–17 win over Ireland in Dublin in 1992, was awarded the captaincy during 1993 in the absence of Michael Lynagh. Ewen skippered the Wallabies in the 25–10 Bledisloe Cup loss to New Zealand, and rather more memorably throughout the home series win over South Africa. Lynagh returned thereafter

Touchlines: Trying to find ways to spend more time with my wife

Merle, O.   France

Full Name: Olivier Merle
Club: Grenoble
Position: Lock
Height: 6ft 6in (1.98m)
Weight: 20st (124kg)
Occupation: Rugby development officer with Isère Council
Born: Chamalieres, 14.11.65
Former clubs: Blanzat, Montferrand, Vichy
International debut: South Africa 20, France 20, 1993
Five Nations debut: France 35, Ireland 15, 1994
Notable landmarks in rugby career: An extraordinary athletic specimen, Olivier only took up rugby four years ago, having been one of his country's most promising shot-putters. He boasts the ability to achieve an 80cm standing jump in full gear. Weighing in at an even 20st, and the owner of size-17 boots, his progress up rugby's representative ladder was swift. Joining Grenoble at the start of the 1992/93 season, he powered them to

France (1993)

Last Season 1994	10 caps	10 pts
	Tour to Canada/NZ	
Career	10 caps	10 pts

Caps (10): **1993** SA(1,2), R(b), A(1,2) **1994** I, W, E, S, C

Points (10 – 2t): **1993** R(b:1t) **1994** I(1t)

the French Club Championship final, where they lost 14–11 to Castres (Paris, 5.7.92), and he was promptly invited to bolster France's challenge in South Africa during the summer of 1993. The former lumberjack proved invaluable, playing in both Tests as the French won a series in the Republic for the first time since 1958. Thereafter he was a regular, playing in all of France's Test matches in 1993/94 – the shared series with world champions Australia, the 51–0 thrashing of Romania and the 1994 Five Nations Championship – before hitting the road again for the summer tour of Canada and New Zealand

Milne, K. S.   Scotland

Full Name: Kenneth Stuart Milne
Club: Heriot's FP
Position: Hooker
Height: 6ft (1.83m)
Weight: 15st 12lb (101kg)
Occupation: Sales manager with
P.E.C. Barr, Printers of Leith
Born: Edinburgh, 1.12.61
Family: Eleanor (wife), Stuart (son)
and Jenny (daughter)
Family links with rugby: Iain
(brother) played for Heriot's,
Scotland and British Lions; David
(brother) plays for Heriot's and
Scotland
International debut: Scotland 23,
Wales 7, 1989
Five Nations debut: As above
Best moment in rugby: 1990
Grand Slam
Worst moment in rugby: Losing
15–51 to New Zealand, 1993
Most embarrassing moment:
Accidentally flooring the referee
when the front rows of Heriot's and
Jed-Forest squared up. He let me off
Most respected opponent: Gary
Callender (Kelso & Scotland)
Biggest influence on career:
Brothers Iain and David

Scotland (1989)

Last Season	5 caps	0 pts
Career	30 caps	12 pts
Lions 1993	1 Test	0 pts

Caps (30): **1989** W, E, I, F, Fj, Ro **1990**
I, F, W, E, NZ(2), Arg **1991** F,
W, E wc–Z **1992** E, I, F, W, A(1)
1993 I, F, W, E. Lions–NZ(1).
NZ **1994** W, E, I, F

Points (12 – 3t): **1989** Fj(1t) **1990**
Arg(2t)

Best memory last season: Not a lot to cheer about except being picked for
first Lions Test
Should rugby's amateur rules be revised? Yes
To what degree should players benefit? Trust funds should be set up for
promotional work, dinners etc. We should be paid compensation whilst on
tours, though that too should be left in a trust fund until we retire. But no
payment for playing rugby
Should referees be rewarded? Should be compensated for time they devote,
but I can't think it would improve standards
Advice for International Board: Leave rules alone. Make penalties between
goal line and 22 worth 3 points, between 22 and 10-metre line 2 points, and
beyond 10-metre line 1 point. (It seems stupid that you can lose a game on a
technical offence 45 metres out.) People would be encouraged to run ball more

and make for more exciting spectacle. Then you wouldn't get an ordinary side with a good kicker winning the game

Suggestions to improve rugby: On-field – stop changing the rules; Scottish Inter-District Championship should be broadened to include likes of Bath and Leicester; a British League of sorts, with stronger opposition, must be the way forward. Off-field – clarification of amateurism issue is desperately needed; more could be done for the players (rewards are very minimal, especially in Scotland)

Notable landmarks in rugby career: Earned British Lions recognition on 1993 tour to New Zealand, beating English rival Brian Moore to No 2 jersey for first Test, an occasion marred from the British standpoint by Grant Fox's controversial injury-time penalty winner (lost 20–18, Christchurch, 12.6.93). Emigration to South Africa of long-time Scottish rival John Allan, after 1991 World Cup (in which Kenny made only one appearance), left way clear for Kenny to take cap tally to 30 for the five-year period since his debut in 1989. Scored first international try against Fiji in October 1989, and became first Scotland hooker to score two tries in an international when bagging a brace in 49–3 defeat of Argentina (Murrayfield, 10.11.90), in the same year as he had been ever-present through triumphant Grand Slam campaign. Toured with Scotland to North America (1985 & 1991), New Zealand (1990), Australia (1992) and Argentina (1994). On aforementioned Australia tour, Kenny lasted just ten minutes in the 12–27 first-Test defeat in Sydney before injury forced him out of fray. He was an absentee the following week as the Aussies completed a 2–0 series win at Ballymore, and was again missing when a shadow Scotland side warmed up for the 1993 Five Nations campaign with a 22–17 win over Italy A at Melrose. However, he was in situ by time of Championship. The youngest of the three-capped Milne brothers (they once played together for Barbarians in Mobbs Memorial Match), Kenny has six Scotland B appearances to his name

Touchlines: Fly fishing (salmon & trout)

Montlaur, P.   France

Full Name: Pierre Montlaur
Club: Agen
Position: Outside-half
Height: 5ft 8 ½ in (1.74m)
Weight: 11st 12lb (70.7kg)
Occupation: Joinery contractor
Born: Castelsarrasin, 7.2.63
Former club: Castelsarrasin
International debut: France 13,
England 31, 1992
Five Nations debut: As above
**Notable landmarks in rugby
career:** Extended his international
career to 44 minutes when he came
on as a 52nd-minute replacement
against Scotland in final game of
France's distinctly ordinary 1994
Five Nations campaign. As he took
over from Thierry Lacroix, he also
assumed goalkicking responsibilities,
and was called upon to convert the
interception try scored by new
captain Philippe Saint-André; he
made no mistake. His only previous
cap had been as a 64th-minute
replacement for the concussed Jean-
Luc Sadourny against England two years previously.

France (1992)

Last Season	1 cap	0 pts
Career	2 caps	2 pts

Caps (2): **1992** E(R) **1994** S(R)

Points (2 – 1c): **1994** S(R:1c)

The long-time half-back partner of French coach Pierre Berbizier at Agen, he was one of three replacements deployed by Berbizier, the coach, in that traumatic 13–31 Five Nations loss at Parc des Princes. Prior to that he had displayed prolific form for France B during the 1990/91 season, with 19 points (2c,4p,1dg from eight pots at goal) in the comprehensive 31–10 defeat of Scotland B at Hughenden, and six points (2dg) in the 10–6 win over England's second string at Bristol. Spent his formative years representing France Juniors and the French Armed Forces before helping Agen to win the 1988 French Club Championship and reach the final two years later. He also represented the French Barbarians against the All Blacks (27.10.90), landing a dropped goal and conversion in a 23–13 losing cause. Came close to guiding South West France to a famous win over the 1993 Wallabies (20.10.93), kicking 14 points (1c,4p) in a 19–20 loss

Moon, R. H. St J. B.   Wales

Full Name: Rupert Henry St John Barker Moon
Club: Llanelli
Position: Scrum-half
Height: 5ft 11in (1.81m)
Weight: 13st 7lb (86kg)
Occupation: TV researcher/production manager and presenter with Rugby Vision (Cardiff)
Born: Birmingham, 1.2.68
Family: Single
Family links with rugby: Brother (Richard) plays scrum-half for Rosslyn Park. Sister (Estelle) plays scrum-half/back row for Wasps Ladies
Former clubs: Walsall, Abertillery, Neath
International debut: France 26, Wales 10, 1993
Five Nations debut: As above
Best moments in rugby: Kicking conversion from each touchline playing for Barbarians at 1991 Hong Kong Sevens; captaining Barbarians against Cork Constitution on centenary tour; selection to Wales team (1993); being shouldered off Stradey Park after Llanelli beat 1992 Wallabies

Wales (1993)		
Last Season	10 caps	5 pts
Career	14 caps	15 pts

Caps (14): **1993** F, Z(1,2), Na, J, C **1994** S, I, F, E. wc(q)–Sp. C, Fj, WS

Points (15 – 3t): **1993** Z(1:1t), Na(1t), J(1t)

Worst moment in rugby: Head-high tackle by Gloucester's Dave Sims which dislocated my shoulder
Most embarrassing moments: Saying my full name on national television; losing kicking competition to Llanelli club mates Phil Davies and Gary Jones
Most respected opponents: David Bishop (ex-Pontypool & Wales) and brother Richard (Rosslyn Park & England B)
Biggest influence on career: Alfie the fruitbat Brickell (Abertillery coach) – inspired to me go further at age of 18
Serious injuries: Popped rib cartilage, shoulder dislocation
Other sporting achievements: Cricket for Walsall; soccer for Midlands Schools
Best memory last season: Winning Five Nations Championship – the style of play and atmosphere at Cardiff Park against Scotland was incredible

Should rugby's amateur rules be revised? Should be clarified, so that all people across the world are aware of where they stand

To what degree should players benefit? Sould be compensated, and free to earn from off-the-field activities – but no, I don't want to see a wage for internationals

Should referees be rewarded? Yes, they should, and it would improve standards. It would make them more professional

Advice for International Board: I'm very unsure as to what they actually do, but I'm confident that new chairman Vernon Pugh will make sure they do the right thing. As for the amateur regulations, they make them without any idea of the effect they will have on the rest of the world. It is a game for players, not committees. Give all student rugby players free food vouchers (but never money). Organize cheap nose jobs for people with big noses when they've finished playing career

Notable landmarks in rugby career: Three tries and a part in Wales's 1994 Five Nations title triumph represented a pretty good return for Rupert last season. But anything less would have seen him slip from the heights of 1992/93. Two of his tries came on 1993 summer tour of Zimbabwe and Namibia, one against each nation, and the third was all but lost in the points avalanche that submerged hapless Japan (Cardiff, 16.10.93). Other career highs include being shouldered off Stradey Park after captaining Llanelli to a 13–9 defeat of the touring Wallabies (14.11.92), and then leading Scarlets to 1992/93 league and cup double. Declared his allegiance to Wales in 1991/92, having sat on bench for England Schools and stood on pitch for England Colts, Under-21s (scored try in inaugural match: Romania 13, England 54, Bucharest, 13.5.89), Students (as captain and in 1988 Students World Cup) and B grades. Made his Test debut on 20 March 1993, displacing British Lion Robert Jones for the match against France in Paris (lost 10–26). Had been ever-present bench reserve prior to that. Joined Llanelli in 1990/91, and was promptly selected for four England B games against Emerging Australians, Ireland B, France B and Spain. Scored two tries in Kingsholm defeat of Spain. Picked up Man-of-the-Match awards in both 1990/91 and 1991/92 Schweppes Challenge Cup finals, when Llanelli beat Pontypool and Swansea respectively. Captained England Students against pre-World Cup England XV. Selected to England's development squad, but then switched to Wales, saying: 'After six years of living in Wales, I have found myself being deeply affected by the passion for, and commitment to, the game as shown by the whole community'.

Touchlines: Watching educational videos, eating out, ballet, theatre, star gazing, grass counting

Moore, B. C.   England

Full Name: Brian Christopher
Moore
Club: Harlequins
Position: Hooker
Height: 5ft 9in (1.76m)
Weight: 14st 3lb (90kg)
Occupation: Commercial litigation
partner with Edward Lewis
Solicitors
Born: Birmingham, 11.1.62
Family: Dr Penny Sowden (wife)
Former clubs: Old Crossleyans,
Nottingham
International debut: England 21,
Scotland 12, 1987
Five Nations debut: As above
Best moment in rugby: 1991
Grand Slam decider against France
Worst moment in rugby: Wales
16, England 3, 1987 World Cup
quarter-final
Most embarrassing moment:
Being forced to watch pre-match
team talks on video
Most respected opponent: Kenny
Milne (Heriot's FP & Scotland)
Biggest influence on career: Alan
Davies (Nottingham coach)
Serious injuries: Fractured ego v
Scotland, Murrayfield, 17.3.90
Other sporting achievements:
Intermediate swimming certificate
Best memory last season: England
15, New Zealand 9

England (1987)

Last Season	7 caps	0 pts
1994	Tour to South Africa	
Career	52 caps	4 pts
Lions 1989	3 Tests	0 pts
1993	2 Tests	0 pts

Caps (52): **1987** S wc–A, J, W(b) **1988**
F, W, S, I(1,2), A(a1,a2), Fj,
A(b) **1989** S, I, F, W, Ro, Fj.
Lions–A(1,2,3) **1990** I, F, W, S,
Arg(a1,a2) **1991** W, S(a), I, F(a),
Fj, A(a) wc–NZ, It, F(b), S(b),
A(b) **1992** S, I, F, W, SA **1993** F,
W, S, I. Lions–NZ(2,3). NZ
1994 S, I, F, W, SA(1,2)

Points (4 – 1t): **1989** I(1t)

**Should rugby's amateur rules be
revised?** Revised! – they don't even exist in half the world!
To what degree should players benefit? As far as possible
Should referees be rewarded? Yes. But what we desperately need is more
consistent refereeing, and even more importantly, more consistent refereeing
selections, so that experienced officials always handle big matches, and so that
referees serve their time going up a proper ladder. What we have at present are
referees taking charge of Pilkington Cup semi-finals, then Old Haberdashers,
then a school game, then an International – that shouldn't happen

Advice for International Board: Redefine the role of the IB, but don't disband it. Somewhere has to be found for our senile geriatrics. Nothing wrong with IB structure that couldn't be corrected by the right people. It's become a dumping ground for old administrators who have an artificial perception of the game because they don't speak to players and coaches. Look at their decision to keep maul law, the practical consequences of which are totally counter-productive. Once the maul is stationary, the defence's job is complete and they can spread out across the field, so negating the whole purpose of the exercise. Off the field, rugby still desperately requires parity between northern and southern hemisphere in what is allowed under the amateur regulations. Why is there no uniform interpretation? I don't necessarily think the Wallabies and All Blacks are receiving broken-time payments, but their earnings allowance from sponsorship for off-the-field activities is far more liberally interpreted than ours

Notable landmarks in rugby career: World's most-capped hooker (jointly with Scotland's Colin Deans, 1978-87), having won 52nd cap in second-Test defeat by South Africa (11.6.94) in Cape Town – well clear of previous English record holder John Pullin (42 caps, 1966-76). Brian produced some of his best rugby in 1993/94, and particularly delighted in 15–9 Twickenham defeat of New Zealand (27.11.93) – opponents to whom he had lost out with '93 British Lions. Has only missed four of England's last 54 internationals dating back to his debut against Scotland in 1987. Former captain of Nottingham and England B (on first appearance), he represented England Students in 1982, and toured Romania and Spain with England U-23s. First played for Nottingham in 1981, and left them for Quins prior to 1990/91 season. Voted 1990/91 Whitbread/Rugby World Player of Year. Ever-present in 1989 Lions 2–1 series win over Australia. Toured with England to Australia/Fiji (1988), Argentina (1990), Fiji/Australia (1991) and South Africa (1994)

Touchlines: Opera, theatre, cooking, training, tennis, golf

Morgan, G. J.   Australia

Full Name: Garrick Jay Morgan
State: Queensland
Club: Southern Districts
Position: Flanker, No 8
Height: 6ft 6in (1.98m)
Weight: 17st (108kg)
Occupation: Sales representative with Castlemaine Perkins XXXX
Born: 25.1.70
Family: Monique (mother), John (father), Evette (sister)
Family links with rugby: Father (John 'Pogo' Morgan) played rugby league for Australia
Former clubs: None. Souths since 1989
International debut: Australia 16, New Zealand 15, 1992
Best moment in rugby: Scoring two tries for Queensland v 1992 All Blacks
Worst moment in rugby: Going off injured v Monmouthshire at Ebbw Vale (1992)
Most embarrasssing moment: Being wrongly sent off during match with Munster on 1992 Irish tour

Australia (1992)

Last Season	10 caps	5 pts
Career	13 caps	5 pts

Caps (13): **1992** NZ(1R,3R), W **1993** T, NZ, SA(1,2,3), C, F(1,2) **1994** I(1,2)

Points (5 – 1t): **1993** T(1t)

Most respected opponent: Michael Jones (Auckland & New Zealand)
Serious injuries: Groin and pelvis (Wales Test 1992)
Other sporting achievements: Basketball for Queensland Country
Suggestions to improve rugby: On-field – get representative players to go to schools etc. We need to get to grass roots of rugby and fertilize. Off-field – compensate players for lost revenue due to heavy representative commitments
Notable landmarks in rugby career: Enjoyed by far his most prosperous year in international terms in 1993, due mainly to the long-term injury suffered by Queensland team mate and Wallaby rival John Eales. In his absence, Garrick was an ever-present throughout the eight-match campaign, sharing the engine room duties equally with Rod McCall. An added bonus came in Brisbane on 3 July, when he claimed his first Test try during Australia's 52–14 win against Tonga. Benefited hugely from being moved from blindside, where he had had an unsuccessful time on tour in South Africa the previous year. Named Player of the Tour in France, with Wallaby coach Bob Dwyer saying, 'He has taken this country by storm'. Chosen for Queensland in 1990 without having played

a first-grade match, he made a name for himself in the Australian Sevens team that same year. In 1991 he toured with the Wallabies to New Zealand, as a replacement for Tim Gavin, and played against Counties. In 1992, again as a replacement (in the 77th minute for Sam Scott-Young), he made his international bow in the 16–15 Test defeat of New Zealand in Sydney. A second cap followed in the third-Test loss, this time as a 33rd-minute replacement for John Eales, before he was granted the luxury of the entire match against Wales, at Cardiff, in the final Test of the season. Other appearances on tour in 1992 came against Western Transvaal (scored try), Eastern Province, Munster, Connacht, Wales B (scored try) and Monmouthshire

Touchlines: Surfing, basketball, golf, swimming

Morris, C. D.   England

Full Name: Colin Dewi Morris
Club: Orrell
Position: Scrum-half
Height: 6ft (1.83m)
Weight: 13st 7lb (86kg)
Occupation: Sales executive with Hallbridge of Warrington, Sport and Leisure Wear
Born: Crickhowell, Wales, 9.2.64
Family: Penny (wife)
Former clubs: Brecon, Crewe & Alsager College, Winnington Park, Liverpool St Helens
International debut: England 28, Australia 19, 1988
Five Nations debut: England 12, Scotland 12, 1989
Best moments in rugby: Scoring try on England debut and winning. Scoring winning try for North in 15–9 defeat of Australia (October 1988). Winning 1992 Grand Slam. 1993 Lions selection
Worst moment in rugby: Losing 9–12 to Wales at Cardiff (March 1989), and being dropped thereafter
Most embarrassing moment: Being dropped by North for match against US Eagles after five

England (1988)		
Last Season	4 caps	0 pts
1994	Tour to South Africa	
Career	19 caps	21 pts
Lions 1993	3 Tests	0 pts

Caps (19): **1988** A **1989:** S, I, F, W **1992** S, I, F, W, C, SA **1993** F, W, S, I. Lions–NZ(1,2,3) **1994** F, W, SA(1,2)

Points (21 – 5t): **1988** A(1t) **1992** S(1t), I(1t), F(1t), SA(1t)

consecutive international caps and five consecutive divisional caps

Most respected opponent: Richard Hill (Bath & England)

Biggest influence on career: Mickey Skinner (Blackheath & England) – for his team talks

Serious injuries: Broken nose (three times), serious ligament damage to left shoulder, both knees and right ankle, dislocated finger, damaged shoulder (1993)

Other sporting achievements: Gwent Schools Under-19 County cricket finalists

Best memory last season: Beating France in Paris, again, on my Test recall. It was like my first cap all over again – we kept our discipline and they hated it

Should rugby's amateur rules be revised? Yes

To what degree should players benefit? All we ask is to be treated like everyone else. Allow advertising on jerseys, like in Australia, South Africa and New Zealand. Let us endorse products, speak at dinners. It won't make much difference, but every little bit helps

Should referees be rewarded? Yes, standards will surely improve as a result, and they need to, as discipline becomes increasingly important

Advice for International Board: Make sure rules are adhered to by everyone. Too much is left to interpretation

Notable landmarks in rugby career: 1993/94 an up-and-down season for Dewi: having played all three Test matches for the '93 British Lions in New Zealand, he returned home and promptly fell off a scrambler, so missing the North of England's contest with the touring All Blacks. Looked to have recovered in time for international itself, but went down with flu in week of game and had to pass jersey over to young pretender Kyran Bracken. A brave performance by his Bristol rival meant that Dewi had to take his tally of bench-reserve 'caps' to 22 before being recalled after England's dismal defeat against Ireland. Immediately re-established himself with strong showing in Paris, where England yet again beat France, and followed up by helping to bury Wales's Grand Slam hopes. An unused replacement throughout 1991 World Cup, he replaced Richard Hill for 1992 Five Nations Championship and responded with tries in first three games, against Scotland, Ireland and France. Disappeared as quickly as he had risen when dropped by England after 1989 Five Nations loss in Wales. Dewi had graduated from junior rugby to international level in six months, via Winnington Park, Liverpool St Helens, Lancashire and North and England B. Scored three tries to inspire Lancashire to 32–9 victory over Middlesex in 1990 County Championship final. Toured with England to Argentina (1990), Australia (1991) and South Africa (1994)

Touchlines: Motocross, holidays spent on lazy beaches

Morrison, I. R.   Scotland

Full Name: Iain Robert Morrison
Club: London Scottish
Position: Flanker
Height: 6ft 1in (1.86m)
Weight: 15st 7lb (98kg)
Occupation: Money broker,
Director of Bond Sales with Swiss
Bank Corporation
Born: Linlithgow, 14.12.62
Family: Courtenay (child)
Family Links with rugby: Father
captained Melville College FP
Former clubs: Linlithgow,
Cambridge University
International debut: Scotland 15,
Ireland 3, 1993
Five Nations debut: As above
Best moment in rugby: Winning
1991 Middlesex Sevens
Worst moment in rugby: Breaking
leg in 1988 during qualifying for
Middlesex Sevens
Most respected opponent: Stuart
Barnes (Bath & England)
Biggest influence on career: Tony
Rodgers (Cambridge University coach)

Scotland (1993)

Last Season	1 cap	0 pts
Career	5 caps	0 pts

Caps (5): **1993** I, F, W, E **1994** W

Points Nil

Serious injuries: Broken right leg (plate attached with ten screws); knee
cartilage operation (1993); broken left leg (two places, 1994)
Best memory last season: There wasn't one
Should rugby's amateur rules be revised? Yes
To what degree should players benefit? Compensation for time given up to
rugby. There will soon come a time when international players will not have a
decent job. I am losing out dramatically: a large part of my salary is
performance-related bonus, so if I am away I am losing out
Should referees be rewarded? Yes
Notable landmarks in rugby: Iain's injury jinx struck once again last season,
when he broke his left leg in two places in opening quarter of Scotland's 29–6
defeat by Wales in Cardiff (15.1.94). To make matters worse, it was the Anglo's
first international appearance of 1993/94, having been mighty unlucky to have
missed out on a place on the 1993 British Lions tour to New Zealand following
impressive debut series in '93 Five Nations. Such a bad break ensured that Iain
missed remainder of season, not to mention the summer tour to Argentina. A
latecomer to international rugby, he had turned 30 when he made his first

311

appearance for Scotland A, in the 22–13 win over Ireland A (28.12.92). He then played in his first Scotland Trial, and was promptly given his full debut (16.1.93) in the 15–3 defeat of Ireland. He retained his openside berth for duration of Championship. During his formative days at Glenalmond School, he had represented Scotland 16 Group at Sevens and toured with them to Zimbabwe. Joined Linlithgow aged 16. Varsity appearances ensued for Cambridge in 1983 and 1984, during which time he also toured to Japan and the USA. Regular for London Scottish and Anglo-Scots since 1985. Scored try in Anglo Scots' 19–16 win over touring French in 1987. Helped London Scottish to five London Floodlit Sevens titles, and was also twice on winning sides at Dubai Sevens – most recently in 1992/93 with Scotland

Touchlines: Collects antique glasses

Müller, P. G. South Africa

Full Name: Pieter Gysbert Müller
Club: College Rovers
Province: Natal
Position: Centre
Height: 6ft 3in (1.90m)
Weight: 14st 2lb (90kg)
Occupation: Sales executive
Born: Bloemfontein, 5.5.69
Family links with rugby: Brother (Helgard) played for Orange Free State and won two caps – 1986 Cv(4R) 1989 Wd(1R)
Former Province: Orange Free State
International debut: South Africa 24, New Zealand 27, 1992
Notable landmarks in rugby career: One of only two players (James Small being the other) to have played in all 14 Tests since the Springboks returned to the international sporting fraternity in 1992, Pieter was acclaimed as the best player in South African rugby in '92. A big and powerful midfield presence, he claimed his second international try in the 28–20 second-Test reversal at the hands of Australia (Brisbane, 14.8.93), during a season in which he was permanently

South Africa (1992)		
Last Season	9 caps	5 pts
Career	14 caps	10 pts

Caps (14): 1992 NZ, A, F(1,2), E **1993** F(1,2), A(1,2,3), Arg(1,2) **1994** E(1,2)

Points (10 – 2t): **1992** NZ(1t) **1993** A(2:1t)

partnered in the centres by Heinrich Fuls. On tour in Australia, he also turned out against South Australia, New South Wales and Queensland, and he featured in five of the six autumn engagements in Argentina. Born and educated in Bloemfontein, he represented South African Schools before making his provincial bow for Orange Free State in 1990. After 27 matches for OFS, he switched allegiances to Natal, with whom he picked up a Currie Cup winners medal in '92, following the 14–13 final win over Transvaal at Ellis Park, Johannesburg on 12 September. It was in the same arena that he had made his international debut a month earlier, in the 24–27 defeat by New Zealand. His place in the XV which took the Springboks back into genuine Test rugby for the first time in 11 years was won with a fine performance for Natal in the 25–43 loss to the All Blacks at King's Park, Durban (1.8.92). He marked his debut in South African colours with a try to go with the two bagged by fellow centre Danie Gerber. The following week he was required at Newlands in Cape Town for the visit of Australia, who ran riot with a historic 26–3 win. Pieter retained his berth alongside Gerber throughout the tour of France and England, playing in all three Tests

Munro, D. S. Scotland

Full Name: Donald Shade Munro
Club: Glasgow High/Kelvinside
Position: Lock
Height: 6ft 6in (1.98m)
Weight: 17st (103kg)
Occupation: Student (BA in Sport in the Community) at Strathclyde University
Born: Paisley, 19.11.66
Family: Single
Family links with rugby: Grandfather played for Scotland (1919–28)
International debut: Wales 29, Scotland 6, 1994
Five Nations debut: As above
Best moment in rugby: Making successful recovery from what I thought was a career-ending injury
Best memory last season: Winning first cap
Notable landmarks in rugby career: A remarkable comeback from a career-threatening injury was

Scotland (1994)

Last Season	6 caps	0 pts
Career	6 caps	0 pts

Caps (6): **1994** W, E, I, F, Arg(1,2)

Points Nil

completed last season when Shade cemented himself in Scotland's 1994 Five Nations Championship plans. Playing, ironically, in a charity match (for David Millar) for a Scotland XV against West of Scotland in 1990, he shattered his knee so severely that he required a bone graft, the insertion of pins and two years away from rugby. That would have been enough for most of us, but Shade, a Scotland Under-19 and Under-21, was built of sterner stuff. He got himself fit again, and after a spell of club rugby in New Zealand, returned to representative rugby in Scotland. A-team appearances against Ireland and France in 1992/93, and against New Zealand (Glasgow, 13.11.93), propelled him into Test consideration. He had also toured with weakened national squad to Fiji, Tonga and Western Samoa in 1993, turning out against Fiji Juniors, Tongan President's XV and in the non-cap Test against Western Samoa (lost 11–28, Apia 12.6.93). Test call-up followed a further two A-team outings, against Italy (lost 15–18, Rovigo 28.12.93) and Ireland. In the latter match (Ayr, 28.12.93), he scored a try in the 24–9 win. Scotland's senior side could have done with a win as they headed towards the '94 Wooden Spoon. After helping Glasgow High/Kelvinside to their Scottish division-two title, he toured with Scotland to Argentina last summer, playing against Cuyo (lost 11–25) and in both Test defeats

Murdoch, A. R.   Australia

Full Name: Alistair Richard Murdoch
State: New South Wales
Club: Gordon
Position: Winger
Height: 5ft 10in (1.78m)
Weight: 15st 3lb (92kg)
Occupation: Solicitor
Age: 27
Family: single
International debut: France 16, Australia 13, 1993
Best moment in rugby: Playing first Test match against France at Bordeaux
Worst moment in rugby: Losing the above
Most respected opponent: James Small (Natal & South Africa)
Serious injuries: Thigh calcification (1992), broken bones in hand (1990 and 1993)
Best memories last season: Playing for Australia; scoring two tries against

South Africa for New South Wales; winning 1993 Premiership with Gordon

Suggestions to improve rugby: On-field – change back to old maul rule; decrease points for field goals and penalties; anything to encourage

Australia (1993)		
Last Season	1 cap	0 pts
Career	1 cap	0 pts

Caps (1): **1993** F(1)

Points Nil

more running of the ball and less kicking. Off-field – the game is now professional in some places: let's acknowledge this, and organize it in much the same way as cricket, so that the amateur spirit of the game is retained

Notable landmarks in rugby career: Gordon's try-scorer in their 23–19 Sydney Grand Final defeat of Warringah in 1993, Alistair continued the trend on Australia's autumn tour to North America and France that year. It was a memorable trip for the NSW wing flier, as he made his Test debut in the first international against France. The Wallabies did lose 16–13 in Bordeaux (30.10.93), but by then he had already claimed a hatful of tries. In his first tour match, against Canada B (Calgary, 6.10.93), he donated two tries to a commanding 40–3 win. Then it was on to France, where Aquitaine could not contain him, Alistair bagging a try in the 30–15 win (Dax, 16.10.93). He repeated the feat at Narbonne against Languedoc (won 35–18, 23.10.93), before the supply finally dried up against a French Selection at Grenoble (26.10.93), where he appeared at centre. He finished the tour as a replacement for Constable in the 15–21 loss to Côte-d'Azur (Toulon, 2.11.93). Alistair had twice previously come up against the '93 Springboks: in Sydney (24.7.93), where New South Wales won 29–28; and at Penrith (18.8.93), where Sydney were on the wrong end of a 31–20 scoreline

Touchlines: Watching foreign films, golf, gym, dancing

Scotland's Shade Munro outjumps England's Martin Johnson.

Irish Number 10 Eric Elwood doing what he does best.

315

Nicol, A. D. — Scotland

Full Name: Andrew Douglas Nicol
Club: Dundee High School FP
Position: Scrum-half
Height: 5ft 11 ½ in (1.82m)
Weight: 13st (78kg)
Occupation: Business Studies student at University of Abertay, Dundee
Born: Dundee, 12.3.71
Family: Single
Family links with rugby: Alastair (brother) plays for Scotland U-18s, Army and Dundee HSFP; George Ritchie (grandfather) played for Scotland against England at Twickenham (1932: lost 3–16)
Former club: Heriot's FP
International debut: Scotland 7, England 25, 1992
Five Nations debut: As above
Best moments in rugby: Winning first cap against England; scoring try against Ireland; representing World XV in New Zealand
Worst moments in rugby: Dislocating collarbone in Scotland B's 19–29 loss to Ireland B (28.12.91) and thus missing 1992 Scotland Trial; Scotland's defeat by All Blacks – the whole game was a nightmare

Scotland (1992)

Last Season	2 caps	0 pts
Career	8 caps	4 pts

Caps (8): **1992** E, I, F, W, A(1,2) **1993** NZ **1994** W

Points (4 – 1t): I(1t)

Most embarrassing moment: Ripping shorts open in a club game against Perthshire; trying to change them and the ball coming back to me
Most respected opponents: Gary Armstrong (Jed-Forest & Scotland) and Nick Farr-Jones (NSW & Australia)
Biggest influence on career: Sandy Hutchison (Dundee High School PE teacher and coach)
Serious injuries: Sprung collarbone (five weeks out), medial ligament, dislocated elbow, concussion, torn medial ligaments in right knee (Alloa Brewery Cup final v Boroughmuir '94 – cost place on Tour)
Other sporting achievements: Cricket for Dundee High School CC
Best memory last season: Being appointed Scotland captain for 1993 tour to South Seas; captaining Pringle Presidents Seven, winners of the Hawick Sevens
Should rugby's amateur rules be revised? Yes
To what degree should players benefit? Should be compensated for time

lost, able to benefit from off-the-field activities, and receive some form of payment for an international game

Should referees be rewarded? Top referees should – it might improve standards. But make payment performance-related

Advice for International Board: On the whole I am happy with the job they do; it's the unions that are the problem. Some stick to the laws more than others. There should be either universal adherance or the laws should be changed. Please clarify what players can and cannot do. I believe, too, that administrators should be able to alter new laws immediately should they be seen not to work, rather than having to wait a year, and more

Notable landmarks in rugby career: Captained Scotland to South Seas in 1993, and did so with such style that the British Lions thought 'We'll have a bit of that'. So, having led Scotland in non-cap Tests against Fiji, Tonga and Western Samoa, he made the short hop to New Zealand as a temporary replacement, and justified trip by coming on as a 77th-minute replacement for Robert Jones in 49–25 defeat of Taranaki (New Plymouth, 16.6.93). Played three seasons for Scotland Schools. Captained Schools and Scotland Under-19s (great honour). One game for Scotland Under-21s (concussed against Combined Services) before earning Scotland B call-up in 1990/91 for 10–31 loss to France B at Hughenden (2.3.91). Scored Scots' solitary try that day. Toured North America with Scotland (1991), scoring a try on each of three appearances (v Alberta, Rugby East and Ontario). Not included in World Cup squad, but good performances for Scottish Students (against Oxford University) and Scotland B (against Ireland B: another try) prompted selection for 1992 Five Nations Championship in place of knee-ligament victim Gary Armstrong. Scored try against Ireland on second outing. Concluded amazing season (also helped Dundee HSFP gain promotion) with selection to World XV for Test series in New Zealand to celebrate centenary of NZRFU. Also represented Barbarians in 1992 Hong Kong Sevens, and toured Australia (1992) with Scotland, playing in both Tests. However, return of Armstrong in 1993, allied to a succession of injuries, has restricted Andy to just two caps since – both last season and both resulting in heavy defeats for Scotland (against New Zealand and Wales). Rounded off miserable season by being stretchered of with knee-ligament damage 38 minutes into Alloa Brewery Cup final, in whic.. Dundee HSFP, celebrating second-division promotion, were spanked 42–18 by Boroughmuir

Touchlines: Golf (handicap 18), cricket, cinema

N'Tamack, E. France

Full Name: Emile N'Tamack
Club: Toulouse
Position: Fulback, wing
Height: 6ft 2in (1.88m)
Weight: 14st 3lb (85.7kg)
Occupation: Student
Born: Lyon, 25.6.70
International debut: Wales 24, France 15, 1994
Five Nations debut: As above
Best moments in rugby: Scoring first Test try v Canada (1994); helping Toulouse win 1994 French championship
Former clubs: Meyzieu, Lavaur
Notable landmarks in rugby career: Emile claimed his first Test try against Canada in Ottawa (4.6.94), but there was little celebrating, as France crashed to an 18–16 defeat which left Canadian coach Ian Birtwell beaming: 'This victory is the most meaningful for us, even better than our wins over England and Wales'. Emile's debut had also ended in disappointment in

France (1994)

Last Season	2 caps	5 pts
1994	Tour to Canada/NZ	
Career	2 caps	5 pts

Caps (2): **1994** W,C

Points (5 – 1t): **1994** C(1t)

the cauldron of Cardiff Arms Park. A trapped nerve in Philippe Bernat-Salle's neck gave the Toulouse flier his chance, but he didn't receive another once the game got underway, as a marvellous Welsh performance handed France their first defeat at the hands of the boys from the Principality in 13 contests. Lost his place to Bordeaux University's William Techoueyres for the championship closer against Scotland, but was included in France's summer tour squad (while the garçon Techoueyres was not). Regarded by many as the new Serge Blanco, Emile played a central role in Toulouse's 22–16 win over Montferrand in the 1994 French Club Championship final, a year after appearing in the successful French Under-23 side

Nucifora, D. V.   Australia

Full Name: David Vincent Nucifora
State: Queensland
Club: Queensland University
Position: Hooker
Height: 5ft 11in (1.82m)
Weight: 15st 10lb (95kg)
Occupation: Auctioneer
Family: Annabel (wife)
Born: 15.1.62
International debut: Australia 32, Argentina 19, 1991
Best moment in rugby: Coming on for Test debut as replacement against Argentina in 1991 World Cup
Worst moment in rugby: NSW Inter-State series 1991
Most embarrassing moment: Being called 'Mr Nucifora' by one of the young guys in the University side
Most respected opponent: All front-rowers respect each other
Serious injuries: Usual front-row legacies – back, neck, hamstring
Best memory last season: Beating NSW 37–15 at Ballymore

Australia (1993)

Last Season	1 cap	0 pts
Career	2 caps	0 pts

Caps (2): **1991** wc–Arg(R) **1993** C(R)

Points Nil

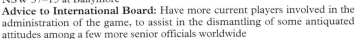

Advice to International Board: Have more current players involved in the administration of the game, to assist in the dismantling of some antiquated attitudes among a few more senior officials worldwide
Notable landmarks in rugby career: Has had the misfortune to peak at the same time as New South Waless Phil Kearns, who has rather monopolized the Wallabies' No 2 jersey with 36 appearances to Nucci's two, each as replacement. Toured England and Europe in 1990 with the Emerging Wallabies, and became first choice in the Queensland side that same year. The following season he made his Test bow at the World Cup, replacing the injured Kearns 50 minutes into Australia's 32–19 defeat of Argentina at Llanelli in south Wales (4.10.91). Remained a bench-warmer for almost exactly two years before getting his second chance, again following injury to Kearns, against Canada in Calgary (9.10.93). The Aussies won 43–16. Renowned for his busy forward play and accurate lineout throwing.
Touchlines: Beach, surfing, golf

O'Connell, K. D.   Ireland

Full Name: Kenneth Denis O'Connell
Club: Sunday's Well
Position: Flanker
Height: 6ft 2in (1.88m)
Weight: 15st 7lb (98kg)
Occupation: Medical representative with Pinewood Healthcare
Born: Cork, 25.7.68
Family: Single
Family links with rugby: Father (Des) and brothers (Brian and Eoin) played for Sunday's Well
Former clubs: PBC Cork, Lansdowne
International debut: France 35, Ireland 15, 1994
Five Nations debut: As above
Best moment in rugby: Running out at Paris for Test debut
Worst moment in rugby: Missing 1991/92 season with left shoulder injury, which required pin and plate insertion
Most embarrassing moment: Asking my boss for time off for Ireland's 1994 tour to Australia and then not being picked (later called out as replacement)
Most respected opponent: Wayne Shelford (ex-Northampton & New Zealand)
Serious injuries: Shoulder (1991/92)
Best memory last season: Captaining Sunday's Well to first Munster Senior Cup in 41 years
Should rugby's amateur rules be revised? Yes
To what degree should players benefit? Should be compensated for working time devoted to rugby, but should not be paid for off-field activities or receive wage for playing; these smack of professionalism
Should referees be rewarded? No
Advice for International Board: None, very happy
Notable landmarks in rugby career: Feared he would become a one-cap wonder when he was dropped (in favour of fit-again Denis McBride) after his debut against France last season (15.1.94). He was therefore most relieved to come on as a temporary replacement for Brian Robinson in Ireland's 13–12

Ireland (1994)		
Last Season	2 caps	0 pts
1994	Tour to Australia	
Career	2 caps	0 pts

Caps (2): **1994** F, E(TR)

Points Nil

defeat of England at Twickenham (19.2.94). Called out late to join Ireland's tour of Australia, he played against Australia B and NSW Country. Won Munster Senior and Junior Cup medals during his formative days with PBC Cork, and after playing for Ireland Schools, played twice for Under-21s and skippered side to 13–13 draw with a New Zealand XV (Donnybrook, 19.11.89). Four months later turned out for Ireland Under-25s against US Eagles in Limerick (10.3.90), having played for Munster against touring All Blacks at Musgrave Park before Christmas. The following season he won another Under-25 cap in 36–17 win over Spain at Thomond Park. Injury then sidelined him for more than a year before he finally broke into the top flight last season. Impressive provincial displays for Munster, together with a useful Irish trial, led to debut in Paris.

Touchlines: Travelling, fishing

Ofahengaue, V.   Australia

Full Name: Viliame Ofahengaue
State: New South Wales
Club: Manly
Position: Flanker, No 8
Height: 6ft 4in (1.93m)
Weight: 16st 7lb (105kg)
Occupation: Pile driver for Emanon Pty Ltd (Manly, NSW)
Born: 3.5.68
Family: Heleni (wife), Lavinia (mother), Sione (father), Sione Kata (brother), Epalahame (brother), Talia (sister)
Former clubs: Manly since 1989
International debut: New Zealand 21, Australia 6, 1990
Best moments in rugby: Being picked to play for Wallabies and winning 1991 World Cup
Worst moment in rugby: Being left in Australia by the New Zealand team when I toured Oz with them in 1988
Most respected opponent: Everyone
Serious injuries: Knee (1989)
Suggestions to improve rugby: On-field – improve discipline

Australia (1990)

Last Season	0 caps	0 pts
Career	17 caps	16 pts

Caps (17): **1990** NZ(1,2,3) **1991** W(a), E(a), NZ(a1,a2). wc–Arg,W(b), I, NZ(b), E(b) **1992** – S(1,2), SA, I, W

Points (16 – 4t): **1990** NZ(2:1t) **1991** W(a:1t), E(a:2t)

Notable landmarks in rugby career: 'Willie O' was without doubt one of the characters of 1992, and without doubt one of the most sorely missed in 1993 as injury ruled him out for almost all of the season. The big man had developed a sizeable fan club during Australia's tour to Ireland and Wales in '92. Missed the Bledisloe Cup series win over New Zealand due to a knee injury, but came back strongly (very strongly) in the Tests against South Africa, Ireland and Wales. Other appearances on tour came against Western Transvaal, Eastern Province, Leinster, Ulster, Wales B, Llanelli and the Barbarians. Tongan-born and Auckland-educated, he toured New Zealand in 1990 as a late inclusion for Jeff Miller. Two years earlier he had been in the New Zealand Schools side, but because of visa difficulties he was refused re-entry into the land of the Kiwi and headed back to Oz to live with his uncle. New Zealand's loss was Australia's gain, as he has quickly amassed 17 caps and developed a fearsome reputation as an explosive runner and bone-crunching defender. Represented the World XV against New Zealand in the 1992 Centenary Series and helped Australia reach the 1993 World Cup Sevens final in Edinburgh

Touchlines: Music, movies

O'Hara, P. T.   Ireland

Full Name: Patrick Thomas O'Hara
Club: Cork Constitution
Position: Flanker
Height: 6ft 2in (1.88m)
Weight: 15st 7lb (94kg)
Occupation: Sales director with Architectural and Metal Systems Ltd (Cork)
Born: Essex, England, 4.8.61
Family: Marie (wife), Darren (son) and Grian (son)
Former club: Sunday's Well
International debut: Ireland 49, Western Samoa 22, 1988
Five Nations debut: Ireland 21, France 26, 1989
Best moment in rugby: Beating England (Dublin, 1993)
Worst moment in rugby: Not being at Twickenham (1994)

Most embarrassing moment: Playing in front of provincial selectors in 1984/85, ended up in centre and attempted long pass to wing that was intercepted for try

Most respected opponent: Finlay Calder (Stewart's-Melville & Scotland) –

great reader of game, very street wise, and always willing to advise

Biggest influence on career: Father (Tom)

Serious injuries: Two years of foot and shoulder ligament damage; torn groin muscle; left knee operation (13 weeks off)

Other sporting achievements: Won a number of cross-country races in Essex

Best memory last season: Ireland's win at Twickenham

Should rugby's amateur rules be revised? Yes

To what degree should players benefit? Should be compensated for time lost to work, and permitted to benefit from off-the-field activities. But no wage for playing

Should referees be rewarded? Yes

Advice for International Board: Happy with them in general, fairly well in tune, and no need for same rule for all. However, stop messing about with the rules. Leave game alone. Allow playing ball on ground, within reason

Notable landmarks in rugby career: Injury-wrecked season in 1993/94 alleviated only by place amongst reserves for 25–3 defeat of Romania (Dublin, 14.11.93). Had made Sunday's Well debut in 1979, aged 18, and following year helped them win Cork Charity Cup. Won first Munster provincial cap in 1983, and went on to represent them against 1984 Wallabies and 1989 All Blacks. Toured with Ireland to France (1988), North America (1989) and Namibia (1991). Had to wait until 15 minutes from end of 1988 game against Western Samoa to replace Phil Matthews and win first cap. Voted 1989/90 Irish Player of the Year. Foot and shoulder injuries forced him to miss entire 1991 Championship, though he recovered in time to make Ireland B debut at Old Belvedere (1.3.91), where England B were beaten 24–10. Solitary appearance in 1991/92 came in 32–16 World Cup tie against Japan in Dublin (9.10.91), an occasion he marked with his first international try. Further injury again sidelined him thereafter until he enjoyed respite in February 1993. He wasted little time returning to the international fray at blindside, and played a key role in Ireland's late-season resurgence, when they upset the odds by beating Wales and England

Touchlines: About to become a serious gardener

Ireland (1988)		
Last Season	0 caps	0 pts
Career	14 caps	4 pts

Caps (14): **1988** WS(R) **1989** F, W, E, NZ **1990** E, S, F, W **1991** Na(1) wc–J **1993** F, W, E

Points (4 – 1t): **1991** wc–J(1t)

Ojomoh, S. O.   England

Full Name: Stephen Oziegbe Ojomoh
Club: Bath
Position: No 8, flanker
Height: 6ft 2in (1.88m)
Weight: 16st 7lb (100kg)
Occupation: Business/finance student at University of West of England
Born: Benin City, Nigeria, 25.5.70
Family: Single
International debut: England 12, Ireland 13, 1994
Five Nations debut: As above
Best moment in rugby: Walking out onto Parc des Princes pitch in England jersey
Worst moment in rugby: Final whistle of 1994 defeat against Ireland
Most respected opponent: Chris Sheasby (Harlequins & England A)
Biggest influence on career: Laurence Whittle-Williams (school coach)
Serious injuries: Ankle and knee ligament damage

England (1994)

Last Season	4 caps	0 pts
1994	Tour to South Africa	
Career	4 caps	0 pts

Caps (4): **1994** I, F, SA(1R,2)

Points Nil

Other sporting achievements: South West decathlon champion (1988). Runner-up in 1988 English Schools discus championship. South West long-jump and triple-jump champion. Third in All-England decathlon championship
Best memory last season: Bath's league win over Northampton – had a lot to prove, and delivered
Should rugby's amateur rules be revised? Yes
To what degree should players benefit? Players should be allowed to gain from off-field activities. We shouldn't be in the position where we can see New Zealanders and others benefit from the sport while we lose out
Should referees be rewarded? Yes, we must do something to raise standards
Advice for International Board: Be a stronger governing body. Eliminate loopholes that exist in certain regulations
Notable landmarks in rugby career: Unable to win a regular place in Bath's first team, but remarkably that did not stop Steve breaking into the full England side in 1994; on tour in South Africa he was arguably the outstanding player.

A brilliant natural athlete, he has worked the skills that brought him schoolboy honours in the decathlon disciplines into his rugby, and has become a very dynamic performer. Drafted into England side for visit of Ireland (19.2.94), and although England, lost his performance earned praise. So much so, in fact, that he retained his place for the trip to Paris a fortnight later, and played a central role in the fine win. When Dean Richards then announced himself fit again, the selectors only reluctantly moved Steve onto the bench for title decider against Wales. Previously played for England at 18-Group, Colts and Under-21 levels, and joined Bath from Rosslyn Park in 1989. Toured with England A to New Zealand (1992) and Canada (1993), and last summer was recruited onto England's tour party for the trip to South Africa, where he appeared in both Tests. Made three appearances against 1993 All Blacks, for South West England (as a late replacement), England A (temporary replacement for Nigel Redman) and Emerging England

Touchlines: Basketball

Olivier, J. South Africa

Full Name: Jacques Olivier
Club: Tukkies
Province: Northern Transvaal
Position: Wing
Height: 5ft 10 ½ in (1.79m)
Weight: 13st 3lb (84kg)
Occupation: Law student
Born: Pretoria, 13.11.68
Family links with rugby: Nephew of Springbok legend Jan Ellis
International debut: France 15, South Africa 20, 1992
Notable landmarks in rugby career: Lost Test place to Western Province's Chester Williams for South Africa's final outing of 1993, against Argentina in Buenos Aires (13.11.93), but prior to that had worn Springbok No 11 jersey in all six starts, encompassing series against France and Australia, and first match against the Pumas. Scored his one and only Test try in 20–28 second-Test loss to Wallabies (Brisbane, 14.8.93). His total of nine caps leaves him 29 short of legendary

South Africa (1992)

Last Season	6 caps	5 pts
Career	9 caps	5 pts

Caps (9): **1992** F(1,2), E **1993** F(1,2), A(1,2,3), Arg(1)

Points (5 – 1t): **1993** A(2:1t)

father Jan, whose 38 caps at flanker between 1965 and 1976 remains unsurpassed by any of his compatriots. Jacques, a former Junior Springbok, made his provincial bow in 1991. Included in South Africa's party for the 1992 tour to France and England. On that trip he developed into the first-choice left wing, playing in all three Tests – two against France and the 16–33 loss to England at Twickenham (14.11.92). In the other games he scored four tries in five games, with only the French Barbarians denying him a try. His touchdowns came against Aquitaine (won 29–22, Pau, 7.10.92), Midi-Pyrénées (won 18–15, Toulouse, 15.10.92), Provence-Côte d'Azur (won 41–12, Marseille, 13.10.92), and on the British leg of the tour, England B in the Springboks' thrilling 20–16 victory at Bristol (7.11.92). Jacques's other big game of 1992 was for the Blue Bulls against the world-champion Wallabies at Loftus Versfeld, Pretoria (14.8.92), where the tourists won 24–17. In Australia (1993) he also turned out against South Australia, New South Wales and Queensland, while in Argentina he played in five of the six engagements

---

O'Shea, C. M. P. Ireland

Full Name: Conor Michael Patrick O'Shea
Club: Lansdowne
Position: Fullback, outside-half
Height: 6ft 2in (1.88m)
Weight: 14st 6lb (92kg)
Occupation: Lending executive with Ulster Investment Bank
Born: Limerick, 21.10.70
Family: Single
Family links with rugby: Brothers (Donal and Diarmid) play for Terenure College
International debut: Ireland 25, Romania 3, 1993
Five Nations debut: France 35, Ireland 15, 1994
Best moment in rugby: Lansdowne beating Terenure to win 1990/91 Senior Cup

Worst moment in rugby: Lansdowne having to settle for third place in 1990/91 All-Ireland League after making slow start
Most respected opponent: Kenny Murphy (Cork Constitution & Ireland)
Best memory last season: Beating England at Twickenham
Advice for International Board: Nothing. Game is running well
Notable landmarks in rugby career: Established himself in Ireland side

326

during 1993/94, three years after making his Irish Under-21 debut against Netherlands (lost 7–21, Leiden 21.9.90) and England. Took his Under-21 cap tally to four the following season, with appearances against Wales (lost 15–22, Newport 16.10.91) and England (won 19–10, Dublin 23.10.91), scoring a try in the latter. Broke into Leinster senior side in 1992/93, having previously represented province at Under-19 (two years) and Under-20 (two years). Came on as 22nd-minute replacement for Jim Staples in 1993 Irish trial, and celebrated with try. But cracked left ankle the following week ruled him out of Test contention until he embarked on Irish development squad's summer tour to Zimbabwe, Namibia and South Africa. Tour displays earned him starting spot in Irish side last season, displacing Colin Wilkinson and Ciaran Clarke, who had shared duties in 1992/93 campaign, and his penetrating running combined with sound defence ensured that he remained a permanent member of the side through five internationals. Broke his Test scoring famine with 11 points in two internationals against 1994 Wallabies

Touchlines: Golf, tennis

Ireland (1993)		
Last Season	7 caps	11 pts
1994	Tour to Australia	
Career	7 caps	11 pts

Caps (7): **1993** R **1994** F, W, E, S, A(1,2)

Points (11 – 1c,2p,1dg): **1994** A(1:1p), A(2:1c,1p,1dg)

Pears, D.   England

Full Name: David Pears
Club: Harlequins
Position: Outside-half
Height: 5ft 10in (1.78m)
Weight: 12st 6lb (74kg)
Occupation: Eurobond broker
Born: Workington, 6.12.67
Family: Single
Family links with rugby: Father (Reg) played Rugby League for Cumbria
Former clubs: Aspatria, Sale
International debut: Argentina 12, England 25, 1990
Five Nations debut: France 13, England 31, 1992
Best moment in rugby: Winning first full England cap in Buenos Aires

Worst moments in rugby: Returning home from 1994 South African tour after just one game

Most embarrassing moment: On England B trip to Italy in 1989, asking Gary Pearce 36 England caps whether it was his first international

Most respected opponent: Ian Hunter (Northampton & England)

England (1990)		
Last Season	1 cap	0 pts
1994	Tour to South Africa	
Career	4 caps	0 pts

Caps (4): **1990** Arg(1,2) **1992** F(R) **1994** F

Points Nil

Biggest influence on career: My father

Serious injuries: Too numerous to mention

Other sporting achievements: Cumbria Schools soccer captain

Best memory last season: Recall to England side to play France in Paris, having played hardly any rugby during 1993/94

Should rugby's amateur rules be revised? Yes!

To what degree should players benefit? Cash payments for international games, trust funds for players and product endorsements in clothing

Should referees be rewarded? Yes

Advice for International Board: Stop meddling with laws. It takes three to four years to get a full understanding of new laws, by which time you can bet they will have changed them again

Notable landmarks in rugby career: One of rugby's most injury-prone players, David spent more than 17 months on the sidelines after winning his first two England caps against Argentina on 1990 tour. An experienced bench reserve, from where he watched 1991 World Cup and three-quarters of 1992 Five Nations Championship, he finally returned to fray in 35th minute of match against France in Paris (15.2.92), replacing injured Rob Andrew at outside-half. Further spate of injuries ruled him out of contention for another two years before coming back, again against France in Paris, in 1994. In the interim he had undergone three operations and he had only made three appearances for Harlequins during the season. But he was selected all the same, as a fullback. Did his good fortune last? Did it heck! By the time of the next Test, the title decider against Wales, he was sidelined again, with Ian Hunter having to switch to No 15 at the last moment. Fit to tour South Africa last summer, but then came perhaps the cruellest cut of all when he suffered damaged ribs on first appearance, against Natal, and had to return home. Had also toured with England to Australia/Fiji in 1991 (playing against Victoria Select, Fiji B and Emerging Australians). Made England B debut in 9–37 loss to 1988 Wallabies, and kicked all 12 points (4p) for England B in draw with Emerging Australians (Wasps, 4.11.90). Contributed a conversion to 50–6 defeat of Spain (Gloucester, 20.1.91), and two penalty goals in 6–10 loss to France B (Bristol, 15.3.91). Member of original England Under-21 XV (kicked conversion in 54–13 defeat of Romania Under-21s, Bucharest 13.5.89), he represented Harlequins in 1991 and 1992 Pilkington Cup final, but missed out in 1993 through injury

Touchlines: Golf, tennis, swimming

Penaud, A.   France

Full Name: Alain Penaud
Club: Brive
Position: Outside-half
Height: 5ft 11in (1.81m)
Weight: 14st 2lb (90kg)
Born: Juillac, 19.7.69
Former club: Objat
Occupation: Student
International debut: Wales 9, France 12, 1992
Five Nations debut: As above
Notable landmarks in rugby career: Just when he seemed to have firmly established himself as France's first-choice outside-half, Alain let himself down against England in Paris (5.3.94), and was dropped from the side at the close of the 1994 championship at Murrayfield (with Thierry Lacroix stepping in). Neither was he selected to tour Canada and New Zealand last summer. Had landed crucial dropped goal in Johannesburg (3.7.93) as France clinched the Test series with a 18–17 defeat of South Africa, and repeated the feat during France's shock 16–13 defeat of world champions Australia in Bordeaux (30.10.93). Had drawn rave reviews from French team

France (1992)

Last Season	8 caps	6 pts
Career	19 caps	39 pts

Caps (19): **1992** W, E, S, I, R, Arg(a1,a2), SA(1,2), Arg(b) **1993** R(a), SA(1,2), R(b), A(1,2) **1994** I, W, E

Points (39 – 6t,4dg): **1992** W(1dg), E(1t), I(2t), Arg(a1:1dg), SA(1:2t), SA(2:1t) **1993** SA(2:1dg), A(1:1dg)

manager Robert Paparemborde for his performances on the 1992 tour of Argentina. Penaud confirmed his status as the best fly-half in France, said the team manager. He continued to shine in the home series against South Africa, scoring two tries in the 15–20 defeat at Lyon (17.10.92), and another the following week as France gained her revenge by winning 29–16 in Paris. Was then moved to centre for the visit to Nantes of Argentina (14.11.92), and when the Pumas recorded their first ever win on French soil, Alain was caught in the clearout. Didier Camberabero returned for the 1993 Championship, which France won. Alain had made a strong impression after being given his chance out of the blue by new coach Pierre Berbizier in the '92 Championship. Having dropped a goal in France's three-point defeat of Wales in Cardiff on his debut (1.2.92), he managed a try against England in a 31–13 losing cause next time out (15.2.92) after charging down Will Carling's attempted clearance in the 66th minute. He drew a blank in Edinburgh, but ended the season with a two-try flourish against Ireland, starting and finishing the seven-try rout with touchdowns in the second and 85th minutes. Originally made a name for himself when guiding French Schools to the 1987 'Triple Crown' with 18 points in wins against Scotland, Wales and England. From there he graduated to France A and the 1989/90 FIRA Championship, in which he tasted triumph when scoring the try that inspired a 22–14 victory over the Soviet Union and gave France A the title on try difference

Pene, A. R. B.   New Zealand

Full Name: Arran Rawi Brett Pene
Province: Otago
Position: No 8
Height: 6ft 3 ½ in (1.91m)
Weight: 16st 6lb (104kg)
Occupation: Student
Born: 26.10.67
International debut: New Zealand 14, World XV 28, 1992
Most embarrasing moment in rugby: Trying to chip kick down the line and missing ball altogether
Notable landmarks in rugby career: Returned to New Zealand's Test side in 1993 after shining against the touring British Lions both for Otago and the New Zealand Maoris, of whom he captained the latter. Pressed into action in the third-Test decider (Auckland, 3.7.93) in place of Auckland's Zinzan Brooke, and was one of the outstanding figures in the All Blacks' 30–13 win. Kept his place thereafter on autumn tour to England and Scotland; in addition to both Tests, he turned out in the Saturday games against London, South West

New Zealand (1992)

Last Season	5 caps	0 pts
Career	12 caps	16 pts

Caps (12): **1992** Wd(1R,2,3), I(1,2),A(1,2R) **1993** BL(3), A, WS, S, E

Points (16 – 4t): **1992** Wd(2:1t), Wd(3:1t), I(2:2t)

England, England A, Scotland A and the Barbarians. A member of Otago's outstanding All Black back row which took Otago to the 1992 National Championship final, Arran was one of a number of players who owed his All Black jersey to an outstanding '92 trial perfomance. Ultimately, though, his

Test selection was down to Mike Brewer, his Provincial captain and fellow back-rower, whose calf injury ruled him out of selection and the national captaincy. Arran grabbed his chance with both hands, and after coming on as a 35th-minute replacement for Michael Jones in the 14–28 first Test defeat by the World XV, monopolized the No 8 berth throughout the rest of the centenary series and the two-Test visit of Ireland. Four tries in his first four Tests did his cause no harm. Little surprise that he won selection to the '92 All Black squad for Australia and South Africa, but injuries – in particular a broken hand – led to him losing his first-choice spot to the aforementioned Brooke for the second Test against Australia. Despite coming on as a replacement for Kevin Schuler in that game, he failed to win back his place for the third 'dead' leg of the Bledisloe Cup series, or for the victory over South Africa in Johannesburg

Perego, M. A. Wales

Full Name: Mark Angelo Perego
Club: Llanelli
Position: Flanker
Height: 6ft (1.83m)
Weight: 14st 7lb (92kg)
Occupation: Fireman with Dyfed Powys Brigade
Born: Winchester, Hants, 8.2.64
Family: Married
Family links with rugby: Father played for Llanelli, Army and Wales Youth
Former club: South Wales Police
International debut: Wales 9, Scotland 13, 1990
Five Nations debut: As above
Best moment in rugby: Llanelli's 1992/93 campaign
Worst moment in rugby: Llanelli losing to Cardiff in 1989/90 Cup (first Cup-tie defeat with club)
Most respected opponent: Jonathan Griffiths (ex-Llanelli & Wales)
Serious injuries: Torn neck muscles, concussion (twice)
Other sporting achievements: Golf (8 handicap)
Best memory last season: Beating France in Cardiff

Wales (1990)

Last Season	5 caps	0 pts
Career	9 caps	0 pts

Caps (9): 1990 W 1993 F, Z(1), Na(R) 1994 S, I, F, E. wc(q)–Sp

Points Nil

Suggestions to improve rugby: Increase emphasis on schoolboy rugby

Notable landmarks in rugby career: Capitalized upon Richard Webster's defection to Rugby League (Salford RLFC), taking over blindside wing-forward berth in Wales team and contributing mightily to Waless 1994 Five Nations title triumph as part of the all-Llanelli back row also comprising Emyr Lewis and Scott Quinnell. English-born Mark had returned to his best form in 1992/93 as part of the Stradey Park 'red machine' which monopolized domestic honours in the Principality, winning the league and cup double. Mark, who had also collected a Cup winners medal in 1988 when Neath succumbed 28–13, turned domestic bliss into the international variety last season after a successful 1993 summer tour to Zimbabwe and Namibia, on which he won two caps. Previously a member of Wales B side beaten 11–24 by Australia at Cardiff (7.11.92), but gained quick revenge the following weekend when Llanelli beat the tourists 13–9 at Stradey. He retained his place in the second-string side, now rechristened Wales A, for the 57–12 win over Holland in Den Bosch (6.2.93), and was then upgraded onto the senior bench for the 14–19 defeat by Ireland in Cardiff (6.3.93). That result prompted changes, and Mark, who had previously represented Wales at U-15, U-16, U-18 and Youth levels, came in on the blindside (instead of Emyr Lewis, who switched to No 8) for the 10–26 loss to France (20.3.93). Returned to Llanelli, where he had started his career, after two-year spell at South Wales Police

Touchlines: River and mountain running, golf

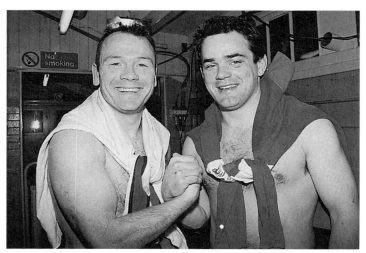

Everyone's a winner: Ievan Evans (left) and Will Carling celebrate victory at Twickenham. England won the match but Wales took the championship.

Pienaar, F.   South Africa

Full Name: François Pienaar
Province: Transvaal
Position: Flanker
Height: 6ft 4in (1.92m)
Weight: 17st 1lb (104kg)
Occupation: Businessman
Born: 2.1.67
International debut: South Africa
20, France 20, 1993
**Notable landmarks in rugby
career:** Transvaal captain who was
appointed to skipper South Africa
on his Test debut in 1993. The
occasion was the first Test against
France in Durban (26.6.93), for
which the Springboks had made no
fewer than ten changes, two
positional, from the side beaten by
England on its previous outing, at
Twickenham seven months earlier.
In spite of South Africa's wholesale
alterations, or perhaps because of
them, the game ended in a 20–20
draw, and France went on to nick
the series with an 18–17 win on his
home Ellis Park pitch in

South Africa (1993)

Last Season	9 caps	5 pts
Career	9 caps	5 pts

Caps (9): **1993** F(1,2), A(1,2,3),
Arg(1,2) **1994** E(1,2)

Points (5 – 1t): **1993** A(3:1t)

Johannesburg the following week. Enjoyed greater success with Transvaal, who
completed a sensational Currie Cup-Super 10 double, and with Springboks in
South America, where Argentina were handed a 2–0 whitewash during their
Autumn series. François played in only the two Tests, as he had suffered
concussion playing in the 21–15 Currie Cup final defeat of Natal, and
according to IB regulations was forced to spend three weeks on the sidelines.
Had enjoyed rather more game time in Australia, during July and August,
making three appearances (against Western Australia, New South Wales and
Queensland) in addition to the three internationals. His one and only try for
South Africa, thus far, came in the series-deciding third Test at Sydney
(21.8.93), but Australia still won 19–12. Enjoyed further significant success in
1994, when his Transvaal side beat touring England 24–21. However, the big
man's joy was shortlived, as the following week he captained South Africa to a
humiliating 15–32 loss to the very same England side in Pretoria. Perilously
close to losing his place, he survived a night of the long knives to skipper
Springboks to glorious 27–9 second-Test win over England, their first home
triumph since returning to international fold

Popplewell, N. J.　　　　　　　Ireland

Full Name: Nicholas James Popplewell
Club: Greystones
Position: Loosehead prop
Height: 5ft 10in (1.78m)
Weight: 17st (103kg)
Occupation: Retail manager with Argus Furniture
Born: Dublin, 6.4.64
Family: Rachel (wife)
Former club: Gorey
International debut: Ireland 6, New Zealand 23, 1989
Five Nations debut: Ireland 15, Wales 16, 1992
Best moments in rugby: Winning first cap against 1989 All Blacks; 1993 Lions second-Test win over New Zealand
Worst moment in rugby: Losing first Test with Lions to New Zealand due to controversial last-minute penalty award
Most respected opponent: Olo Brown (Auckland & New Zealand)
Serious injuries: Broken ribs (twice), cruciate knee ligaments (operation, May 1994)

Ireland (1989)

Last Season	5 caps	0 pts
Career	23 caps	8 pts

Caps (23): **1989** NZ **1990** Arg **1991** Na(1,2) wc–Z,S,A **1992** W, E, S, F, NZ(1,2), A **1993** S, F, W, E, R **1994** F, W, E, S

Points (8 – 2t): **1991** wc–Z(2t)

Other sporting achievements: Hockey for Irish Schools (three caps)
Best memory last season: Beating England at Twickenham
Should rugby's amateur rules be revised? Yes
To what degree should players benefit? Should be compensated for working time lost to rugby (reduce hassle in claiming legitimate expenses), but I disagree with notion of receiving a wage for playing
Should referees be rewarded? Yes
Advice for International Board: You're getting there, but a bit slowly. Decrease value of penalty goal to two points. Scrap 90-degree scrum wheel law
Notable landmarks in rugby career: In only his second full season as Ireland's first-choice loosehead prop, Nick gained selection for 1993 British Lions and spent his second successive summer in New Zealand; was solitary Irishman in Test side (playing in all three internationals). An ever-present in 1993/94 campaign, also turning out for Barbarians in 12–25 loss to touring All Blacks (Cardiff, 4.12.93). Missed 1994 tour to Australia in order to have

operation on cruciate knee ligaments. Had taken over the Irish No 1 jersey during 1991/92 season, following 1991 tour to Namibia, where he played in both Tests. Made great start to 1991 World Cup by scoring two tries in 55–11 Pool win over Zimbabwe in Dublin (6.10.91). With exception of Japan game, when John Fitzgerald took his turn, he retained his slot for remainder of tournament and then throughout 1992 Five Nations Championship, before touring with Ireland to New Zealand. Returned with his reputation enhanced, and was one of only three permanent fixtures (along with Vinnie Cunningham and Paddy Johns) throughout seven-Test Irish programme. That meant that he experienced the lows – heavy defeats by New Zealand (second Test), Australia, and to a lesser extent Scotland – and the highs – a great first-Test showing against the All Blacks, and the wins over Wales and England. Previously, Nick had been a member of the Irish party which toured France (May 1988) and North America (1989), where he played in 24–21 defeat of Canada. Retired injured after 20 minutes of full debut against 1989 All Blacks, and lost place for 1990 Championship. Redundant thereafter, except for 1990 Argentina game (won 20–18), before heading off to Namibia. Helped train Presentation Juniors Bray Under-15s to two Leinster Junior Cups in three years. Represented Ireland Under-25s v US Eagles (1990). Scored one of Ireland B's four tries in 24–10 win over England B (Old Belvedere, 1.3.91)
Touchlines: Golf (18 handicap), tennis, squash

Preston, J. P.   New Zealand

Full Name: Jon Paul Preston
Province: Wellington
Club: Burnside
Position: Stand-off, scrum-half, centre
Height: 5ft 9in (1.75m)
Weight: 12st 8lb (80kg)
Occupation: Promotions officer with the NZRFU
Born: Dunedin, 15.11.67
Former province: Canterbury
International debut: New Zealand 46, USA 6, 1991
Serious injuries: Dislocated shoulder (1992)
Suggestions to improve rugby: Introduce a law making certain players carry 20kg weights during games – then I might be able to keep up

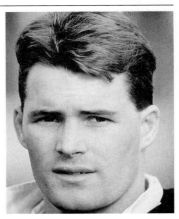

Notable landmarks in rugby career: An outside-half turned scrum-half, Jon joined David Kirk's Wellington as captain in 1993, but the move did little to further his Test prospects, as he lost the No 9 jersey to Otago rival Stu Forster on the autumn tour to England and Scotland, where he had to make do with outings against the English

New Zealand (1991)

Last Season	4 caps	0 pts
Career	7 caps	28 pts

Caps (7): **1991** wc–US, S **1992** SA(R) **1993** BL(2,3), A, WS

Points (28 – 1t,4c,5p): **1991** wc–US(4c,2p), S(3p) **1993** BL(3:1t)

Midlands and South West, South of Scotland, Scottish Development XV, an Emerging England XV and the Combined Services. He at least had the satisfaction of emerging victorious on each occasion. Prior to the trip he had succeeded Ant Strachan as scrum-half for the second and third Tests against the Lions, scoring a try in the latter, and retained his place through the Bledisloe Cup wins over Australia and Western Samoa. His 1992 tour of Australia and South Africa had been a tale of two shoulder dislocations. Sustaining the injury in the opening tour fixture against Western Australia (having scored a try, two conversions and a penalty), he was sidelined for four games before marking his return against a Victorian XV with three conversions in the 53–3 win. However, he was unable to recover his best form. But just when hope appeared lost, Strachan dislocated his shoulder 16 minutes into the Test against South Africa in Johannesburg. Enter Mr Preston for a mightily impressive afternoon's work in tandem with halfback partner Grant Fox. Jon was first seen in Britain with the 1984 New Zealand Schools touring party, and after visiting Canada on the 1990 development tour and helping a New Zealand XV stroll past the Soviet Union 56–6 in 1991, he returned to the United Kingdom for the World Cup, selected as reserve halfback in preference to Simon Mannix and Paul McGahan. He was employed at outside-half for the 46–6 pool win over the United States, kicking 14 points, and returned in the third-place play-off game against Scotland in Cardiff, slotting three penalty goals in a 13–6 victory. Claimed a New Zealand record of 20 conversions in a single match as West Coast were routed 128–0 by Canterbury in 1992
Touchlines: Fishing, water sports

Proctor, W. T.   Wales

Full Name: Wayne Thomas Proctor
Club: Llanelli
Position: Wing, fullback
Height: 6ft (1.83m)
Weight: 12st 2lb (77kg)
Occupation: Student at Swansea Institute of Higher Education
Born: Bridgend, 12.6.72
Family: Single
Former club: Cardigan Youth
International debut: Wales 6, Australia 23, 1992
Five Nations debut: Wales 10, England 9, 1993
Best moment in rugby: Beating England on Five Nations debut (6.2.93)
Worst moment in rugby: Broken jaw suffered against Ireland (1994)
Most embarrassing moment: Being interviewed by the BBC for the first time
Most respected opponent: Tony Underwood (Leicester & England)
Other sporting achievements: Represented Wales 11 times at athletics; third in 1988 British Schools 400m hurdles
Serious injuries: Broken jaw (1994)
Best memory last season: Wales's Five Nations title

Wales (1992)

Last Season	5 caps	0 pts
1994	Tour to Canada/South Seas	
Career	11 caps	10 pts

Caps (11): 1992 A 1993 E, S, Z(1,2), Na, C 1994 I, C, Fj,WS

Points (10 – 2t): 1993 Z(1:1t), Na(1t)

Advice for International Board: Introduce alternative to the scrum to help quicken up the game. Sell the game better. Televise more live games at different levels

Notable landmarks in rugby career: Last season was marred for Wayne by the broken jaw he suffered playing for Wales against Ireland in Dublin (5.2.94). It was only his second start of the campaign (he had also figured in the 24–26 pre-Christmas loss to Canada), and promptly sidelined him until the summer tour. It was a shame, as he had discovered his try-scoring knack on 1993 tour of Zimbabwe and Namibia, claiming a try against each host. Rapidly progressed into Wales senior side in 1992/93, only seven months after having made debut for Welsh Under-21s in 28–19 win over Scotland (Stirling, 18.4.92). And he got to know the touring Wallabies well in the process, as he followed an outing for Wales B against them (Australia won 24–11, Cardiff,

7.11.92) with another the following weekend as Llanelli won 13–9 at Stradey. Seven days later he made his Test debut in the 6–23 loss to the men from Down Under at the National Stadium. Wayne, who had previously won four Welsh Youth caps and three Wales Under-19 caps (touring with the latter to Canada), kept his place for the first two matches of the 1993 Five Nations Championship, sharing in the euphoria which surrounded the 10–9 defeat of England at Cardiff and then the dejection which followed their 0–20 shutout at Murrayfield. It was then that the selectors turned to the pace of Olympic hurdler Nigel Walker. Partook in Llanelli's league and cup double in 1992/93, having turned out in the 16–7 finals defeat of Swansea the previous season

Touchlines: Athletics, tennis, badminton

Purvis, G. H. New Zealand

Full Name: Graham Herbert Purvis
Province: Waikato
Club: Hamilton Old Boys
Position: Tighthead prop
Height: 6ft (1.83m)
Weight: 17st (18kg)
Born: 12.10.61
International debut: New Zealand 46, USA 6, 1991
Most embarrassing moment: Running out of toilet paper in the grandstand at Taumaranui, then being handed a telephone book by one of the officials, who asked me not to use the Te Kuiti pages
Biggest influence on career: My optometrist Adrian Paterson, who suggested I wear soft contact lenses
Best memory last season: Winning Ranfurly Shield at Auckland's expense
Notable landmarks in rugby career: If Graham knows how to foster good relations on a long overseas tour, he is keeping it to

New Zealand (1991)

Last Season	1 cap	0 pts
Career	2 caps	4 pts

Caps (2): 1991 wc–US 1993 WS

Points (4 – 1t): 1991 wc–US(1t)

himself. Prior to New Zealand's 1993 visit to England and Scotland, he broke the jaw of fellow tourist Mark Allen when Waikato met Taranaki. He was sent off on that occasion, but the pair spent the 13–match tour playing in the same dirt trackers team, same front row. An experienced campaigner, Graham has been involved in every New Zealand tour dating back to 1989, when he was brought to Wales and Ireland. Amongst his other ports of call have been France, Argentina, Australia and South Africa. But his scrapbook of Test memories remains thin. Save for his debut, at Kingsholm, Gloucester, in the 1991 World Cup, where he scored a try against the Americans on 8 October, his only other appearance came on 31 July 1993, when Western Samoa fronted up to the All Blacks in an international for the first time. Auckland's Olo Brown was unfit, and Graham received the call. Among his collection of provincial memories, in over 100 appearances for the Waikato club, are the 1992 national championship (after an overwhelming 40–5 final defeat of Otago at Hamilton on 4 October), and the 17–6 Ranfurly Shield upset in 1993 against Auckland, who had held the trophy for eight years and 62 matches. Unfortunately, he missed the 38–10 rout of the '93 Lions (29.6.93)

Touchlines: Fishing, eating cottage cheese (with chives)

Quinnell, L. S. Wales

Full Name: Leon Scott Quinnell
Club: Llanelli
Position: No 8, flanker
Height: 6ft 4in (1.93m)
Weight: 17st (103kg)
Occupation: Sales representative with Chemtreat and Aquatreat Ltd (Llanelli)
Born: 20.8.72
Family: Nicola (wife), Samantha (daughter)
Family links with rugby: Father (Derek) played for Wales (23 caps: 1972-80) and British Lions (5 Tests: 1971-80); uncle (Barry John) played for Wales (25 caps: 1966-72) and British Lions (5 Tests: 1968-71)
International debut: Wales 24, Canada 26, 1993
Five Nations debut: Wales 29, Scotland 6, 1994
Best moment in rugby: Try scored v France (1994)
Worst moment in rugby: Losing 1994 Swalec Cup final to Cardiff
Most respected opponent: Buck Shelford (ex-Northampton & New Zealand)

Wales (1993)

Last Season	9 caps	15 pts
1994	Tour to Canada/South Seas	
Career	9 caps	15 pts

Caps (9): **1993** C **1994** S, I, F, E. wc(q)–P, Sp. C, WS

Points (15 – 3t): **1994** F(1t). wc(q)–P(1t), Sp(1t)

Biggest influence on career: Father

Best memory last season: Winning first cap

Should rugby's amateur rules be revised? Yes

To what degree should players benefit? Anything that can alleviate pressure on players. We must keep up with Australian and New Zealand players

Should referees be rewarded? Yes, give them something so they can concentrate on rugby. At present they take a lot of stick for no reward

Advice for International Board: None. They make the laws. I just play by them

Notable landmarks in rugby career: Sixteen years after father Derek had shared in the last Welsh Grand Slam, son Scott came mighty close last season, as Wales ended a dark period by winning the 1994 Five Nations title. Scott was no bit-part player either, impressing to such an extent that he was acclaimed as the best young international player of the season. There could be few dissenters, especially not Frenchmen. It was against France (19.2.94) that he scored one of the finest forward tries ever seen at the Arms Park, bursting through a lineout on the French ten-metre line and shrugging off three tackles en route to the try-line. The score inspired Wales's first win over France in 13 attempts dating back to 1982. He bagged his second and third Test tries in the World Cup qualifying wins over Portugal (17.5.94) and Spain (21.5.94). With such explosive pace over the first five metres, Scott was rarely the wrong side of the gain line, and Wales reaped the benefit. It was hard to believe that the young man only turned 21 in August 1993, two months before his Test debut against Canada (Cardiff, 10.11.93), where he appeared thanks to Stuart Davies' withdrawal through injury. Wales lost the game 24–26, but coach Alan Davies kept faith with Scott, though he moved him from blindside to No 8 for the Five Nations campaign. Scott had been previously capped at Schools, Youth, Under-19, Under-21 and A levels (scored try in 61–5 defeat of Japan, Llanelli 29.9.93). Toured with Wales Under-18s to New Zealand in 1990 (they became the first side ever to roam through NZ unbeaten), and with Wales Under-19s to Canada in 1991. First played for Llanelli as an Under-8

Touchlines: None

Rayer, M. A.   Wales

Full Name: Michael Anthony Rayer
Club: Cardiff
Position: Fullback
Height: 5ft 10in (1.78m)
Weight: 13st 3lb (78kg)
Occupation: Sales representative
with Dimex Ltd
Born: Cardiff, 21.7.65
Family: Debra (wife), Abigail (3)
and Lloyd (1)
Family links with rugby: Father
(Alec) played for Penarth, Cardiff
Athletic and Llandaff North
Former club: Llandaff North
International debut: Wales 13,
Western Samoa 16, 1991
Five Nations debut: England 24,
Wales 0, 1992
Best moments in rugby: Landing
dropped goal in extra time of 1987
Schweppes Cup final against
Swansea to put Cardiff in winning
position; scoring a try during
Cardiff's victory in the 1994
Swayleck Cup Final
Worst moment in rugby: Being
dropped by Wales (1993), which
scuppered Lions chances
Most embarrassing moment:
Aquaplaning 20 feet with ball in
sodden conditions at St Helen's playing for Cardiff against Swansea

Wales (1991)

Last Season	9 caps	20 pts
1994	Tour to Canada/South Seas	
Career	19 caps	23 pts

Caps (19): **1991** wc–WS(R), Arg, A(R) **1992** E(R), A **1993** E, S, I, Z(1), Na, J(R) **1994** S(R), I(R), F, W. wc(q)–P. C, Fj, WS

Points (23 – 4t,1p): **1991** wc–Arg(1p) **1993** J(R:1t) **1994** S(R:2t), Fj (1t)

Most respected opponent: Jean-Baptiste Lafond (Begles & France)
Serious injuries: Dislocated elbow (1988), sprung shoulder joint, damaged ribs, torn hamstring, ankle and knee ligaments
Other sporting achievements: Captained Wales B baseball team (1990/91)
Best memories last season: Scoring two tries against Scotland; beating France and the 1994 Swalec Cup win
Should rugby's amateur rules be revised? Yes
To what degree should players benefit? Should be compensated for time lost, and most certainly allowed to benefit from off-the-field activities, and should definitely be paid a wage for playing in an international
Should referees be rewarded? Yes, there is definitely a case for referees being paid

341

Advice for International Board: I'm not happy. Obviously they are promoting the game better, but they need to discuss law changes with the players. We should be more involved

Suggestions to improve rugby: Develop more professional attitude. Disband 'old school tie' committees and stop living in past

Notable landmarks in rugby career: Topped 1994 Five Nations try-scoring charts (along with compatriot Nigel Walker and Frenchman Philippe Saint-André) thanks to two touchdowns he scored after coming on as a replacement against Scotland (Cardiff, 15.1.94). Had started season as second-choice fullback behind Tony Clement, and it was not until the last two games (against France and England) that he finally displaced his Swansea rival. Not that Mike missed out, as he was also deployed as a replacement against Japan (scoring try) and Ireland. More of a disappointment to him was being dropped for final international of 1993 Five Nations campaign against France, as it wrecked his Lions ambitions. Instead Clement was picked, and Mike spent summer with Wales in Zimbabwe and Namibia. Captained Wales Youth (1983-85) at fullback before joining Cardiff in 1984/85. Played twice for Wales B, as a replacement against France B at Begles (lost 0–26, 17.10.87), and then from the start against the same opposition at La Teste two years later (won 28–15, 12.11.89). Toured Namibia with Wales (1990), but was unable to shift Paul Thorburn from fullback slot, despite scoring 28 points in 67–9 defeat of North Region (Tsumeb, 6.6.90). Top-scored on tour, with 64 points in three appearances. Knee surgery in August 1991 further delayed his entry into big time, but day finally arrived when he replaced Clement during World Cup defeat by Western Samoa. Third and fourth Wales B appearances came in 1992/93 against North of England (scoring try in 21–13 win at Pontypool, 14.10.93) and Australia (7.11.92)

Ben Clarke, England's back row colossus, is oblivious to Nigel Walker's tackle during England's 15–8 defeat of Wales.

Scotland lock Andy Reed makes a textbook two-handed catch against France at Murrayfield.

Redman, N. C.   England

Full Name: Nigel Charles Redman
Club: Bath
Position: Lock
Height: 6ft 4in (1.93m)
Weight: 17st 2lb (104kg)
Occupation: Technical
representative with Halfem-Unistrut
Born: Cardiff, 16.8.64
Family: Lorinda (wife), Rhys (son)
Family links with rugby: Younger
brother (Paul) plays No 8 for
Weston-super-Mare
Former club: Weston-super-Mare
International debut: England 3,
Australia 19, 1984
Five Nations debut: Scotland 33,
England 6, 1986
Best moments in rugby: England
15, New Zealand 9, 1993; achieving
League and Cup double with Bath
(1993/94)
Worst moments in rugby:
Being left out of Bath Cup final team
in 1988/89 after playing in all other
games (being dropped by club is
harder to take than by country,
because that is your bread and
butter). Breaking hand v Harlequins
(1993) a week after England beat
All Blacks

England (1984)

Last Season	5 caps	0 pts
1994	Tour to South Africa	
Career	18 caps	4 pts

Caps (18): **1984** A **1986** S(R) **1987** I, S
wc–A, J, W(b) **1988** Fj **1990**
Arg(1,2) **1991** Fj. wc–It, US **1993**
NZ **1994** F, W, SA(1,2)

Points (4 – 1t): **1987** wc–J(1t)

Most embarrassing moment: South Australia v England (1988) – the only
occasion in which English team was not on pitch while National Anthem was
being played, because I was on the toilet
Most respected opponent: Paul Ackford (ex-Harlequins & England)
Biggest influence on career: Jack Rowell (Bath coach)
Serious injuries: Having both elbows operated on after England's 1990 tour
of Argentina; broken hand (1993)
Best memories last season: Being with wife when she gave birth to Rhys;
gaining place in England side on merit
Should rugby's amateur rules be revised? Yes
To what degree should players benefit? We should be compensated in full
for any loss of earnings – it is not as though the RFU lose out. Most definitely
allow us to benefit from off-field activities. Anything we can do, whether rugby-

343

related or not, is fine by me. No payment for playing

Should referees be rewarded? Treat them in same way as players. Should be marketed better. Follow English referee Tony Spreadbury's example of going round schools, promoting refereeing as an exciting alternative to playing

Advice for International Board: A lot of driftwood in IB. We're getting disillusioned in England over amateur situation. Unfortunately for us, RFU is a stickler for tradition, very conservative. They don't see change as being good, and we are losing out. Work harder to establish uniformity in refereeing interpretations. During 1991 World Cup all the referees looked out of the same pair of eyes, and there was not a dull game as a result of the players knowing where they stood. Times have changed. We didn't know what was going on most of the time in South Africa last summer

Notable landmarks in rugby career: Arguably England's outstanding forward last season in his five Tests. Four of the five were England's best displays of the campaign – against New Zealand, France (away), Wales and the first Test in South Africa – and that was no coincidence. His return in defeat of All Blacks (27.11.93) ended two years in the wilderness, and while it might have been prompted largely by the retirements of Paul Ackford and Wade Dooley, as well as injury to Martin Bayfield, there is no doubt Nigel took his chance with both hands. A broken bone in his hand cost him some of his momentum, but should not have cost him his place against first Scotland and then Ireland. That was a mistake on the selectors part, for which they paid. But once his considerable ball-winning skills had been recalled at Bayfield's expense, England were at the races again. Previously played in both World Cup tournaments, scoring the only international try in 60–7 defeat of Japan in Sydney, Australia, during 1987 event. Toured with England to Argentina (1990), Australia/Fiji (1991) and South Africa (1994). Has played in seven out of a possible eight Cup final wins since joining Bath in 1983 (84, 85, 86, 87, 90, 92 and 94). Played in 1984 final against Bristol aged only 19, scored two tries in 19–12 finals defeat of Wasps (1987), and one try in 48–6 finals defeat of Gloucester (1990). Captained England Under-23 to 15–10 win over Spain (Twickenham, 9.4.86)

Touchlines: Basketball, swimming, golf

Redpath, B. W.   Scotland

Full Name: Bryan William Redpath
Club: Melrose
Position: Scrum-half
Height: 5ft 7in (1.70m)
Weight: 11st 4lb (67kg)
Occupation: Joiner with W T McLeish
Born: Galashiels, 2.7.71
Family: Single
Family links with rugby: Andrew (brother) has played for Melrose and Scotland U-21s, Craig (brother) for Melrose, Scotland U-21s and B, and Lynne (sister) for Scotland Women U-21s
International debut: Scotland 15, New Zealand 51, 1993
Five Nations debut: Scotland 14, England 15, 1994
Best moment in rugby: Being selected for first start v France (1994)
Most respected opponent: Gary Armstrong (Jed-Forest & Scotland)
Biggest influence on career: Rob Moffat

Scotland (1993)

Last Season	5 caps	0 pts
1994	Tour to Argentina	
Career	5 caps	0 pts

Caps (5): **1993** NZ(TR) **1994** E(TR), F, Arg(1,2)

Other sporting achievements: Represented South of Scotland at cricket (also St Boswells) and athletics
Best memory last season: Winning Scottish title again with Melrose
Should rugby's amateur rules be revised? Yes
To what degree should players benefit? Anything short of being paid to play
Should referees be rewarded? Same should apply as to players
Advice for International Board: Rules must apply equally to everyone, irrespective of geography. Reduce value of penalty goal to make for more entertaining spectacle
Notable landmarks in rugby career: Graduated into Scotland side on back of consistently outstanding displays for Melrose's back-to-back championship winning side. Achieved first two caps by taking advantage of new temporary replacement ruling. His debut, at Murrayfield on 20.11.93, followed an injury to scrum-half incumbent Andy Nicol which required medical treatment off the field. And Bryan was again required to fill the breach temporarily when Gary Armstrong popped off for attention during Scotland's heartbreaking 14–15 Calcutta Cup loss to England (5.2.94). Finally, the diminutive Borderer won

345

selection in his own right, for the 1994 Wooden Spoon decider against France, again in Edinburgh (19.3.94). Scotland lost 12–20, but his services were retained for the summer tour to Argentina, on which he played in both Test defeats. Bryan also turned out in 1993/94 for Scotland A against New Zealand, Italy A and France A, as well as for South of Scotland on the day they were slaughtered 84–5 by the touring All Blacks. He originally surfaced on the representative scene as a replacement for Scotland Under-18s and Under-19s. Made his Under-21 debut in loss to Wales at Llanelli (20.4.91). Added second cap against Welsh at Bridgehaugh, Stirling (lost 19–28, 18.4.92). First played for Melrose as an 18-year old in October 1989
Touchlines: Golf, cricket

Reece-Edwards, H.   South Africa

Full Name: Hugh Reece-Edwards
Club: Crusaders
Province: Natal
Position: Fullback
Height: 6ft 2 ½ in (1.89m)
Weight: 15st 2lb (96kg)
Occupation: Representative
Born: Johannesburg, 5.1.61
International debut: France 15, South Africa 20, 1992
Notable landmarks in rugby career: Lost Springbok No 15 jersey to Transvaal rival Theo van Rensburg and then fellow Natalian Andre Joubert last season; his only outing was in 28–20 second Test loss to Australia (Brisbane, 14.8.93). Possesses one of the most prolific boots in South African rugby, having scored well over 1,000 points in first-class rugby. Kicked nine points in 1992 Currie Cup final, when his three penalty goals contributed mightily to Natal's 14–13 victory over Transvaal (Ellis

South Africa (1992)

Last Season	1 cap	0 pts
Career	3 caps	0 pts

Caps (3): **1992** F(1,2) **1993** A(2)

Points Nil

Park, Johannesburg, 12.9.92) – their second Cup success in three years. New Zealand also experienced his potency when they visited Kings Park, Durban on 1 August. Hugh landed six penalty goals and the conversion of a penalty try for a 20-point haul, but the All Blacks still beat Natal 43–25. Educated at Northlands in Durban, he made his provincial debut for Natal in 1982. He went on to represent the Junior Springboks before earning Test recognition at the age of 31 during the Springboks' tour of France and England. He played in both internationals against the French – the 20–15 win in Lyon on 17 October, and the 16–29 reversal in Paris the following weekend – before losing the No 15 jersey to Transvaal's Theo van Rensburg (who had occupied the berth in the home Tests against New Zealand and Australia) for the final international against England at Twickenham on 14 November. His other tour appearances were against France B (lost 17–24, Bordeaux, 4.10.92), Provence-Côte d'Azur (kicked 16 points (5c,2p) in 41–12 win, Marseille, 13.10.92), the French Barbarians (lost 20–25, Lille, 31.10.92) and the Northern Division (landed 14 points (1c,4p) in 19–3 win, Leeds, 10.11.92)

Reed, A. I. Scotland

Full Name: Andrew Ian Reed
Club: Bath
Position: Lock
Height: 6ft 7in (2.01m)
Weight: 18st (109kg)
Occupation: Unemployed
Born: St Austell, Cornwall, 4.5.69
Family: Sarah (wife)
Family links with rugby: Father played in Royal Navy; brother (Alec) played for Hong Kong Islanders
Former clubs: Bodmin, Camborne, Plymouth Albion
International debut: Scotland 15, Ireland 3, 1993
Five Nations debut: As above
Best moments in rugby: Winning first cap; Cup Final winners with Bath
Worst moments in rugby: Cornwall's two County Championship final defeats v Durham (1988/89) and Lancashire (1991/92); second half of the Lions Tour; lost place in Test side after playing badly

Scotland (1993)		
Last Season	5 caps	0 pts
1994	Tour to Argentina	
Career	9 caps	0 pts
Lions 1993		

Caps (9): **1993** I, F, W, E **1994** E, I, F, Arg(1,2)

Points Nil

Most embarrassing moment:
Dropping ball in front of clubhouse, playing for Bath United, when over for try; club captain John Hall was standing in the crowd, and he was first person I saw

when I looked up

Most respected opponent: Olivier Roumat (Agen & France)

Biggest influence on career: The whole Bath experience

Serious injuries: Torn ankle ligaments, a/c shoulder joint, torn quadricep tendon in both knees (right knee – Jan '93, left knee – June '93, first Test with Lions)

Best memories last season: Being informed of selection to British Lions; winning my first Cup Final with Bath and then a few days later being told I was captain on the Scottish tour

Other sporting achievements: Goalkeeper for Cornwall Schools

Should rugby's amateur rules be revised? To a great extent. I stopped work in December because I wasn't earning enough. Since then I have tried desperately to find a job, but as yet no luck. It is difficult, what with club and international commitments. In this age, who wants to employ a freeloader? Rugby has always come first, but I've reached the point where I have to start thinking about settling down, getting a home

To what degree should players benefit? Everyone should receive some form of compensation for time lost – you have to. Why shouldn't we benefit from off-the-field activities. Murrayfield can house nearly 70,000, all paying around £20.00 a ticket. What do the players get? A load of free kit, which doesn't even fit. The Unions make an absolute fortune out of the players. There must be a realistic appreciation of how much time and effort is put into playing top-level rugby. I don't want to make money from playing rugby – I enjoy playing and building friendships through the sport – but I want to see that our commitment is appreciated. It takes me more than six hours to get to Murrayfield for training, and I still have to get home

Should referees be rewarded? It is not a nice environment for referees. Like the players, they have to devote a lot of time to the sport as well as keep down a job. They should definitely receive something for their time and effort. It is a fact of life, bad refereeing can cost you a game

Advice for International Board: I don't know what they do apart from change the rules without consulting the players. The sames rules should apply across the board. Everyone, however, has their own interpretation, and some countries are prepared to bend the rules more than others. New Zealand is forward-thinking, it has to be. There is a lot of competition between Union and League rugby, and Union are trying hard to appear more attractive

Notable landmarks in rugby career: Meteoric rise up representative ladder saw him advance from second-choice club player at start of 1992/93 season to British Lion by the end. Touring with the Lions in New Zealand, Andy played in first-Test defeat (Christchurch, 12.6.93), as well as turning out against North Auckland, Canterbury, Southland, Hawke's Bay and Waikato. Played in Cornwall's County Championship side in three Twickenham finals in four years from 1989 to 1992 (beating Yorkshire, 29–20, in 1990/91). Prior to his Scotland debut in 1993, Andy's only international experience had come in the colours of England Colts. All that changed when a series of impressive televised displays for Bath alerted first the Anglo-Scots, for whom he turned out in the

1992/93 Inter-District Championship, then Scotland. His switch of allegiances came courtesy of an Edinburgh-born mother and a Hearts football scarf, which a Scottish spy spotted him wearing when watching a rugby match in Plymouth. The news was relayed back up north, and on 16 January 1993, having played in Scotland A's 22–13 win in Dublin, the former Bodmin Town goalkeeper (South Western League), made his debut in the 15–3 win over Ireland at Murrayfield – a 1,200-mile round trip from his home. A member of Bath, whom he joined for their 1990 tour to Australia, Andy shared in their league and cup double last season, as well as becoming Scotland's pack leader
Touchlines: Watersports

Richards, D.   England

Full Name: Dean Richards
Club: Leicester
Position: No 8
Height: 6ft 4in (1.93m)
Weight: 17st 8lb (kg)
Occupation: Police officer
Born: Nuneaton, 11.7.63
Family: Nicky (wife)
Family links with rugby: Father (Brian) played for Nuneaton
Former club: Roanne (France)
International debut: England 25, Ireland 20, 1986
Five Nations debut: As above
Best moment in rugby: Winning decisive third Test with 1989 Lions
Worst moments in rugby: Losing four front teeth whilst in action; England losing to Wales in Cardiff (1989)
Most respected opponent: Brian Moore (Harlequins & England)
Biggest influence on career: My work
Serious injuries: Recurring dislocated shoulder
Best memories last season: Beating Bath in the league and Wales in the Championship
Should rugby's amateur rules be revised? Yes
To what degree should players benefit? As much as possible
Should referees be rewarded? Yes
Advice for International Board: Redefine your role, for all our sakes
Suggestions to improve rugby: On-field – Home Unions must guard against taking on new laws just because they suit the Southern Hemisphere nations.

Off-field – reduce maximum age of committee men to 55; allow players to prosper from non-rugby-related activities, as they do everywhere else in the world

Notable landmarks in rugby career: Selected to tour with 1993 British Lions despite not figuring in England's plans for '93 Five Nations Championship, Dean played in all three Tests against New Zealand, and then, much to their chagrin, returned to England's side to inspire a 15–9 defeat of the touring All Blacks. Injury to Deano spared Scotland, Ireland and France, but he was back for the 1994 championship decider against Wales, and although there had been some concerns as to his match fitness, he produced a typically dictatorial performance to snuff out Wales's Grand Slam aspirations. It was his 36th Test appearance, and strengthened his position as England's most-capped No 8. Had lost jersey in 1993 to Ben Clarke, whose ultra-mobile style of play was perfectly suited to new laws, but returned after Clarke was turned into an openside flanker. Deano joined Leicester in 1982 after a season playing in France. Played for England Schools at lock, before graduating to England U-23s (against Romania). Has also represented Leicestershire and Midlands Division. Scored two tries on international debut against Ireland, but it was one of my worst performances. Played in 1987 World Cup and returned to Australia with 1989 Lions, playing in all three Tests of 2–1 series win. Shoulder injury ruled out 1989/90 season. Lynchpin of England's 1991 Grand Slam success. Scored one of England XV's two tries in 18–16 defeat of centenary Barbarians at Twickenham (29.9.90). Voted 1990/91 Whitbread/Rugby World Player of Year. Toured Fiji/Australia (1991), and played in three World Cup Pool games before Mike Teague took over at No 8 for knock-out stages. Returned in 1992 Five Nations Championship, helping England to second Grand Slam

Touchlines: Squash, five-a-side soccer

England (1986)		
Last Season	3 caps	0 pts
1994	Tour to South Africa	
Career	37 caps	24 pts
Lions 1989	3 Tests	0 pts
1993	3 Tests	0 pts

Caps (37): **1986** I, F **1987** S wc–A, J, US, W **1988** F, W, S, I(1), A(a1,a2), Fj, A(b) **1989** S, I, F, W, Ro. Lions–A(1,2,3) **1990** Arg **1991** W, S, I, F, Fj, A(a) wc–NZ, It, US **1992** S(R), F, W, C **1993** Lions–NZ(1,2,3). NZ **1994** W, SA(1)

Points (24 – 6t): **1986** I(2t) **1987** wc–J(1t) **1988** A(a2:1t) **1989** I(1t), Ro(1t)

Richter, A.   South Africa

Full Name: Adriaan Richter
Club: Harlequins (Pretoria)
Province: Northern Transvaal
Position: No 8
Height: 6ft 5in (1.96m)
Weight: 15st 6lb (98kg)
Occupation: Accountant
Born: Roodepoort, 10.5.66
Former Province: Transvaal
International debut: France 15,
South Africa 20, 1992
**Notable landmarks in rugby
career:** Returned to South African
Test team for second Test against
England last summer. The move
helped the Springboks turn a 32–15
first-Test reversal into a 27–9 win
(Cape Town, 11.6.94). Two years
previously, had started the
Springboks' tour to France and
England as a flanker, had a game at
lock, and finished up as No 8 in the
Test against England. During the
course of the trip he developed into
a first-choice player, deposing

South Africa (1992)

Last Season	1 cap	0 pts
Career	4 caps	0 pts

Caps   (4): **1992** F(1,2), E **1994** E(2)

Points Nil

Transvaal's Ian Macdonald as breakaway wing-forward in the two
internationals against France – the 20–15 win in Lyon on 17 October and the
16–29 loss in Paris' Parc des Princes the following weekend. His other tour
appearances came against Aquitaine (won 29–22, Pau, 7.10.92), Midi-
Pyrenées (won 18–15, Toulouse, 15.10.92), French Universities (lost 13–18,
Tours, 28.10.92) the French Barbarians (lost 20–25, Lille, 31.10.92), the
Midlands Division (won 32–9, Leicester, 4.11.92) and England B (scored try
in 20–16 win, Bristol, 7.11.92). Although he missed out on selection for the two
home Tests against New Zealand and Australia in August, he did captain
Northern Transvaal against the All Blacks (lost 17–24) at Loftus Versfeld,
Pretoria on 14 August. Four years earlier (1988) he had made his provincial
debut for rivals Transvaal, with whom he played 27 times, before switching to
the Blue Bulls

Robinson, B. F.   Ireland

Full Name: Brian Francis Robinson
Club: Ballymena
Position: No 8, flanker
Height: 6ft 4in (1.94m)
Weight: 15st (95kg)
Occupation: Development officer with IRFU
Born: Belfast, 20.3.66
Family: Single
Former club: London Irish
International debut: Ireland 13, France 21, 1991
Five Nations debut: As above
Best moment in rugby: Breaking Irish single-match try-scoring record with four against Zimbabwe in 1991 World Cup
Worst moment in rugby: Tearing cruciate and medial ligaments in first match after touring Zimbabwe with Ulster (1986/87) and missing next 18 months
Most respected opponent: Zinzan Brooke (Auckland & New Zealand)
Serious injuries: As above
Best memory last season: Scoring try against Wales
Should rugby's amateur rules be revised? Yes
To what degree should players benefit? So that we do not lose out financially in any way from playing rugby
Advice for International Board: Relax amateur rules to allow players to earn money away from rugby. Reimburse employers for time lost

Ireland (1991)

Last Season	7 caps	0 pts
1994	Tour to Australia	
Career	25 caps	25 pts

Caps (25): **1991** F, W, E, S, Na(1,2) wc–Z, S, A **1992** W, E, S, F, NZ(1,2), A **1993** W, E, R **1994** F, W, E, S, A(1,2)

Points (25 – 6t): **1991** S(1t) wc–Z(4t) **1993** W(1t)

Notable landmarks in rugby career: Holds world record for most tries scored by a forward in a single international, with the four he bagged against Zimbabwe in the 55–11 World Cup defeat of Zimbabwe at Lansdowne Road (6.10.91). It also represented a record for any Irish player, surpassing the hat-tricks claimed by half a dozen names, including Keith Crossan (v Romania, 1986) and Brendan Mullin (v Tonga, 1987). Switched clubs in 1992/93 season from Ballymena (to which he has subsequently returned) to London Irish, but his injury problems followed him across the Irish Sea, and having played both Tests in New Zealand over the summer and against Australia (31.10.92), he then missed the Five Nations losses to Scotland and France. Made an immediate impact on his return, however, bagging Ireland's try in the 19–14 win at Cardiff (6.3.93), and also figuring in the famous 17–3 defeat of England (Dublin, 20.3.93). Again helped rub England's noses in the turf, this time at Twickenham, last season, having been moved to blindside flanker from No 8, the position in which he had started campaign against Romania and France. Brian played for Combined Irish Provinces as a 20-year old, for Irish Wolfhounds seven in Sicily (1989/90), for Ireland U-25s against US Eagles (1989/90) and for Ulster against 1989 All Blacks. Made Ireland B debut in 22–22 draw with Scotland B (1989/90)

Touchlines: Sub-aqua diving, keep-fit

Rodber, T. A. K. — England

Full Name: Timothy Andrew Keith Rodber
Clubs: Northampton & Army
Position: Flanker, No 8
Height: 6ft 6in
Weight: 16st 7lb
Occupation: Officer serving with Green Howards
Born: Richmond, Yorkshire, 2.7.69
Family: Single
Family links with rugby: Father played
Former clubs: Oxford Old Boys, Petersfield
International debut: Scotland 7, England 25, 1992
Five Nations debut: As above
Best moment in rugby: Beating South Africa in first Test (1994)
Worst moment in rugby: Being sent off against Eastern Province (1994)
Most respected opponent: Dean Richards (Leicester & England) – awesome in every department
Serious injuries: Popped ribs
Other sporting achievements: Hampshire Schools County hockey and cricket
Best memory last season: Performance against Springboks in Pretoria
Suggestions to improve rugby: Anything to take away stagnant play
Notable landmarks in rugby career: An officer and a gentleman, widely

England (1992)

Last Season	6 caps	5 pts
1994	Tour to South Africa	
Career	8 caps	5 pts

Caps (8): 1992 S, I 1993 NZ 1994 I, F, W, SA(1,2)

Points (5 – 1t): 1994 W(1t)

353

considered to be heir-apparent to Will Carling's England captaincy as and when the post becomes vacant. Came on in leaps and bounds last season, combining with Dean Richards and Ben Clarke to form a powerful back-row unit. He was particularly outstanding in England's heroic 32–15 first-Test defeat of South Africa (Pretoria, 4.6.94). But tarnished his image somewhat when dismissed for fighting against Eastern Province (the only other player ever to be sent off in an English jersey was Mike Burton back in 1975), though under extreme provocation from a disgrace of an opposition team. Having been selected as a No 8 in his first two international outings, against Scotland and Ireland during England's 1992 Grand Slam run, Tim was moved to blindside flanker last season. An impressive showing against the touring All Blacks secured his place, but a ripped hamstring then put him out of the Calcutta Cup clash and a return to where he had made his debut (18.1.92). However, once he was fit, John Hall was dropped to accommodate his return. Had represented England's inaugural Under-21 side in 54–13 defeat of Romania in Bucharest (13.5.89), and after helping an England XV beat Italy 33–15 in May 1990, he toured with full England squad to Argentina that summer, turning out against Tucumán Selection (won 19–14), Cuyo Selection (lost 21–22) and Córdoba Selection (won 15–12). In 1990/91 he scored tries for England B in 31–16 defeat of Namibia and in 10–24 loss to Ireland B, and represented Northampton in 1991 Pilkington Cup final, losing to Harlequins in extra time. On a happier note, he helped England win 1993 World Cup Sevens title in Edinburgh, and scored one of only two England tries in entire 1993/94 campaign as Wales were beaten (19.3.94)

Roebuck, M. C. Australia

Full Name: Martin (Marty) Clive Roebuck
State: New South Wales
Club: Eastwood
Position: Fullback, five-eighth, centre
Height: 5ft 10in (1.77m)
Weight: 12st 8lb (80kg)
Occupation: Marketing executive with Linfox Distribution Group
Born: 10.1.65
Family: Su (wife), Kiah (daughter), Mary (mother), Pat (father), Louise (sister), Anne (sister), Mike (brother), Tim (brother)
Former clubs: None. Eastwood since 1983

354

International debut: Australia 63, Wales 6, 1991
Best moment in rugby: Winning 1991 World Cup
Worst moment in rugby: Any loss to New Zealand
Most embarrassing moment: Being told my haircut has given inspiration to people with bad haircuts all over the world!
Most respected opponents: John Kirwan/Grant Fox (both Auckland & New Zealand)
Serious injuries: Ankle reconstructions (right in 1990, left in 1991), fractured left ankle (1993)

Australia (1991)

Last Season	6 caps	73 pts
Career	23 caps	114 pts

Caps (23): **1991** – W(a), E(a), NZ(a1,a2). wc–Arg, WS, W(b), I, NZ(b), E(b) **1992** S(1,2), NZ(2,3), SA, I, W **1993** T, SA(1,2,3), C, F(2)

Points (114 – 5t,12c,23p): **1991** W(a:1t), E(a:1t). wc–W(b:2t) **1992** I(4c,3p), W(1c,2p) **1993** T(3c,3p), SA(1:4p), SA(2:2c,3p), SA(3:1c,4p), F(2:1t,1c,4p)

Other sporting achievements: Once sat through half an hour of motor racing
Suggestions to improve rugby: On-field – award 'mark' for any catch (whether in the air or not) to discourage over-kicking; limit lineout to five. Off-field – remove men only culture when organizing social/official functions; give more thought to providing for player compensation for tours and time off work generally
Notable landmarks in rugby career: Twice dropped from Test side in 1993, and Australia lost both games, to New Zealand and France. In the latter case, the Wallaby management chose to play young fullback Matthew Burke, and let Michael Lynagh kick and captain. It was a mistake, and after the 16–13 loss in Bordeaux Marty was summoned for the Paris finale. He responded with a 19-point match-winning display, as well as providing a more solid presence in the last line of defence. Returned to side after sitting out the Bledisloe Cup defeat, when rival Tim Kelaher suffered a ruptured stomach. Marty has himself been dogged by injury, namely dodgy ankles, which caused him to miss virtually all of 1990. But since his debut against the hapless Welsh tourists in 1991, when he opened his scoring account with a try, he has been rated among the world's very best fullbacks. He toured Canada and France in 1989, appearing four times for the Wallabies in provincial games. Having won New South Wales player -of-the-year award in 1991, he embarked on a splendid 1992 campaign. Injury robbed him of a place in the first-Test defeat of New Zealand in Sydney, but he returned for the second and third legs of what turned out to be a triumphant Bledisloe Cup series. In South Africa he kicked 16 points (2c,4p) as Western Transvaal were routed 46–13, and also played in the historic Test with the Republic, before turning his attentions towards Great Britain, landing 25 points in the Test wins against Wales and Ireland
Touchlines: Playing with Kiah

Roumat, O.   France

Full Name: Olivier Roumat
Club: Dax
Position: Lock
Height: 6ft 6in (1.98m)
Weight: 17st 5lb (111kg)
Occupation: Surveyor
Born: Mont-de-Marsan, 16.6.66
Family links with rugby: Father played in Mont-de-Marsan back row
International debut: New Zealand 34, France 20, 1989
Five Nations debut: Wales 19, France 29, 1990
Notable landmarks in rugby career: Captained France to their first series win in South Africa since 1958 during summer of 1993, after 'regular' skipper Jean-François Tordo had been stamped out of the tour. France drew first Test 20–20 (Durban, 26.6.93) before winning second Test 18–17 (Johannesburg, 3.7.93). Olivier was magnifique, both as a player and a captain, opined Tordo generously. He retained captaincy on return home, leading France to 51–0 rout of Romania and to a share of home series against world champions Australia (after Wallabies had slumped to shock 13–16 loss in Bordeaux, 30.10.93). However,

France (1989)
Last Season	9 caps	5 pts
1994	Tour to Canada/NZ	
Career	43 caps	18 pts

Caps (43): **1989** NZ(2R), BL **1990** W, E, S, I, Ro, A(1,2,3), NZ(1,2) **1991** S, I, W, E, Ro, US(1), W wc–Ro, Fj, C, E **1992** W(R), E(R), S, I, SA(1,2), Arg(b) **1993** E, S, I, W, R(a), SA(1,2), R(b), A(1,2) **1994** I, W, E, C

Points (18 – 4t): **1991** W(1t) wc–Ro(1t) **1992** SA(2:1t) **1994** W(1t)

fortunes dipped during 1994 Five Nations Championship. He scored a try against Wales (Cardiff, 19.2.94), and was then dropped after England won again in Paris (5.3.94), missing 20–12 win in Scotland, but returning for summer tour to Canada and France. Became the first French forward to score a five-point try when touching down against South Africa (Paris, 24.10.92). It helped France salvage a share of the series, and cemented Olivier's place for the triumphant 1993 Five Nations campaign. His 1992 summer had been spoiled by the dismissal he incurred playing against New Zealand for a World XV at Athletic Park, Wellington. It was the second Test, and the Dax surveyor lasted only nine minutes before Kiwi referee David Bishop dismissed him for illegal use of the shoe. He was banned for four weeks, and did not tour to Argentina with the French side. However, he did play in the return match at Nantes (14.11.92), where Argentina won on French soil for the first time, and was one of the few players not to be dropped as a result. Partnered Abdel Benazzi in the second row throughout '93 Championship campaign. That was in marked contrast to the previous season, when despite being France's only genuine quality lineout jumper, he lost out to Begless Christophe Mougeot in the selection stakes for the 1992 Tournoi des Cinq Nations. It did not cost him a cap, though, as Mougeot failed to last the course against Wales and England, and Olivier was sent into the fray in the 40th and 64th minutes respectively. Thereafter, he started the games against Scotland and Ireland. Formerly a flanker – his position against the British Lions XV who helped celebrate the bicentenary of the French Revolution in 1989 – he built himself an impressive reputation in the 1988 Student World Cup, and helped France B beat Wales B 28–15 in La Teste (12.11.89), four months after replacing Marc Cecillon against New Zealand in Auckland for his first cap

Sadourny, J.-L. France

Full Name: Jean-Luc Sadourny
Club: Colomiers
Position: Wing, fullback
Height: 6ft 1in (1.86m)
Weight: 13st 9lb (86.5kg)
Occupation: Sales representative
Born: Toulouse, 26.8.66
International debut: Wales 9, France 22, 1991
Five Nations debut: France 13, England 31, 1992
Notable landmarks in rugby career: One of four fullbacks employed by France during 1992/93 season, Jean-Luc had to wait until 1993/94 to finally establish himself as the successor to Serge Blanco, playing in all ten Tests (scoring a try against Scotland at Murrayfield,

19.3.94, and a dropped goal in the 16–13 defeat of Australia at Bordeaux, 30.10.93) before heading off on summer tour to Canada and New Zealand. He had deposed Stephane Ougier on the 1992 summer tour of Argentina, after coming on as a 42nd-minute replacement for the Toulouse player in the 27–12 first-Test win in Buenos Aires (4.7.92). Retained his place for second Test the following week, and took his cap tally to nine, with appearances in both legs of the drawn series with South Africa back home in October. However, Sébastien

Viars was then selected to wear the No 15 jersey against Argentina in Nantes, and Jean-Baptiste Lafond took over after that humiliating loss. Being dropped was not the first knock-out blow Jean-Luc had suffered in his Test career. For he suffered concussion in the 10–6 win over England B at Bristol in 1991, having previously marked his B debut with a try in the 31–10 win over Scotland at Hughenden. Lightning struck twice as he lasted just nine minutes on his Five Nations debut against England in Paris (15.2.92). Having replaced injured captain Philippe Sella in the 55th minute, he was then involved in a head-on collision with outside-half Alain Penaud attempting a scissors movement, and was led groggily from the arena. His first cap (following the 1991 US tour, during which he scored two tries against USA B) came as a 76th-minute replacement for Blanco in the floodlit international against Wales at the Arms Park (4.9.91). Scored first Test try in 44–12 win over Ireland (1992)

France (1991)

Last Season	10 caps	8 pts
1994	Tour to Canada/NZ	
Career	20 caps	12 pts

Caps (20): **1991** W(R) wc–C(R) **1992** E(R), S, I, Arg(a1R,a2), SA(1,2) **1993** R(a), SA(1,2), R(b), A(1,2) **1994** I, W, E, S, C

Points (12 – 2t,1dg): **1992** I(1t) **1993** A(1:1dg) **1994** S(1t)

Saint-André, P.   France

Full Name: Philippe Saint-André
Club: Montferrand
Position: Wing
Height: 5ft 11in (1.80m)
Weight: 13st 6lb (85kg)
Occupation: Self-employed sponsorship agent
Born: Romans, 19.4.67
Former clubs: Romans, Clermont-Ferrand
International debut: France 6, Romania 12, 1990
Five Nations debut: Ireland 13, France 21, 1991
Notable landmarks in rugby career: Appointed France captain for 1994 Five Nations finale against Scotland (won 20–12, Murrayfield, 19.3.94) in succession to Olivier

Roumat, who was dropped after defeat by England a fortnight previously. In so doing, Philippe, nicknamed 'le goret' (the piglet), became the first wing to

captain France since Christian Darrouy 27 years ago. Celebrated with his second try of the championship, his first having come against Ireland (won 35–15, Paris, 15.1.94). Has become one of world rugby's most potent finishers, with 15 Test tries in the past three years. His finest moment came at Twickenham (16.1.91), when he scored the Try against England in a thrilling Grand Slam decider. The move was initiated by Serge Blanco, and fed via Jean-Baptiste Lafond, Didier Camberabero, Philippe Sella and then Camberabero's boot behind enemy lines, where Philippe, who has clocked 10.9sec over 100m, scorched through to apply the coup de grace. Claimed championship high of three tries – against England (two) and Ireland – as France won 1993 Five Nations Cup. He also toured to Argentina with the French side, crossing in the 33–9 second-Test win in Buenos Aires (11.7.92), and turned out on both occasions against South Africa (in Lyon and Paris). A prolific try-scorer in French club rugby for Montferrand, he also represented France A and B before stepping into the top flight at Stade Patrice Brocas, Auch (24.5.90), as a centre for the visit of Romania, who triumphed (12–6) on French soil for the first time

France (1990)

Last Season	9 caps	15 pts
1994	Tour to Canada/NZ	
Career	36 caps	67 pts

Caps (36): **1990** R, A(3), NZ(1,2) **1991** I(R), W(a), E(a), US(1,2), W(b) wc–R(b), Fj, C, E(b) **1992** W, E, S, I, R, Arg(a1,a2), SA(1,2) **1993** E, S, I, W, SA(1,2), A(1,2) **1994** I, W, E, S, C

Points (67 – 15t): **1991** W(a:1t), E(a:1t), US(1:1t), W(b:1t) wc–R(b:1t), C(1t) **1992** W(1t), R(1t), Arg(a2:1t) **1993** E(2t), I(1t), SA(1:1t) **1994** I(1t), S(1t)

Alain Penaud escapes the clutches of Welshmen Gareth Llewellyn and Neil Jenkins during France's defeat in Cardiff.

Schmidt, U. L.

South Africa

Full Name: Uli Schmidt
Province: Northern Transvaal
Position: Hooker
Height: 5ft 11in (1.81m)
Weight: 14st 8lb (92kg)
Occupation: Doctor
Born: 10.7.61
International debut: South Africa 21, NZ Cavaliers 15, 1986
Notable landmarks in rugby career: Managed to avoid the attention of British fans, having missed South Africa's tour to France and England in 1992, and having then been replaced by Natal's former Scotland hooker John Allan (who had long maintained Uli was the world's best hooker) by the time England arrived in the New Republic last summer. He was the man the Springboks turned to when they returned to the international fold in '92 against the touring All Blacks, following 11 years of isolation. He packed down between Heinrich Rodgers and Lood Muller at Ellis Park, Johannesburg (15.8.92), but unhappily for them,

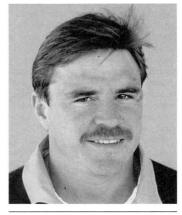

South Africa (1986)

Last Season	5 caps	0 pts
Career	13 caps	9 pts

Caps (13): **1986** Cv(1,2,3,4) **1989** Wd(1,2) **1992** NZ, A **1993** F(1,2), A(1,2,3)

Points (9 – 2t): **1986** Cv(3:1t) **1993** F(1:1t)

New Zealand won 27–24. A week later, inside Cape Town's Newlands stadium, he was unable to prevent the Wallabies running riot and inflicting a world-record defeat on South Africa. That was Uli's eighth cap, although his first six had been won against controversial opposition. He was an ever-present through the four-Test series against the rebel New Zealand Cavaliers in 1986, scoring a try in the 33–18 third-Test victory in Pretoria (24.5.86) as the Springboks headed towards a 3–1 series win. Three years later, when the First National Bank XV toured as part of the SARB's centenary celebrations, he played in each of the Republic's two wins: (1) won 20–19, Cape Town, 26.8.89; (2) won 22–16, Johannesburg, 1.9.89. At the start of 1993 Uli recaptured the No 2 jersey from Willie Hills and played in the two-Test series against France (scored try in 20–20 first Test, Durban, 26.6.93) and throughout the three-international campaign against Australia. Whilst Down Under he also turned out against South Australia, New South Wales and Queensland

Seigne, L.   France

Full Name: Laurent Seigne
Club: Merignac
Position: Prop
Height: 5ft 10in (1.78m)
Weight: 16st 9lb (106kg)
Occupation: Travelling salesman
Born: Tulle, 12.8.60
International debut: France 27, British Lions 29, 1989
Five Nations debut: England 16, France 15, 1993
Former clubs: Brive, Montferrand, Cognac, Agen, Narbonne
Notable landmarks in rugby career: Laurent was an ever-present in the French front row during the 1993 Five Nations Championship, and so impressed that the French media voted him prop of the Year. The campaign, which culminated in France winning the championship title, was in marked contrast to the rest of his Test career, which has been a stop-start affair. Last season, for example, he had three spells in the side, adding four caps (against Romania, Australia (twice) and Scotland) to his tally before

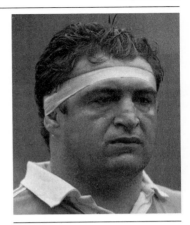

France (1989)

Last Season	4 caps	0 pts
1994	Tour to Canada/NZ	
Career	12 caps	0 pts

Caps (12): **1989** BL, A(1) **1990** NZ(1) **1993** E, S, I, W, R(a), A(1,2) **1994** S, C

Points Nil

embarking on the summer tour of Canada and New Zealand. Debut came against the British Lions XV in the Parc des Princes (4.10.89) in a match staged to celebrate the bicentenary of the French Revolution. But the Lions had the last roar, winning a thriller 29–27. Laurent retained his place for the next international, the first Test against Australia in Strasbourg (4.11.89), but when France lost a match they were red-hot favourites to win (15–32), heads rolled, among them his. Still, he returned in Nantes the following season when New Zealand were the visitors for the first of two Tests (3.11.90). A match for which the French front row allegedly prepared by head-butting each other ended in 3–24 defeat, and Laurent was again sent packing. This time it was two and a half years before he re-emerged, but when he did – called into the squad as a replacement for calf injury victim Philippe Gallart – he hung around long enough to share in France's '93 title triumph

Sella, P.   France

Full Name: Philippe Sella
Club: Agen
Position: Centre
Height: 5ft 11in (1.80m)
Weight: 13st 4lb (84kg)
Occupation: Businessman
Born: Clairac, 14.2.62
International debut: Romania 13, France 9, 1982
Five Nations debut: England 15, France 19, 1983
Notable landmarks in rugby career: Sent off against Canada (5.6.94) on world-record 99th international appearance for (allegedly) punching as France slumped to a shock 18–16 defeat at Elms Park, Ontario. Philippe, who had captained France between February and May 1992, was subsequently banned for one match. Dropped for France's tour to Argentina in 1992, but reclaimed midfield berth (14.11.92) for disastrous return against Pumas in Nantes. His only consolation in a game which saw Argentina secure their first ever win on French soil was his 26th Test try. The 27th and most recent came in the 21–6 win over Ireland in Dublin (20.2.93) as France completed the third leg of their 1993 Championship win. Philippe succeeded compatriot Serge Blanco (93) as world's most-capped player during 1993/94 campaign, his tally having been amassed since his debut in the 1982 defeat by Romania. On his next appearance, in the first Test against Argentina, he scored the first two of his 29 international tries. He played 45 consecutive Tests until injury

France (1982)

Last Season	10 caps	10 pts
1994	Tour to Canada/NZ	
Career	99 caps	120 pts

Caps (99): 1982 Ro, Arg(1,2) **1983** E, S, I, W, A(1,2), Ro **1984** I, W, E, S, NZ(1,2), Ro **1985** E, S, I, W, Arg(1,2) **1986** S, I, W, E, Ro(a), Arg(1,2), A, NZ, Ro(b), NZ(1,2) **1987** W, E, S, I wc–S, Ro, Z(R), Fj, A, NZ **1988** E, S, I, W, Arg(a1,a2), Arg(b1,b2), Ro **1989** I, W, E, S, NZ(1,2), BL, A(1,2) **1990** W, E, S, I, A(1,2,3) **1991** W, E, Ro, US(1,2), W, Fj, C, E **1992** W, E, S, I, Arg(b) **1993** E, S, I, W, R(a), SA(1,2), R(b), A(1,2) **1994** I, W, E, S, C

Points (120 – 29t): 1982 Arg(1:2t) **1983** E(1t) **1984** I(1t), W(1t), E(1t), Ro(1t) **1986** S(1t), I(1t), W(1t), E(1t), Ro(a:1t), Arg(2:1t), A(1t), NZ(1:1t) **1987** E(1t), wc–S(1t), Ro(1t), A(1t) **1988** I(1t), Arg(4:1t) **1990** W(1t) **1991** W(1t), Fj(2t) **1992** Arg(b:1t) **1993** I(1t), R(b:1t) **1994** W(1t)

ruled him out of the 49–3 win over Romania, a match played on his own Agen pitch (11.11.87). It was but a temporary blip for a man who had also represented France at Schools, Juniors and Universities grade. In 1986 he scored a try in every Championship match, equalling a feat achieved only by compatriot Patrick Esteve (1983), Johnny Wallace (Scotland, 1925) and Carston Catcheside (England, 1924). That same year he was alone in playing all 12 French internationals, and represented the Five Nations in a 13–32 defeat by the Overseas Unions in the IRB Centenary match at Twickenham (19.4.86). The next season he played a key role in France's run to the 1987 World Cup final. A torn thigh muscle accounted for his absence from the 1991 World Cup opener against Romania, but typically he returned with two dazzling tries in the following match against Fiji

Sharp, A. V. Scotland

Full Name: Alan Victor Sharp
Club: Bristol
Position: Loosehead prop
Height: 5ft 10in (1.78m)
Weight: 17st 4lb (105kg)
Occupation: Builder with Alan Richardsom Construction (Bedminster)
Born: Bristol, 17.10.69
Family: Zoe (daughter)
International debut: Scotland 14, England 15, 1994
Five Nations debut: As above
Best moment in rugby: Winning first cap
Worst moment in rugby: Having to pull out of Scotland team to play Ireland (1993) less than 48 hours before what would have been my debut, when found I had a broken leg
Most respected opponent: Paul Burnell (London Scottish & Scotland)
Biggest influence on career: Derek Eves (Bristol)
Serious injuries: Broken leg
Best memory last season: Putting on Scotland jersey for first time
Suggestions to improve rugby: More money must be pumped into grass-

Scotland (1994)

Last Season	5 caps	0 pts
1994	Tour to Argentina	
Career	5 caps	0 pts

Caps (5): **1994** E, I, F, Arg(1,2)

Points Nil

roots rugby to give everyone a chance of coming through

Notable landmarks in rugby career: Began his representative life as a Scotsman (playing for the Under-21s), then became an Englishman (winning England B honours against Spain as a 20-year-old in 1989, and being included in England's Development Squad), then switched back to the land of the kilt – a decision I have not regretted for one minute. Qualified by virtue of having a grandmother in Brechin. A Scottish Exile, Alan was chosen to play for his adopted nation without representing the second-string XV, but had to postpone his debut after learning he had a broken leg two days before Ireland visited Murrayfield. Had declared himself fit, but a hard midweek scrummaging session resurrected his uncertainty, and an Edinburgh Hospital X-ray (after dye had been injected into the bone) revealed a crack. No matter: he satisfied himself with A-team appearances against Italy and Ireland in '93, before hitting the big time in 1994: replacing Boroughmuir's Peter Wright in the No 1 jersey after Scotland's heavy defeat in Cardiff, and wearing it with distinction against England, Ireland and France. Toured Argentina last summer, playing in both Tests, as well as in the 24–24 draw with Buenos Aires (25.5.94)

Touchlines: Coaching Southmead RFC

Shiel, A. G. Scotland

Full Name: Andrew Graham Shiel
Club: Melrose
Position: Outside-half, centre
Height: 5ft 10lb (1.78m)
Weight: 12st 10lb (81kg)
Occupation: Stonemason with Historic Scotland (Melrose)
Born: Galashiels, 13.8.70
Family: Single
Family links with rugby: Father (Andrew) played for Melrose GS
Former club: Manly (Aus)
International debut: Scotland 24, Ireland 15, 1991
Five Nations debut: Scotland 15, Ireland 3, 1993
Best moment in rugby: Scoring winning try against Ireland on Scotland debut after coming on as 43rd-minute replacement in 1991 World Cup match at Murrayfield

Worst moment in rugby: Missing majority of 1993/94 season through injury
Most embarrassing moment: Ball toppled over in front of posts before I

kicked it during 1990 Hawick Sevens

Most respected opponent: Sean Lineen (Boroughmuir & Scotland)

Biggest influences on career: Ian McGeechan and Jim Telfer

Serious injuries: Straining inner and exterior quadriceps and adductor muscle (1988/89), and missing over four months of rugby; pelvic strain (November 1990) – three months out; knee ligaments (1993/94) – six months out; flaked bone in ankle trapping nerve

Other sporting achievements: Athletics for Borders Schools and Borders AAA

Best memory last season: Earning selection for Scotland's summer tour to Argentina after being so long out with injury

Should rugby's amateur rules be revised? Yes

To what degree should players benefit? Allow players at very top to earn from off-field activities as reward for so much time-consuming commitment

Should referees be rewarded? Match fee for top officials, as rugby is just as competitive and time-consuming for them as for players

Advice for International Board: Rules must be made for everyone, regardless of geography. Communicate better. Players are not sure what the rules are in relation to amateurism, for example. They have changed so much. Make us more aware

Suggestions to improve Scottish rugby: Playing standards need to be improved at club level – inferior to England and Wales. Still too forward-orientated in Scotland (lack of running ability)

Notable landmarks in rugby career: An exciting young talent whose 1993/94 season was blighted by injury. Graham reckons he only played in 3 out of 12 months due to damaged anterior cruciate ligaments in left knee (caused him to miss Scotland's 1992 tour to South Seas) and a trapped nerve in his ankle caused by a flaked bone. Between injuries he fitted in one Test cap, as centre in 51–15 loss to New Zealand (Murrayfield, 20.11.93). Run of bad luck started at the end of a season in which he had established himself as heir-apparent to Sean Lineen alongside Scott Hastings in Scottish midfield. He played in all four legs of the 1993 Five Nations Championship, after a Trial in which he started for the possibles and finished with the probables. Represented Scottish Schools (three times), Scotland U-19s and U-21s (twice). Scored six points in 1989/90 defeat (10–24) by Wales Under-21s, and played in 15–23 loss to same opposition (1990/91). Toured with Scotland to New Zealand (1990), North America and Canada (1991), Australia (1992) and Argentina (1994), the latter trip ending his injury nightmare as he appeared at centre in both Tests. Represented European Saltires against South Pacific Barbarians in XVs prior to 1991 Hong Kong Sevens. Having been included in Scotland's 1991 World Cup squad, he was given debut against Ireland as a 43rd-minute replacement for outside-half Craig Chalmers. A fairytale scenario saw him score a try as

Scotland (1991)		
Last Season	3 caps	0 pts
1994	Tour to Argentina	
Career	9 caps	4 pts

Caps (9): **1991** wc–I(R), WS **1993** I, F, W, E, NZ **1994** Arg(1,2)

Points (4 – 1t): **1991** wc–I(R:1t)

Scotland came from behind to win. Seven days later, he won second cap (as centre) in quarter-final against Western Samoa, when knee injury ruled out Lineen. Remained in Australia after 1992 tour to spend summer playing with Manly

Touchlines: Social golf, cricket, swimming

Slattery, P. J. Australia

Full Name: Peter John Slattery
State: Queensland
Club: Queensland University
Position: Scrum-half
Height: 5ft 9in (1.76m)
Weight: 12st 4lb (78kg)
Occupation: Sales representative with Rugby Products of Australia
Born: 6.6.65
Family: Single
Former clubs: Wests (1983-86); Queensland University since 1987
International debut: Australia 67, USA 9, 1990
Best moments in rugby: Winning 1991 World Cup; beating Wales (1992)
Worst moment in rugby: Pre-season training
Most embarrassing moment: Driving to training in my car
Serious injuries: Broken arm (1987)
Suggestions to improve rugby: Ban kicking ball out on full inside your own 22
Notable landmarks in rugby career: Assigned the considerable task of filling the Wallaby No 9

Australia (1990)

Last Season	6 caps	0 pts
Career	14 caps	8 pts

Caps (14): **1990** US(R) **1991** W(aR), E(aR). wc–WS(R), W(b),I(R) **1992** I, W **1993** T, C, F(1,2) **1994** I(1,2)

Points (8 – 2t): **1990** US(1t) **1991** wc–W(b:1t)

jersey worn by Nick Farr-Jones, after the long-time skipper and inspiration hung up his boots having claimed the scalp of South Africa. But after successfully steering the Wallabies past Ireland and Wales in the autumn of 1992, Peter sustained broken ribs playing against Tonga in the curtain-opener for the 1993 Test campaign (Brisbane, 3.7.93). The upshot was the recall from retirement of Farr-Jones for the Bledisloe Cup match and three-Test home series with South Africa. Fit again, Slattery returned for the autumn tour to

North America and France, but did not produce his best form, notably in the first-Test defeat by France in Bordeaux, when he spilled two scoring passes. A Test reserve on and off since 1985, he bagged a try on his international debut in 1990 after coming on as a replacement for Farr-Jones in the 67-9 defeat of the United States Eagles. The following year he replaced his perennial rival on a further four occasions, twice during the Wallabies' triumphant World Cup campaign. In 1992 he captained Queensland to victory in the prestigious Super Six Championship, and skippered the Aussies twice on tour in South Africa.
Touchlines: Sleeping, eating and surfing

Small, J. T.   South Africa

Full Name: James Terence Small
Club: Wits
Province: Natal
Club: College Rovers
Position: Wing
Height: 6ft (1.82m)
Weight: 13st 3lb (84kg)
Occupation: Representative
Born: Cape Town, 10.2.69
Family links with rugby: None.
Son of former Springbok soccer
player Vernon Small (1956)
Former province: Transvaal
International debut: South Africa
24, New Zealand 27, 1992
**Notable landmarks in rugby
career:** Most prolific try-scorer in
world rugby during 1993, with seven
scores in a six-Test spell.
Unfortunately he sullied his
reputation by being sent off for
verbally abusing English referee Ed
Morrison during South Africa's
20–28 second-Test defeat by
Australia (Brisbane, 14.8.94). 'The
Springboks blazer means more to
me than most things in life, and I let
it down. I've also let down my team
mates. It will be a while before I can
look them in the eye'. Not too long, actually, as the ex-South African Schools

South Africa (1992)

Last Season	7 caps	35 pts
Career	14 caps	40 pts

Caps (14): **1992** NZ, A, F(1,2), E **1993** F(1,2), Arg(1,2), A(1,2,3) **1994** E(1,2)

Points (40 – 8t): **1992** F(1:1t) **1993** F(2:1t), Arg(1:2t), Arg(2:1t), A(1:2t), A(3:1t)

player weighed in with a try in the final Test, having bagged a match-winning brace in the first match. Petulance got the better of him in the first Test against

England last summer, and he was quite fortunate to last the duration. Formerly a superb soccer player – a talent which he inherited from his father, a 1956 international – James was included in the first Springbok side selected after the ending of the international boycott. He played not only against New Zealand but also against Australia the following week, before turning out for Transvaal in the 1992 Currie Cup final. Unhappily for the player, victory went to Natal by the odd point in 27 (he later moved to Natal in 1993 and – would you believe? – lost to Transvaal in the 1993 final), but his smile was restored when he scored one of South Africa's two tries in their 20–15 victory over France (Lyon, 17 10.92), and he also retaining his place for the next two Test engagements against France (lost 16–29, Paris, 24.10.92) and England (lost 16–33, Twickenham, 14.11.92). Ever-present through 1993 campaign (as he has been since South Africa's return to the international fold), scoring a try against France in the second Test of the home series (lost 17–18, Johannesburg, 3.7.93), and bagging three tries in the two away Test wins over Argentina in the autumn

---

Smith, D. P. P. Australia

Full Name: Damian Paul Peter Smith
State: Queensland
Club: Brisbane
Position: Wing
Height: 6ft 2in (1.88m)
Weight: 14st 9lb (93kg)
Occupation: Property consultant for Colliers Jardine
Born: 1.2.69
International debut: Australia 12, South Africa 19, 1993
Best moment in rugby: Playing for my state and country
Worst moments in rugby: Losing first Test for Australia against South Africa; kicking a ball 20 metres backwards with a gale-force wind behind me against Welsh Students on 1992 Wales/Ireland Tour
Most respected opponent: James Small (Natal & South Africa)
Best memory last season: Winning second Test 28–20 against South Africa at Ballymore

Australia (1993)

Last Season	7 caps	10 pts
Career	7 caps	10 pts

Caps (7): **1993** SA(1,2,3), C, F(2) **1994** I(1,2)

Points (10 – 2t): **1993** C(1t) **1994** I(1:1t)

Serious injuries: Broken wrist and arm (1990)

Notable landmarks in rugby career: Broke into Queensland side in 1992, and quickly graduated into the Wallaby squad which toured Wales and Ireland. Having missed the 1990 season with a broken arm, he was not about to let his chance slip, and he responded with eight starts out of a possible 13, scoring three tries. However, a Test place eluded him until 1993, when the strong-running winger was drafted in for the three-match home series against South Africa – their first visit Down Under since 1971. Damian occupied the right wing berth in each of the Tests as Australia came from behind to edge a 2–1 decision. The next goal to be fulfilled was his first international try, achieved during Canada's 43–16 beating in Calgary (9.10.93) in the early throes of an autumn tour which also incorporated two Tests against France. Damian lost out to young NSW flier Alistair Murdoch in the first-Test selection stakes, but after France triumphed 16–13 in Bordeaux, he was recalled for the second match, which yielded a 24–3 series-levelling scoreline. Keeping his place into 1994, he wore the Wallaby No 14 jersey through the 2–0 series sweep of Ireland

Touchlines: Water skiing, mountineering, surfing and parachuting.

Smith, I. R. Scotland

Full Name: Ian Richard Smith
Club: Gloucester
Position: Flanker
Height: 6ft (1.83m)
Weight: 14st (89kg)
Occupation: Civil engineer with Sir William Halcrow Ltd
Born: Gloucester, 16.3.65
Family: Karen (wife)
Family links with rugby: Father (Dick) was an England triallist who played for (and captained) Gloucester and Barbarians
Former club: Longlevens, Wollongong (Aus, 1988)
International debut (England): Spanish Select 15, England B 32, 1989
International debut (Scotland): Scotland 7, England 25, 1992
Five Nations' debut: As above
Best moment in rugby: Running out at Murrayfield for first Scotland cap against England
Worst moment in rugby: Losing 1989/90 Pilkington Cup final 6–48 to Bath

Most embarrassing moment:
Above match – we were humiliated
Most respected opponent: Lyn
Jones (Treorchy & Wales)
Biggest influences on career:
Father and Derek Cook (coach at
Longlevens)
**Should rugby's amateur rules be
revised?** Yes

Scotland (1992)
Last Season	5 caps	0 pts
1994	Tour to Argentina	
Career	10 caps	0 pts

Caps (10): **1992** E, I, W, A(1,2) **1994**
E(R), I, F, Arg(1,2)

Points Nil

To what degree should players benefit? Reimburse employers for
employee's time lost to rugby. It's not that we want to profit from rugby: it's
that we and our bosses don't want to be out of pocket
Should referees be rewarded? Yes, if it leads to greater consistency. I'm in
favour of setting up refereeing seminars where they can get together with
players and coaches to work things out
Advice for International Board: Relax amateurism laws
Notable landmarks in rugby career: Recalled to Scotland side in 1993/94
after injury forced out Rob Wainwright. Ian replaced him 66 minutes into 1994
Calcutta Cup clash at Murrayfield (5.2.94), a match which England won 15–14
with last kick of game. He held his place for final two games of the Wooden
Spoon campaign, against Ireland and France, before departing for summer
tour to Argentina. Two years earlier had toured Australia, appearing at
openside in both Test defeats. A former England 18-Group triallist, who played
200th game for Gloucester in 1990 Pilkington Cup final, Ian spent the 1988
Australian season playing in Wollongong. Toured Spain with England B
(1990) and was selected to England's 1991 World Cup squad, having spent
1990 off-season on standby for Argentina tour, but then decided to switch
allegiances to Scotland (Scottish grandparents on father's side), and played
twice for Scotland B in 1990/91 (v Ireland and France) before leading side in
19–29 home loss to Ireland in 1991/92, a season in which he also captained
Gloucester (as in 1992/93) and broke into Scotland team for Five Nations
Championship; he missed only the French visit to Murrayfield, due to a badly
cut hand, but then was absent throughout 1993 Championship, displaced by
another Anglo-Scot, London Scottish's Iain Morrison., Before losing his place,
Ian had been tipped in some quarters as a successor to national captain David
Sole – after all, he did skipper Scotland against New South Wales (lost 15–35,
Sydney, 6.6.92) – but a place in the shadow Scotland XV which struggled to
beat Italy at Melrose (19.12.92) was as near as he came to the national side in
any capacity
Touchlines: Shooting, squash, trout fishing

Stanger, A. G.   Scotland

Full Name: Anthony George Stanger
Club: Hawick
Position: Wing
Height: 6ft 2in (1.88m)
Weight: 15st 2lb (96kg)
Occupation: New Business representative with Royscott Trust (Edinburgh)
Born: Hawick, 14.5.68
Family: Bridget (wife)
Family links with rugby: Peter (brother) plays for Hawick and Scotland U-18s
Former club: Warringah (Aus)
International debut: Scotland 38, Fiji 17, 1989
Five Nations debut: Ireland 10, Scotland 13, 1990
Best moment in rugby: Scoring winning try in 1990 Grand Slam decider against England
Worst moment in rugby: Getting dropped by Scotland on 1992 Australia tour
Most respected opponents: Keith Crossan (Instonians & ex-Ireland) and Patrice Lagisquet (Bayonne & ex-France)
Other sporting achievements: Hawick High School athletics champion (three times)

Scotland (1989)

Last Season	5 caps	0 pts
Career	35 caps	61 pts

Caps (35): **1989** Fj, Ro **1990** I, F, W, E, NZ(1,2), Arg **1991** F, W, E, I, Ro wc–J, Z, I, WS, E, NZ **1992** E, I, F, W, A(1,2) **1993** I, F, W, E, NZ **1994** W, E, I, F

Points (61 – 15t): Fj(2t), Ro(3t) **1990** E(1t), NZ(2:1t), Arg(2t) **1991** I(1t) wc–J(1t), Z(1t), WS(1t) **1992** I(1t) **1993** I(1t)

Best memory last season: Long-awaited resurgence of Hawick
Should rugby's amateur rules be revised? Yes
To what degree should players benefit? As far as they can without being paid to play
Should referees be rewarded? Yes – anything which improves standards gets my vote
Advice for International Board: Everyone must adhere to the same rulebook. So many are bending the laws at present, and we get upset when we're being made to look stupid
Notable landmarks in rugby career: An ever-present in Scotland's side from his debut against Fiji in 1989 – 35 matches ago – until he missed last summer's

tour to Argentina through unavailability. Requires three more caps to surpass Iwan Tukalo (37: 1985-92) as Scotland's most-capped wing. Scored six tries in first six internationals (two on debut against Fiji, three against Romania and one against England in 1990 Grand Slam decider). Toured with Scotland to Japan (1989), New Zealand (1990), North America (1991), Australia (1992) and Argentina (1994). Made debut for Hawick as a 17-year-old student. Earned five caps for Scottish Schools at centre in 1985/86, followed by two for Scotland U-21s. Began 1990/91 season with two tries in 49–3 defeat of Argentina, taking try tally to nine in as many games. Could not sustain that prolific pace through 1991/92 season's 11-game schedule, but did not do badly, managing four tries: three in World Cup and one against Ireland in Championship for second consecutive season. Also turned out for Scotland A in 36–16 win over Spain (Murrayfield, 28.12.91). Made second A-team appearance in 22–13 win over Ireland (28.12.92), scoring two tries to book his Five Nations place. Celebrated with great try in Championship opener against Ireland to join Tukalo as Scotland's second-top try scorer (15). Injury cost him a place in Scotland's World Cup seven (1993)
Touchlines: Social golf

Staples, J. E.   Ireland

Full Name: James (Jim) Edward Staples
Club: London Irish
Position: Fullback, wing
Height: 6ft 2in (1.88m)
Weight: 13st 9lb (86kg)
Occupation: Employé with French bank Société Générale
Born: London, 20.10.65
Family: Single
Family links with rugby: Younger brother (David) plays for Westcombe Park
Former clubs: St Mary's, Bromley, Sidcup
International debut: Wales 21, Ireland 21, 1991
Five Nations debut: As above
Best moment in rugby: Making Ireland debut in Cardiff (1991)

Worst moments in rugby: Michael Lynagh's last-gasp try for Australia in our World Cup quarter-final. Missing out on promotion to English First Division with London Irish in 1988/89, after losing 22–21 to last-minute dropped goal by Blackheath, having led 21–0 at half-time

Most embarrassing moment: Missing flight home from Spain on first county senior trip

Most respected opponent: Gavin Hastings (Watsonians & Scotland) – strong, fast and always a threat

Biggest influence on career: John O'Driscoll (Connacht: got me involved in the provincial scene)/Roy White (schoolteacher: took me along to Sidcup where he was captain)

Ireland (1991)

Last Season	0 caps	0 pts
1994	Tour to Australia	
Career	14 caps	21 pts

Caps (14): **1991** W, E, S, Na(1,2) wc–Z, J, S, A **1992** W, E, NZ(1,2), A

Points (21 – 4t,2c): **1991** W(1t), Na(2:1t,2c) wc–J(1t) **1992** NZ(1:1t)

Serious injuries: Prolapsed disc in back, broken nose, damaged knee ligaments (missed whole of 1993/94 season)

Other sporting achievements: Played in same Greenwich Borough forward line as Arsenal and England striker Ian Wright

Best memory last season: Watching Simon Geoghegan score Irish try at Twickenham

Should rugby's amateur rules be revised? Yes

To what degree should players benefit? Unions should pay a third of players' working salaries to employers to reduce stress in workplace. They must realize that without sympathetic employers, we could not afford to play. But I don't want to be paid to play

Should referees be rewarded? No, I don't think payments would improve standards

Advice for International Board: Some of the Southern Hemisphere unions are doing exactly as they like, and some more traditional unions are letting them get away with it for fear that the objections they make will force the more radical unions to split and go and play elsewhere. It doesn't matter if game is professional or amateur as long as rules are same for everyone. The IB as an institution has failed. Last year I feared that increasing the try value meant the ball wouldn't come out and there would be a lot more penalties conceded – and that is what has come to pass

Notable landmarks in rugby career: Test career blighted by injury ever since he damaged his knee in Irish trial preceding 1993 Five Nations campaign. Before that had been first-choice fullback. He toured with Ireland to New Zealand over the summer of 1992, weighing in with one of the three tries which so nearly proved good enough to beat the All Blacks in the first Test at Dunedin (30.5.92). Also played in second Test in Wellington, and against Australia in Dublin (31.10.92). Took over from former Ireland fullback Hugo MacNeill at No 15 in London Irish team, and followed his footsteps into Ireland side in 1991. Represented Connacht against 1989 All Blacks and Irish Wolfhounds in 1988/89 Hong Kong Sevens. Played twice for Ireland Under-25s before reaching B grade in 1989/90, with appearance in 22–22 draw with Scotland. Selected for senior bench against France in 1991 Five Nations opener before playing in next three games, scoring try in 21–21 draw with Wales. Toured with Ireland to Namibia (1991), New Zealand (1992) and last summer – to the delight of his long-waiting fans – in Australia, playing in five of the eight matches: against Western Australia, New South Wales, ACT, Australia B and NSW Country

Touchlines: Soccer, most other sports

Stensness, L.   New Zealand

Full Name: Lee Stensness
Province: Auckland
Position: Centre
Height: 5ft 11in (1.80m)
Weight: 14st (89kg)
Occupation: Student
Born: 24.12.70
International debut: New Zealand 30, British Lions 13, 1993
Most respected opponent: Marty Berry (Wellington & All Blacks)
Biggest influence on career: Manawatu coach Mark Donaldson
Notable landmarks in rugby career: One of the most exciting young talents in world rugby, Lee made a name for himself in the colours of second-division Manawatu. In 1992 he scored two tries as his province ripped apart Ireland 58–24 at Palmerston North (2 June). A fullback that day, his brace of scores took his try tally to 22 in 25 outings for a side that reached the semi-finals in the end-

New Zealand (1993)

Last Season	3 caps	5 pts
Career	3 caps	5 pts

Caps (3): 1993 BL(3), A, WS

Points (5 – 1t): 1993 WS(1t)

of-season play-offs. He also graced the New Zealand Students line-up and that of the New Zealand XV which dispensed with Stuart Barnes' England B side 2–0 in their series in June and July. Not surprisingly, Lee was lured away from Manawatu at the season's end to join the mighty Auckland, for whom he was transformed into a centre and quickly went on to win full international honours. His debut came against the 1993 British Lions, on his home Eden Park field, in the tense third-Test series decider (3 July). He acquitted himself well, sparking New Zealand's revival from a 10–0 deficit with a 27th-minute chip through which Frank Bunce collected to touch down the hosts' first points. He produced another strong performance two weeks later in Dunedin, as the All Blacks regained the Bledisloe Cup from world champions Australia with a commanding 25–10 result, before celebrating his first international try with a splendid burst against Western Samoa back in Auckland on 31 July. On such form he was a certainty for the autumn tour to England and Scotland, but perhaps surprisingly he was unable to keep his place in the first-choice line-up. A knee injury had forced him to miss Auckland's Ranfurly Shield defeat by Waikato, and perhaps took the edge fractionally off his game. Matthew Cooper took his place in the Test against Scotland, and when he was injured Eroni Clarke was drafted in. Lee had to make do with appearances against the English Midlands, South of Scotland, Scottish Development XV, Emerging England, Combined Services and the Barbarians

Touchlines: Playing video games

Strachan, A. D. New Zealand

Full Name: Anthony (Ant) Strachan
Province: North Harbour
Position: Scrum-half
Height: 5ft 9in (1.75m)
Weight: 13st (82kg)
Born: Te Awamutu, 7.6.66
Former Provinces: Otago, Auckland
International debut: New Zealand 54, World XV 26, 1992
Serious injuries: Dislocated shoulder (1992)
Notable landmarks in rugby career: Made the All Black scrum-half position his own with a brilliant 1992 campaign, but then lost out to Jon Preston and Stu Forster in '93. His prodigious clearance speed earned him a national call-up after just eight first-class games for Auckland, where he was back-up to Jason Hewett. It was an injury to Hewett which gave him his ticket to the big time, ahead of Paul McGahon and Kevin Putt. And

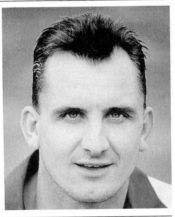

New Zealand (1992)

Last Season	1 cap	0 pts
Career	9 caps	8 pts

Caps (9): **1992** Wd(2,3), I(1,2), A(1,2,3), SA **1993** BL(1)

Points (8 – 2t): **1992** Wd(2:1t), I(2:1t)

although his squad selection was as second-string scrum-half, he was given his Test debut as early as the second leg of the centenary series, following New Zealand's 14–28 first-Test defeat in Christchurch. Brought in for Graeme

Bachop, he responded with a try in the 54–26 Wellington win. A product of Auckland Grammar School, Ant kept his place as New Zealand completed their come-from-behind series win in Auckland and through the two-Test Ireland visit, contributing another try in the 59–6 second-Test victory in Wellington. In Australia and South Africa, on New Zealand's three-month, 16-match tour, no one surpassed Ant's tally of ten appearances, nor his consistently high standard of performance. His one disappointment came in the 27–24 defeat of South Africa at Ellis Park, Johannesburg, where he lasted just 16 minutes before dislocating his shoulder and making way for Preston. Strachan reassumed control at the start of the Lions series in 1993, but lost his place after an unconvincing performance in the first Test at Christchurch and never re-emerged thereafter. A member of New Zealand's Student World Cup-winning squad in 1988, he enjoyed remarkably little provincial action before crossing the bridge from Auckland to North Harbour in 1992, having started out with Otago in 1987

Stransky, J. South Africa

Full Name: Joel Stransky
Province: Natal
Club: College Rovers
Position: Outside-half
Height: 5ft 11in (1.80m)
Weight: 13st 5lb (80kg)
Occupation: Representative
Born: 16.7.67
International debut: Australia 12, South Africa 19, 1993
Notable landmarks in rugby career: Accomplished playmaker who vied with Transvaal's Hennie le Roux for South Africa's No 10 jersey throughout 1993. Le Roux got first shot, but when the Springboks won neither Test against France with him at the helm, Joel was brought in for the country's first tour to Australia in 22 years. Glad to report that his debut (Sydney, 31.7.93) saw a famous 19–12 win for the visitors against shell-shocked world champions. Joel took over the goalkicking duties for the second Test (Brisbane, 14.8.93), after Theo

South Africa (1993)

Last Season	4 caps	26 pts
Career	4 caps	26 pts

Caps (4): 1993 A(1,2,3), Arg(1)

Points (26 – 1t,6c,3p): 1993 A(2:1t,2c,2p), A(3:1c), Arg(1:3c,1p) van Rensburg had been forced to return home for emergency surgery on a groin hernia, and responded with 15 points (1t,2c,2p), though Australia still won 28–20. One Stransky conversion in the deciding third Test was insufficient to stop the series staying in Oz. Still, he finished the tour with 58 points, (1t,22c,3p) – a figure reached with appearances against Western Australia (eight conversions), Victoria (nine conversions) and Queensland (two conversions and a penalty). Joel then kicked five penalty goals in the Currie Cup final (Kings Park, Durban, 16.10.93), but Natal lost 15–21 to Transvaal. He then headed off to Argentina, where he lost his Test place after kicking nine points (3c,1p) in a 29–26 first-Test defeat of the Pumas (Buenos Aires, 6.11.93). His successor was Henry Honiball, who promptly nicked his provincial No 10 jersey for the 1994 Super-10 final defeat by Queensland and famous 21–6 win against touring England

---

Strauss, C. P.   South Africa

Full Name: Christiaan (Tiaan) Petrus Strauss
Club: Northerns-Tygerberg-College
Province: Western Province
Position: No 8
Height: 6ft 1in (1.86m)
Weight: 15st 6lb (98kg)
Occupation: Articled clerk with Cape Town law firm
Born: Uppington, 28.6.65
International debut: France 15, South Africa 20, 1992
Notable landmarks in rugby career: Spearhead of South Africa's pack, Tiaan was one of only two Springbok forwards to play in all seven Tests during 1993 (the other being skipper François Pienaar), saving his most productive performance for last, bagging two tries in the 52–23 defeat of Argentina (Buenos Aires, 13.11.93) which completed a 2–0 series whitewash away from home. He had also claimed a try hat-trick in the opening 55–37 victory over Córdoba (27.10.93) and finished the six-match tour as top try-scorer.

South Africa (1992)

Last Season	8 caps	10 pts
Career	11 caps	15 pts

Caps   (11): **1992** F(1,2), E **1993** F(1,2), A(1,2,3), Arg(1,2) **1994** E(1)

Points (15 – 3t): **1992** E(1t) **1993** Arg(2:2t)

Appeared in all six big tour games in Australia, and skippered the side to their biggest win of that tour: a 90–3 rout of hapless South Australia (Adelaide, 17.7.93). However, lost his place after England had swept the first Test match of 1994, 32–15 in Pretoria. Had captained Junior Springboks side which played against both Namibia and New Zealand (lost 15–20) in 1992, a year in which he made a favourable impression on the tour of France and England (with whom he renewed acquaintance last summer), playing in all three Tests and five other games besides: against France B, Aquitaine, Midi-Pyrenées, French Barbarians and England B. A powerful man – the legacy of his days on the family farms in the Kalahari and Namibia – he was pulled from the under-20 ranks to make his senior debut for Western Province in 1986. Scored South Africa's only try in 16–33 loss to England (14.11.92). Capped 120 times by his union before the accomplished Jannie Breedt retired, vacating a berth in the back row for him to make his Test bow in the 20–15 defeat of France in Lyon (17.10.92). Not that he had sat around idly waiting for his chance. He had spent the late 1980s and early 1990s in Italy playing with Noceto – a second-division outfit to be found near Parma. Such experience stood him in good stead during the Springboks' long stay in Europe in '92

Strydom, H. South Africa

Full Name: Hannes Strydom
Province: Transvaal
Position: Lock
Height: 6ft 6 ½ in (1.99m)
Weight: 18st 5lb (112kg)
Occupation: Medical representative
Born: 13.7.65
International debut: South Africa 17, France 18, 1993
Notable landmarks in rugby career: One of three forwards drafted in to bolster South Africa's flagging challenge against France, after the 1993 tourists had sent shockwaves throughout the Republic by sharing the first Test 20–20 (Durban, 26.6.93). The injection of new blood made no odds as South Africa crashed 18–17 in Ellis Park,

Johannesburg (3.7.93). Hannes was retained despite the setback, and played the full three-Test complement in Australia over the next two months, on each occasion in second-row partnership with Western Province's Nico Wegner. He remained first-choice lock throughout the tour, turning out in the other 'biggies'

against South Australia (won 90–3, Adelaide, 17.7.93), New South Wales (lost 28–29, Sydney, 24.7.93) and Queensland (won 17–3, Brisbane, 8.8.93). On a provincial note, 1993 was a red-letter year for Transvaal, who captured both the prestigious Super-10 trophy (beating Auckland 20–7 in final at Ellis Park,

South Africa (1993)

Last Season	7 caps	0 pts
Career	7 caps	0 pts

Caps (7): 1993 F(2), A(1,2,3), Arg(1,2) **1994** E(1)

Points Nil

Johannesburg on 22.5.93) and the Currie Cup (beating Natal 21–15 at Kings Park, Durban in final on 16.10.93). After the latter, Hannes departed with Springboks for Argentina, where he played in four of the six tour missions: both Test wins, the 28–27 loss to Buenos Aires, and the 40–12 'battle' of Tucumán. The latter contest (2.11.93) brought shame on the player, as he was one of four dismissed. However, lady luck treated him kindly, as he and fellow Springbok Keith Andrews were handed nothing more than suspended sentences, and so were free to play in the first Test a mere four days later. Started 1994 in Springboks side, but lost place after England's shock 32–15 win in Pretoria (4.6.94)

Styger, J. J. South Africa

Full Name: Johannes (Johann) Jakobus Styger
Club: Oud-Studente
Province: Orange Free State
Position: Prop
Height: 6ft (1.82m)
Weight: 16st 7lb (105kg)
Occupation: Dentist
Born: Bloemfontein, 31.1.62
Former Province: Northern Transvaal
International debut: South Africa 24, New Zealand 27, 1992
Notable landmarks in rugby career: An aggressive dentist is bad news for everyone other than Springbok fans. Johann, who tends to teeth by profession, is a tough customer in the colours of both

Orange Free State and South Africa, though he saw little action for the latter in 1993, his game time being restricted to 35 minutes in the series-deciding third Test against Australia (Sydney, 21.8.93) after he had replaced broken-nose

victim Balie Swart; Australia won 19–12. Johann's other seven tour appearances were for the midweek dirt-trackers against Western Australia (won 71–8, Perth, 14.7.93), Victoria (won 78–3, Melbourne, 21.7.93); NSW Country (won 41–7, Orange, 27.7.93), ACT (won 57–10, Canberra, 4.8.93), Queensland Country (won 65–5, Mackay, 11.8.93) and Sydney (won 31–20, Penrith, 18.8.93). Previous to all that, he had quickly graduated from the replacements' bench (where he started the 1992 international campaign against New Zealand) to first-choice loosehead prop. His cause was helped by the 51st-minute injury suffered by Transvaal's Heinrich Rodgers against the All Blacks, which allowed him into the fray at Ellis Park. But once in the spotlight he did not depart. Indeed, when Rodgers returned to the side fully fit, for the two Tests in France, he did so on the other side of the scrum. Born and educated (at Grey College) in Bloemfontein, Johann played 13 matches for Northern Transvaal following his debut in 1983, before switching to Free State. Other starts on the 1992 European tour came against Aquitaine, Languedoc-Roussillon, the French Barbarians and England B

South Africa (1992)

Last Season	1 cap	0 pts
Career	6 caps	0 pts

Caps (6): 1992 NZ(R), A, F(1,2), E 1993 A(3R)

Points Nil

Swart, B.   South Africa

Full Name: Balie Swart
Province: Transvaal
Position: Prop
Height: 6ft ½ in (1.84m)
Weight: 18st 1lb (110kg)
Occupation: Motor salesman
Born: 18.5.64
International debut: Australia 12, South Africa 19, 1993
Notable landmarks in rugby career: Enjoyed a triumphant debut in Sydney (3.7.93) when South Africa celebrated their return to Australia (after a 22-year absence) with a 19–12 defeat of the Wallabies. Balie would almost certainly have made his bow earlier but for an emergency appendectomy, which forced him out of the reckoning for

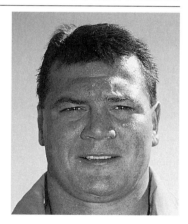

the two-Test series with France in June and July of the same year. Still, he made up for lost time in Australia, turning out in eight of the 13 engagements, including each leg of the three-Test series, which the world champions came from behind to win at Sydney on 31 July. His other starts were against Western Australia (won 71–8, Perth, 14.7.93), New South Wales (lost 28–29, Sydney, 24.7.93), ACT (won 57–10, Canberra, 4.8.93), Queensland (won 17–3, Brisbane, 8.8.93) and Queensland Country (won 65–5, Mackay, 11.8.93). Came off 45 minutes into decisive third Test (Sydney, 31.8.93) with a broken nose. A member of the Transvaal side which in 1993 won the inaugural Super-10 tournament (beating Auckland 20–7 in final at Ellis Park, Johannesburg, 22.5.93) and the Currie Cup (beating Natal 21–15 in final at Kings Park, Durban, 16.10.93). He also toured with the Springboks to Argentina in the autumn, but was replaced by Western Province's Keith Andrews at tighthead for the second Test in Buenos Aires – a city where he had appeared in the first international the previous weekend, and whose team had beaten the Springboks 28–27 (30.10.93). Despite his omission from the rest of the South American tour, he was restored to the Test side for the visit of England last summer, and was superb in the second Test once he had switched to his favoured tighthead berth

South Africa (1993)

Last Season	6 caps	0 pts
Career	6 caps	0 pts

Caps (6): 1993 A(1,2,3), Arg(1) **1994** E(1,2)

Points Nil

Tabua, I. Australia

Full Name: Ilie Tabua
State: Queensland
Club: Brothers
Position: Flanker
Height: 6ft 5in (1.96m)
Weight: 16st 4lb (104kg)
Occupation: Student of town planning at Armidale
Born: Fiji, 30.9.64
Family: single
International debut: Australia 28, South Africa 20, 1993
Best moments in rugby: Test debut against South Africa at Ballymore; World Cup Sevens in Edinburgh when I made my Australia debut
Worst moment in rugby: Canterbury verses Old

(Christchurch) in 1992 – nearly died of hypothermia

Best memory last season: Test debut

Serious injuries: None

Advice for International Board: Legalize lifting in the lineout

Australia (1993)

Last Season	6 caps	10 pts
Career	6 caps	10 pts

Caps (6): 1993 SA(2,3), C, F(1) **1994** I(1,2)

Points (10 – 2t): 1994 I(1:1t), I(2:1t)

Notable landmarks in rugby career: One to watch in 1995 World Cup, Ilie first came to the notice of British audiences when playing for Australia in 1993 World Cup Sevens in Edinburgh (16–18 April). The Fijian-born Brothers flanker, then uncapped in the XV-man sphere, helped the Wallabies reach the final, where he was spared the agony of losing 21–17 to unfancied England. Among his team mates in that tournament were David Campese and Matt Burke, with whom he made his Test debut against South Africa in Brisbane (14.8.93). His call-up was prompted by the Wallabies' shock 12–19 loss in the first Test in Sydney, and his arrival more than redressed the balance. The world champions won the next two Tests. Ilie then embarked on the autumn tour to North America and France, scoring a try in the 26–22 non-cap Test victory over the United States in sweltering California (2.10.93), before appearing against Canada and then France in the surprise 13–16 first-Test loss in Bordeaux. It was an especially painful afternoon for Ilie, as he broke his left arm midway through the game and was put out of action for the remainder of the season. Made a typically positive return in 1994, scoring a try in each of the two Test wins over Ireland, confirming himself a powerhouse in the 'Willie O' mould

Touchlines: Relaxing, reading, sleeping

Spot the ball: French scrum-half Aubin Hueber gathers possession despite the presence of five Wallabies. To no avail, France lost 24–3.

Taylor, H. T.   Wales

Full Name: Hemi Takatou Taylor
Club: Cardiff
Position: Flanker, No 8
Height: 6ft 2in (1.88m)
Weight: 14st 7lb (87.5kg)
Occupation: Rugby development
officer for Cardiff RFC
Born: Morrinsville, New Zealand,
17.12.64
Family: Wife and child
Former provinces/clubs: Waikato
(NZ), Wairarapa Bush (NZ),
Newbridge (Wal), East Brisbane
(Aus)
International debut: Portugal 11,
Wales 102, 1994
Five Nations debut: None
**Notable landmarks in rugby
career:** Became first New Zealander
to represent Wales at Test level
when given debut in World Cup
qualifier against Portugal (Lisbon,
17.5.94). The former New Zealand
Colt, whose allegiances in the Land
of the Long White Cloud were to
Waikato and Wairarapa Bush,
celebrated the occasion with a try in

Wales (1994)

Last Season	5 caps	5 pts
1994	Tour to Canada/South Seas	
Career	5 caps	5 pts

Caps (5): **1994** wc(q)–P. C, Fj, T, WS (R)

Points (5 – 1t): **1994** wc(q)–P(1t)

the 102–11 rout. Although he did not play in the second leg of the Iberian trip, against Spain four days later, he was included in the national squad for the summer tour of Canada, Fiji, Tonga and Western Samoa. Picked up his second cap in the 33–15 'revenge' victory over the Canucks in Toronto (11.6.94) and collected caps in the next three 'Island' Tests. An ever-present in Wales A's 1994 5-match 'Grand Slam', he appeared in the wins over Japan (won 61–5, Llanelli, 29.9.93), North of England (scored try in 24–8 win, Pontypool, 13.10.93), Ireland A (won 20–10, Donnybrook, 4.2.94), Canada A (won 42–11, Cardiff, 12.3.94) and France A (won 21–8, Cardiff, 18.3.94). Cardiff fans voted him their Player of the Year in 1992/93, and it was with the same club that he picked up a Swalec Cup winners medal last season

Techoueyres, W.　　　　　　　France

Full Name: William Techoueyres
Club: Bordeaux University
Position: Wing
Height: 6ft ½ in (1.84m)
Weight: 13st 6lb (80.7kg)
Occupation: Café owner
Born: Bordeaux, 12.2.66
International debut: France 14, England 18, 1994
Five Nations debut: As above
Best moments in rugby: Getting capped; helping Begles win 1991 French Championship
Notable landmarks in rugby career: William's debut proved to be a baptism of fire, as it coincided with England's 1994 defeat of France in Paris. Being a winger, he was an easy target for a Parc des Princes crowd looking to vent their displeasure. Not that he deserved the abuse – a point confirmed by the selectors, who retained his services for the next international, against Scotland (Murrayfield, 19.3.94).

France (1994)		
Last Season	2 caps	0 pts
Career	2 caps	0 pts

Caps (2): **1994** E, S

Points Nil

That game ended on a happier note for France, as a 20–12 victory staved off the dreaded Wooden Spoon. William, who did not tour to Canada and New Zealand last summer, is the first Bordeaux University player since Michael Celaya, 33 years ago, to receive full international recognition. He joined the club last season after a lengthy spell at Begles (Bordeaux's other major club), with whom he won a French Championship medal in 1991, when Toulouse were sent packing after losing the final 19–10

Timu, J. K. R.   New Zealand

Full Name: John Kahukura Raymond Timu
Club: University
Province: Otago
Position: Fullback, wing
Height: 5ft 11in (1.80m)
Weight: 13st 10lb (87kg)
Occupation: PE student
Born: Dannevirke, Hawke's Bay, 8.5.69
International debut: Argentina 14, New Zealand 28, 1991
Best memory in rugby: Being called into All Black squad to replace injured John Kirwan
Notable landmarks in rugby career: Hailed as the new John Gallagher following his spectacularly successful switch from wing to fullback in 1991. Indeed, John has been one of New Zealand's most prized assets ever since he made the Otago team in 1988 in his first year out of school, immediately shattering the province's try-scoring record. His tally of 16 bettered the previous record established back in 1948, and won him a place on the 1988 NZ Maoris' world tour. By the age of 22

New Zealand (1991)

Last Season	7 caps	0 pts
Career	20 caps	21 pts

Caps   (20): **1991** Arg(1), A(1,2). wc–E, US, C, A **1992** Wd(2), I(2), A(1,2,3), SA **1993** BL(1,2,3), A, WS, S, E

Points (21 – 5t): **1991** wc–US(1t), C(2t) **1992** I(2:1t), A(2:1t)

he had become Otago's all-time leading try-scorer, with 54 tries in 63 games, and quickly showed he was not afraid to cross the international try-line either. The year before he toured Australia with New Zealand Colts, and helped beat the Wallabies 24–21, John had been flown to Britain to join the New Zealand senior squad's 1989 tour of Wales and Ireland as a replacement. He bagged a try on his All Black debut against Newport, and two more next time out against Leinster. In 1990 he also visited France with the national squad, but it was not until the 1991 tour of Argentina that he picked up his first cap, standing in for the injured John Kirwan. He failed to score in that first Test, but crossed nine times in the seven tour games he appeared in. Such prolific form brought him back to Britain for the World Cup and four more caps, the pick being his two-try display from fullback in the 29–12 quarter-final defeat of Canada in Lille. Scored further tries in the second Tests against Ireland and Australia in 1992, the latter on a tour which he began with four tries against Western Australia.

Finished year with one of All Blacks' three Test tries in Johannesburg, taking his try count to 25 in 37 appearances prior to the '93 tour to England and Scotland. He remained first-choice full-back throughout, though surprisingly his only All Black try of the entire year came in the 26–12 win over England A (Gatsehead, 7.11.93).

Touchlines: Surfing, snowboarding, golf, tennis, hunting

Tordo, J.-F. France

Full Name: Jean-François Tordo
Club: Nice
Position: Flanker, hooker
Height: 6ft 1in (1.86m)
Weight: 14st 10lb (93kg)
Occupation: Building foreman
Born: Nice, 1.8.64
Former club: Toulon
International debut: United States 9, France 41, 1991
Five Nations debut: Wales 9, France 12, 1992
Notable landmarks in rugby career: A wretched year for 'Jeff': nothing went right after he had captained France to the 1992 Five Nations Championship title. Leading his side on tour in South Africa, his tour was abruptly halted by a vicious injury suffered in the 12–6 win over Western Province in Cape Town (12.6.93). Home prop Garry Pagel was cited by his own union after stamping on the Frenchman's face, inflicting an injury which required 50 stitches to his mouth, nose and cheek in a two-hour plastic surgery operation. If

France (1991)

Last Season	0 caps	0 pts
1994	Tour to Canada/NZ	
Career	15 caps	0 pts

Caps (15): **1991** US(1R) **1992** W, E, S, I, R, Arg(a1,a2), SA(1), Arg(b), **1993** E, S, I, W, R(a)

Points Nil

that wasn't enough, Jean-François was ruled out of the 1994 Five Nations campaign after sustaining another injury which required surgery (this time knee-related) whilst playing for Nice. In happier times he had succeeded Marc Cecillon as national captain following the 1992 summer tour to Argentina, on which he played both Tests at breakaway. But not before he had been dropped from the side following the 16–29 defeat by South Africa in Lyon, a game in which he appeared at blindside. His debut as captain coincided with

Argentina's first ever win on French soil, in Nantes (14.11.92). However, coach Pierre Berbizier kept faith with the Nice man while moving him to hooker for the 1993 International Championship. Four games later, and France collected the inaugural Five Nations Cup. At home in either front or back row, Jean-François hooked France B to a 28–15 win over Wales B at La Teste (12.11.89), reverted to back row for France B's 31–10 defeat of Scotland B at Hughenden (2.3.91), but then reclaimed the No 2 jersey for the 10–6 win over England B a fortnight later. He had been promoted to the senior XV on the 1991 tour of the United States, and made his debut as a 73rd-minute replacement for Michel Courtiols in the 41–9 win at Denver (13.7.91). Although excluded from the French World Cup squad, he returned for the 1992 Tournoi des Cinq Nations, occupying the No 6 jersey throughout the campaign. He tasted the high life as a teenager when, aged 18, he won a runner-up medal after coming on as a second-half replacement for Nice in the 1983 French Club Championship final. Thereafter, joined Toulon, but returned to the French Riviera and Nice in September 1990, having toured New Zealand with France in 1989

Townsend, G. P. J.   Scotland

Full Name: Gregor Peter John Townsend
Club: Gala
Position: Outside-half, centre
Height: 5ft 11in (1.81m)
Weight: 13st 6lb (80.7kg)
Occupation: History/politics student at Edinburgh University
Born: Edinburgh, 26.4.73
Family: Single
Family links with rugby: Father (Peter) played twice for South of Scotland
International debut: England 26, Scotland 12, 1993
Five Nations debut: As above
Best moment in rugby: Playing in Australia for Warringah
Worst moment in rugby: 1993 World Cup Sevens – I was looking forward to it so much, and then played terribly and got dropped
Most embarrassing moment: Giving try-scoring 'pass' to French winger Philippe Saint-André at

Scotland (1993)

Last Season	6 caps	6 pts
1994	Tour to Argentina	
Career	7 caps	6 pts

Caps (7): **1993** E(R) **1994** W, E, I, F

Points (3 – 1dg): **1994** E(1dg), Arg(2:1dg)

Murrayfield (1994)

Most respected opponent: Rob Andrew (Wasps & England)

Biggest influence on career: My father (Peter)

Serious injuries: Sprung ribs at 1992 Hong Kong Sevens, damaged knee ligaments in 1993 Scotland Trial; broken bone in hand (September 1993 v Boroughmuir: out for 12 weeks)

Best memory last season: Playing at Cardiff Arms Park – amazing atmosphere, even though we got beaten

Should rugby's amateur rules be revised? Yes

To what degree should players benefit? Should be compensated for time lost and allowed to benefit from off-field activities, but a playing wage would not be appropriate

Should referees be rewarded? Yes, although I don't know if it would improve standards

Advice for International Board: Consult players before introducing new laws. Encourage greater integration between top and bottom level of game (massive difference between club and international level in terms of facilities etc)

Notable landmarks in rugby career: Gregor proved an exciting prospect, but rather prone to errors as he continued to learn his trade. A case in point was last summer, when Scotland coach Dougie Morgan directly blamed the Gala youngster's decision-making for Argentina's 16–15 first-Test win (Buenos Aires, 4.6.94). Nonetheless, Gregor's have-a-go style brightened up a largely tedious international stage in 1994. Started Five Nations campaign as a centre against Wales, moving to stand-off after an injury to Craig Chalmers. Scotland instantly looked a different side, and Gregor dropped a goal, only to have it ruled out by French referee Patrick Robin, who didn't think it had gone over. He did get off the mark in next game, with a spectacular last-minute dropped goal which looked to have won Calcutta Cup match against England (Murrayfield, 5.2.94). But Jon Callard struck decisive blow for England in injury time, and Scotland lost 14–15. Toured Argentina last summer, having previously gone with Scotland to Fiji, Tonga and Western Samoa (1993: playing in the latter two Tests and top-scoring on tour with 30 points) and Australia (1992), appearing in eight games. Then helped Scotland win Dubai Sevens and turned out for Scotland A against Spain, Italy and Ireland. But knee-ligament damage sustained in Scotland Trial ruled him out of Test contention. Gregor recovered in time to earn his first cap as a 26th-minute replacement for arm-break victim Craig Chalmers in the 12–26 Twickenham loss to England (6.3.93). Turned out for Irish Wolfhounds at 1992 Hong Kong Sevens, having quickly progressed through Gala U-14, U-15 and U-16 ranks, and in 1991/92 played for Scotland U-21 and Scotland B

Touchlines: Golf (9 handicap)

Turnbull, D. J.   Scotland

Full Name: Derek James Turnbull
Club: Hawick
Position: Flanker
Height: 6ft 4in (1.93m)
Weight: 15st 6lb (98kg)
Occupation: Police Officer with
Lothians and Borders Police
Born: Hawick, 2.10.61
Family: Angie (wife)
Family links with rugby: Father
(Jim) is past president of Hawick
Trades RFC
Former clubs: Hawick PSA,
Hawick Trades
International debut: New Zealand
30, Scotland 3, 1987 (World Cup)
Five Nations debut: Scotland 23,
France 12, 1988
Best moment in rugby: Coming
on as a replacement in the 1990
Grand Slam decider against England
at Murrayfield
Worst moment in rugby: Missing
1992 Five Nations Championship
due to broken jaw; missing New
Zealand game and being dropped
after game against Wales

Scotland (1987)

Last Season	1 cap	0 pts
Career	11 caps	4 pts

Caps (11): **1987** wc–NZ **1988** F, E
1990 E(R) **1991** F, W, E, I, Ro
wc–Z **1994** W

Points (4 – 1t): **1991** wc–Z(1t)

Most embarrassing moment: Leading a Hawick Sevens side out at Gala
Sports on 1 April 1989 – the rest of the side stayed in the dressing room until I
was out on the pitch all by myself!
Most respected opponent: Wayne Shelford
Biggest influences on career: Derrick Grant (Hawick & ex-Scotland coach),
my father and Norman Suddon
Other sporting achievements: Completed London Marathon in 1982
Serious injuries: Numerous, but include broken wrist (1982) and broken jaw
(1991/92)
Best memories last season: Scoring try in win over Wales; South winning
District Championship
Should rugby's amateur rules be revised? Should be scrapped
To what degree should players benefit? Should be compensated for time lost
and able to benefit from off-the-field activities. SRU must compensate
employers for the time their employees give up to rugby. Its not just the
monetary aspect – you lose your holidays too

Should referees be rewarded? Yes, but standards are improving anyway

Advice for International Board: Restrict law changes. New mauling law is too negative for my liking. Don't allow anyone to kick the ball outside their own 22. Teams then would have to run, and rugby would demand a more mobile approach. More liberal interpretations from referees, like those in Southern Hemisphere. Other than that, I'm happy with job IB are doing

Notable landmarks in rugby career: Test-wise, the 1993/94 season left Derek with bit of a headache. Played in just one international, a 6–29 loss to Wales (Cardiff, 15.1.94), in which he received a haymaker early on which prompted a Scottish solicitor to file a complaint with South Wales Police. Was not required to tour to Argentina last summer, but has previously visited North America (1985), France and Spain (1986), World Cup (1987), Zimbabwe (1988), Japan (1989) and New Zealand (1990) with Scotland. Made his Hawick debut as a 17-year-old against Alnwick (December 1978), and nine years later came on as replacement for John Jeffrey for first cap in 1987 World Cup quarter-final against New Zealand. He scored his first international try in 55–12 defeat of Zimbabwe (Murrayfield, 9.10.91), and added another in 1992 Five Nations Championship as Wales were routed 20–0 at Murrayfield (20.2.93). He has picked up six B caps (including his debut match in 1989) and helped Hawick win the 1992 Gala Sevens. After turning out for Scotland A in 35–14 defeat of Spain in Madrid (12.9.92), he regained his blindside berth in the Test side and held onto it through 1993 Championship before finishing the season at Murrayfield in World Cup Sevens action for Scotland

Touchlines: Enjoy golf – especially the 19th hole (handicap 18)

Ubogu, V. E. England

Full Name: Victor Eriakpo Ubogu
Club: Bath
Position: Tighthead prop
Height: 5ft 9in (1.76m)
Weight: 16st 2lb (102.5kg)
Occupation: London-based company director with Cobrawatch, a family-owned security firm
Born: Lagos, Nigeria, 8.9.64
Family: Single
Former clubs: Moseley, Richmond
International debut: England 26, Canada 13, 1992
Five Nations debut: Scotland 14, England 15, 1994
Best moments in rugby: Being capped by England; Bath beating

Toulouse in 1989/90

Worst moment in rugby: England losing 21–6 to Natal in Durban (1994)

Best memories last season: Beating South Africa in first Test; Bath's League and Cup double

Should rugby's amateur rules be revised? Yes

To what degree should players benefit? For off-field activities, including promotional work

Should referees be rewarded? No

Advice for International Board: Must be refined so we have the same game in either hemisphere. Too many vague interpretations of what is, and is not, okay, and no consistency in refereeing. You've also made a hash of the laws

Notable landmarks in rugby career: Wembley debuts are few and far between, but Victor, a member of Oxford's beaten Varsity team in 1987, made his in the shadow of the twin towers when selected ahead of Jeff Probyn against Canada on 17 September 1992 (Twickenham was unavailable due to reconstruction). England won the game 26–13, and yer man, who had impressed on England B's 1992 summer tour to New Zealand (playing in the 18–24 first 'Test' loss at Hamilton, 28.6.92), kept his place for the visit of the Springboks to Twickenham on 14 November. Although the school wing turned international prop lost his place to Probyn for the 1993 Five Nations campaign, his time came last season, when he was ever-present throughout. Adept on either side of the scrum, he won a Pilkington Cup winners medal with Bath in 1990, after helping demolish arch-rivals Gloucester 48–6 at Twickenham, and added a second last season as the West Country giants completed league and cup double. Had also picked up championship medal in 1992/93 before embarking with England A on summer tour to Canada. Toured to South Africa with England last summer, playing in both Tests

England (1992)

Last Season	7 caps	0 pts
1994	Tour to South Africa	
Career	9 caps	0 pts

Caps (9): **1992** C, SA **1993** NZ **1994** S, I, F, W, SA(1,2)

Points Nil

Underwood, R.   England

Full Name: Rory Underwood
Club: Leicester & RAF
Position: Wing
Height: 5ft 9in (1.76m)
Weight: 14st (84kg)
Occupation: RAF pilot
Born: Middlesbrough, 19.6.63
Family: Wendy (wife), Rebecca (daughter) and Alexandra (daughter)
Family links with rugby: Brother (Tony) plays for Leicester, England and British Lions
Former club: Middlesbrough
International debut: England 12, Ireland 9, 1984
Five Nations debut: As above
Best moment in rugby: Winning first (1991) Grand Slam with England
Worst moment in rugby: England's 9–12 loss to Wales at Cardiff (1989)
Most embarrassing moment: Making error which led to Wales scoring crucial try against England in above match
Most respected opponent: Patrice Lagisquet (Bayonne & France)
Biggest influence on career: Geoff Cooke (ex-England manager)
Other sporting achievements: Swam and played cricket for Barnard Castle School, which England team mate Rob Andrew also attended
Best memory last season: Beating New Zealand
Should rugby's amateur rules be revised? Yes
To what degree should players benefit? We should be compensated for time lost away from work, and

England (1984)

Last Season	7 caps	5 pts
1994	Tour to South Africa	
Career	67 caps	150 pts
Lions 1986		
1989	3 Tests	0 pts
1993	3 Tests	5 pts

Caps (67): **1984** I, F, W, A **1985** Ro, F, S, I, W **1986** W, I, F **1987** I, F, W, S wc–A, J, W **1988** F, W, S, I(1,2), A(a1,a2), Fj, A(b) **1989** S, I, F, W. Lions–A(1,2,3). Ro, Fj **1990** I, F, W, S, Arg(b) **1991** W, S, I, F, Fj, A wc–NZ, It, US, F, S, A **1992** S, I, F, W, SA **1993** F, W, S, I. Lions–NZ(1,2,3). NZ **1994** S, I, F, W, SA(1,2)

Points (150 – 37t): **1984** F(1t) **1985** I(1t) **1987** wc–J(2t) **1988** I(1:2t), I(2:1t), A(a1:1t), A(a2:1t), Fj(2t), A(b:2t) **1989** Fj(5t) **1990** I(1t), F(1t), W(2t), Arg(b:3t) **1991** I(1t), F(1t), Fj(1t) wc–It(1t), US(2t), F(1t) **1992** S(1t), I(1t), F(1t) **1993** S(1t). Lions–NZ(2:1t) **1994** W(1t)

allowed to benefit from off-field activities, but I would not like to see payment for playing

Should referees be rewarded? Yes, it would be likely improve standards

Advice for International Board: I'm not happy with IB. I don't feel they have the players' interests in mind in any way. A lot of them are out of touch with reality. IB must make unambiguous rulings concerning amateurism

Notable landmarks in rugby career: England's most-capped player (67) and record try-scorer (37). Scored two tries for Leicester against Barbarians in 1983, and three months later was in England team. Missed tour to Argentina in summer of 1990 due to RAF commitments, having already become England's most-capped back and highest try-scorer during 1989/90 season. RAF duties also took precedence over tours to South Africa (1984) and New Zealand (1985). Equalled Dan Lambert's 1907 England record of five tries in an international, against Fiji (won 58–23, Twickenham, 4.11.89). Previously played for England Colts, U-23 and B teams. Toured Australia with 1989 Lions, playing in all three Tests. Held his place on 1993 tour to New Zealand, where he scored winning try in second Test. Rates his 26th Test try (scored in 16–7 defeat of Ireland during 1991 Grand Slam run) as most important of career. Also scored in 21–19 win over France (1991 Grand Slam decider). In 1991/92 he notched a further eight tries, including four en route to World Cup final and three in 1992 Grand Slam campaign. Retired from international arena once back-to-back Grand Slams were safely in the bag, but did a Frank Sinatra and returned in 1992/93 after missing Wembley opener against Canada. Ever-present from then onwards, scoring glorious try against Scotland (6.3.93) – his 36th, but the first to be worth five points – and then adding No. 37 a year later against Wales. He and Tony are first brothers to have appeared in the same England championship side since the Wheatley brothers packed down against Scotland in 1938. Toured South Africa with England (1994)

Touchlines: Crosswords, reading

Underwood, T.   England

Full Name: Tony Underwood
Clubs: Leicester, Cambridge University
Position: Wing
Height: 5ft 9in (1.76m)
Weight: 13st 7lb (81kg)
Occupation: Asian Equity broker with Lehman Brothers
Born: Ipoh, Malaysia, 17.2.69
Family: Single
Family links with rugby: Brother Rory is England's record try-scorer and most-capped player (67 caps – 37 tries, 150 points)
International debut: England 26, Canada 13, 1992
Five Nations debut: England 26, Scotland 12, 1993
Best moments in rugby: 1993 Lions selection; South Africa 15, England 32, 1994
Worst moments in rugby: England's 12–13 loss to Ireland (1994)
Most embarrassing moment: Post-try behaviour following my late score in 1991 Varsity match

England (1992)

Last Season	6 caps	0 pts
1994	Tour to South Africa	
Career	10 caps	10 pts
Lions 1993		

Caps (10): 1992 C, SA 1993 S, I, NZ 1994 S, I, W, SA(1,2)

Points (10 – 2t): 1992 SA(1t) 1993 S(1t)

Most respected opponents: Ian Hunter (Northampton & England B) and David Campese (Randwick & Australia)
Biggest influence on career: My mother (Anne)
Serious injuries: Broken jaw, torn hamstring and damaged knee cartilage – all in second half of 1989/90 season
Best memory last season: Beating New Zealand and Wales at Twickenham
To what degree should players benefit? Players should be remunerated for working time given up to rugby, be allowed to endorse products and benefit from any off-field activities. There should be a greater representation of players' views in Union
Should referees be rewarded? Should be treated the same as players. It would be nice to think this would have a dramatic effect on standards
Advice for International Board: A governing body needs to govern. So while the principle of the IB is sound, in practice the Board has a lack of standing
Notable landmarks in rugby career: Finished 1994 Championship strongly

after disappointing mid-term lull which saw him dropped after England's shock home defeat by Ireland. Replaced by Ian Hunter against France and Wales, but in the latter case scrambled back in through back door: injury to Stuart Barnes brought Tony onto bench, from where David Pears's subsequent injury in run-up to game led to Hunter moving to fullback and Tony being reprieved. A midweek British Lion in 1993, Tony had returned home to make England No 14 jersey his own against All Blacks, Scotland and Ireland. But shared in criticism of England's try-scoring failure – ironic, as he has been such a prolific scorer at B and A level. Played for England Schools (18 Group) before graduating to England team for inaugural Student World Cup (1988), for Barbarians in 10–21 defeat by 1989 All Blacks at Twickenham, and for England in 18–16 win over Barbarians (1990/91). Also represented Irish Wolfhounds in 1989 Hong Kong Sevens. Went on to represent Combined Students, England B, North of England, and latterly England in 1990 summer tour of Argentina (v Tucumán, Cuyo and Córdoba Selections). Previous year had made B debut (in 12–20 loss to Fiji) and scored five tries in four B games in 1991/92 campaign (including three in 47–15 defeat of Ireland B, Richmond, 31.1.92). Toured with B team to New Zealand (1992), where he played in both 'Tests', scoring a try in the 18–26 second-leg defeat in Pukekohe (5.7.92). Claimed another four B tries in 1992/93, and added 13th cap in last season's 8–20 loss to France A (5.3.94). In among these prolific exploits, Tony fitted in his Test debut against Canada (Wembley, 17.10.92) and his first top-level try in the 33–16 defeat of South Africa (Twickenham, 14.11.92). Lost place for first two games of 1993 Championship, but returned (on opposite flank to brother Rory) to score try against Scotland (Twickenham, 6.3.93). Helped Leicester win 1992/93 Pilkington Cup, and played in 1993/94 final loss to Bath, before enjoying impressive tour to South Africa
Touchlines: Cricket, squash, golf, tennis

England wing Tony Underwood stretches his legs against Ireland.

Van der Westhuizen, J.　　South Africa

Full Name: Joost van der Westhuizen
Province: Northern Transvaal
Position: Scrum-half
Height: 6ft 1½ in (1.86m)
Weight: 13st 9lb (82kg)
Occupation: Student
Born: 20.2.71
International debut: Argentina 26, South Africa 29, 1993
Notable landmarks in rugby career: One of South Africa's new breed, and the current jewel in Northern Transvaal's crown, scoring tries by the bucket-load. Joost made an extraordinary Springbok debut, scoring four tries against Western Australia (WACA, 14.7.93); granted the opposition was not up to much – they crashed 71–8 – but his remained an outstanding opening effort. And he continued in the same prolific vein, crossing New South Wales' line during the 29–28 defeat (Waratah, 24.7.93), repeating the feat against NSW Country (won

South Africa (1993)

Last Season	4 caps	10 pts
Career	4 caps	10 pts

Caps (4): **1993** Arg(1,2) **1994** E(1,2R)

Points (10 – 2t): **1993** Arg(1:1t), Arg(2:1t)

41–7, Orange, 31.7.93), and bagging try-braces against both Australian Capital Territory (won 57–10, Bruce Stadium, 4.8.93) and Queensland Country (won 63–5, Mackay, 11.8.93). He completed a cracking first tour with a try on his final outing against Sydney (Penrith, 18.8.93), to return home top try-scorer with 11. Little wonder he was promptly redirected to Argentina for the Springboks' autumn visit, and little wonder either that he graduated into the Test XV during the trip. The Pumas could not contain Joost either: he claimed a try in each game (first Test won 29–26, Buenos Aires, 6.11.93; second Test won 52–23, Buenos Aires, 13.11.93) as South Africa completed a 2–0 series whitewash. He retained his place in 1994 for South Africa's opening mission against England (Pretoria, 2.6.94), and despite looking lively was dropped for the Cape Town return as the management changed the gameplan, preferring Johan Roux's style. Still, he picked up his cap, as a 30th-minute replacement for injured wing Chester Williams

Van Rensburg, J. T. J. South Africa

Full Name: Jan Theodorus (Theo)
Jansen Van Rensburg
Club: RAU
Province: Transvaal
Position: Fullback
Height: 5ft 10in (1.78m)
Weight: 12st 4lb (78kg)
Occupation: Law student
Born: Carletonville, 26.8.67
Former province: Northern
Transvaal
International debut: South Africa
24, New Zealand 27, 1992
**Notable landmarks in rugby
career:** Kicked Transvaal to 24–21
victory over England in Pretoria
(28.5.94), with four penalty goals
and a conversion, but it proved
insufficient to earn his recall to the
Springbok Test side, which he
graced on six occasions in 1992 and
1993. The selectors' decision, one
suspects, was no indictment on his
performance at Ellis Park. Theo had
simply lost his place in the queue
after suffering a groin hernia during
the '93 tour of Australia and being

South Africa (1992)

Last Season	3 caps	31 pts
Career	6 caps	31 pts

Caps (6): **1992** NZ, A, E **1993** F(1,2), A(1)

Points (31 – 2c,9p): **1993** F(1:5p), F(2:4p), A(1:2c)

forced to return home for emergency surgery. His absence allowed Natal's
André Joubert and Transvaal rival Gavin Johnson to share the Test duties on
the autumn tour of Argentina. Educated at Potchefstroom Gymnasium, Theo
made his provincial bow in 1989 for Northern Transvaal, with whom he played
28 matches before moving to Johannesburg. When South Africa was welcomed
back into the international sporting fold in 1992, he went straight into the Test
side for the historic return against New Zealand. With Naas Botha also in
harness, there were few goalkicking opportunities for Theo, though he still
rattled up 48 points on the autumn '92 tour to France and England, during
which he turned out against France B, Acquitaine, Midi-Pyrenées, Languedoc-
Roussillon, French Universities, English Midlands, England B and England
(Twickenham, 14.11.92). He was omitted from the two Tests against France
in favour of Natal's Hugh Reece-Edwards. However, by the time France came
to the Republic the following summer, he was back in the side and revved up
to take the pot-shots at goal. But despite his landing nine penalty goals in the
two matches, South Africa won neither game and lost the series. Rather more

joy came in Sydney (31.7.93), where he kicked two conversions as world champions Australia were downed 19–12. It was his first Test win in six attempts

Viars, S. France

Full Name: Sebastien Viars
Club: Brive
Position: Wing
Height: 5ft 10½ in (1.79m)
Weight: 11st 11lb (70kg)
Occupation: Student
Born: Aurillac, 24.6.71
International debut: Wales 9, France 12, 1992
Five Nations debut: As above
Notable landmarks in rugby career: A late call-up for France's tour of Canada and New Zealand last summer, Sebastien came on as a replacement for captain Philippe Saint-André during the Test opener in Ontario (5.6.94), where Canada won 18–16. His appearance ended a year in international wilderness since his previous outing, in 37–20 defeat of Romania in Bucharest, back in May 1993. Previously he had been France's find of 1992, marking his debut in Cardiff with a penalty goal in the 12–9 win over Wales before notching his first try (as well as a penalty and conversion) on his Paris debut against England (lost 13–31) a fortnight later. Topped it all by then

France (1992)

Last Season	1 cap	0 pts
1994	Tour to Canada/NZ	
Career	5 caps	53 pts

Caps (5): **1992** W, E, I **1993** R(a) **1994** C(R)

Points (53 – 3t,10c,7p): **1992** W(1p), E(1t,1c,1p), I(2t,5c,2p) **1993** R(a:4c,3p)

claiming a Five Nations record 24 points in the 44–12 win over Ireland on a delightful sunny afternoon in Parc des Princes. His history-making haul included two tries, five conversions and two penalty goals. Sebastien had hinted at this potential when he had scored a quite outstanding try in France B's 10–6 win over England B at Bristol (15.3.91), having represented French second string in the 31–10 win over Scotland B at Hughenden, two weeks earlier. Not required for duty during the World Cup – although he toured to North America in July 1991, scoring four tries against Western Unions and USA B. His very early career featured Schools caps in 1989, Junior honours in 1990 (landing four goals against Wales Youth) and appearance at 1991 Hong Kong Sevens with France

Visagie, R. G.   South Africa

Full Name: Rudie Visagie
Province: Natal
Position: Lock
Height: 6ft 6in (1.98m)
Weight: 20st 5lb (130kg)
Occupation: Transnet clerk
Born: 27.6.59
International debut: South Africa
33, England 15, 1984

South Africa (1993)

Last Season	1 cap	0 pts
Career	5 caps	0 pts

Caps (5): **1984** E(1,2), SAm(1,2) **1993** F(1)

Points Nil

Notable landmarks in rugby career: Came back into international reckoning in 1993, nine years after making his Test debut against England in Port Elizabeth. That date was 2 June 1984, and South Africa had triumphed by the crushing margin of 33–15 (little did they suspect then that exactly ten years and two days later England would turn the tables, winning 32–15 in Pretoria, but Rudie wasn't playing on that occasion). The big man followed up his debut by helping the Springboks thrash England again, this time 35–9 in Johannesburg, and completed the '84 international campaign by turning out in the two equally convincing wins over the South American Jaguars: 32–15 in Pretoria (20.10.84) and 22–13 in Cape Town (27.10.84). Much had changed in his homeland by the time he picked up his fifth cap in Durban (26.6.93). This time France were the visitors, and held their hosts to a 20–20 draw. Rudie did not figure in the Springbok side thereafter, although the former Orange Free State player did join in the tour to Australia in July 1993, turning out against South Australia (won 90–3, Adelaide, 17.7.93), Victoria (won 78–3, Melbourne, 21.7.93), NSW Country (won 41–7, Orange, 27.7.93) and ACT (won 57–10, Canberra, 4.8.93). His one try of the trip came in the rout of South Australia

Wainwright, R. I. Scotland

Full Name: Robert Iain Wainwright
Club: Edinburgh Academicals
Position: Flanker
Height: 6ft 5in (1.95m)
Weight: 15st 4lb (97kg)
Occupation: Army doctor
Born: Perth, 22.3.65
Family: Single
Family links with rugby: Father (J. F. Wainwright) a 1956 Cambridge Blue
Former club: Cambridge University
International debut: Ireland 10, Scotland 18, 1992
Five Nations debut: As above
Best moment in rugby: Replacing Neil Edwards against Ireland (1992) to win first cap
Worst moment in rugby: Cambridge University v Durham University (January 1988)
Most respected opponent: John Jeffrey (Kelso & ex-Scotland)
Other sporting achievements: Boxing Blue at Cambridge University

Scotland (1992)

Last Season	3 caps	5 pts
Career	7 caps	9 pts

Caps (7): 1992 I(R), F, A(1,2) 1993 NZ 1994 W, E

Points (9 – 2t): 1992 A(1:1t) 1994 E(1t)

Serious injuries: Broken cheekbone (January 1990), ankle (September 1990)
Best memory last season: Scoring try against Australia in Sydney
Notable landmarks in rugby career: Appointed Scotland captain for last summer's tour to Argentina, despite missing half of 1994 Five Nations campaign after sustaining broken cheekbone 66 minutes into 15–14 Calcutta Cup defeat by England (5.2.94) – a Murrayfield match in which he had scored solitary try on 28 minutes. But injury once again thwarted his ambitions, and Rob had to hand the captain's armband over to Andy Reed before the plane left for South America. One of Scotland's most versatile players, his seven caps have come at No 8 (three), flanker (three) and replacement lock (one, on debut). Representative career really took off in 1991/92 season, when he captained Scotland B, broke into senior side and toured Australia in summer, playing in both Tests and claiming Scotland's only try in 12–27 Sydney loss (13.6.92). First cap had come four months earlier when he replaced Neil Edwards for last two minutes against Ireland in Dublin (15.2.92). He then played the full 80 minutes in the 10–6 win over France (7.3.92). Injury deprived

him of a Test run on his return from Down Under in 1992. Having appeared in three consecutive Varsity matches (1986–88), he made his Scotland B debut in 26–3 win over Italy at L'Aquila. Won further B caps against Ireland (lost 0–16, 22.12.90), and as captain against France (lost 18–27, Albi, 3.2.92); he scored a try in the latter contest. Other career landmarks include participation on Barbarians Easter tour (1988), Hong Kong Sevens (1988 and 1989), and 1989 tour to Japan with Scotland (two games, two tries).

Touchlines: Wildlife, fishing, photography, whisky

Walker, N. K. — Wales

Full Name: Nigel Keith Walker
Club: Cardiff
Position: Wing
Height: 5ft 11in (1.81m)
Weight: 12st 2lb (73kg)
Occupation: Development officer with Sports Council of Wales; also part-time Radio Wales presenter of `Walker-ound Sport'
Born: Cardiff, 15.6.63
Family: Mary (wife), Rebecca (daughter)
International debut: Wales 14, Ireland 19, 1993
Five Nations debut: As above
Best moment in rugby: Scoring try v France (1994)
Worst moments in rugby: Conceding try in 1994 Swalec Cup final (thankfully Cardiff still won); being helped off pitch with concussion against Scotland (1994)
Most respected opponent: Ieuan Evans (Llanelli & Wales)
Serious injuries: Torn ankle ligaments, sprained wrist, concussion (1994)

Wales (1993)

Last Season	6 caps	35 pts
Career	8 caps	40 pts

Caps (8): **1993** I, F, J **1994** S, F, E. wc(q)–P, Sp

Points (40 – 8t): **1993** F(1t) **1994** F(1t), E(1t). wc(q)–P(4t), Sp(1t)

Other sporting achievements: 110m hurdles semi-finalist in 1984 Los Angeles Olympics, having clocked 14.07sec in heat
Best memory last season: Cardiff's Swalec Cup final defeat of Llanelli
Should rugby's amateur rules be revised? They are constantly being revised. If changes in the game keep going at this pace, then no problem. But if they go any quicker, that will be a recipe for disaster

401

To what degree should players benefit? I see no problem with international players being rewarded for the commitment demanded of them, but it should be a reward for sacrifices made, not for playing

Should referees be rewarded? Why not?

Advice for International Board: Clear up the many grey areas which currently exist in rulebook. It's absolute chaos at present. Put greater thought into changes. Referees must interpret rules in uniformed manner

Notable landmarks in rugby career: Olympic hurdler who equalled Welsh try-scoring record when he bagged four in 102–11 World Cup qualifying defeat of Portugal in Lisbon (17.5.94). Made eight tries in eight Tests, with one against Spain four days later. But shoulder operation forced him out of last summer's tour to Canada and the South Pacific. Reached the top in his second sport when capped against Ireland on 6 March 1993 at Cardiff. In the following Test, against France, he became the first Welshman to cross the try-line at Parc des Princes since Jeff Squire ten years earlier. Had returned to rugby at the age of 29, following a conversation with Cardiff's Mark Ring, having gained a Welsh Schools trial in 1981. Made an immediate impression last season, getting among the try leaders in the Heineken Championship, appearing in the East-West match at Cardiff in December, and scoring a try hat-trick in Den Bosch on 6 February as Wales A walloped Holland 57–12. His ambition is to 'maximize my potential and to become an automatic choice in the Wales side'. Went some way to achieving his goal towards end of last season, when he marked his recall to the Test arena with tries in last two games against France and England. The first, a match-sealing effort against France, all but lifted the roof off the Arms Park, while the second, at Twickenham (19.3.94) ensured that Wales clinched the 1994 Five Nations title. Nigel, who had been unable to tour with Wales to Zimbabwe and Namibia in the summer of '93, also turned out against Japan and Scotland, but was injured in the latter. Ended 1993/94 on a high, helping Cardiff lift Swalec Cup after beating holders Llanelli in final

Touchlines: No time

Wallace, R. M.   Ireland

Full Name: Richard Michael Wallace
Club: Garryowen
Position: Wing
Height: 5ft 11in (1.80m)
Weight: 13st 7lb (86kg)
Occupation: Partner with K Walshe & Associates
Born: Cork, 16.1.68
Family: Single
Former club: Cork Constitution
International debut: Namibia 15, Ireland 6, 1991
Five Nations debut: Ireland 15, Wales 16, 1992
Best moment in rugby: 1993 Lions call-up and defeat of England
Most respected opponent: Philippe Saint-André (Montferrand & France)
Serious injuries: Broken right leg (1994)
Other sporting achievements: Sailed (Laser class) for Ireland at 1990 European Championships (France)
Best memories last season: Beating England at Twickenham; Garryowen winning All-Ireland Championship for second time in three years

Ireland (1991)		
Last Season	5 caps	0 pts
Career	15 caps	13 pts
Lions 1993		

Caps (15): 1991 Na(1R) 1992 W, E, S, F, A 1993 S, F, W, E, R 1994 F, W, E, S

Points (13 – 3t): 1991 W(1t), S(1t) 1992 A(1t)

Should rugby's amateur rules be revised? Rules need ongoing scrutiny
To what degree should players benefit? Should receive compensation for loss of earnings, but that too is an ongoing process, and I'm quite happy with it
Should referees be rewarded? Only in same way as players. You can't pay referees and not players
Advice for International Board: Resist calls for professionalism. It is not right, as we know what we're getting into when we opt to play rugby. If we want to play a professional sport, then we are free to do so. Its right not to force every union to obey laws to the letter, because each nation has different circumstances, so needs to be given bit of freedom to perceive laws as it sees fit
Notable landmarks in rugby career: Missed out on tour to Australia last summer after breaking leg playing for Garryowen against Shannon. Great shame, as had been ever-present in Ireland side throughout 1993/94 campaign.

Had spent previous two off-seasons in New Zealand, each trip providing a tale of the unexpected. In 1992 he had only just overcome the jet-lag following the trip out with Ireland when he was punched while playing against Canterbury, sustained a hairline fracture of the jaw and was flown home. In 1993 he was minding his own business in Moscow when Ian Hunter was injured in the British Lions' first engagement against North Auckland, and he was summoned post haste as a replacement. Once in place, he turned out against Canterbury, Taranaki, Southland, Hawke's Bay and Waikato. Richard had taken his first step up the representative ladder when appearing for Munster Under-18s and Under-21s (1988). A member of the 1987/88 Irish Colleges XV, he scored a try in the 24–10 defeat of England B at Old Belvedere on only his second outing for Ireland B (1.3.91). Broke into Ireland senior XV on 1991 tour of Namibia, replacing Simon Geoghegan in 74th minute of first Test (Windhoek, 20.7.91). Scored tour-high five tries in Namibia. Marked Five Nations debut with try in Dublin loss to Wales (18.1.92), and retained place throughout Championship (also crossing against Scotland) before ill-fated trip to the land of the All Blacks. Third and most recent Test try came in 17–42 loss to Australia (Dublin, 31.10.92), before helping Ireland reach semi-finals of inaugural World Cup Sevens (Murrayfield, April 1993)

Touchlines: Flying (hold private licence), sailing, reading, music

---

Walton, P.   Scotland

Full Name: Peter Walton
Club: Northampton
Position: Flanker, No 8
Height: 6ft 3in (1.90m)
Weight: 18st (110kg)
Occupation: Livestock fieldsman
Born: Alnwick, 3.6.69
Family: Diana (wife)
Family links with rugby: Brother (Michael) played for Scottish Schools
Former clubs: Alnwick, Gosforth
International debut: Scotland 14, England 15, 1994
Five Nations debut: As above
Best moment in rugby: Winning first cap
Worst moment in rugby: Losing to England with last kick of game

Most embarrassing moment: Passing to Leicester's Rory Underwood in Cup quarter-final. I thought he was a team-mate – you know, similar hooped

shirt, that sort of thing. Cost us scoring position

Most respected opponent: Dean Richards (Leicester)/Tim Rodber (Northampton)

Biggest influence on career: Brother Michael, who had to give up rugby aged 22 through injury after playing for Scotland Schools and England Colts

Serious injuries: Shoulder operation five years ago, after which told I couldn't play rugby again. Returned to the game three months later

Advice for International Board: IB has seen sense with ruck law, but should have revised maul regulation at same time

Notable landmarks in rugby career: Played for and captained Scotland Schools six times (1986-87) in sides which also included Tony Stanger, Craig Chalmers, Andy Nicol and Carl Hogg. But then played at prop for England Colts in 1988, there being Scottish alternative, alongside Neil Back and fellow Scot Andy Reed. First represented Northumberland in 1989, but it was in colours of Scottish Exiles last season (against Leinster, Munster and Auckland) that he earned his Test call-up. Bench replacement for Scotland A against touring All Blacks (Glasgow, 13.11.93). A fine display three days later in Edinburgh for Scottish Development XV against same opposition (lost 12–31) won him starts in A team against Italy (lost 15–18, Rovigo, 18.12.93) and Ireland A (won 24–9, Ayr, 28.12.293). After Scotland's dismal showing against Wales in 1994 Five Nations opener, Peter was among the newcomers drafted in for Calcutta Cup clash. England were given the shock of their lives, and Peter retained blindside berth throughout remainder of campaign and on summer tour to Argentina

Touchlines: Horse racing (Newcastle & Kelso)

Scotland (1994)		
Last Season	5 caps	0 pts
1994	Tour to Argentina	
Career	5 caps	0 pts

Caps (5): **1994** E, I, F, Arg(1,2)

Points Nil

Watt, A. G. J.   Scotland

Full Name: Alan Gordon James Watt
Club: Glasgow High/Kelvinside
Position: Prop, lock
Height: 6ft 5in (1.96m)
Weight: 18st ½ lb (113kg)
Occupation: Student (BA in sport) at Jordanhill College
Born: Glasgow, 10.7.67
Family: Single
Family links with rugby: Father (Gordon) played for Jordanhill FP, grandfather (Jimmy Cairney) played for Hutchesons
International debut: Scotland 51, Zimbabwe 12, 1991
Five Nations debut: Scotland 15, Ireland 3, 1993
Best moment in rugby: Winning first cap
Worst moment in rugby: Scotland's 51–15 thumping by New Zealand (1993)
Most embarrassing moment: Sprinting into a goalpost during training and knocking myself out
Most respected opponent: Stewart Hamilton (Stirling County)
Biggest influences on career: Jim Telfer/Richie Dixon
Best memory last season: GHK beating Newport at their place
Should rugby's amateur rules be revised? Yes

Scotland (1991)

Last Season	2 caps	0 pts
1994	Tour to Argentina	
Career	4 caps	0 pts

Caps (4): 1991 wc–Z 1993 S, NZ 1994 Arg(2R)

Points Nil

To what degree should players benefit? We should be free to benefit from off-the-field activities. There should be less restrictions on what we can do
Advice for International Board: Every country should live by the same rules. New mauling rule is a nonsense. Use scrummage to restart game. Bring back double banking in lineout, as second rows would be then left alone and the whole set-piece would be a lot tidier
Notable landmarks in rugby career: Not a memorable Test campaign for big Wattie in 1993/94. He played twice: first Scotland were shredded 51–15 by New Zealand (Murrayfield, 20.11.93), then they were beaten 19–17 by Argentina (Buenos Aires, 11.6.94) in a game in which he played as a replacement. His selection against New Zealand followed his contribution to a good Scotland A team effort against same opponents (lost 9–20, Glasgow,

13.11.93). Omitted from Scotland tour to Fiji, Tonga and Western Samoa (1993), having turned out for Scotland A against Spain (won 35–14, Madrid, 12.9.92) and Ireland A (won 22–13, Dublin, 28.12.92). When Bristol's former England B prop Alan Sharp pulled out of national side picked to play Ireland in 1993 Five Nations curtain-raiser, Alan was drafted in for his debut (though typically of his luck, it was too late to get a mention in matchday programme). After a satisfactory performance he was retained for trip to Paris three weeks later, but pulled out six days beforehand suffering with the ubiquitous mystery virus. Missed the remainder of the campaign, and was then overlooked for the South Seas trip – manager Alan Hosie explained that Alan appears to be in the process of going back to playing in the second row (the position he occupied most competently before the selectors decided to turn him into a prop). Previously represented Scotland Schools, scoring try against Wales in 1987, and Scotland U-21s (twice v Wales, 1987-88). Called into Scotland A team as prop for 39–7 defeat of Spain in Seville (1990) even though club position was lock. Also given Scotland B debut, in 10–31 defeat by France at Hughenden (2.3.91), before touring North America with Scotland (1991) and playing against US Eagles (won 41–12) and Canada (lost 19–24) in non-cap Tests. Scored two tries in 76–7 win over Alberta, and one in 24–12 defeat of Rugby East. Included in Scottish World Cup squad, and played against Zimbabwe (9.10.91)

Touchlines: Pool

Waugh, W. W. Australia

Full Name: Warwick William Waugh
State: New South Wales
Club: Randwick
Position: Lock
Height: 6ft 7in (2.01m)
Weight: 18st 8lb (118kg)
Occupation: Sales rep with Timberland
Born: 17.9.68
Family: single
International debut: Australia 12, South Africa 19, 1993
Best moment in rugby: Scoring in my first Wallaby game with my first touch of the ball, Western Transvaal v Australia 1992.
Worst moment in rugby: Breaking my leg (New South Wales v Wales 1991)

Most respected opponent: Ian Jones

Best memory last season: My first Test (Australia v SA)

Suggestions to improve rugby: More ex-players refereeing the game

Notable landmarks in rugby career: Wallaby debut came two years later than had been widely anticipated, after Warwick broke his leg playing for New South Wales against touring Wales in 1991. He had formed a highly successful partnership with Steve Cutler, soon after making his debut for the state in Argentina, and was seen as a genuine international contender. However, the leg break put such thoughts on hold. A powerful scrummager and noted lineout jumper, he was selected to tour South Africa in the summer of 1992, and marked his debut with a try against Western Transvaal (won 46–13, Potchefstroom, 11 August). He also turned out in the 34–8 victory over Eastern Province in Port Elizabeth seven days later. On to Wales and Ireland, where he gained further experience with starts against Munster, Connacht, Swansea, Monmouthshire and Welsh Students. His apprenticeship complete, Wallaby coach Bob Dwyer finally gave him his first cap on 31 July 1993, in the first Test against South Africa in Sydney. Unhappily for Warwick, the Springboks won 19–12, and it was back to bench duties for the remainder of the series

Touchlines: Cars, music, skiing, running, golf

Australia (1993)		
Last Season	1 cap	0 pts
Career	1 cap	0 pts
Caps (1): 1993 SA(1)		
Points Nil		

Wegner, N.   South Africa

Full Name: Nico Wegner

Province: Western Province

Position: Lock

Height: 6ft 8in (2.02m)

Weight: 18st 12lb (115kg)

Occupation: Student

Born: 3.12.68

International debut: South Africa 17, France 18, 1993

South Africa (1993)		
Last Season	4 caps	0 pts
Career	4 caps	0 pts
Caps (4): 1993 F(2), A(1,2,3)		
Points Nil		

Notable landmarks in rugby career: One of three Western Province forwards in the Springbok pack during 1993 (along with prop Keith Andrews and back row Tiaan Strauss), Nico was brought in as the selectors hit the panic button after France shocked South Africa by holding her to a 20–2 draw in Durban (26.6.93). The second row was vacated by Kobus Wise and Rudie Visagie, and in came Nico and Transvaal's Hannes Strydom – for all the good it did. France won the second Test 18–17 at Ellis park, Johannesburg (3.7.93). But at least Nico was given an extended run, touring to Australia soon after and appearing in each of the three internationals, all alongside Strydom. South

Africa won the first (19–12, Sydney, 31.7.93), but the world champions rebounded strongly to take the series with wins in Brisbane (28–20, 14.8.93) and back in Sydney (19–12, 21.8.93). In addition to the Tests, Nico turned out against Western Australia (won 71–8, Perth, 14.7.93), New South Wales (lost 28–29, Sydney, 24.7.93) and Queensland (won 17–3, Brisbane, 8.8.93). He lost his Test place to Natal's Steve Atherton on the autumn tour to Argentina, having to make do with outings against Córdoba (won 55–37, 27.10.93), Buenos Aires (lost 27–28, 30.10.93) and Rosario (won 40–26, 9.11.93)

Weir, G. W. Scotland

Full Name: George Wilson (Doddie) Weir
Club: Melrose
Position: No 8, lock
Height: 6ft 6in (1.98m)
Weight: 16st 2lb (98kg)
Occupation: Farmer with John W. Weir
Born: Edinburgh, 4.7.70
Family: Single
Family links with rugby: Father (John) played for Gala; brother (Tom) plays for Scottish Schools and Gala; brother (Christopher) plays for Melrose
International debut: Scotland 49, Argentina 3, 1990
Five Nations debut: Scotland 7, England 25, 1992
Best moment in rugby: Getting capped against Argentina
Worst moments in rugby: Getting beaten by 1993 All Blacks on more than one occasion
Most embarrassing moment: Trying to kick clear and then dive on a loose ball, and missing it both times, in 1991 Melrose Sevens first-round loss to Hawick

Scotland (1990)

Last Season	5 caps	0 pts
Career	23 caps	4 pts

Caps (23): **1990** Arg **1991** Ro wc–J, Z, I, WS, E, NZ **1992** E, I, F, W, A(1,2) **1993** I, F, W, E, NZ **1994** W(R), E, I, F

Points (4 – 1t): **1991** wc–Z(1t)

Most respected opponents: John Eales (Queensland & Australia) and Ian Jones (North Auckland & New Zealand)
Biggest influence on career: Jim Telfer (Melrose coach) – told me what to do, when and how

Other sporting achievements: Stow sprint champion. Completing Thirlestone cross-country (horses); 1991 Scottish Horse Trials (intermediate class)

Best memory last season: Melrose winning third straight League title

Should rugby's amateur rules be revised? Yes

To what degree should players benefit? Allow us to benefit from off-field activities, and though I'm against being paid to play, a new house and car would be nice

Should referees be rewarded? Yes, it would improve standards

Advice for International Board: Rules should be tightened so that we all play by same rules. Sort out lineout. There is supposed to be a one-metre gap, but no one bothers with it. Better education of referees to allow game to flow better. Abolish conversions and instead increase value of tries

Notable landmarks in rugby career: Played in each of Scotland's five Tests in 1993/94, although was not selected for '94 Five Nations opener against Wales. Came on as 18th-minute replacement after Iain Morrison had broken his left leg in two places. Unbroken sequence of appearances in Test side now stands at 22. Toured New Zealand with Scottish Schools (1988) and Scotland (1990). Represented South of Scotland in Inter-District Championship, Scotland U-19, Scotland U-21s (v Wales, 1990 and 1991) and Scotland B, becoming youngest forward to represent them (at 19) in 22–22 draw with Ireland B (Murrayfield, 9.12.89). Also played in annual Scotland A game against Spain for three years (1990-93), and for full Scotland side masquerading as A team against Italy (19.12.92). His one A-team outing last season resulted in a 24–9 defeat of Ireland (Ayr, 28.12.93). Made full debut against touring Pumas (10.11.90). With Scotland toured North America in 1991 (playing in all six matches, including two non-cap Tests against US Eagles and Canada), Australia in 1992 (appearing at lock in both Tests), South Pacific in 1993 (playing in non-cap Tests against Fiji, Tonga and Western Samoa), and Argentina in 1994. Helped Melrose win McEwan's Scottish Club Championship for fourth time in five seasons in 1993/94

Touchlines: Horse riding (one-day eventing), clay pigeon shooting, training six days per week

Wiese, K.   South Africa

Full Name: Kobus Wiese
Province: Transvaal
Position: Lock
Height: 6ft 6in (1.98m)
Weight: 20st 1lb (125kg)
Occupation: Businessman
Born: 16.5.64
International debut: South Africa 20, France 20, 1993
Notable landmarks in rugby career: Made a big impression on England's tourists last summer, his bullish runs and immense strength guiding both Transvaal and South Africa B to accomplished wins. Indeed, such an impact did he make that he was conspicuous by his absence in Pretoria, where South Africa were trounced in the first Test. Unhappily for Kobus, his international career is but 80 minutes long, as he was one of the victims of the selectors' purge after France had the temerity to draw the first Test of the 1993 series 20–20 in

South Africa (1993)

Last Season	1 cap	0 pts
Career	1 cap	0 pts

Caps (1): **1993** F(1)

Points Nil

Durban (26.6.93). Along with engine-room partner, Natal's Rudie Visagie, he was given his cards and replaced by Nico Wegner and Hannes Strydom for the second Test, which France proceeded to win. A member of the 1993 Transvaal side that won the inaugural Super-10 tournament (beating Auckland 20–7 in the final at Ellis Park, Johannesburg, 22.5.93) and the Currie Cup (beating Natal 21–15 in the final at Kings Park, Durban, 16.10.93). Between the two he toured Australia with the Springboks, turning out against Western Australia (won 71–8, Perth, 14.7.93), Victoria (won 78–3, Melbourne, 21.7.93); NSW Country (won 41–7, Orange, 27.7.93), ACT (won 57–10, Canberra, 4.8.93), Queensland Country (won 65–5, Mackay, 11.8.93) and Sydney (won 31–20, Penrith, 18.8.93). But he was not required when the selectors took an inexperienced party to Argentina in the autumn

Williams, C. M.   South Africa

Full Name: Chester Williams
Province: Western Province
Position: Wing
Height: 5ft 8 ½ in (1.74m)
Weight: 13st 4lb (80kg)
Occupation: Soldier
Born: 9.8.70
International debut: Argentina 23, South Africa 52, 1993
Notable landmarks in rugby career: One of the new breed of Springboks to come through in 1993. Picked to tour Australia, he played in seven of the 13 matches: against Western Australia (won 71–8, Perth, 14.7.93), South Australia (won 90–3, Adelaide, 17.7.93), Victoria (won 78–3, Melbourne, 21.7.93), NSW Country (won 41–7, Orange, 27.7.93), ACT (won 57–10, Canberra, 4.8.93), Queensland Country (won 65–5, Mackay, 11.8.93) and Sydney (won 31–20, Penrith, 18.8.93). Chester weighed

South Africa (1993)

Last Season	3 caps	5 pts
Career	3 caps	5 pts

Caps (3): **1993** Arg(2) **1994** E(1,2)

Points (5 – 1t): **1993** Arg(2:1t)

in with seven tries, including a hat-trick against Victoria. The remainder were against ACT (2), Western Australia and Queensland Country. His services were retained on the autumn trip to Argentina, where the hosts were handed a 2–0 series whitewash in the first ever games between the sides (although South Africa did play eight Tests against a predominantly Argentine side masquerading as the South American Jaguars in the early 1980s). Chester was deployed in four of the six games, and responded with three tries. One of these came on his international debut in the second Test against the Pumas in Buenos Aires (13.11.93), as South Africa ran out convincing 52–23 winners. He was given his chance after Jacques Olivier withdrew from the side with flu. His other tries came against Córdoba (won 55–37, 27.10.93) and Tucumán (won 40–12, 2.11.93), though the latter contest was more memorable for the four sendings-off, two from each side. Collected his second cap in Pretoria on 4 June 1994, when England ran riot, winning 32–15. Was stretchered off with neck injury 30 minutes into second Test (Cape Town, 11.6.94)

Wilson, D. J.   Australia

Full Name: David John Wilson
State: Queensland
Club: Eastern Districts
Position: Flanker
Height: 6ft 2in (1.88m)
Weight: 14st 11lb (94kg)
Occupation: Area manager with BP Oil
Born: 4.1.67
Family: June (mother), Keith (father), Peter (brother) and Paul (brother)
Former clubs: None. Easts since 1986
International debut: Australia 27, Scotland 12, 1992
Best moment in rugby: Second Test win over All Blacks which secured 1992 Bledisloe Cup series
Worst moment in rugby: Missing the 1990 tour to New Zealand due to broken ankle
Most respected opponent: Michael Jones (Auckland & New Zealand)
Serious injuries: Knee reconstruction (1987), broken ankle (1990), broken collarbone (1992)

Australia (1992)

Last Season	10 caps	5 pts
Career	18 caps	10 pts

Caps (18): **1992** S(1,2), NZ(1,2,3), SA, I, W **1993** T, NZ, SA(1,2,3), C, F(1,2) **1994** I(1,2)

Points (10 – 2t): **1992** W(1t) **1994** I(2:1t)

Other sporting achievements: Bettering 105 for a round of golf
Suggestions to improve rugby: On-field – penalty and dropped goal should be worth only two points. Off-field – players at representative level should be financially rewarded
Notable landmarks in rugby career: Another of the current crop of Wallabies who emerged on the 1989 tour to Canada and France, David's progress was slowed by a fractured ankle which kept him out of the 1990 tour to New Zealand. However, he had recovered in time to tour Europe with the Emerging Wallabies later that year, along with the likes of Jason Little, John Eales and Willie Ofahengaue. A highly valued member of the Test side since his debut against Scotland in 1992, he has in fact been ever-present in the last 18 Tests, scoring a try in the defeat of Wales at Cardiff Arms Park, and again in the 32–18 second-Test win over Ireland (Brisbane, 11.6.94). In addition to his front-line Test duties David, a dual winner in 1989 and 1991 of the Queensland Rothmans Medal, featured in the non-cap international against the

USA, scoring a try in the 26–22 win (California, 2.10.93)
Touchlines: Surfing, golf, fishing

Wilson, J.   New Zealand

Full Name: Jeffrey (Jeff) William
Wilson
Province: Otago
Position: Wing, full-back
Height: 5ft 11 ½ in (1.81m)
Weight: 14st 6lb (91kg)
Occupation: Student teacher
Born: 24.10.73
International debut: Scotland 15,
New Zealand 51, 1993
Best moment in rugby: Scoring
hat-trick of tries on Test debut
Most respected player: Serge
Blanco (ex-Biarritz & France), the
greatest fullback ever to play the
game
**Notable landmarks in rugby
career:** One of those individuals
who is horribly good at everything
he turns his hand to. At the age of 16
he clocked 11sec over 100m. While
still at High School he played
provincial rugby and cricket, and he
finished the 1992 season as the star
of the New Zealand Secondary
Schools rugby side. Let's not forget

New Zealand (1993)

Last Season	2 caps	26 pts
Career	2 caps	26 pts

Caps   (2): **1993** S,E

Points (26 – 3t,1c,3p): **1993** S(3t,1c),
E(3p)

either that in June '92 he scored 66 points (nine tries and 15 conversions) for
Cargill High School, Invercargill – in just one match. But all that was nothing
compared with 1993. He began the year with a call-up to the New Zealand one-
day cricket side against Australia (he has since taken his tally of one-day caps
to four), and, after an impressive bowling performance stroked the winning
runs. Swapping flannels for Black, he became an All Black at the age of 19,
scoring two tries on his first start against London (won 39–12, Twickenham,
23.10.93). No doubt he followed up by marking his Test debut with a hat-
trick of tries against Scotland? Right again – and a touchline conversion to boot. 'My
aim was to get through the game without making a mistake', he said. However,
his bubble deflated a little on his second Test outing, when after an injury to
first-choice goalkicker Matthew Cooper he was assigned his duties against
England at Twickenham. Five penalty misses out of eight effectively cost New

Zealand the match. But it was a rare off-day for the young man, who moved from Invercargill to Dunedin to attend teaching college, joined Otago and made an immediate impression, scoring a last-minute try in their victory over Auckland, and then kicking a last-minute touchline conversion to clinch a draw with Wellington. He is nicknamed 'Goldie' by Otago and New Zealand team mates alike – short, of course, for Golden Boy

Touchlines: Cricket, basketball

Wood, K. G. M. Ireland

Full Name: Keith Gerald Mallinson
Club: Garryowen
Position: Hooker
Height: 6ft (1.83m)
Weight: 15st 12lb (101kg)
Occupation: Bank official with Irish Permanent Building Society
Born: Limerick, 27.1.72
Family links with rugby: Father (Gordon) played for Ireland (29 times: 1954-61) and 1959 British Lions (first and third Tests v New Zealand)
International debut: Australia 33, Ireland 13, 1994
Five Nations debut: None
Notable landmarks in rugby career: Ireland's most valuable player on last summer's tour of Australia, Keith finally broke into the Test ranks, appearing in both internationals, and despite the defeats impressing all with his pace and mobility. A bench replacement since 1992, his path to progress blocked at both provincial (Munster)

Ireland (1994)

Last Season	2 caps	0 pts
1994	Tour to Australia	
Career	2 caps	0 pts

Caps (2): **1994** A(1,2)

Points Nil

and national level by Dolphin's Terry Kingston, Keith helped Garryowen win 1991/92 and 1993/94 All-Ireland League titles. As recently as the 1992/93 season, he was playing for the Ireland Under-21 side, and as recently as October 1993, he turned out for them against the New Zealand Rugby News Under-21 XV which won 22–6 at Donnybrook. A year previously he had been selected for the senior bench against the '92 Wallabies, but an injury frustrated him over the remainder of the season. The next time he encountered Australia, in their own backyard, he opposed them on the field, first at Ballymore, Brisbane

(5.6.94) and then in Sydney (11.6.94), where the Wallabies wrapped up a 2–0 series win with a 32–18 victory. Gerry Murphy, Ireland's coach, said of Keith: He has been our outstanding player in both Tests, and has the potential to be world class. His other tour outings were against Western Australia and Queensland, scoring a try in the 29–26 loss to the latter

Wright, P. H.   Scotland

Full Name: Peter Hugh Wright
Club: Boroughmuir
Position: Prop
Height: 6ft (1.83m)
Weight: 17st 2lb (109kg)
Occupation: Blacksmith with MacDonald & Ross, Structural Engineers
Born: Bonnyrigg, 30.12.67
Family: Audrey (wife)
Family links with rugby: Graham (brother) and David (brother) play for Lasswade
Former club: Lasswade
International debut: Australia 27, Scotland 12, 1992
Five Nations debut: France 11, Scotland 3, 1993
Best moment in rugby: Being told I was in the British Lions squad
Worst moment in rugby: Tearing medial and cruciate knee ligaments
Most respected opponent: Tony Daly (NSW & Australia) and most French props
Biggest influence on career: Bruce Hay (Boroughmuir coach)

Scotland (1992)

Last Season	1 cap	0 pts
Career	6 caps	0 pts

Lions 1993

Caps (6): **1992** A(1,2) **1993** F, W, E **1994** W

Points Nil

Serious injuries: Torn medial and cruciate knee ligaments (October 1989: out for 18 months)
Best memories last season: Avoiding relegation with Boroughmuir and winning Scottish Cup
Should rugby's amateur rules be revised? Yes
To what degree should players benefit? Give us opportunity to make money outwith the game. Anything short of being paid to play I would favour
Should referees be rewarded?: Yes. I don't know if standards would improve drastically, but it certainly could do no harm. At present they get away with an

awful lot. If there were rewards, the bad officials would be forced to drop out of the system

Advice for International Board: Stop chopping and changing rules – it is difficult to keep adapting. And when you've decided on them, make sure every nation adheres to them

Notable landmarks in rugby career: A British Lion in 1993, although he failed to reproduce the same form last season, playing just the once for Scotland (against Wales, 15.1.94) and being dropped thereafter. The seventh player from the Boroughmuir club to be capped, Peter appeared on both sides of the Scottish front row in 1992/93, making his debut on the tour to Australia in the first-Test defeat in Sydney (13.6.92). Retained place the following week at Ballymore, when the world champion Wallabies ran out 37–13 winners, but was deposed by Paul Burnell for the 1993 Five Nations Championship. That would have been that but for the fact that the Scots were having something of a crisis at loosehead in the wake of David Sole's retirement. Bristol's Alan Sharp was picked but withdrew injured, and after one cap his replacement, GHK's Alan Watt, also pulled out of contention. Peter was offered the job, and did so well against France, Wales and England that he was picked to tour New Zealand with the Lions, playing against North Auckland, NZ Maoris, Southland, Taranaki, Hawke's Bay and Waikato. During a previous Lions tour in 1989 he was to be found in Japan with Scotland, where he made appearances against Kanto and Japan Under-23. Indeed, Peter is no strange to representative rugby, having played for Scotland at Under-15, Under-18, Under-19 and Under-21 levels. He also skippered Edinburgh Under-21s. He played his first senior game for Boroughmuir at the age of 18, and his Scotland B bow in the 14–12 win over France B at Melrose in 1989. Added to his A caps with outings last season against Italy, Ireland and France

Touchlines: Golf, all sports

Wyllie, D. S.   Scotland

Full Name: Douglas Stewart Wyllie
Club: Stewart's-Melville FP
Position: Centre, outside-half
Height: 6ft 1in (1.85m)
Weight: 13st 10lb (82.5kg)
Occupation: Scottish sales representative for Russell Athletic
Born: Edinburgh, 20.5.63
Family: Jennifer (wife)
International debut: Scotland 12, Australia 37, 1984
Five Nations debut: Scotland 21, Wales 25, 1985
Best moment in rugby: Winning 1982 Middlesex Sevens at Twickenham with Stewart's Melville as an 18-year-old
Worst moment in rugby: Playing in Scotland XV which lost 1989 'Test' 24–28 to Japan in Tokyo – we took them for granted
Most respected opponent: Maurice Fields (Ireland)
Biggest influence on career: Dougie Morgan (ex-Stew-Mel coach)
Best memories last season: Being back in the Scotland squad on a regular basis; captaining the Scotland 'A' side that came quite close to beating the All Blacks; I scored two drop goals

Scotland (1984)

Last Season	5 caps	0 pts
Career	18 caps	3 pts

Caps (18): **1984** A **1985** W(R), E **1987** I, F wc–F, Z, R, NZ **1989** R **1991** R wc–J(R), Z **1993** NZ(R) **1994** W(R), E, I, F

Points (3 – 1dg): **1991** wc–Z(1dg)

Should rugby's amateur rules be revised? Should be scrapped. I'd love to have been a professional rugby player…
To what degree should players benefit? …And I would love to have been paid for it. It will happen one day. In the meantime we should get compensated for time off work, and should definitely be able to benefit from off-the-field activities. It's a great honour to play for your country, but I would still like to have been paid
Should referees be rewarded? If you want more professional referees, then you have to consider paying them. Where you can afford to pay referees, standards will definitely benefit
Advice for International Board: I don't know what they do
Notable landmarks in rugby career: Appeared in all five of Scotland's Tests in 1993/94, having come on as a replacement in first two against New Zealand

and Wales. Selected at centre against England, Ireland and France before touring Argentina over summer. Impressive showing when captaining Scotland A to 9–20 defeat against All Blacks (dropping two goals), just three days after tourists had humiliated South of Scotland 84–5. Also made A-team appearances in 15–18 loss to Italy (Rovigo, 18.12.93). First called into full Scotland squad aged 19, having twice represented Scotland B in 1982. Selected to Scotland bench in 1983. Spent early years in England, where was educated at Dulwich College in South London. Did not take up rugby until aged 14. Ever-present for Scotland in 1987 World Cup, moving from centre to outside-half after John Rutherford broke down in opening match. Captained Scotland on 1991 tour to North America, playing in all six games (including non-cap Tests v US Eagles and Canada). Represented Scotland A against Spain in 1990 and 1991, scoring try on latter occasion. Having turned out for Scotland in 12–18 loss to Romania (Bucharest, 31.8.91), he played twice in 1991 World Cup, against Japan and Zimbabwe. Dropped goal against Zimbabwe (Murrayfield 9.10.91) to claim first senior Scotland points in seven years of trying

Touchlines: Golf (handicap 14), football and all other sports

Ireland's match winner Simon Geoghegan closes in for the kill against England.

APPENDIX

ACCOCEBERRY, Guy. **Status:** France tour squad. **Position:** Scrum-half. **Club:** Begles-Bordeaux. **Debut:** France A 18, England A 23, 1992. **Caps:** 4A. **1993/94:** 3A. **Born:** 5.5.67. **Height:** 5ft 11 ½ in. **Weight:** 12st 6lb. **Occupation:** Chemist. **Notes:** Toured Canada/NZ (1994) with France. Captained France A on each appearance

ADEBAYO, Adedayo Adeyemi. **Status:** England tour squad. **Position:** Wing. **Club:** Bath. **Debut:** England A 50, Spain 6, 1991. **Caps:** 5A. **Points:** 13A (3t). **1993/94:** 2A (5pts:1t). **Born:** 30.11.70. **Height:** 5ft 11in. **Weight:** 14st. **Occupation:** Student. **Notes:** Toured South Africa (1994) with England, playing v Free State, South Africa B and Eastern Province

ANDREWS, Mark. **Status:** South Africa full. **Position:** Flanker. **Province:** Natal. **Debut:** South Africa 27, England 9, 1994. **Caps:** 1. **Points:** 0. **Age:** 22. **Height:** 6ft 7in. **Weight:** 17st 10lb. **Notes:** Outstanding debut v England (11.6.94). Reserve v Argentina (both Tests) on 1993 tour. Springbok v Córdoba, Buenos Aires and Rosario. Helped Natal beat England 21–6 (22.5.94). **Record (1):** 1994 E(2)

ATHERTON, Stephen. **Status:** South Africa squad. **Position:** Lock. **Province:** Natal. **Club:** Pinetown. **Debut:** Argentina 26, South Africa 29, 1993. **Caps:** 4. **Points:** 0. **Born:** England, 17.3.65. **Height:** 6ft 7in. **Weight:** 18st 8lb. **Notes:** Made six appearances on Springboks' 1992 tour to France and England, and was a considerable presence in 1994 Test series with England. **Record (4):** 1993 Arg(1,2) 1994 E(1,2)

BACHOP, Stephen John. **Status:** New Zealand squad. **Position:** Fly-half. **Club:** Otago. **Debut:** Wales 13, Western Samoa 16, 1991. **Caps:** 4 (for WS). **Points:** 7. 1993: 6 apps in E/S (3t,1dg). **Born:** 2.4.66. **Height:** 5ft 10in. **Weight:** 13st 3lb. **Notes:** Brother (Graeme) played for All Blacks (19 caps, 8pts). **Record (W Samoa–4):** 1991 wc–W, A, Arg(1t), S(1dg)

BACK, Matthew. **Status:** Wales A. **Position:** Fullback. **Club:** Bridgend. **Debut:** Wales A 61, Japan 5, 1993. **Caps:** 2A. **Points:** 5(1t). **1993/94:** 2A(J,NoE). **Born:** 5.4.70. **Height:** 6ft 0in. **Weight:** 14st 7lb. **Occupation:** Student. **Notes:** Marked debut with try against Japan at Stradey Park, Llanelli (29.9.93)

BARNES, Stuart. **Status:** England squad. **Position:** Outside-half. **Club:** Bath. **Debut:** England 3, Australia 19, 1984. **Caps:** 10. **Points:** 34 (5c,7p,1dg). **1993/94:** 1A (vNZ). **Born:** 22.11.62. **Height:** 5ft 6in. **Weight:** 11st 12lb. **Occupation:** Building society branch manager. **Notes:** Toured NZ with 1993 Lions; England bench reserve (1993/94). **Record (10):** 1984 A(1p) 1985 Ro(R), NZ(1:1c,1p), NZ(2:2c,1dg) 1986 S(R), F(R:2p) 1987 I(R) 1988 Fj(2c,3p) 1993 S,I

BARRY, Liam John Patrick. **Status:** New Zealand squad. **Position:** Flanker. **Province:** North Harbour. **Caps:** 0. **1993:** 5 apps in E/S (1t). **Born:** 15.3.71. **Height:** 6ft 4 ½ in. **Weight:** 14st 13lb. **Notes:** Father and grandfather were All Blacks. Capt & No 8 of '92 NZ Colts. Scored 4 tries v Taranaki on day '93 NZ tour to Eng/Scot was picked

BATES, Steven Michael. **Status:** England A. **Position:** Scrum-half. **Club:** Wasps. **Debut:** Romania 3, England 58, 1989. **Caps:** 1F. **Points:** 0. **1993/94:** 1A. **Born:** 4.3.63. **Height:** 5ft 10in. **Weight:** 13st. **Occupation:** Teacher. **Notes:** Toured South Africa (1994) with England, playing five times and scoring try v Eastern Province (7.6.94). **Record (1):** 1989 R

BEAL, Nick David. **Status:** England A. **Position:** Wing. **Club:** Northampton. **Debut:** Ireland A 18, England A 22, 1993. **Caps:** 0. **1993/94:** 3A. **Born:** 2.12.70. **Height:** 6ft 2in. **Weight:** 13st 8lb. **Occupation:** Life assurance clerk with Equity & Law. **Notes:** Helped England win 1993 World Cup Sevens. A caps last season v It,F,I

BELL, Jonathan. **Status:** Ireland full. **Position:** Fullback. **Club:** Ballymena and Loughborough University. **Debut:** Australia 33, Ireland 13, 1994. **Caps:** 1. **Points:** 0. **1993/94:** 1F. **Born:** 7.2.74. **Height:** 5ft 11in. **Weight:** 14st 7lb. **Notes:** Ex-Ireland U-21 cap, selected to tour Australia (1994) with full side, playing six games and scoring one try. **Record (2):** 1994 A(1,2)

BERRY, Marty Joseph. **Status:** New Zealand squad. **Position:** Centre. **Province:** Wellington. **Debut:** NZ 9, Australia 22, 1986. **Caps:** 1F(R). **Points:** 0. 1993: 5 apps in E/S(1t). **Born:** 13.7.66. **Height:** 6ft 2in. **Weight:** 14st 13lb. **Notes:** 1985 NZ Colt who had spell at Glasgow Accies and who boasts 5-second Test career. **Record (1):** 1986 A(3R)

BLACKMORE, Andrew George. **Status:** England A. **Position:** Lock. **Club:** Bristol. **Debut:** England A 16, South Africa 20, 1992. **Caps:** 10A. **Points:** 0. **1993/94:** 3A. **Born:** 1.11.65. **Height:** 6ft 7in. **Weight:** 17st 8lb. **Notes:** Took his tally of A caps into double figures with 1993/94 apps v Italy, France and Ireland

BLOND, Xavier. **Status:** France squad. **Position:** Flanker. **Club:** Racing Club de France. **Debut:** Australia 19, France 28, 1990. **Caps:** 5. **Points:** 0. **1993/94:** 1A. **Born:** 28.8.67. **Height:** 6ft 3in. **Weight:** 15st 3lb. **Occupation:** Sales rep. **Notes:** Bench reserve in '94 Five Nations. RCF captain who helped France A beat England A 20–8 in home city. **Record (5):** 1990 A(3) 1991 S, I, W(a), E

BROTHERSTONE, Steve. **Status:** Scotland tour squad. **Position:** Hooker. **Club:** Melrose. **Caps:** 0. **1993/94:** Toured with Scotland to Argentina (1994), playing three times. **Born:** 16.4.71. **Height:** 6ft. **Weight:** 16st 6lb. **Occupation:** Student. **Notes:** Helped Melrose win 1993/94 Scottish title before going to South America

BUCKETT, Ian. **Status:** Wales Full. **Position:** Prop. **Club:** Swansea. **Debut:** Tonga 9, Wales 18, 1994. **Caps:** 1F, 5A. **Points:** 0. **1993/94:** 2A. **Born:** 23.12.67. **Height:** 6ft 1in. **Weight:** 16st. **Occupation:** Student. **Notes:** 1993/94 A-team outings in wins over Ireland and France. Toured with Wales in 1990 and '94, making Test debut vs Tonga. **Record (1):** 1994 T

BURKE, Paul Anthony. **Status:** Ireland A. **Position:** Fly-half. **Club:** London Irish. **Debut:** Ireland A 10, Wales A 20, 1994. **Caps:** 1A. **Points:** 5(1c,1p). **1993/94:** 1A(5pts). **Born:** London, 1.5.73. **Height:** 5ft 8in. **Weight:** 12st. **Occupation:** Student. **Notes:** Toured Africa with '93 Irish Development squad; played for England and Ireland at U-21 level

CAMPAN, Olivier. **Status:** France full. **Position:** Fullback. **Club:** Agen. **Debut:** South Africa 20, France 20, 1993. **Caps:** 2. **Points:** 0. **1993/94:** 2. **Born:** 15.3.70. **Height:** 5ft 11in. **Weight:** 12st 8lb. **Occupation:** Student. **Notes:** Replacement in both Tests in South Africa (also in 18–17 win, Jo'burg, 3.7.93). Helped France win last Students World Cup. **Record (2):** 1993 SA(1R,2R)

CAMPBELL, Stewart Joseph. **Status:** Scotland tour squad. **Position:** Lock. **Club:** Dundee HSFP. **Debut:** France A 9, Scotland A 12, 1994. **Caps:** 1A. **Points:** 0. **1993/94:** 1A. **Born:** 25.4.72. **Height:** 6ft 6in. **Weight:** 16st 11lb. **Occupation:** Architectural student. **Notes:** Toured with Scotland to Argentina (1994) after helping A team win in Rennes

CHALLINOR, Andrew Paul. **Status:** England A. **Position:** Outside-half. **Club:** Harlequins. **Debut:** England A 29, France A 17, 1992. **Caps:** 4A. **1992/93:** 4A(vF,It,Sp,I). **Points:** 29(1t,3c,6p). **Born:** Wolverhampton, 5.12.69. **Height:** 6ft. **Weight:** 13st 2lb. **Note:** 14pts v France, 10pts v Italy, 5pts v Spain

CLARK, Christopher John. **Status:** England A. **Position:** Prop. **Club:** Swansea. **Debut:** England A 59, Italy A 0, 1993. **Caps:** 5A, 2u/21. **Points:** 0. **1993/94:** 2Ax. **Height:** 6ft. **Weight:** 16st. **Notes:** Combined England U-21 duties in 1992/93 with A team outings v France, Italy and Spain; A-team loosehead v Italy and Ireland

CLARKE, Ciaran Paul. **Status:** Ireland A. **Position:** Fullback. **Club:** Terenure. **Debut:** Ireland 6, France 21, 1993. **Caps:** 3. **Points:** 3(1dg). **1993/94:** 1A(vS). **Born:** 8.3.69. **Height:** 6ft 1in. **Weight:** 14st 9lb. **Occupation:** Sales executive with Playboy. **Notes:** Dropped goal in 19–14 defeat of Wales (Cardiff, 6.3.93). **Record (3):** 1993 F,W(1dg),E

COEURVEILLE, Christian. **Status:** France A. **Position:** Centre. **Club:** Biarritz. **Debut:** Argentina 12, France 27, 1992. **Caps:** 2F. **Points:** 0. **1993/94:** 1A. **Born:** 26.3.68. **Height:** 6ft. **Weight:** 12st 8lb. **Occupation:** Student. **Notes:** Played in both Tests on tour of Argentina (1992). A game v Scotland (20.2.94). **Record (2):** 1992 Arg(1R,2)

COLLINS, Richie Graham. **Status:** Wales Full. **Position:** Flanker. **Club:** Cardiff. **Debut:** Wales 19, England 12, 1987. **Caps:** 21. **Points:** 0. **1993/94:** 4(5pts). **Born:** 2.3.62. **Height:** 6ft 1in. **Weight:** 14st 4lb. **Occupation:** Policeman. **Record (21):** 1987 E(R), I(a). wc–I(b), E, NZ. US 1988 E, S, I, F, R 1990 E, S, I 1991 A, F(b). wc–WS 1994 C, Fj(1t)T, WS

CORKERY, David. **Status:** Ireland full. **Position:** Flanker. **Club:** Cork Constitution. **Debut:** Australia 33, Ireland 13, 1994. **Caps:** 1. **Points:** 0. **1993/94:** 1F. **Born:** 6.11.72. **Height:** 6ft 4in. **Weight:** 14st 5lb. **Notes:** Outstanding on debut Ireland tour to Australia (1994), playing five times. **Record (2):** 1994 A(1,2)

COSTELLO, Victor Carton Patrick. **Status:** Ireland A. **Position:** No 8, lock. **Club:** St Mary's College. **Debut:** England A 29, Ireland A 14, 1994. **Caps:** 1A, 3u/21. **Points:** 4u/21(1t). **1993/94:** 1A. **Born:** 23.10.70. **Height:** 6ft 5 ½ in. **Weight:** 18st. **Occupation:** Student. **Notes:** Irish Olympic shot-putter; toured to Australia (1994), playing four times

COUFFIGNAL, Herve. **Status:** France A. **Position:** Centre. **Club:** Colomiers. **Debut:** Romania 20, France 37, 1993. **Caps:** 1. **Points:** 0. **1993/94:** 1A. **Notes:** Having teamed up with Philippe Sella for full debut in Bucharest (20.5.93), he played for A team in 8–21 loss to Wales A (18.3.94). **Record (1):** 1993 R(a)

DALGLEISH, Chris Stephen. **Status:** Scotland tour squad. **Position:** Wing. **Club:** Gala. **Caps:** 0. **1993/94:** Toured to Argentina with full Scotland squad. **Born:** 10.4.74. **Height:** 5ft 11in. **Weight:** 13st 2lb. **Occupation:** Sales administrator. **Notes:** Late call-up for summer tour (playing four times and scoring two tries)

DALLAGLIO, Lawrence Bruno. **Status:** England tour squad. **Position:** No 8, flanker. **Club:** Wasps. **Debut:** France A 20, England A 8, 1994. **Caps:** 1A. **Points:** 0. **1993/94:** 1A. **Born:** 10.8.72. **Height:** 6ft 4in. **Weight:** 15st 7lb. **Notes:** Toured South Africa (1994) with England, playing three times. Also represented Emerging England XV

DAVIDSON, Jeremy. **Status:** Ireland tour squad. **Position:** Lock. **Club:** Dungannon. **Debut:** England U-21 22, Ireland U-21 15, 1993. **Born:** 28.4.74. **Height:** 6ft 6in. **Weight:** 16st 3lb. **Notes:** Toured with Ireland to Australia (1994), playing against Western Australia, ACT, Australia B and NSW Country

DAWE, Richard Graham Reed. **Status:** England squad. **Position:** Hooker. **Club:** Bath. **Debut:** Ireland 17, England 0, 1987. **Caps:** 4F,11A. **Points:** 0. **1993/94:** 1A. **Born:** Plymouth, 4.9.59. **Height:** 5ft 11in. **Weight:** 13st 3lb. **Note:** A team beaten 26–12 by All Blacks (7.11.93), 1994 5N reserve. Toured South Africa (1994), playing four times. **Record (4):** 1987 I, F, W wc–US

DAWSON, Matthew. **Status:** England squad. **Position:** Scrum-half. **Club:** Northampton. **Debut:** England A 29, France A 17, 1993. **Caps:** 6A. **Points:** 20A(4t). **1993/94:** 2A(1t). **Height:** 5ft 10in. **Weight:** 13st. **Notes:** England bench reserve in 15–9 win over New Zealand (27.11.93); '94 A apps v Italy and Ireland (1t)

DE ROUGEMONT, Marc. **Status:** France A. **Position:** Hooker. **Club:** Toulon. **Debut:** France A 20, England A 8, 1994. **Caps:** 2A. **Points:** 0. **1993/94:** 2A. **Born:** 24.5.72. **Height:** 5ft 9in. **Weight:** 14st 7lb. **Occupation:** Hotel owner. **Notes:** A-team games against England and Wales (as 50th-min rep). Tour to Canada/NZ (1994)

DEVERGIE, Thierry. **Status:** France A. **Position:** Lock. **Club:** Nîmes. **Debut:** Romania 12, France 16, 1988. **Caps:** 15F. **Points:** 0. **1993/94:** 1A. **Born:** 27.7.66. **Height:** 6ft 6in. **Weight:** 17st 4lb. **Occupation:** PR officer. **Notes:** Dropped from senior XV before 1991 World Cup, but played for A team in 8–21 loss to Wales (Cardiff, 18.3.94). **Record (15):** 1988 R 1989 NZ(1,2), BL, A(2) 1990 W, E, S, I, R, A(1,2,3) 1991 US(2), W

DIPROSE, Anthony. **Status:** England A. **Position:** Lock. **Club:** Saracens. **Debut:** England A 29, Ireland A 14, 1994. **Caps:** 2A. **Points:** 5(1t). **1993/94:** 2A(5pts). **Height:** 6ft 5in. **Weight:** 16st. **Occupation:** Student. **Notes:** Scored try on A-team debut v Ireland (18.2.94), also played for U-21s and Emerging England

DIRKS, Chris. **Status:** South Africa squad. **Position:** Fullback. **Province:** Transvaal. **Caps:** 0. **Age:** 27. **Height:** 6ft 2in. **Weight:** 14st 12lb. **Notes:** Toured to Argentina (1993), playing against Córdoba (won 55–37, 27.10.93) and Tucumán (won 40–12, 2.11.93), scoring a try in each game; broken hand v Tucumán ended his tour. 1993 Currie Cup winner

DOOLEY, Dan. **Status:** Ireland A. **Position:** Wing. **Club:** London Irish. **Debut:** Scotland A 24, Ireland A 9, 1993. **Caps:** 1A. **Points:** 0. **1993/94:** 1A. **Born:** 18.10.68. **Height:** 6ft 1in. **Weight:** 15st 4lb. **Notes:** Made A debut at Ayr (28.12.93)

DROTSKE, Naka. **Status:** South Africa full. **Position:** Hooker. **Province:** Orange Free State. **Debut:** Argentina 23, South Africa 52, 1993. **Caps:** 1. **Points:** 0. **1993/94:** 1F. **Age:** 22. **Height:** 5ft 11 ½ in. **Weight:** 15st 10lb. **Notes:** Springbok v Córdoba, Tucumán and Rosario in Argentina (1993). Injury v England in Natal (17.5.94) put him out of Test contention. **Record (1):** 1993 Arg(2)

DUNN, Kevin Anthony. **Status:** England A. **Position:** Hooker. **Club:** Wasps. **Debut:** England A 9, Australia 37, 1988. **Caps:** 11A (also 89:F,It,Fj; 93:F,It,Sp,I; 94:It,F,I). **Points:** 9A(2t). **1993/94:** 3A. **Height:** 5ft 9in. **Weight:** 13st 10lb. **Notes:** Tries v France (1989) and Spain (1993)

EKERT, Anthony. **Status:** Australia squad. **Position:** Scrum-half. **Club:** Gordon. State: NSW. **Caps:** 0. Age: 25. **Height:** 5ft 10in. **Weight:** 12st. **Occupation:** Student. **Notes:** Played v Munster, Connacht, Wales B, Monmouthshire and Welsh Students during 1992 Ireland/Wales tour

ETHERIDGE, John. **Status:** Ireland A. **Position:** Lock. **Club:** Northampton. **Debut:** Wales A 28, Ireland A 29, 1993. **Caps:** 4A. **Points:** 0. **1993/94:** 2A. **England A caps:** 2 (1989 It, USSR). **Points:** 0. **Born:** Gloucester, 8.6.65. **Height:** 6ft 6in. **Weight:** 16st 7lb. **Notes:** Played v Wales A and England A in 1992/93 and 1993/94

FABRE, Philippe. **Status:** France A. **Position:** Wing. **Club:** Toulouse. **Debut:** France A 9, Scotland A 12, 1994. **Caps:** 1A. **Points:** 0. **1993/94:** 1A. **Born:** 25.4.64. **Height:** 6ft 1in. **Weight:** 13st 1lb. **Occupation:** Restauranteur. **Notes:** A-team debut in 12–9 loss to Scotland (Rennes, 20.2.94)

FERGUSON, Steve William. **Status:** Scotland tour squad. **Position:** Prop. **Club:** Peebles. **Caps:** 0. **1993/94:** Tour to Argentina, playing three times. **Born:** 18.6.65. **Height:** 6ft 1in. **Weight:** 17st 8lb. **Occupation:** Lumberjack. **Notes:** Career almost ended when a tree he was chopping down landed on his knee

FITZGERALD, John Joseph. **Status:** Ireland full. **Position:** Prop. **Club:** Young Munster. **Debut:** Ireland 22, Scotland 18, 1988. **Caps:** 12. **Points:** 4(1t). **1993/94:** 2. **Born:** 31.8.61. **Height:** 5ft 11in. **Weight:** 16st 4lb. **Occupation:** Business development executive. **Notes:** Toured Australia in 1994, ending three years in Test wilderness. **Record (10):** 1988 S, F 1990 S(1t), F, W 1991 F, W, E, S(a) wc–J 1994 A(1,2)

FROMONT, Richard Trevor. **Status:** New Zealand squad. **Position:** Lock. **Province:** Auckland. **Caps:** 0. 1993: 6 apps in E/S. **Born:** 7.9.69. **Height:** 6ft 8in. **Weight:** 16st 10lb. **Notes:** Biggest of '93 NZ tourists, who earned selection after just four games for Auckland since debut against Natal in '93 Super-10. Favourite film is *White Men Can't Jump!*

FULCHER, Gabriel Mark. **Status:** Ireland full. **Position:** Lock. **Club:** Constitution. **Debut:** Australia 32, Ireland 18, 1994. **Caps:** 1. **Points:** 0. **1993/94:** 1. **Born:** 27.11.69. **Height:** 6ft 5in. **Weight:** 16st 7lb. **Notes:** Made four apps (NSW, Queensland, Australia B) in Australia, including second Test (Sydney, 11.6.94). **Record (1):** 1994 A(2)

GARFORTH, Darren James. **Status:** England A. **Position:** Prop. **Club:** Leicester. **Debut:** England A 66, Spain 5, 1993. **Caps:** 4A. **Points:** 0. **1993/94:** 1A. **Born:** 9.4.66. **Height:** 5ft 10in. **Weight:** 16st 10lb. **Occupation:** Tubular technician. **Notes:** A-team app as 63rd-minute rep for Gary Holmes in 20–8 away loss to France

GIBBS, Andrew. **Status:** Wales A. **Position:** Flanker. **Club:** Newbridge. **Debut:** Ireland A 10, Wales A 20, 1994. **Caps:** 1A. **Points:** 0. **1993/94:** 1A. **Born:** 20.3.72. **Height:** 6ft 3in. **Weight:** 15st 10lb. **Occupation:** Mechanical engineer/fitter. **Notes:** Represented Wales at Youth, U-19 and U-21 levels

GREENWOOD, Matthew. **Status:** England A. **Position:** Flanker. **Club:** Wasps. **Debut:** Spain 3, England A 34, 1992. **Caps:** 8A (92:Sp, I, F, It; 93:NZ1, It, I; 94:F). **Points:** 0. **Born:** 25.9.64. **Height:** 6ft 6in. **Weight:** 16st 8lb. **Occupation:** Building surveyor with Thames Water. **Notes:** Toured with England A to Canada (1993)

HALVEY, Eddie Oliver. **Status:** Ireland A. **Position:** Flanker. **Club:** Shannon. **Debut:** Scotland A 9, Ireland A 24, 1993. **Caps:** 2A. **Points:** 0. **1993/94:** 2A. **Born:** 11.7.70. **Height:** 6ft 4in. **Weight:** 15st 8lb. **Occupation:** Aer Rianta employee. **Notes:** A-team outings against Scotland (at Ayr) and Wales (lost 10–20, Dublin)

HENDERSON, Paul. **Status:** New Zealand squad. **Position:** Flanker. **Province:** Southland. **Debut:** Argentina 14, NZ 21, 1991. **Caps:** 6F. **Points:** 4(1t). **1993:** 5 apps in E/S. **Born:** 21.9.64. **Height:** 6ft 2in. **Weight:** 14st 13lb. **Notes:** Toured Eng/Scot in '93 after Michael Jones picked up freak injury on eve of departure. Replacement in both Tests. **Record (6):** 1991 Arg(1) wc–C 1992 Wd(1,2,3), I(1:1t)

HERBERT, Daniel. **Status:** Australia full. **Position:** Centre. **Club:** GPS (Brisbane). **State:** Queensland. **Debut:** Australia 32, Ireland 18, 1994. **Caps:** 1. Points 5 (1t). **1993/94:** 1 (5pts). **Age:** 20. **Height:** 5ft 11 ½ in. **Weight:** 15st 5lb. **Occupation:** Student. **Notes:** Within three minutes of debut (11.6.93) scored try v Ireland. **Record (1):** 1994 I(2:1t)

HEWITT, Norm. **Status:** New Zealand squad. **Position:** Hooker. **Province:** Hawke's Bay. **Caps:** 0. 1993: 6 apps (3 tries) in E/S. **Born:** 11.11.68. **Height:** 5ft 10in. **Weight:** 17st. **Notes:** Outstanding for NZ Maoris and Hawke's Bay v '93 Lions. Two tries in 84–5 win v South of Scotland (10.11.93). Once scored try on 22 line!

HODGE, Duncan William. **Status:** Scotland tour squad. **Position:** Outside-half. **Club:** Watsonians. **Caps:** 0. **Points:** 0. **1993/94:** Toured to Argentina with Scotland. **Born:** 18.8.74. **Height:** 5ft 11½ in. **Weight:** 13st 13lb. **Occupation:** Student. **Notes:** Three outings in Argentina v Cuyo, Córdoba and Rosario, scoring eight points (1t,1dg)

HOGAN, Niall Andrew. **Status:** Ireland A. **Position:** Scrum–half. **Club:** Terenure. **Debut:** Scotland A 9, Ireland A 24, 1993. **Caps:** 2A. **Points:** 0. **1993/94:** 2A. **Born:** 20.4.71. **Height:** 5ft 8in. **Weight:** 11st 7lb. **Occupation:** Medical student. **Notes:** Captained Ireland at U-21 level and v Scotland and Wales at A level in 1993/94

HOGAN, Paul John. **Status:** Ireland A. **Position:** Flanker, No 8. **Club:** Garryowen. **Debut:** France 44, Ireland 12, 1992. **Caps:** 1. **Points:** 0. **1993/94:** 1A. **Born:** 25.6.68. **Height:** 6ft 3in. **Weight:** 16st. **Occupation:** Sales rep with Frank Hogan Ltd. **Notes:** Played in A team's 14–29 loss to England (1993/94); toured to Australia (1994), playing v ACT. **Record (1):** 1992 F

HOLMES, Gary. **Status:** England A. **Position:** Prop. **Club:** Wasps. **Debut:** England A 31, Namibia 16, 1990. **Caps:** 5A. **Points:** 0. **1993/94:** 1A. **Born:** 7.7.65. **Height:** 5ft 11in. **Weight:** 16st. **Occupation:** General manager for packaging company. **Notes:** Late selection for 1986 Cup final. A team v France (1993/94). London bench v NZ

HOPLEY, Damian Paul. **Status:** England A. **Position:** Centre. **Debut:** England A 12, Emerging Australians 12, 1990. **Caps:** 12A. **Points:** 9A(2t). **1993/94:** 4A. **Club:** Wasps. **Born:** 12.4.70. **Height:** 6ft 2in. **Weight:** 14st 11lb. **Notes:** A-team ever-present since 1992. Helped England win 1993 World Cup Sevens. Toured with England to Oz (1991) and South Africa (1994: 4 games, 2 tries)

HOWARTH, Shane Paul. **Status:** New Zealand squad. **Position:** Fullback. **Province:** Auckland. **Caps:** 0. **1993:** 6 apps in E/S. **Born:** 8.7.68. **Height:** 5ft 10in. **Weight:** 13st 5lb. **Notes:** Protégé of Grant Fox who broke neck in teenage diving accident. Top scorer on NZ's '93 tour of Eng/Scot with 81 points (3t,15c,12p)

HOWE, Tyrone Gyle. **Status:** Ireland A. **Position:** Wing. **Club:** Dungannon. **Debut:** Ireland A 10, Wales A 20. **Caps:** 2A. **Points:** 0. **1993/94:** 2A. **Born:** 2.4.71. **Height:** 6ft. **Weight:** 13st. **Occupation:** Student. **Notes:** No age-group provincial rugby before making senior Ulster debut. A-team apps v Wales and England in 1993/94

HOWLEY, Robert. **Status:** Wales tour squad. **Position:** Scrum-half. **Club:** Bridgend. **Debut:** Holland 12, Wales A 57, 1993. **Caps:** 5A. **Points:** 10A(2t). **1993/94:** 5A(5pts). **Born:** 13.10.70. **Height:** 5ft 10½in. **Weight:** 12st 5lb. **Notes:** Scored try on A-team debut in Den Bosch (6.2.93). Toured with Wales in 1993-4; try v Canada A (12.3.94)

HUMPHREYS, David George. **Status:** Ireland A. **Position:** Fly-half. **Club:** QUB. **Debut:** Wales A 28, Ireland A 29, 1993. **Caps:** 3A. **Points:** 19A. **1993/94:** 1A. **Born:** 10.9.71. **Height:** 5ft 10in. **Weight:** 11st 12lb. **Occupation:** Student. **Notes:** Marked A-team debut with 19 points (1t,1c,2p,2dg). Played twice v England A

HURLEY, Henry. **Status:** Ireland A. **Position:** Loosehead prop. **Club:** Old Wesley. **Debut:** Scotland A 24, Ireland A 9, 1993. **Caps:** 1A. **Points:** 0. **1993/94:** 1A. **Born:** 28.12.65. **Height:** 5ft 10in. **Weight:** 16st 5lb. **Notes:** Made A-team debut at Ayr (18.12.93)

JENKINS, Rory Harry John. **Status:** England A. **Position:** Flanker. **Club:** London Irish. **Debut:** Italy A 9, England A 15, 1994. **Caps:** 2A. **Points:** 0. **1993/94:** 2A. **Born:** 29.6.70. **Height:** 6ft 2in. **Weight:** 15st 10lb. **Occupation:** Law student. **Notes:** Scored one of only five tries conceded by 1993 All Blacks in London's 12–39 loss

JOHN, Paul. **Status:** Wales full. **Position:** Scrum-half. **Club:** Pontypridd. **Debut:** Tonga 9, Wales 18, 1994. **Caps:** 1F, 4A. **Points:** 5(1t). **1993/94:** 3A. **Born:** 25.1.70. **Height:** 5ft 9in. **Weight:** 11st 7lb. **Occupation:** Teacher. **Notes:** Test debut vs Tonga (18.6.94). **Record** (1): 1994 T

JOINER, Craig Alexander. **Status:** Scotland full. **Position:** Centre, wing. **Club:** Melrose. **Debut:** Argentina 16, Scotland 15, 1994. **Caps:** 2. **Points:** 0. **1993/94:** 2. **Born:** 21.4.74. **Height:** 5ft 10in. **Weight:** 14st 6lb. **Occupation:** Student. **Notes:** Made Test debut on wing in both Tests v Argentina (1994) after helping steer Melrose to another Scottish title. **Record** (2): 1994 Arg(1,2)

JONES, Derwyn. **Status:** Wales A. **Position:** Lock. **Club:** Cardiff. **Debut:** Wales A 24, North of England 8, 1993. **Caps:** 4A. **Points:** 0. **1993/94:** 4A. **Born:** 14.11.70. **Height:** 6ft 10in. **Weight:** 18st 7lb. **Occupation:** Student. **Notes:** Played in four of Wales A's five wins in 1993/94. One of rugby's tallest men

JONES, Ian Wyn. **Status:** Wales A. **Position:** Wing, fullback. **Club:** Llanelli. **Debut:** Wales A 11, Australia 24, 1992. **Caps:** 6A. **points:** 15A(3t). **1993/94:** 3A(2t). **Born:** 12.5.71. **Height:** 5ft 10in. **Weight:** 12st 4lb. **Occupation:** Student. **Notes:** 2t v Canada A (Cardiff, 12.3.94); toured with Wales to Oz (1991) and Africa (1993)

JORGENSEN, Peter. **Status:** Australia full. **Position:** Wing, fullback. **State:** NSW. **Debut:** Australia 27, Scotland 12, 1992. **Caps:** 2. **Points:** 0. **Born:** 30.4.73. **Height:** 5ft 11in. **Weight:** 12st 7lb. **Occupation:** Futures market trainee. **Notes:** Toured Britain with Australia U-19s in 1991/92; both caps came v Scotland (1992). **Record** (2): 1992 S(1,2)

KEBBLE, Guy. **Status:** South Africa full. **Position:** Loosehead prop. **Province:** Natal. **Debut:** Argentina 26, South Africa 29, 1993. **Caps:** 2. **Points:** 0. **1993:** 2. **Age:** 27. **Height:** 6ft 1in. **Weight:** 20st. **Notes:** Springbok v Córdoba and Tucumán in Argentina (1993) as well as playing in both Tests (6 & 13.11.93). **Record** (2): 1993 Arg(1,2)

LABIT, Laurent. **Status:** France A. **Position:** Fullback. **Club:** Castres. **Debut:** Scotland A 19, France A 29, 1993. **Caps:** 4A. **Points:** 23(1c,7p). **1993/94:** 3A(21pts). **Born:** 16.6.69. **Height:** 5ft 9in. **Weight:** 12st 4lb. **Occupation:** Technico Commercial. **Notes:** Scored in every A game played: 1993 S(1c) 1994 E(3p), S(3p), W(1p)

LANDREAU, Fabrice. **Status:** France squad. **Position:** Hooker. **Club:** Grenoble. **Caps:** 1A. **Debut:** France A 18, England A 22, 1992. **Born:** 1.8.68. **Height:** 5ft 10in. **Weight:** 15st 9lb. **Occupation:** Travelling salesman. **Notes:** Former flanker/centre who toured Argentina with France in 1992. 1994 Five Nations replacement; A team v Scotland (20.2.94)

LARSEN, Blair Peter. **Status:** New Zealand squad. **Position:** Lock. **Province:** North Harbour. **Debut:** NZ 54, World XV 26, 1992. **Caps:** 3F. **Points:** 4(1t). 1993: 8 apps in E/S. **Born:** 20.1.69. **Height:** 6ft 6in. **Weight:** 16st 12lb. **Notes:** Scored try on his debut. Toured Eng/Scot (1993), 8 apps but only replacement in Tests. **Record (3):** 1992 Wd(2:1t), Wd(3), I(1)

LAWLOR, Philip. **Status:** Ireland A. **Position:** No 8. **Club:** Bective Rangers. **Debut:** Ireland 20, Argentina 18, 1990. **Caps:** 1. **Points:** 0. **1993/94:** 1A. **Born:** 2.7.65. **Height:** 6ft 5in. **Weight:** 16st 3lb. **Occupation:** Farmer. **Notes:** Five Nations bench reserve in 1992. A-team outing in 9–24 loss to Scotland (28.12.93). **Record (1):** 1990 Arg

LEFLAMAND, Laurent. **Status:** France A. **Position:** Wing. **Club:** Lyon. **Debut:** France A 9, Scotland A 12, 1994. **Caps:** 3A. **Points:** 5(1t). **1993/94:** 3A(5pts). **Born:** 4.4.68. **Height:** 6ft 1½in. **Weight:** 14st 7lb. **Occupation:** Technician. **Notes:** Scored try v Wales A (18.3.94). Toured Canada/NZ (1994) with France

LEMEUR, Yann. **Status:** France full. **Position:** Lock. **Club:** Racing Club de France. **Debut:** Romania 20, France 37, 1993. **Caps:** 1F, 2A. **Points:** 0. **1993/94:** 1F. **Born:** 29.3.67. **Height:** 6ft 7in. **Weight:** 16st 8lb. **Occupation:** Cadre EDF. **Notes:** Made full debut in Bucharest (20.5.93); toured SA (1993). **Record (1):** 1993 R(a)

LE ROUX, André-Henry. **Status:** South Africa full. **Position:** Prop. **Province:** Orange Free State. **Debut:** South Africa 15, England 32, 1994. **Caps:** 2. **Points:** 0. **1993/94:** 2. **Age:** 21. **Height:** 6ft 2in. **Weight:** 18st. **Notes:** Toured Argentina (1993) with SA, playing v Buenos Aires, Tucumán and Rosario. Impressive in OFS's defeat of England (17.5.94). **Record (2):** 1994 E(1,2)

LEWIS, Steele Lloyd. **Status:** Wales A. **Position:** Centre. **Club:** Pontypridd. **Debut:** France A 28, Wales A 15, 1989. **Caps:** 5A. **Points:** 0. **1993/94:** 3A. **Born:** 29.10.64. **Height:** 5ft 10in. **Weight:** 13st 2lb. **Occupation:** Tiler. **Notes:** Toured Australia with Wales (1991); A games v Ireland, Canada and France in 1993/94

LHERMET, Jean-Marc. **Status:** France tour squad. **Position:** Lock, back row. **Club:** Montferrand. **Debut:** Scotland 21, France 0, 1990. **Caps:** 3. **Points:** 0. **Born:** 14.8.67. **Height:** 6ft 4in. **Weight:** 15st 3lb. **Occupation:** Engineer. **Notes:** Played six times for France A. Recalled to full side in Bucharest (20.5.93) after three-year gap. **Record (3):** 1990 S, I 1993 R(a)

LIEVREMONT, Marc. **Status:** France A. **Position:** Back row. **Club:** Perpignan. **Debut:** France A 20, England A 8, 1994. **Caps:** 1A. **Points:** 0. **1993/94:** 1A. **Born:** 28.10.68 (Dakar, Senegal). **Height:** 5ft 11½in. **Weight:** 13st 8lb. **Occupation:** Moniteur EPS. **Notes:** A-team debut at flanker against England

LLEWELLYN, Glyn, David. **Status:** Wales A. **Position:** Lock. **Club:** Neath. **Debut:** Namibia 9, Wales 18, 1990. **Caps:** 9. **Points:** 0. **1993/94:** 1A. **Born:** 9.8.65. **Height:** 6ft 6in. **Weight:** 17st 10lb. **Occupation:** Sales executive with Terotech (Dorking). **Notes:** A-team outing in 24–8 defeat of North of England (Pontypool, 13.10.93). **Record (9):** 1990 Na(1,2), Ba 1991 E, S, I, F(a), A(a),F(b)

McBRYDE, Robin Colin. **Status:** Wales full. **Position:** Hooker. **Club:** Swansea. **Debut:** Fiji 8, Wales 23, 1994. **Caps:** 1F, 4A **1993/94:** 1F, 2A, 4A. **Points:** 0. **1993/94:** 2A(vNoE,C). **Born:** 3.7.70. **Height:** 6ft. **Weight:** 14st 7lb. **Occupation:** Electrician. **Notes:** 1994 Five Nations bench reserve. **Record (1):** 1994 Fj

McDONALD, John Parker. **Status:** Ireland A. **Position:** Hooker. **Club:** Malone. **Debut:** Ireland 46, Canada 19, 1987. **Caps:** 4. **Points:** 0. **1993/94:** 2A (capt vW,E). **Born:** 9.4.60. **Height:** 5ft 10in. **Weight:** 12st 12lb. **Occupation:** Civil servant. **Notes:** Withdrew from Ireland side 15 mins before Wales 1990 after tearing calf muscle warming up. **Record (4):** 1987 C 1990 E(R), S, Arg

McGOWAN, Alan Noel. **Status:** Ireland squad. **Position:** Fly-half. **Club:** Blackrock. **Debut:** Ireland A 9, Scotland A 24, 1993. **Caps:** 1A. **Points:** 9(3p). **1993/94:** 1A(9pts). **Born:** 2.1.72. **Height:** 5ft 10in. **Weight:** 12st. **Occupation:** Student. **Notes:** Senior bench reserve throughout 1993/94. Toured Australia with Ireland (1994), kicking 33 points (11p) in three games

McINTOSH, Dale Lynsay Manawa. **Status:** Scotland A. **Position:** Flanker. **Club:** Pontypridd. **Debut:** Scotland A 19, Ireland B 29, 1991. **Caps:** 1A, 2B, 1u-21. **Points:** 0. **1993/94:** 1A. **Born:** 23.11.69 (Turangi, NZ). **Height:** 6ft 3in. **Weight:** 16st. **Occupation:** Labourer. **Notes:** 1993 Scotland Trial injury robbed him of Test cap; A team v Italy (18.12.93)

McKEE, Kevin John. **Status:** Ireland A. **Position:** Flanker. **Club:** Instonians. **Debut:** Ireland A 13, Scotland A 22, 1992. **Caps:** 3A. **Points:** 5(1t). **1993/94:** 2A. **Born:** 13.9.69. **Height:** 6ft 2in. **Weight:** 14st 7lb. **Occupation:** Student. **Notes:** Toured Africa with Irish Development squad (1993); try v England A last season (lost 14–29)

McKENZIE, Kevin Duncan. **Status:** Scotland full. **Position:** Hooker. **Club:** Stirling County. **Debut:** Argentina 16, Scotland 15, 1994. **Caps:** 2F,8A. **Points:** 0. **1993/94:** 4A. **Born:** 22.1.68. **Height:** 5ft 6in. **Weight:** 14st 1lb. **Occupation:** Sales rep. **Notes:** Represented Scotland at every level; captained A team v I (won 24–9, 28.12.93); 1994 Five Nations bench reserve; toured Arg (1994). **Record (2):** 1994 Arg(1,2)

MALLETT, John. **Status:** England A. **Position:** Prop. **Club:** Bath. **Debut:** France A 20, England A 8, 1993. **Caps:** 2A. **Points:** 0. **1993/94:** 2F,4A. **Born:** 28.5.70. **Height:** 6ft 1in. **Weight:** 16st. **Occupation:** Area manager with Contemporary Leisure. **Notes:** Capt Eng Colts (1989); Emerging England v 1993 All Blacks; toured SA with Eng (1994), playing four times

MANLEY, David. **Status:** Wales A. **Position:** Wing. **Club:** Pontypridd. **Debut:** Ireland A 10, Wales A 20, 1994. **Caps:** 3A. **Points:** 5(1t). **1993/94:** 3A(I,C,F). **Born:** 8.11.68. **Height:** 5ft 11in. **Weight:** 14st. **Occupation:** Teacher. **Notes:** 1993/94 top try-scorer in Welsh rugby; marked A debut with try v Ireland (4.2.94)

MARTENS, Hennie. **Status:** South Africa squad. **Position:** Scrum-half. **Province:** Orange Free State. **Caps:** 0. **Age:** 22. **Height:** 5ft 10in. **Weight:** 12st 10lb. **Notes:** Bench reserve in both Tests v Argentina (1993), playing v Córdoba, Tucumán and Rosario

MENIEU, Emmanuel. **Status:** France A. **Position:** Prop. **Club:** Montferrand. **Debut:** Wales A 21, France A 8, 1994. **Caps:** 1A. **Points:** 0. **Born:** 23.7.69. **Height:** 6ft 1in. **Weight:** 18st 12lb. **Occupation:** Employé ASM. **Notes:** Late call-up for France tour to SA (1993), playing v E Province and SA Dev XV. Sent off v Wales A (18.3.94)

MERCERON, Gerald. **Status:** France A. **Position:** Outside-half. **Club:** Toulon. **Debut:** France A 9, Scotland A 12, 1994. **Caps:** 2A. **Points:** 0. **1993/94:** 2A. **Born:** 25.2.73. **Height:** 5ft 9in. **Weight:** 12st 1lb. **Occupation:** Student. **Notes:** Debut as replacement v Scotland (20.2.94); started at fly-half in 20–8 win over England A

MILLAR, Peter. **Status:** Ireland A. **Position:** Tighthead prop. **Club:** Ballymena. **Debut:** England A 47, Ireland A 15, 1992. **Caps:** 6A. **Points:** 0. **1993/94:** 2A. **Born:** 8.6.62. **Height:** 6ft 1in. **Weight:** 16st 6lb. **Occupation:** Bank official with Northern Bank. **Notes:** 1993/94 A-team outings v Wales & England

MILLIGAN, Kenneth R. **Status:** Scotland A. **Position:** Wing, centre. **Club:** Stewart's-Melville FP. **Debut:** Scotland A 19, France A 29, 1993. **Caps:** 4A. **Points:** 0. **1993/94:** 3A. **Born:** 19.7.72. **Height:** 5ft 10in. **Weight:** 12st 7lb. **Notes:** A-team outings on right wing v Italy, Ireland and France

MITCHELL, John E. P. **Status:** New Zealand squad. **Position:** No 8. **Province:** Waikato. **Caps:** 0. **1993:** 6 apps in E/S (captain 3 times). **Born:** 23.3.64. **Height:** 6ft 3in. **Weight:** 17st. **Notes:** Captained Waikato to historic Ranfurly Shield defeat of eight-year holders Auckland (1993). Never even a trial before selection for 1993 NZ tour

MONI, Christophe. **Status:** France A. **Position:** No 8, flanker. **Club:** Nice. **Debut:** France A 9, Scotland A 12, 1994. **Caps:** 3A. **Points:** 0. **1993/94:** 3A. **Born:** 15.1.72. **Height:** 6ft 3in. **Weight:** 14st 8lb. **Occupation:** Student. **Notes:** Ever-present for France A in 1993/94 v Scotland, England and Wales

MULLINS, Andrew Richard. **Status:** England A. **Position:** Prop. **Club:** Harlequins. **Debut:** England 58, Fiji 23, 1989. **Caps:** 1F, 15A/B. **Points:** 0. **1993/94:** 2A. **Born:** 12.12.64. **Height:** 5ft 11in. **Weight:** 16st 1lb. **Occupation:** Accountant. **Note:** Played both A Tests in NZ (1992) and 1993/94 A-team games v NZ, It. **Record (1):** 1989 Fj

MURRAY, Patrick Vincent. **Status:** Ireland A. **Position:** Fullback. **Club:** Shannon. **Debut:** Scotland A 22, Ireland A 22, 1989. **Caps:** 2A. **Points:** 4(1t). **1993/94:** 1A(vW). **Born:** 12.10.63. **Height:** 6ft 1in. **Weight:** 13st 7lb. **Occupation:** TSB bank official. **Notes:** Five years between A caps; winger's try on debut

MUSTOE, Lyndon. **Status:** Wales A. **Position:** Prop. **Club:** Cardiff. **Debut:** Netherlands 12, Wales A 57, 1993. **Caps:** 7A. **Points:** 0. **1993/94:** 5A. **Born:** 30.1.69. **Height:** 5ft 11in. **Weight:** 15st. **Occupation:** Bricklayer. **Note:** Ever-present in Wales A's five-match Grand Slam in 1993/94 (including temp repl v Japan)

NICHOL, Scott, Alan. **Status:** Scotland full. **Position:** Centre. **Club:** Selkirk. **Debut:** Argentina 19, Scotland 17, 1994. **Caps:** 1F, 5A. **Points:** 0. **1993/94:** 1F, 3A. **Born:** 18.6.70. **Height:** 5ft 10in. **Weight:** 11st 7lb. **Occupation:** Fireman. **Notes:** Recovered from serious injury to win 3 A caps last season before touring Argentina (1994) with full side, making Test debut (11.6.94). **Record (1):** 1994 Arg(2R)

O'CONNOR, Matthew. **Status:** Australia full. **Position:** Centre. **Club:** Royals. **State:** ACT. **Debut:** Australia 32, Ireland 15, 1994. **Caps:** 1. **Points:** 0. **1993/94:** 1. **Age:** 23. **Height:** 5ft 8in. **Weight:** 14st 4lb. **Occupation:** Teacher. **Notes:** Outstanding for ACT v Ireland (1994); earned Test debut (5.6.94) but knee injury curtailed progress. **Record (1):** 1994 I(1)

OOSTHUYSEN, Deon Eugene. **Status:** South Africa squad. **Position:** Wing. **Province:** Northern Transvaal. **Caps:** 0. **Born:** 4.12.63. **Height:** 5ft 8in. **Weight:** 11st 10lb. **Occupation:** Bank official. **Notes:** Blue Bulls' record try-scorer; six apps on '93 tour of Australia, scoring three tries v S Australia, NSW Country and Queensland Country

PAGES, Gilbert. **Status:** France A. **Position:** Back row. **Club:** Castres. **Debut:** France A 9, Scotland A 12, 1994. **Caps:** 1A. **Points:** 0. **Born:** 24.12.61. **Height:** 6ft 3in. **Weight:** 15st 3lb. **Occupation:** Life assurance executive. **Notes:** Wore No 6 jersey against Scots at Rennes on 20 February but lost place after defeat

PALFREY, Adam John. **Status:** Wales A. **Position:** Fullback. **Club:** Cardiff. **Debut:** Ireland A 10, Wales A 20, 1994. **Caps:** 1A. **Points:** 0. **1993/94:** 1A. **Born:** 3.11.71. **Height:** 5ft 10in. **Weight:** 12st 9lb. **Occupation:** Student. **Notes:** Replacement in Dublin (4.2.94); Cambridge Blue in 1993 Varsity match

PARKER, Gary. **Status:** Scotland A. **Position:** Wing. **Club:** Melrose. **Debut:** Scotland A 9, NZ 20, 1993. **Caps:** 1A. **Points:** 0. **1993/94:** 1A(vNZ). **Born:** 3.3.66. **Height:** 5ft 6in. **Weight:** 13st 6lb. **Occupation:** former pro footballer with Hearts, Berwick & Napier City (NZ). **Notes:** Distinction of being only Scotsman to score try v 1993 All Blacks for South in 5–84 loss!

PELOUS, Fabien. **Status:** France A. **Position:** Lock. **Club:** Graulhet. **Debut:** France A 9, Scotland A 12, 1994. **Caps:** 2A. **Points:** 0. **1993/94:** 2A. **Born:** 7.12.73. **Height:** 6ft 7in. **Weight:** 17st 4lb. **Occupation:** Soldier. **Notes:** Twice second row in 1993/94, beating England (20–8) and losing to Scotland (9–12)

PINI, Matthew. **Status:** Australia full. **Position:** Fullback. **Club:** Wests (Brisbane). State: Queensland. **Debut:** Australia 33, Ireland 15, 1994. **Caps:** 1. **Points:** 0. **1993/94:** 1. **Age:** 25. **Height:** 5ft 11 ½ in. **Weight:** 14st 12lb. **Occupation:** Plumber. **Notes:** Ex-Aussie U-21 who sustained hamstring in training after full debut (Ballymore 5.11.94). **Record (1):** 1994 I(1)

POOLE, Matthew David. **Status:** England tour squad. **Position:** Lock. **Club:** Leicester. **Debut:** Romania U-21 13, England U-21 54, 1989. **Caps:** 3u–21. **Points:** 0. **Born:** 6.2.69. **Height:** 6ft 7in. **Weight:** 17st 7lb. **Occupation:** Office equipment machines manager. **Notes:** Toured South Africa (1994) with England; played for Tigers in 1994 Cup final

POTTER, Stuart. **Status:** England tour squad. **Position:** Centre. **Club:** Leicester. **Debut:** England A 59, Italy A 0, 1993. **Caps:** 6A. **Points:** 10A(2t). **1993/94:** 3A. **Born:** 11.11.67. **Height:** 5ft 11in. **Weight:** 13st 8lb. **Occupation:** Insurance broker. **Notes:** Two tries on debut v Italy (Bath, 3.2.93); also v Sp, I, It, F, I; toured SA with Eng (1994)

PRETORIUS, Petrus (Piet) Ingenas Lourens. **Status:** South Africa squad. **Position:** Flanker, lock. **Club:** Pretoria. **Province:** Northern Transvaal. **Caps:** 0. **Born:** 17.8.64. **Height:** 6ft 3in. **Weight:** 16st 1lb. **Occupation:** Technician. **Notes:** Six apps on '92 tour to France and England

PROSSER, Greg. **Status:** Wales A. **Position:** Lock. **Club:** Pontypridd. **Debut:** Wales A 42, Canada A 11, 1994. **Caps:** 1A. **Points:** 0. **1993/94:** 1A. **Born:** 21.5.66. **Height:** 6ft 7 ½ in. **Weight:** 17st 2lb. **Occupation:** Policeman. **Notes:** Partnered Swansea's Paul Arnold in engine room as Canadians were scuppered at Cardiff (12.3.94)

REID, Stuart James. **Status:** Scotland A. **Position:** No 8, flanker. **Club:** Boroughmuir. **Debut:** USA 12, Scotland 41, 1991. **Caps:** 2xv, 6A. **Points:** 12xv(3t) **1993/94:** 1A(vF). **Born:** Kendal, 31.1.70. **Height:** 6ft 3 ½ in. **Weight:** 15st 11lb. **Occupation:** Bank officer. **Notes:** 3 tries for '91 Scotland XV v USA(2) and Canada(1)

RICHARDSON, Jeremy Francis. **Status:** Scotland tour squad. **Position:** Lock. **Club:** Edinburgh Acads. **Caps:** 0. **1993/94:** Scotland squad for Argentina. **Born:** 7.9.63 (Crawley). **Height:** 6ft 6in. **Weight:** 16st 13lb. **Occupation:** Investment manager. **Notes:** Captained Scotland's mid-week side in Argentina

RIDGE, Martin Patrick. **Status:** Ireland tour squad. **Position:** Centre. **Club:** Blackrock College. **Debut:** Scotland A 19, Ireland A 29, 1991. **Caps:** 3A. **Points:** 8A(2t). **1993/94:** Ireland squad to Australia. **Born:** 8.10.70. **Height:** 6ft 1 ½ in. **Weight:** 13st 3lb. **Notes:** Toured NZ (1992); A tries v S,I ('91/'92); 54th-min A rep v E (19.3.93)

RIGNEY, Brian Joseph. **Status:** Ireland A. **Position:** Lock. **Club:** Greystones. **Debut:** Ireland 13, France 21, 1991. **Caps:** 6. **Points:** 0. **1993/94:** 1A(vS). **Born:** 22.9.63. **Height:** 6ft 4in. **Weight:** 17st 8lb. **Occupation:** Brewers' rep. **Notes:** Test career hampered by severe knee-ligament injury suffered in Namibia (1991). **Record (6):** 1991 F, W, E, S, Na(1) 1992 F

ROLLAND, Alain Colm Pierre. **Status:** Ireland tour squad. **Position:** Scrum-half. **Club:** Blackrock. **Debut:** Ireland 20, Argentina 18, 1990. **Caps:** 1F, 3A. **Points:** 0. **1993/94:** 1A. **Born:** 22.8.66. **Height:** 5ft 10in. **Weight:** 11st 9lb. **Occupation:** Financial consultant. **Notes:** A games v Scotland (1990), England (1992) and England (1994); three apps in Australia (1994). **Record (1):** 1990 Arg

ROWNTREE, Graham Christopher. **Status:** England squad. **Position:** Prop. **Club:** Leicester. **Debut:** Canada 15, England A 12, 1993. **Caps:** 3A. **Points:** 0. **1993/94:** 1A. **Born:** 18.4.71. **Height:** 6ft. **Weight:** 16st 10lb. **Occupation:** Insurance broker. **Notes:** Played both Tests in Canada (1993) and v NZ tourists; Five Nations bench warmer and SA tourist (1994), playing four times

RUSH, Eric James. **Status:** New Zealand squad. **Position:** Wing. **Province:** North Harbour. **Caps:** 0. **1993:** 6 apps in E/S. **Born:** 11.2.65. **Height:** 6ft. **Weight:** 13st 5lb. **Occupation:** Solicitor. **Notes:** Openside flanker turned wing who plays Sevens anytime, anywhere. Regular Barbarian. Toured Aus/SA 1992, Eng/Scot 1993

RYAN, Dean. **Status:** England squad. **Position:** Flanker, No 8. **Club:** Wasps. **Debut:** Argentina 12, England 25, 1990. **Caps:** 3. **Points:** 4(1t). **1993/94:** 2A(1tvI). **Born:** 22.6.66. **Height:** 6ft 6in. **Weight:** 16st 13lb. **Occupation:** Manager with DHL couriers. **Notes:** 1994 – England A captain v It, I; bench reserve v France; England midweek captain in SA, breaking hand v East Province. **Record (3):** 1990 Arg(a1:1t), Arg(a2) 1992 C

SAUNDERS, Rob. **Status:** Ireland squad. **Position:** Scrum-half. **Club:** London Irish. **Debut:** Ireland 13, France 21, 1991. **Caps:** 11F, 2A, 1u/21. **Points:** 0. **Born:** 5.8.68. **Height:** 5ft 10in. **Weight:** 13st. **Occupation:** Marketing executive. **Notes:** Captained Ireland on debut but dropped after 11 straight apps; 1993/94 bench reserve. **Record (11):** 1991 F, W, E, S, Na(1,2) wc–Z, J, S, A 1992 W

SCHUTTE, Philip. **Status:** South Africa squad. **Position:** Lock. **Province:** Northern Transvaal. **Debut:** None. **Age:** 24. **Height:** 6ft 7½in. **Weight:** 19st 9lb. **Notes:** Pulled off SA development tour in Western Samoa to join Springboks in England (1992) when Adri Geldenhuys withdrew. Played v Midlands and North

SHEASBY, Chris. **Status:** England A. **Position:** Flanker, No 8. **Club:** Harlequins. **Debut:** Italy A 9, England A 15, 1994. **Caps:** 1A. **Points:** 5(1t). **1993/94:** 1A(5pts). **Born:** 30.11.66. **Height:** 6ft 3in. **Weight:** 16st. **Occupation:** Student. **Notes:** Helped England win 1993 World Cup Sevens; marked A-team debut with try in Piacenza (4.2.94)

SHEPHERD, Rowen James Stanley. **Status:** Scotland A. **Position:** Centre. **Club:** Edinburgh Acads. **Debut:** France A 9, Scotland A 12, 1994. **Caps:** 1A. **Points:** 0. **1993/94:** 1A. **Born:** 25.12.70. **Height:** 6ft. **Weight:** 13st 8lb. **Occupation:** PE student. **Notes:** Toured North America (1991) and Argentina (1994: 24 points – 1t,2c,5p) with Scotland; A debut in Rennes (20.2.94)

SIMS, David. **Status:** England A. **Position:** Lock. **Club:** Gloucester. **Debut:** Spain 3, England A 34, 1992. **Caps:** 6A. **Points:** 0. **1993/94:** 2A. **Born:** 22.11.69. **Height:** 6ft 7in. **Weight:** 17st 3lb. **Occupation:** Fruit & veg wholesaler. **Notes:** Played for South West and England A v 1993 All Blacks; also A team v Italy in Piacenza

SODEN, Philip Joseph. **Status:** Ireland tour squad. **Position:** Loosehead prop. **Club:** Cork Constitution. **Debut:** Ireland A 16, Scotland A 0, 1990. **Caps:** 7A,2u-21. **Points:** 0. **1993/94:** 2A. **Born:** 6.9.69. **Height:** 6ft. **Weight:** 16st 10lb. **Occupation:** Owns dry-cleaning business. **Notes:** A team caps v Wales and England before touring with full squad to Oz (1994)

STARK, Derek Alexander. **Status:** Scotland squad. **Position:** Wing. **Club:** Boroughmuir. **Debut:** Scotland 15, Ireland 3, 1993. **Caps:** 4. **Points:** 5(1t). **1993/94:** 3A(vIt,I,F). **Born:** 13.4.66. **Height:** 6ft 2in. **Weight:** 13st 12lb. **Occupation:** Chef. **Notes:** Try with first touch in Test rugby (16.1.93); rep v W, E (1994). **Record (4):** 1993 I(1t), F, W, E

TEICHMANN, Gary. **Status:** South Africa squad. **Position:** No 8. **Province:** Natal. **Caps:** 0. **1993:** Tour to Argentina. **Age:** 27. **Height:** 6ft 2in. **Weight:** 16st. **Notes:** Springbok v Buenos Aires and Rosario (scoring try in 40–26 win, 9.11.93); helped Natal beat England 21–6 (May 1994)

TOLAND, Liam Thomas. **Status:** Ireland A. **Position:** Flanker. **Club:** Old Crescent. **Debut:** Wales A 29, Ireland A 28, 1993. **Caps:** 3A, 2u-21. **Points:** 0. 1993/94: 1A. **Born:** 18.6.72. **Height:** 6ft 2in. **Weight:** 14st 7lb. **Notes:** Turned out for A team v Wales (5.3.93), England (19.3.93) and Scotland (28.12.93). U-21 caps also v Wales and England (1991)

 TWEED, David Alexander. **Status:** Ireland A. **Position:** Lock. **Club:** Ballymena. **Debut:** Ireland A 13, Scotland A 22, 1992. **Caps:** 6A. **Points:** 0. 1993/94: 3A. **Born:** 13.11.59. **Height:** 6ft 5in. **Weight:** 18st 2lb. **Occupation:** Railway engineer. **Notes:** A-team ever-present last season v Scotland, Wales and England

VELO, Frédéric. **Status:** France A. **Position:** Centre. **Club:** Grenoble. **Debut:** England A 16, France A 35, 1989. **Caps:** 6A. 1993/94: 3A(5pts). **Born:** 4.1.66. **Height:** 6ft½in. **Weight:** 13st 13lb. **Occupation:** Employé. **Notes:** kicked 11 points in A win over England (1990); ever-present for France A last season; try v England in 20–8 win

WALLACE, Fergus Steve. **Status:** Scotland tour squad. **Position:** Flanker, No 8. **Club:** Glasgow High/Kelvinside. **Caps:** 0. 1993/94: Toured Argentina (1994) with Scotland. **Born:** 2.2.65. **Height:** 6ft 3in. **Weight:** 15st 12lb. **Occupation:** Chief surveyor. **Notes:** Played against Cuyo, Córdoba and Rosario in Argentina

 WALSH, Brian Andrew. **Status:** Ireland tour squad. **Position:** Centre. **Club:** Constitution. **Debut:** Ireland A 13, Scotland A 22, 1992. **Caps:** 5A. **Points:** 5(1t). 1993/94: 2A(vW,E). **Born:** 21.10.69. **Height:** 6ft 1in. **Weight:** 13st 8lb. **Occupation:** TSB bank official. **Notes:** Scored try in 29–28 defeat of Wales A (5.3.93); three apps in Oz (1994)

 WILKINS, Gwilym. **Status:** Wales full. **Position:** Wing. **Club:** Bridgend. **Debut:** Tonga 9, Wales 18, 1994. **Caps:** 1F, 4A. **Points:** 10A(2t). 1993/94: 4A(J,I,C,F). **Born:** 4.5.67. **Height:** 5ft 10in. **Weight:** 12st 2lb. **Occupation:** Steelworker. **Notes:** Try-scoring debut as repl v Japan (29.9.93); 2nd try v France (18.3.94); toured with Wales to Canada and South Seas (1994). Makry Test debut vs Tonga. **Record** (1): 1994 T

 WILLIAMS, Barrie Hugh. **Status:** Wales squad. **Position:** Hooker. **Club:** Neath. **Debut:** Ireland A 10, Wales A 20, 1993. **Caps:** 2A. **Points:** 0. 1993/94: 2A(vI,F). **Born:** 6.1.74. **Height:** 5ft 11in. **Weight:** 15st. **Occupation:** Labourer. **Notes:** Senior bench reserve for Scotland (15.1.94); Wales Youth cap record holder (10)

 WILLIAMS, David Aled. **Status:** Wales A. **Position:** Fly-half. **Club:** Swansea. **Debut:** Namibia 30, Wales 34, 1990. **Caps:** 1F. **Points:** 0. 1993/94: 2A. **Points:** 14A. **Born:** 26.1.64. **Height:** 5ft 5in. **Weight:** 11st. **Occupation:** Groundwork surveyor. **Notes:** A-team games v North of England (2c) & Ireland (1t,1c,1p) last season. **Record** (1): 1990 Na(2R)

WILLIAMS, Steven Michael. **Status:** Wales full. **Position:** No 8. **Club:** Neath. **Debut:** Tonga 9, Wales 18, 1994. **Caps:** 1F, 3A. **Points:** 5(1t). **1993/94:** 1F, 2A(1t). **Born:** 3.10.70. **Height:** 6ft 5in. **Weight:** 17st. **Occupation:** Student. **Notes:** Capt Wales U-21 for two seasons; try in 42–11 win over Canada A (Cardiff, 12.3.94). **Record** (1): 1994 T

 WILLIAMS-JONES, Hugh. **Status:** Wales squad. **Position:** Prop. **Club:** Llanelli. **Debut:** Scotland 23, Wales 7, 1990. **Caps:** 15. **Points:** 0. **1993/94:** 3F, 1A(vJ). **Born:** 10.1.63. **Height:** 5ft 11in. **Weight:** 16st 6lb. **Occupation:** Police sergeant. **Notes:** Member of Wales's 1994 Five Nations Trophy-winning squad. **Record** (15): 1989 S(R) 1990 F(R), I 1991 A(a) 1992 S, A 1993 E, S, I, F, Z(1), Na 1994 Fj, T, WS (R)

 WILSON, Roger Kyle. **Status:** Ireland A. **Position:** No 8. **Club:** Instonians. **Debut:** Ireland A 10, Wales A 20, 1994. **Caps:** 2A. **Points:** 0. **1993/94:** 2A(vI,E). **Born:** 5.5.72. **Height:** 6ft 5in. **Weight:** 15st 7lb. **Occupation:** Medical student. **Notes:** Toured to Australia with Ireland (1994); 1990 Irish Schools Triple Crown

 WINTLE, Matthew Edward. **Status:** Wales A. **Position:** Centre. **Club:** Llanelli. **Debut:** Ireland A 10, Wales A 20, 1994. **Caps:** 1A. **Points:** 0. **1993/94:** 1A. **Born:** 13.2.72. **Height:** 6ft. **Weight:** 14st 4lb. **Occupation:** Student. **Notes:** Member of triumphant Wales Schools U-18s in NZ (1990); capt Wales U-19s; 3 apps for U-21s

 WOODS, Niall. **Status:** Ireland full. **Position:** Wing. **Club:** Blackrock. **Debut:** Australia 33, Ireland 13, 1994. **Caps:** 1F, 6A. **Points:** 5A(1t). **1993/94:** 1F,3A (5pts). **Born:** 21.6.71. **Height:** 5ft 11in. **Weight:** 11st 8lb. **Notes:** A-team apps v S, W, E (1992-94); try v Wales (4.2.94); toured Zim/Nam/SA (1993) and Australia (1994) with Ireland. **Record** (2): 1994 A(1,2)

1995 WORLD CUP

SCHEDULE

Date		k–o	Venue	Pool	
May	25	1430	Cape Town	A	Australia v South Africa
	26	1600	Rustenburg	D	Scotland v Ivory Coast
		1800	Pretoria	D	France v Tonga
		2000	Port Elizabeth	A	Canada v Europe 3
	27	1300	East London	B	Western Samoa v Europe 2
		1500	Bloemfontein	C	Europe 1 v Asia
		1700	Durban	B	England v Argentina
		2000	Johannesburg	C	New Zealand v Ireland
	30	1230	East London	B	Western Samoa v Argentina
		1430	Cape Town	A	South Africa v Europe 3
		1800	Rustenburg	D	France v Ivory Coast
		2000	Pretoria	D	Scotland v Tonga
	31	1300	Port Elizabeth	A	Australia v Canada
		1500	Bloemfontein	C	Ireland v Asia
		1700	Durban	B	England v Europe 2
		2000	Johannesburg	C	New Zealand v Europe 1
Jun	3	1300	Potchefstroom	D	Tonga v Ivory Coast
		1500	Stellenbosch	A	Australia v Europe 3
		1700	Pretoria	D	Scotland v France
		2000	Port Elizabeth	A	Canada v South Africa
	4	1300	East London	B	Argentina v Europe 2
		1500	Bloemfontein	C	New Zealand v Asia
		1700	Johannesburg	C	Ireland v Europe 1
		2000	Durban	B	England v Western Samoa
	10	1300	Durban	(E)	Winners D v Runners-Up C
		1500	Johannesburg	(F)	Winners A v Runners-Up D
	11	1300	Cape Town	(H)	Winners B v Runners-Up A
		1500	Pretoria	(G)	Winners C v Runners-Up D
	17	1430	Durban	s/f	Winners E v Winners F
	18	1430	Cape Town	s/f	Winners G v Winners H
	22	1430	Pretoria	3/4	Losers E/F v Losers G/H
	24	1430	Johannesburg	Final	Winners E/F v Winners G/H

QUALIFYING ROUNDS

EUROPE

EUROPEAN (WESTERN) ZONE PRE-QUALIFYING TOURNAMENT (Andorra): Denmark 0, Andorra 3; Denmark 8, Switzerland 3; Switzerland 14, Andorra 0

	P	W	D	L	F	A	Pts
Switzerland	2	1	0	1	17	8	4
Denmark	2	1	0	1	8	6	4
Andorra	2	1	0	1	3	14	4

Switzerland progress to Europe (Western) Zone qualifying tournament

EUROPEAN (WESTERN) ZONE QUALIFYING TOURNAMENT (11–16 May 1993, Lisbon, Portugal): Spain 40, Switzerland 0; Belgium 3, Portugal 8; Belgium 3, Spain 67; Portugal 32, Switzerland 0; Portugal 15, Spain 37; Belgium 42, Switzerland 3

	P	W	D	L	F	A	Pts
Spain	3	3	0	0	144	18	9
Portugal	3	2	0	1	55	40	7
Belgium	3	1	0	2	48	78	5
Switzerland	3	0	0	3	3	114	3

Spain and Portugal progress to European (Western) Zone

EUROPEAN (WESTERN) ZONE: Portugal 11, Wales 102 (Lisbon, 17.5.94); Spain 0, Wales 54 (Madrid, 22.5.94); Spain 35, Portugal 19 (Madrid, 29.5.94)

	P	W	D	L	F	A	Pts
Wales	2	2	0	0	156	11	6
Spain	2	1	0	1	35	73	4
Portugal	2	0	0	2	19	137	2

Wales qualify for World Cup finals (pool to be determined by European play-offs)

EUROPEAN (EASTERN) ZONE QUALIFYING TOURNAMENT (A): Germany 31, Lithuania 5 (Berlin, 1.5.93); Latvia 5, Germany 27 (Riga, 8.5.93); Lithuania 6, Latvia 7 (Siaulia, 29.5.93)

	P	W	D	L	F	A	Pts
Germany	2	2	0	0	58	10	6
Latvia	2	1	0	1	12	33	4
Lithuania	2	0	0	2	11	38	2

Germany progress to European (Eastern) Zone

EUROPEAN (EASTERN) ZONE QUALIFYING TOURNAMENT (B): (24–29 May 1993, Gdansk, Poland) Russia 15, Georgia 9; Poland 23, Georgia 6; Russia 41, Poland 5

	P	W	D	L	F	A	Pts
Russia	2	2	0	0	56	14	6
Poland	2	1	0	1	28	47	4
Georgia	2	0	0	2	15	38	2

Russia progress to European (Eastern) Zone

EUROPEAN (EASTERN) ZONE (Bucharest, Romania, 2–7 May 1994): Russia 67, Germany 5 (2.5.94); Romania 60, Germany 6 (5.5.94); Romania 30, Russia 0 (7.5.94)

	P	W	D	L	F	A	Pts
Romania	2	2	0	0	90	6	6
Russia	2	1	0	1	67	35	4
Germany	2	0	0	2	11	127	0

Romania qualify for World Cup finals (pool to be determined by European play-offs)

EUROPEAN (CENTRAL) ZONE QUALIFYING TOURNAMENT: Hungary 8, Israel 67 (Budapest, 30.5.93); Israel 10, Sweden 26 (Den Haag, 31.10.93); Netherlands 42, Czech Republic 6 (Den Haag, 31.10.93); Netherlands 56, Israel 0 (Apeldoorn, 3.11.93); Czech Republic 34, Sweden 7 (Apeldoorn, 3.11.93); Netherlands 31, Sweden 6 (Amsterdam, 6.11.93); Czech Republic 28, Israel 0 (Amsterdam, 6.11.93)

	P	W	D	L	F	A	Pts
Netherlands	3	3	0	0	129	12	9
Czech Republic	3	2	0	1	68	49	7
Sweden	3	1	0	2	39	75	5
Israel	3	0	0	3	10	110	3

Netherlands and Czech Republic join Italy in European (Central) Zone

EUROPEAN (CENTRAL) ZONE (Italy, 15–21 May 1994): Netherlands 33, Czech Republic 9 (14.5.94); Italy 104, Czech Republic 8 (17.5.94); Italy 63, Netherlands 9 (21.5.94).

	P	W	D	L	F	A	Pts
Italy	2	2	0	0	167	17	6
Netherlands	2	1	0	1	42	72	4
Czech Republic	2	0	0	2	17	137	2

Italy qualify for World Cup finals (pool to be determined by European play-offs)

EUROPEAN PLAY-OFFS (September-October 1994, all three Zone winners guaranteed qualification): Romania v Wales (Bucharest, 17.9.94); Italy v Romania (Italy, 1.10.94); Wales v Italy (Cardiff, 12.10.94) Winner progresses into Pool C, runner-up into Pool B, third-placed into Pool A

PACIFIC

PACIFIC ZONE: Fiji 11, Tonga 24 (Suva, 12.6.93); Tonga 10, Fiji 15 (Nuku'alofa, 17.6.93)

	P	W	D	L	F	A	PD
Tonga	2	1	0	1	34	26	+12
Fiji	2	1	0	1	26	34	−8

Tonga (into Pool D) qualify for finals

AFRICA

AFRICAN PRE-QUALIFYING TOURNAMENT (A: 3–10 July 1993, Nairobi, Kenya): Zimbabwe 50, Gulf States 21; Namibia 64, Gulf States 20; Kenya 9, Namibia 60; Kenya 7, Zimbabwe 42; Kenya 24, Gulf States 23; Namibia 41, Zimbabwe 16

	P	W	D	L	F	A	Pts
Namibia	3	3	0	0	165	45	9
Zimbabwe	3	2	0	1	108	69	7
Kenya	3	1	0	2	40	125	5
Gulf States	3	0	0	3	64	138	3

Namibia and Zimbabwe progress to African Zone

AFRICAN PRE-QUALIFYING TOURNAMENT (B: 26 October 1993, Tunis, Tunisia): Tunisia 16, Ivory Coast 19; Tunisia 5, Morocco 6; Morocco 3, Ivory Coast 15

	P	W	D	L	F	A	Pts
Ivory Coast	2	2	0	0	34	19	6
Morocco	2	1	0	1	9	20	4
Tunisia	2	0	0	2	21	25	2

Ivory Coast and Morocco progress to African Zone

AFRICAN ZONE TOURNAMENT (Casablanca, Morocco, 12–19 June 1994): Ivory Coast 17, Zimbabwe 10; Morocco 16, Namibia 16; Ivory Coast 13, Namibia 12; Morocco 9, Zimbabwe 21; Morocco 17, Ivory Coast 9; Namibia 25, Zimbabwe 20.

	P	W	D	L	F	A	Pts
Ivory Coast	3	2	0	1	39	39	7
Namibia	3	1	1	1	53	49	6
Morocco	3	1	1	1	42	46	6
Zimbabwe	3	1	0	2	51	51	5

Ivory Coast (into Pool D) qualify for World Cup Finals.

AMERICAS

AMERICAN ZONE (SOUTH) QUALIFYING TOURNAMENT: Chile 24, Paraguay 25 (Santiago, 26.9.93); Paraguay 3, Uruguay 67 (Asunción, 2.10.93); Uruguay 14, Chile 6 (Montevideo, 9.10.93); Argentina 70, Chile 7 (11.10.93); Argentina 51, Paraguay 3 (Buenos Aires, 16.10.93); Uruguay 10, Argentina 19 (Montevideo, 23.10.93)

	P	W	D	L	F	A	Pts
Argentina	3	3	0	0	140	20	9
Uruguay	3	2	0	1	91	28	7
Paraguay	3	1	0	2	31	141	4
Chile	3	0	0	3	37	109	3

Argentina progress to American Zone play-off

AMERICAN ZONE (NORTH) PLAY-OFF: Bermuda 3, USA 60 (Bermuda, 12.3.94)

AMERICAN ZONE PLAY-OFF: USA 22, Argentina 28 (Long Beach, California, 28.5.94); Argentina 16, USA 11 (Buenos Aires, 20.6.94)
Argentina (into Pool B) qualify for World Cup finals

ASIA

ASIAN ZONE (Malaysia, 21–29 October 1994): Republic of China, Hong Kong, Korean RU, Japan, Malaysia, Singapore, Sri Lanka, Thailand
Winner (into Pool C) qualifies for World Cup finals

POOL A

Programme:

May	25	Australia v South Africa (Cape Town, 1430)	
	26	Canada v Europe 3 (Port Elizabeth, 2000)	
	30	South Africa v Europe 3 (Cape Town, 1430)	
	31	Australia v Canada (Port Elizabeth, 1300)	
Jun	3	Australia v Europe 3 (Stellenbosch, 1500)	
	3	Canada v South Africa (Port Elizabeth, 2000)	

Pool pointers: When Australia last played in Cape Town (22.8.92), South Africa were handed a record 26–3 beating. However, since then the Springboks have won a Test in Sydney (31.7.93), and while the Wallabies recovered to take that series, there is now precious little to choose between the two countries. The Pool opener, therefore, should also be the decider, with the loser qualifying as runner-up. The Wallabies beat Canada 43–16 in Calgary (9.10.93), and despite the speed with which the Canucks are improving (witness wins over Wales and France in 1993–94), I would not expect them to overcome the Southern Hemisphere giants.

AUSTRALIA

Qualification: Holders. **Colours:** Gold jersey, green shorts

World Cup record: 1987 – Semi-finalists. Australia's problem was one of endurance. 79 minutes was okay, but the full 80 minutes became a problem later in the tournament. Wins over England (19–6), the United States (47–12) and Japan (42–23) augured well for the knock-out stage, but after dismantling Ireland 33–15 in Sydney to reach the semi-finals, they bowed out at the same venue to France. In what is remembered as one of the greatest games ever, the Wallabies succumbed to a last-gasp try from Serge Blanco (lost 24–30). They then met Wales in the third-place play-off, and lost out to a final-minute penalty by Paul Thorburn (21–22). **1991 – Winners.** No question, Bob Dwyer's Wallabies were the best after an imperious campaign in Britain. Made light work of Argentina (32–19) and Wales (38–3), with a relatively close shave against surprise packets Western Samoa (9–3) sandwiched in between. But it was quarter-final opponents Ireland, on their home patch in Dublin, who gave them the shock of their lives, leading 18–15 before Michael Lynagh's last-minute try saved their bacon (19–18). After that, anything was going to be easier, even a semi-final against holders New Zealand (16–6). The Aussies attacked with elan, scoring brilliant tries through David Campese and Tim Horan, and then built a brick wall along their own line to deny any All Black comeback. The Twickenham final (12–6) against England was another memorable affair, with England removing their conservative shackles and spinning the ball wide. Ironically, the game's only try went to Aussie prop Tony Daly.

Results since 1991 World Cup (P20 W16 D0 L4): 1992 – Australia 27, Scotland 12; Australia 37, Scotland 13; Australia 16, New Zealand 15; Australia 19, New Zealand 17; Australia 23, New Zealand 26; South Africa 3, Australia 26; Ireland 17, Australia 42; Wales 6, Australia 23. 1993 – Australia 52, Tonga 14; New Zealand 25, Australia 10; Australia 12, South Africa 19; Australia 28, South Africa 20; Australia 19, South Africa 12; Canada 16, Australia 43; France 16, Australia 13; France 3, Australia 24. 1994 – Australia 33, Ireland 13; Australia 32, Ireland 18; Australia 23, Italy 20; Australia 20, Italy 7.

Survivors from 1991 squad: David Campese, Troy Coker, Dan Crowley, Tony Daly, John Eales, Anthony Herbert, Tim Horan, Phil Kearns, Jason Little, Michael Lynagh, Rod McCall, Ewen McKenzie, David Nucifora, Willie Ofahengaue, Peter Slattery, Richard Tombs.

Previous form:

1987 Pool performance:	P	W	D	L	F	A	Pts
AUSTRALIA*	3	3	0	0	108	41	6
England	3	2	0	1	100	32	4
United States	3	1	0	2	39	99	2
Japan	3	0	0	3	48	123	0

* Semi-finalists.

1991 Pool performance:	P	W	D	L	F	A	Pts
AUSTRALIA*	3	3	0	0	79	25	9
Western Samoa	3	2	0	1	54	34	7
Wales	3	1	0	2	32	61	5
Argentina	3	0	0	3	38	83	3

* Winners.

CANADA

Qualification: 1991 quarter-finalists. **Colours:** Red jerseys, white shorts

World Cup record: 1987 – Opened account in impressive form when trouncing Tonga 37–4 in Napier, scoring seven tries in the process. Unable to reproduce winning form against Ireland (19–46) or Wales (9–40), but nevertheless had good reason to be proud of their campaign. **1991** – Qualified as winners of Americas zone. However, the 100-per-cent record, which had seemed assured after two wins over Argentina and an away triumph in the United States, eluded them when the Eagles scored a surprise win in Seattle. Had the misfortune to be drawn in Pool 4 at finals – the one French-based group – but it did not affect their performance, as they beat Fiji (13–3) in Bayonne and Romania (19–11) in Toulouse before giving France an uncomfortable time in Agen (13–19) in the Pool decider. Deservedly through to the quarter-finals, their luck with the draw failed them again: holders New Zealand in sodden Lille. Canada again performed with great credit, especially their forwards, but the task proved beyond them.

Major Results since 1991 World Cup: 1992 – England 26, Canada 13. 1993 – Canada 15, England A 12; Canada 14, England A 19; Wales 24, Canada 26; Canada 16, Australia 43. 1994 – Canada 18, France 16; Canada 15, Wales 33.

Survivors from 1991 World Cup: Al Charron, Glen Ennis, Eddie Evans, John Graf, Stephen Gray, Dan Jackart, David Lougheed, Gord MacKinnon, Gareth Rees, Scott Stewart, Karl Svoboda.

Previous form:

1987 Pool performance:	P	W	D	L	F	A	Pts
Wales	3	3	0	0	82	31	6
Ireland	3	2	0	1	84	41	4
CANADA	3	1	0	2	65	90	2
Tonga	3	0	0	3	29	98	0

1991 Pool performance:	P	W	D	L	F	A	Pts
France	3	3	0	0	82	25	9
CANADA*	3	2	0	1	45	33	7
Romania	3	1	0	2	31	64	5
Fiji	3	0	0	3	27	63	3

* Quarter-finalists.

SOUTH AFRICA

Qualification: Hosts. **Colours:** Green and gold jerseys, white shorts

World Cup record: None. Due to the international sporting boycott, South Africa missed out on both the 1987 and 1991 tournaments. However, they will be no fresh-faced novices – witness their 27–9 second-Test backs-to-the-wall destruction of England (11.6.94), after they had already beaten France (17.10.92) and world champions Australia (31.7.93). The England win was especially significant as it ended their home jinx. It was the Springboks' first Test victory in the Republic since their return in 1992. The real acid Test of their progress comes in New Zealand this summer.

Results since 1991 World Cup (P14 W5 D1 L8): 1992 – South Africa 24, New Zealand 27; South Africa 3, Australia 26; France 15, South Africa 20; France 29, South Africa 16; England 33, South Africa 16. 1993 – South Africa 20, France 20; South Africa 17, France 18; Australia 12, South Africa 19; Australia 28, South Africa 20; Australia 19, South Africa 12; Argentina 26, South Africa 29; Argentina 23, South Africa 52. 1994 – South Africa 15, England 32; South Africa 27, England 9.

Players to watch: André Joubert (fullback), James Small (wing), Pieter Müller (centre), Hennie le Roux (outside-half), Joost van der Westhuizen (scrum-half), Balie Swart (prop), Mark Andrews (lock), François Pienaar (flanker), Tiaan Strauss (No 8).

EUROPEAN ZONE 3 QUALIFIER (see pp 448)

POOL B

Programme:

May	27	Western Samoa v Europe 2 (East London, 1300)
		England v Argentina (Durban, 1700)
	30	Western Samoa v Argentina (East London, 1230)
	31	England v Europe 2 (Durban, 1700)
Jun	4	Argentina v Europe 2 (East London, 1300)
		England v Western Samoa (Durban, 2000)

Pool pointers: England, runners-up in 1991, should top this group, having won 13 of their 17 games since the memorable Twickenham final with Australia. But we shouldn't forget that their tour to South Africa last summer yielded only three wins from eight starts. Argentina, despite their series sweep of a very weak Scotland side last summer, are no great shakes, relying greatly on goalkicker Santiago Meson – while Western Samoa have lost to New Zealand the mainstays of their side (including Frank Bunce and Steve Bachop), which proved the surprise packets of 1991 by reaching the quarter-finals. However, with the supporting cast still in place, I would expect them to repeat the feat. They beat Scotland last year, and won seven of their nine games on tour in New Zealand, scoring 455 points and conceding just 131, before thrashing Wales last summer

ENGLAND

Qualification: 1991 Runners-up. **Colours:** White jerseys with red rose, white shorts

World Cup record: 1987 – Quarter-finalists. Lost controversial opening match to Australia (6–19), but rebounded well to account for Japan (60–7) and the United States (34–6) and book a quarter-final tie against Wales. The match proved disastrous for England as they lost 3–16, although Wales's later feat of beating Australia in the third-place play-off showed England's defeat in a slightly more favourable light. **1991 – Runners-up.** Swept along on a wave of public emotion, England utilized home advantage to the full, but no one could ever say they had it easy. They opened up with defeat by holders New Zealand (12–18), which cost them the Pool, but wins over Italy (36–6) and the USA (37–9) booked their place in the last eight – in Paris. England triumphed brilliantly in the Parc des Princes (19–10), and then went to Murrayfield, where Scotland had not lost in three years, and won with Rob Andrew's late dropped goal (9–6). Thus far their progress had been forward-based, and in the build-up to the final against Australia (6–12), England's squad had the critics on their back. Come the final, they dispensed with the more conservative approach. It made for an exciting spectacle, but arguably played into the Wallabies pouch.

Results since 1991 World Cup (P17 W13 L4): 1992 – Scotland 7, England 25; England 38, Ireland 9; France 13, England 31; England 24, Wales 0; England 26, Canada 13; England 33, South Africa 16. 1993 – England 16, France 15; Wales 10, England 9; England 26, Scotland 12; Ireland 17, England 3; England 15, New Zealand 9. 1994 – Scotland 14, England 15; England 12, Ireland 13; France 14, England 18; England 15, Wales 8; South Africa 15, England 32; South Africa 27, England 9.

Survivors from 1991 World Cup: Rob Andrew; Will Carling, Jeremy Guscott, Jason Leonard, Brian Moore, Dewi Morris, David Pears, Nigel Redman, Dean Richards, Rory Underwood.

Previous form:

1987 Pool performance:	P	W	D	L	F	A	Pts
Australia	3	3	0	0	108	41	6
ENGLAND*	3	2	0	1	100	32	4
USA	3	1	0	2	39	99	2
Japan	3	0	0	3	48	123	0

* Quarter finalists

1991 Pool performance:	P	W	D	L	F	A	Pts
New Zealand	3	3	0	0	95	39	9
ENGLAND*	3	2	0	1	85	33	7
Italy	3	1	0	2	57	76	5
USA	3	0	0	3	24	113	3

* Quarter finalists

WESTERN SAMOA

Qualification: 1991 quarter-finalists. **Colours:** Blue jersey, white shorts

World Cup record: 1987 – Reserves. 1991 – Qualified by winning Asian/Pacific pool with 100-per-cent record against Japan (37–11), Tonga (12–3) and Korea (74–7). Once in the finals, they were a revellation. With the likes of Frank Bunce, Timo Tagaloa, Stephen Bachop, Apollo Perelini, Pat Lam and Peter Fatialofa, the South Sea Islanders relished the big stage – as Wales need no reminding. The Samoans triumphed in Cardiff (16–13), then gave Australia the fright of their lives (3–9), before being edged out at wet Pontypool and then trouncing Argentina (35–12) by six tries to one at Pontypridd. That booked their quarter-final berth and a trip to Murrayfield, where the dream finally ended (28–6).

Major results since 1991 World Cup: 1993 – New Zealand 35, Western Samoa 13; Western Samoa 28, Scotland XV 11. 1993 Super 10: Western Samoa 27, Queensland 19; Natal 56, Western Samoa 13; Auckland 18, Western Samoa 10; Western Samoa 30, Otago 20. 1994 – Western Samoa 34, Wales 9.

Survivors from 1991 World Cup: Andrew Aiolupo, Brian Lima, To'o Vaega, Keneti Sio, Filipo Saena, Matthew Vaea, Tu Nu'ualitia, Stan To'omalatai, Vili Alalatoa, Mark Birtwhistle, Matt Keenan, Sila Vaifale, Peter Fatialofa, Danny Kaleopa.

Previous form:

1991 Pool performance:	P	W	D	L	F	A	Pts
Australia	3	3	0	0	79	25	9
WESTERN SAMOA*	3	2	0	1	54	34	7
Wales	3	1	0	2	32	61	5
Argentina	3	0	0	3	38	83	3

* Quarter-finalists.

ARGENTINA

Qualification: Americas zone winners. **Colours:** Light blue and white hooped jersey, white shorts
World Cup record: 1987 – Sandwiched defeat of Italy (25–16) between losses to Fiji (9–28) and New Zealand (15–46). 1991 – Disappointing performance when qualifying from pressure-free American zone, in which all three competing nations were guaranteed a passage to finals. Despite twice defeating the United States (23–6 and 13–6), they failed to get the better of pool winners Canada at either of their meetings. After going down 6–15 away from home, the Pumas failed to gain revenge at home, losing 15–19. Always struggled in the final stages, losing a lively opener (19–32) to eventual champions Australia, giving Wales their only respite from a dreary campaign (7–16), and being pasted (12–35) by Western Samoa in a match in which Pedro Sporleder was dismissed. 1995 – Qualified through American Zone South, beating Chile 70–7, Paraguay 51–3 and Uruguay 19–10, before beating 1991 finalists USA over two legs in Americas Play-off.

Major results since 1991 World Cup: 1992 – Argentina 12, France 27; Argentina 9, France 33; France 20, Argentina 24. 1993 – Argentina 26, South Africa 29; Argentina 23, South Africa 52. 1994 – Argentina 70, Chile 7; Paraguay 3, Argentina 51; Argentina 19, Uruguay 10; USA 22, Argentina 28; Argentina 16, Scotland 15; Argentina 19, Scotland 17.

Survivors from 1991 World Cup: Lisandro Arbizu, Gonzalo Camardon, Ricardo le Fort, Guillermo Jos del Castillo, German Llanes, Diego Cuesta Silva, Gustavo Jorge, Martin Teran, Santiago Meson, Pedro Sporleder, Jose Santamarina.

Previous form:

1987 Pool Performance:	P	W	D	L	F	A	Pts
New Zealand	3	3	0	0	190	34	6
Fiji	3	1	0	2	56	101	2
ARGENTINA	3	1	0	2	49	90	2
Italy	3	1	0	2	40	110	2
1991 Pool performance:	**P**	**W**	**D**	**L**	**F**	**A**	**Pts**
Australia	3	3	0	0	79	25	9
Western Samoa	3	2	0	1	54	34	7
Wales	3	1	0	2	32	61	5
ARGENTINA	3	0	0	3	38	83	3

EUROPEAN ZONE RUNNERS-UP (see pp 448)

POOL C

Programme:

May	27	Europe 1 v Asia (Bloemfontein, 1500)
		New Zealand v Ireland (Johannesburg, 2000)
	31	Ireland v Asia (Bloemfontein, 1500)
		New Zealand v Europe 1 (Johannesburg, 2000)
Jun	4	New Zealand v Asia (Bloemfontein, 1500)
		Ireland v Europe 1 (Johannesburg, 1700)

Pool pointers: As New Zealand made nine changes from the side beaten by England (November '93) for the next Test, against France (June '94), it's not easy to predict how competitive the All Blacks will be in the very top tier. With respect, however, Pool C is not the very top tier. And although Ireland will cling to the memory of their Twickenham win last season, they are most unlikely to prove an immovable obstacle. Wales will probably qualify into this pool, and providing they can forget recent horrors against New Zealand (which won't be easy), could give them more of a game and (as in the 1987 competition) get the better of the Irish to nick the runners-up slot.

NEW ZEALAND

Qualification: 1991 semi-finalists. **Colours:** Black jerseys with silver fern, black shorts
World Cup record: 1987 – Webb Ellis Trophy winners. Qualified from Pool 3 with maximum points and a points difference of plus 156, courtesy of wins over Italy (70–6), Fiji (74–13) and Argentina (46–15). Never troubled by either Scotland in Christchurch quarter-final (30–3) or Wales in Brisbane semi-final (49–6). Even the French were powerless as New Zealand, steered by the unerring boot of Grant Fox (17 points in final, 126 overall), won the Auckland final 29–9. **1991 – Third place.** The tournament came just too close to the holder's sell-by date. While they swept through their group, beating England at Twickenham in front of the Queen (18–12), and USA (46–6), they were no better than workmanlike in snuffing out little Italy (31–21). Canada succumbed in a wet quarter-final (29–13), but the spectre of invincibility, prevalent in 1987, was conspicuously absent from the Blacks game. And come the semi-finals, arch-rivals Australia found them out (16–6). New Zealand took third place by beating Scotland (13–6) in Cardiff.

Results since 1991 World Cup (P18 W11 L7): 1992 – New Zealand 14, World XV 28; New Zealand 54, World XV 26; New Zealand 26, World XV 15; New Zealand 24, Ireland 21; New Zealand 59, Ireland 6; Australia 16, New Zealand 15; Australia 19, New Zealand 17; Australia 23, New Zealand 26; South Africa 24, New Zealand 27. 1993 – New Zealand 20, British Lions 18; New Zealand 7, British Lions 20; New Zealand 30, British Lions 13; New Zealand 25, Australia 10; New Zealand 35, Western Samoa 13; Scotland 15, New Zealand 51; England 15, New Zealand 9. 1994 – New Zealand 8, France 22; N Zealand 20, France 23.

Survivors from 1991: Zinzan Brooke, Sean Fitzpatrick, Steve Gordon, Paul Henderson, Ian Jones, Michael Jones, John Kirwan, Walter Little, Jon Preston, Graham Purvis, John Timu.

Previous form:

1987 Pool performance:	P	W	D	L	F	A	Pts
NEW ZEALAND*	3	3	0	0	190	34	6
Fiji	3	1	0	2	56	101	2
Argentina	3	1	0	2	49	90	2
Italy	3	1	0	2	40	110	2

* Winners.

1991 Pool performance:	P	W	D	L	F	A	Pts
NEW ZEALAND*	3	3	0	0	95	39	9
England	3	2	0	1	85	33	7
Italy	3	1	0	2	57	76	5
USA	3	0	0	3	24	113	3

* Third place.

IRELAND

Qualification: Automatic. **Colours:** Green jerseys, white shorts
World Cup record: 1987 – Quarter-finalists. Having lost 6–13 to Wales in their opening game, Ireland collected wins over Canada (46–19) and Tonga (32–9) to qualify as runner-up. That earned them the doubtful privilege of facing Australia in Sydney for a place in the semi-finals; Ireland lost 33–15. **1991 –Quarter-finalists.** So close and yet so far. Ireland had to make do with the runners-up slot in their qualifying pool: Brian Robinson's record four-try haul accounted for Zimbabwe (55–11), and doughty Japan hung tough before losing out (32–16), but Scotland won an epic at Murrayfield (24–15). So the men in green headed home to Dublin for a quarter-final against Australia, and amazingly, with no time left on the clock, led 18–15 – only for Michael Lynagh's late try to break their hearts.

Results since 1991 World Cup (P18 W4 D1 L13): 1992 – Ireland 15, Wales 16; England 38, Ireland 9; Ireland 10, Scotland 18; France 44, Ireland 12; New Zealand 24, Ireland 21; New Zealand 59, Ireland 6; Ireland 17, Australia 42. 1993 – Scotland 15, Ireland 3; Ireland 6, France 21; Wales 14, Ireland 19; Ireland 17, England 3; Ireland 25, Romania 3. 1994 – France 35, Ireland 15; Ireland 15, Wales 17; England 12, Ireland 13; Ireland 6, Scotland 6; Australia 33, Ireland 15; Australia 32, Ireland 18.

Survivors from 1991 World Cup: Vinnie Cunningham, Phil Danaher, John Fitzgerald, Neil Francis, Mick Galwey, Simon Geoghegan, Garrett Halpin, Terry Kingston, Pat O'Hara, Nick Popplewell, Brian Robinson, Jim Staples.

Previous form:

1987 Pool performance:	P	W	D	L	F	A	Pts
Wales	3	3	0	0	82	31	6
IRELAND*	3	2	0	1	84	41	4
Canada	3	1	0	2	65	90	2
Tonga	3	0	0	3	29	98	0

* Quarter-finalists.

1991 Pool performance:	P	W	D	L	F	A	Pts
Scotland	3	3	0	0	122	36	9
IRELAND*	3	2	0	1	102	51	7
Japan	3	1	0	2	77	87	5
Zimbabwe	3	0	0	3	31	158	3

* Quarter-finalists.

EUROPEAN ZONE WINNERS (see pp 448)
ASIAN ZONE WINNERS (see pp 451)

POOL D

Programme:

May	26	Scotland v Ivory Coast (Rustenburg, 1600)
		France v Tonga (Pretoria, 1800)
May	30	France v Ivory Coast (Rustenburg, 1800)
		Scotland v Tonga (Pretoria, 2000)
Jun	3	Tonga v Ivory Coast (Potchefstroom, 1300)
		Scotland v France (Pretoria, 1700)

SCOTLAND

Qualification: 1991 Semi-finalist. **Colours:** Navy blue jerseys, white shorts

World Cup record: 1987 – Quarter-finalists. To lose the inspirational John Rutherford in the opening Pool match against France and to be paired with New Zealand in the quarter-finals were two factors which conspired against the Scots. However, they had the satisfaction of sharing a 20–20 draw with the French, who had just won a splendid Grand Slam and were en route for the World Cup final. Comprehensive wins over Zimbabwe (60–21) and Romania (55–28) ensured that the Scots qualified unbeaten, but they lost that tag to the All Blacks next time out (30–3). **1991 – Fourth place.** Enjoyed themselves immensely at Fortress Murrayfield where they played every game up until the final, which they missed altogether after England's late drama semi-final win had silenced Edinburgh (9–6). Previously, the Scots had impressed in coming through their pool unblemished, routing Japan (47–9) and Zimbabwe (51–12) before edging past Ireland in a titanic forward contest (24–15). Astute tactics accounted for Western Samoa (28–6) in a command quarter-final performance but then came England ... and the Scots had to make do with fourth place, beaten (13–6) by New Zealand in the third place play-off.

Results since 1991 World Cup (P20 W6 D1 L13): 1992 – Scotland 7, England 25; Ireland 10, Scotland 18; Scotland 10, France 6; Wales 15, Scotland 12; Australia 27, Scotland 12; Australia 37, Scotland 13. 1993 – Scotland 15, Ireland 3; France 11, Scotland 3; Scotland 20, Wales 0; England 26, Scotland 12; Fiji 10, Scotland XV 21; Tonga 5, Scotland XV 23; Western Samoa 28, Scotland XV 11; Scotland 15, New Zealand 51. 1994 – Wales 29, Scotland 6; Scotland 14, England 15; Ireland 6, Scotland 6; Scotland 12, France 20; Argentina 16, Scotland 15; Argentina 19, Scotland 17.

Survivors from 1991: Gary Armstrong, Paul Burnell, Craig Chalmers, Damian Cronin, Gavin Hastings, Scott Hastings, Kenny Milne, Graham Shiel, Tony Stanger, Alan Watt, Doddie Weir, Doug Wyllie.

Previous form:

1987 Pool performance:	P	W	D	L	F	A	Pts
France	3	2	1	0	145	44	5
SCOTLAND*	3	2	1	0	135	69	5
Romania	3	1	0	2	61	130	2
Zimbabwe	3	0	0	3	53	151	0

* Quarter-finalists.

1991 Pool performance:	P	W	D	L	F	A	Pts
SCOTLAND*	3	3	0	0	122	36	9

Ireland	3	2	0	1	102	51	7
Japan	3	1	0	2	77	87	5
Zimbabwe	3	0	0	3	31	158	3

* Fourth place.

FRANCE

Qualification: 1991 quarter-finalist. **Colours:** Blue jerseys, white shorts

World Cup record: 1987 – **Runners-up.** Unbeaten in Pool 4 although held to a draw by Scotland (20–20) in opening game. Progressed after beating Romania (55–12) and Zimbabwe (70–12). Better points difference assured them of avoiding New Zealand until final, whereas Scotland were obliged to play them in last eight. Beat Fiji (31–16) quarter-finals before squeezing past Australia 30–24 in Sydney semi-final which many believed to be the greatest ever international. Serge Blanco's last minute try pipped the hosts to the final berth. Against New Zealand, who had been given a far easier semi-final ride by Wales, France were unable to rescale the heights attained against Australia, and Grant Fox (17 points) condemned France to the runners-up spot. **1991 – Quarter Finalists.** Unable to call upon the magic of '87, France stuttered to the quarter-finals, beating Romania (30–3) and Fiji (33–9) easily enough but then struggling to subdue Canada (19–13). Their reward for topping the pool was England in Paris (far from a favourite French fixture these days). Violence on (Blanco and Eric Champ on Nigel Heslop) and off the field (coach Daniel Dubroca on Kiwi referee David Bishop in the tunnel afterwards) marred a game which France lost (10–19).

Results since 1991 World Cup (P27 W17 D1 L9): 1992 – Wales 9, France 12; France 13, England 31; Scotland 10, France 6; France 44, Ireland 12; France 25, Romania 6; Argentina 12, France 27; Argentina 9, France 33; France 15, South Africa 20; France 36; France 20, Argentina 24. 1993 – England 16, France 15; France 11, Scotland 3; Ireland 6, France 21; France 26, Wales 10; Romania 20, France 37; South Africa 20, France 20; South Africa 17, France 18; France 51, Romania 0; France 16, Australia 13; France 3, Australia 24. 1994 – France 35, Ireland 15; Wales 24, France 15; France 14, England 18; Scotland 12, France 20; Canada 18, France 16, New Zealand 8, France 22; New Zealand 20, France 23.

Survivors from 1991 World Cup: Louis Armary, Abdel Benazzi, Philippe Benetton, Laurent Cabannes, Marc Cecillon, Fabien Galthie, Thierry Lacroix, Franck Mesnel, Olivier Roumat, Jean-Luc Sadourny, Philippe Saint-André, Philippe Sella.

Previous form:

1987 Pool performance:	P	W	D	L	F	A	Pts
FRANCE*	3	2	1	0	145	44	5
Scotland	3	2	1	0	135	69	5
Romania	3	1	0	2	61	130	2
Zimbabwe	3	0	0	3	53	151	0

* Finalists.

1991 Pool performance:	P	W	D	L	F	A	Pts
FRANCE*	3	3	0	0	82	25	9
Canada	3	2	0	1	45	33	7
Romania	3	1	0	2	31	64	5
Fiji	3	0	0	3	27	63	3

* Quarter-finalists.

TONGA

Qualification: Pacific Zone winners.

World Cup record: 1987 –Failed to win a match in inaugural tournament after being thumped 37–4 by weakest rival Canada in the Pool 2 opener at Napier. Put up a better display against Wales, who would eventually finish the event third, restricting the margin of defeat to 13 points (16–29), but bade farewell with a 9–32 loss at the hands of Ireland. 1991 – Obliged to qualify through the Asia/Pacific zone, Tonga failed, finishing behind winners Western Samoa (lost 3–12) and Japan (lost 16–28). A 45–22 defeat of Korea was of little consolation. 1995 – Made no mistake this time, narrowly topping the two-team Pacific Zone on points difference from 1991 finalists Fiji, winning 24–11 in Suva (12.6.93) and losing the return 15–10 in Nuku'Alofa (17.6.93).

Notable results since 1991 World Cup: 1993 – Australia 52, Tonga 14 (Aussies gaining revenge for catastrophic 16–11 loss to Tongans at Ballymore in 1973)

Previous form:

1987 Pool performance:	P	W	D	L	F	A	Pts
Wales	3	3	0	0	82	31	6
Ireland	3	2	0	1	84	41	4
Canada	3	1	0	2	65	90	2
TONGA*	3	0	0	3	29	98	0

* Failed to qualify.

IVORY COAST

Qualification: African Zone winners.
World Cup record: 1987 – Did not enter. **1991** – Did not qualify. **1995** – Qualifed as shock African Zone winners. Progressed into final qualifying tournament courtesy of a 19–16 defeat of Tunisia, followed by a 15–3 win over Morocco. The Moroccans gained revenge on the Ivorians in Casablanca, rebounding 17–9, but the Ivory Coast refused to be affected by the setback. Instead, they surprised favourites Namibia, scraping home 13–12 to punish an opponent who had over-confidently rested a number of its first-choice players and blooded six new caps. 1991 finalists Zimbabwe were next to be upset (17–10) with the Ivorians turning in an ultra-tactically aware display (winning by a goal and two tries to a goal and a penalty). In a thrilling tournament, Namibia would have gone through to the finals had not Morocco recovered a 16–0 deficit to dramatically draw 16–16 and instead allow the Ivory Coast to become the first ever qualifiers from French Africa.

EUROPEAN QUALIFIERS
(winners into Pool C; runners-up Pool B; third Pool A)

ITALY

Qualification: European (Central) zone winners. **Colours:** Blue shirts, white shorts
World Cup record: 1987 – After being crushed by New Zealand (6–70) in Pool opener, Italy improved markedly against Argentina (lost 16–25) before scoring one of the tournament's biggest upsets by beating Fiji (18–15). **1991** – Qualified by winning European pool (played in Italy) with 100-per-cent record against Spain (30–6), Netherlands (24–11) and Romania (29–21). Placed in tough pool alongside holders New Zealand and England, but covered themselves in credit by only losing narrowly (21–31) to the All Blacks. Marcello Cuttitta's try at Twickenham couldn't prevent them losing to their hosts (6–36), but they did have the satisfaction of beating the USA convincingly at Otley (30–9). **1995** – Qualified for the finals by way of European (Central) Zone, which they topped after registering a World Cup record win against the Czech Republic (104–8) and then trouncing the Netherlands (63–9).

Notable results since 1991 World Cup: 1992 – Wales XV 43, Italy 12. 1993 – Italy 18, Scotland A 15. 1994 – Italy 104, Czech Republic 8; Italy 63, Netherlands 9, Australia 23, Italy 20; Australia 20, Italy 7.

Survivors from 1991 World Cup: Stefano Barba, Massimo Bonomi, Alessandro Bottacchiara, Carlo Checchinato, Giambattista Croci, Marcello Cuttitta, Massimo Cuttitta, Diego Dominguez, Ivan Francescato, Giovanni Grespan, Francesco Pietrosanti, Giancarlo Pivetta, Franco Properzi-Curti, Roberto Saetti, Luigi Troiani, Paolo Vaccari, Edgardo Venturi.

Previous form:

1987 Pool performance:	P	W	D	L	F	A	Pts
New Zealand	3	3	0	0	190	34	6
Fiji	3	1	0	2	56	101	2
Argentina	3	1	0	2	49	90	2
ITALY*	3	1	0	2	40	110	2

* Failed to qualify.

1991 Pool performance:	P	W	D	L	F	A	Pts
New Zealand	3	3	0	0	95	39	9
England	3	2	0	1	85	33	7
ITALY*	3	1	0	2	57	76	5
USA	3	0	0	3	24	113	3

* Failed to qualify.

ROMANIA

Qualification: European (Eastern) zone runners-up. **Colours:** Yellow jerseys, blue shorts, red socks
World Cup record: 1987 – Struggled to beat Zimbabwe (21–20) in opening match, and not allowed to find rhythm thereafter, losing heavily to both France (12–55) and Scotland (28–55). **1991** – Qualified as

runners-up in European zone, beating Spain (19–6) and Netherlands (45–7), but going down to Italy (21–29). Never really got going in France, where they were based for the finals, after being pummelled (30–3) by the host nation first time up. Then lost to surprise packets Canada (11–19) before squeezing past Fiji (15–17). It was too little, too late. 1995 – Topped the European (Eastern) Zone after beating Germany (60–6) and Russia (30–0).

Notable results since 1991 World Cup: 1992 – France 25, Romania 6. 1993 – Romania 20, France 37; France 51, Romania 0; Ireland 25, Romania 3. 1994 – Romania 60, Germany 0; Romania 30, Russia 0.

Survivors from 1991 World Cup: Constantin Cojocariu, Lucian Colceriu, Haralambie Dumitras, Marian Dumitru, Mihai Foca, Nicolae Fulina, Cristian Gheorghe, Gheorghe Ion, Gheorghe Leonte, Nicusor Marin, Gabriel Vlad.

Previous form:

1987 Pool performance:	P	W	D	L	F	A	Pts
France	3	2	1	0	145	44	5
Scotland	3	2	1	0	135	69	5
ROMANIA*	3	1	0	2	61	130	2
Zimbabwe	3	0	0	3	53	151	0

* Failed to qualify.

1991 Pool performance:	P	W	D	L	F	A	Pts
France	3	3	0	0	82	25	9
Canada	3	2	0	1	45	33	7
ROMANIA*	3	1	0	2	31	64	5
Fiji	3	0	0	3	27	63	3

* Failed to qualify.

WALES

Qualification: European (Western) Zone winners

World Cup record: 1987 – Third place. Wales headed Down Under as joint holders (with England) of the Wooden Spoon, but produced a memorable month of performances to claim the Bronze. They were made to work for their place in the second stage, winning Pool 2 only after close matches against Ireland (won 13–6) and Tonga (won 29–16) and a less taxing 46–19 win over Canada, thanks largely to four tries from Ieuan Evans. However, that achieved, Wales were good value for their 16–3 quarter-final triumph over a sub-par England. The 49–6 beating handed out by New Zealand in the semi-final looked to have shattered Wales, but to their enormous credit they regrouped and defeated Australia 22–21 in a thrilling third-place play-off in which Paul Thorburn converted from the touchline in the final minute. **1991** – A campaign to forget, as unknown Western Samoa and Australia both brought down Wales's colours in Cardiff, winning 16–13 and 38–3 respectively. Sandwiched between these disappointments was a 16–7 win over Argentina, but it was not enough to save Wales's bacon. **1995** – Born-again Wales (Five Nations champions) cruised through the 'humiliating' qualifying progress, trouncing Portugal in Lisbon (102–11) and Spain in Madrid (54–0).

Results since 1991 World Cup (P25 W16 L9): 1992 – Ireland 15, Wales 16; Wales 9, France 12; England 24, Wales 0; Wales 15, Scotland 12; Wales 43, Italy 12; Wales 6, Australia 23. 1993 – Wales 10, England 9; Scotland 20, Wales 0; Wales 14, Ireland 19; France 26, Wales 10; Zimbabwe 14, Wales 35; Zimbabwe 13, Wales 42; Namibia 23, Wales 38; Wales 55, Japan 5; Wales 24, Canada 26. 1994 – Wales 29, Scotland 6; Ireland 15, Wales 17; Wales 24, France 15; England 15, Wales 8; Portugal 11, Wales 102; Spain 0, Wales 54; Canada 15, Wales 33; Fiji 8, Wales 23; Tonga 9, Wales 18; Western Samoa 34, Wales 9.

Survivors from 1991 World Cup: Paul Arnold, Anthony Clement, Richie Collins, Adrian Davies, Phil Davies, Ieuan Evans, Mike Hall, Garin Jenkins, Robert Jones, Emyr Lewis, Mike Rayer, Hugh Williams-Jones.

Previous form:

1987 Pool performance:	P	W	D	L	F	A	Pts
WALES*	3	3	0	0	82	31	6
Ireland	3	2	0	1	84	41	4
Canada	3	1	0	2	65	90	2
Tonga	3	0	0	3	29	98	0

* Third place.

1991 Pool performance:	P	W	D	L	F	A	Pts
Australia	3	3	0	0	79	25	9
Western Samoa	3	2	0	1	54	34	7
WALES*	3	1	0	2	32	61	5
Argentina	3	0	0	3	38	83	3

* Failed to qualify.

ASIAN QUALIFIER
(into Pool C):

To be decided – candidates:
Republic of China, Hong Kong, Korean RU, Japan, Malaysia, Singapore, Sri Lanka, Thailand

WORLD CUP RECORDS

Most points in World Cup rugby:
150	G Fox	(New Zealand)
148	M Lynagh	(Australia)
123	G Hastings	(Scotland)
99	J Webb	(England)

Most points in single tournament:
126	G Fox	(New Zealand, 1987)
82	M Lynagh	(Australia, 1987)
68	R Keyes	(Ireland, 1991)
66	M Lynagh	(Australia, 1991)

Most points in a match:
74   New Zealand v Fiji (1987)

Most points in a match (individual):
30   D Camberabero   (France v Zimbabwe, 1987)

Most tries in single tournament:
6	C Green	(New Zealand, 1987)
	J Kirwan	(New Zealand, 1987)
	D Campese	(Australia, 1991)
	J-B Lafond	(France, 1991)

Most tries in a single match:
13   France v Zimbabwe (1987)

Most tries in a single match (individual):
4	I Evans	(Wales v Canada, 1987)
	C Green	(New Zealand v Fiji, 1987)
	J Gallacher	(New Zealand v Fiji, 1987)

Most conversions in single tournament:
30   G Fox   (New Zealand, 1987)

Most conversions in single match:
10   New Zealand v Fiji (1987)

Most conversions in single match (individual):
10   G Fox   (New Zealand v Fiji, 1987)

Most penalty goals in single tournament:
21   G Fox   (New Zealand, 1987)

Most penalty goals in match:
6   New Zealand   (v Scotland/Argentina)

Most penalty goals in match (individual):
6   G Fox   (New Zealand v Scotland/Argentina)

Most dropped goals in single tournament:
3   J Davies   (Wales, 1987)

Most dropped goals in a match (team):
3   Fiji v Romania (1991)

Most dropped goals in a match (individual):
2	J Davies	(Wales v Ireland, 1987)
	L Arbizu	(Argentina v Australia, 1991)
	T Rabaka	(Fiji v Romania, 1991)

THE YEAR IN REVIEW

SOUTH AFRICA TO AUSTRALIA
July-August 1993: P12 W9 D0 L3 F527 A147

South Africa stun the cock-sure world champions by capturing the first leg of the three-Test series, but Australia rally to overcome the deficit. However, all is not milk and honey. David Campese accuses the Springboks of unneccesarily violent play in the first two Tests. Referring to the middle match, in which South African winger James Small is sent off for twice abusing English referee Ed Morrison during Australia's 28-20 win (only their third in 11 home meetings with SA), Campo says scrum-half Robert du Preez and hooker Uli Schmidt might also have walked. 'Some of the things that went on out there would have got eight weeks' suspension in Rugby League', he claims, adding: 'If players were sent off more often, it would stop this sort of thing straight away'. Small, the first Springbok ever to be sent off, receives only a one-match ban, which means that, thanks to an existing midweek engagement (one in which he would probably not have otherwise played), he is available for the third Test. The Natal speedster, who made a first Test-winning, two-try contribution as Australia were downed 19-12 under the Sydney floodlights, responds with another touchdown in the decider, but it is not enough to deny victory to the home side, who triumph 19-12. Australia could be satisfied enough, considering the absence of Michael Lynagh, Willie Ofahengaue and John Eales, but South African coach Ian McIntosh at least had the solace of a 8–4 try count in his side's favour: 'It shows that we are on the right tracks. When we get the first-phase ball we will be hard to beat'.

PARTY: J Allan (Natal – 1,3,5,6,7,9,11); K Andrews (Western Province – 2,3,5,6,8,9,10,12); S Atherton (Natal – 9,11); R du Preez (Natal – 2,3,6,8,10,12); H Fuls (Eastern Province – 1,4,6,8,10,12); W Hills (Northern Transvaal – 2,4,6); H Honiball (Natal – 1,2,3,4,5,7,9,11,12); A Joubert (Natal – 9,11,12); R Kruger (Free State – 2,3,5,7,9,11); H le Roux (Transvaal – 2,4,5,7,9,11); T Linee (Western Province – 3,5,7,9,11); D Lotter (Transvaal – 2,4,6,7,8,10,11); I Macdonald (Transvaal – 1,3,5,7,9,11); P Müller (Natal – 2,4,6,8,10,12); J Olivier (Northern Transvaal – 2,4,6,8,10,12); D Oosthuysen (Northern Transvaal – 2,3,5,7,9,11); F Pienaar (Transvaal, capt – 1*,4*,6*,8*,10*,12*); H Reece-Edwards (Natal – 1,2,5,7,8,10); A Richter (Northern Transvaal – 1,3*,5*,7*,8,9*,11*); H Rodgers (Transvaal – 9,11); U Schmidt (Transvaal – 2,4,6,8,10,12); J Small (Natal – 1,4,6,8,10,12); J Stransky (Natal – 1,3,6,8,10,12); T Strauss (Western Province – 2*,4,6,8,10,12); H Strydom (Transvaal – 2,4,6,8,10,12); J Styger (Free State – 1,3,5,7,8,9,11,12); B Swart (Transvaal – 1,4,6,7,8,9,10,12); J van der Westhuizen (Northern Transvaal – 1,4,5,7,9,11); T van Rensburg (Transvaal – 3,4,6); R Visagie (Natal – 2,3,5,7); N Wegner (Western Province – 2,3,5,7,9,11); K Wiese (Transvaal – 1,3,5,7,9,11); C Williams (Western Province – 1,2,3,5,7,9,11). Manager: J Engelbrecht. Coach: I McIntosh. Assistant coach: G Pienaar.

Results: (1) Western Australia 8, Springboks 71 (Perth, 14 July); (2) South Australia 3, Springboks 90 (Adelaide, 17 July); (3) Victoria 3, Springboks 78 (Melbourne, 21 July); (4) New South Wales 29, Springboks 28 (Sydney, 24 July); (5) NSW Country 7, Springboks 41 (Orange, 27 July); (6) first Test: Australia 12, South Africa 19 (Sydney, 31 July); (7) ACT 10, Springboks 57 (Canberra, 4 August); (8) Queensland 3, Springboks 17 (Brisbane, 8 August); (9) Queensland Country 5, Springboks 65 (Mackay, 11 August); (10) second Test: Australia 28, South Africa 20 (Brisbane, 14 August); (11) Sydney 20, Springboks 31 (Penrith, 18 August); (12) third Test: Australia 19, South Africa 12 (Sydney, 21 August).

Scorers (527 – 75t,49c,18p): Reece-Edwards 73 (3t,17c,8p), Stransky 58 (1t,22c,3p), van der Westhuizen 55 (11t), Kruger 45 (9t), du Preez 40 (8t), Williams 35 (7t), Joubert 30 (2t,4c,4p), Small 25 (5t), Van Rensburg 22 (1t,4c,3p), Macdonald 20 (4t), Richter 20 (4t), Allan 15 (3t), Olivier 15 (3t), Oosthuysen 15 (3t), Le Roux 14 (2t,2c), Muller 10 (2t), Linee 5 (1t), Lotter 5 (1t), Pienaar 5 (1t), Schmidt 5 (1t), Strauss 5 (1t), Visagie 5 (1t), Wiese 5 (1t).

Western Australia 8, Springboks 71
Perth, 14 July 1993

Western Australia: R Smith; P Morton, D Hamilton, S Bunce, E Saaga; T Fearn, M Ryburn; S Porter,

A Box, M Hudson, G Thompson, T Thomas, G Thomas, P Roberts (capt), H Nguruve.
Scorers – *Try:* Hamilton. *Penalty goal:* Fearn.

Springboks: Reece-Edwards; Small, Fuls, Honiball, Williams; Stransky, van der Westhuizen; Styger, Allan, Swart, Wiese, Wegner, Pienaar (capt), Macdonald, Richter.
Scorers – Tries: van der Westhuizen 4, Small 2, Macdonald 2, Williams, Wiese, Richter. *Conversions:* Stransky 8.

Referee: W Erickson.

South Australian XV 3, Springboks 90
Adelaide, 17 July 1993

South Australia: A Lawson; R Sadler, S Elliott, R Tuhou, S Fonua; D Emtage, M Catchpole; W Matthews, N Edwards, M Florey, N Porter, J Hyland, D Rees (capt), B Pillinger, P Jackson.
Scorer – *Penalty goal:* Emtage.

Springboks: Reece-Edwards; Olivier, Honiball, Müller, Oosthuizen; le Roux (Williams), du Preez; Hills, Schmidt, Andrews, Strydom, Visagie, Kruger, Lotter, Strauss (capt).
Scorers – *Tries:* du Preez 4, Kruger 2, Reece-Edwards, Visagie, Lotter, Strauss, Olivier, Müller, Oosthuizen, le Roux. *Conversions:* Reece-Edwards 10.

Referee: S Young.

Victoria 3, Springboks 78
Melbourne, 21 July 1993

Victoria: P Gascoigne; T Hogan, J Goodman, R Saunders, C MacGregor; P Hanara, J Dix; N Raikuna, C Smith, M L'Hullier, S Hughes, C Clyng, D Williams (capt), C Freighter, N Potae.
Scorer – *Penalty goal:* Goodman.

Springboks: van Rensburg; Oosthuizen, Honiball, Linee, Williams; Stransky, du Preez; Andrews, Allan, Styger, Visagie, Wiese, Kruger, Macdonald, Richter (capt).
Scorers – Tries: du Preez 4, Williams 3, Richter 2, Kruger 2, Allan. *Conversions:* Stransky 9.

Referee: J Allan.

New South Wales 29, Springboks 28
Sydney, 24 July 1993

NSW: T Kelaher; D Campese, M Burke, R Tombs, A Murdoch; S Bowen, N Farr-Jones (S Payne); T Daly, P Kearns (capt), E McKenzie, T Kava, W Waugh, M Brial, T Dempsey, T Gavin.
Scorers – *Tries:* Murdoch 2, Tombs, Kelaher. *Conversions:* Kelaher 3. *Penalty goal:* Kelaher.

Springboks: van Rensburg; Small, Müller (Honiball), Fuls, Olivier; le Roux, van der Westhuizen; Hills, Schmidt, Swart, Strydom, Wegner, Pienaar (capt), Lotter, Strauss.
Scorers – *Tries:* le Roux, van der Westhuizen, van Rensburg. *Conversions:* van Rensburg 2. *Penalty goals:* van Rensburg 3.

Referee: B Leask.

NSW Country 7, Springboks 41
Orange, 27 July 1993

NSW Country: D Munday; M Crawford, P O'Brien, C Coffey, D Earp; J Trevaskis, S Merrick; M Prior, J Ives, K Whiteman, N Cobcroft, J Nowland, A McCalman (capt), J Langford, J Fenwicke.
Scorers – *Try:* O'Brien. *Conversion:* Trevaskis.

Springboks: Reece-Edwards; Oosthuizen, Honiball, Linee, Williams; le Roux, van der Westhuizen; Andrews, Allan, Styger, Wiese, Visagie, Macdonald, Kruger, Richter (capt).
Scorers – *Tries:* Reece-Edwards 2, Oosthuizen, van der Westhuizen, Kruger. *Conversions:* Reece-Edwards 2. *Penalty goals:* Reece-Edwards 4.

Referee: K O'Halloran.

Australia (9) 12, South Africa (14) 19
first Test: Sydney, 31 July 1993

Australia: M Roebuck (NSW); D Smith (Queensland), J Little (Queensland), T Horan (Queensland), D Campese (NSW); S Bowen⁺ (NSW), N Farr-Jones (NSW); A Daly (NSW), P Kearns (NSW), E McKenzie (capt, NSW), R McCall (Queensland), W Waugh (NSW), D Wilson (Queensland), T Gavin (NSW).
Scorer – *Penalty goals:* Roebuck 4.

South Africa: van Rensburg; Small, Müller, Fuls, Olivier; Stransky, du Preez; Hills, Schmidt, Swart, Wegner, Strydom, Pienaar (capt), Lotter, Strauss.
Scorers – *Tries:* Small 2, Müller. *Conversions:* van Rensburg 2.

Referee: L McLachlan (New Zealand). **Attendance:** 41,000.
Series score: Played 30, Australia 8, South Africa 22, Drawn 0.

Australian Capital Territory 10, Springboks 57
Canberra, 4 August 1993

ACT: A Apps; D Grimmond, J Swan (G Didier), P Cornish, V Crowe; R Hayes, G Gregan; A Hayes, J Taylor (capt), C Hutchinson (D McLachlan), A Harley, M McGuiness, J Ross, P Docherty, G Emmery.
Scorers – *Try:* Hayes. *Conversion:* Cornish. *Penalty goal:* Cornish.

Springboks: Reece-Edwards; Oosthuizen, Honiball, Linee, Williams; le Roux, van der Westhuizen; Andrews, Allan, Styger, Wiese, Visagie, Macdonald, Kruger, Richter (capt).
Scorers – *Tries:* van der Westhuizen 2, Williams 2, Allen, Kruger, Richter. *Conversions:* Reece-Edwards 5. *Penalty goals:* Reece-Edwards 4.

Referee: A Cole.

Queensland 3, Springboks 17
Brisbane, 8 August 1993

Queensland: M Pini (A Herbert); D Smith, J Little, T Horan, P Carozza (B Fielke); P Howard, P Slattery (capt); M Ryan, D Nucifora, D Crowley, R McCall, G Morgan, D Wilson, I Tabua (R Korst), S Scott-Young.
Scorer – *Penalty goal:* Pini.

Springboks: Reece-Edwards; Small, Müller, Fuls, Olivier; Stransky, du Preez; Andrews, Schmidt, Styger (Swart), Strydom, Wegner, Pienaar (capt) (Richter), Lotter, Strauss.
Scorers – *Tries:* Schmidt, Olivier. *Conversions:* Stransky 2. *Penalty goal:* Stransky.

Referee: P Marshall.

Queensland Country 5, Springboks 63
Mackay, 11 August 1993

Queensland Country: R Leeson; B Lea, M Hood, R Constable, B Fielke; M Catchpole, A Gold; G Brown, M Holt, R Blackley, R Korst, S Thorn, G Hislop, M Murray, M Cockbain.
Scorer – *Try:* Constable.

Springboks: Joubert; Oosthuizen, Honiball, Linee, Williams; le Roux, van der Westhuizen; Swart (Andrews), Allan, Rodgers, Wiese, Atherton, Macdonald, Kruger, Richter (capt).
Scorers – *Tries:* Joubert 2, van der Westhuizen 2, Kruger 2, Allan 2, Williams, Oosthuizen, Macdonald. *Conversions:* Joubert 2, le Roux 2.

Referee: B Fienberg.

Australia (10) 28, South Africa (10) 20
second Test: Brisbane, 14 August 1993

Australia: M Roebuck (NSW); D Smith (Queensland), J Little (Queensland), T Horan (Queensland), D Campese (NSW); S Bowen (NSW), N Farr-Jones (NSW); A Daly (NSW), P Kearns (NSW), E McKenzie (capt, NSW), R McCall (Queensland), I Tabua⁺ (Queensland), D Wilson (Queensland), T Gavin (NSW). *Repl:* A Herbert (Queensland) for Little, 35 mins.
Scorers – *Tries:* Little 2, Horan. *Conversions:* Roebuck 2. *Penalty goals:* Roebuck 3.

South Africa: Reece-Edwards; Small, Müller, Fuls, Olivier; Stransky, du Preez; Andrews, Schmidt, Swart, Wegner, Strydom, Pienaar (capt), Lotter, Strauss. Sent off: Small (70 minutes, verbal abuse).
Scorers – *Tries:* Olivier, Stransky. *Conversions:* Stransky 2. *Penalty goals:* Stransky 2.

Referee: E Morrison (England). **Attendance:** 28,878.
Series score: Played 31, Australia 9, South Africa 22.

Sydney 20, Springboks 31
Penrith, 18 August 1993

Sydney: M Burke (R Muik); D Junee, A Murdoch, R Tombs (capt), P Jorgensen; T Wallace, A Ekert; M Hartill, M Bell, A Blades, W Waugh, J Hearn, S Talbot, T Dempsey, M Guberina.
Scorers – *Tries:* Murdoch, Wallace, Ekert. *Conversion:* Wallace. *Penalty goal:* Burke.

Springboks: Joubert; Oosthuizen, Honiball, Linee, Williams; le Roux, van der Westhuizen; Styger, Allan, Rodgers, Wiese (Macdonald), Atherton, Lotter, Kruger, Richter (capt).
Scorers – *Tries:* Linee, van der Westhuizen, Macdonald. *Conversions:* Joubert 2. *Penalty goals:* Joubert 4.

Referee: M Keogh.

Australia (6) 19, South Africa (5) 12
third Test: Sydney, 21 August 1993

Australia: M Roebuck (NSW); D Smith (Queensland), J Little (Queensland), T Horan (Queensland), D Campese (NSW); S Bowen (NSW), N Farr-Jones (NSW); A Daly (NSW), P Kearns (NSW), E McKenzie (capt, NSW), R McCall (Queensland), I Tabua (Queensland), D Wilson (Queensland), T Gavin (NSW). Repl: M Burke* (NSW) for Smith, 38 mins.
Scorers – *Try:* Horan. *Conversion:* Roebuck. *Penalty goals:* Roebuck 4.

South Africa: Joubert; Small, Müller, Fuls, Olivier; Stransky, du Preez; Andrews, Schmidt, Swart, Wegner, Strydom, Pienaar (capt), Macdonald, Strauss. Repl: Styger for Swart, 45 mins; Honiball for Müller, 48 mins.
Scorers – *Tries:* Small, Pienaar. *Conversion:* Stransky.

Referee: E Morrison (England) **Attendance:** 41,877.
Series score: Played 32, Australia 10, South Africa 22.

IRELAND DEVELOPMENT SQUAD TO ZIMBABWE, NAMIBIA AND SOUTH AFRICA
July-August 1993: P7 W6 D0 L1 F219 A103 (no caps awarded)

PARTY: A Adair (Instonians), P Burke (London Irish), C Clarke (Terenure College), M Corcoran (London Irish), B Cronin (Garryowen), B Cusack (Bective Rangers), D Dooley (Saracens), G Fulcher (Cork Constitution), B Glennon (Lansdowne), I Gray (QUB), N Hogan (Terenure College), P Hogan (Garryowen), D Humphreys (QUB), H Hurley (Old Wesley), G Longwell (QUB), M McCall (Bangor), A McKeen (Lansdowne), K McKeen (Instonians), A Matchett (Ballymena), W Mulcahy (Skerries), C O'Shea (Lansdowne), A O'Sullivan (Old Crescent), K Potts (St Mary's College, capt), P Soden (Cork Constitution), L Toland (Old Crescent), P Wallace (UCC), B Walsh (Cork Constitution), A White (St Mary's College), R Wilson (QUB), N Woods (Blackrock College).

Fixtures: (1) Mashonaland 10, Irish XV 22 (Harare, 21 July); (2) Zimbabwe A 6, Irish XV 20 (Harare, 24 July); (3) Namibia B 21, Irish XV 38 (Windhoek, 28 July); (4) Namibia A 33, Irish XV 19 (Windhoek, 31 July); (5) South African Rural Development XV 18, Irish XV 23 (Nelspruit, 4 August); (6) South African Central Provinces XV 15, Irish XV 53 (Pietersburg, 7 August); (7) South African Development XV 0, Irish XV 44 (Brakpan, 11 August).

SOUTH AFRICA TO ARGENTINA
October-November 1993: P5 W4 D0 L1 F243 A142

South Africa claim their first series win since returning to the international fold in 1992, when they captured both Tests in Argentina. The first Test is a narrow squeak, as the Pumas rally from 10–29 at half-time to 26–29 with Santiago Meson's last-minute penalty kick at the goal to come. The wise money is on him, as he has already pocketed 21 points including four penalties, but his 55-metre effort falls short, and Argentina lose for the first time in 11 Tests. In the second Test South Africa acclaim a new hero in fullback Gavin Johnson, who equals Gerald Bosch's national record (set in 1975 v France) with 22 points on his debut (1t,4c,3p), as the much-changed Springboks run riot, winning 52–23. Despite that, the Springboks are largely unconvincing in the country's first visit to the Pampas since the Junior Springboks in 1932.

PARTY: J Allan (Natal – 2,4,6R); K Andrews (Western Province – 1,3,4,5,6); M Andrews (Natal – 1,2,5); S Atherton (Natal – 1,3,4,6); W Bartmann (Natal – 2*,3,5*); C Dirks (Transvaal – 1,3); N Drotske (Free State – 1,3,5,6); H Fuls (Eastern Province – 1,3,4,5,6); H Honiball (Natal – 1,3,6); G Johnson (Transvaal – 5,6); A Joubert (Natal – 2,4,5R); G Kebble (Natal – 1,3,4,6); R Kruger (Free State – 1,3,4,5,6); H le Roux (Transvaal – 1,2,3,5); O le Roux (Free State – 2,3,5); H Martens (Free State – 1,3,5); P Müller (Natal – 2,3,4,5,6); J Olivier (Northern Transvaal – 1,2,3,4,5); F Pienaar (capt, Transvaal – 4*,6*); J Small (Natal – 2,3,4,6); J Stransky (Natal – 2,4,5); T Strauss (Western Province – 1*,3*,4,6); H Strydom (Transvaal – 2,3,4,6); B Swart (Transvaal – 2,4); G Teichmann (Natal – 2,5); J van der Westhuizen (Northern Transvaal – 2,4,6); N Wegner (Western Province – 1,2,5); C Williams (Western Province – 1,3,5,6).

Results: (1) Córdoba 37, Springboks 55 (Córdoba, 27 October); (2) Buenos Aires 28, Springboks 27 (Buenos Aires, 30 October); (3) Tucumán 12, Springboks 40 (Tucumán, 2 November); (4) first Test: Argentina 26, South Africa 29 (Buenos Aires, 6 November); (5) Rosario 26, Springboks 40 (Rosario, 9 November); (6) second Test: Argentina 23, South Africa 52 (13 November).

Scorers (243 – 32t,22c,12p,1dg): Honiball 35 (10c,5p), Stransky 31 (8c,4p,1dg), Johnson 27 (2t,4c,3p), Strauss 25 (5t), Olivier 20 (4t), Small 20 (4t), Williams 15 (3t), Dirks 10 (2t), Joubert 10 (2t), Kruger 10 (2t), H le Roux 10 (2t), van der Westhuizen 10 (2t), Fuls 5 (1t), Martens 5 (1t), Müller 5 (1t), Teichmann 5 (1t).

Córdoba 37, Springboks 55
Córdoba, 27 October 1993

Córdoba: J Luna; A Tomalino, I Merle, G Sagrera, M Caldo (J Dragotto); H Herrera, C Barrea; A Rodriguez Arya, I Ferreyra, P Sanchez, D Pereyra, J Simes, M Viola, S Irazoqui, D Rotondo.
Scorers – *Tries:* Irazoqui, Dragotto 2, Sagrera. *Conversions:* Luna 4. *Penalty goals:* Luna 3.

Springboks: Dirks; Olivier, Fuls, H le Roux, Williams; Honiball, Martens; Kebble, Drotske, K Andrews, Atherton, Wegner, Kruger, M Andrew, T Strauss (capt).
Scorers – *Tries:* Strauss 3, Olivier, Dirks, Williams, Kruger, le Roux. *Conversions:* Honiball 6. *Penalty goal:* Honiball.

Referee: G Savio. **Attendance:** 6,000.

Buenos Aires 28, Springboks 27
Buenos Aires, 30 October 1993

Buenos Aires: D Cuesta Silva; H Rivarola, M Loffreda, S Salvat, G Jorge; L Arbizu, N Fernandez Miranda; M Corral, J Jose Angillo, D Cash (capt), P Sporledor, G Llandes, R Martin, A Villalonga, G Ugartemendia.
Scorers – *Try:* Villalonga. *Conversion:* Arbizu. *Penalty goals:* Arbizu 7.

Springboks: Joubert; Olivier, Müller, H le Roux, Small; Stransky, van der Westhuizen; O le Roux, Allan, Swart, Strydom, Wegner, Bartmann (capt), M Andrews, Teichmann.
Scorers – *Tries:* Olivier 2, Joubert, Müller. *Conversions:* Stransky 2. *Penalty goal:* Stransky.

Referee: P Blackwedell. **Attendance:** 30,000.

Tucumán 12, Springboks 40
Tucumán, 2 November 1993

Tucumán: S Meson; M Pfister, L Herrera, P Meson, M Teran; R Sauze, G Hamilton; J Coria, R le Fort, L Molina, P Buabse, C Gentile, F Buabse, J Santemarina, A Macome. Sent off: Molina and P Buabse.
Scorer – *Penalty goals:* Meson 4.

Springboks: Dirks (Olivier); Williams, Müller (H le Roux), Fuls, Small; Honiball, Martens; Kebble,

Drotske, K Andrews, Strydom, Atherton, Bartmann (temp: Kruger), Kruger (O le Roux), Strauss (capt). Sent off: Strydom and Andrews.
Scorers – *Tries:* Dirks, Martens, Williams, Olivier. *Conversions:* Honiball 4. *Penalty goals:* Honiball 4.

Referee: E Sklar. **Attendance:** 22,000.

Argentina (10) 26, South Africa (29) 29
first Test: Buenos Aires, 6 November 1993

Argentina: S Meson; G Jorge, D Cuesta Silva, S Salvat, M Teran; L Arbizu (capt), G Camardon; M Corral, R le Fort (S Peratti 63), P Noriega, G Llanes, P Sporledor, R Perez, P Fernandez Bravo, G Ugartsmendia.
Scorers – *Try:* Cuesta Silva, Meson. *Conversions:* Meson 2. *Penalty goals:* Meson 4.

South Africa: Joubert; Olivier, Fuls, Müller, Small; Stransky, van der Westhuizen; Kebble, Allan, Swart, Strydom, Atherton, Pienaar (capt), Kruger, Strauss.
Scorers – *Tries:* Small 2, Joubert, van der Westhuizen. *Conversions:* Stransky 3. *Penalty goal:* Stransky.

Referee: W D Bevan (Wales). **Attendance:** 30,000.
Series score: Played 1, Argentina 0, South Africa 1.

Rosario 26, Springboks 40
Rosario, 9 November 1993

Rosario: L Bouzza; A Caffaro Rossi, F de Castillo, M Molina, G Romero Acura; G de Castillo, R Crexell (capt); C Promancio, D Silvetti, H Cespedes, R Perez, N Boskovich, M Carmona, P Baraldi, C Oviedo.
Scorers – *Tries:* Oviedo, de Castillo. *Conversions:* Crexell 2. *Penalty goals:* Crexell 4.

Springboks: Johnson (Joubert); Olivier, Müller (Fuls), H le Roux, Williams; Stransky, Martens; O le Roux, Drotske, K Andrews, M Andrews, Wegner, Bartmann (capt), Kruger, Teichmann.
Scorers – *Tries:* H le Roux, Johnson, Kruger, Teichmann, Fuls. *Conversions:* Stransky 3. *Penalty goals:* Stransky 3.

Referee: J Rolandi. **Attendance:** 4,000.

Argentina (3) 23, South Africa (27) 52
second Test: Buenos Aires, 13 November 1993

Argentina: S Meson; G Jorge, D Cuesta Silva, S Salvat (temp: L Cricuolo), M Teran; L Arbizu (capt), G Camardon (temp: R Bullrich); M Corral, R le Fort, P Noriega, G Llanes, P Sporledor, M Bertranou, P Fernandez Bravo, G Ugartemendia.
Scorers – *Tries:* Camardon, Jorge. *Conversions:* Meson 2. *Penalty goals:* Meson 2. *Dropped goal:* Arbizu.

South Africa: Johnson; Williams, Müller, Fuls, Small; Honiball, van der Westhuizen; Kebble, Drotske, K Andrews, Strydom, Atherton, Kruger, Pienaar (capt) (Allan 52), Strauss.
Scorers – *Tries:* Johnson, van der Westhuizen, Williams, Small 2, Strauss 2. *Conversions:* Johnson 4. *Penalty goals:* Johnson 3.

Referee: W D Bevan (Wales). **Attendance:** 30,000.
Series score: Played 2, Argentina 0, South Africa 2.

AUSTRALIA TO NORTH AMERICA AND FRANCE
October–November 1993: P11 W9 D0 L2 F313 A182

Wallaby coach Bob Dwyer prepares for his third tour to France in ten years by telling his squad that 'I would rate touring France harder than a tour of New Zealand … they currently have better running and support skills than we do'. Suitably warned, Australia go out and share the two-Test series, though how they lose the first match 13–16 in Bordeaux only they can know. It is one of two defeats suffered (Côte d'Azur enjoyed a 21–15 win three days later) by a young squad which includes new faces Alistair Murdoch, Barry Lea, Mark Catchpole, Fili Finau, Michael Brial, Tim Kava and Mark Hartill. Australia's biggest win comes against Canada, thanks largely to David Campese's second-half try hat-trick, but Dwyer still criticizes his team for playing without any real fire as Canada grab an almost equal share the lineouts.

SQUAD: Bell (2,7R); S Bowen (NSW – 2,4); M Brial (NSW – 2,5,7,8R,9,10R); M Burke (NSW – 1,2,5,6,8,10); D Campese (NSW – 3,4,6,8,9,10,11); M Catchpole (Queensland – 2,5,7,9,11); D Crowley (Queensland – 2R,3R,4,5,7,9,); A Daly (NSW – 1,3,5R,6,8,10,11); Dempsey (2,4,7); F Finau (NSW – 1,4,7,9,11); T Gavin (NSW – 2*,3,5,6,8,10,11); M Hartill (NSW – 2,4,7,9); T Horan (Queensland – 2,3,5,6,8,10,11); P Howard (Queensland – 1,4,5R,7,9); T Kava (NSW – 2,5,7*,9*); P Kearns (NSW – 3,4*,6,8,10); B Lea (Queensland – 1,2,5,7,11); J Little (Queensland – 1,3,4,6,7R,8,10,11); M Lynagh (Queensland – 1*,3*,5*,6*,8*,10*,11*); R McCall (Queensland – 3,5,6,8,10,11); E McKenzie (NSW – 1,3,5,6,8,10,11); G Morgan (Queensland – 2,3,4,6,7R,8,10,11); A Murdoch (NSW – 2,4,6,7,8,9R,10); D Nucifora (Queensland – 1,3R,5,7,9,11); Robinson (9); M Roebuck (NSW – 2,3,4,6R,7,9,10,11); Skeggs (2); P Slattery (Queensland – 1,3,4,6,8,9TR,10); D Smith (Queensland – 1,2R,3,5,7,9); I Tabua (Queensland – 1,4,6,8,10); T Wallace (9); W Waugh (NSW – 1,3,4,7,9); D Wilson (Queensland – 1,3,5,6,8,10,11).

Results: (1) non-cap Test: USA 22, Australia 26 (California, 2 October); (2) Canada A 3, Wallabies 40 (Calgary, 6 October); (3) Test: Canada 16, Australia 43 (Calgary, 9 October); (4) Aquitaine XV 15, Wallabies 30 (Dax, 16 October); (5) South West 19, Wallabies 20 (Agen, 20 October); (6) Languedoc XV 18, Wallabies 35 (Narbonne, 23 October); (7) French Select 23, Wallabies 24 (Grenoble, 26 October); (8) first Test: France 16, Australia 13 (Bordeaux, 30 October); (9) Côte d'Azur 21, Wallabies 15 (Toulon, 2 November); (10) second Test: France 3, Australia 24 (Paris, 6 November); (11) French Barbarians 26, Wallabies 43 (Clermont Ferrand, 11 November).

Scorers (313 – 32t,18c,39p) – Roebuck 104 (2t,8c,26p), Lynagh 57 (9c,13p), Lea 25 (5t), Campese 20 (4t), Murdoch 20 (4t), Morgan 15 (3t), Gavin 10 (2t), Horan 10 (2t), Smith 10 (2t), Little 7 (1t,1c), Bowen 5 (1t), Burke 5 (1t), Catchpole 5 (1t), Daly 5 (1t), Howard 5 (1t), Tabua 5 (1t), Wilson 5 (1t).

United States 22, Australia 26
non-cap: California, 2 October 1993

Australia: Burke, Smith, Little, Howard, Lea; Lynagh (capt), Slattery; Daly, Nucifora, McKenzie, Waugh, McCall, Tabua, Wilson, Finau.
Scorers – *Tries:* Wilson, Howard, Tabua, Lea. *Conversions:* Lynagh 3

Series score: Played 6, USA 0, Australia 6.

Canada A 3, Wallabies 40
Calgary, 6 October 1993

Wallabies: Roebuck; Murdoch, Burke, Horan, Lea (Smith); Bowen, Catchpole; Skeggs, Bell, Hartill (Crowley), Kava, Morgan, Brial, Dempsey, Gavin.
Scorers – *Tries:* Murdoch 2, Smith, Morgan, Lea, Roebuck. *Conversions:* Roebuck 2. *Penalty goals:* Roebuck 2.

Canada (8) 16, Australia (24) 43
Test: Calgary, 9 October 1993

Canada: S Stewart (UBC OB); J Loveday (Calgary Irish), M Williams (Meralomas), S Gray (Kats), I Stuart (Vancouver RC, capt); J Graf UBC OB; I McKay (Vancouver Kats); P Szabo (Britannia Lions), I Kennedy (Meralomas), D Jackart (UBC OB), A Charron (Ottawa Irish), C Whittaker (James Bay), I Gordon (James Bay), J Hutchinson (York Yeomen), C McKenzie (UBC OB). Repl: M Cardinal (James Bay) for Kennedy, 59 mins.
Scorers – *Tries:* Kennedy, Jackart. *Penalty goals:* Graf 2.

Australia: Roebuck; Smith, Little, Horan, Campese; Lynagh (capt), Slattery; Daly, Kearns, McKenzie, McCall, Morgan, Waugh, Wilson, Gavin. Repl: Crowley for Daly, 59 mins; Nucifora for Kearns, 67 mins.
Scorers – *Tries:* Campese 3, Horan, Daly, Smith. *Conversions:* Lynagh 2. *Penalty goals:* Lynagh 3.

Referee: W D Bevan (Wales).
Series score: Played 3, Canada 0, Australia 3.

Aquitaine 15, Wallabies 30
Dax, 16 October 1993

Wallabies: Roebuck; Campese, Little, Howard, Murdoch; Bowen, Slattery; Crowley, Kearns (capt),

Hartill, Waugh, Morgan, Dempsey, Tabua, Finau.
Scorers – *Tries:* Murdoch, Little, Bowen. *Conversions:* Roebuck 3. *Penalty goals:* Roebuck 3.

South West France 19, Wallabies 20
Agen, 20 October 1993

Wallabies: Burke; Smith, Constable (Howard), Horan, Lea; Lynagh (capt), Catchpole; Crowley (Daly), Nucifora, McKenzie, Kava, McCall, Brial, Wilson, Gavin.
Scorers – *Try:* Horan. *Penalty goals:* Lynagh 5.

Languedoc 18, Wallabies 35
Narbonne, 23 October 1993

Wallabies: Burke (Roebuck); Campese, Horan, Little, Murdoch; Lynagh (capt), Slattery; Daly, Kearns, McKenzie, McCall, Morgan, Tabua, Wilson, Gavin.
Scorers – *Tries:* Morgan 2, Murdoch, Burke. *Conversions:* Lynagh 3. *Penalty goals:* Lynagh 3.

French Selection 23, Wallabies 24
Grenoble, 26 October 1993

Wallabies: Roebuck; Smith, Murdoch, Howard, Lea; Bowen (Little), Catchpole; Hartill, Nucifora (Bell), Crowley, Waugh, Kava (capt), Brial, Dempsey (Morgan), Finau.
Scorers – *Tries:* Lea 2. *Conversion:* Roebuck. *Penalty goals:* Roebuck 4.

France (13) 16, Australia (10) 13
first Test: Bordeaux, 30 October 1993

France: J-L Sadourny (Colomiers); P Bernat-Salles (Pau), P Sella (Agen), T Lacroix (Dax), P Saint-André (Montferrand); A Penaud (Brive), A Hueber (Toulon); L Armary (Lourdes), J-M Gonzalez (Bayonne), L Seigne (Merignac), O Merle (Grenoble), O Roumat (capt, Dax), P Benetton (Agen), A Benazzi (Agen), M Cecillon (Bourgoin).
Scorers – *Try:* Hueber. *Conversion:* Lacroix. *Penalty goal:* Lacroix. *Dropped goals:* Penaud, Sadourny.

Australia: Burke; Murdoch*, Little, Horan, Campese; Lynagh (capt), Slattery; Daly, Kearns, McKenzie, McCall, Morgan, Tabua, Wilson, Gavin. Repl: Brial* for Tabua, 40 mins.
Scorers – *Try:* Gavin. *Conversion:* Lynagh. *Penalty goals:* Lynagh 2.

Referee: D Bishop (NZ).
Series score: Played 24, France 13, Australia 9, Drawn 2.

Côte d'Azur 21, Wallabies 15
Toulon, 2 November 1993

Wallabies: Roebuck; Campese, Constable (Murdoch), Howard, Smith; Wallace, Catchpole (temp: Slattery); Crowley, Nucifora, Hartill, Kava (capt), Waugh, Brial, Robinson, Finau.
Scorers – *Penalty goals:* Roebuck 5.

France (3) 3, Australia (13) 24
second Test: Paris, 6 November 1993

France: J-L Sadourny (Colomiers); P Bernat-Salles (Pau), P Sella (Agen), T Lacroix (Dax), P Saint-André (Montferrand); A Penaud (Brive), A Hueber (Toulon); L Armary (Lourdes), J-M Gonzalez (Bayonne), L Seigne (Merignac), O Merle (Grenoble), O Roumat (capt, Dax), P Benetton (Agen), A Benazzi (Agen), M Cecillon (Bourgoin). Repl: S Graou (Auch) for Seigne, 75 mins.
Scorer – *Penalty goal:* Lacroix.

Australia: Roebuck; Smith, Little, Horan, Campese; Lynagh (capt), Slattery; Daly, Kearns, McKenzie, McCall, Morgan, Brial, Wilson, Gavin.
Scorers – *Tries:* Roebuck, Gavin. *Conversion:* Roebuck. *Penalty goals:* Roebuck 4.

Referee: D Bishop (NZ).
Series score: Played 25, France 13, Australia 10, Drawn 2.

French Barbarians 26, Wallabies 43
Clermont-Ferrand, 11 November 1993

Wallabies: Roebuck; Campese, Little, Horan, Lea; Lynagh (capt), Catchpole; Daly, Nucifora, McKenzie, McCall, Morgan, Wilson, Finau, Gavin.

Scorers – *Tries:* Lea, Catchpole, Campese. *Conversions:* Roebuck, Little. *Penalty goals:* Roebuck 8.

One comment made by Tour captain Sean Fitzpatrick provides the lingering memory of the 1993 All Blacks. It is uttered on the eve of the Test against England, at which time New Zealand have played ten and won ten. They have shredded Scotland by a record 51–15 along the way. But Fitzpatrick says: 'If we lose to England, everything we have achieved so far is out of the window'. It is an extraordinary comment, but wholly in keeping with the New Zealand psyche. Winning for them is not just everything, it is the only thing. In a way they are to be envied for such singlemindedness – in another, pitied. For such a do-or-die attitude puts inexorable pressure on the shoulders of an All Black and at times pushes him into playing a cynical game in the quest of the only outcome acceptable. Perhaps that is why the '93 Blacks will be remembered less for the fact they score 42 tries and concede a miserly five than for the way they go about their business. Phil de Glanville is lucky not to lose an eye after being stamped on in a ruck playing for the South West (requires 15 stitches), while Kyran Bracken's England debut is marred by a gratuitous stamp on his right ankle by Jamie Joseph. 'They will be remembered mostly as a dirty side ... I feel sad for the damage they have done to rugby's reputation', Will Carling is quoted as having said. To which Fitzpatrick retorts: 'We did not set out to give away penalties, and we are not a dirty side'. Still, it's good box office. The 13-match tour grosses more than £4 million in gate receipts alone. Among the main attractions is young wing Jeff Wilson, who claims a try hat-trick against Scotland on his debut. Ironically, though, his goalkicking failures contribute to England's 15-9 win, of which home fly-half Rob Andrew remarks: 'It was better than two Grand Slams by miles'.

PARTY: M Allen (Taranaki – 2,4,6,7R,8,10,12); S Bachop (Otago – 1,3,6,8,10,12); L Barry (North Harbour – 2,4,8,10,12); M Berry (Wellington – 1,4,6,10,12); Z Brooke (Auckland – 1TR,2*,3R,4*,5,6*,9,11,13); O Brown (Auckland – 1,3,5,7,9,11,13); F Bunce (Auckland – 1,3,5,7,9,11,13); E Clarke (Auckland – 2,4,6,8,9R,10,11,12); M Cooper (Waikato – 1,2R,3,5,7,9); C Dowd (Auckland – 1,3,5,7,9,11,13); M Ellis (Otago – 2,4,5,6R,7,9,11,13); S Fitzpatrick (Auckland, capt – 1*,3*,5*,7*,9*,11*,13*); S Forster (Otago – 1,4,5,7,9,11,13); R Fromont (Auckland – 2,4,6,8,10,12); S Gordon (Waikato – 1,3,5,6,7,9,11,13); P Henderson (Southland – 1,3,7,10,12); N Hewitt (Hawke's Bay – 2,4,6,8,10,12); S Howarth (Auckland – 2,4,6,8,10,12); I Jones (North Auckland – 1,2,3,5,7,9,11,13); J Joseph (Otago – 1,3,7,8,9,11); B Larsen (North Harbour – 4,5,6,7R,8,10,12,13); J Mitchell (Waikato – 2,4,6,8*,10*,12*); A Pene (Otago – 1,3,5,7,9,11,13); J Preston (Wellington – 2,3,6,8,10,12); G Purvis (Waikato – 2,4,6,8,10,12); E Rush (North Harbour – 2,4,6,8,10,12); L Stensness (Auckland – 2,6,8,10,12,13); J Timu (Otago – 2,3,5,7,9,11,13); V Tuigamala (Auckland – 1,3,5,7,9,11,13); J Wilson (Otago – 1,3,4,5,7,8,9,11,13). Manager: N Gray (Waikato). Coach: L Mains (Otago). Assistant coach: E Kirton (Wellington).

Results: (1) London 12, All Blacks 39 (Twickenham, 23 October); (2) Midlands 6, All Blacks 12 (Leicester, 27 October); (3) South-West 15, All Blacks 19 (Redruth, 30 October); (4) North 21, All Blacks 27 (Liverpool, 2 November); (5) England A 12, All Blacks 26 (Gateshead, 7 November); (6) South of Scotland 5, All Blacks 84 (Galashiels, 10 November); (7) Scotland A 9, All Blacks 20 (Glasgow, 13 November); (8) Scottish Development XV 12, All Blacks 31 (Edinburgh, 16 November); (9) Test: Scotland 15, New Zealand 51 (Edinburgh, 20 November); (10) Emerging England Players 19, All Blacks 30 (Gloucester, 23 November); (11) Test: England 15, New Zealand 9 (Twickenham, 27 November); (12) Combined Services 3, All Blacks 13 (Devonport, 30 November); (13) Barbarians 12, All Blacks 25 (Cardiff, 4 December).

Scorers (386 – 42t, 31c, 36p, 2dg) – Howarth (3t,15c,12p) 81, Cooper (11c,18p) 76, Wilson (6t,5c,6p) 58, Ellis (6t,1dg) 33, Brooke (5t) 25, Hewitt (4t) 20, Bachop (3t,1dg) 18, Rush (3t) 15, Mitchell (2t) 10, Barry (1t) 5, Berry (1t) 5, Bunce (1t) 5, Clarke (1t) 5, Dowd (1t) 5, Jones (1t) 5, Joseph (1t) 5, Preston (1t) 5, Timu (1t) 5, Tuigamala (1t) 5.

London & SE Division 12, All Blacks 39
Twickenham, 23 October 1993

London: H Davies (Wasps); T Underwood (Leicester), W Carling (Harlequins), D Hopley (Wasps), C Oti (Wasps); R Andrew (Wasps, capt), S Bates (Wasps); J Leonard (Harlequins), B Moore (Harlequins), J Probyn (Wasps), A Snow (Harlequins), D Ryan (Wasps), M Greenwood (Wasps), R Jenkins (London Irish), C Sheasby (Harlequins).
Scorers – *Tries:* Jenkins, Oti. *Conversion:* Andrew.

All Blacks: Cooper; Wilson, Bunce, Berry, Tuigamala; Bachop, Forster; Dowd, Fitzpatrick (capt), Brown, Jones, Gordon, Joseph, Henderson (temp: Brooke), Pene.
Scorers – *Tries:* Bachop 2, Wilson 2, Berry. *Conversion:* Cooper 4. *Penalty goals:* Cooper 2.

Referee: P Thomas (France). **Attendance:** 56,400.

Midlands Division 6, All Blacks 12
Leicester, 26 October 1993

Midlands: J Steele (Northampton); S Hackney (Leicester), S Potter (Leicester), I Bates (Leicester), H Thorneycroft (Northampton); P Challinor (Harlequins), M Dawson (Northampton); G Rowntree (Leicester), J Olver (Northampton), G Pearce (Northampton), M Johnson (Leicester), S Lloyd (Moseley), J Wells (Leicester), N Back (Leicester), D Richards (Leicester, capt).
Scorer – *Penalty goals:* Steele 2.

All Blacks: Howarth; Timu, Clarke, Stensness (Cooper 50), Rush; Ellis, Preston; Allen, Hewitt, Purvis, Jones, Fromont, Brooke (capt), Barry, Mitchell.
Scorers – *Penalty goals:* Howarth 2, Cooper 2.

Referee: B Stirling (Ireland). **Attendance:** 14,500.

South West Division 15, All Blacks 19
Redruth, 30 October 1993

South West: J Callard (Bath); P Hull (Bristol), P de Glanville (Bath), N Beal (Northampton), A Lumsden (Bath); M Catt (Bath), K Bracken (Bristol); C Clark (Oxford Univ), G Dawe (Bath), V Ubogu (Bath), N Redman (Bath), A Blackmore (Bristol), J Hall (Bath, capt), A Robinson (Bath), B Clarke (Bath). Repl: P Holford (Gloucester) for de Glanville, 15 mins; S Ojomoh (Bath) for Robinson, 66 mins; D Sims (Gloucester) for Blackmore, 79 mins.
Scorers – *Penalty goals:* Callard 4. *Dropped goal:* Hull.

All Blacks: Timu; Wilson, Bunce, Cooper, Tuigamala; Bachop, Preston; Dowd, Fitzpatrick (capt), Brown, Jones, Gordon, Joseph (Brooke 77), Henderson, Pene.
Scorers – *Try:* Joseph. *Conversion:* Cooper. *Penalty goals:* Cooper 4.

Referee: C Thomas (Wales). **Attendance:** 15,000.

North Division 21, All Blacks 27
Liverpool, 2 November 1993

North: I Hunter (Northampton); J Mallinder (Sale), M Fielden (Northampton), K Simms (Liverpool St Helens, capt), R Underwood (Leicester); P Grayson (Northampton), D Scully (Wakefield); M Hynes (Orrell), G French (Orrell), S McMain (Sheffield), J Dixon (West Hartlepool), D Baldwin (Sale), T Rodber (Northampton), N Ashurst (Orrell), A Macfarlane (Sale). Repl: C Cusani (Orrell) for Baldwin, 40 mins.
Scorer – *Penalty goals:* Grayson 7.

All Blacks: Howarth; Wilson, Clarke, Berry, Rush; Ellis, Forster; Allen, Hewitt, Purvis, Larsen, Fromont, Brooke (capt), Barry, Mitchell.
Scorers – *Tries:* Ellis 2, Hewitt, Rush. *Conversions:* Wilson 2. *Penalty goal:* Wilson.

Referee: J Fleming (Scotland). **Attendance:** 24,636.

England A 12, All Blacks 26
Gateshead, 7 November 1993

England A: J Callard (Bath); I Hunter (Northampton), D Hopley (Wasps), M Catt (Bath), P Hull (Bristol); S Barnes (Bath), K Bracken (Bristol); G Rowntree (Leicester), G Dawe (Bath), A Mullins (Harlequins), N Redman (Bath), D Sims (Gloucester), J Hall (Bath, capt), N Back (Leicester), T Rodber (Northampton). Temp repl: S Ojomoh (Bath) for Redman, 61-63 mins.
Scorer – *Penalty goals:* Callard 4.

All Blacks: Timu; Wilson, Bunce, Cooper, Tuigamala; Ellis, Forster; Dowd, Fitzpatrick (capt), Brown, Jones, Gordon, Larsen, Brooke, Pene.
Scorers – *Tries:* Wilson, Timu. *Conversions:* Cooper 2. *Penalty goals:* Cooper 3. *Dropped goal:* Ellis.

Referee: R Megson (Scotland). **Attendance:** 19,100.

South of Scotland 5, All Blacks 84
Galashiels, 10 November 1993

South: M Dods (Gala); T Stanger (Hawick), S Nichol (Selkirk), G Shiel (Melrose), G Parker (Melrose); C Chalmers (Melrose), B Redpath (Melrose); G Isaac (Gala), J Hay (Hawick), H Hunter (Gala), R Brown (Melrose, capt), G Weir (Melrose), D Turnbull (Hawick), J Amos (Gala), B Renwick (Hawick). Repl: S McColm (Selkirk) for Hunter, 6 mins.
Scorer – *Try:* Parker.

All Blacks: Howarth; Clarke, Berry, Stensness, Rush; Bachop, Preston; Allen, Hewitt, Purvis, Gordon, Fromont, Larsen, Brooke (capt), Mitchell. Repl: Ellis for Berry, 26 mins.
Scorers – *Tries:* Brooke 4, Hewitt 2, Howarth 2, Ellis, Bachop, Preston, Mitchell. *Conversions:* Howarth 9. *Penalty goals:* Howarth 2.

Referee: D Matthews (England). **Attendance:** 7,000.

Scotland A 9, All Blacks 20
Glasgow, 13 November 1993

Scotland A: M Dods (Gala); K Logan (Stirling Co), S Nichol (Selkirk), I Jardine, G Parker (Melrose); D Wyllie (capt, Stewart's-Melville FP), B Redpath (Melrose); A Watt (Glasgow H/K), K McKenzie (Stirling Co), D Herrington (Dundee HSFP), S Munro (Glasgow H/K), A Macdonald (Heriot's FP), D McIvor (Edinburgh Acads), R Wainwright (Edinburgh Acads), C Hogg (Melrose).
Scorers – *Penalty goal:* Dods. *Dropped goals:* Wyllie 2.

All Blacks: Timu; Wilson, Bunce, Cooper, Tuigamala; Ellis, Forster; Dowd (Allen 14), Fitzpatrick (capt), Brown, Jones, Gordon (Larsen 30), Joseph, Henderson, Pene.
Scorers – *Try:* Ellis. *Penalty goals:* Cooper 5.

Referee: A Spreadbury (England). **Attendance:** 10,000.

Scottish Development XV 12, All Blacks 31
Edinburgh, 16 November 1993

Scottish XV: C Glasgow (Heriot's FP); D Stark (Boroughmuir), F Harrold (London Scottish), R MacNaughton (Northampton), C Dalglish (Gala); K Bray (Harlequins), D Patterson (Edinburgh Acads); J Manson (Dundee HSFP), J Hay (Hawick, capt), D Herrington (Dundee HSFP), S Campbell (Dundee HSFP), N Edwards (Northampton), P Walton (Northampton), I Smith (Gloucester), F Wallace (Glasgow H/K). Repl: S McIntosh (West of Scotland) for Stark, 57 mins.
Scorer – *Penalty goals:* Bray 4.

All Blacks: Howarth; Wilson, Clarke, Stensness, Rush; Bachop, Preston; Allen, Hewitt, Purvis, Fromont, Larsen, Barry, Mitchell (capt).
Scorers – *Tries:* Barry, Rush, Mitchell. *Conversions:* Howarth 2. *Penalty goals:* Howarth 4.

Referee: G Black (Ireland). **Attendance:** 5,000.

Scotland 15, New Zealand 51
Edinburgh, 20 November 1993

Scotland: G Hastings (Watsonians, capt); T Stanger (Hawick), I Jardine[+] (Stirling County), G Shiel (Melrose); C Chalmers (Melrose), A Nicol (Dundee HSFP); A Watt (Glasgow H/K), K Milne (Heriot's FP), P Burnell (London Scottish), D Cronin (London Scottish), A Macdonald (Heriot's FP), D McIvor (Edinburgh Academicals), R Wainwright (Edinburgh Academicals), G Weir (Melrose). Repl: D Wyllie (Stewart's-Melville FP) for Chalmers, 59 mins; C Hogg (Melrose) for Cronin, 62 mins. Temp repl: B Redpath (Melrose) for Nicol, K Logan (Stirling County) for G Hastings.
Scorers – *Penalty goals:* G Hastings 4, Chalmers.

New Zealand: Timu; Wilson[+], Bunce, Cooper, Tuigamala; Ellis*, Forster; Dowd, Fitzpatrick (capt), Brown, Jones, Gordon, Joseph, Z Brooke, Pene. Repl: E Clarke for Cooper, 78 mins.
Scorers – *Tries:* Wilson 3, Ellis 2, Brooke, Bunce. *Conversions:* Cooper 4, Wilson. *Penalty goals:* Cooper 2.

Referee: F Burger (South Africa) **Attendance:** 34,000.
Series score: Played 17, Scotland 0, New Zealand 15, Drawn 2.

Emerging England XV 19, All Blacks 30
Gloucester, 23 November 1993

Emerging England: P Challinor (Harlequins); P Holford (Gloucester), N Beal (Northampton), D Hopley (Wasps), M Catt (Bath); M Dawson (Northampton); C Clark (Oxford Univ), K Dunn (Wasps), J Mallett (Bath), D Sims (Gloucester), R West (Gloucester), C Sheasby (Harlequins), S Ojomoh (Bath), D Ryan (Wasps, capt).
Scorers – *Tries:* Sims, Challinor. *Penalty goals:* Challinor 3.

All Blacks: Howarth; Clarke, Berry, Stensness, Rush; Bachop, Preston; Allen, Hewitt, Purvis, Larsen, Fromont, Barry, Henderson, Mitchell (capt).
Scorers – *Tries:* Rush, Clarke, Howarth. *Conversions:* Howarth 3. *Penalty goals:* Howarth 2. *Dropped goal:* Bachop.

Referee: D Mene (France). **Attendance:** 13,000.

England (6) 15, New Zealand (0) 9
Twickenham, 27 November 1993

England: J Callard[+] (Bath); T Underwood (Leicester), W Carling (capt, Harlequins), P de Glanville (Bath), R Underwood (Leicester); R Andrew (Wasps), K Bracken[+] (Bristol); J Leonard (Harlequins), B Moore (Harlequins), V Ubogu (Bath), M Johnson (Leicester), N Redman (Bath), T Rodber (Northampton), B Clarke (Bath), D Richards (Leicester).
Scorer – *Penalty goals:* Callard 5.

New Zealand: Timu; Wilson, Bunce, Clarke, Tuigamala; Ellis, Forster; Dowd, Fitzpatrick (capt), Brown, Jones, Gordon, Joseph, Brooke, Pene.
Scorer – *Penalty goals:* Wilson 4.

Referee: F Burger (South Africa). **Attendance:** 68,000
Series score: Played 17, England 4, New Zealand 13.

Combined Services 3, All Blacks 13
Devonport, 30 November 1993

Combined Services: P Hull (RAF); S Bartliff (Army), G Sharpe (RAF), D Sibson (RN), R Underwood (RAF); A Johnson (RAF), S Worrall (Army, capt); A Billett (RAF), J Brammer (Army), J Fowers (Army), R Armstrong (RN), B Richardson (Army), C Moore (RAF), M Watson (Army), R Wainwright (Army). Repl: S Berryman (Army) for Watson.
Scorer – *Penalty goal:* Worrall.

All Blacks: Howarth; Clarke, Berry, Stensness, Rush; Bachop, Preston; Allen, Hewitt, Purvis, Larsen, Fromont, Barry, Henderson, Mitchell (capt).
Scorers – *Try:* Hewitt. *Conversion:* Howarth. *Penalty goals:* Howarth 2.

Referee: D Davies (Wales). **Attendance:** 8,000.

Barbarians 12, New Zealand 25
Cardiff, 4 December 1993

Barbarians: A Clement (Wales); A Stanger (Scotland), S Gibbs (Wales), S Hastings (Scotland), N Walker (Wales); E Elwood (Ireland), G Armstrong (Scotland); N Popplewell (Ireland), T Kingston (Ireland), E McKenzie (Australia), P Johns (Ireland), O Roumat (France), R Wainwright (Scotland), N Back (Leicester), S Quinnell (Wales).
Scorer – *Penalty goals:* Elwood 4.

New Zealand: Timu; Wilson, Bunce, Stensness, Tuigamala; Ellis, Forster; Dowd, Fitzpatrick (capt), Brown, Jones, Gordon, Larsen, Brooke, Pene.
Scorers – *Tries:* Dowd, Tuigamala, Jones. *Conversions:* Wilson 2. *Penalty goals:* Wilson 2.

Referee: P Robin (France). **Attendance:** 51,000.

JAPAN TO WALES
October 1993: P6 W3 D0 L3 F111 A197

RESULTS: (1) Wales A 61, Japan 5 (Llanelli, 29 September); (2) Dunvant 23, Japan 24 (Dunvant, 2 October); (3) East Wales 38, Japan 12 (Abertillery, 6 October); (4) West Wales 10, Japan 26 (Narbeth, 9 October); (5) Wales 3rd/4th Division XV 10, Japan 39 (Pontypridd, 12 October); (6) Test: Wales 55, Japan 5 (Cardiff, 16.10.93).

Wales (29) 55, Japan (0) 5
Cardiff, 16 October 1993

Wales: A Clement (Swansea); I Evans (capt, Llanelli), S Gibbs (Swansea), N Jenkins (Pontypridd), N Walker (Cardiff); A Davies (Cardiff), R Moon (Llanelli); M Griffiths (Cardiff), A Lamerton (Llanelli), J Davies (Neath), T Copsey (Llanelli), G O Llewellyn (Neath), S Davies (Swansea), L Jones (Neath), E Lewis (Llanelli). Repl: M Rayer (Cardiff) for Walker, 27 mins; R Bidgood (Newport) for Evans, 73 mins.
Scorers – *Tries:* Evans 2, Gibbs 2, Clement, Jenkins, Moon, Lewis, Rayer. *Conversions:* Jenkins 5.

Japan: T Matsuda (Toshiba); I Williams* (Kobe Steel), M Fujikake+ (World), E Kutsuki (Toyota Motor), Y Yoshida (Isetan); S Aoki (Richmond), Y Nagatomo+ (Suntory); P Ota (NEC), M Kunda (Toshiba Fuchu, capt), R Takashi (Toyota Motor), S Kaleta (Ricoh), Y Sakuraba (Nippon Steel), B Ferguson+ (Hino Motor), H Ouchi (Ryukoku Univ), S Lato (Sanyo).
Scorer – Williams.

Referee: E Morrison (England).
Series score: Played 1, Wales 1, Japan 0.

Ireland (19) 25, Romania (0) 3
Dublin, 14 November 1993

Having lost 51-0 to France on their previous outing, and indeed 60-0 on their last visit to Lansdowne Road in 1986, Romania can be fairly satisfied with this effort in front of 20,000 rain-drenched fans in Dublin. For their hosts, Eric Elwood equals Ollie Campbell's 11-year-old national record of six penalty goals in a match, and his 20-point haul is within three of Ralph Keyess record single-match total. The game's only try is a nifty effort from Simon Geoghegan, capitalizing on his one pass of the day.

Ireland: C O'Shea (Lansdowne); R Wallace (Garryowen), V Cunningham (St Mary's College), P Danaher (Garryowen), S Geoghegan (London Irish); E Elwood (Lansdowne), M Bradley (capt, Cork Constitution); N Popplewell (Greystones), T Kingston (Dolphin), G Halpin (London Irish), P Johns (Dungannon), N Francis (Old Belvedere), M Galwey (Shannon), D McBride (Malone), B Robinson (London Irish). Repl: P McCarthy (Cork Constitution) for Popplewell, 76 mins.
Scorers – *Try:* Geoghegan. *Conversion:* Elwood. *Penalty goals:* Elwood 6.

Romania: V Brici (Farul Constanta); C Sasu (Farul Constanta), G Solomie (Universitate Timisoara), N Fulina (Farul Constanta), L Colceriu (Steaua Bucharest); S Rosu (Forest Sibiu), D Neaga (Dinamo Bucharest); G Leonte (Vienne), C Gheorghe (Grivita Bucharest), G Vlad (Grivita Bucharest), A Girbu (Farul Constanta), T Oroian (Steaua Bucharest), H Dumitras (Pau, capt), A Guranescu (Dinamo Bucharest), T Brinza (Universitate Cluj). Repl: C Cojocariou (Bayonne) for Girbu, 43 mins. Temp rel: N Marin (Farul Constanta) for Cojocariu.

Scorer – *Penalty goal:* Rosu.

Referee: R Yeman (Wales).
Series score: Played 2, Ireland 2, Romania 0.

Wales 24, Canada 26
Cardiff, 10 November 1993

A shattering blow to morale in Wales as the sturdy foundations built in Africa over the summer sink into the Cardiff turf. 'Alan [coach Davies] and I both believe it is time for some home truths', says manager Bob Norster after Gareth Rees wins the game for the Canucks, World Cup quarter-finalists in 1991, with the last kick of the game, converting Al Charron's try. Wales, for whom centre Neil Jenkins has kicked a world-record-equalling eight penalty goals, can have few complaints. 'Canada drew us into a game we didn't want to play, but that is our own fault', reflects Davies. Insult to injury is provided by Canadian coach Ian Birtwell's assertion that 'We played well below our best'.

Wales: A Clement (Swansea); I Evans (capt, Llanelli), S Gibbs (Swansea), N Jenkins (Pontypridd), W Proctor (Llanelli); A Davies (Cardiff), R Moon (Llanelli); M Griffiths (Cardiff), G Jenkins (Swansea), J Davies (Neath), A Copsey (Llanelli), G O Llewellyn (Neath), S Quinnell* (Llanelli), L Jones (Llanelli), E Lewis (Llanelli).
Scorer – *Penalty goals:* N Jenkins 8.

Canada: M Williams (Meralomas); R Toews* (Meralomas), S Gray (Kats), I Stuart (capt, Vancouver RC), D Stewart (UBC OB); G Rees (Oak Bay Castaways & Oxford Univ), C Tynan (Meralomas & Cambridge Univ); P Szabo (Pocomo), I Kennedy (Meralomas), D Jackart (UBC OB), J Knauer (Meralomas), A Charron (Ottawa Irish), I Gordon (James Bay), J Hutchinson (York Yeomen), C McKenzie (UBC OB).
Scorers – *Tries:* Stuart, Charron. *Conversion:* Rees 2. *Penalty goals:* Rees 4.

Referee: O E Doyle (Ireland).
Series score: Played 2, Wales 1, Canada 1.

1994 FIVE NATIONS CHAMPIONSHIP

It has been a while in coming, but Wales are back. Yet how ironic that their first Five Nations title since they shared the honour with France in 1988 should come in a season in which they also suffer their greatest ever humiliation – having to pre-qualify for the World Cup. England deny their arch-rivals a Grand Slam (their first since 1978) and Triple Crown (their first since 1988) by snuffing out the dragon's fire on the last day of the championship, to finish equal on three wins. But points difference, a new innovation in Five Nations rugby, intervenes on Wales's behalf, allowing them to lose at Twickenham but still win. The shock of the campaign (and there are many) is Ireland's victory in England; the most dramatic moment Jon Callard's injury-time penalty winner at Murrayfield; the most compelling performance that of Scott Quinnell and Wales ending a run of 12 straight defeats by France in Cardiff.

Wales (12) 29, Scotland (3) 6
Cardiff, 15 January 1994

It is a little hard to know which side is in the worst shape coming into this match. Both are coming off shocking autumn losses, and there is about much confidence on the Arms Park turf as there is dry ground. But one of the worst day's weather Cardiff has known in recent memory stimulates the home side into a remarkable performance. Forget the defeat by Canada, Wales are full of life and belief, and wholesale credit must go to the Davies-Norster management combination, which has been lucky to survive the WRUs New Year night of the long knives. Truth to tell, Scotland are woeful. Craig Chalmers is a shadow of his former self, and only when Gregor Townsend moves to stand-off in his place late on do the visitors regroup. Too late though. There is only one side in this one, as two Welsh tries in the last couple of minutes (including replacement Mike Rayer's second) confirms. Townsend drops a goal for Scotland, but referee Patrick Robin says it doesn't go through the posts. How the Scots would like to send him home tae think again!

Wales: A Clement (Swansea); I Evans (capt, Llanelli), N Davies (Llanelli), M Hall (Cardiff), N Walker (Cardiff); N Jenkins (Pontypridd), R Moon (Llanelli); R Evans (Llanelli), G Jenkins (Swansea), J Davies (Neath), P Davies (Llanelli), G O Llewellyn (Neath), E Lewis (Llanelli), M Perego (Llanelli), S Quinnell (Llanelli). Repl: M Rayer (Cardiff) for Walker, 12 mins.
Scorers – *Tries:* Rayer 2, I Evans. *Conversion:* N Jenkins. *Penalty goals:* N Jenkins 4.

Scotland: G Hastings (capt, Watsonians); T Stanger (Hawick), S Hastings (Watsonians), G Townsend (Gala), I Jardine (Stirling County); K Logan (Stirling County); C Chalmers (Melrose), A Nicol (Dundee HSFP); P Wright (Boroughmuir), K Milne (Heriot's FP), P Burnell (London Scottish), N Edwards (Northampton), S Munro* (Glasgow H/K), D Turnbull (Hawick), I Morrison (London Scottish), R Wainwright (Edinburgh Acads). Repl: G Weir (Melrose) for Morrison, 18 mins; D Wyllie (Stewart's-Melville FP) for Chalmers, 53 mins.
Scorer – *Penalty goals:* G Hastings 2.

Referee: P Robin (France).
Series score: Played 98, Wales 54, Scotland 42, Drawn 2.

France (16) 35, Ireland (12) 15
Paris, 15 January 1994

Ireland are rather accustomed to having their backsides tanned in Paris. What is it, 24 years since the Tricolors has been lowered by the men in green? No change likely this time either, although at least this time the Irish are sensible enough to take some points with them. Eric Elwood dutifully hoists them onto the Parc des Princes scoreboard, with five penalty goals from seven attempts – but it cannot disguise the fact that France are unhesitatingly the better side. That said, the end result flatters them, as it is only nailed down with two tries in the last three minutes. Not quite a moral victory for the visitors, but not a record defeat either.

France: J-L Sadourny (Colomiers); P Bernat-Salles (Pau), P Sella (Agen), T Lacroix (Dax), P Saint-André (Montferrand); A Penaud (Brive), F Galthie (Colomiers); L Armary (Lourdes), J-M Gonzalez (Bayonne), P Gallart (Béziers), O Merle (Grenoble), O Roumat (Dax), P Benetton (Agen), A Benazzi (Agen), M Cecillon (Bourgoin).
Scorers – *Tries:* Benetton, Lacroix, Saint-André, Merle. *Conversions:* Lacroix 3. *Penalty goals:* Lacroix 3.

Ireland: C O'Shea (Lansdowne); R Wallace (Garryowen), V Cunningham (St Mary's College), P Danaher (Garryowen), S Geoghegan (London Irish); E Elwood (Lansdowne), M Bradley (capt, Cork Constitution); N Popplewell (Greystones), T Kingston (Dolphin), P O'Clohessy (Young Munster), P Johns (Dungannon), N Francis (Old Belvedere), M Galwey (Shannon), K O'Connell* (Sunday's Well), B Robinson (London Irish).
Scorers – *Penalty goals:* Elwood 5.

Referee: J Fleming (Scotland).
Series score: Played 67, France 37, Ireland 25, Drawn 5.

Ireland (9) 15, Wales (8) 17
Dublin, 5 February 1994

There is a theory doing the rounds before kick-off that this will be a tale of two goalkickers. Eric Elwood will do the business for Ireland and Neil Jenkins for Wales, and everyone else will stand around and show their appreciation. A touch simplistic but basically spot-on. Putting aside the memory of his nightmare in the corresponding fixture the previous year, Jenkins claims 17 points with a try and four penalties. (In 1993 he missed with seven kicks as Ireland won.) The hero of '93, yer man Elwood, sets off like a steam train, bagging five penalty goals for an Irish record contribution to the fixture. Yet he ends up a loser, which is remarkable given that Ireland lead 15–8 after 45 minutes. That they mess up is entirely their own fault, as two try-scoring positions are criminally spurned by the blunt instrument that is their attack. At least when all else fails, they can turn to Eric. Not this time they cannot. He slams his easiest attempt against an upright, and Ireland lament. Victory provides solace to a Welsh side battered if not bowed. Wayne Proctor (broken jaw), Nigel Davies and Ieuan Evans all sustain injuries which will keep them out of the France game in a fortnight.

Ireland: C O'Shea (Lansdowne); R Wallace (Garryowen), M McCall* (Bangor), P Danaher (Garryowen), S Geoghegan (London Irish); E Elwood (Lansdowne), M Bradley (capt, Cork Constitution); N Popplewell (Greystones), T Kingston (Dolphin), P Clohessy (Young Munster), M

Galwey (Shannon), N Francis (Old Belvedere), B Robinson (London Irish), D McBride (Malone), P Johns (Dungannon).
Scorers – *Penalty goals:* Elwood 5.

Wales: A Clement (Swansea); I Evans (capt, Llanelli), N Davies (Llanelli), M Hall (Cardiff), W Proctor (Llanelli); N Jenkins (Pontypridd), R Moon (Llanelli); R Evans (Llanelli), G Jenkins (Swansea), J Davies (Neath), P Davies (Llanelli), G O Llewellyn (Neath), E Lewis (Llanelli), M Perego (Llanelli), S Quinnell (Llanelli). Repl: S Hill[*] (Cardiff) for Proctor, 44 mins; M Rayer (Cardiff) for Clement, 51 mins; R Jones (Swansea) for N Davies, 71 mins.
Scorers – *Try:* N Jenkins. *Penalty goals:* Jenkins 4.

Referee: T Spreadbury (England).
Series score: Played 97, Ireland 33, Wales 58, Drawn 6.

Scotland (5) 14, England (3) 15
Edinburgh, 5 February 1994

This match will be remembered for one decision, and one decision alone. Time is up on the clock when New Zealand whistler Lyndsay McLachlan sees illegal hands in a ruck 40-odd metres from the Scottish posts. He regards the offending mitts as Scottish, and Jon Callard boldly belts home the resultant penalty goal to overturn a Scottish lead gained by Gregor Townsend's wonderful last-minute dropped goal. But the Scots cry foul – blue cuffs, they say, are English not ours. The debate rumbles on … and on. 'I will never agree with it', says Scotland skipper Gavin Hastings in his review on page 38. 'The harsh and cruel manner of that defeat totally knocked the stuffing out of us'.

Scotland: G Hastings (sent off, Watsonians); T Stanger (Hawick), S Hastings (Watsonians), D Wyllie (Stewart's-Melville FP), K Logan (Stirling County); G Townsend (Gala), G Armstrong (Jed-Forest); A Sharp[*] (Bristol), K Milne (Heriot's FP), P Burnell (London Scottish), S Munro (Glasgow H/K), A Reed (Bath), P Walton[*] (Northampton), R Wainwright (Edinburgh Acads), G Weir (Melrose). Repl: I Smith (Gloucester) for Wainwright, 66 mins; I Jardine (Stirling County) for S Hastings, 71 mins.
Scorers – *Try:* Wainwright. *Penalty goals:* G Hastings 2. *Dropped goal:* Townsend.

England: J Callard (Bath); T Underwood (Leicester), W Carling (sent off, Harlequins), P de Glanville (Bath), R Underwood (Leicester); R Andrew (Wasps), K Bracken (Bristol); J Leonard (Harlequins), B Moore (Harlequins), V Ubogu (Bath), M Johnson (Leicester), M Bayfield (Northampton), J Hall (Bath), N Back[*], B Clarke (Bath).
Scorers – *Penalty goals:* Callard 5.

Referee: L McLachlan (New Zealand).
Series score: Played 111, Scotland 39, England 55, Drawn 17.

England (6) 12, Ireland (10) 13
Twickenham, 19 February 1994

England pay the ultimate price for kidding themselves that their Murrayfield experience was a one-off by turning in an even more disappointing show. As England sent off Will Carling admits, in his review of the season on page 10: 'We thought we could almost play it off the cuff … we'd forgotten that you have to refocus before each game'. Ireland take full advantage, Simon Geoghegan's 38th-minute try securing the visitors' first win at Twickenham since 1982. Defeat for England is their first at home in the Five Nations Championship for six years. The *Daily Telegraph's* John Mason refers to England as 'a shambling muddle in which known skills departed with disconcerting rapidity in the face of aggressive defence'. Enough said!

England: J Callard (Bath); T Underwood (Leicester), W Carling (sent off, Harlequins), P de Glanville (Bath), R Underwood (Leicester); R Andrew (Wasps), K Bracken (Bristol); J Leonard (Harlequins), B Moore (Harlequins), V Ubogu (Bath), M Johnson (Leicester), M Bayfield (Northampton), T Rodber (Nottingham), N Back (Leicester), S Ojomoh[*] (Bath).
Scorer – *Penalty goals:* Callard 4.

Ireland: C O'Shea (Lansdowne); R Wallace (Garryowen), M Field[*] (Malone), P Danaher (Garryowen), S Geoghegan (London Irish); E Elwood (Lansdowne), M Bradley (capt, Cork Constitution); N Popplewell (Greystones), T Kingston (Dolphin), P Clohessy (Young Munster), M Galwey (Shannon), N Francis (Old Belvedere), B Robinson (London Irish), D McBride (Malone), P Johns (Dungannon).
Scorers – *Try:* Geoghegan. *Conversion:* Elwood. *Penalty goals:* Elwood 2.

Referee: P Thomas (France).
Series score: Played 107, England 61, Ireland 38, Drawn 8.

Wales (11) 24, France (3) 15
Cardiff, 19 February 1994

The match of the championship, and surely the best Northern Hemisphere contest since the law changes were implemented in 1992. This was a fixture Wales had forgotten how to win – 12 straight defeats dating back to 1982 providing proof of this particular pudding. No member of the Welsh team had ever beaten France, no Frenchman had ever lost to Wales. Against that lopsided backdrop there can only be one result, and it's not Wales by nine points! Oh yes it is, thanks to a truly Herculean performance by Scott Quinnell, and 14 other worthy displays. Quinnell, at 21 the youngest man on the park, sets the tone with an immense try early doors – muscling his way through the French lineout 40 metres out, gathering a loose ball and running through three defenders en route to the try-line. Neil Jenkins misses the conversion, but that's all.

Wales: M Rayer (Cardiff); S Hill (Cardiff), M Hall (Cardiff), A Clement (Swansea), N Walker (Cardiff); N Jenkins (Pontypridd), R Moon (Llanelli); R Evans (Llanelli), G Jenkins (Swansea), J Davies (Neath), P Davies (Llanelli), G O Llewellyn (capt, Neath), E Lewis (Llanelli), M Perego (Llanelli), S Quinnell (Llanelli).
Scorers – *Tries:* Quinnell, Walker. *Conversion:* Jenkins. *Penalty goals:* Jenkins 4.

France: J-L Sadourny (Colomiers); E N'Tamack' (Toulouse), P Sella (Agen), T Lacroix (Dax), P Saint-André (Montferrand); A Penaud (Brive), F Galthie (Colomiers); L Armary (Lourdes), J-M Gonzalez (Bayonne), P Gallart (Béziers), O Merle (Grenoble), O Roumat (Dax), P Benetton (Agen), A Benazzi (Agen), M Cecillon (Bourgoin).
Scorers – *Tries:* Roumat, Sella. *Conversion:* Lacroix. *Penalty goal:* Lacroix.

Referee: L McLachlan (New Zealand).
Series score: Played 68, Wales 37, France 28, Drawn 3.

Ireland (3) 6, Scotland (0) 6
Dublin, 5 March 1994

What a belter this one isn't. A swirling wind proves a pain, but neither side has the innovative nouse to sidestep it. Scotland captain Gavin Hastings says his Murrayfield heartbreak is behind him, and proves the point by snapping up both penalty chances to match Eric Elwood's brace from five attempts. Hastings receives four staples for his troubles, courtesy of an accidental head-butt by team mate Gary Armstrong – the scrum-half's sole blemish on a stunning afternoon's work. 'You just wonder sometimes whether he's from the same planet', says Scottish coach Dougie Morgan, indebted to the Border terrier for ending a three-match losing sequence since his succession of Ian McGeechan. A couple of punchy runs restore Simon Geoghegan's reputation as Ireland's most exciting player, but Ireland, only 3–0 up after a first half played with the elements more in their favour, are happy enough to share the spoils.

Ireland: C O'Shea (Lansdowne); R Wallace (Garryowen), M Field (Malone), P Danaher (Garryowen), S Geoghegan (London Irish); E Elwood (Lansdowne), M Bradley (capt, Cork Constitution); N Popplewell (Greystones), T Kingston (Dolphin), P Clohessy (Young Munster), M Galwey (Shannon), N Francis (Old Belvedere), B Robinson (London Irish), D McBride (Malone), P Johns (Dungannon).
Scorer – *Penalty goals:* Elwood 2.

Scotland: G Hastings (capt, Watsonians); T Stanger (Hawick), S Hastings (Watsonians), D Wyllie (Stewart's Melville FP), K Logan (Stirling County); G Townsend (Gala), G Armstrong (Jed-Forest); A Sharp (Bristol), K Milne (Heriot's FP), P Burnell (London Scottish), S Munro (Glasgow H/K), A Reed (Bath), P Walton (Northampton), I Smith (Gloucester), G Weir (Melrose). Temp repl: M Dods' (Gala) for G Hastings.
Scorer – *Penalty goals:* G Hastings.

Referee: E Morrison (England).
Series Score: Played 106, Ireland 45, Scotland 55, Drawn 5, Abandoned 1.

France (0) 14, England (3) 18
Paris, 5 March 1994

There is a twin-edged recent history to this one. The *entente* is always dis-*cordiale* and England always wins … well ever since 1988. And even though the Le Crunch aspect is removed by the fact that both teams have been beaten a fortnight earlier, the feeling is the same. All is sweetness and light until French coach Pierre Berbizier accuses England hooker Brian Moore of being the *agent provocateur* in recent violent clashes between the nations. Moore responds by branding Berbizier 'bizarre and irresponsible', and the stage is set. In the event Rob Andrew, who rarely shoots his mouth off about anything, decides the contest in England's favour with an imperious kicking display. Recalled to goalkicking duties, he lands five penalty goals and a dropped goal, and promptly pays a debt of gratitude to Dave Alred, a kicker with American football outfit Minnesota Vikings in the 1970s, who has honed his technique. France rally from 0–12 to 11–12, thanks largely to Abdel Benazzi's try, but England – despite extending their tryless run to 427 minutes – are not to be denied.

France: J-L Sadourny (Colomiers); W Techoueyres* (Bordeaux), P Sella (Agen), T Lacroix (Dax), P Saint-André (Montferrand); A Penaud (Brive), F Galthie (Colomiers); L Benezech (Racing Club de France), J-M Gonzalez (Bayonne), P Gallart (Béziers), O Merle (Grenoble), O Roumat (Dax), A Benazzi (Agen), L Cabannes (Racing Club de France), P Benetton (Agen).
Scorers – *Try:* Benazzi. *Penalty goals:* Lacroix 3.

England: D Pears (Harlequins); I Hunter (Northampton), W Carling (capt, Harlequins), P de Glanville (Bath), R Underwood (Leicester); R Andrew (Wasps), D Morris (Orrell); J Leonard (Harlequins), B Moore (Harlequins), V Ubogu (Bath), M Johnson (Leicester), N Redman (Bath), T Rodber (Nottingham), B Clarke (Bath), S Ojomoh (Bath).
Scorers – *Penalty goals:* Andrew 5. *Dropped goal:* Andrew.

Referee: S Hilditch (Ireland).
Series score: Played 70, France 24, England 39, Drawn 7.

England (7) 15, Wales (3) 8
Twickenham, 19 March 1994

Not since 1959 have England last gone through a Five Nations campaign without a try, yet here they are within 80 minutes of such a dubious feat. However, with arch-rivals Wales homing in on the Grand Slam and Triple Crown, this is a day on which the result can wholly justify whatever means by which it is achieved. Moreover, remarkably, England can still win the championship, given a 16-point winning margin. Wales coach Alan Davies warns England that his boys will definitely score a try at Twickenham, to the delight of the Welsh punter, who stands to win £20,000 from a £200 bet at 100 to 1 on Wales's first Grand Slam in 16 years – and indeed they do, with Nigel Walker touching down late on. But it is too late as – shock horror – England have already managed two tries. First Rory Underwood, superbly rounding off a rare three-quarter move in the left corner, then Tim Rodber, plucking a Welsh throw-in at the front of the lineout and plunging over the adjacent try-line. England are 15–3 ahead and with only 54 minutes on the clock, their Sweet Chariot is purring like a Rolls. But almost as suddenly as they have found their form, it deserts them in the last quarter. Wales lose but win the title, and there is the faintly ridiculous sight of the vanquished receiving the spoils from Her Majesty the Queen.

England: I Hunter (Northampton); T Underwood (Leicester), W Carling (capt, Harlequins), P de Glanville (Bath), R Underwood (Leicester); R Andrew (Wasps), D Morris (Orrell); J Leonard (Harlequins), B Moore (Harlequins), V Ubogu (Bath), M Johnson (Leicester), N Redman (Bath), T Rodber (Nottingham), B Clarke (Bath), D Richards (Leicester). Repl: M Catt* (Bath) for Andrew, 76 mins.
Scorers – *Tries:* R Underwood, Rodber. *Conversion:* Andrew. *Penalty goal:* Andrew.

Wales: M Rayer (Cardiff); I Evans (capt, Llanelli), M Hall (Cardiff), N Davies (Llanelli), N Walker (Cardiff); N Jenkins (Pontypridd), R Moon (Llanelli); R Evans (Llanelli), G Jenkins (Swansea), J Davies (Neath), P Davies (Llanelli), G O Llewellyn (Neath), E Lewis (Llanelli), M Perego (Llanelli), S Quinnell (Llanelli). Repl: A Copsey (Llanelli) for Lewis, 49 mins.
Scorers – *Try:* Walker. *Penalty goal:* N Jenkins.

Referee: J Fleming (Scotland).
Series score: Played 100, England 40, Wales 48, Drawn 12.

Scotland (9) 12, France (13) 20
Edinburgh, 19 March 1994

Continuing the bizarre story of this season's Five Nations Championship right to the end, Scotland dutifully collect the dreaded Wooden Spoon after losing the decider to a French side who should have never been in the neighbourhood of such kitchen cutlery. Nothing particularly bizarre in the result, you may think, even if it is France's first win at Murrayfield since 1978. But look at the statistics: Scotland win 60% of lineout ball, 67% of scrums, 63% of ball in set play, 71% in loose play, and they have 55% of overall possession. Funny old game!

Scotland: G Hastings (capt, Watsonians); T Stanger (Hawick), S Hastings (Watsonians), D Wyllie (Stewart's-Melville FP), K Logan (Stirling County); G Townsend (Gala), B Redpath (Melrose); A Sharp (Bristol), K Milne (Heriot's FP), P Burnell (London Scottish), S Munro (Glasgow H/K), A Reed (Bath), P Walton (Northampton), I Smith (Gloucester), G Weir (Melrose).
Scorer – *Penalty goals:* G Hastings 4.

France: J-L Sadourny (Colomiers); W Techoueyres (Bordeaux), P Sella (Agen), Y Delaigue[+] (Toulon), P Saint-André (Montferrand); T Lacroix (Dax), A Macabiau[+] (Perpignan); L Benezech (Racing Club de France), J-M Gonzalez (Bayonne), L Seigne (Merignac), O Merle (Grenoble), O Brouzet (Grenoble), A Benazzi (Agen), L Cabannes (Racing Club de France), P Benetton (Agen). Repl: P Montlaur (Agen) for Lacroix, 52 mins.
Scorers – *Tries:* Sadourny, Saint-André. *Conversions:* Lacroix, Montlaur. *Penalty goals:* Lacroix 2.

Referee: D Bevan (Wales).
Series score: Played 65, Scotland 30, France 32, Drawn 3.

THE 1994 FIVE NATIONS CHAMPIONSHIP TABLE
(1993 positions in brackets)

		P	W	D	L	F	(t,c,p,dg)	A	(t,c, p,dg)	Pts	+/-
Wales	(5)	4	3	0	1	78	7,2,13,0	51	4,2,9,0	6	+27
England	(3)	4	3	0	1	60	2,1,15,1	49	4,1,8,1	6	+11
France	(1)	4	2	0	2	84	9,6,9,0	69	2,1,18,1	4	+15
Ireland	(4)	4	1	1	2	49	1,1,14,0	70	5,3,13,0	3	−21
Scotland	(2)	4	0	1	3	38	1,0,10,1	70	5,3,13,0	1	−32

WORLD CUP QUALIFIERS

Portugal 11, Wales 102
Lisbon, 17 May 1994

Records tumble as Wales cruise through a World Cup qualifier they should never have got themselves involved with in the first place. That they are, however, serves as a reminder as to how far they have come this season. In sweeping aside Portugal they establish the biggest winning margin in a senior international (overtaking New Zealand's 70–6 defeat of Italy in 1987), while their score represents the highest ever in a senior international (bettering NZ's 74–13 win over Fiji in '87 World Cup), although in World Cup qualifying terms it is not a record-breaker. In pre-qualifying for the 1991 tournament, Japan beat Thailand 108–7, and Korea dispatched Malaysia 102–0. Nigel Walker equals the Welsh single-match try-scoring record with four, while Ieuan Evans' 19th start as captain is another national record, bettering the 18 outings of former skipper Arthur 'Monkey' Gould.

Portugal: M Vilar-Gomes; P Murinello, R Pereira, N Mourao, T Morais; J Queimado (capt), P Netto Fernandes, S Perreira (E Macedo 53), M Batista, P Domingos, A Pecas, A Andrade, P Arsenio, P Eusebio, J Pires.
Scorers – *Try:* Murinello. *Penalty goals:* Vilar-Gomes 2.

Wales: M Rayer (Cardiff); I Evans (capt, Llanelli), M Hall (Cardiff), N Davies (Llanelli), N Walker (Cardiff); N Jenkins (Pontypridd), R Jones (Swansea); R Evans (Llanelli), G Jenkins (Swansea), J Davies (Neath), A Copsey (Llanelli), G O Llewellyn (Neath), H Taylor (Cardiff), E Lewis (Llanelli), S Quinnell (Llanelli).
Scorers – *Tries:* Quinnell, Llewellyn, Walker 4, Hall 3, Jones 2, I Evans 3, Taylor (penalty try). *Conversions:* Jenkins 11.

Referee: B Leask (Australia).
Series score: Played 1, Portugal 0, Wales 1.

Spain (0) 0, Wales (16) 54
Madrid, 21 May 1994

Wales's Iberian experience comes to a profitable end when victory over a hard-working Spain, following hard on the heels of their Portuguese romp, confirms the Principality's place in the World Cup finals. Ieuan Evans' second try hat-trick in four days takes him to within one try of the Welsh record held jointly by Gareth Edwards and Gerald Davies, while wing counterpart Nigel Walker also crosses to make his personal tally eight tries in eight Tests.

Spain: J Azkargorta; P Martin, A Mino, A Emciso, J Torres; F Puertas, J Hernandez-Gil; J Alvarez (S Espina 40), J Aguiar, J Diez (J Delazaro 45, O Salano 51), A Malo, M Villau, J Etxeberria (F Calle 68), J Lopez, J Gutierrez (capt).

Wales: A Clement (Swansea); I Evans (Llanelli, capt), M Hall (Cardiff), N Davies (Llanelli), N Walker (Cardiff); N Jenkins (Pontypridd), R Moon (Llanelli); R Evans (Llanelli), G Jenkins (Swansea), J Davies (Neath), P Arnold (Swansea), G O Llewellyn (Neath), M Perego (Llanelli), S Quinnell (Llanelli), E Lewis (Llanelli). Repl: A Copsey (Llanelli) for Lewis, 40 mins.

Scorers – *Tries:* Quinnell, I Evans 3 (penalty try), Walker, G Jenkins. *Conversions:* N Jenkins 5. *Penalty goals:* N Jenkins 3.

Referee: D Bishop (New Zealand).

1994 SUPER-10 TOURNAMENT

Final: Natal 10, Queensland 21
Kings Park, Durban, 14 May 1994

Natal: A Joubert (Durban Harlequins); J Small (College Rovers), P Müller (College Rovers), J Thomson (College Rovers), C van der Westhuizen (Durban Harlequins); H Honiball (Pietermaritzburg Police), R du Preez (Crusaders); G Keble (College Rovers), J Allan (Glenwood OB), A Garvey (Crusaders), S Atherton (Crusaders), J Slade (Crusaders), W Bartmann (Crusaders, capt), A Blakeway (Durban HSOB), G Teichmann (College Rovers). Repl: A Marinos (Crusaders) for Müller, 36 mins; S Payne (Crusaders) for Thomson, 40 mins.

Scorers – *Try:* van der Westhuizen. *Conversion:* Joubert. *Penalty goal:* Joubert.

Queensland: M Pini (Wests); B Lea (Souths), J Little (Souths), T Horan (Souths), D Smith (Souths); M Lynagh (University), P Slattery (University, capt); C Lillicrap (University), M Foley (Souths), A Skeggs (Souths), R McCall (Brothers), G Morgan (Souths), I Tabua (Brothers), D Wilson (Easts), S Scott-Young (Souths). Repl: A Herbert (GPS) for Horan, 44 mins; P Carozza (Wests) for Little, 59 mins; J Eales (Brothers) for Tabua, 59 mins.

Scorers – *Tries:* Lea, Scott-Young. *Conversion:* Lynagh. *Penalty goals:* Lynagh 2. *Dropped goal:* Lynagh.

Referee: G Wahlstrom (New Zealand).

IRELAND TO AUSTRALIA
May-June 1994: P8 W2 D0 L6 F177 A252

Not a memorable tour for the Irish, who are whitewashed 2–0 in the Test series and win just two of the other six games, even if the 64-8 Tour-opening defeat of Western Australia is a national best Down Under. The bonuses are Garryowen hooker Keith Wood, who shows signs of becoming a major player in the world game, and the Constitution forward pairing of flanker David Corkery and lock Gabriel Fulcher.

SQUAD: J Bell (Loughborough Univ – 2,3R,4,5,6,8); M Bradley (capt, Constitution – 1*,2*,4*,5R,6*,8*); S Byrne (Blackrock – 3,5R); P Clohessy (Young Munster – 1,3,4,6,8); D Corkery (Constitution – 1,3,4,6,8); V Costello (St Mary's – 1,3R,5,7); B Cronin (Garryowen – 7); P Danaher (Garryowen – 2,4,6,8); J Davidson (Dungannon – 1,3,5,7); E Elwood (Lansdowne – 1,2,4,6,8); M Field (Malone – 1,3,5,6R,7); J Fitzgerald (Young Munster – 1,4,6,8); N Francis (Old Belvedere – 2,4,6,8); G Fulcher (Constitution – 2,4,5,8); M Galwey (Shannon – 1,2R,3*,6); S Geoghegan (London Irish – 1,2,4,6,8); G Halpin (London Irish – 2,3,4R,5,7); N Hogan (Terenure – 7); P Hogan (Garryowen – 3); P Johns (Dungannon – 1,3,4,6,8); T Kingston (Dolphin – 1R,2,5*,7*); D McBride (Malone – 2,5,6R,7); A McGowan (Blackrock – 3,5,7); K O'Connell (Sunday's Well – 5,7); C O'Shea (Lansdowne – 1,4,5R,6,8); M Ridge (Blackrock – 1,3,5,7); B Robinson (Ballymena – 1R,2,4,5R,6,8); A Rolland (Blackrock – 3,5); P Soden (Constitution – 2,5,7); J Staples (London Irish – 1,2,3,5,7); B Walsh

470

(Constitution – 3,5,7); R Wilson (Instonians – 2); K Wood (Garryowen – 1,4,6,8); N Woods (Blackrock – 2,3,4,6,7,8).

Results: (1) Western Australia 8, Ireland 64 (Perth, 18 May); (2) New South Wales 55, Ireland 18 (Waratah, 22 May); (3) ACT 22, Ireland 9 (Canberra, 25 May); (4) Queensland 29, Ireland 26 (Brisbane, 29 May); (5) Australia B 57, Ireland 9 (Mount Isa, 1 June); (6) **first Test:** Australia 33, Ireland 13 (Brisbane, 5 June); (7) NSW Country 18, Ireland 20 (Lismore, 8 June); (8) **second Test:** Australia 18, Ireland 32 (Sydney, 11 June).

Scorers (177 – 17t,13c,20p,2dg): Elwood 35 (10c,4p,1dg), McGowan 33 (11p), O'Shea 29 (1t,3c,5p,1dg), Field 15 (3t), Francis 10 (2t), Johns 10 (2t), Kingston 10 (2t), Bell 5 (1t), Clohessy 5 (1t), Costello 5 (1t), Davidson 5 (1t), Geoghegan 5 (1t), Staples 5 (1t), Wood 5 (1t).

Western Australia 8, Ireland 64
Perth, 18 May 1994

Western Australia: R Smith; G Hamilton, D Hamilton, S Bunce, D Dunbar; T Fearn, M Ryburn (G Johnson 40); J Tepania, P Roberts (capt), G Thompson, T Thomas, S Vitali, R Walters, J O'Callaghan, D Gleghorn.
Scorers – *Try:* O'Callaghan. *Penalty goal:* Fearn.

Ireland: O'Shea; Geoghegan, Field, Ridge, Staples; Elwood, Bradley (capt); Fitzgerald, Wood (Kingston 31), Clohessy, Galwey, Davidson, Costello (Robertson 39), Corkery, Johns.
Scorers: *Tries:* Costello, Kingston 2, Davidson, Field 3, Johns, O'Shea. *Conversions:* Elwood 8. *Penalty goal:* Elwood.

Referee: A Cole (Australia).

New South Wales 55, Ireland 18
Waratah, 22 May 1994

New South Wales: T Kelaher; D Junee, M Burke, R Tombs, D Campese; T Wallace, S Payne; T Daly, P Kearns (capt), M Hartill, T Dempsey, T Kava, M Brial, S Domoni, W Waugh.
Scorers – *Tries:* Campese 2, Payne 2, Tombs 2, Brial, Waugh. *Conversions:* Wallace 6. *Penalty goal:* Wallace.

Ireland: Staples; Geoghegan, Bell, Danaher, Woods; Elwood, Bradley (capt); Soden, Kingston, Halpin, Francis, Fulcher, Wilson (Galwey 38), McBride, Robinson.
Scorers – *Tries:* Bell, Francis. *Conversion:* Elwood. *Penalty goals:* Elwood 2.

Referee: B Leask (Queensland).

Australian Capital Territory 22, Ireland 9
Canberra, 25 May 1994

ACT: R Kafer; D McLachlan, J Swan (L O'Connor 38), M O'Connor (capt), D Grimmond; P Cornish, G Gregan; M Harley, M Caputo, D Hutchinson, F Mafi, C Sweeny, B Jones, I Fenukitau, C Bretton.
Scorers – *Tries:* Grimmond, M O'Connor, Swan. *Conversions:* M O'Connor 2. *Penalty goal:* M O'Connor.

Ireland: Staples; Walsh, Field (Bell 51), Ridge, Woods; McGowan, Rolland; Halpin, Byrne, Clohessy, Galwey (capt) (temp: Costello 25), Davidson, Hogan (Costello 38), Corkery, Johns.
Scorer – *Penalty goals:* McGowan 3.

Referee: B Kinsey (NSW).

Queensland 29, Ireland 26
Brisbane, 29 May 1994

Queensland: M Pini; B Lea (P Carozza 56), A Herbert, D Herbert, D Smith; M Lynagh, P Slattery (capt) (B Johnstone 41); C Lillicrap, M Foley, A Skeggs, R McCall, G Morgan (temp: M Connors 7), J Eales, D Wilson, S Scott-Young.
Scorers – *Tries:* Slattery, Herbert. *Conversions:* Lynagh 2. *Penalty goals:* Lynagh 5.

Ireland: O'Shea; Geoghegan, Bell, Danaher, Woods; Elwood, Bradley (capt); Fitzgerald, Wood,

Clohessy (Halpin 75), Fulcher, Francis, Robinson, Corkery, Johns.
Scorers – *Tries:* Geoghegan, Wood. *Conversions:* O'Shea 2. *Penalty goals:* O'Shea 3. *Dropped goal:* Elwood.

Referee: W Erickson (NSW).

Australia XV 57, Ireland 9
Mount Isa, 1 June 1994

Australian XV: A Apps; A Murdoch, J Roff, P Cornish (P Howard 67), R Constable; T Mandrusiak, M Catchpole; D Crowley (capt), T Walton, G Websdale, J Nowlan, R Korst, W Ofahengaue (R Harry 48), B Robinson, F Finau (O Finegan 6).
Scorers – *Tries:* Catchpole 3, Apps, Dalton, Howard, Mandrusiak, Murdoch, Ofahengaue. *Conversions:* Mandrusiak 3. *Penalty goals:* Mandrusiak 2.

Ireland: Staples; Walsh (O'Shea 51), Field, Ridge, Bell, McGowan, Rolland (Bradley 38); Soden, Kingston (capt), Halpin, Fulcher (Robinson 60, Byrne 70), Davidson, O'Connell, McBride, Costello.
Scorer – *Penalty goals:* McGowan 3.

Referee: P Marshall (NSW).

Australia 33, Ireland 13
first Test: Brisbane, 5 June 1994

Australia: M Pini (Queensland); D Campese (NSW), M Burke (NSW), M O'Connor (ACT), D Smith (Queensland); M Lynagh (Queensland, capt), P Slattery (Queensland); T Daly (NSW), P Kearns (NSW), E McKenzie (NSW), J Eales (Queensland), G Morgan (Queensland), D Wilson (Queensland), I Tabua (Queensland), T Gavin (NSW).
Scorers – *Tries:* Tabua, Lynagh, Campese, Burke, Smith. *Conversion:* Lynagh. *Penalty goals:* Lynagh 2.

Ireland: O'Shea (Field 39); Geoghegan, Bell, Danaher, Woods; Elwood, Bradley (capt); Fitzgerald, Wood, Clohessy, Galwey (McBride 28), Francis, Robinson, Corkery, Johns.
Scorers – *Try:* Johns. *Conversion:* Elwood. *Penalty goals:* Elwood, O'Shea.

Referee: J Dume (France).
Series score: Played 15, Australia 9, Ireland 6.

NSW Country 18, Ireland 20
Lismore, 8 June 1994

NSW Country: T Eddy; M Sykes, P O'Brien, C Coffey, S Rutledge; S Salter, S Merrick; A Baldwin, J Ives, G Clarke (W Petty 51), J Nowlan, J Langford, N Cobcroft, A McCalman (capt), H Williams.
Scorers – *Tries:* Sykes, Nowlan, Rutledge. *Penalty goal:* Salter.

Ireland: Staples; Walsh, Field, Ridge, Woods; McGowan, Hogan; Soden, Kingston (capt), Halpin, Costello, Davidson, O'Connell, McBride, Cronin.
Scorers – *Try:* Staples. *Penalty goals:* McGowan 5.

Referee: K O'Halloran (Queensland).

Australia 32, Ireland 18
second Test: Sydney, 11 June 1994

Ireland: O'Shea; Geoghegan, Bell, Danaher, Woods; Elwood, Bradley (capt); Fitzgerald, Wood, Clohessy, Fulcher, Francis, Robinson, Corkery, Johns.
Scorers – *Tries:* Clohessy, Francis. *Conversion:* O'Shea. *Penalty goal:* O'Shea. *Dropped goal:* O'Shea.

Australia: M Burke (NSW); D Campese (NSW), R Tombs (NSW), D Herbert+ (Queensland), D Smith (Queensland); M Lynagh (Queensland, capt), P Slattery (Queensland); T Daly (NSW), P Kearns (NSW), E McKenzie (NSW), J Eales (Queensland), G Morgan (Queensland), D Wilson (Queensland), I Tabua (Queensland), T Gavin (NSW). Repl: R Constable+ for Smith, 78 mins.
Scorers – *Tries:* Herbert, Wilson, Tabua. *Conversion:* Lynagh. *Penalty goals:* Lynagh 5.

Referee: J Dume (France).
Series score: Played 16, Australia 10, Ireland 6.

A dramatic tour which starts oh so badly, features one glorious day in Pretoria, and ends with two horrors in Port Elizabeth and Cape Town. The good news is the sensational 32-15 first-Test victory at Loftus Versfeld (at altitude!), and the tour displays of fullback Paul Hull and back-row Steve Ojomoh. The bad news is the appalling local refereeing, which permits some appalling acts of violence to be perpetrated. The worst incidents come in the 'Battle of Port Elizabeth', highlighted (though that is hardly the word) by the fact that Jon Callard's head needs 25 stitches after he is blatantly stamped upon. Neither are England immune friom criticism as Tim Rodber is dismissed for retaliation against Eastern Province, Rodber become only the second England player ever to be sent off (Mike Burton 1975 being the other). South Africa, to their credit, rebound wonderfully well in the second Test, at Newlands in Cape Town, having made six changes during an eight-hour selection meeting.

SQUAD: A Adebayo (Bath – 1,5,7); R Andrew (Wasps – 2,4,6,8); S Barnes (Bath – 1,2R,3,5); S Bates (Wasps – 1,3,4R,5,7); M Bayfield (Northampton – 1,3,4,6,8); J Callard (Bath – 3R,5,7); W Carling (Harlequins, capt – 2*,3*,4*,6*,8*); M Catt (Bath – 1,5,7); B Clarke (Bath – 2,3,4,6,8); L Dallaglio (Wasps – 1,5,7); G Dawe (Bath – 1,3,5,7); P de Glanville (Bath – 2,4,6,8); D Hopley (Wasps – 1,3,5,7); P Hull (Bristol – 1,3,4,6,7,8); M Johnson (Leicester – 2); J Leonard (Harlequins – 2,4,6,8); J Mallett (Bath – 1,3,5,7); B Moore (Harlequins – 2,4,6,8); D Morris (Orrell – 2,4,6,8); S Ojomoh (Bath – 1,2R,3,5,6R,7,8); D Pears (Harlequins – 2); M Poole (Leicester – 1,5,7); S Potter (Leicester – 1,3,5,7); N Redman (Bath – 2,3,4,6,8); D Richards (Leicester – 2,4,6); T Rodber (Nottingham – 2,4,6,7R,8); G Rowntree (Leicester – 1,3,5,7); D Ryan (Wasps – 1*,3*,5*,7*); S Shaw (Bristol – 5,7); V Ubogu (Bath – 2,4,6,7R,8); R Underwood (Leicester – 2,4,6,7R,8); T Underwood (Leicester – 1R,2,3,4,6,8).

Results: (1) Orange Free State 22, England 11 (Bloemfontein, 18 May); (2) Natal 21, England 6 (Durban, 21 May); (3) Western Transvaal 24, England 26 (Pretoria, 25 May); (4) Transvaal 24, England 21 (Pretoria, 28 May); (5) South Africa B 19, England 16 (Kimberley, 31 May); (6) first Test: South Africa 15, England 32 (Pretoria, 4 June); (7) Eastern Province 13, England 31 (Port Elizabeth, 7 June); (8) second Test: South Africa 27, England 9 (Cape Town, 11 June).

Scorers (152 – 11t,8c,26p,1dg): Andrew 58 (2t,3c,13p,1dg), Barnes 22 (2c,6p), Callard 17 (1c,5p), Catt 10 (2c,2p), Hopley 10 (2t), Hull 10 (2t), T Underwood 10 (2t), Bates 5 (1t), Clarke 5 (1t), R Underwood 5 (1t).

Orange Free State 22, England 11
Bloemfontein, 18 May 1994

OFS: A Pawson; C Badenhorst, E Lubbe, B Venter, D van Rensburg; F Smith, H Martens; O le Roux, N Drotske (C Marais 2), D Heymans, R Opperman, B Els, A Venter (J Coetzee 65), A Cloete, J von Solms.
Scorers – *Tries:* Badenhorst 2, A Venter, Coetzee. *Conversion:* van Rensburg.

England: Hull; Hopley, Potter, Catt (T Underwood 65), Adebayo; Barnes, Bates; Rowntree, Dawe, Mallett, Poole, Bayfield, Dallaglio, Ojomoh, Ryan (capt).
Scorers – *Try:* Hopley. *Penalty goals:* Barnes 2.

Referee: P Lombard (Natal).

Natal 21, England 6
Durban, 21 May 1994

Natal: A Joubert; C van der Westhuizen (A Marinos 51), R Muir, P Müller; J Enslin; H Honiball, K Putt; G Kebble (D Morkel 9), J Allan, A Garvey, S Atherton, M Andrews, W Bartmann (capt), A Blakeway, G Teichmann.
Scorers – *Penalty goals:* Joubert 4, Honiball 3.

England: Pears (Barnes 63); R Underwood, de Glanville, Carling (capt), T Underwood; Andrew, Morris; Leonard, Moore, Ubogu, Johnson, Redman, Rodber, Clarke, Richards (Ojomoh 40).
Scorer – *Penalty goals:* Andrew 2.

Referee: M Franken (Griqualand West).

Western Transvaal 24, England 26
Pretoria, 25 May 1994

Western Transvaal: J Blaauw; A Vermeulen, D Swart, J van Wyck, D Basson; E Hare (capt), A Pretorius, E Grobler, L Boshoff, M Proudfoot, P Oosthuizen, P Herbst, A Kriek, M van Greunen, S Bekker.
Scorers – *Tries:* Basson, van Greunen. *Conversion:* Basson. *Penalty goals:* Basson 4.

England: Hull; Hopley, Carling (capt), Potter, T Underwood; Barnes (Callard 75), Bates; Rowntree, Dawe, Mallett, Bayfield, Redman, Ryan, Clarke, Ojomoh.
Scorers – *Tries:* T Underwood 2, *Conversions:* Barnes 2. *Penalty goals:* Barnes 4.

Referee: N Heilbron (Cape Town).

Transvaal 24, England 21
Pretoria, 28 May 1994

Transvaal: T van Rensburg; J Louw, C Schultz, J Mulder, P Hendriks; H le Roux, J Roux; B Swart (I Hatting 78), J Dalton, J le Roux, H Strydom, K Wiese, F Pienaar (capt), I Macdonald, R Streuli.
Scorers – *Tries:* H le Roux, Louw. *Conversion:* van Rensburg. *Penalty goals:* van Rensburg 4.

England: Hull; T Underwood, Carling (capt), de Glanville, R Underwood; Andrew, Morris (Bates 51); Leonard, Moore, Ubogu, Johnson, Redman, Rodber, Clarke, Richards.
Scorers – *Tries:* Andrew, R Underwood. *Conversion:* Andrew. *Penalty goals:* Andrew 3.

Referee: I Rogers (Natal).

South Africa B 19, England 16
Kimberley, 31 May 1994

South Africa B: C Dirks (Transvaal); S Berridge (Western Province), C Scholtz (Transvaal), J Mulder (Transvaal), C van der Westhuizen (Natal); J Stransky (Western Province), J Roux (Transvaal); G Pagel (Western Province), J Dalton (Transvaal), J le Roux (Transvaal), K Wiese (Transvaal), K Otto (Northern Transvaal), F van Heerden (Western Province), A Venter (Orange Free State), A Richter (Northern Transvaal, capt).
Scorers – *Tries:* Scholtz, Stransky. *Penalty goals:* Stransky 2. *Dropped goal:* Stransky.

England: Callard; Hopley, Potter, Catt, Adebayo; Barnes, Bates; Rowntree, Dawe, Mallett, Shaw, Poole, Dallaglio, Ojomoh, Ryan (capt).
Scorers – *Try:* Hopley. *Conversion:* Callard. *Penalty goals:* Callard 3.

Referee: S Neethling (Wellington, Boland).

South Africa (3) 15, England (23) 32
first Test: Pretoria, 4 June 1994

South Africa: A Joubert (Natal); J Small (Natal), P Müller (Natal), B Venter (Orange Free State), C Williams (Western Province); H le Roux (Transvaal), J van der Westhuizen (Northern Transvaal); A-H le Roux (Orange Free State), J Allan (Natal), S Swart (Natal), J Strydom (Natal), S Atherton (Natal), F Pienaar (Transvaal, capt), F van Heerden (Western Province), C Strauss (Western Province).
Scorer – *Penalty goals:* Joubert 5.

England: Hull; T Underwood, Carling (capt), de Glanville, R Underwood; Andrew, Morris; Leonard, Moore, Ubogu, Bayfield, Redman, Rodber, Clarke, Richards (Ojomoh 55).
Scorers – *Tries:* Clarke, Andrew. *Conversions:* Andrew 2. *Penalty goals:* Andrew 5. *Dropped goal:* Andrew.

Referee: C Hawke (New Zealand).
Series score: Played 11, South Africa 6, England 4, Drawn 1.

Eastern Province 13, England 31
Port Elizabeth, 7 June 1994

Eastern Province: A Fourie; A Markow (D Marshall 57), R Potgieter, F Crouse, M van Vuuren; B Kruger, A Coetzee (R Lurie 79); G Halford, J Kirsten, W Meyer, A Geldenhuys, E van der Bergh, M Mastert (capt), S Tremain, H Karele. Sent off: Tremain.

Scorers – *Try:* Fourie. *Conversion:* Kruger. *Penalty goals:* Kruger 2.

England: Callard (R Underwood 28); Hull, Hopley, Potter, Adebayo; Catt, Bates; Rowntree (Ubogu 22), Dawe, Mallett, Poole, Shaw, Dallaglio, Ojomoh, Ryan (capt, Rodber 12).
Scorers – *Tries:* Bates, Hull 2. *Conversions:* Catt 2. *Penalty goals:* Callard 2, Catt 2.

Referee: P van Blommenstein (Western Province).

South Africa (3) 27, England (3) 9
second Test: Cape Town, 11 June 1994

South Africa: A Joubert (Natal); J Small (Natal), P Müller (Natal), B Venter (Orange Free State), C Williams (Western Province); H le Roux (Transvaal), J Roux+ (Transvaal); S Swart (Transvaal), J Allan (Natal), A-H le Roux (Orange Free State), M Andrews (Natal), S Atherton (Natal), F Pienaar (Transvaal, capt), I Macdonald (Transvaal), A Richter (Northern Transvaal). Repl: J van der Westhuizen (Northern Transvaal) for Williams, 30 mins; F van Heerden (Western Province) for Macdonald, 67 mins.
Scorers – *Tries:* H le Roux, Joubert. *Conversion:* Joubert. *Penalty goals:* H le Roux 3, Joubert 2.

England: Hull; T Underwood, Carling (capt), de Glanville, R Underwood; Andrew, Morris; Leonard, Moore, Ubogu, Bayfield, Redman, Rodber, Clarke, Ojomoh.
Scorer – *Penalty goals:* Andrew 3.

Referee: C Hawke (New Zealand).
Series score: Played 12, South Africa 7, England 4, Drawn 1.

A tour to forget for a Scottish side always thought likely to struggle after the call-off of so many essential players (the Hastings brothers and Gary Armstrong, to name but three). The Scots manage just one win, against Córdoba, and an opening draw against Buenos Aires. But when they return to the capital for the two Tests the news is all bad. Poor decision making and equally bad goalkicking combines to hand victory, on both occasions, to the home Pumas.

SQUAD: S Brotherstone (Melrose – 2,3,5); P Burnell (London Scottish – 2,4,6); S Campbell (Dundee HSFP – 2,3,5); C Dalgleish (Gala – 1,2,3R,5); M Dods (Gala – 1,4,6); S Ferguson (Peebles – 1,3,5); D Hodge (Watsonians – 2,3,5); C Hogg (Melrose – 3,4,6); I Jardine (Stirling Co – 2,3,4,6); C Joiner (Melrose – 1,2,3,4,6); K Logan (Stirling Co – 2,3,4,5,6); D McIvor (Edinburgh Acads – 2,3,5); K McKenzie (Stirling Co – 1,4,6); S Munro (Glasgow H/K – 2,4,6); S Nichol (Selkirk – 1,3,5,6R); D Patterson (Edinburgh Acads – 1,5); B Redpath (Melrose – 2,3,4,6); A Reed (Bath, capt – 1*,4*,6*); S Reid (Boroughmuir – 1,2,5); J Richardson (Edinburgh Acads – 1,3*,5*); A Sharp (London Scottish – 1,4,6); R Shepherd (Edinburgh Acads – 2,3,5); G Shiel (Melrose – 1,4,6); I Smith (Gloucester – 1,4,6); G Townsend (Gala – 1,4,5,6); F Wallace (Glasgow H/K – 2,3,5); P Walton (Northampton – 1,4,6); A Watt (Glasgow H/K – 2,3,5,6R). Manager: F McLeod. Coaches: D Morgan, R Dixon.

Results: (1) Buenos Aires 24, Scotland 24 (Buenos Aires, 25 May); (2) Cuyo 25, Scotland 11 (Mendoza, 28 May); (3) Córdoba 14, Scotland 40 (Córdoba, 31 May); (4) first Test: Argentina 16, Scotland 15 (Buenos Aires, 4 June); (5) Rosario 27, Scotland 16 (Rosario, 7 June); (6) second Test: Argentina 19, Scotland 17 (Buenos Aires, 11 June).

Scorers (106 – 12t,2c,13p,1dg): Dods 24 (8p), Shepherd 24 (1t,2c,5p), Dalgleish 10 (2t), Logan 10 (2t), Watt 10 (2t), Hodge 8 (1t,1dg), Jardine 5 (1t), Joiner 5 (1t), McIvor 5 (1t), Nichol 5 (1t).

Buenos Aires 24, Scotland 24
Buenos Aires, 25 May 1994

Buenos Aires: R Bullrich; H Rivarola, F Garcia, E Laborde, D Albanese; D Forrester, F Salvat; G Holingren, M Bosch, H Grotte, M Lerga, G Ugartemendia (capt), P Traini, P Camerlinckx, D Devries.
Scorers – *Tries:* Lerga, Rivarola. *Conversion:* Forrester. *Penalty goals:* Forrester 4.

Scotland: Dods; Joiner, Nichol, Shiel, Dalgleish; Townsend, Patterson; Sharp, McKenzie, Ferguson, Richardson. Reed (capt), Walton, Smith, Reid.
Scorers – *Tries:* Dalgleish 2, Nichol. *Penalty goals:* Dods 3.

Referee: S Borsani (Rosario).

Cuyo 25, Scotland 11
Mendoza, 28 May 1994

Cuyo: M Brandi; E Saurina, P Cremaschi, P Capitelli (capt), M Roby; L Andia, M Diaz, R Grau, F Bartolini, M Miranda, P Pascual, P Lambert, M Cassone, C Correa-Llano, M Bertranau.
Scorers – *Tries:* Bartranau, Cassone, Diaz. *Conversions:* Capitelli 2. *Penalty goal:* Capitelli. *Dropped goal:* Andia.

Scotland: Logan; Joiner, Shepherd, Jardine, Dalgleish; Hodge, Redpath; Watt, Brotherstone, Burnell, Munro, Campbell, Wallace, McIvor, Reid.
Scorers – *Try:* Hodge. *Penalty goals:* Shepherd 2.

Referee: E Sklar (Arura).

Córdoba 14, Scotland 40
Córdoba, 31 May 1994

Scotland: Shepherd; Joiner (Dalgleish 68), Nichol, Jardine, Logan; Hodge, Redpath; Watt, Brotherstone, Ferguson, Richardson (capt), Campbell, Wallace, McIvor, Hogg.
Scorers – *Tries:* Jardine, Joiner, Logan, McIvor, Shepherd, Watt. *Conversions:* Shepherd 2. *Penalty goal:* Shepherd. *Dropped goal:* Hodge.

Córdoba: J Luna; G Tomalino, G Ussher, I Merlo, F Pereyra; F Grangretto, J Dragott; F Zarate, I Ferreyra, P Sanchez, D Pereyra (capt), J Sunes, G Piergentili, D Rotondo, S Irazoqui.
Scorers – *Tries:* Dragott 2. *Conversions:* Luna 2.

Referee: E Casanave (AURA).

Argentina 16, Scotland 15
first Test: Buenos Aires, 4 June 1994

Argentina: S Meson; M Teran, D Cuesta-Silva, M Loffreda (capt), G Jorge; G del Castilla, N-F Miranda; M Corral, J-J Angelillo, P Noriego, P Sporleder, G Llanes, C Viel, P Temperley, P Camerlinckx.
Scorers – *Try:* Teran. *Conversion:* Meson. *Penalty goals:* Meson 3.

Scotland: Dods; Joiner+, Jardine, Shiel, Logan; Townsend, Redpath; Sharp, McKenzie+, Burnell, Munro, Reed (capt), Walton, Smith, Hogg.
Scorer – *Penalty goals:* Dods 5.

Referee: W Erickson (Australia).
Series score: Played 2, Argentina 1, Scotland 1.

Rosario 27, Scotland 16
Rosario, 7 June 1994

Rosario: E Jurado; L Bouza, A Caffaro-Rossi, F del Castillo, G Acuna; G del Castillo, R Crexell; S Pietrobon, C Promanzio, H Cespedes, R Perez, N Boiscovich, M Carmona, C Oviedo, P Baraldi.
Scorers – *Tries:* Caffaro-Rossi, Crexell. *Conversion:* Crexell. *Penalty goals:* Crexell 2. *Dropped goals:* del Castillo 3.

Scotland: Shepherd; Dalgleish, Townsend, Nichol, Logan; Hodge, Patterson; Watt, Brotherstone, Ferguson, Richardson, Campbell, Wallace, McIvor, Reid.
Scorers – *Tries:* Logan, Watt. *Penalty goals:* Shepherd 2.

Referee: R Bordcoch (Córdoba).

Argentina 19, Scotland 17
second Test: Buenos Aires, 11 June 1994

Argentina: S Meson; M Teran, D Cuesta-Silva, M Loffreda (capt), G Jorge; G del Castilla, N-F Miranda; R Grau, J-J Angelillo, P Noriego, P Sporleder, G Llanes, R Martin, P Temperley, J Santamarina.
Scorers – *Try:* Martin. *Conversion:* Meson. *Penalty goals:* Meson 3. *Dropped goal:* del Castilla.